100 Classic Graphic Design Books

Bibliographic

Jason Godfrey

Foreword by Steven Heller

For
Angela and Orson,
Wendy and Michael

First published in Great Britain in 2009
This paperback edition first published in 2011 by Laurence King Publishing Ltd
361-373 City Road
London EC1V 1LR
United Kingdom
Tel: +44 20 7841 6900
Fax: +44 20 7841 6910
Email: enquiries@laurenceking.com
www.laurenceking.com

A catalogue record for this book is available from the British Library.

ISBN: 978 1 85669 765 1

Designed by Jason Godfrey,
www.godfreydesign.co.uk

Printed in China

Contents

GRAPHIC STYLE

STEVEN HELLER &
SEYMOUR CHWAST
ABRAMS
Thoughts on Design: Paul Rand
Wittenborn

THE COMPLETE TADANORI YOKOO
KODANSHA
Emil Ruder Typographie Typography Typography
Niggli
Weingart : TYPO GRAPHY
Lars Müller Publishers
A sign systems manual
Crosby/Fletcher/Forbes
Praeger
Living by design Pentagram
Lund Humphries London
Whitney Library of Design New York
Graphic design: visual comparisons by Fletcher/Forbes/Gill
Studio Books
Alphabet Thesaurus Nine Thousand
STOLTZ
PHOTO-LETTERING
216 East Forty-fifth Street New York Murray Hill 2-2346
Karel Martens printed matter | drukwerk
Hyphen

Design Books: Not Just Eye Candy

By Steven Heller

Scanning the graphic design books that Jason Godfrey has amassed for this unique volume should provoke in me an intense case of design-book envy, the need to own them all – that is, if I did not actually own them all already (and even wrote one of them). What *Bibliographic* triggers instead is a case of severe angst. The problem it brings into vivid focus is this: I honestly don't know where many of my prized copies of the titles reproduced herein are hiding. If you saw my personal library – a separate apartment where I store most of my books – you would understand that the sheer volume of my holdings and the colossal paucity of shelf space, which forces me to stack my books in high piles in front of the bookcases, prevents me finding the vast majority of titles precisely when I need them. Of course, when I don't need them or am not looking for them they routinely appear as if by magic. I know it's irrational, but I feel the books are in cahoots to prohibit my access to them, yet they enjoy toying with my brain in a bibliographic cat-and-mouse hide-and-seek game. Damn them! It's as if these books have their own devilish intelligence (rather than being the mere repositories of intelligences). But enough paranormal, paranoid speculation; suffice to say that without an effective system for cataloguing design books it is easy to become overwhelmed. Which is why I envy Mr Godfrey's penchant for organization and appreciate his useful taxonomy.

Before you is the cream of the design books to have been published over a span of the twentieth and twenty-first centuries. Given how comparatively unimportant graphic design has been to scholars of art and culture, it is fascinating that so many volumes were published on so many general and arcane aspects of graphic design. Yet I recall that over 20 years ago, when I started writing books on the subject, editors were extremely cautious about what to publish lest they flood what was perceived to be a very small market. Only the most carefully vetted books would see the light of day. Currently, an increasing number of publishers worldwide are issuing many more titles per year, everything from conventional 'how-to' and process books to esoteric monographs on design 'culture'. I am convinced that the number of volumes devoted to design and related themes over the course of the past couple of years is near or equal to the number of books published throughout the entire 1930s, or even the 1980s.

This makes the task of culling – separating the wheat from the chaff, so to speak – somewhat daunting. While there are obviously some inferior books out there, and others that have been made irrelevant by the passage of time, many vintage design books are important building blocks of graphic design history. The 1926 catalogue for Fonderies Deberny & Peignot, the Parisian type foundry and design wellspring that launched the careers of A.M. Cassandre and Alexey Brodovitch, among others, is a significant historical document that, while long out of print, chronicles a critical period in typographic history. Similarly, Robert Massin's 1970 *Letter and Image* is essential for every student of pictorial typography. What many designers are doing with the layering of type and image in the computer age began in the pre-computer era. Massin, known as a typographic experimenter, collected the historic roots and traced the routes of this phenomenon. Even the practical handbooks like Joseph Binder's 1934 *Colour in Advertising* and Alfred Tolmer's 1931 *Mise en Page* are critical pieces in the patchwork that is the design legacy because of the way in which each book addressed the stylistic and formal concerns of its respective period.

These vintage books are untapped repositories of design knowledge, as relevant today as they were when first published. The 1952 *Seven Designers Look at Trademark Design* edited by Egbert Jacobson may survey the work of designers like the late Paul Rand, Herbert Bayer, Will Burtin and Alvin Lustig, but in some cases the logos are still extant and in others they provide valuable case studies in success and failure. The 1963 *Graphic Design: Visual Comparisons* by Alan Fletcher, Colin Forbes and Bob Gill during their pre-Pentagram days, a collection of disparate yet corresponding images, is as inspiring for young designers now as it was back then.

It is eye-opening to see how design books have evolved since the days when colour was an expensive extravagance. When Paul Rand's *Thoughts on Design* was released in 1947 few pages were in colour, but his 1985 *A Designer's Art* is awash with it (and the printing and paper are better quality, too). Even such a stickler as Rand accepted that back in the late 1940s and 1950s design-book production was at its low ebb. A potentially colourful book like John Lewis's 1962 *Printed Ephemera* suffered from its monochromatic reproductions (although it is still a useful record). But today books like Rick Poynor and Edward Booth-Clibborn's ground-breaking 1991 *Typography Now*, the first survey of the 'new deconstructivist typography', and Alan Fletcher's 2001 *The Art of Looking Sideways* could not be effectively marketed without full-colour printing.

Design books are too often unfairly designated 'eye candy', and while a proportion of those published each year are pictorial inspiration for other designers, the majority of books represented here, from Henry Dreyfuss's 1972 *Symbol Sourcebook* to Herbert Spencer's 1969 *Pioneers of Modern Typography*, are essential to design practice and cultural study. Although most graphic design books are usually produced for a professional or student audience, even this should not limit their readership. This collection brilliantly reveals that the most significant of these books are reliquaries of popular culture.

Introduction

By Jason Godfrey

Bibliographic is a library dedicated to the subject of graphic design. It's not a history of graphic design through its books, and it does not pretend to be the definitive list of 100 books on the subject. Instead, it represents a cross-section of books that would be a welcome addition on any studio's shelves. They are titles that have become sources of visual inspiration and vital objects for practising graphic designers. Condensed from the thousands of graphic design books published, many are linchpins of the profession, either as seminal historical publications and points of reference or as symbolic of certain eras or styles. Some books are of their time, others benefit from hindsight. Moreover, as befits a book on graphic design, the books included are for the most part fine examples of the craft of book design itself.

Designers have always given great prominence to their libraries; they are a living and working part of the studios they occupy. I've been lucky enough to have had my passion for books encouraged by college professors, and to have spent the early years of my career in environments where the availability and use of a library was seen as important, and I've no doubt that this influenced my subsequent interest in building a collection of books.

Such collections are almost always accessible and seemingly in constant use, and often say more about the designer than their portfolio of work. The range of books will be wide. It is rarely confined to graphic design titles, invariably including books from many creative fields, especially fine arts and photography. This book, for the sake of expediency, concentrates on graphic design. It was also decided to omit the design annuals standard on many shelves, as they are so numerous that they probably deserve a survey in their own right and, as the product of judged competitions, they often lack an editorial perspective.

The selection of books was not an easy task, and of necessity ultimately produced a list arbitrary in nature. As an illustrated book it was important that the books should be visually interesting. This effectively removed many volumes dedicated to the critical analysis of graphic design, which tend to be text-heavy and include few images. There are notable exceptions to this – László Moholy-Nagy's *Vision in Motion* (1947) and György Kepes's *Language of Vision* (1944) were both dynamic books that preached a new way forward for design and reflected this in their layouts.

The need to photograph all the titles meant that the books had to be accessible. Many of the books in *Bibliographic* are still in print and others are not difficult to find in the second-hand book trade. This has caused the list to be weighted in favour of books published after the Second World War, partly because this period coincides with the growth of graphic design as a profession, but also because books produced before this date are rarer to find and are now often confined to museums. This is particularly true for books related to the typographic revolutions of the 1920s and 1930s, which thankfully are extremely well recorded in Herbert Spencer's exemplary and peerless *Pioneers of Modern Typography* (1969), Eckhard Neumann's *Functional Graphic Design in the 20's* (1967) and Gerd Fleischmann's *Bauhaus: Drucksachen, Typografie, Reklame* (1984).

Some pre-war books were included because they were deemed so important to the history of graphic design: Jan Tschichold's *Die Neue Typographie* (1928) and Alfred Tolmer's *Mise en Page* (1931) were both highly influential books that changed the design landscape. They appear in this book thanks to the generosity of the St Bride Printing Library in London, their scarcity meaning that such institutions are among the few places volumes like these can be studied. Hopefully *Bibliographic* can give an impression of the physical presence of these often-quoted books.

Even in the post-war period, graphic design books, with a few exceptions, have never printed in huge quantities. As the industry has grown, more and more designers try to obtain copies of early design publications, and this has inevitably made some titles harder to find, particularly those that were never reprinted, such as Ladislav Sutnar's *Visual Design in Action* (1961) and Bradbury Thompson's *The Art of Graphic Design* (1988). For students, the school library is now one of the few avenues available to get hold of these books.

The earliest books featured in *Bibliographic* are two typographic specimen books, the first from the American Type Founders Company (ATF) and the second from French type founders Deberny & Peignot. There were many companies producing such catalogues to advertise their typographic wares to the printing trade. The two selected for this book provide a contrast in styles. The ATF 1906 specimen book, with its bold gothics and workmanlike serif typefaces such as Bookman and Cheltenham, is a book rooted in the nineteenth-century jobbing printing industry. Deberny & Peignot's 1926 catalogue shows a company aware of new trends in the French graphic arts in the 1920s, employing designers in its production and marketing directly to their needs. The value of these specimens and the others routinely found in graphic design libraries is not one confined to their use as historical typographic reference tools but also as reminders of the origins of their profession. Other such examples in this book include the mammoth *Alphabet Thesaurus Nine Thousand* (1960) from Photo-Lettering Inc. and the *Letraset* book of types (c.1970s) that, because of the product's use in the general art trade, was often the first book to inspire a career in graphic design during the 1970s.

The structure of *Bibliographic* is not too dissimilar to the arrangement of any studio library. Books on typography, whether they are pure specimens or explorations on the subject, tend to gravitate to each other. As a specialized area within graphic design, 'Typography' is a natural home to collections of types such as Rob Roy Kelly's extensively researched and brilliantly presented *American Wood Type: 1828–1900* (1969) and Imre Reiner's more idiosyncratic compilation *Modern and Historical Typography* (1946). Designers' experiments with type are seen in the classical elegance of *A Constructed Roman Alphabet* (1982) by David Lance Goines and Takenobu Igarashi's sculptural letterforms in *Igarashi Alphabets* (1987). These sit comfortably alongside works dedicated to the study of particular typefaces, of which Lars Müller's pocketbook *Helvetica: Homage to a Typeface* (2002) and Colin Banks's *London's Handwriting* (1994), an oversize tribute to the typeface Johnston, are among the best.

On a day-to-day basis, perhaps the most used section of the graphic designers library would be the 'Sourcebooks'. This is the visual repository of signs, symbols and ideas that is often the backbone of the research and execution of any project. Clarence P. Hornung's *Handbook of Designs and Devices* (1932), a book that remains in print over 70 years after its original publication, is a catalogue of forms that have been the foundation of many a corporate logo. Henry Dreyfuss's *Symbol Sourcebook* (1972) and Rudolf Modley's *Handbook of Pictorial Symbols* (1976) are both explorations into the process of finding an internationally recognizable system of signs, and are indispensable sources of graphic symbols. Collections of logos and logotypes have been regularly published since the 1970s – one of the earliest and perhaps without equal is Yasaburo Kuwayama's *Trade Marks & Symbols* (1973), which is organized in alphabetical and pictorial groupings, complete with a thorough cross-referenced index.

The need to educate has been a constant in graphic design publishing, and thanks to the revolving door of students in need of guidance these books remain in demand. The most successful 'Instructional' books have been authored by some of the foremost design educators; Armin Hofmann's *Graphic Design Manual* (1965) offers the purest analysis of graphic form published and a system of graphic exercises that still resonates in teaching today. His colleague at the Allgemeine Gewerbeschule in Basel, Emil Ruder, wrote the book *Typography* (1967), which became the defining textbook on the subject. W.A. Dwiggins's *Layout in Advertising* (1928) was one of the first books to explain the role and methods of the new graphic design profession, a template for design that, excepting the impact of technological advances in production, has changed remarkably little in the intervening years. A small format guide to fundamental graphic standards, John Lewis's *Typography: Basic Principles* (1963) was an important book, in no small part because of Lewis's belief that an understanding of the history of graphic design was needed before embarking on the design itself.

It would be 20 years before a fully fledged account of the origins and development of graphic design was published. *A History of Graphic Design* (1983) by Philip B. Meggs is the benchmark for all subsequent histories of the subject, tracing the full story of graphic design from the earliest forms of writing to the present day. Lesser in scope and more compact in size, Richard Hollis's *Graphic Design: A Concise History* (1994) is essential reading, and benefits from its well-conceived integration of text and image. As a pictorial survey, the visual feast of Edward Booth-Clibborn and Daniele Baroni's *The Language of Graphics* (1990) is hard to top, its super-saturated colour pages containing top-to-bottom images throughout.

Compiling the work of graphic designers with a common purpose creates books that are contemporary in character. The best of these books in the 'Anthologies' section foster their own historical context; the growing awareness of corporate identity is captured in *Seven Designers Look at Trademark Design* (1952) edited by Egbert Jacobson, and the start of a diverse international design industry is to be found in *Graphic Design: Visual Comparisons* (1963) by Alan Fletcher, Colin Forbes and Bob Gill, which pairs different design solutions with common problems. *Typography Now* (1991), written by Rick Poynor, with its collection of deconstructed typography, signalled a revolution in type design and layout in the 1990s.

In 1947 Paul Rand published *Thoughts on Design*, a seminal book that proclaimed his unique mixture of art and advertising, setting the standard for graphic design monographs to follow. Work not only had to be of a high standard, it had to come with a point of view and sense of purpose, elevating the contents above a mere portfolio of work. Milton Glaser's *Graphic Design* (1973) and George Lois's *The Art of Advertising* (1977) not only showcase their respective subjects' prodigious talents, they are also records of American popular culture. Stories remain important, whether Wolfgang Weingart's journeys through typography in *Weingart: Typography* (2000), Paula Scher's urge to reinvent herself creatively in *Make it Bigger* (2002) or the tragic tale of Robert Brownjohn's lifelong battle with addiction told in Emily King's *Robert Brownjohn: Sex and Typography* (2005).

A portion of a book's success must also be attributed to its packaging and layout. It comes as no surprise that the books in *Bibliographic* are excellent examples of their craft. Changing use of formats, different paper stocks and new binding techniques are all in evidence. The quality of printing, particularly from the Swiss publishers such as Arthur Niggli in the 1960s, is matched by the production values behind books from publishers such as Lars Müller Publishers and Hyphen Press today.

Trying to present the correct bibliographical details has been an arduous task. For each book there is information on the original publication: title, author, publisher, date and place of publication. Page trim size is given, height first, then width, together with a total page count, measured from endpaper to endpaper including all frontmatter and endmatter. Where it is provided, the designer's credit is listed. In the cases of books published simultaneously in multiple locations we have listed the credits on the pictured book and mentioned other known editions within the text – any updates are welcome. Within each section the books are arranged in chronological order by their publication dates.

Bibliographic is a book about experiencing books, not about collecting. The books were nearly all supplied from designers' libraries. They have been regularly used and many show the scars of these labours. Some are missing jackets and, while an effort has been made to try and obtain original editions of each title, some of the books pictured are from subsequent reprints in which no significant changes have been made to the fabric of the book. They are important assets in the understanding of graphic design and valuable tools in the shaping of its future.

Typography

RAILROAD GOTHIC

120 Point 3 A $11 25

CAMEO

96 Point 3 A $9 00

LEMONS

84 Point 3 A $6 85

FOUNDING

72 Point 3 A $5 40

HORSE CAR

60 Point 3 A $4 75

GOLD MINERS

54 Point 4 A $4 25

CHIMES MUSIC

406

RAILROAD GOTHIC

48 Point 4 A $3 75

BEST MECHANIC

42 Point 5 A $3 25

TRADING PRINTER

36 Point 6 A $2 75

SHINING DAUGHTERS

30 Point 8 A $2 50

RAILROAD CHANGES TIME

24 Point 11 A $2 50

PERFECTION IN TYPEFOUNDING

18 Point 15 A $2 00

ADAPTED TO HIGHEST CLASS OF WORK
PLAIN GOTHICS ESSENTIAL

14 Point 19 A $1 75

MEMBERS OF CONGRESS PROCLAIMING REFORMS
TARIFF REVISION BEING AGITATED

12 Point 20 A $1 50

PRINTING OFFICES SUPPLIED WITH MODERN IDEAS
EXPENSES $1234567890& REDUCED

10 Point No. 2 24 A $1 40

KEEPS PACE WITH DEVELOPED
IDEAS OF MODERN ART
AND EXISTING CONDITIONS

10 Point No. 1 30 A $1 40

HANDSOME BURLESQUE PERFORMER
DEMANDS RECOGNITION
OF UNAPPRECIATIVE AUDIENCE

8 Point No. 2 26 A $1 25

DISCUSSING INTERESTING PROPOSITIONS
FRENCH DIPLOMATS AND
REPRESENTATIVE AMERICAN MEN

8 Point No. 1 30 A $1 25

REMARKABLE KLEPTOMANIAC PERFORMANCES
PRACTICED BY PICKPOCKETS
DURING HOLIDAY SEASON PURCHASES

6 Point No. 5 36 A $1 00

PROFESSOR LIGHTFOOT ANNOUNCES A SERIES OF LESSONS IN
THE GRACEFUL ART OF TERPSICHORE
TO WHICH ALL AWKWARD BUMPKINS ARE INVITED FREE

6 Point No. 4 42 A $1 00

BRAINS AND MONEY WHEN JUDICIOUSLY EXPENDED IN ADVERTISING
BRING RESULTS FAR MORE BENEFICIAL THAN
USUALLY ACCOUNTED TO THE SPLATTERING HAPHAZARD

6 Point No. 3 and 6 Point No. 2 in preparation

407

HEADING CONDENSED

MEANDERING CANDIDATE

DOUBTING THOMAS PRESENT

STORMY WEATHER PREDICTIONS

ABSORBING PRESIDENTAL ELECTIONS

MUCH INTEREST DISPLAYED BY DELEGATION

MUCH REMODELED BEFORE HEADED BY MERCHANTS

QUICK DELIVERIES MADE FROM MANY SELLING HOUSES
ENABLE PRINTERS TO REPLENISH

THOROUGHNESS IN DETAIL BECOMES SECOND NATURE TO MANY
CAREFUL AND THOUGHTFUL PRINTERS

THERE IS FAR MORE VALUE IN DISTINCTIVE TYPES THAN MERE CHANCE
OF CHARACTERISTIC DISPLAY MASTER PRINTER

AMERICAN PRINTERS ARE IN THE LEAD WORKING WITH AMERICAN TYPES AND IN A
LAND WHERE GOOD PRINTING FLOWS LIKE MILK AND HONEY

420

HEADING CONDENSED

NEW MONEY FOR OLD
AT SUB-TREASURY

KIND UNCLE SAM HAS EXPRESSED THERE $3,000,000
FOR CHRISTMAS PRESENTS

A Christmas gift in cash, whether to your wife or your bootblack, is received with greater appreciation when the banknotes are crisp or the coin new and shining.

Uncle Sam, who is a sort of Santa Claus, knows this, so he has sent $3,000,000 in freshly-engraved yellow and greenbacks and newly-coined gold pieces to the Wall street Sub-Treasury.

"New money for old" is now the Aladdin-like cry there. But no one can get more than $300 in new money without paying a small premium—the express charges on it from the mints to the Sub-Treasury.

Uncle Sam, who loves all his children, demands this premium so that any fellow will have a chance to get a bright $5 gold piece and put it in baby's bank.

SUNDAY THRONG IN HOT CHASE

ROBBERS CAUGHT AT WORK IN A WOODLAWN HOTEL FLEE, WITH BULLETS FROM
PURSUING POLICE FLYING ALL ABOUT THEM

PROPRIETOR HAS APOPLECTIC STROKE FROM SHOCK AND FRIGHT

TO OBTAIN BEST RESULTS USE
HOOSIER
BAKING
POWDER
THE GROCERYMAN SELLS IT

RUNAWAY DRIVES
THROUGH WINDOW

HORSE CRASHES THROUGH PLATE GLASS
AND POKES NOSE IN DRUG STORE
SHOW WINDOW

While Adolph Slotskin, a druggist at the corner of Park and Bond streets, was chatting with two men in his store yesterday morning a big gray horse entered the place by crashing through the large plate glass window filled with all

Body in 8 Point Century Expanded

421

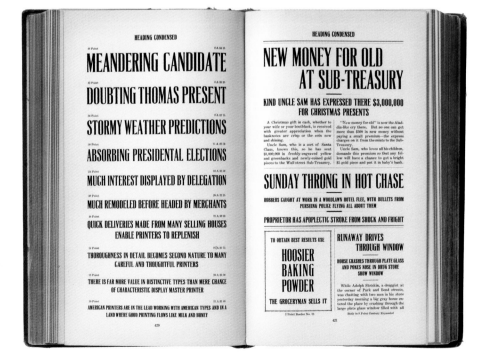

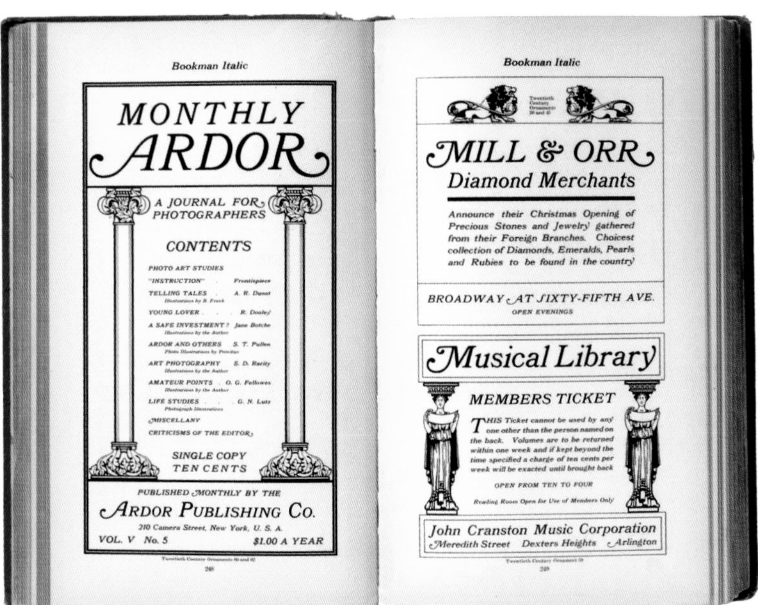

Potential applications of Bookman Italic are displayed to aid buyers in their choice of typeface. The designs also promote the decorative material ATF had on offer.

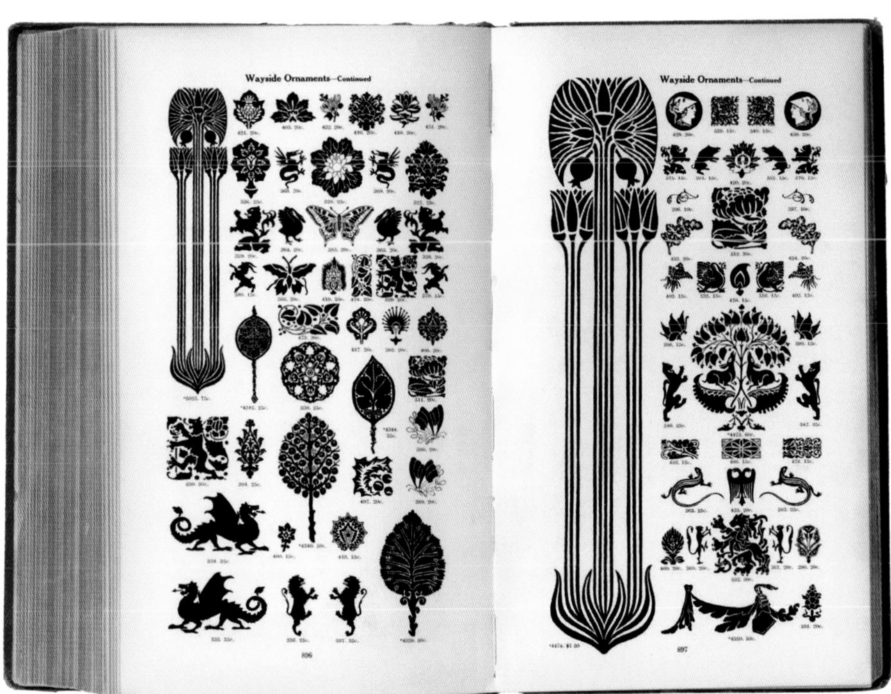

Decorative material and borders are displayed in a section at the rear of the book.

American Line Type Book

Borders and Ornaments, Price-List, Printing Machinery and Material
American Type Founders Company, New York, 1906
1184 pages
262 × 155 mm (10.25 × 6 in)

Formed in 1892 as an amalgam of 23 type foundries, by the turn of the century the American Type Founders Company (ATF) had become the world's leading producer of type. Its first large specimen book was produced in 1896 and further versions were issued in 1906, 1912 and 1923. The catalogues contained a prodigious amount of material: type specimens, rules, borders and ornaments, alongside a range of printing tools and machinery.

To fit in all this material the catalogues were inevitably substantial – the 1912 version, often referred to as 'Big Red', contained over 1300 pages and was the largest the company produced. Despite their size they did not list all the available ATF typefaces; rather, they reflected what was popular in the marketplace.

The 1906 book has its feet still planted firmly in the nineteenth century; its ornate cover with black lettertype and an image of an early printer by his printing press studying a book is pure Victoriana. The page layouts are highly decorative and skilfully composed, with type displayed both in sample text and through renderings of fictitious advertisements, trade cards and newspaper columns. An extensive section on decorative materials includes borders, ornaments and numerous cuts and decorated initials.

ATF was keen to promote the relatively novel concept of font 'families'. Typefaces such as Cheltenham, Century Expanded, Copperplate Gothic, Alternate Gothic and Jenson were all offered in multiple variations. Wood type and borders were still available but were placed discreetly towards the rear of the book.

Mac McGrew's *American Metal Typefaces of the Twentieth Century* (The Myriade Press, New Rochelle, 1986; revised 1996) and Alexander Lawson's *Anatomy of a Typeface* (David R. Godine, Publisher, Boston, 1990) provide excellent commentaries on the specimens of the many American type foundries in the early twentieth century.

Spécimen Général: Tome 1
Fonderies Deberny & Peignot, Paris, 1926
Unpaginated
250 × 180 mm (9.875 × 7.125 in)
Designed by Maximilien Vox

Probably the most elegant type specimen book ever produced, the 1926 catalogue for the French type foundry Deberny & Peignot is a stunning showcase of the company's numerous fonts, cuts and borders. It was issued shortly after the 1925 'Exposition Internationale des Arts Décoratifs et Industriels Modernes' in Paris, from which Art Deco took its name, and shows how the foundry was at the forefront of this contemporary trend, offering a range of modern typefaces and decorative materials to supplement its large range of classic fonts.

The company's artistic direction was headed by its proprietor Charles Peignot (1897–1983), who forged links with France's leading commercial artists. He wanted the advances in other forms of the arts to be repeated in Deberny & Peignot's typographic output – in particular, the kind of decorative modern letterforms seen in the ground-breaking work of poster artists such as A.M. Cassandre (who would later design the Peignot font named after Charles) and Jean Carlu.

Peignot collaborated closely with the art director and critic Maximilien Vox (1894–1974), who designed the 1926 catalogue. Most notable are his striking designs in a mixture of hand-drawn lettering, illustrations and set type that decorate the tabulated dividers for each of the ten sections. Vox would later work with Peignot on the elaborate specimen guides *Les Divertissements Typographiques* first produced by the foundry in 1928; circulated in the printing trade, these were an important influence on the graphic arts of the time.

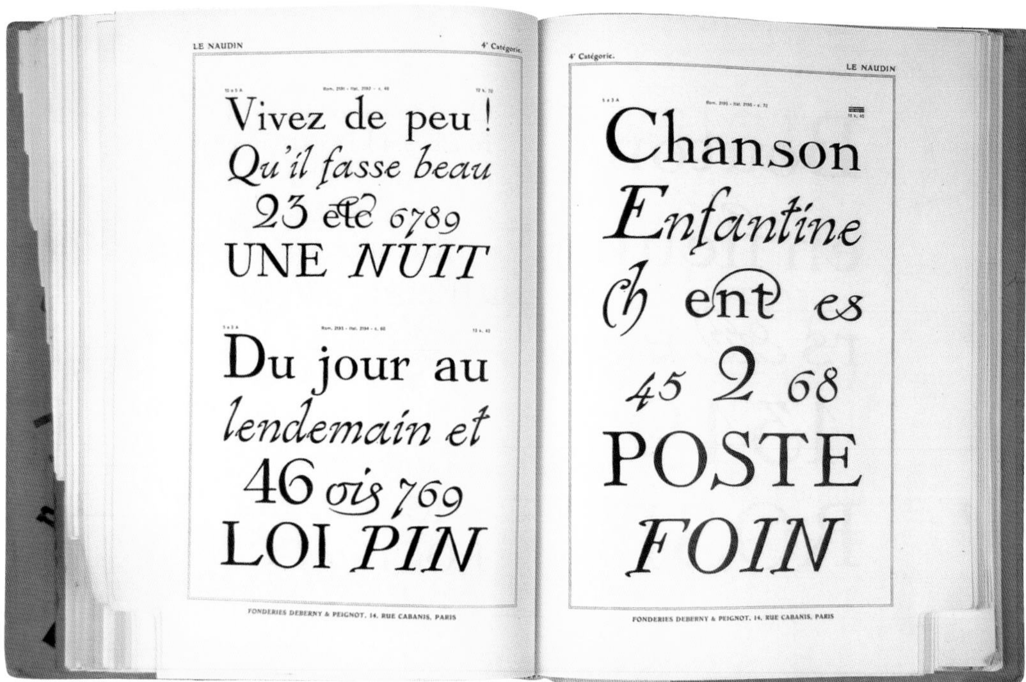

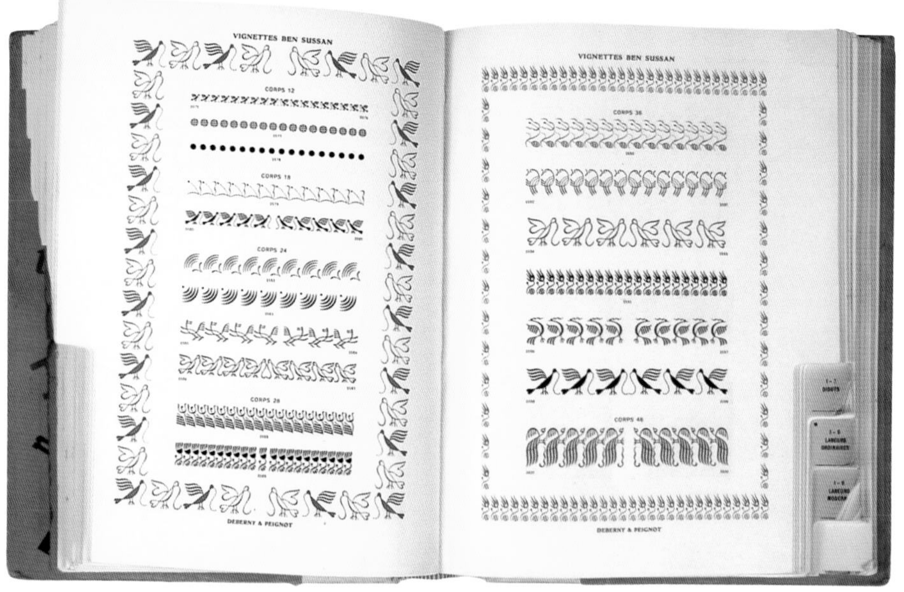

The tabulated section dividers are a highlight of the catalogue – more can be seen in Steven Heller and Louise Fili's French Modern *(Chronicle Books, San Francisco, 1997).*

Typomundus 20, The International Center for the Typographic Arts (ITCA), Reinhold Publishing Corporation, New York, 1966
The New Graphic Art, Karl Gerstner, Markus Kutter, Hastings House, New York, 1959
Campo Grafico: 1933–1939, Electa Editrice, Milan, 1983
Typography, Aaron Burns, Reinhold Publishing Corporation, New York, 1961
Ladislav Sutnar, Iva Janáková, Museum of Decorative Arts and Argo Publishers, Prague, 2003
World Geo-Graphic Atlas: A Composite of Man's Environment, Herbert Bayer, Container Corporation of America, Chicago, 1953
Die Deutsche Werbe Graphik, Dr Walter F. Schubert, Verlag Francken & Lang, Berlin, 1927
Bauhaus: Drucksachen, Typografie, Reklame, Gerd Fleischmann, Edition Marzona, Dusseldorf, 1984
Spécimen Général: Tome 1, Fonderies Deberny & Peignot, Paris, 1926
The Encyclopaedia of Type Faces, W. Turner Berry, A.F. Johnson, W.P. Jaspert, revised edition, Blandford Press, London, 1958

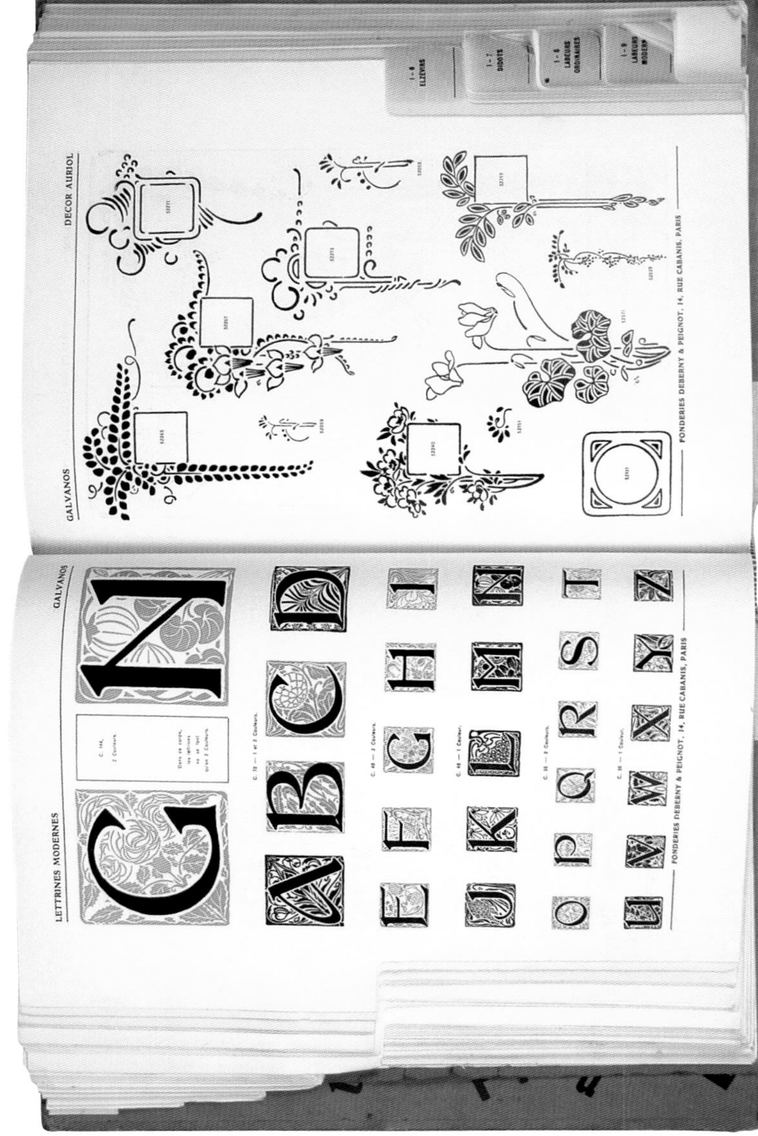

The decorative endpapers designed by Maximilien Vox used the range of typefaces on offer from Deberny & Peignot.

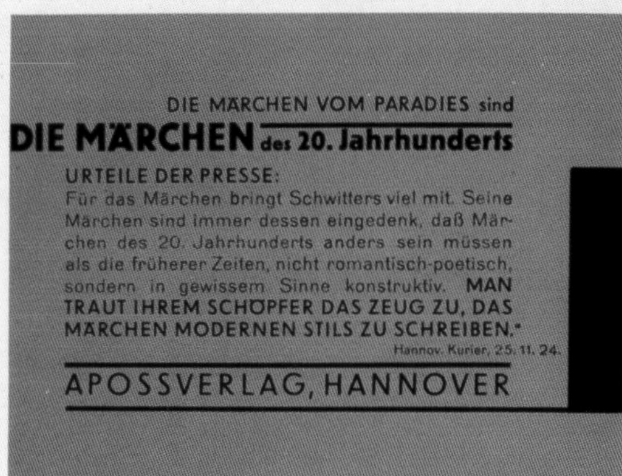

DIE MÄRCHEN VOM PARADIES sind
DIE MÄRCHEN des 20. Jahrhunderts
URTEILE DER PRESSE:
Für das Märchen bringt Schwitters viel mit. Seine Märchen sind immer dessen eingedenk, daß Märchen des 20. Jahrhunderts anders sein müssen als die früherer Zeiten, nicht romantisch-poetisch, sondern in gewissem Sinne konstruktiv. MAN TRAUT IHREM SCHÖPFER DAS ZEUG ZU, DAS MÄRCHEN MODERNEN STILS ZU SCHREIBEN."
Hannov. Kurier, 25. 11. 24.
APOSSVERLAG, HANNOVER

KURT SCHWITTERS:
Werbezettel (Originalformat). Schwarze Schrift auf blauem Papier.

und auch dies bietet viele Vorteile. Grundsätzlich sind als Formate für Werbsachen alle Größen der A-Reihe gegeben; indessen ist eine Beschränkung auf wenige notwendig. Die Hauptformate sind auch hier A 4 (210×297 mm) und A 5 (148×210 mm).

Die künstlerischen Möglichkeiten werden durch das Normformat, das ein sehr gutes Seitenverhältnis zeigt, nicht eingeschränkt. Das beweist nicht zuletzt die große Menge von Abbildungen nach Drucksachen im Normformat, die dieses Buch enthält. Jedenfalls ist es meist ein Zeichen von mangelnden Fähigkeiten, wenn man „aus künstlerischen Gründen" an der Forderung eines bestimmten Nicht-Normformats unbedingt festhält.

Formgestaltung

Die graphische Gestalt einer Werbsache hängt in hohem Maße von der werblichen Qualität des Textes ab. Man sollte die Textgestaltung stets einem Werbefachmann anvertrauen; denn die Reklame ist heute eine Wissenschaft geworden, deren Gebiete der Laie nicht ungestraft betritt. Ein schlechter Text kann die Wirksamkeit des Ganzen in Frage stellen.

Beschränkt sich die Werbsache auf die bloße Schrift, so kommt es darauf an, eine wirksame und neuartige typographische Form zu finden. Die ausgezeichnete Werbekarte für die Kubin-Ausstellung von Walter Dexel beweist,

156

KUNSTVEREIN JENA
PRINZESSINNENSCHLÖSSCHEN
3. BIS 31. MAI 1925

ALFRED KUBIN
AQUARELLE
ZEICHNUNGEN
LITHOGRAPHIEN

MITTWOCHS UND SONNABENDS 3—5 SONNTAGS 11—1
AUSSER DER ZEIT FÜHRUNG DURCH DEN HAUSMEISTER

WALTER DEXEL: Werbekarte im Normformat A 6. Original: Schwarze Schrift auf blauem Karton.

157

Examples of the contrived layouts and over-elaborate letterforms of which Tschichold disapproved.

Die Neue Typographie

Jan Tschichold

Verlag des Bildungsverbandes der Deutschen Buchdrucker, Berlin, 1928
240 pages
210 × 148 mm (8.25 × 5.875 in)
Designed by Jan Tschichold

Written and designed by the German designer Jan Tschichold (1902–1974), *Die Neue Typographie* ('The New Typography') is the definitive text on the movement that bears its name, and is a landmark in graphic design history.

Trained as a calligrapher, Tschichold had become a convert to the new typographical style of sans serif type and asymmetric layouts emanating from the Bauhaus. He had also been dismayed by the outmoded state of the printing trade, and *Die Neue Typographie* is a practical handbook for printers as well as a study of the history and theory of this young movement in typography.

Tschichold illustrates his discussion of the basic elements of the New Typography with examples of his own work, and also with designs by Kurt Schwitters, Willi Baumeister, Piet Zwart and Paul Schuitema, among others. He assesses the use of white space and contrast in layout; the importance of photography as a communication medium; and promotes standardization through the adoption of the DIN (Deutsche Industrie Norm or German Industrial Standard) formats of paper sizes. Lessons in asymmetric design include diagrams that show how not to lay out a page.

This original edition is in German only. The first English-language version, translated by Ruari McLean, was published as late as 1995 by the University of California Press, and included a scholarly introduction by Robin Kinross. A reprint in 1987 by Verlag Brinkman und Bose is a faithful reproduction of the original, packaged inside a grey slipcase with a supplement containing illustrated essays by Tschichold, Werner Doede and Gerd Fleischmann.

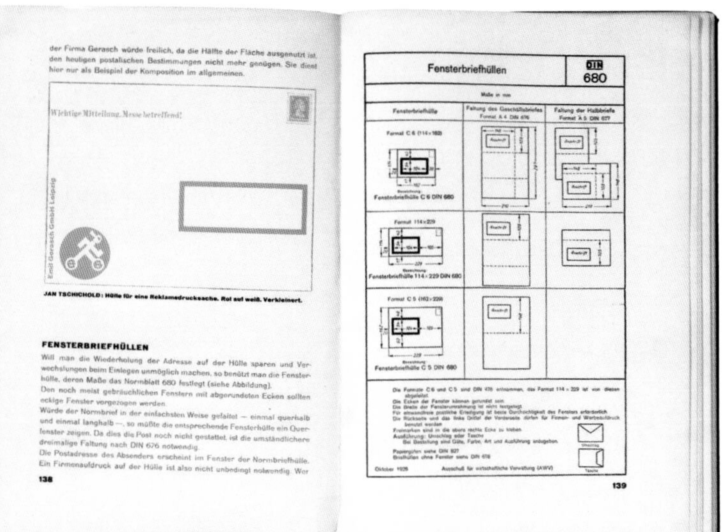

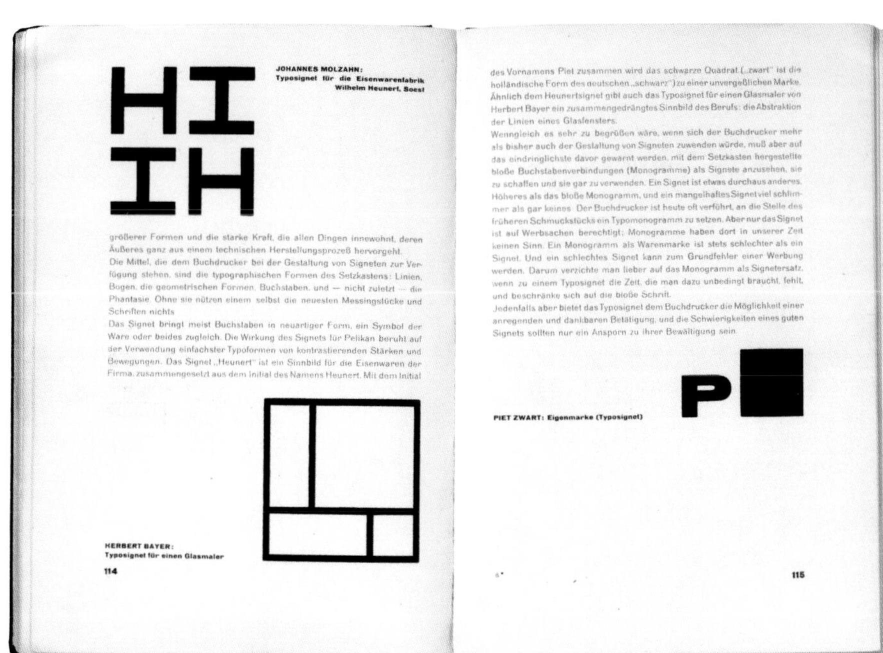

Trademarks and symbols by Johannes Molzahn, Herbert Bayer and Piet Zwart.

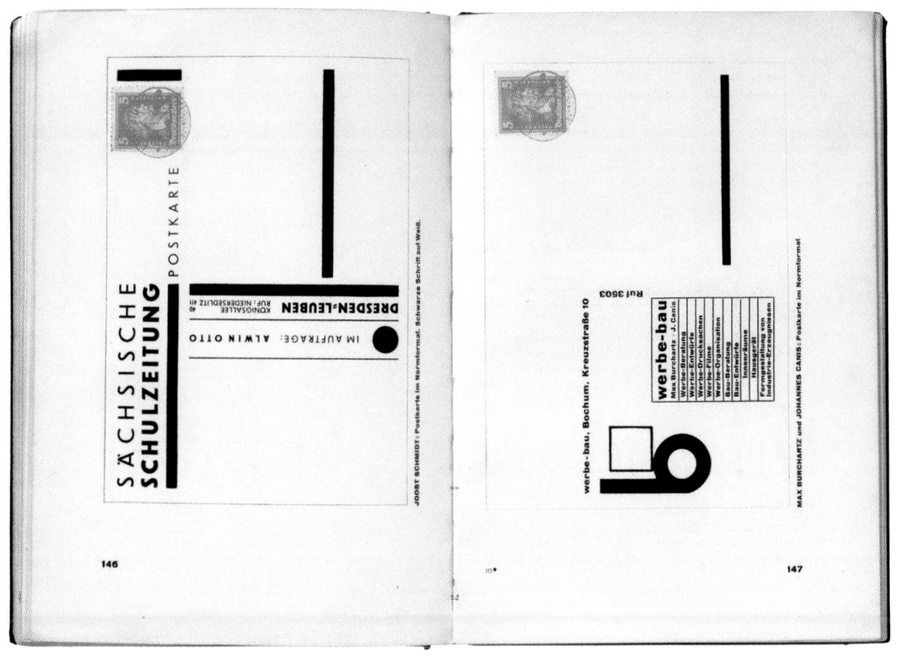

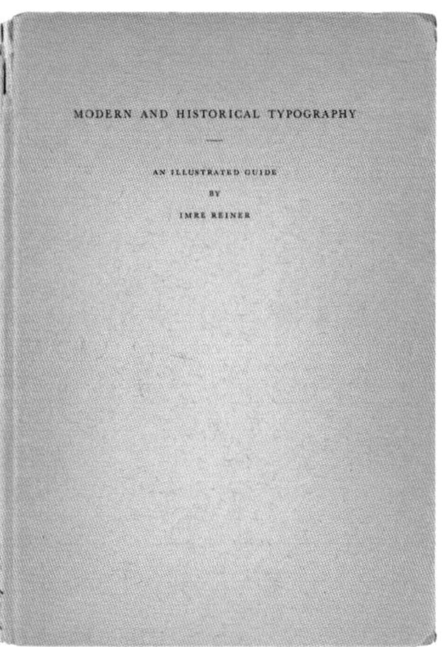

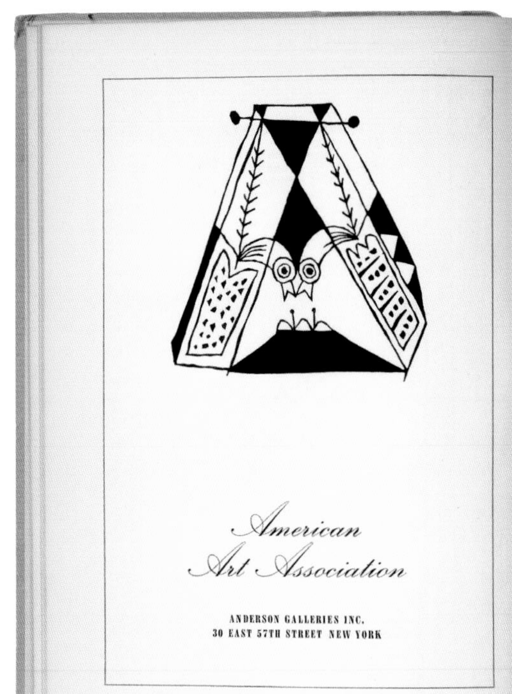

American
Art Association
ANDERSON GALLERIES INC.
30 EAST 57TH STREET NEW YORK

Cover of a booklet

TRADE AND BUSINESS CARDS

Trade and business cards are the representatives of commercial firms or their proxies. They come as ambassadors and must be designed to enhance the reputation of the firms they represent, at the same time illustrating the character and special features of a company's business.

The designer of a business card is faced with the task of combining its psychological and typographic purposes and effects. Every sketch of a projected business card must be judeged both for its practical and for its aesthetic values. Thus, the business card of an industrial firm which deals chiefly with architects and builders should make use of the latest techniques and be clear and concise, much more so than the card of a storekeeper who looks for customers among all classes of society. In both these cases, however, a clear-cut layout of the text is essential.

Often business cards must be designed for firms whose goods are to be recommended as "hailing from the good old times." This frequently occurs in the case of tobaccos, wines and spirits, certain kinds of cosmetics (eau de Cologne and lavender water, for example), handmade paper, linen and even a considerable number of pharmaceutical products, especially old household remedies. Most of these firms, take pride in their old, established traditions. This means, of course, the application of specific typographic media in the design of their business cards, to assure the effect of age and tradition.

Sometimes the use of an illustration, such as a signet or a registered trade-mark, is required or seems desirable. The figure and the printed matter in such cases should be made to fit together with an appropriate type style and matching colors.

To facilitate the organization of the layout, it is advisable first to cut the copy apart into units. Then an outline of the actual size and shape of the card should be sketched. By moving the cut-out units of copy around within this outline, the typographer can easily obtain the desired impression.

Business cards should be given more care and thought than any other kind of stationery except letter-heads. There are few things which give a salesman more con-

27

Reiner's distinctive calligraphic letterforms and woodcuts are scattered throughout the book.

SHENVAL PRESS NEWS LETTER

2

CONTENTS

EDITORIAL, FINE PAPERS FOR PRINT

RE-PLAN BOOK MAKING

WHO DESIGNS TYPOGRAPHY

THE SHENVAL PRESS, HERTFORD, HERTS.

ENGLAND

Front of news letter

Kardomah
KEE-MUN
An elegant
Drawing Room China Tea
4/4 per Pound

Packaging

Modern and Historical Typography
An Illustrated Guide
Imre Reiner
Paul A. Struck, New York, 1946
128 pages
239 × 170 mm (9.375 × 6.75 in)

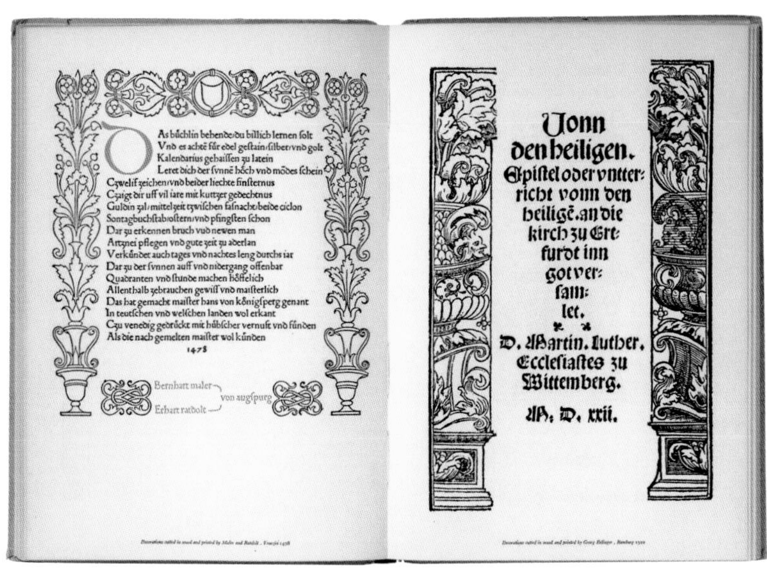

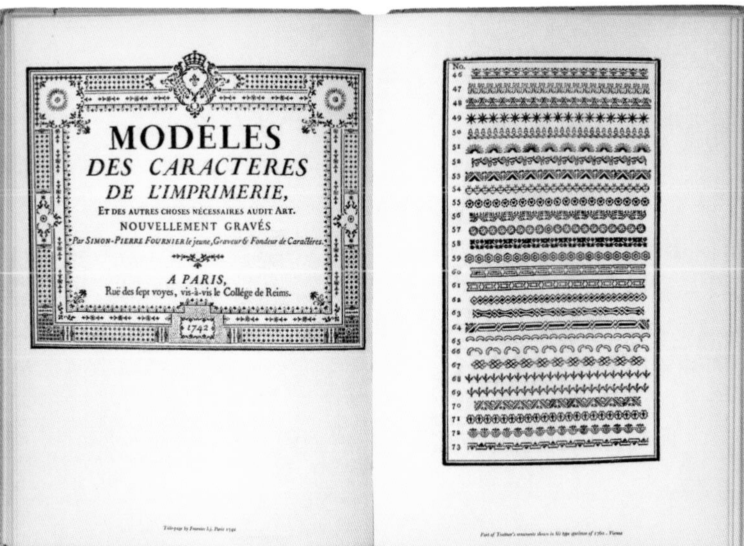

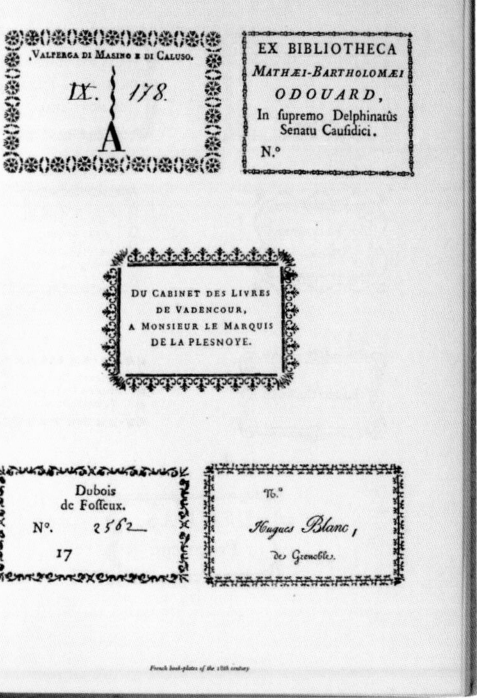

A spread of eighteenth-century French bookplates showing varying degrees of ornamentation.

A forgotten man in graphic design histories, Imre Reiner (1900–1987) was a craftsman with multiple talents in the graphic arts. Born in Hungary, he lived in Europe and the United States before settling in Switzerland in 1931. He was a calligrapher, type designer, illustrator, wood engraver, graphic designer and author.

Reiner was not part of any discernible trend, and deliberately avoided being labelled as such. He believed that a modern approach to design should be achieved not by a rejection of the past but through work of lasting significance that was unafraid to reference it. He positively embraced ornament as a design element without ever allowing it to overpower his measured layouts. The whimsically constructed calligraphic letterforms he drew are the most noteworthy items in his prolific output and are much in evidence in the book.

Modern and Historical Typography places his work among that of his antecedents in the history of the printed arts. It is split into chapters, each of which has a brief introduction by Reiner and deals with a different aspect of a designer's work, such as title pages, trade cards and billheads. Illustrations of historical typography are followed, in some cases, by examples of Reiner's work in the relevant subject area.

Printed letterpress in black and Reiner's trademark vermilion, this is an arbitrary and engaging collection of mostly jobbing printing, together with some fine typographic specimens from varying sources that give a clue to Reiner's creative influences. His own work sits comfortably in these surroundings without being derivative.

The Letter as a Work of Art

Observations and Confrontations with Contemporaneous Expressions of Art from Roman Times to the Present Day

Dr Gerard Knuttel

Amsterdam Typefoundry, Amsterdam, 1951

272 pages

360 × 265 mm (14.125 × 10.5 in)

Published in 1951 to coincide with the centennial of the Amsterdam Typefoundry (formerly known as N. Tetterode), *The Letter as a Work of Art* is a collection of historical typographic specimens that have been carefully paired with cultural artworks of the relevant eras. As the splendid subtitle suggests, the aim was to put typography in an artistic perspective where it could be compared and contrasted with works of art and architecture.

There can be no doubt that this was a serious academic venture on the part of the author, but the book's real value is measured in artistic terms. Both the typographic specimens and artworks have been expertly selected, and the pairings take on an ethereal quality that needs little explanation.

In many cases the links between typeface and artwork are clear: a 1783 specimen of 'Early French-classicistic roman' in a book on art printed by François-Ambroise Didot sits next to a painting of 1800 by the neoclassical artist Jacques-Louis David. Other pairings are implied rather than immediately obvious, but are nevertheless effective. For example, there is a compositional similarity between a specimen of roman text by William Caslon, printed by the Clarendon Press in 1750, and the London fireplace built between 1686 and 1688 that it faces, but little else concrete to link the two – yet both seem to work well in unison.

This unique viewpoint, which looks at a rarely explored historical aspect of the place of typography in the cultural landscape, is helped considerably by high production values. The illustrations are printed in gravure and the reproductions have been carefully balanced to keep similar tonal ranges throughout the book.

Originally published in a Dutch-language format, the book contains five chapters that study letters in chronological order from Roman inscriptions to mid-twentieth-century examples.

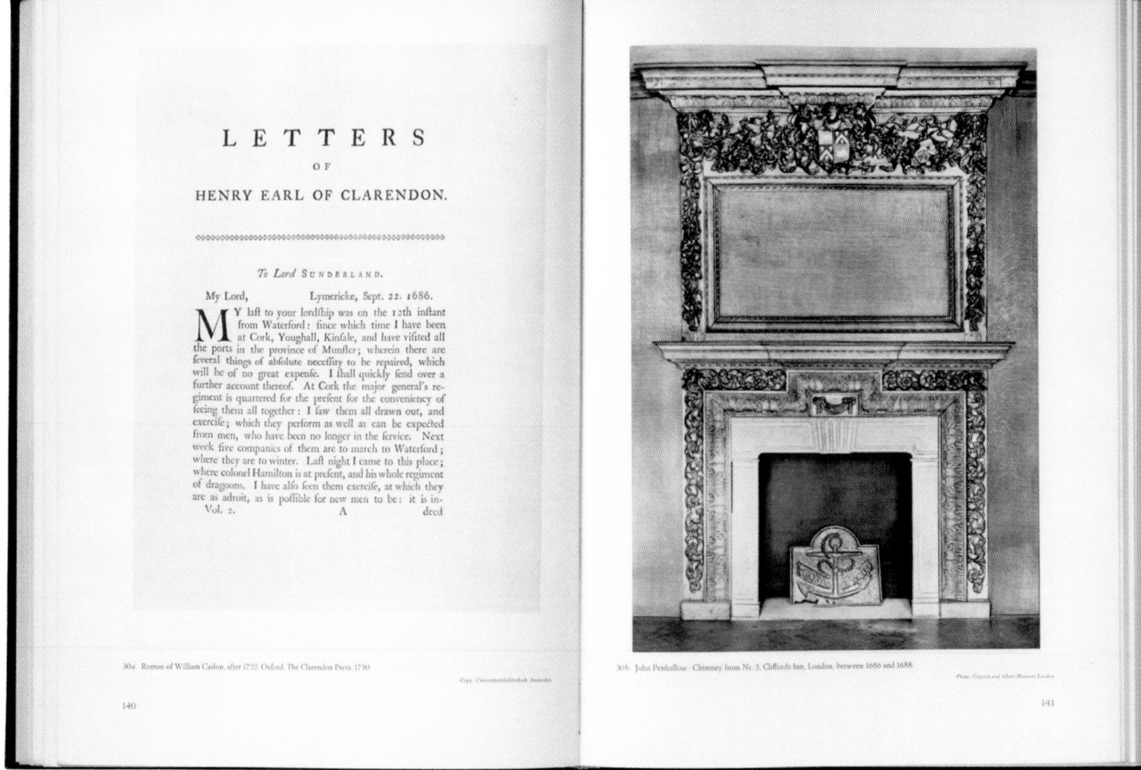

LETTERS
OF
HENRY EARL OF CLARENDON.

To Lord SUNDERLAND.

My Lord, Lymericke, Sept. 22. 1686.

MY laſt to your lordſhip was on the 12th inſtant from Waterford: ſince which time I have been at Cork, Youghall, Kinſale, and have viſited all the ports in the province of Munſter; wherein there are ſeveral things of abſolute neceſſity to be repaired, which will be of no great expenſe. I ſhall quickly ſend over a further account thereof. At Cork the major general's regiment is quartered for the preſent for the conveniency of ſeeing them all together: I ſaw them all drawn out, and exerciſe; which they perform as well as can be expected from men, who have been no longer in the ſervice. Next week five companies of them are to march to Waterford; where they are to winter. Laſt night I came to this place; where colonel Hamilton is at preſent, and his whole regiment of dragoons. I have alſo ſeen them exerciſe, at which they are as adroit, as is poſſible for new men to be: it is in-

Vol. 2. A deed

30*a*. Roman of William Caslon, after 1722. Oxford, The Clarendon Press, 1730

140

30*b*. John Penhallow: Chimney from Nr. 3, Cliffords Inn, London, between 1686 and 1688

141

The illustrated spreads all follow the same format: left-hand pages contain a type specimen and right-hand pages a contemporary piece of art or architecture. Below is an example by Firmin Didot from 1807, placed with Anne-Louis Girodet de Roucy-Trioson's Burial of Atala *of 1808.*

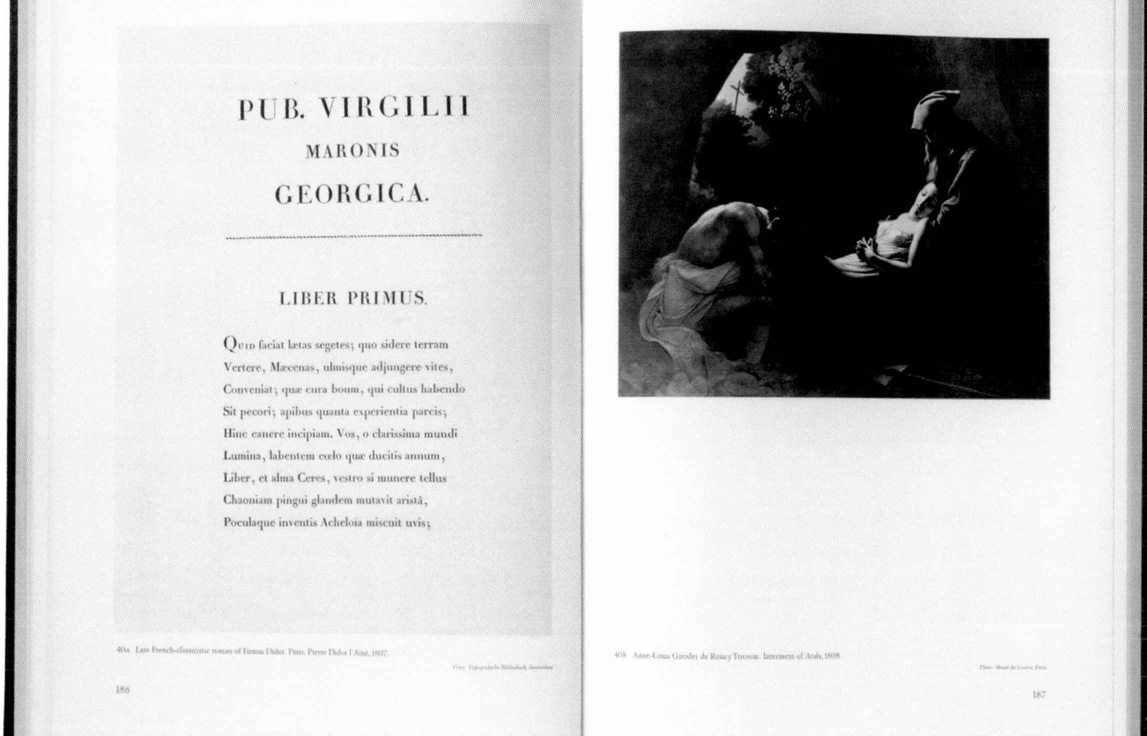

PUB. VIRGILII
MARONIS
GEORGICA.

LIBER PRIMUS.

Quid faciat lætas segetes; quo sidere terram
Vertere, Mæcenas, ulmisque adjungere vites,
Conveniat; quæ cura boum, qui cultus habendo
Sit pecori; apibus quanta experientia parcis;
Hinc canere incipiam. Vos, o clarissima mundi
Lumina, labentem cœlo quæ ducitis annum,
Liber, et alma Ceres, vestro si munere tellus
Chaoniam pingui glandem mutavit aristâ,
Poculaque inventis Acheloia miscuit uvis;

40*a*. Late French-classicistic roman of Firmin Didot. Paris, Pierre Didot l'Aîné, 1807.

186

40*b*. Anne-Louis Girodet de Roucy Trioson: Interment of Atala, 1808

187

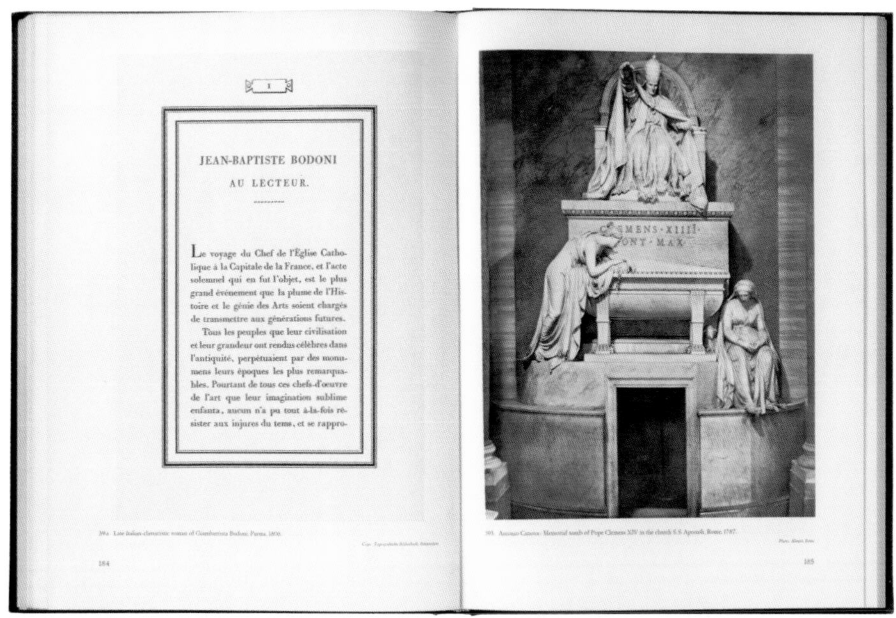

1

JEAN-BAPTISTE BODONI

AU LECTEUR.

Le voyage du Chef de l'Église Catholique à la Capitale de la France, et l'acte solemnel qui en fut l'objet, est le plus grand événement que la plume de l'Histoire et le génie des Arts soient chargés de transmettre aux générations futures.

Tous les peuples que leur civilisation et leur grandeur ont rendus célèbres dans l'antiquité, perpétuaient par des monumens leurs époques les plus remarquables. Pourtant de tous ces chefs-d'oeuvre de l'art que leur imagination sublime enfanta, aucun n'a pu tout à-la-fois résister aux injures du tems, et se rappro-

The cover has been finished with gold foil and blind-debossed letterforms.

The first page from Milton's Areopagitica *with a title designed by Edward Johnston (Doves Press, Hammersmith, 1907) has been placed next to The Homestead, Frinton-on-Sea, by English architect Charles Voysey (c.1905).*

THEY WHO TO STATES AND GOVERNOURS OF THE COMMONWEALTH DIRECT THEIR SPEECH, HIGH COURT OF PARLAMENT, or wanting such accesse in a private condition, write that which they foresee may advance the publick good; I suppose them as at the beginning of no meane endeavour, not a little alter'd & mov'd inwardly in their mindes: Some with doubt of what will be the successe, others with feare of what will be the censure; some with hope, others with confidence of what they have to speake. And me perhaps each of these dispositions, as the subject was whereon I enter'd, may have at other times variously affected; & likely might in these formost expressions now also disclose which of them sway'd most, but that the very attempt of this addresse thus made, and the thought of whom it hath recourse to, hath got the power within me to a passion, farre more welcome then incidentall to a Preface. Which though I stay not to confesse ere any aske, I shall be blamelesse, if it be no other, then the joy & gratulation which it brings to all who wish and promote their Countries liberty; whereof this whole Discourse propos'd will be a certaine testimony, if not a Trophey. For this is not the liberty which wee can hope, that no grievance ever should arise in the Commonwealth, that let no man in this

8

Art Without Boundaries: 1950–1970, Gerald Woods, Philip Thompson, John Williams, Thames & Hudson, London, 1972
Cultural Calendar of the Twentieth Century, Edward Lucie-Smith, Phaidon Press, London, 1979
Fraktur Mon Amour, Judith Schalansky, Hermann Schmidt, Mainz, 2006
Pioneers of Modern Typography, Herbert Spencer, Lund Humphries, London, 1969
Jan Tschichold: Typographer, Ruari McLean, Lund Humphries, London, 1975
Art as Design, Design as Art: A Contemporary Guide, Sterling McIlhany, Studio Vista, London, 1970
Piet Zwart, Fridolin Müller (editor), Verlag Niggli, Teufen, 1966
The Letter as a Work of Art, Dr Gerard Knuttel, Amsterdam Typefoundry, Amsterdam, 1951
Leaving the Twentieth Century: The Incomplete Work of the Situationist International, Christopher Gray (editor), Free Fall, London, 1974
The Development of Writing, Hans Eduard Meyer, Graphis Press, Zurich, 1977

Zapf used a total of 60 typefaces in Manuale Typographicum, *all sourced from the D. Stempel AG type foundry in Frankfurt.*

ABCDEFGHIKLMN

RICHARD von SICHOWSKY Eine gute Druckschrift ist das Werk eines künstlerischen Menschen. Sie hat, so seltsam es klingen mag, eine eigene Lebendigkeit mitbekommen, oder besser, sie hat die Kraft mitbekommen, eine bestimmte, ihr entsprechende Lebendigkeit in dem Lesenden auszulösen

OPQRSTUVWXYZ

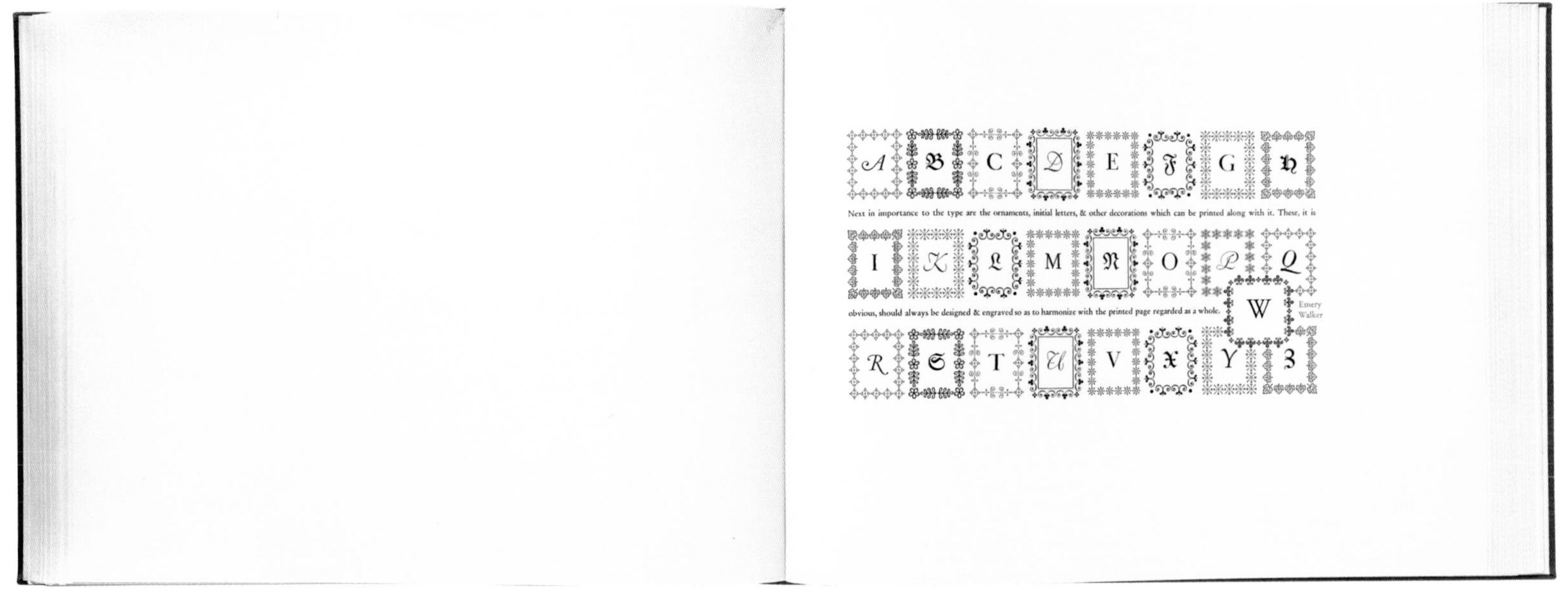

This copy of the Manuale Typographicum *is in the St Bride Printing Library in London. Given by Zapf to the typographer Stanley Morison, it comes enclosed in a hand-painted box with foiled lettering. The book itself is cloth-bound with a leather spine.*

Manuale Typographicum

Hermann Zapf

Georg Kurt Schauer,
Frankfurt am Main, 1954
114 pages
226 × 302 mm (9 × 11.875 in)
Designed by Hermann Zapf

Hermann Zapf (1918–) taught himself calligraphy. An admirer of fellow German calligrapher Rudolf Koch, he developed his talent to become one of the pre-eminent type designers of the twentieth century. His faces, such as Palatino, Melior and Optima, have been widely used – the last is often seen as overused. Although the traditional nature of his work was not in line with the constructed typography that was becoming dominant in Switzerland and Germany after the Second World War, Zapf's designs were thoroughly modern in outlook.

A tour de force of book design, *Manuale Typographicum* contains 100 quotes on typography from an arbitrary assortment of writers and designers, including Stanley Morison, Peter Behrens, Charles Dickens, W.A. Dwiggins, Victor Hugo and Eric Gill.

Zapf arranged each quote meticulously, using typefaces from the D. Stempel AG type foundry in Frankfurt. There are 60 faces in total and the quotes are in their original languages. Confined to the same area on each page, the designs are richly varied. An alphabet is effortlessly combined with each quotation. Information on the typeface used is given in an index at the back of the book.

Manuale Typographicum is printed letterpress on uncoated art paper, in black and China red with a third colour used solely for the pagination. There have been three main publications of the book, in 1954, 1968 and 1970. Some of these were also available in limited editions and with a variety of cover designs, making them hard for librarians to catalogue.

The Encyclopaedia of Type Faces
W. Turner Berry, A.F. Johnson, W.P. Jaspert
Blandford Press, London, 1953
Revised and enlarged edition (pictured), 1958
360 pages
247 × 182 mm (9.75 × 7.125 in)

The Encyclopaedia of Type Faces was first published partly because of the paucity of specimen catalogues being printed by type foundries after the Second World War. The large specimen books that advertised a foundry's wares were too expensive to produce in such austere times, so an audience of designers and printers was left with no clear way of knowing who was offering a particular typeface and what the type looked like.

It says much for the efforts of the encyclopaedia's three authors that it remains in print 50 years after it was first published. They decided not to try and produce a definitive collection (which could have been an endless task) but rather to 'classify representative specimens of every main type family'. Typical of the groupings they originally used are Venetian Romans, Old Faces and Eighteenth Century Transition Types. Typefaces are arranged alphabetically under the relevant headings.

Nor did they want to produce a history of typefaces, although, usefully, the entry for each one lists its origins, foundry and any available design credits (an index of designers was added to later editions). The authors' main interest, however, was in the distinguishing features of each specimen: noteworthy or unusual letterforms and similarities with other types are described in the brief accompanying text.

The centred layout is simple and functional: printed in black and white only, it clearly displays each typeface. Complete character sets are shown where possible, and, to add to the book's authenticity, efforts were made to have specimens printed directly from materials supplied by the foundries that produced them.

Originally jacketed, the boards of the second edition have a debossed 'a' on the front and 'z' on the back.

PLACARD

Monotype

A condensed sans serif with very short ascenders and descenders. The **M** is slightly splayed. The **g** has an open tail and the **t** is a cross. There are various weights, and a Titling.

For those interested in the Art of Fine Printing, there is nothing

PLACARD EXTRA LIGHT

For those interested in the Art of Fine Printing, there is

PLACARD MEDIUM

For those interested in the Art of Fine Printing

PLACARD BOLD No. 1

For those interested in the Art of Fine

PLACARD No. 2

RAZIONALE

Nebiolo

A condensed sans serif titling which is negative on a square mesh background. There are two versions, one with the background flush with the tops and feet of the letters, and the other one extending above and below the letters.

EDAD MODERNA

ALDO PIO MANUZIO IL VECCHIO

RAZIONALE

FREGIO RAZIONALE

FREGIO RAZIONALE

REFORM GROTESQUE

Stempel

The **A** has a low bar, **E** and **F** are wide, **M** is square and **R** has a wide and short bowl. There is a slight variation of colour in the lower case—but not in the light face. There are four weights, with some italics, condensed and extended faces. The design was modernised in the 1930's.

ABCDEFGHIJKLMNOPQRS

abcdefghijklmnopqrstuvz1234

REFORM GROTESQUE

190

ABCDEFGHIJKLMNOPQRST

REFORM GROTESQUE ITALIC

DEFGHIJKLMNOPQRSTUVWXY

abcdefghijklmnopqrstuvw1234567

ABCDEFGHIJKLMNOPQRSTUVW

REFORM GROTESQUE LIGHT

ABCDEFGHIJKLMNOPQR

abcdefghijklmnopq12345

REFORM GROTESQUE SEMI-BOLD

ABCDEFGHIJKLMNOPQRS

abcdefghijklmnopqr1234567

ABCDEFGHIJKLMNOPQRS

defghijklmnopqrst 1234567

REFORM GROTESQUE BOLD

ABCDEFGHIJKLMNOPQR

bcdefghijklmno 12345678

REFORM GROTESQUE EXTRA BOLD

ABCDEFGHIJKLMNOPQRSTUVWXYZ

abcdefghijklmnopqrstuvwxyz

REFORM GROTESQUE EXTRA BOLD CONDENSED

191

Expressing their interest only 'with the superficial impression made by the type when pressed onto paper', the authors describe each typeface with attention to its defining characteristics.

ABCDEFGHIJKLMNO

PQRSTUVWXYZ1234

BAUER EXCELLENT*

FESTIVAL

Monotype 1951

Specially designed to commemorate the Festival of Britain and for Festival advertising by Phillip Boydell and his associates of the London Press Exchange. Based upon condensed sans italic capitals it has a three-dimensional form making it suitable for use in exhibition display typography. Capitals and numerals only.

THE QUICK LAZY FOX

SCANDINAVIAN

FESTIVAL

FIGGINS SHADED

Stevens Shanks

Three-dimensional capitals and figures with white faces. Probably designed by A. Bessemer, the letter first appeared in Bessemer and Catherwood's specimen of 1825, although Vincent Figgins has shown a 24 point of different design as early as 1815. The first specimen shown here is slightly heavier and more oblique in shading than the original 24 point.

ABCDEFGHIJKLMNOPQRSTUVW

XYZŒÆ&£1234567800

FIGGINS SHADED

ABCDEFG

24 POINT FIGGINS SHADED

FILM

Deberny & Peignot 1934

Designed by Marcel Jacno. Sans serif capitals and figures. The face of the letters is in white and they are three-dimensional. They are placed on a criblé ground.

278

ABCDEFGHIJKLM

NOPQRSTUVXYZ

FILM

FLORIDE

Deberny & Peignot 1939

Designed by Imre Reiner. Three-dimensional, sans serif capitals and figures, in which the faces of the letters are horizontally shaded.

ABCDEFG

VWXYZ12345

INITIALES FLORIDES

FORTUNA

Trennert 1930

Designed by Friedrich Bauer. An inline series of roman capitals. The line passes right through vertical strokes. Serifs are very small. In the **M** the middle strokes stop short of the line. *Cf.* DALIA.

GEISENHEIM

FORTUNA

FORUM

Weber

Designed by Georg Trump. An Egyptian face with light (FORUM I) and heavy (FORUM II) shading. The **M** is pointed at the bottom, and in the bold version (FORUM II) the shading of many letters at the foot of the line is continuous. Several letters are similar to SUPERBA ILLUSTRA.

279

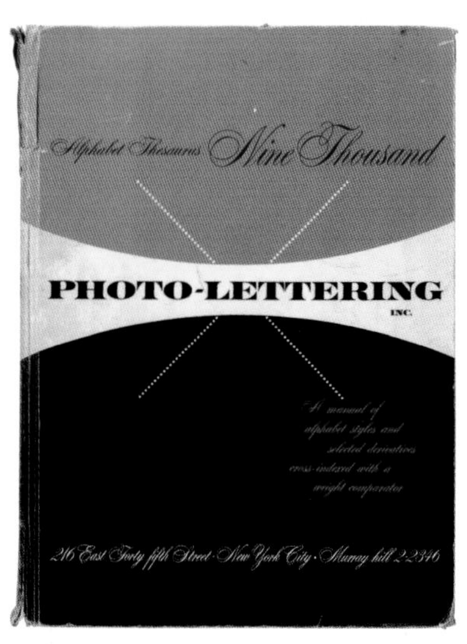

Oliental Arphabet VELY GOOD, Most Rik
HONESTY IS THE BASIS OF PERSONAL
OPEN OR CLOSED IT IS ALL THE SAMI
THEY CALLED HIM PEIPING TOMB
ALWAYS PLAYING TO THE BALCO
YOU GET THE blue pagoda when
692

THE SCENARIO WRITER often calls ona
GOOD RISK IS ALWAYS IN THE BLI
DESIGN finish
BLAST OFF AND ROCKET AHI
VERY OFTEN TAKEN FORT
CORNY BUT PRIZE WIZ
16
693

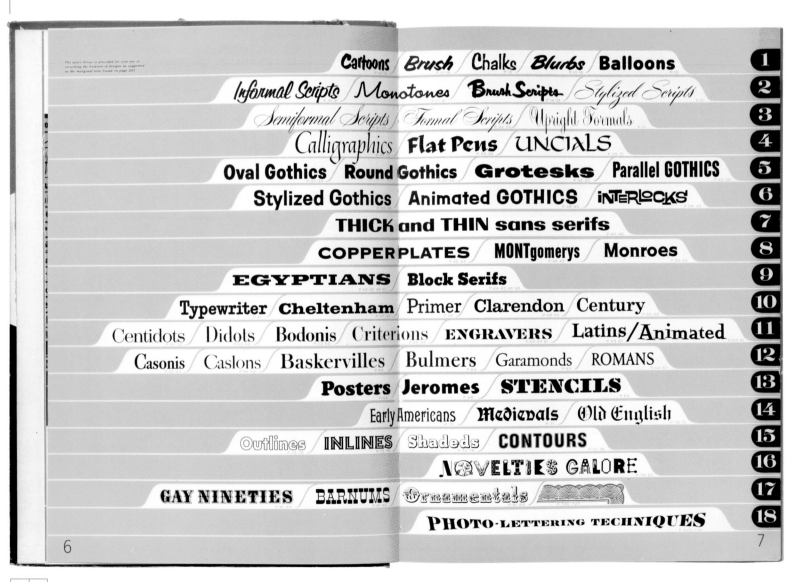

The contents spread is an effective point of departure for making a choice of typeface.

Cartoons / Brush / Chalks / Blurbs / Balloons 1
Informal Scripts / Monotones / Brush Scripts / Stylized Scripts 2
Semiformal Scripts / Formal Scripts / Upright Formals 3
Calligraphics / Flat Pens / UNCIALS 4
Oval Gothics / Round Gothics / Grotesks / Parallel GOTHICS 5
Stylized Gothics / Animated GOTHICS / INTERLOCKS 6
THICK and THIN sans serifs 7
COPPERPLATES / MONTgomerys / Monroes 8
EGYPTIANS / Block Serifs 9
Typewriter / Cheltenham / Primer / Clarendon / Century 10
Centidots / Didots / Bodonis / Criterions / ENGRAVERS / Latins/Animated 11
Casonis / Caslons / Baskervilles / Bulmers / Garamonds / ROMANS 12
Posters / Jeromes / STENCILS 13
Early Americans / Medievals / Old English 14
Outlines / INLINES / Shadeds / CONTOURS 15
NOVELTIES GALORE 16
GAY NINETIES / BARNUMS / Ornamentals 17
PHOTO-LETTERING TECHNIQUES 18
6 7

Alphabet Thesaurus Nine Thousand

Photo-Lettering Inc.
and Reinhold Publishing
Corporation, New York, 1960
740 pages
304 × 226 mm (12 × 9 in)
Designed by Ed Benguiat
Cover designed by
Herman Beeber

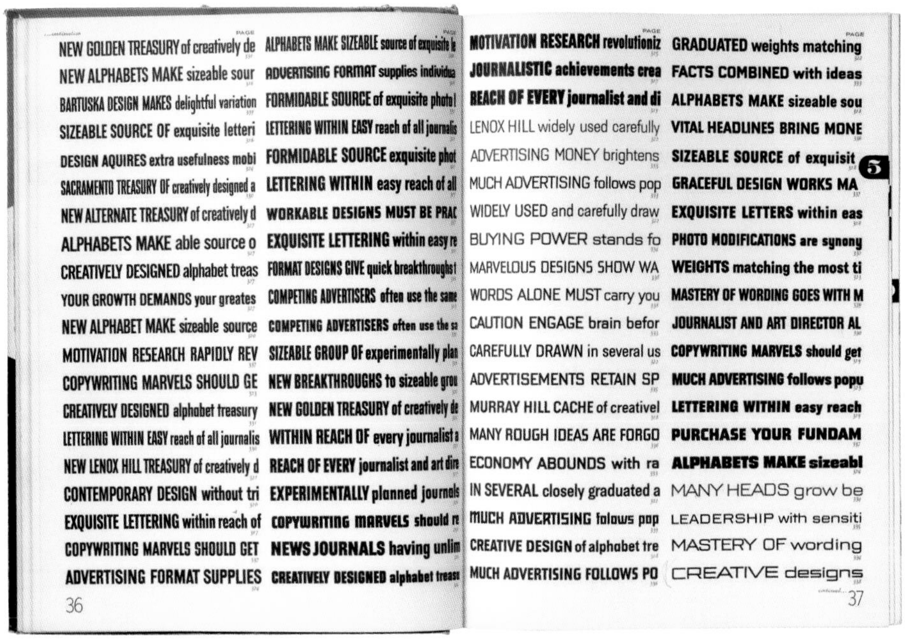

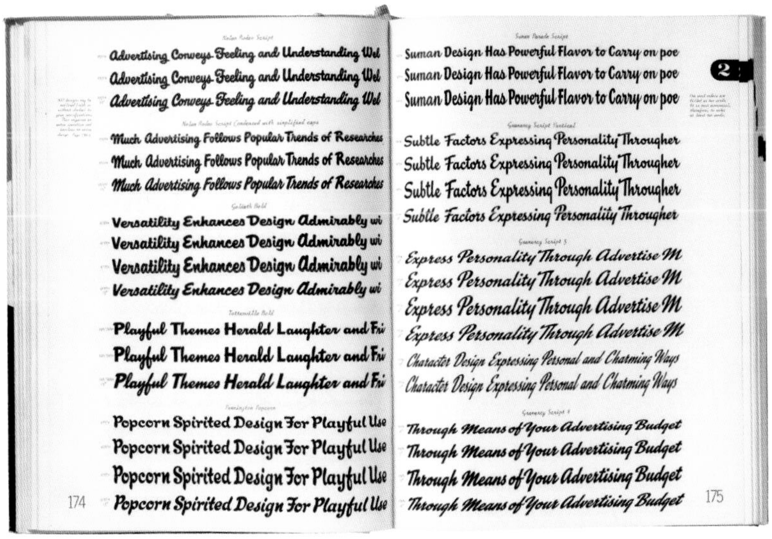

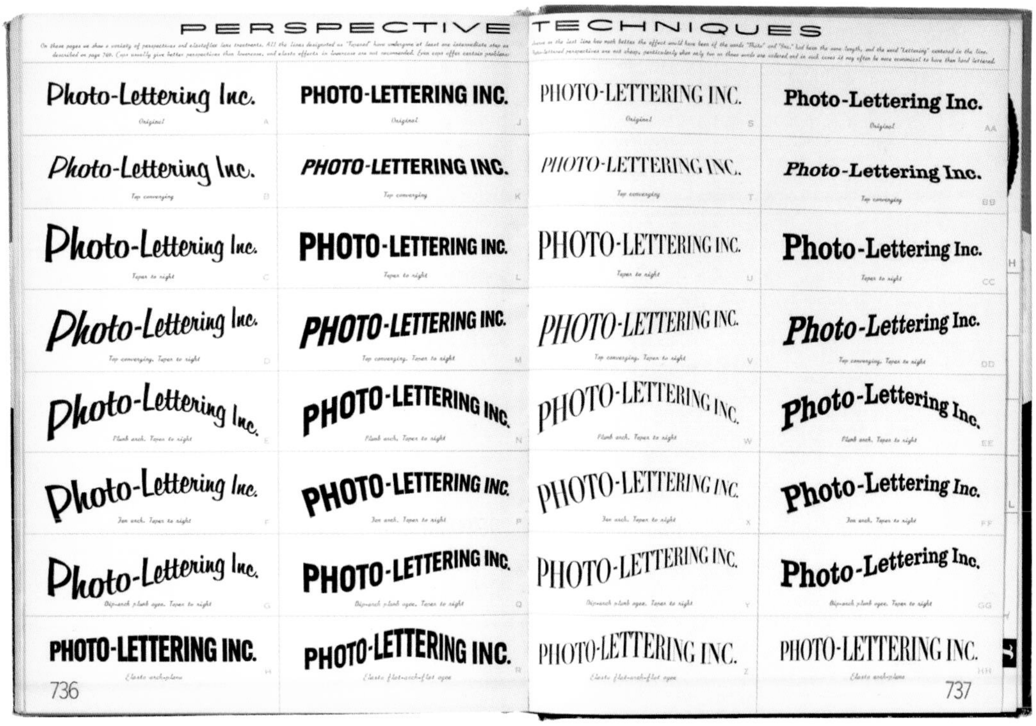

Photo-Lettering Inc. was the pre-eminent American phototypesetter in the early 1960s, and, being a typical New York company, it was unafraid to show it. It described the *Alphabet Thesaurus Nine Thousand* as 'replete with style … as exciting and diversified as Fifth Avenue from Washington Square to Fifty-ninth'. Its extensive range of typefaces lives up to the billing.

Over 100 'participating letterers' are credited in the thesaurus, including F.H.K. Henrion, Imre Reiner, Josef Albers, Alexey Brodovitch and Victor Caruso, but it was the type designer Ed Benguiat (1927–) who was most closely involved with the creative output of Photo-Lettering. He designed numerous alphabets and was also in charge of the many catalogues the company produced.

Originally developed in the 1920s, phototypesetting involved the letter-by-letter exposure of type from a photographic plate. With the use of varying lenses and optical devices an array of sizes and type styles could be achieved. Primarily used for headline fonts (type was billed by the word), phototypesetting had some significant benefits over the metal equivalent. Letters could be kerned negatively, which was particularly successful with the script and interlocking typefaces on offer. Producing a font was also much easier, cheaper and quicker than producing a metal typeface – the reason for the huge variety of styles displayed in the thesaurus.

Selecting a style of type on the book's contents spread sends the reader to a page with a selection of typefaces in that style; and after choosing the desired type he or she is sent to a further page where other sizes and weights are on display. Notes in the margins prompt readers to try other fonts and push the limits of their designs, with added visual techniques illustrated at the end of the thesaurus.

Photolettering offered many different optical techniques; seen below is a variety of choices for output in perspective. Other pages show options for outlining and type on a curve.

A selection of letterforms from Giovanni Battista Bodoni's Manuale Tipografico *(Parma, 1818). The choice of letters was based on their ability to illustrate the defining characteristics of any typeface.*

Ex Libris
Matthew Carter

The Elements of Typographic Style, Version 3.0, Robert Bringhurst, Hartley & Marks, Vancouver, 2004
A View of Early Typography: Up to about 1600, Harry Carter, revised edition, Hyphen Press, London, 2002
Types of the De Vinne Press, Theodore L. De Vinne & Co., New York, 1907
Die Neue Haas Grotesk Satzklebebuch, Haas'schen Schriftgießerei, Basel, 1960
Modern Typography: An Essay in Critical History, Robin Kinross, second edition, Hyphen Press, London, 2004
The Nymph and the Grot, James Mosley, Friends of the St Bride Printing Library, , London, 1999
An Atlas of Typeforms, James Sutton, Alan Bartram, Lund Humphries, London, 1968
Letters of Credit: A View of Type Design, Walter Tracy, Gordon Fraser, London, 1986
Meisterbuch der Schrift, Jan Tschichold, Otto Maier Verlag, Ravensburg, 1952
Printing Types, Daniel Berkeley Updike, second edition, Harvard University Press, Cambridge, Massachusetts, 1937

Photography is used for type specimens – they are often positioned across a spread for a trompe l'œil effect.

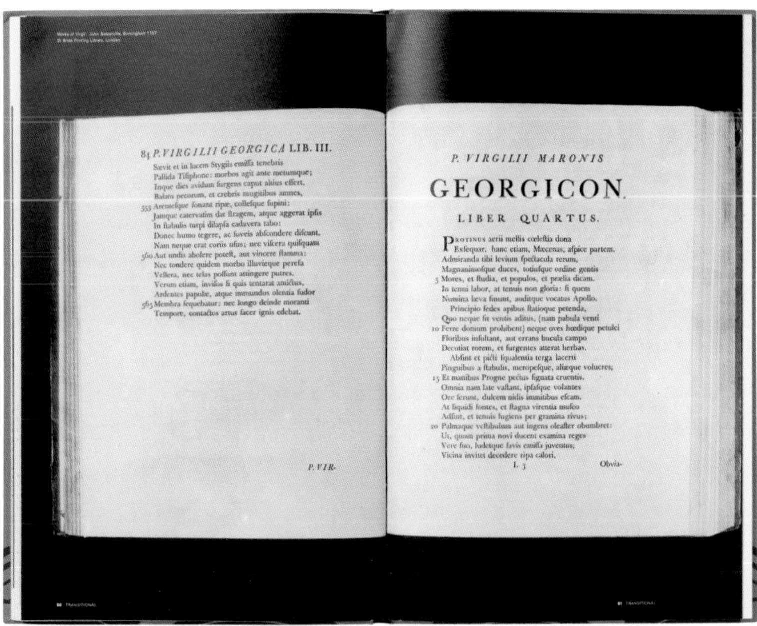

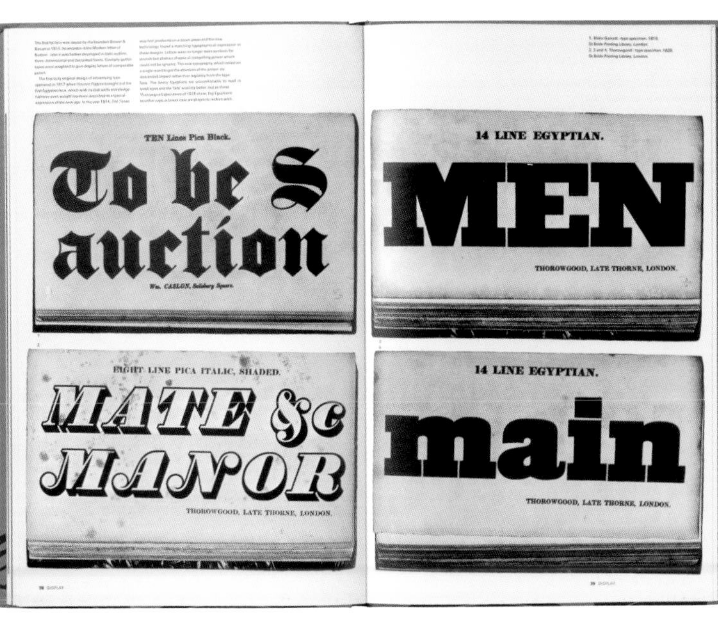

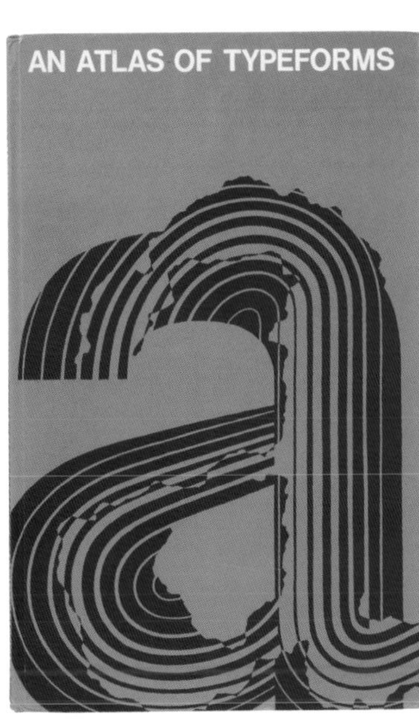

An Atlas of Typeforms

James Sutton,
Alan Bartram

Lund Humphries, London, 1968
122 pages
406 × 254 mm (16 × 10 in)
Designed by Alan Bartram

Calling this history of typeforms over 500 years an atlas was a comment on both its impressively large format and the predominantly visual presentation of materials. The authors were determined that it should be primarily a book of pictorial reference and not one of words.

A clue to their methodology can be seen in the bold cover design, composed of two superimposed lower-case 'a's, one a modern sans serif, the other a magnified Venetian from the fifteenth century. In the book, letterforms are analyzed by comparing original examples of usage. This is largely accomplished through the use of enlarged specimens, allowing the viewer to make a detailed study of the letters. Emphasis is placed on describing the shapes, outline and variation of weight of the letters.

The same process is applied to the modern versions of these typefaces. At the time of publication these were available to designers in metal, and the authors chose to show them as complete typefaces at 30-point size as well as in enlarged form for more detailed comparisons.

The chapters are arranged in type classifications, such as Venetian, Old Face Italian, Old Face French, etc. Photographs of historical typographic specimens and other printed matter are displayed alongside the enlarged text.

The designer and co-author Alan Bartram often placed the images of open books so that their gutters were exactly on the actual gutter in the layout. It is an effective trick that works well in this oversized format.

Wood 2
Morgan Press Printers and Typographers, Hastings-on-Hudson, New York, c.1965
156 pages
278 × 210 mm (11 × 8.25 in)
Designed by John Alcorn

Building on a collection started by their father, the publisher Willard D. Morgan, brothers Lloyd and Douglas Morgan had amassed about 2000 metal fonts and more than 200 wood ones by 1960, rescued from print workshops around the United States and saved from being melted down or thrown away.

These fonts represented the great burgeoning of the printing industry in the middle of the nineteenth century, which created ever more varied and fanciful types at the request of an insatiable advertising industry. The advent of cheaper offset lithography and photo-composition sounded the death knell for the wood-type market.

The brothers founded the Morgan Press and offered these long-forgotten types to designers, including those of the New York-based Push Pin Studio, who found they were a perfect fit for the exploration into graphic styles they pioneered in the late 1950s and the 1960s. The revival of interest in the types led the Morgan Press to commission one-time Push Pin member John Alcorn to design their specimen books.

Wood 2 concentrates on the wood types, which by the mid-1960s had grown to around 400. Alcorn used a combination of alternating orange, red and olive-green uncoated stock to exhibit the fonts. Types are labelled according to their availability as caps, lower case and figures, and there is information about missing letters. As well as details about how to order the types, there is a useful primer on their history, features and manufacture.

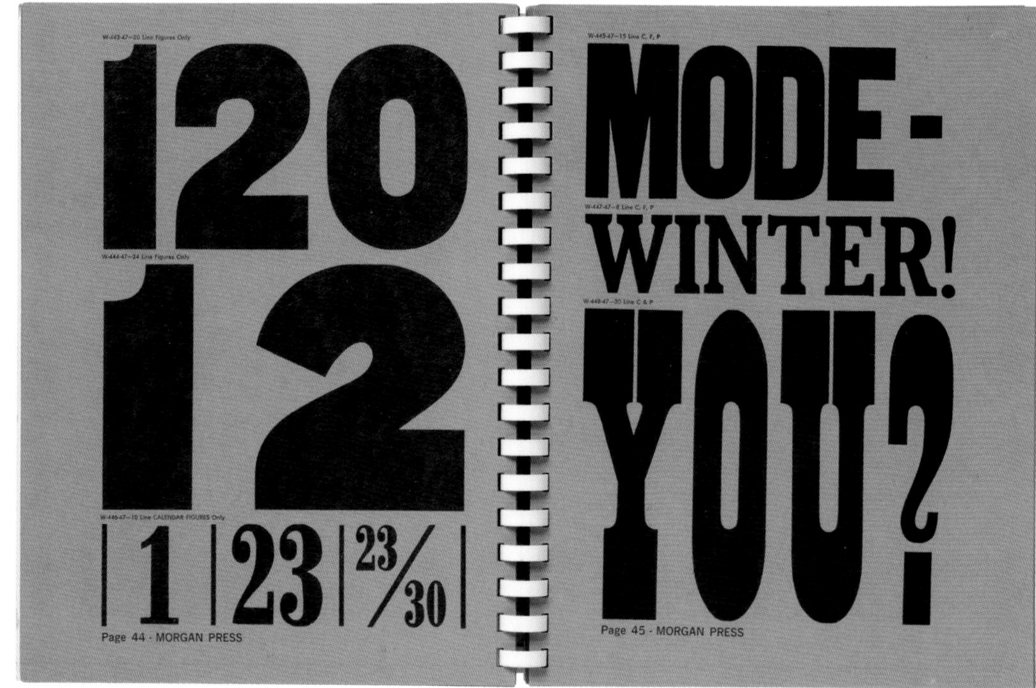

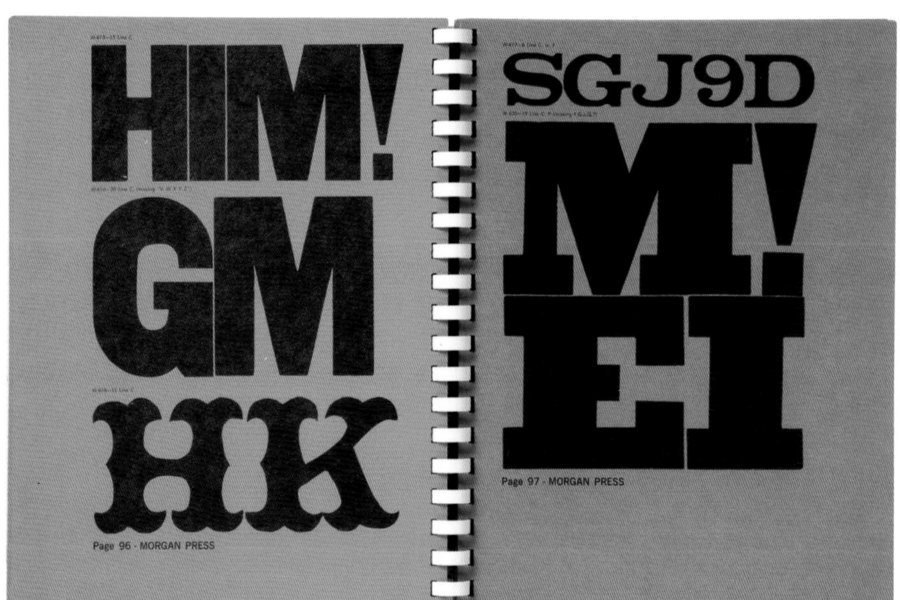

Reproduced at their actual size, the typefaces are represented by only a few characters, resulting in bold graphic layouts.

Wood 2 was one of a series of Morgan Press specimen books designed by artist and designer John Alcorn.

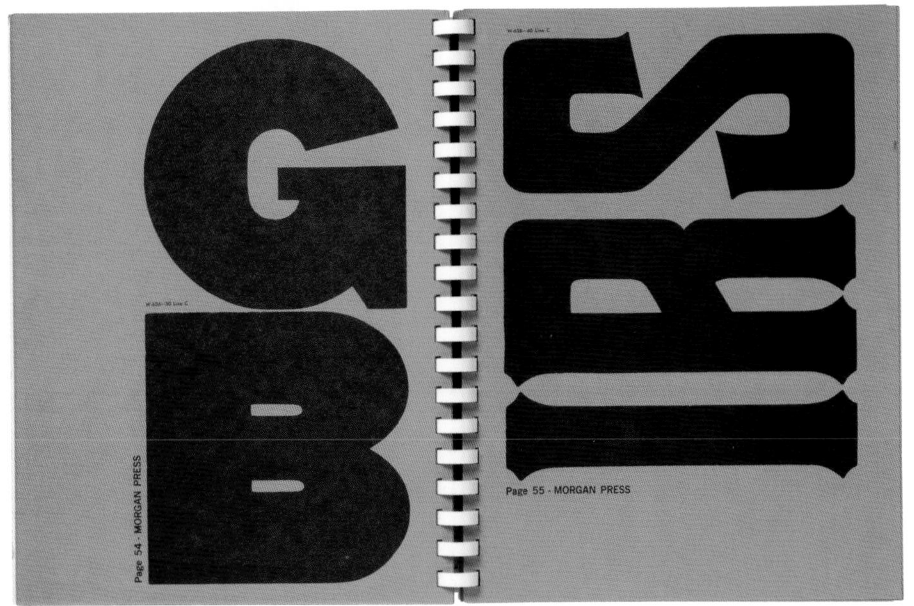

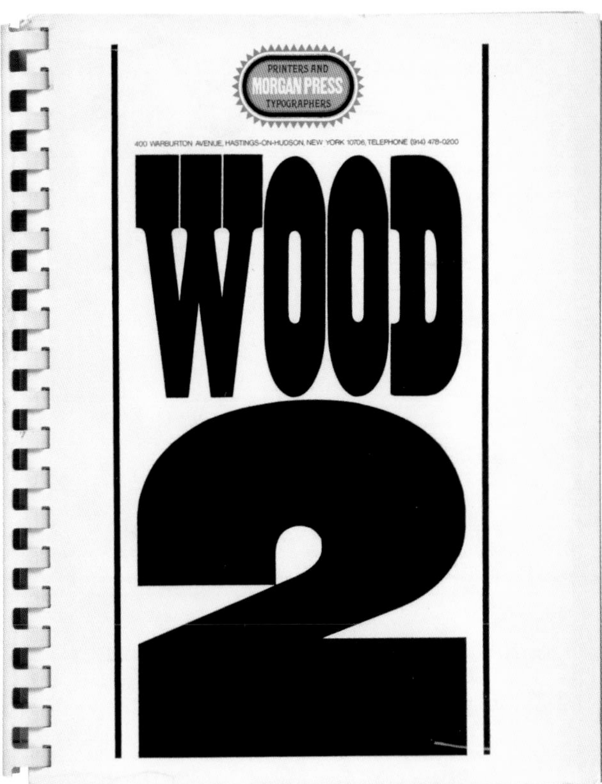

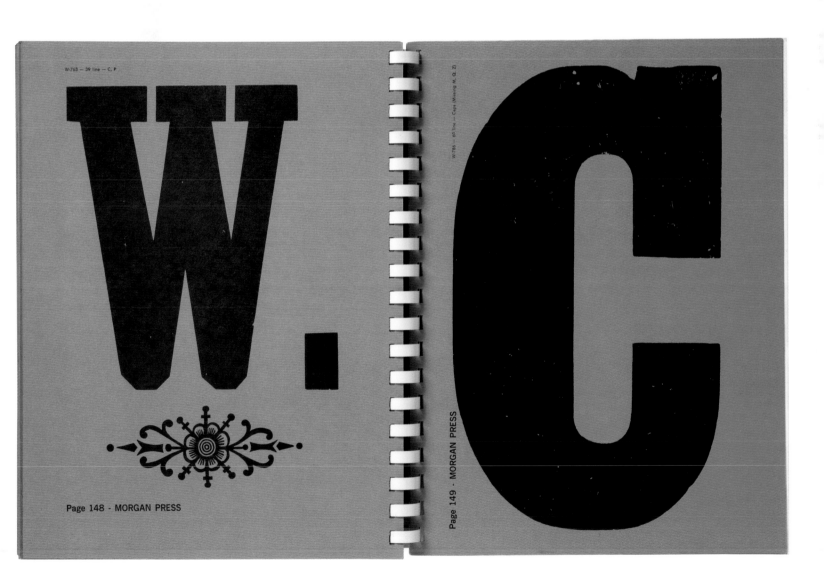

American Wood Type: 1828–1900

Notes on the Evolution of Decorated and Large Types and Comments on Related Trades of the Period

Rob Roy Kelly

Van Nostrand Reinhold Company, New York, 1969
350 pages
302 × 225 mm (11.875 × 9 in)
Designed by Rob Roy Kelly

In the late 1950s, unable to find a history or classification of American wood types, Rob Roy Kelly (1925–2004) took it upon himself to spend the next 11 years researching the subject. Records were widespread and disparate; Kelly scoured small-town printers for type and libraries with specimen books in order to fill this gap in typographic history.

The resulting book catalogues more than 600 type styles and provides a detailed history of the evolution of American wood types. The story begins after 1828, when the printing industry was dominated by the influence of European type, skills and technology. Kelly shows how, over the course of the nineteenth century, Americans developed their own type industry and styles both through advances in manufacture and as a result of the demands of the growing advertising industry. This culminated at the end of the century in the perfection of offset lithography.

The main text is profusely illustrated with meticulously catalogued examples of type, borders and ornaments, and pages from catalogues. Importantly, there are many diagrams detailing how the type is manufactured, together with engravings, photographs of factories and printing presses, and portraits of the industry's main figures.

American Wood Type: 1828–1900 is printed in black throughout on uncoated stock. A rear section shows more than 100 type specimens grouped in three main families: Roman, Antique and Gothic. An extensive bibliography completes this most impressive book.

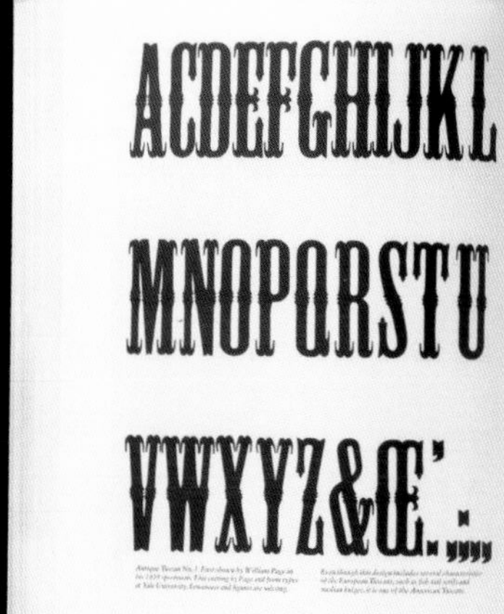

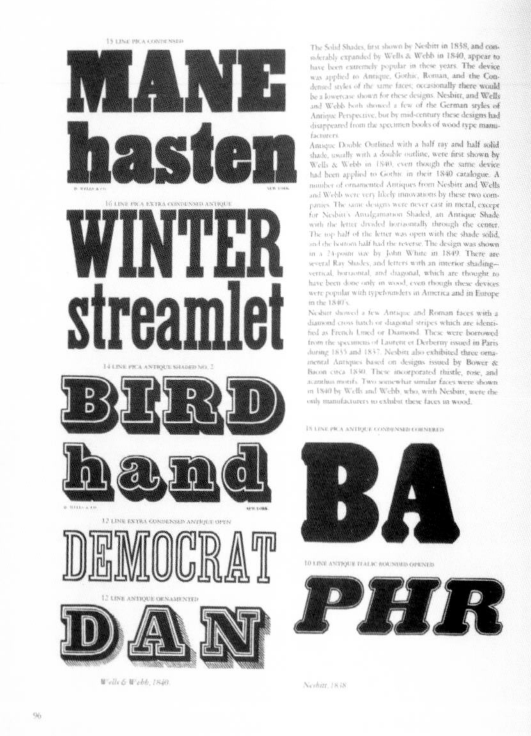

Whole specimens of wood type are available in a section at the back of the book.

24 LINE GERMAN FULL FACE

Ku

24 LINE MUNICH

Ry

14 LINE GERMAN

Fenster

16 LINE BAVARIAN

Boston

24 LINE GERMAN CONDENSED

Numb!

18 LINE PRUSSIAN

Dienstag

24 LINE GERMAN X CONDENSED

Orations!

18 LINE COMPOSITE CONDENSED

Prozeßbes

Page, 1870.

24 LINE POSTER TEXT

10 LINE MUNICH

Outa

Burlington

Vanderburgh, Wells & Co., 1877.

Page, 1870.

144

36 LINE OLD ENGLISH ORNAMENTED NO. 6 (PATENTED)

If

8 LINE GERMAN NO. 2

Stoffe

Vanderburgh, Wells & Co., 1877.

10 LINE BULLETIN SCRIPT

Stensil

20 LINE OLD ENGLISH ORNAMENTED NO. 5 (PATENTED)

Fair

5 LINE ARABESQUE

STEAMS

36 LINE OLD ENGLISH ORNAMENTED NO. 7 (PATENTED)

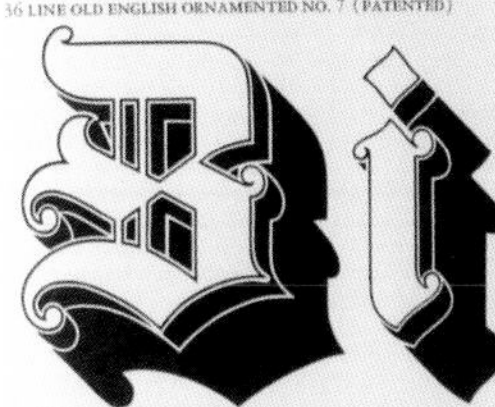

Bi

6 LINE PAGE'S BULLETIN

Printe

TRAIN

Page, 1872.

6 LINE BULLETIN CONDENSED

BULletin

12 LINE OLD ENGLISH ORNAMENTED

Wander

Vanderburgh, Wells & Co., 1877.

15 LINE OLD ENGLISH OPEN

Unbid

Page, 1870.

145

Ornamented No. 2, Bruce, 1837.

Lottery figures (also in 1831 specimens), Bruce, 1837.

Twelve line pica Gothic Condensed Open (Nicolette Gray lists this design for Thorowgood in 1832), Bruce, 1837.

SERM

Gothic Condensed, Bruce, 1837.

festo

Antique Ornamented, Bruce, 1837.

YORK

Ornamented, Bruce, 1837.

SAND

Ornamented, Bruce, 1837.

THING

Skeleton, Bruce, 1837.

ABCDEFGHIJKLMNOPQR

There were a number of new ornamentals, one of which originated with Caslon in 1830, a splayed Tuscan with pearls at the median. Most of the others demonstrated a French influence in ornamentation. Italian, Antique Expanded, and a Roman appeared as small reverses: 2 line English, and 2 line Nonpareil. A Roman No. 1 reminiscent of the intermediate Romans immediately preceding the fat face styles was shown in capitals only and without figures. A great number of wood types were included, both plain faced and ornamental.

In 1842, George Bruce illustrated the first American Roman Extended as metal type in three sizes of 10, 8, and 6 point. The date 1839 included in the sampling may refer to the Roman Extended's first showing. In England this same style was shown by Caslon in 1835. Nesbitt had exhibited it in 1838 as a wood type complete with lowercase and figures. The Bruce specimen did not include a lowercase, and the Caslon design was not listed as having a lowercase. Bruce showed a Roman Extra Condensed which was more condensed than that shown by John White in 1839. It was most like a style initiated by Thorowgood circa 1838. Three sizes of 10, 8, and 6 point Gothic, full faced and a light style, were displayed that were similar to those described for White in 1839, but the irregularities had been eliminated and the drawing of the letterforms was generally better than the White designs. Again, there was no lowercase or figures. In the larger ornamental faces there was a new style of Gothic Shade in perspective–with shade to the left, a Gothic Double Outlined Shade with a Ray Shading around the conventional shade, an Antique Shade, and a Line Shade with interior shading with horizontal emphasis. The designs seem to have been printed from wood letters.

Specimens of Robb for 1844 demonstrated an increasing fascination with the "phantom" look in type design. Figgins had published one of the first of these styles in 1843, which consisted only of parallel ruled lines. Since there was no linear definition of the letter contours, the effect was a light, ghost-like color. Gothic and Antique both were given the same treatment. Also, Ray Shades were found in sufficient numbers to become characteristic of the 1840's. Gothic Condensed of earlier specimens was given a line shade, and the series expanded to include a 22 point size. Many new European ornamented faces displayed for the first time in these specimens incorporated the Ray Shade, or a graded (graduated) interior shading, such as the Zebra of Figgins. Antique Condensed with lowercase was featured in a text arrangement in an 18 point size.

L. Johnson and Company of Philadelphia in its 1844 specimens included a 6 line Roman Light Faced Condensed without lowercase. It was during the 1840's that light face styles began to replace the heavy fat face Romans in the founder's specimen books. They were accompanied by the extremely condensed styles in all three primary families–Gothic, Antique, and Roman, and the overall color of these new styles was light as compared to the boxy, black designs prevailing during the 1820's and 1830's. Some of the first Germans were illustrated in these 1844 specimens, after which they were to be found regularly in all metal and wood specimens until near the end of the century.

John White in 1845 exhibited some recently imported styles of Tuscan, most of which were in outline. Also, a 2 line Small Pica Outline Gothic with two weights of line created an illusion of slight dimension. There were figures, but no lowercase for this design, and it was reasonably well drawn except for the capital G and figures 6 and 9 which were inferior to the others. A substantial number of wood types were included in these specimens. Johnson in 1847 presented the largest number of new styles yet to be introduced at one time. A majority of these were based on the European Tuscans and many were "phantom" designs. Doric Ornamented from France made its first appearance. This design in both metal and wood was to be used extensively from this date through the next 10 years. The first Rustic, with tree limbs or bark as a decorative motif, was shown in a 24 point size, and in the 1880's Page was to cut a like style in wood. This example was somewhat unusual in that the motif had been adapted to a letterform which retained a structure based on type. Most Rustics, formed by arranging boughs into the shape of a letter, were quite irregular. There was a curious Gothic Condensed with Line Shade. Curves were treated as straight lines and counters were mostly angular. In general, it was a clumsy design.

There were seven sizes of Clarendon, the smallest size being Two Line English and the largest 12 pica. It is interesting to note the number of discrepancies in design between the different sizes. The capital E will have a serif on the middle arm on some sizes and not on others; some terminals such as the lowercase a and e will have a slightly bulbous ending and others will be squared off; the dot on the lowercase i will be square in some instances, round in others. It is thought that the larger sizes were printed from wood letters.

Gothic Condensed Round and Tooled was first shown in an American specimen book in a 2 line Great Primer. Nicolette Gray assigns this design, as well as ornamented version of it, to Caslon in 1844.

Up until 1845, almost all specimens were common property among the major American typefounders, and finding a design in one catalogue would almost assure that it could be found in half a dozen other books. Also, as the introduction of new designs was gradual, it is comparatively simple to approximate the dates of their introduction into the American repertory of display designs.

However, by mid-century, when the American typefounder had the machinery, trained workmen, and markets to expand his operations into new levels of production, new designs are increasingly difficult to trace. The quantities of display letters being produced fairly well eliminated the practice of every founder producing the same designs, since it was easier for a founder to take the order and fill it at an agreed price from another founder owning the matrices. One type house advertised that it could fill orders for other founders' designs almost as quickly as for its own. The 1840's and early 1850's saw tremendous numbers of European designs being produced in this country.

One of the first important American typefounding inventions was introduced by David Bruce, Jr. of New York City in 1834. It was a device known then as a squirt machine, a hand force pump attachment for forcing the lead into the mold under pressure. The machine was devised to better cast the ornamental designs, which, according to Theodore De Vinne, owed their popularity to this contrivance. Another invention of Bruce incorporating the force pump was the first successful automatic type caster, initially patented in 1836 but further improved in 1838

Italian, Boston T. & S. F., 1837.

Ornamented, Boston T. & S. F., 1837.

Ornamented, Boston T. & S. F., 1837.

Ornamented, Boston T. & S. F., 1837.

198

199

A selection of predominantly German and Old English designs – the specimens are given with their name, size, date and type foundry of issue. These come from the Page (1870, 1872) and Vanderburgh, Wells & Co. (1877) catalogues.

The contents spread showing the main typefaces in the Letraset catalogue. Typefaces highlighted in cyan were available in special stencil formats that allowed the designer to rub down an outlined letterform, paint in colour and peel away the stencil, leaving a coloured letter.

Letraset

Letraset UK, London,
c.1970s
128 pages
228 × 268 mm (9 × 10.5 in)

For aspiring designers in the 1970s, the Letraset catalogue was often the initial point of contact with the world of letterforms and typography. Available in regular art stores it was easily accessible to young, pre-college students, and for many of them this cornucopia of typefaces and symbols was the first book in their graphic design library.

Letraset manufactured dry transfer characters; fixed on to the back of transparent sheets, these were applied to artworks by burnishing. Its heyday was in the 1970s and 1980s when it was an important product in the graphic arts industry, used primarily for setting headlines. There were many other competitors – among them Artype, C-Thru, Cello-Tak, Chartpak, Normatype, Prestype, Tactype and Zipotone – but it was Letraset that had the largest selection of typefaces (over 225), and its name became synonymous with the product.

A core set of standard typefaces was supplemented with a selection under the banner Letragraphica, chosen by a panel of renowned designers including Derek Birdsall, Roger Excoffon, Colin Forbes, Armin Hofmann, Herb Lubalin and Marcello Minale. The catalogue displayed a complete font for each typeface and a guide to the type sizes available.

While typefaces were the mainstay of Letraset's business, the dry-transfer process lent itself well to symbols, rules, borders, ben-day dot screens, tints and architectural graphics. The company's various catalogues invariably included other graphic art supplies, such as vinyl lettering, special tapes (rules and registration marks) and Pantone colour-matching systems in the form of coloured sheets, film and markers.

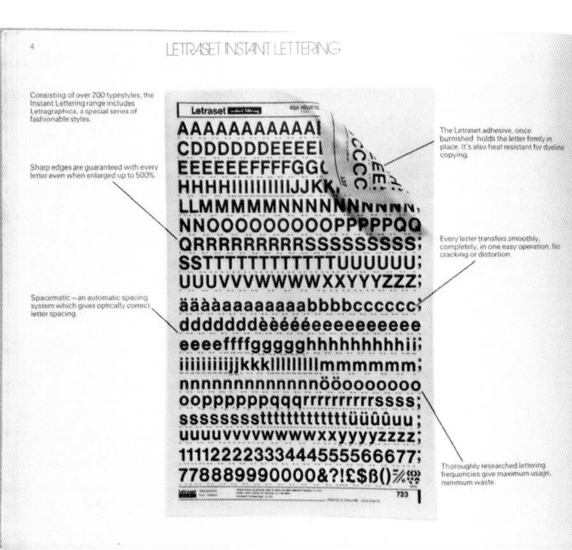

4 LETRASET INSTANT LETTERING

Consisting of over 200 typestyles, the Instant Lettering range includes Letragraphica, a special series of fashionable styles.

Sharp edges are guaranteed with every letter even when enlarged up to 500%.

Spacematic – an automatic spacing system which gives optically correct letter spacing.

The Letraset adhesive, once burnished holds the letter firmly in place. It's also heat resistant for dyeline copying.

Every letter transfers smoothly, completely, in one easy operation. No cracking or distortion.

Thoroughly researched lettering frequencies give maximum usage, minimum waste.

INSTANT LETTERING APPLICATION + HINTS & TIPS 5

How to use Instant Lettering

Remove the siliconized backing paper and position the required lettering using the Spacematic guide.

Press the letter onto the art surface with your finger and then shade lightly over the whole letter with a ballpoint pen, soft pencil, or any other blunt instrument.

Carefully pull away the sheet, making sure that the transfer has been completed.

Repeat until your word is complete. Then place the backing paper over the lettering and burnish moderately hard for firm adhesion with a smooth instrument, such as the cap of a ballpoint pen.

Using the Spacematic Guide

As a guide draw a pencilled line on your artwork ⅛" (3 mm) below the required base line of the text and register the spacemarks exactly with the line.

1 Using the method explained previously transfer the first letter and its **righthand** spacemark.
2 Gently pull away backing sheet.
3 Position the second letter by butting its lefthand spacemark to the spacemark already transferred.
4 Then transfer the second letter with its righthand spacemark.

Continue in this way until your word is complete. It is not necessary to transfer the lefthand spacemarks.

To remove the spacemarks use a rubber cement pick-up, a soft eraser or a piece of adhesive tape.

Notes

1 A few letters when set using the Spacematic system will overlap (e.g. TT LS). When this happens simply move the sheet slightly to the right to leave a hair line of space between the letters.
2 Under some lower case letters with descenders (e.g. j p y) the spacemarks are positioned lower than normal. In this case spacemarks should be aligned visually and not butted.
3 On some sheets containing small point sizes the two Spacematic marks are replaced by single longer spacemarks. In such cases simply transfer the whole spacemark.

General Tips

Transfer. Use light pressure when transferring lettering (about the same as when writing). Shade over with closely spaced lines so that the whole character is covered. Excessive pressure or uneven shading can distort the characters.

Large letters. It is important to press large letters firmly into contact with the art surface before transferring them. Use a broad ended stylus (e.g. the cap of a ballpoint pen) and first shade widely over the letter then repeat using normal shading, paying particular attention to the edges of the character.

Corrections. Instant Lettering is easy to remove. With hard surfaces such as glass, metal or acetate, peel off with adhesive tape. With artboard and paper, use either a soft rubber or adhesive tape.

Dyeline copying. For dyeline copying Instant Lettering should need no further protection.

Protection. To protect Instant Lettering against abrasion from handling and in storage, spray with 101 or Letracote Gloss.

Storage. Always protect Instant Lettering sheets after use with the siliconized backing sheet. Never fold or crease Instant Lettering sheets. Always store them away from heat and humidity.

Difficult surfaces. For uneven and very hard smooth surfaces, use the pre-release technique. Hold the sheet away from the art surface and shade lightly over the letter. It will appear to turn grey. Position the letter carefully on the artwork and then press off the letter with your finger. Remove the sheet, making sure that the transfer has been completed.

Instructions for the application of dry-transfer letters, a standard method for setting headline type for reproduction in the 1970s.

A Constructed Roman Alphabet

A Geometric Analysis of the Greek and Roman Capitals and of the Arabic Numerals

David Lance Goines

David R. Godine, Publisher, Boston, 1982

180 pages

304 × 200 mm (12 × 7.75 in)

Designed by David Lance Goines

In this book, the calligrapher, graphic artist and printer David Lance Goines (1945–) takes on the mantle of sixteenth-century artists and their fascination with the letters of the Roman alphabet. His stunning and thoroughly modern collection of 'majuscules' is a more than worthy addition to the works of Geofroy Tory, Albrecht Dürer, Giambattista Palatino and Desiderius Erasmus. He has joined their search for the underlying harmony and geometric rational of letterforms, and in the process created something uniquely twentieth century.

There is no scholarly introduction; the first half of *A Constructed Roman Alphabet* simply consists of detailed instructions for the geometric assembly of each letterform with, on a facing page, its drawn solution in outline and underneath the completed letter revealed. The two opening chapters – 'To Construct a Square' and 'To find a Distance One-Ninth That of a Given Line' – underpin the construction of all the letters in the alphabet. The formulae for all major letterforms are followed by instructions for the ampersand, ligatures, the Greek characters and, finally, the Arabic numerals. The second half of the book is devoted to the display of the finished Greek and Roman letters, displayed together on a spread and printed one per page in sequence.

Designed by Goines, the book is a sumptuous piece of letterpress printing. Its judicious use of red as a second colour, the classic layout and the selection of an uncoated acid-free stock marry perfectly with the elegant letters to make it an object of distinction.

A B C D E | A B Γ Δ
F G H I J K | E Z H Θ
L M N O P | I K Λ M
Q R S T U | N Ξ O Π
V W X Y Z | P Σ T Y
& Æ · Œ | Φ X Ψ Ω
1 2 3 4 5 | 6 7 8 9 0

A typical spread, in this case for the capital letter 'B', has on the left the meticulous instructions for the geometric assembly of the letter shown on the right.

The Letter B

B Construct first a square ABCD, and bisect AC at E, BD at F, AB at G, and CD at H. Draw the straight lines EF and GH, thereby establishing a point I at their intersection. Using a diameter of one-ninth the distance AB, describe on AE a circle J tangential to AG; a circle from the center B, thereby establishing on BF a point K; a circle from the center E, thereby establishing on JE a point L; a circle from the center F, thereby establishing on KF a point M; on EC a circle N tangential to CH; a circle from the center H, thereby establishing on CH a point O; and a circle from the center D, thereby establishing on FD a point P. Draw the straight lines JK, LM and NP. Draw a straight line tangential to the circles J and N, and produce it to intersect AG at Q and CO at R, thereby establishing on JK a point S. Using the radius AJ, describe on QG a circle QTU, and on RO a circle RVW. Draw the straight line UW. Bisect AE at X and GI at Y. Draw the straight line XY, thereby establishing on UW a point Z. Using the radius AJ, describe on UG a circle *uab*, on ZY a circle *zcd*, and a circle from the center I, thereby establishing on IF a point *e*. Bisect E*e* at *f*. Draw the straight line *ac*, thereby establishing a point *g* on the perimeter of the circle *c*. Draw the straight line ZK, thereby establishing a point *h* on the perimeter of the circle *c*. Using the radius AJ, describe on *h*K a circle *hij*. From the center *h*, describe a circle tangential to SK. From the center *c*, describe a circle tangential to the circle *h* and intersecting LM. From the center *i*, describe a circle tangential to *h*G. From the center *g*, describe a circle tangential to the circle *i* and intersecting LM. Draw the straight line SO. Draw the straight line NF, thereby establishing on SO a point *k*. Draw the straight line *k*P and produce it to intersect ZW at *m*. Using the radius AJ, describe on *mk* a circle *npk*, thereby establishing on S*k* a point *r*. From the center *f*, describe a circle tangential to NP. From the center *k*, describe a circle within the circle *f* and tangential to it. From the center *n*, describe a circle tangential to the circle *k* and to the line EI. From the center *r*, describe a circle tangential to WO. From the center *f*, describe a circle tangential to the circle *r*. From the point C, draw a straight line tangential to the circle *f* just described, and intersecting the circle V.

Q.E.F.

[12]

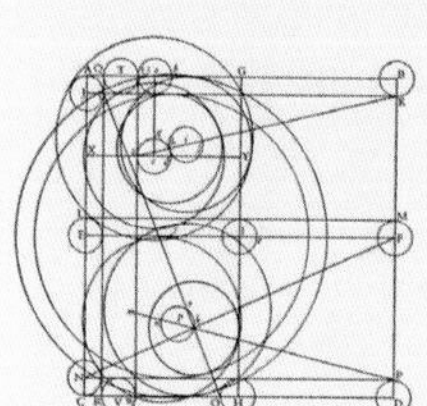

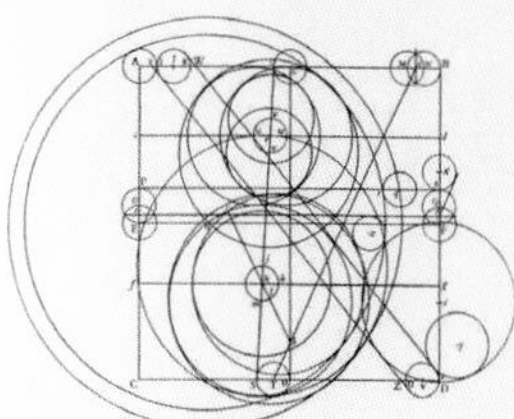

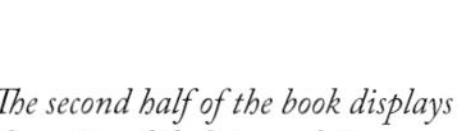

The second half of the book displays the entire alphabet, one letter to a page. The book was printed entirely in letterpress by The Stinehour Press of Lunenburg, Vermont.

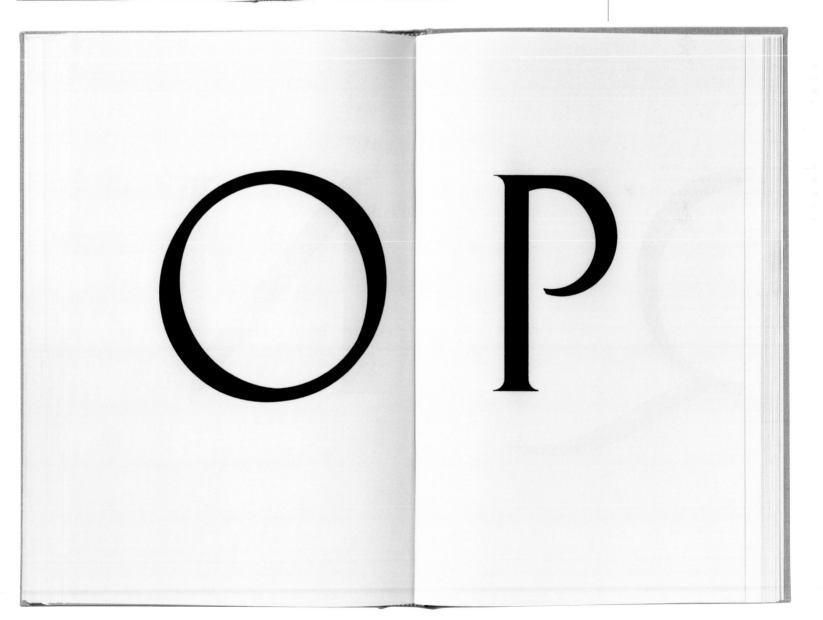

Igarashi Alphabets
From Graphics to Sculptures
Takenobu Igarashi
ABC Edition, Zurich, 1987
152 pages
250 × 254 mm (9.875 × 10 in)
Designed by Debi Shimamoto

Igarashi Alphabets showcases the extracurricular endeavours of the Japanese designer Takenobu Igarashi (1944–), who studied, and opened offices, in Japan and America. Principally an artistic venture, Igarashi's sculptural letterforms fed back into his professional life through projects such as his ten-year calendar for the Museum of Modern Art in New York (each of the 6226 numbers is different) and his monumental *Sculpture 3* for the Michael Peters Group in London (built by Ralph Selby).

Fascinated by what may happen to letterforms outside the two dimensions of the printed page, Igarashi investigated the possible three-dimensional forms that could exist in front of and behind the page. The resulting sculptures were expertly rendered in a series of artworks, each of which explored different themes or materials. *Igarashi Alphabets* is a portfolio of these projects exploring in depth series such as 'Aluminum Alphabet', 'Concrete Alphabet', 'Wood Alphabet' and 'Ori (Folded) Alphabet'.

Igarashi was an early experimenter with computers and robotic machines, using them to aid in drawing and constructing the letterforms. His rather primitive 'Wireframe Alphabet' contrasts with the much more elaborate hand-drawn axonometric typography he produced for posters and magazine covers.

All the images in the book are reproduced in duotone, giving the pages a rich feel and industrial tone. Included are preparatory drawings and photographs of the final sculptures, many of which were shot outdoors.

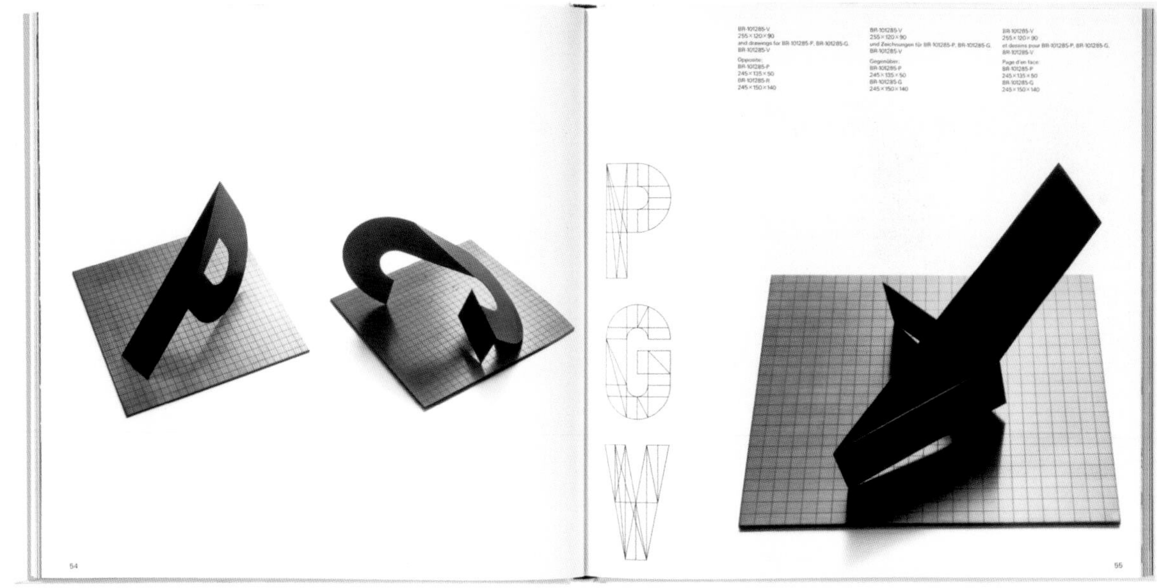

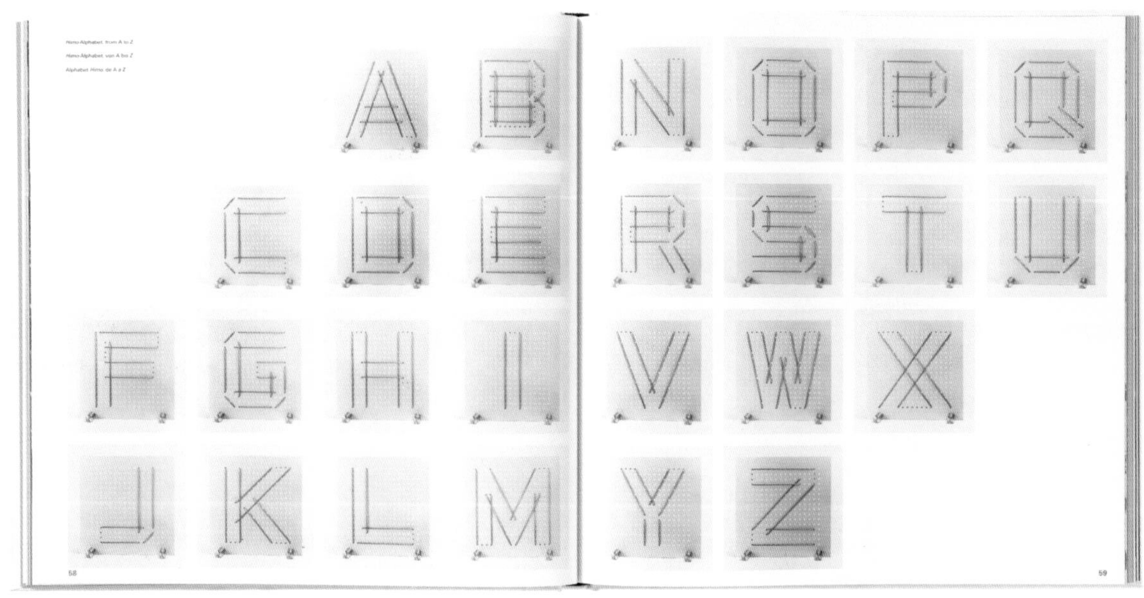

The 'Himo Alphabet', made by passing a vinyl cord through holes in an aluminium plate.

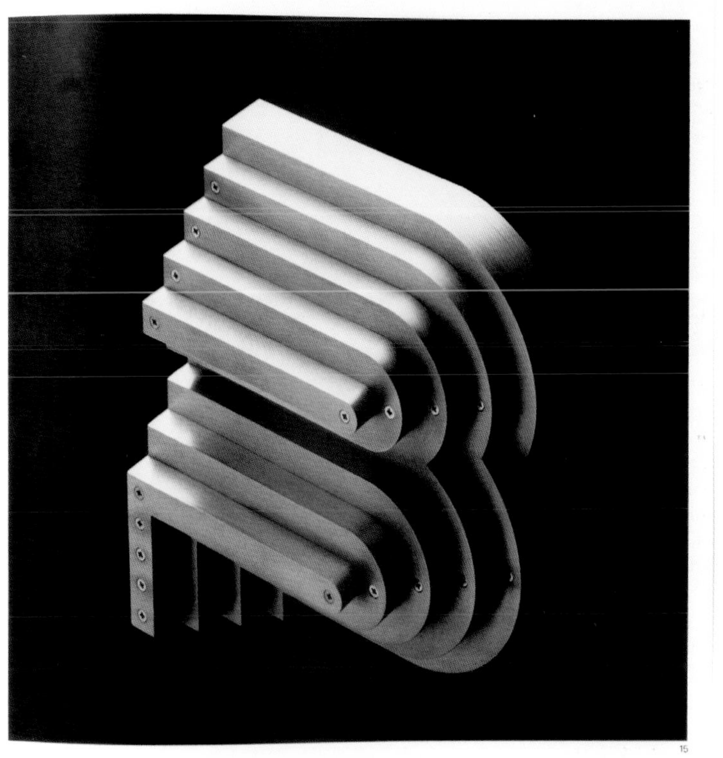

Igarashi experimented with the use of a computer to construct letterforms, drawn on a Fukuchi Cadgraph plotter.

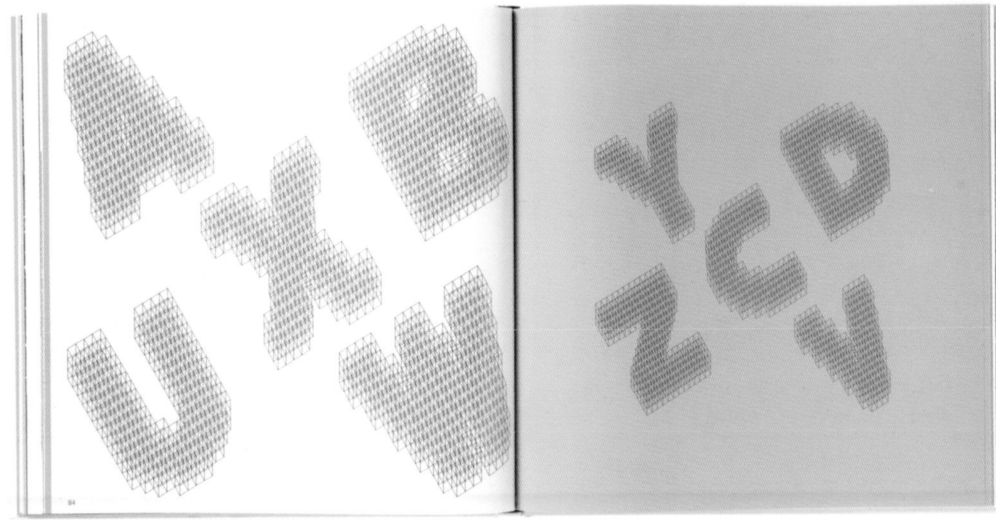

Printed in a mixture of litho and letterpress, the right-hand page here is reproduced from the original Underground Railway Block Letter wood type.

Walter Tracy's drawings for new replacement letter-forms.

HQ411
newgly
Q411 l

Page 33
Underground Railway
Block-Letter Bold
61mm capital height

adapted as necessary to the limitations of the 6 to 12 point range, with companion italic and bold versions … the cost of such a project cannot be trivial … But amortisation might be carried over a long period, because the type is to be in no sense an ephemeral one.'

It is interesting that even Walter Tracy, a man in the centre of the world typesetting business, could not reasonably predict in 1973 that another ten years would bring about a digital revolution, lowering the costs of design origination and accessibility, and challenging the validity of established styles of type and typography.

In 1973, just before Walter Tracy was commissioned, London Transport had asked Berthold Wolpe to design a complementary italic to complete their existing 'Underground' fonts. The design however was rejected by the Design Committee.[9] Although Wolpe's italic did not 'take', it inhibited the Committee – and certainly inhibited Tracy whilst Wolpe was alive – from attempting it again. The first matching italic had to wait another twelve years.

ggg gg gg

From the left this diagram shows three lower case 'g's as designed by Johnston.

A wood letter 'g' and the italic version by Berthold Wolpe, 1973 (not cut).

Walter Tracy's version, December 1973 and the current Banks&Miles version from 1983.

32

FGHIJK
NOPQ
RSTUV
WXYZ
&,.:;''""!?

An example of Edward Johnston's earlier writing, these proportions varied a little in execution for Johnston said that writing between the lines is rather like *'trying to dance in a room your own height'*.

Cap height 8 units
Ascender 5 units
Rossesnight
x height 5 units
Stem width 1.5 units
Descender 4 units

Edward Johnston had hedged his original typeface with principles that had prohibited any further development. Of these, at least three would have to be broken:
1. That the ratio of the width of stroke to the height of a capital letter could not be thicker than 7:1 without sacrificing legibility. This meant for him that bolder letters were not desirable.
2. That the letters should be of mathematically even strokes, not like nineteenth-century grotesque sans where the strokes were thickened and thinned for optical appearance (this is one principle Johnston sometimes neglected in his sketches).
3. That the height of a lower-case 'x' should be in the proportion of 4:7 against the height of a capital 'X'. This kept the lower case relatively small compared to today's display types.

Page 41
Underground Railway
Block-Letter Medium
98mm capital height.

inter
inter

This shows how inter-letter spacing decreases as the spaces within letters are also decreased by the thickening of the stroke forming the letter.

Banks&Miles decreased the ratio of stroke thickness to capital height. The rule about even strokes does not work well visually, as the human eye thinks horizontal strokes are thicker than vertical ones. 'Apparent' evenness of stroke is possible in a lightly drawn sans, but in heavier weights parts of a letter-shape have to be lightened ('modelled') in order to get everything into the drawing, (consider a very heavy '**e**'). The 'x' height was also modified, making it larger than Johnston had decreed. Too strict adherence to the Johnston principles would have inhibited any development; it was better in the 1980s to aim at the 'spirit' of the 1916 achievement. 'New Johnston', as the new type is called, retains all the characteristic shapes of the 1916 original.

Making the 'Medium' slightly heavier than before brought one other benefit: the inter-letter spacing could be reduced. This aspect of 'Underground Railway Block-Letter' caused a lot of problems when it was used as wooden type, for Johnston had set out complex letter-spacing instructions (Appendix 2). The compositors at the four printers who held the London Transport types were used to these spacing requirements, but by the end of the 1980s these skills had declined. Metal letters are fixed and inflexible in the way in which they are spaced, and if made well seldom benefit from adjustment, but film and digital type-

A direct comparison between the same size of 'Underground Railway Block-Letter' and 'New Johnston Medium'. The stroke thickness of the medium font has increased as has the height of lower-case letters in proportion to the height of the capitals.

height x x height

40

RSU
YZ&
2345
7890

London's Handwriting
The Development of Edward Johnston's Underground Railway Block-Letter
Colin Banks
London Transport Museum, London, 1994
52 pages
510 × 375 mm (20 × 14.75 in)
Designed by Banks & Miles

London's Handwriting is the story of the revolutionary lettering designed by the calligrapher Edward Johnston (1872–1944) and first used in 1916 by London Electric Railways. Originally called Underground Railway Block Letter, it was later rolled out across London Transport's vast network of trams, buses, underground trains and stations. This included all signage, posters, publicity and, famously, Harry Beck's diagram of underground lines. Still in use today, the typeface has become synonymous with London.

Written by the designer Colin Banks, the book recalls not only the development of Johnston's typeface but also its influence on later sans serif designs, notably Gill Sans by Johnston's ex-student Eric Gill. Banks's own company, Banks & Miles, was commissioned to redraw Johnston's original typeface in the 1980s, when it was still available only as either metal or wooden type. There is considerable information on this adaptation – called New Johnston, it created a family of weights for the first time and was available for use across modern reproduction techniques.

London's Handwriting is a large-format book. It is very well made: it is housed in a black box embossed with the London Transport roundel, and its red cloth cover and blue endpapers match the London Transport livery. Printed in black on high-quality uncoated stock, it includes letterpress pages with pulls from some of the remaining Underground Railway Block Letter wood type. The largest of these are 98 mm (3.75 in) in cap height, and require the large page size for their display. There are illustrations of Johnston's working drawings and examples of the typeface's usage in signage and posters. Despite his dislike of industry, Johnston would have approved of this book and its craftsmanship.

Published to coincide with the design of the digital typeface New Johnston by Banks & Miles, London's Handwriting *is packaged in its own box.*

Helvetica: Homage to a Typeface

Lars Müller

Lars Müller Publishers, Baden, 2002
240 pages
160 × 120 mm (6.25 × 4.75 in)
Designed by Lars Müller, Sonja Haller, Matilda Plöjel, Hendrik Schwantes

This book is a passionate tribute to the omnipotence of Helvetica. In his sermon-like introduction, its author, the designer and publisher Lars Müller (1955–), calls it 'the shift worker and solo entertainer of typefaces'. He traces the roots of its popularity from its introduction as Neue Haas Grotesk in 1957, and praises its 'forgotten designer' Max Miedinger (1910–1980).

The name was changed to Helvetica, Latin for Switzerland, in 1960 and the typeface and the country became for ever linked. This is reflected in the book's cover design: a cap 'H' on a red background, mimicking the white cross on the Swiss national flag. This association played a part in Helvetica's reputation as a font that was reliable, functional and trustworthy.

In recognition of Helvetica's pre-eminent position as the typeface of choice for many designers, the book consists of examples of work featuring its use in modern-day graphic design.

Müller sees equal merit in the use of the typeface by both professionals and amateurs. Hidden within the French-folded pages of its first edition in 2002, readers will see (should they wish to tear them open) photographs of Helvetica's use as the worldwide typeface of choice for everyday printing, signage and shopfront applications. 'Helvetica is the perfume of the city,' Müller proclaims in his praise of these designs, many of which have been put together without the need of a designer. The second edition, published in 2005, is a paperback with no French folds and has been broken into two separate sections dealing with typographical work and cityscapes.

The top left-hand illustration shows work for Knoll (1966) by Massimo Vignelli, explored in more detail in Design: Vignelli, *Rizzoli, New York, 1990.*

For the observant reader, the book contains seven typefaces apart from Helvetica.

Helvetica communicates with the most legitimate, beautiful, and universal form. Makoto Saito

It was easy to become a designer in those days. I looked to mentors like Josef Müller-Brockmann, Paul Rand, Charles Eames, and Helvetica, and found a path of my own. Edgar Reinhard

Sourcebooks

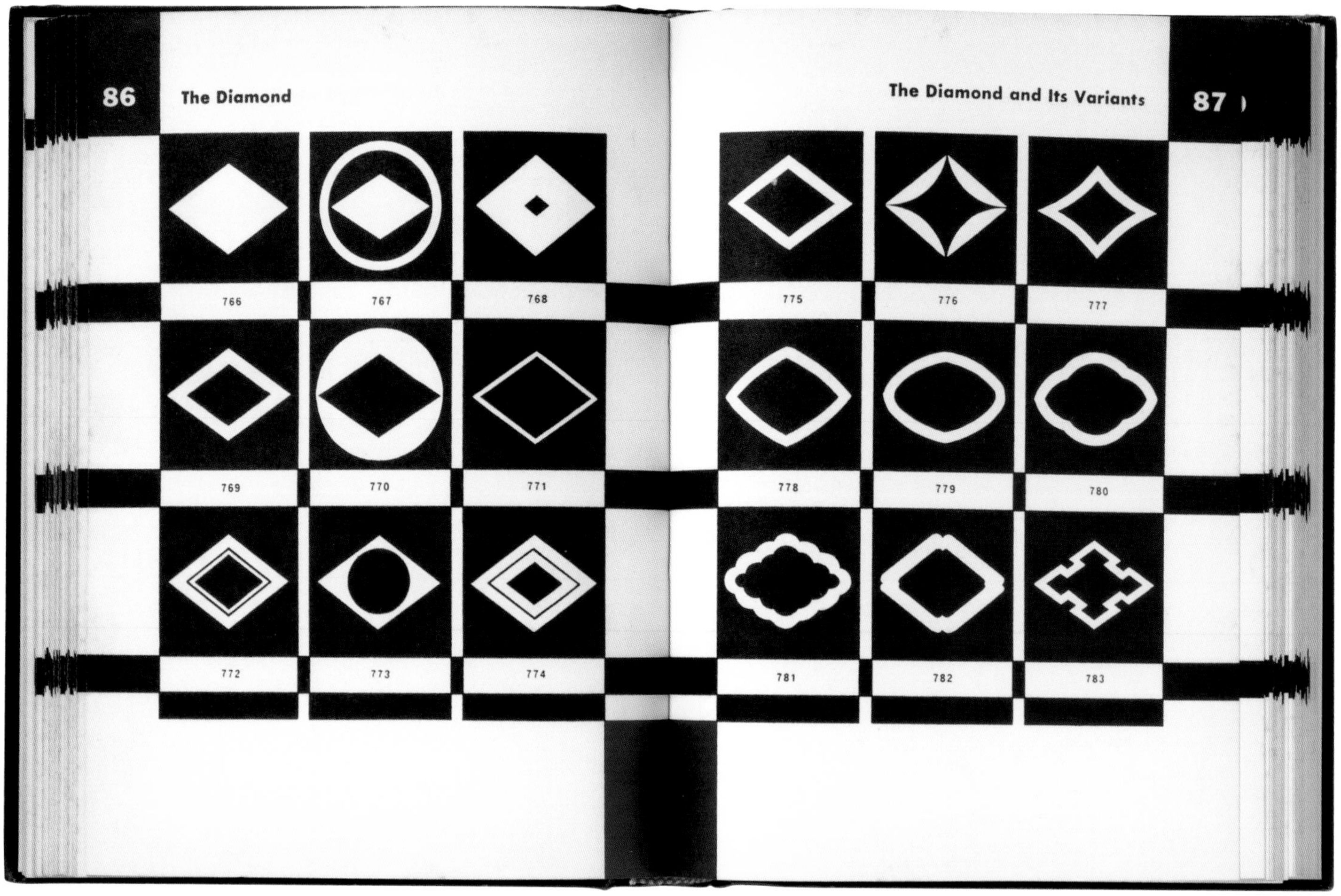

86 The Diamond

The Diamond and Its Variants 87

766	767	768	775	776	777
769	770	771	778	779	780
772	773	774	781	782	783

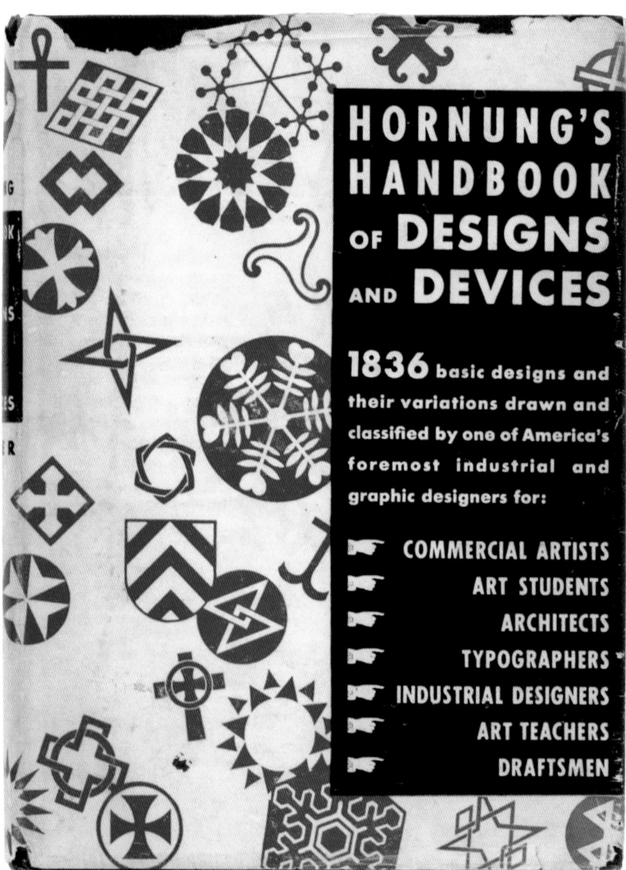

HORNUNG'S
HANDBOOK
OF DESIGNS
AND DEVICES
1836 basic designs and their variations drawn and classified by one of America's foremost industrial and graphic designers for:
COMMERCIAL ARTISTS
ART STUDENTS
ARCHITECTS
TYPOGRAPHERS
INDUSTRIAL DESIGNERS
ART TEACHERS
DRAFTSMEN

Handbook of Designs and Devices

Clarence P. Hornung

Harper and Brothers,
New York, 1932
Second edition (pictured),
Dover Publications,
New York, 1946
240 pages
222 × 162 mm (8.75 × 6.375 in)

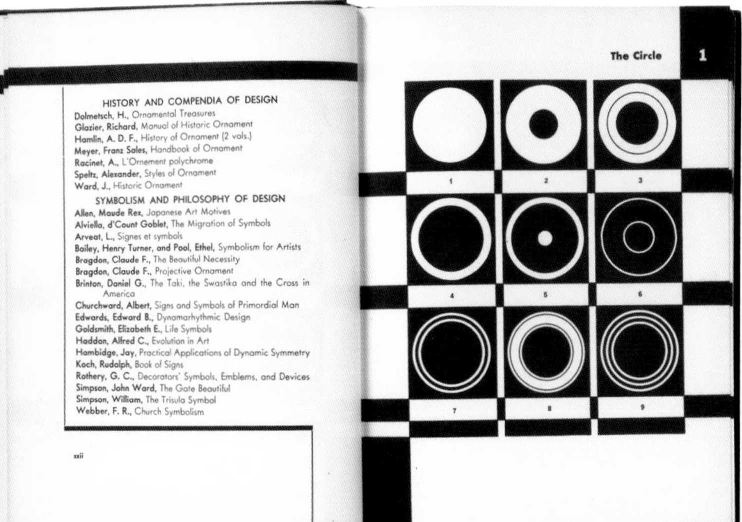

Each page of designs shows the basic form and its derivatives, with nine images to a page.

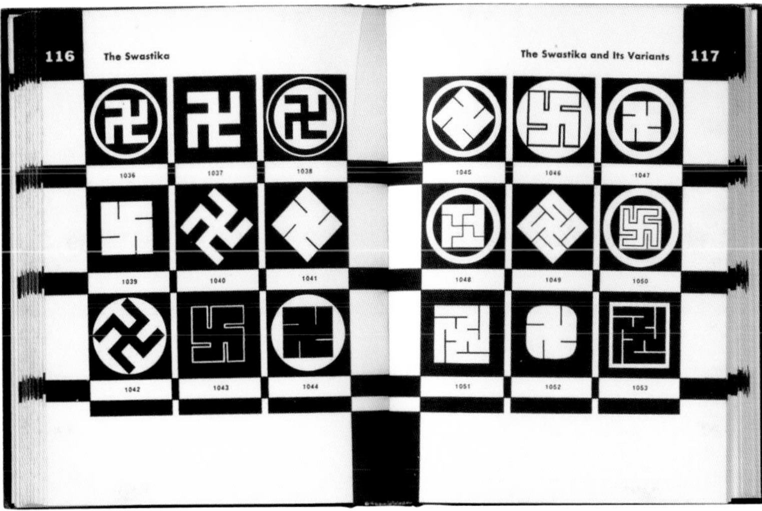

In his preface to the second edition of 1946, Hornung makes reference to the change in meaning of the Swastika through its association with Nazi Germany since the first edition of the book in 1932.

The designer and author Clarence P. Hornung (1899–1997) was inspired by his study of Japanese heraldry to create a resource of geometric designs and their variants for designers. Initially he wanted it to be a practical book rather than a history or an analysis of symbolic meaning, but later editions included a section of notes that provided more historical background.

Handbook of Designs and Devices is divided into chapters according to basic shapes – 'Circle', 'Line' and 'Triangle' – and then subdivided into variations – the Crescent, Sector, Segment, Ring and Trefoil in the case of the circle. The presentation is uniform, which allows clear comparisons to be made between the diverse designs gathered from a multitude of sources including Egyptian, Roman, Arabic and more modern ornament.

By coincidence or not, the all-encompassing corporate identity symbols of the 1950s and 1960s bear a marked resemblance to many of these designs. Regularly in print, the book is still a standard reference tool in design agencies.

Originally published in 1932, the *Handbook of Designs and Devices* was reprinted in 1946 by Dover Publications in a revised edition containing a section of notes at the rear of the book. It was the first art and design title published by this fledgling New York company, which had become a specialist in finding new audiences for overlooked and unfashionable books. Dover became the largest publisher of resource books for graphic designers.

Hornung would later produce two volumes of typographic specimens ('Pictorial' and 'Typographic') as *Hornung's Handbook of Early Advertising Art* for Dover. Among the company's other notable titles were *The 100 Greatest Advertisements* by Julian Lewis Watkins, the many typographic books of Dan X. Solo from his Solotype collection, *1800 Woodcuts By Thomas Bewick and his School*, *The Universal Penman* and the *Handbook of Pictorial Symbols* by Rudolf Modley (see page 58).

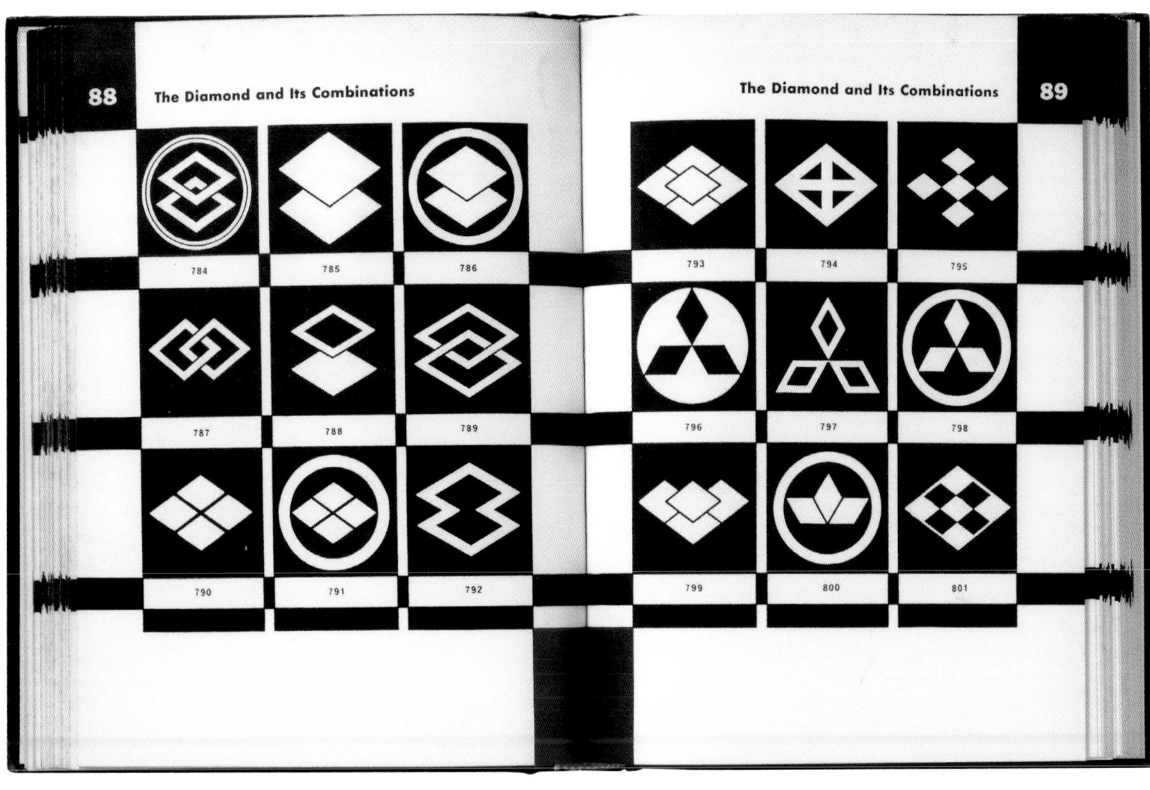

Printed Ephemera
The Changing Uses of Type and Letterforms in English and American Printing
John Lewis
W.S. Cowell, Ipswich, Suffolk, 1962
288 pages
304 × 235 mm (12 × 9.25 in)
Designed by John Lewis

Printed Ephemera is an illustrated history of English and American jobbing printing. Written by the typographer John Lewis (1912–1996), it was the first serious study of the vast amount of ephemera produced over the last 500 years. It is a story distinctly different to that of the well-documented, slowly evolving and scholarly book-printing trade.

Lewis's initial interest was forged when he purchased a collection of ephemera and decided to research the subject by visiting the Bagford Collection at the British Museum. His subsequent research took him to other major collections, including Dr John Johnson's Sanctuary of Printing at Oxford University Press and the Bella C. Landauer Collection at the New York Historical Society. At the same time he started collecting his own ephemera, searching in antiquarian bookshops, printing works, waste-paper baskets and street gutters.

There are two sections of illustrated material. The first and longer, 'Miscellaneous Ephemera', is split into numerous subdivisions such as Trade Cards, Licences and Certificates, Travel Notices, and Receipts, Order Forms and Billheads. The earliest item is an indulgence printed by William Caxton in 1480. There are also twentieth-century examples by designers such as Herbert Bayer, Alvin Lustig, Jan Tschichold and Herbert Spencer, but the majority of the examples are from the great burgeoning of the printing industry in the nineteenth century.

The second section studies the other aspect of the jobbing printer's output: 'Labels and Wrappers'. Here Lewis has edited down the many trades that could have been represented in order to concentrate on a limited selection of subject areas.

Printed Ephemera uses uncoated stock for the prelims and appendix, and coated paper for all the illustrative material. Each of the two main sections has an uncoated, laid, pale olive divider.

Printed in letterpress, the impositions use differing colour schemes, with up to four colours on each, including beige for paper and black for text, giving depth and liveliness to the pages.

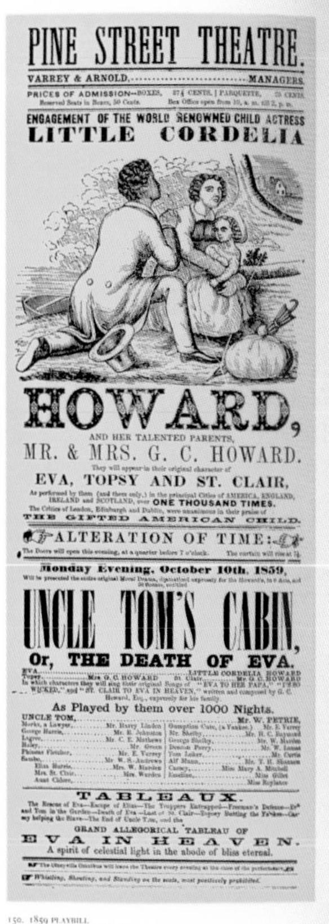

Entertainment notices

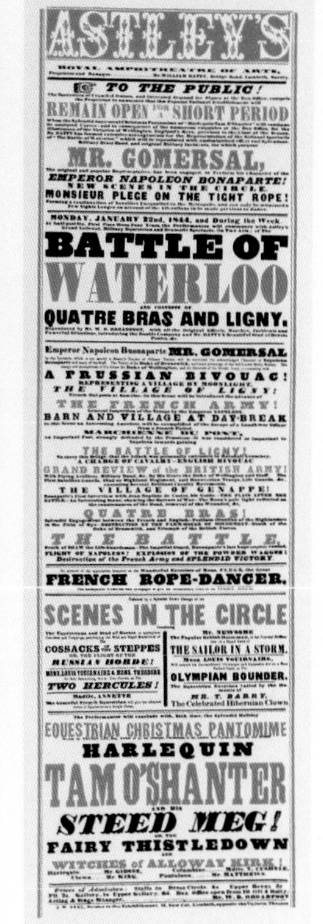

The most visually engaging ephemera are from the nineteenth century, when display typefaces were introduced; according to Lewis, this was a period when 'the jobbing printer or his compositor had the time of their lives, making artless but often brilliant use of an ever-increasing range of display letters'. The numerous attention-seeking playbills with their multiple typefaces and sizes testify to this.

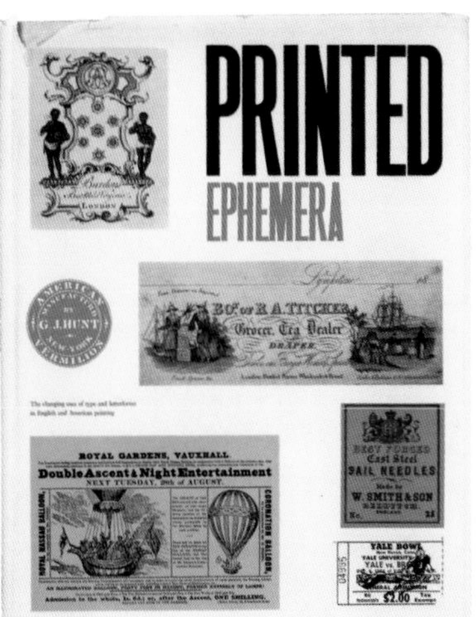

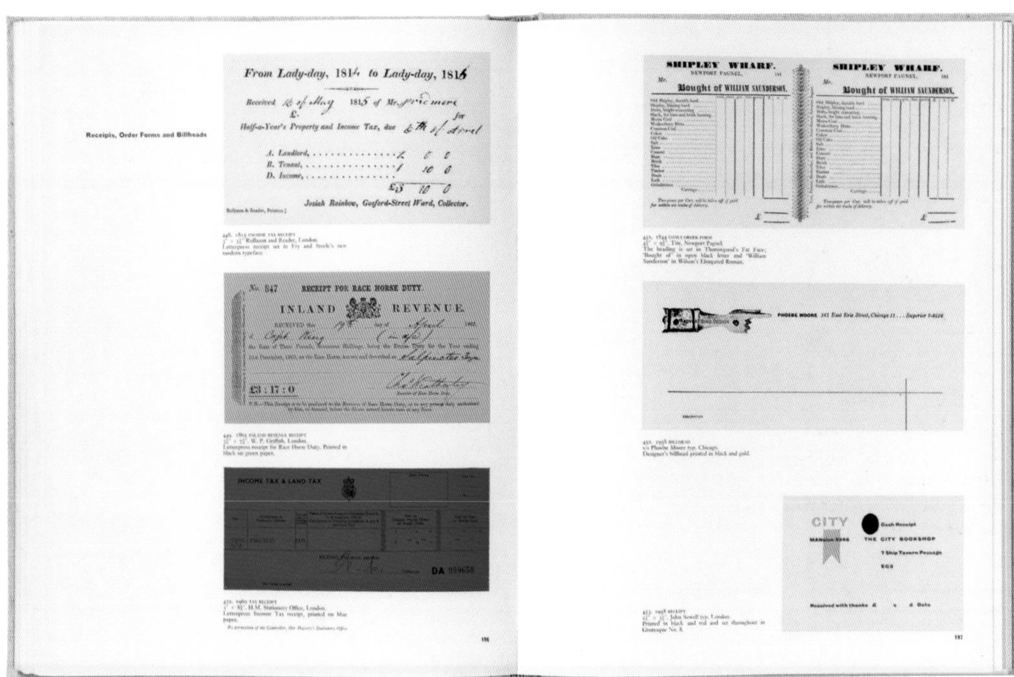

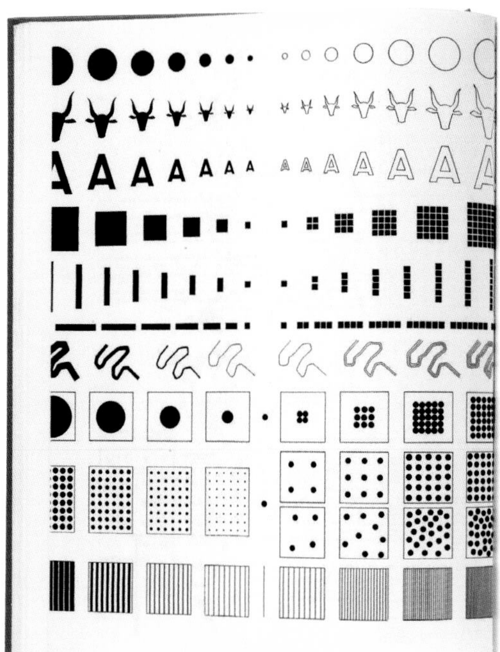

2. CARACTÉRISTIQUES ET PROPRIÉTÉS DES VARIABLES RÉTINIENNES.

LA VARIATION DE TAILLE

Une figure quelconque, de signification ponctuelle ou linéaire peut varier de taille sans pour cela varier de position, de valeur, de grain, de couleur, d'orientation ni de forme.
C'est la variation de surface qui constitue le stimuli sensible de la variation de taille.

L'implantation.
En implantation ponctuelle, la figure peut être quelconque, géométrique ou figurative, elle peut être une colonne de hauteur proportionnelle. La figure peut être formée de parties accolées et dénombrables.
L'extension de la variation est très grande en implantation ponctuelle et l'on peut utilement construire deux points visibles dont l'un a une surface 10 000 fois plus grande que l'autre (p. 182 et 363).
En implantation *linéaire*, une ligne peut varier d'épaisseur. Des lignes parallèles juxtaposées sont dénombrables. L'extension de la variation est souvent limitée par la disposition concourante de lignes, dans un réseau routier par exemple.
En implantation *zonale*, la zone ne peut varier de surface dans le plan. Mais ses constituants, points ou lignes, peuvent varier en taille ou en nombre. L'extension est limitée par la surface de la zone à qualifier. Néanmoins il est possible de construire quelques cercles ou figures plus étendues que celle-ci (p. 373).

La longueur.
En perception quantitative et en perception ordonnée le nombre des paliers possibles est illimité, mais l'œil ne différencie en moyenne pas plus de 20 paliers entre deux points dont les surfaces sont dans le rapport de 1 à 10. Cette limite a permis de proposer la "gamme naturelle des tailles croissantes" qui contient les paliers nécessaires et suffisants pour toute représentation quantitative (p. 369).

La perception.
En perception *sélective*, la variation de taille est courte. Dans des conditions moyennes de dessin, il est imprudent de compter sur plus de 4 ou 5 paliers sélectifs (tels que l'on puisse isoler et définir avec précision la figure formée par tous les points d'une taille donnée).
La variation de taille est dissociative et il n'est pas possible de l'abstraire visuellement. Toute autre variable interférant avec une variation de taille sera dominée par elle, et sa longueur diminuera avec la taille. Dans des points très petits la couleur devient pratiquement insensible.
La combinaison taille valeur. La valeur est aussi dissociative. Aussi la variation de taille ne sera sensible que pour des signes de valeur foncée. A la limite, des signes évidés et blancs font perdre à la variation de taille toutes ses propriétés spontanées.

71

Studies on the visual effects of repeating graphic elements and the resulting vibrating patterns.

L'effet vibratoire en implantation linéaire.
Il est aisé de l'obtenir (2 B, C et D) et de lui dépend la sélectivité du grain en implantation linéaire (de (1) à (3) : variation de valeur; de A à E : variation de grain).

L'effet vibratoire en implantation ponctuelle.
En implantation ponctuelle, et à condition que les signes soient assez grands (plus de 2 mm environ) on approche l'effet vibratoire de deux manières.

1°) par une variation de *complexité interne* dans une forme donnée, suivant (4) ou suivant (5).
Mais parmi toutes les possibilités de construction de (5 c), quelles dimensions de la couronne blanche fournissent le meilleur effet vibratoire ?
Le tableau (7) combine les variations de disposition de la couronne (de gauche à droite) et les variations de valeur (de haut en bas). Répété en construction cyclique (8) il souligne la puissance de l'effet, qui parvient à déformer la variation de valeur; il confirme que c'est dans les valeurs de 50 à 60 % et autour des dessins soulignés par une croix, en (8), que l'effet semble maximum.

2°) par la variation de *complexité externe* d'un signe qui oppose le cercle à l'étoile et dont l'ultime limite est le trait (6).
Cette variation se rapproche, dans ses effets perceptifs de l'effet de grain. Elle tend à créer, dans les limites du signe, une zone de confusion vibratoire et d'ambiguïté. Grâce à cet effet, le cercle, la croix et le trait sont les trois *formes* qui permettent, dans certaines limites, une perception sélective. Mais ces trois signes ne sont pas visuellement ordonnés.

82

Semiologie Graphique

Diagrammes, Réseaux, Cartes

Jacques Bertin

Mouton, Gauthier-Villars, Paris, 1967

432 pages

271 × 209 mm (10.625 × 8.25 in)

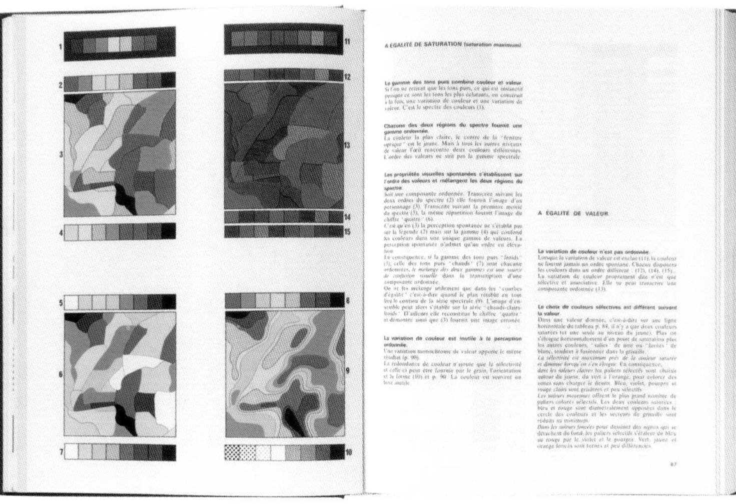

Many of the illustrations depict French subject matter – the spread below shows anamorphic or distorted maps of France.

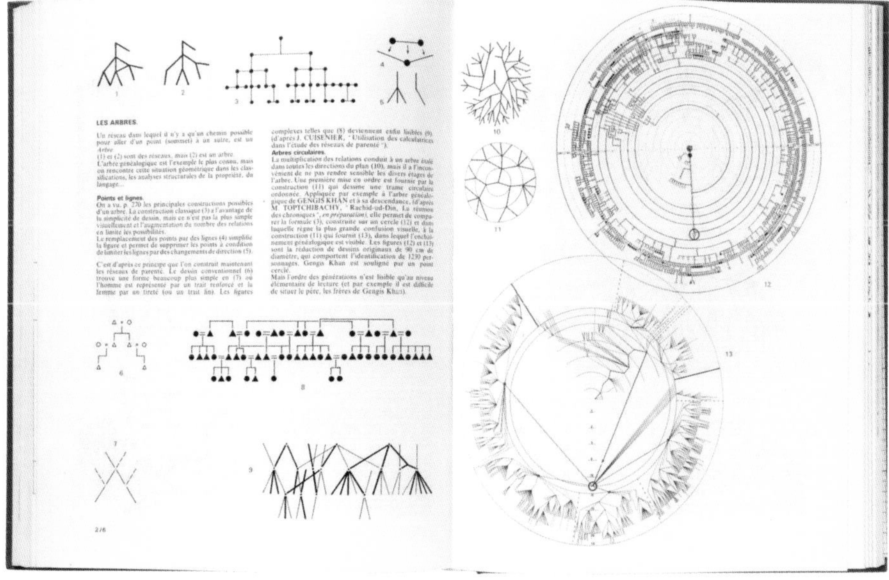

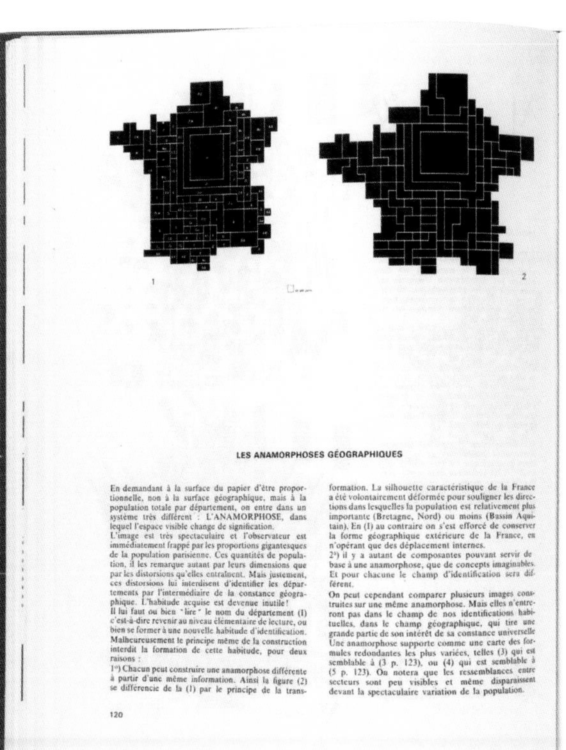

LES ANAMORPHOSES GÉOGRAPHIQUES

En demandant à la surface du papier d'être proportionnelle, non à la surface géographique, mais à la population totale par département, on entre dans un système très différent : L'ANAMORPHOSE, dans lequel l'espace visible change de signification.
L'image est très spectaculaire et l'observateur est immédiatement frappé par les proportions gigantesques de la population parisienne. Ces quantités de population, il les remarque autant par leurs dimensions que par les distorsions qu'elles entraînent. Mais justement, ces distorsions lui interdisent d'identifier les départements par l'intermédiaire de la constance géographique. L'habitude acquise est devenue inutile!
Il lui faut ou bien "lire" le nom du département (1) c'est-à-dire revenir au niveau élémentaire de lecture, ou bien se former à une nouvelle habitude d'identification.
Malheureusement le principe même de la construction interdit la formation de cette habitude, pour deux raisons :
1°) Chacun peut construire une anamorphose différente à partir d'une même information. Ainsi la figure (2) se différencie de la (1) par le principe de la transformation. La silhouette caractéristique de la France a été volontairement déformée pour souligner les directions dans lesquelles la population est relativement plus importante (Bretagne, Nord) ou moins (Bassin Aquitain). En (1) au contraire on s'est efforcé de conserver la forme géographique extérieure de la France, en n'opérant que des déplacement internes.
2°) il y a autant de composantes pouvant servir de base à une anamorphose, que de concepts imaginables. Et pour chacune le champ d'identification sera différent.
On peut cependant comparer plusieurs images construites sur une même anamorphose. Mais elles n'entreront pas dans le champ de nos identifications habituelles, dans le champ géographique, qui tire une grande partie de son intérêt de sa constance universelle. Une anamorphose supporte comme une carte des formules redondantes les plus variées, telles (3) qui est semblable à (3 p. 123), ou (4) qui est semblable à (5 p. 123). On notera que les ressemblances entre secteurs sont peu visibles et même disparaissent devant la spectaculaire variation de la population.

120

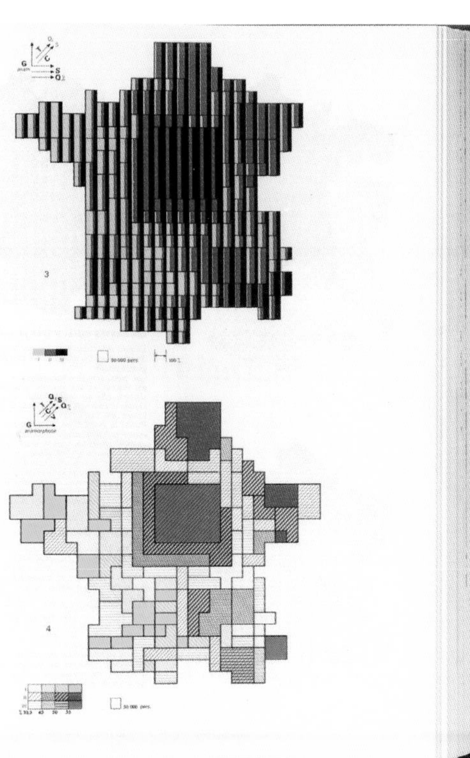

Semiologie Graphique: Diagrammes, Réseaux, Cartes ('Semiology of Graphics: Diagrams, Networks, Maps') is an exhaustive study of the elements and structures involved in the presentation of graphs, diagrams and maps. Written by the French cartographer and educator Jacques Bertin (1918–), this classic book contains thousands of examples of his works and those by his colleagues.

A masterclass in graphic mark-making and diagrammatic techniques, *Semiologie Graphique* is divided into two sections. The first begins with a study of the many different types of network and graphical representation and the best usage for particular kinds of data. This is followed by a detailed look at all the constituent visual elements: colour, shape, pattern, shades, symbols and orientation, and how they can be most effectively utilized. Bertin was less interested in the quality and efficacy of the information on display than with its appearance, and many examples are shown without the aid of context or rationale. The second section examines the best methods of implementation and presentation, with reference to mapping in particular.

Semiologie Graphique is in French only, and most of the illustrations show a natural preponderance of French subject matter. They are mainly black and white, with some dramatic colour pages – these are particularly effective in the parts of the book devoted to the use of colour.

A revised edition of *Semiologie Graphique* was published in English by the University of Wisconsin Press in 1983, as *Semiology of Graphics: Diagrams, Networks, Maps*.

Letter and Image
Robert Massin
Van Nostrand Reinhold Company, New York, 1970
288 pages
270 × 210 mm (10.5 × 8.25 in)
Designed by Robert Massin

The French designer and author Robert Massin (1925–) was an obsessive collector and admirer of all things lettering. The material for this book, his tribute to the symbiotic relationship of the letter and image, was amassed over 15 years. First published as *La Lettre et L'Image* (Editions Gallimard, Paris, 1970), it is a stunning selection of images and literary out-takes – a mighty feat of research and writing.

As a piece of book design its intentionally crude form is not too dissimilar from that of a scrapbook. A surfeit of images is scattered through the pages, a mixture of popular and highbrow, professionally lettered and artisan-made, their diversity reinforced by their informal placement on the page. Massin himself had been experimenting with an expressive form of typography, most notably in his design for *La Cantatrice chauve* ('The Bald Prima Donna') (1964) by Eugène Ionesco, which is illustrated in *Letter and Image*.

A largely visual introductory chapter shows a succession of images to illustrate the concept that letters are at the heart of our environment: a photograph of Times Square, a page reproduced from the *Boston Globe* and a wall of graffiti.

The following chapter is a homage to the letterform, and contains the surreal imaginings in the drawings of J.J. Grandville and Saul Steinberg and the projections of Max Ernst and Robert Brownjohn. There are also whole alphabets, both figurative and decorative, from the marriage of human form and structure in letters of Geofroy Tory's *Champ Fleury* alphabet (1529) to the architectonic alphabet of Johann David Steingruber (1773). Other items include children's book illustrations, logotypes and lettering historically used in design.

Massin devotes a chapter to the calligram, which he describes as 'fusing a visual image and a script'. Guillaume Apollinaire was the first person to use the word, to label his graphic poetry, but Massin traces the tradition back to ancient Greece. The final chapter looks at the letter in painting, and includes examples from works by Paul Klee, Fernand Léger and Georges Braque.

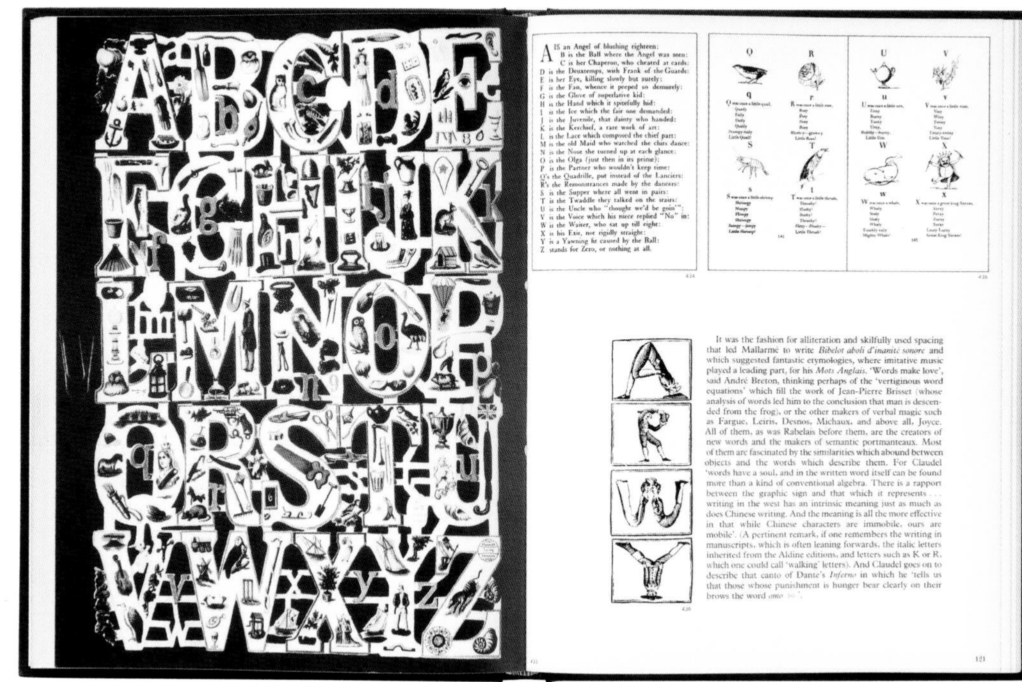

A IS an Angel of blushing eighteen:
B is the Ball where the Angel was seen:
C is her Chaperon, who cheated at cards:
D is the Deuxtemps, with Frank of the Guards:
E is her Eye, killing slowly but surely:
F is the Fan, whence it peeped so demurely:
G is the Glove of superlative kid:
H is the Hand which it spitefully hid:
I is the Ice which the fair one demanded:
J is the Juvenile, that dainty who handed:
K is the Kerchief, a rare work of art:
L is the Lace which composed the chief part:
M is the old Maid who watched the chits dance:
N is the Nose she turned up at each glance:
O is the Olga (just then in its prime):
P is the Partner who wouldn't keep time:
Q's the Quadrille, put instead of the Lanciers:
R's the Remonstrances made by the dancers:
S is the Supper where all went in pairs:
T is the Twaddle they talked on the stairs:
U is the Uncle who "thought we'd be goin'":
V is the Voice which his niece replied "No" in:
W is the Waiter, who sat up till eight:
X is his Exit, not rigidly straight:
Y is a Yawning fit caused by the Ball:
Z stands for Zero, or nothing at all.

It was the fashion for alliteration and skilfully used spacing that led Mallarmé to write *Bibelot aboli d'inanité sonore* and which suggested fantastic etymologies, where imitative music played a leading part, for his *Mots Anglais*. 'Words make love', said André Breton, thinking perhaps of the 'vertiginous word equations' which fill the work of Jean-Pierre Brisset (whose analysis of words led him to the conclusion that man is descended from the frog), or the other makers of verbal magic such as Fargue, Leiris, Desnos, Michaux, and above all, Joyce. All of them, as was Rabelais before them, are the creators of new words and the makers of semantic portmanteaux. Most of them are fascinated by the similarities which abound between objects and the words which describe them. For Claudel 'words have a soul, and in the written word itself can be found more than a kind of conventional algebra. There is a rapport between the graphic sign and that which it represents ... writing in the west has an intrinsic meaning just as much as does Chinese writing. And the meaning is all the more effective in that while Chinese characters are immobile, ours are mobile'. (A pertinent remark, if one remembers the writing in manuscripts, which is often leaning forwards, the italic letters inherited from the Aldine editions, and letters such as K or R, which one could call 'walking' letters). And Claudel goes on to describe that canto of Dante's *Inferno* in which he 'tells us that those whose punishment is hunger bear clearly on their brows the word *omo*'.

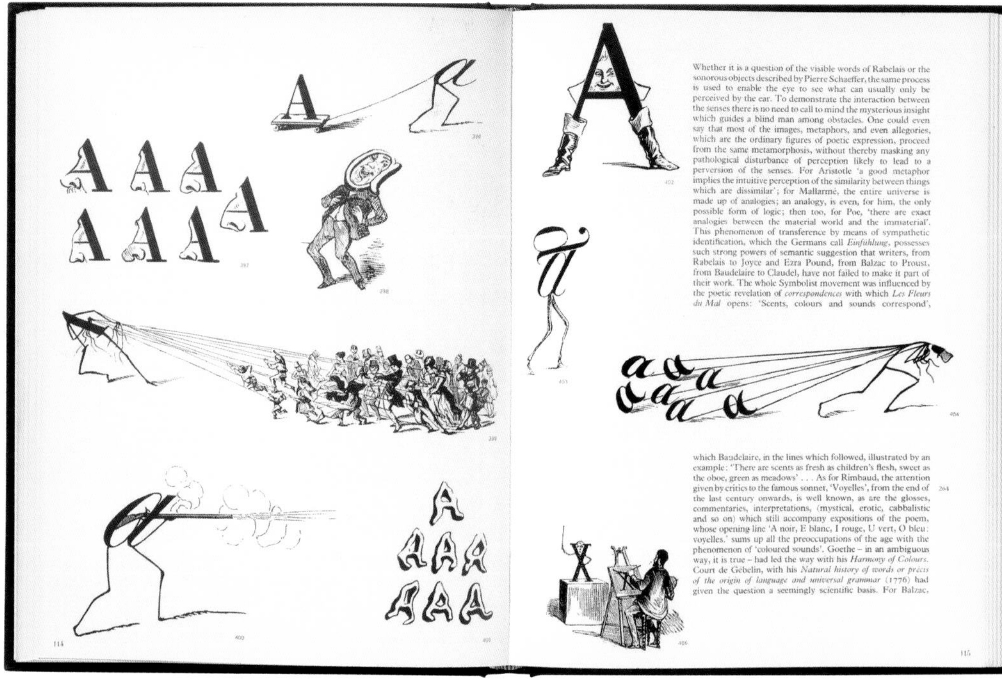

Whether it is a question of the visible words of Rabelais or the sonorous objects described by Pierre Schaeffer, the same process is used to enable the eye to see what can usually only be perceived by the ear. To demonstrate the interaction between the senses there is no need to call to mind the mysterious insight which guides a blind man among obstacles. One could even say that most of the images, metaphors, and even allegories, which are the ordinary figures of poetic expression, proceed from the same metamorphosis, without thereby masking any pathological disturbance of perception likely to lead to a perversion of the senses. For Aristotle 'a good metaphor implies the intuitive perception of the similarity between things which are dissimilar'; for Mallarmé, the entire universe is made up of analogies; an analogy, is even, for him, the only possible form of logic; then too, for Poe, 'there are exact analogies between the material world and the immaterial'. This phenomenon of transference by means of sympathetic identification, which the Germans call *Einfühlung*, possesses such strong powers of semantic suggestion that writers, from Rabelais to Joyce and Ezra Pound, from Balzac to Proust, from Baudelaire to Claudel, have not failed to make it part of their work. The whole Symbolist movement was influenced by the poetic revelation of *correspondences* with which *Les Fleurs du Mal* opens: 'Scents, colours and sounds correspond',

which Baudelaire, in the lines which followed, illustrated by an example: 'There are scents as fresh as children's flesh, sweet as the oboe, green as meadows' ... As for Rimbaud, the attention given by critics to the famous sonnet, 'Voyelles', from the end of the last century onwards, is well known, as are the glosses, commentaries, interpretations, (mystical, erotic, cabbalistic and so on) which still accompany expositions of the poem, whose opening line 'A noir, E blanc, I rouge, U vert, O bleu: voyelles.' sums up all the preoccupations of the age with the phenomenon of 'coloured sounds'. Goethe – in an ambiguous way, it is true – had led the way with his *Harmony of Colours*. Court de Gébelin, with his *Natural history of words or précis of the origin of language and universal grammar* (1776) had given the question a seemingly scientific basis. For Balzac,

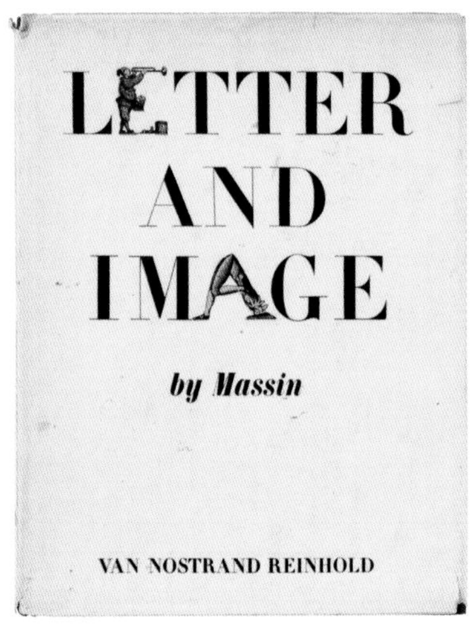

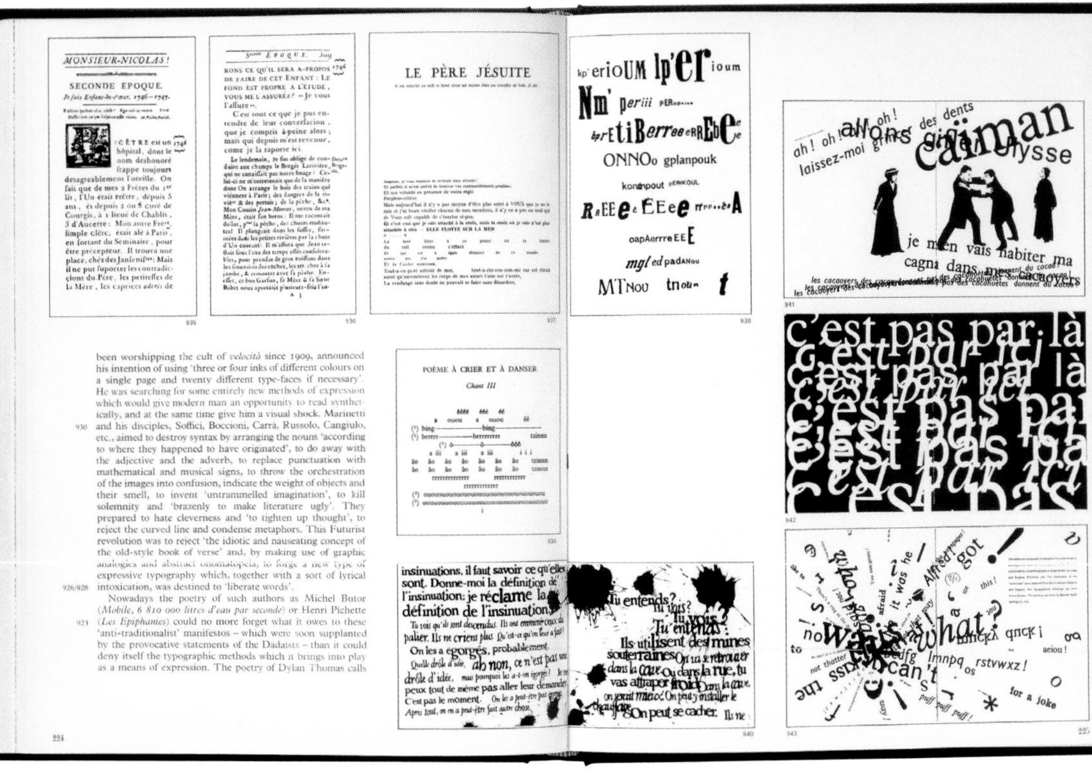

Spreads on the far right from Massin's own typographic designs for La Cantatrice chauve *('The Bald Prima Donna') by Eugène Ionesco show his expressive style. Massin's career is studied in detail in Laetitia Wolff's* Massin, *Phaidon Press, London, 2007.*

De Laudibus Sanctae Crucis, *a manuscript by Hrabanus Maurus, a ninth-century German monk. His grids of text reveal shapes and figures picked out in red lettering. This is one of the few places where Massin allows himself the luxury of a second colour in an otherwise monochrome book.*

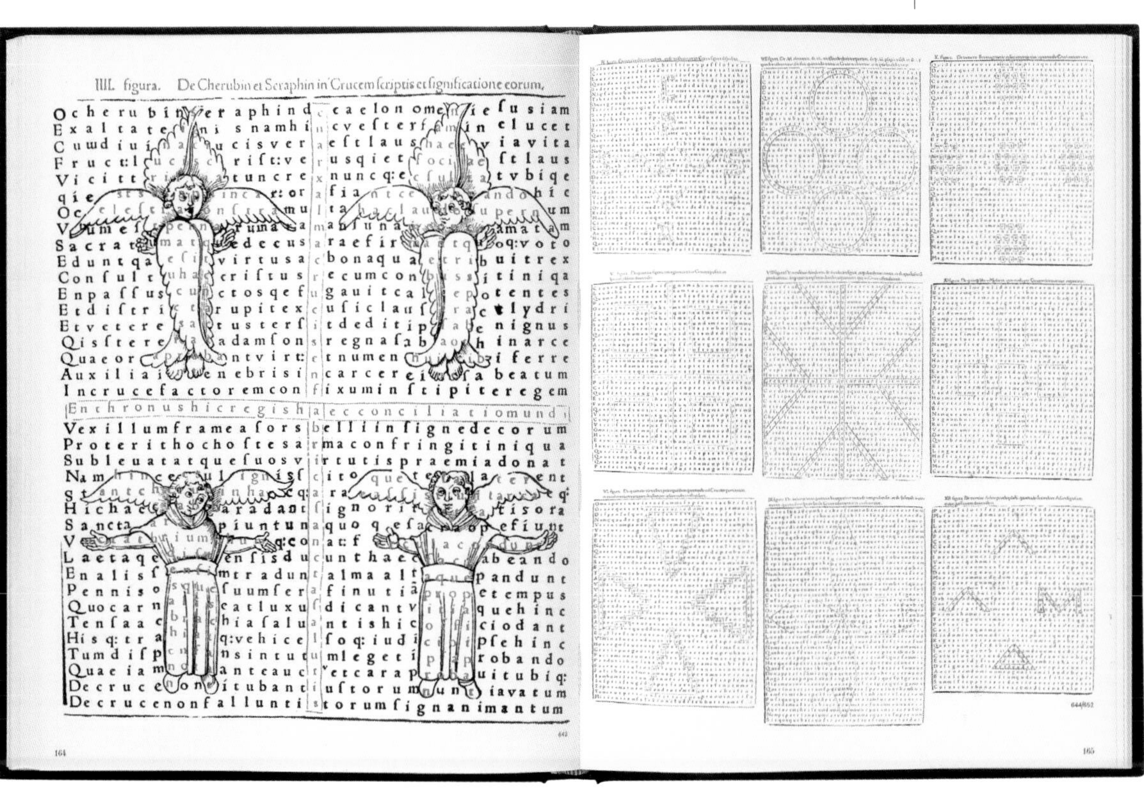

Working Title: Piet Gerards, Graphic Designer, Ben van Melick, Uitgeverij 010, Rotterdam, 2003
Fleckhaus, Michael Koetzle, Carsten M. Wolff, Klinkhardt & Biermann, Munich, 1997
The Compendium, Pentagram, Phaidon Press, London, 1993
Letter and Image, Robert Massin, Studio Vista, London, 1970
Type & Typography: The Designers Type Book, Ben Rosen, Reinhold Publishing Corporation, New York, 1963
Wo Der Buchstabe das Wort Führt, Kurt Weidemann, Hatje Cantz, Ostfildern-Ruit, 1995
Symbol, Handbook of International Signs, Walter Diethelm, second edition, ABC Verlag, Zurich, 1972
Signs & Symbols: Their Design & Meaning, Adrian Frutiger, Ebury Press, London, 1998
Nine Pioneers in American Graphic Design, R. Roger Remington, Barbara J. Hodik, MIT Press, Cambridge, Massachusetts, 1989
Graphic Cosmos: The World of Shin Matsunaga, Shin Matsunaga, Shuiesha, Toyko, 1997

TRADE MARKS
& SYMBOLS
VOLUME 1: Alphabetical Designs
YASABURO KUWAYAMA

Three spreads from Volume 1: Alphabetical Designs *showing, from top to bottom, trademarks based on the letters 'h', 'o', 'p' and 's'.*

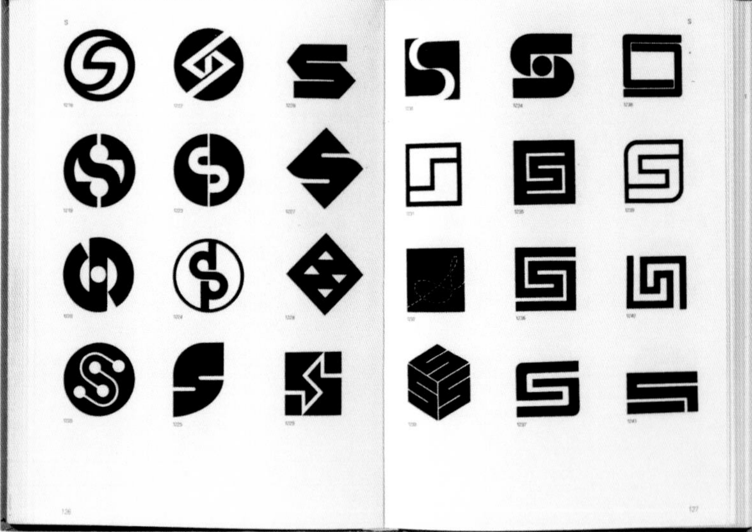

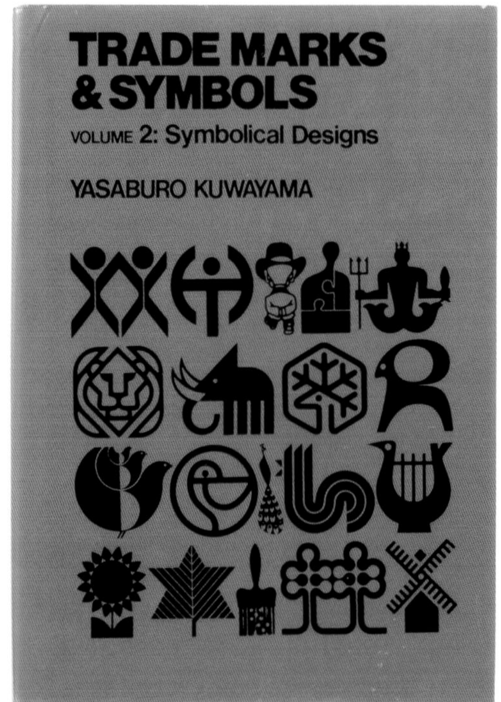

Trade Marks & Symbols

Volume 1: Alphabetical Designs
Volume 2: Symbolical Designs
Yasaburo Kuwayama
Van Nostrand Reinhold Company, New York, 1973
192 pages per volume
253 × 176 mm (10 × 7 in)

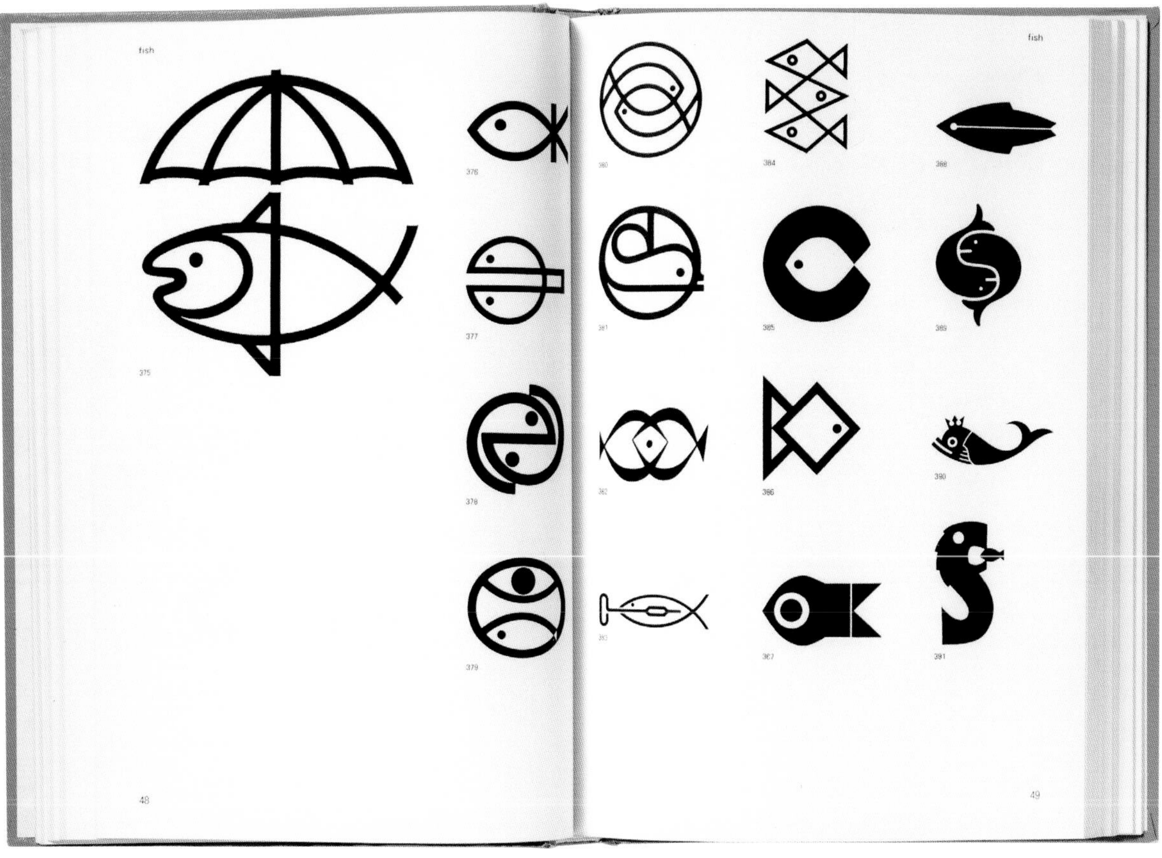

Trademarks based on fish from Volume 2: Symbolical Designs. *Each is numbered, and the main index provides information on its designer and client and the type of industry.*

The two volumes of *Trade Marks & Symbols* by the Japanese designer Yasaburo Kuwayama (1938–) contain over 3000 trademarks. They are a comprehensive study of logo forms and useful visual tools. The trademarks in both volumes are laid out 12 on a page with no captioning and, printed in black only, the spreads have an abstract quality that belies the practical nature of these sourcebooks.

The books – first published in a Japanese-language edition by Kashiwa Shobo in Tokyo – represent an impressive piece of research, with examples of trademarks gathered from across the globe. These include designs by large agencies and by designers working alone. Commissioners range from corporations to much smaller companies, and the trademarks are sourced from many different industries.

The first volume, *Alphabetical Designs*, shows trademarks based on letterforms. There are 26 chapters, one for each letter of the alphabet. The second volume, *Symbolical Designs*, displays trademarks inspired by human and animal forms, objects, geometry, numerals and designs based on Japanese characters.

Usefully, all the information can be cross-referenced through the three indexes at the end of both volumes. Each trademark is identified only by a number, and looking this up in the main index provides information on the designer, client and type of industry. The two remaining indexes group trademarks by industry types, and by the designers and the trademarks they have created.

Label Design
Claude Humbert
Verlag Ernst Wasmuth, Tübingen, 1972
252 pages
271 × 250 mm (10.625 × 9.875 in)
Designed by Claude Humbert

Each of the 1000 labels shown in *Label Design* has been carefully placed in a red keylined box. All the boxes are the same size and the effect is of a serious study in historical classification. However, the book's author and designer, Claude Humbert, had no such pretensions: the design merely facilitated comparison of the similarities and contrasts between labels. His selection was therefore based primarily on visual interest, which makes for a valuable pictorial reference and a diverse creative resource.

Labels dating from the seventeenth century to the early 1970s are illustrated in black and white, and different eras are quite often combined on any one spread. An introductory chapter studies the functions of labels and the impact of different printing techniques and changing typographical styles on their design. The rest of the book is set aside for the labels themselves, which are arranged in six sections.

The first section consists of groups of labels of a similar type, with spreads showing, for example, typographical labels and ones with animals and human figures. The second section relates largely to twentieth-century packaging, and looks at label design across a specific range of goods. The third is concerned with round and oval labels, and the fourth with everyday labels that are ephemeral in nature. The final two sections examine labels in art and in the niche subject area of international and humanitarian organizations.

Most of the labels are by anonymous jobbing printers, but there are ones by designers such as Herb Lubalin, Anton Stankowski and the Swiss firm E. & U. Hiestand. The American Push Pin Studio is particularly well represented; Humbert even displays an example of the envelope in which the company's samples were sent, and the label attached to it.

Examples of food and cosmetic packaging from the 1960s, designed by the Swiss firm E. & U. Hiestand.

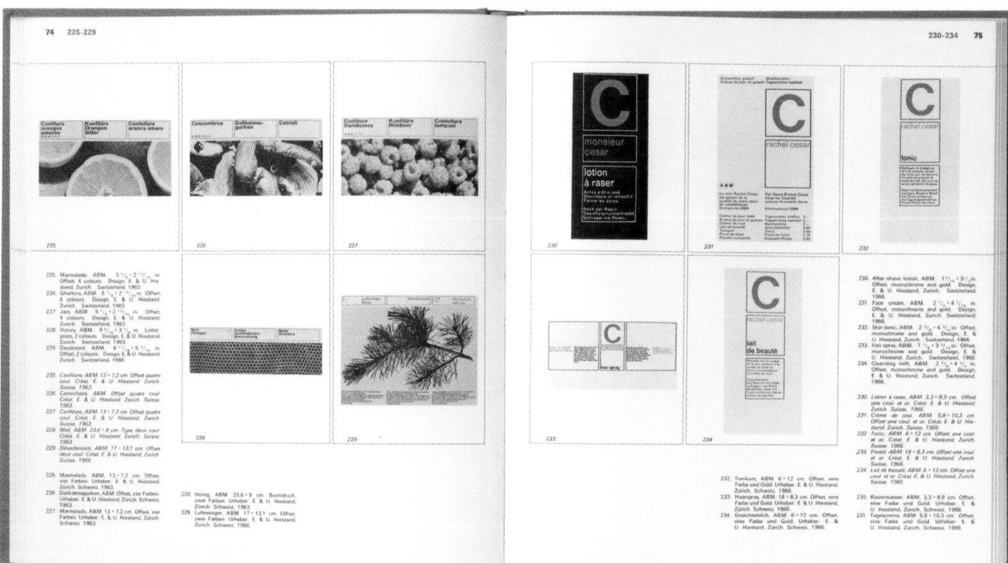

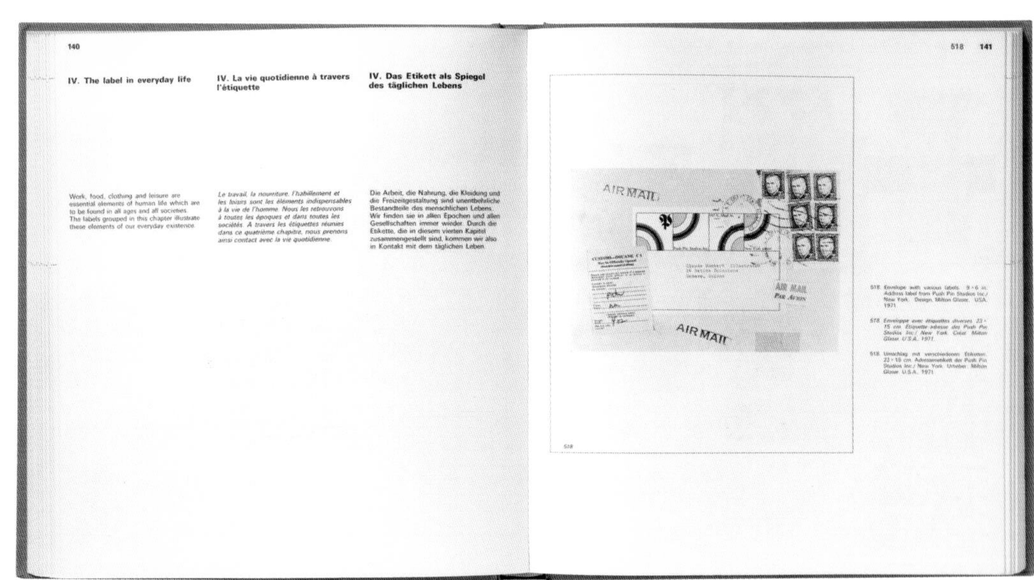

Rebhofweg 24
9500 Wil
Telefon 073 22 52 28

The first section of the book groups together labels that share similar characteristics – in this case simple typographic designs for products ranging from wine labels to ink bottles.

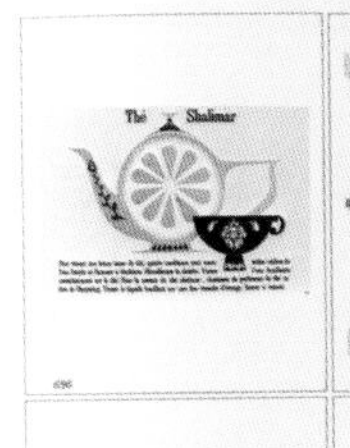

GRAPHIC FORM

Can Be Dry Cleaned, 101
Pole, Electric Distribution, 49
Light Outlet Ceiling, 49
Water Heater, 50
Use, 51
Full Moon, 54
Female, 55

Atomic s Orbital, 68
Attend To Obvious Fault, 73 v
Pressure, 81
Circularity (Roundness), 85
Weld All Around, 85
Alum, 87
Nothing to be Gained Here, 90 v

Village, 92 +
Water Well, 96
Temporary Water, 93
Stop; Off 107
Cylinder Oils B, C, and D, 108
Clear Sky, 121
Still, 126

Buddhism, Zen, Eternal State of Buddha, 138 v
Injury, Non-Fatal, 142
Information Forwarded, 151
Private Aid for Navigation, 155
Off, 157

Restriction, 145
No Vehicles, 146 v

Lubricate every 10 hours, 160
College; University, 95
Emergency Stop; Master Stop, 107
Daily Lubrication, 109
Most Difficult Ski Run, 132

Galactic Cluster, 54
Existing Trees Removed, 51 v
Neutral, 158 v

Traffic Circle Ahead, 143
Circulating Inside Air, 160 v
Traffic Circle, Compulsory, 146 v

Planetary Nebula, 54
Operation; Active; Functioning Properly, 61
Coaxiality and Concentricity, 85
Wind calm, 121

Volume, 63
Shooting Range, 132
Shooting, 136

Systems Device, Fire Alarm, 49

Empty, 158

Scattered Clouds, 0.2 or 0.3, 121 +

Illuminated Exit Sign, 48
Ranger Station, 95 v

Taoism, Yin-Yang, 139

Scattered Clouds, 0.5, 121 +
Contrast, 116 v

Broken Clouds, 0.6, 121

Community Territory, 53

Oil Level Window, 108

Half Full, 158

Broken Clouds, 0.7 or 0.8, 121

Full, 158

Soccer, 136

Overcast, Complete, 121
Human, 51
New Moon, 54
Decimal Sign, 64
Start of Winding, 81
Field Weld, 85
Oil Well, 96
Perennial Water, 93
Tank (Oil, Water), 95
Gold, 105

High Pressure Roller 109 +
Multiplied by, 111
Slight Rain, Intermittent, 120
Staccato, 124
Material Damage, 142
Sound Horn, 152
Position of Buoy, 155

Sunday, 89
Surviving Child with Seed of Life, 90
Radiation Quantities, 115

Sun, 54
Flush Floor Sign Outlet, 48
Existing Trees, 51
Car, 51
Adult (Imago), 55
Sex-Linked Inheritance, 55

Annual, 56
Shift In, 59
Stop, 60
Signal, 64 +
Gold, 86
Named Town within larger urban area, 92
Manganese, 105

Water Ductor Roller, 109
Vector Directed Out of Page, 128
Private Aid for Navigation, 155

magenta
Position of Light, 155

Salt, Sea, 87

Biennial, 56

Core Service Adjacencies, 52

Community Projects Two-Sided, 53

Start and Stop, 107
Odd; Bit Information, 61

Active Male Element, 89
To Switch On, 60
Start, 63
Saltpeter, 87
On, 115
Scattered Clouds, 0.1 or less, 121

168

Broken Clouds, 0.9, 121

Off, 115
To Switch Off, 60

Resonance, 115
Even, 61
Synchronous, 61

Broken Clouds, 121
Isolated; Absolute, 60

Constant Current, 115

Escape, 59
Egg, 55
Finished, 60
Stop Code, 61 v
End of the Information, 62 v
Stop, 63
Salt, 87
Passive Female Element, 89

No Entry, All Vehicles, 146

Input, 60
Complemented, 61 v

Output, 60
Transcribe, 63

Skip, 61
Spark Gap, 115

Step by Step, 61

Indicator, 82

Comparison, 61
AC Adapter, 63

Line for Line, 61

Negative Charge, 128

Mistake, 60

Prohibition, 145

No Parking, 147

Not (Negation), 60
End of Prohibition, 147

Device Control, 59 +
Time, 103 v

Vitriol, 88

Location, 52

Repeater, 72
New Trees, 51
Health Center, 95

Bicycle, 51
Earth; Globular Cluster, 54
Larva, 55
Tetrasporangia, 56
Shift Out, 59
Salt, 87

Creation, 89
Large Hospital, 95
Horizontal Bed, 96
Overcast, 121
Injury, Fatal, 142
1000 Feet (Min.) above Weather, 151

Power, 63

Occupied; (Blocked Up), 60
Citrus Fruit, 40 v
Good Place for a Handout, 90 v
Overcast, Sky Obscured, 121
Railroad Grade Crossing, 146 v
No stopping, 147 v

System, 61

Coral, 96

Cotton Blowing Fan, 161

Torque Converter, 161 v

Siren, 49
Crushing Mill, 46 v
Manual Steering, 108 v

Outdoor Seats, 52

Fulguration, 115

Resection, 115

Foot Switch, 115

Grease, 160 +
Fuel, 158 v
Oil, 160 +

Restaurant, 35

Right-Hand Minus Terminal, 115 +

Council Ring, 130

Change Speed only in motion, 106

169

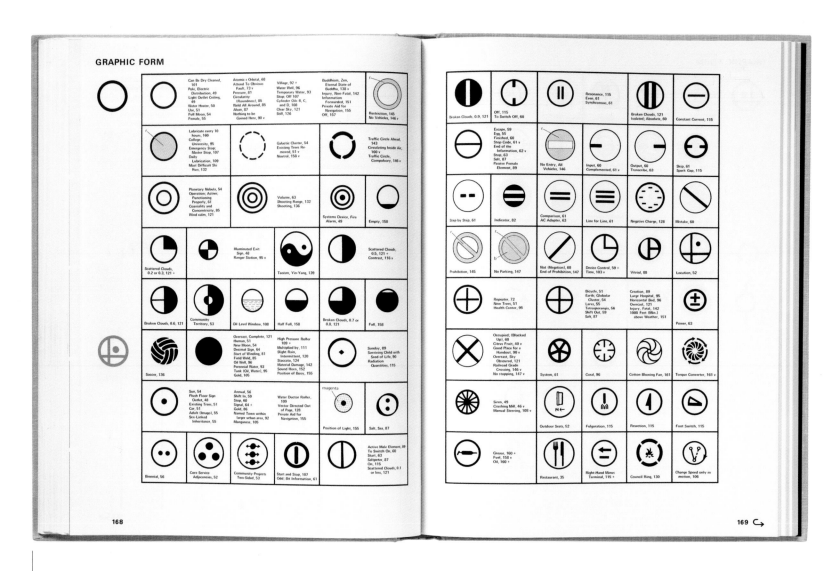

The section 'Graphic Form' groups symbols according to shape – this spread studies the differing circular symbols. Each is referenced with the page number of their appearance under subject area in the 'Disciplines' section.

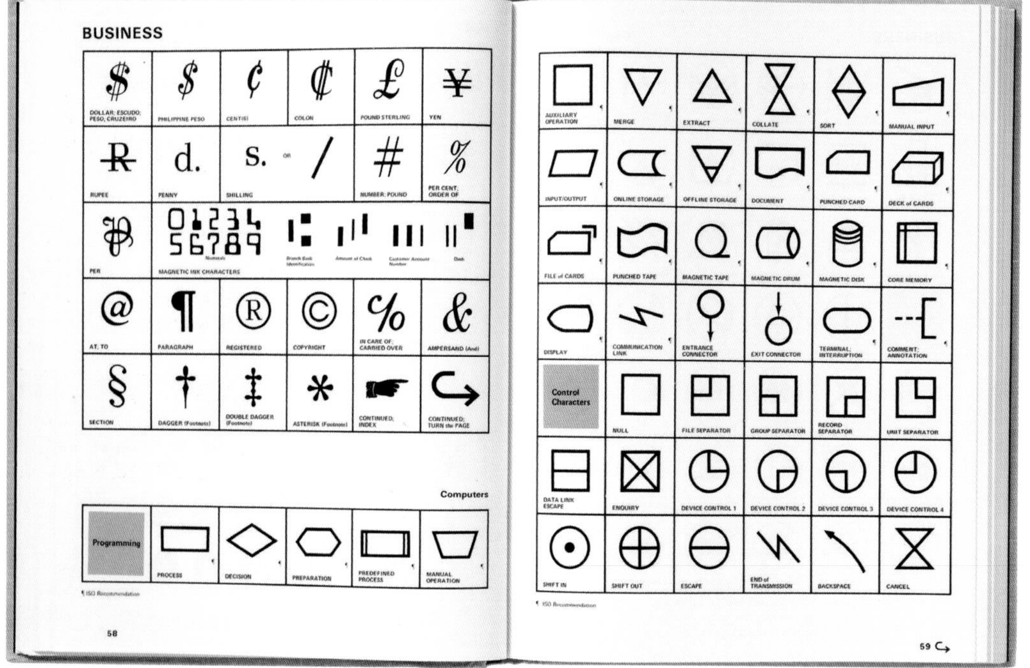

Part of the section devoted to business symbols. It includes the 'continued' symbol used by Dreyfuss alongside the book's pagination (see bottom right) to signal the continuation of a subject area on to the next page.

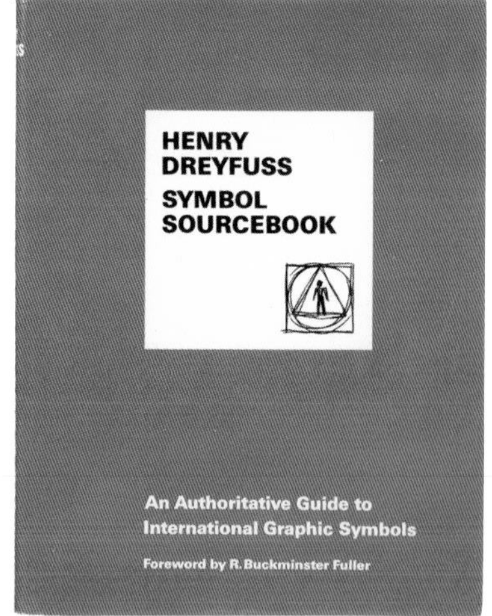

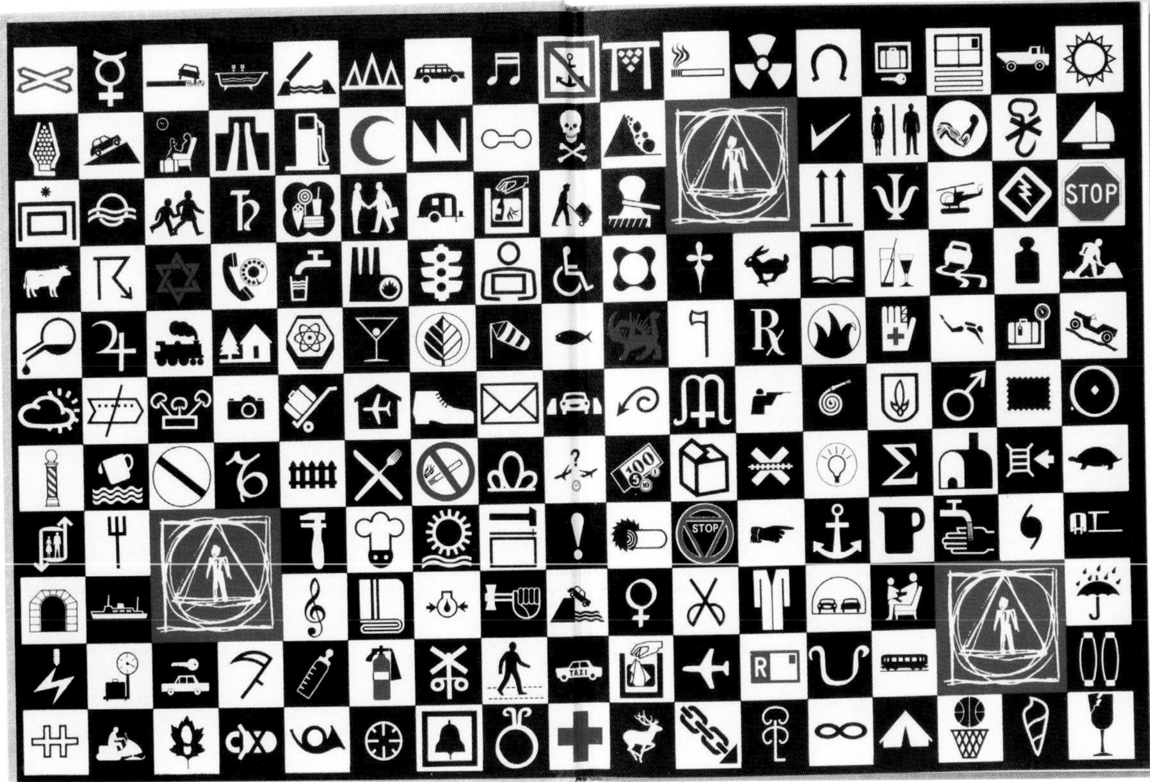

The lively decorative endpapers are in contrast to the systematic layout of the book.

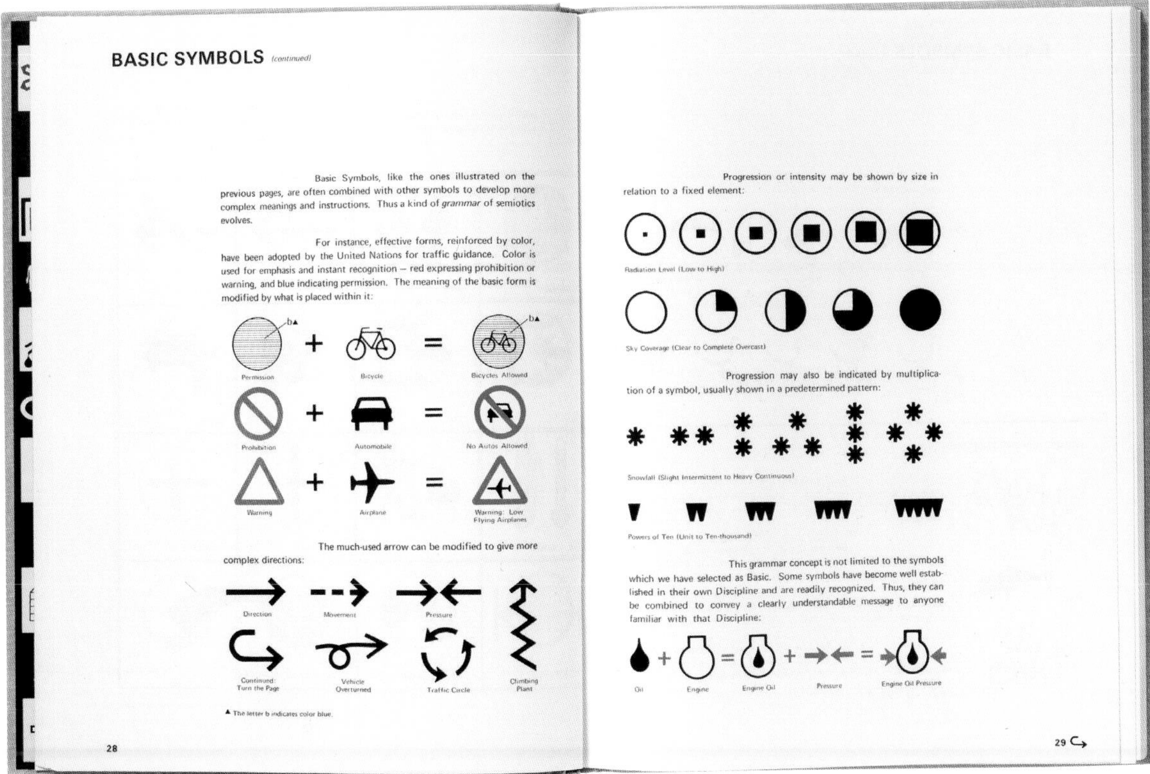
BASIC SYMBOLS *(continued)*

Basic Symbols, like the ones illustrated on the previous pages, are often combined with other symbols to develop more complex meanings and instructions. Thus a kind of *grammar* of semiotics evolves.

For instance, effective forms, reinforced by color, have been adopted by the United Nations for traffic guidance. Color is used for emphasis and instant recognition – red expressing prohibition or warning, and blue indicating permission. The meaning of the basic form is modified by what is placed within it:

The much-used arrow can be modified to give more complex directions:

▲ The letter b indicates color blue.

28

Progression or intensity may be shown by size in relation to a fixed element:

Progression may also be indicated by multiplication of a symbol, usually shown in a predetermined pattern:

This grammar concept is not limited to the symbols which we have selected as Basic. Some symbols have become well established in their own Discipline and are readily recognized. Thus, they can be combined to convey a clearly understandable message to anyone familiar with that Discipline:

29

Symbol Sourcebook

An Authoritative Guide to International Graphic Symbols

Henry Dreyfuss

McGraw-Hill Book Company, New York, 1972

292 pages

278 × 215 mm (11 × 8.5 in)

Designed by Henry Dreyfuss

Henry Dreyfuss's interest in graphic symbols dated back to the 1950s. In the years before *Symbol Sourcebook* was published, he set up a databank as a repository for a collection that by the time of publication had amassed 20,000 symbols from around the world. As one of the most successful industrial designers of the twentieth century, Dreyfuss (1904–1972) recognized the advantage symbols had over the written word on products. There were two reasons for this: the safety of users, as an easily understood colour or form could communicate a function more effectively than a written instruction; and the ability of symbols to break down language barriers, doing away with the need to produce multiple editions, thus opening up new markets.

To avoid publishing multiple versions of the book, and to increase its worldwide reach, the table of contents is in 18 languages. The symbols themselves are placed into two main sections. The first, 'Disciplines', is split into subject areas such as Agriculture, Architecture and Astronomy. The second, 'Graphic Form', groups the same symbols according to their shape, ignoring context. Each symbol is labelled in English.

A foreword by R. Buckminster Fuller extols the efforts of Dreyfuss in his work towards a universal visual language. An essay by Marie Neurath (the wife and colleague of Otto Neurath, who invented the Isotype system of pictorially based symbols) reinforces this need.

Dreyfuss hoped that designers working on new symbols would use this book as a valuable resource for research as well as inspiration. He was careful not to call it a dictionary as he knew that producing the definitive list, even from the symbols he had collected, would have been a daunting, even impossible, task.

Apart from a small section on colour as a symbol and another in the introduction, the book is printed in black only.

Handbook of Pictorial Symbols
3250 Examples from International Sources
Rudolf Modley
Dover Publications, New York, 1976
160 pages
280 × 210 mm (11 × 8.25 in)

Nearly every facet of life, from birth to death and what lies in between, can be represented by one of the 3250 pictorial symbols in this book by Rudolf Modley. Compiled from original sources, including the author's own extensive work in the 1930s and 1940s, it remains a unique if slightly dated resource.

A disciple of Otto Neurath, inventor of the Isotype system of universal pictorial symbols, Modley promoted the use of such symbols in quantitative data and signage systems, and foresaw the demand for a visual language that would cut across language barriers and illiteracy. *Handbook of Pictorial Symbols* was a showcase for some of the finest talent in this field.

The book is split into two sections, the first of which deals with the art of pictographs. The most noteworthy of these are on the pages devoted to Gerd Arntz's work for the Netherlands Statistical Foundation, under the direction of Otto Neurath. The second section looks at public symbols: firstly, at groups of the most common ones, such as telephones, no smoking, toilets, etc.; and then at complete signage systems. Standing out in this section are the pioneering work of Masaru Katsumie for the 1964 Olympic Games in Tokyo, the first system of public symbols that could be read without resorting to multiple languages, and the work of Otl Aicher for the 1972 Olympic Games in Munich, which used a grid and kit of visual elements to construct each pictorial symbol.

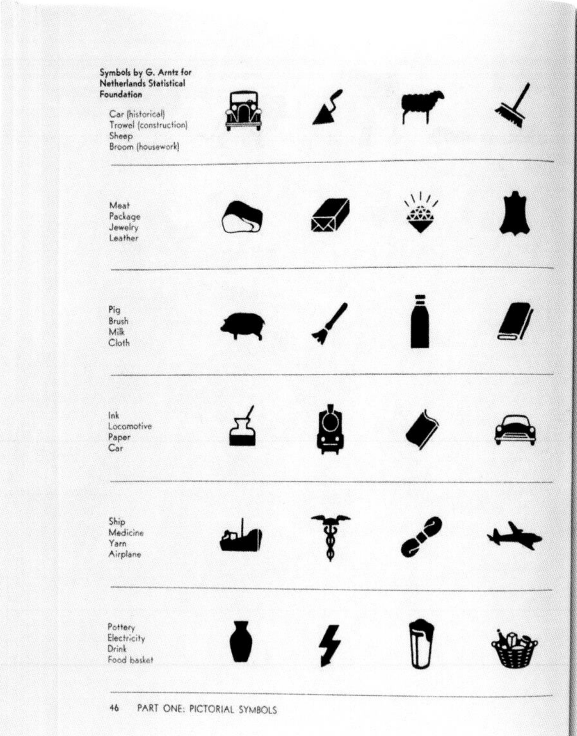
Symbols by G. Arntz for Netherlands Statistical Foundation
Car (historical)
Trowel (construction)
Sheep
Broom (housework)
Meat
Package
Jewelry
Leather
Pig
Brush
Milk
Cloth
Ink
Locomotive
Paper
Car
Ship
Medicine
Yarn
Airplane
Pottery
Electricity
Drink
Food basket
46 PART ONE: PICTORIAL SYMBOLS

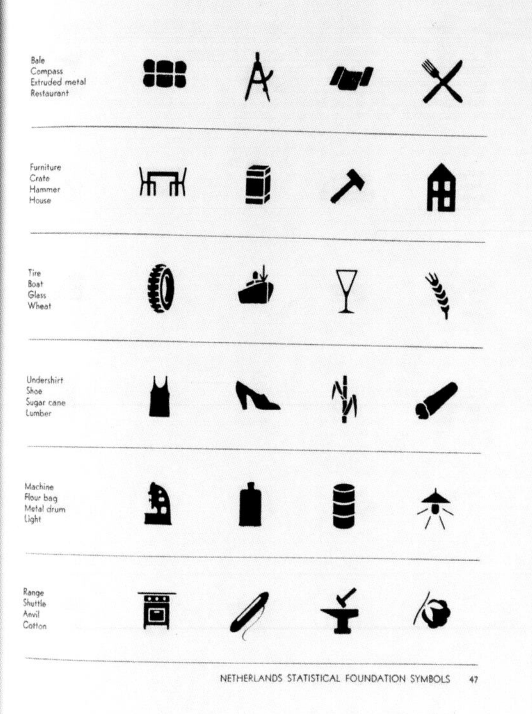
Bale
Compass
Extruded metal
Restaurant
Furniture
Crate
Hammer
House
Tire
Boat
Glass
Wheat
Undershirt
Shoe
Sugar cane
Lumber
Machine
Flour bag
Metal drum
Light
Range
Shuttle
Anvil
Cotton
NETHERLANDS STATISTICAL FOUNDATION SYMBOLS 47

The work of Gerd Arntz for the Netherlands Statistical Foundation.

The designs of Otl Aicher for the 1972 Olympic Games in Munich were extended for the 1976 games in Montreal, as shown below.

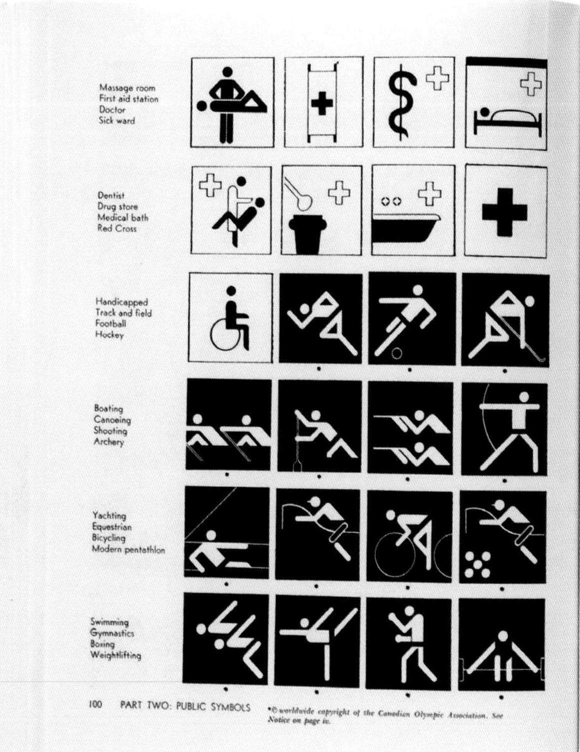
Massage room
First aid station
Doctor
Sick ward
Dentist
Drug store
Medical bath
Red Cross
Handicapped
Track and field
Football
Hockey
Boating
Canoeing
Shooting
Archery
Yachting
Equestrian
Bicycling
Modern pentathlon
Swimming
Gymnastics
Boxing
Weightlifting
100 PART TWO: PUBLIC SYMBOLS
*© worldwide copyright of the Canadian Olympic Association. See Notice on page iv.

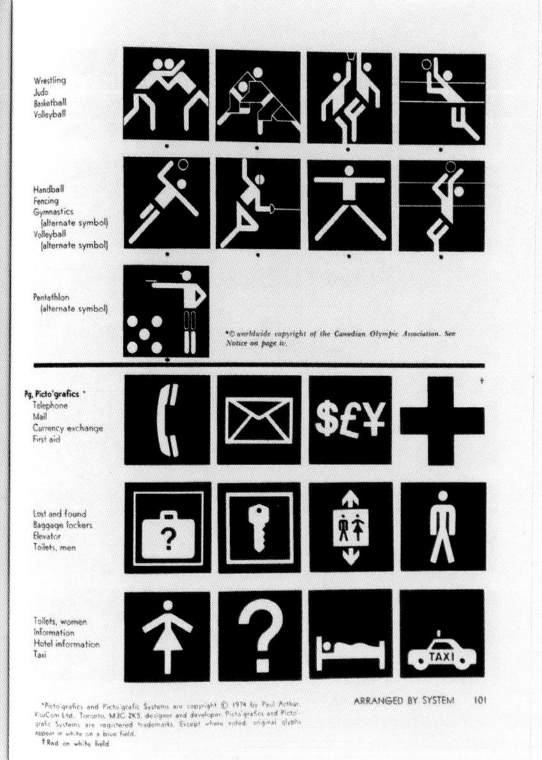
Wrestling
Judo
Basketball
Volleyball
Handball
Fencing
Gymnastics (alternate symbol)
Volleyball (alternate symbol)
Pentathlon (alternate symbol)
*© worldwide copyright of the Canadian Olympic Association. See Notice on page iv.
Pg. Picto'grafics *
Telephone
Mail
Currency exchange
First aid
Lost and found
Baggage lockers
Elevator
Toilets, men
Toilets, women
Information
Hotel information
Taxi

*Picto'grafics and Picto'grafic Systems are copyright © 1974 by Paul Arthur VisuCom Ltd. Toronto, M3C 2K5, designer and developer. Picto'grafics and Picto'grafic Systems are registered trademarks. Except where noted, original glyphs appear in white on a blue field.
†Red on white field
ARRANGED BY SYSTEM 101

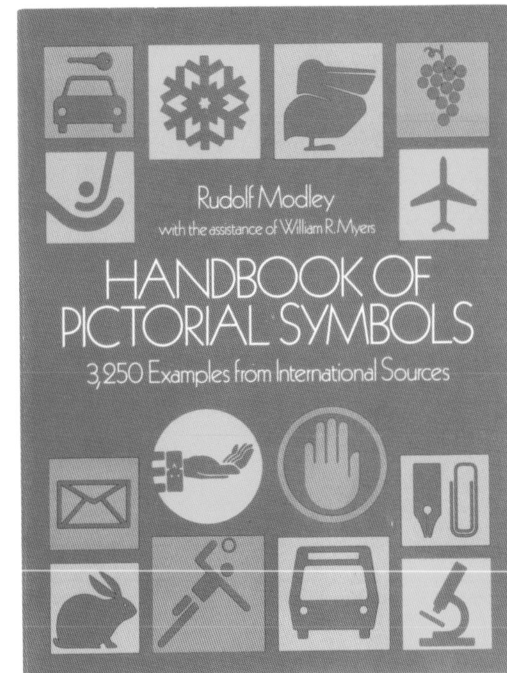

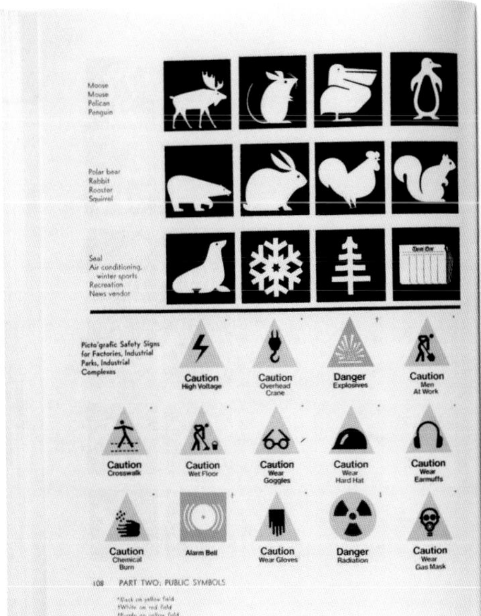

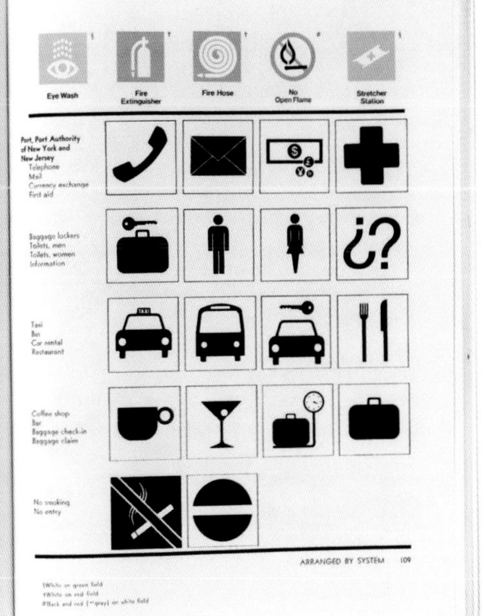

One section of the book groups together similar symbols for comparison. On this spread are toilet symbols taken from the signage systems of numerous projects.

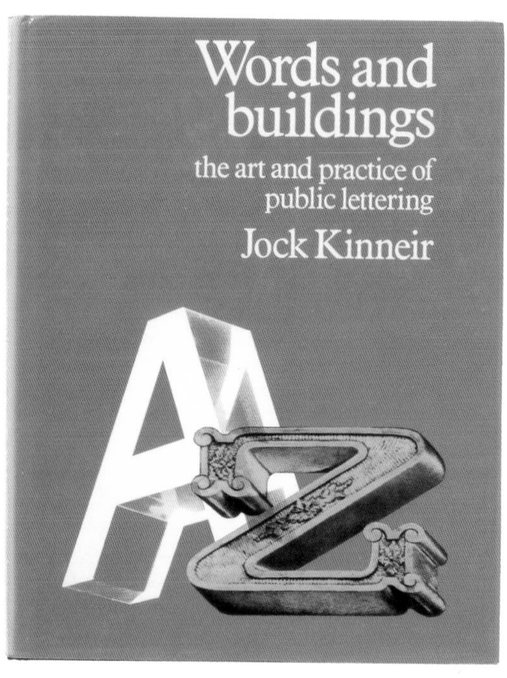

Expressiveness
No one would deny that the art of communication would lose a lot if we only had one universal letterstyle. It is difficult to imagine a popular newspaper set in one face and probable that the monotony would be a contradiction in terms. Yet it is one of the oddities of the professional scene that designers get obsessions with certain letterstyles and use them wholesale irrespective of their appropriateness. The naif, on the other hand, allow their emotions more freedom, and fairground lettering is famous for its expressiveness. Yet this is only a very small—and very obvious and unsubtle—part of the whole area. Sometimes, indeed, expressive is too strong a word and appropriate is enough. A lot of work comes in this category, and at its best, by its interpretation of the mood of the subject, it communicates what it would be impossible to spell out.

Hovering in between is a group of designs which range from visual witticism to subtle analogy; it is a species of concrete poetry and an inexhaustible vein of invention. Perhaps one should also include puposely non-expressive lettering in this group; the fact that it does not speak with its hands is in itself a clear signal to those who are tuned in—see pages 44 and 45.

STARS

133

The light weight titling in the engineering works below is appropriate rather than expressive, and might well be wrong if it was. It suggests precision by avoiding the heavy-handed treatment which is so often meted out to such subjects. But the title over the door of the Parisian night club is vividly evocative of the scatty rhythms of the chanteuse and would have been dead if it wasn't.

Making graphic references is a gambit which can lead to the banal, and the star-spangled theme recurs at intervals; its only justification is that it communicates instantly by being obvious. In *135* the reference is more subtle. The massive letters form part of a bank title, and stand as an analogy with gold ingots.

133 National style. Philadelphia Type Foundry, 1856.
134 Painted in yellow and orange (Waterloo, Iowa).
135 Etched over mica flakes and gilded. The flakes act as a resist and account for the hammered look of the gold deposit (Midland Bank, London).
136 Painted fascia (Paris).

62

63

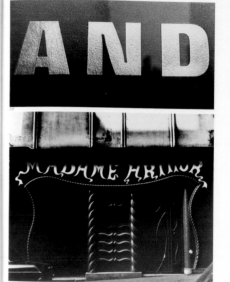

A spread of translucent lettering – the bold graphic layout and dynamic cropping of photography is carried throughout the book.

257

258

136

Translucent lettering
All the lettering shown here is designed in terms of the lighting available, which in every case is a bank of standard fluorescent tubes running the length of the legend and serviced from behind. This is the cheapest and most convenient method short of borrowing room lighting, as in *261*, a method which in many cases does not produce the intensity or crispness necessary.

257 and *259* exploit the ability of clear acrylic to transmit light, a characteristic which has suggested letterforms with deep returns. It is interesting to imagine *242* treated in this way; light is reflected off internal surfaces and could travel even further than this design would demand. In *258* a pattern of holes bring sparkle to the situation in a nearly flush form, thus obviating the level of cleaning necessary in the other examples. It was designed to overcome objections to the use of exposed neon tube at low levels and in a situation where it might have caused interference to other equipment.

The letter T is an even more sparkling style, and being out of doors gets the benefit of some cleaning from the rain. Thick chunks of clear glass usually have a greenish tinge, but this is not noticeable at night.

257 Thick, clear acrylic sheet, edge lit (Paris).
258 Letterstyle composed of holes drilled on a matrix in thin sheet metal (London Heathrow Airport).
259 Clear block acrylic letters (Hettlage store, Ulm, Germany).
260 Fused glass (Hilton Hotel, London).

259

260

137

Words and Buildings
The Art and Practice
of Public Lettering
Jock Kinneir
The Architectural Press,
London, 1980
192 pages
279 × 216 mm (11 × 8.5 in)
Designed by Jock Kinneir

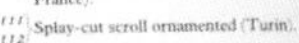

A group of splay-cut letterforms – three-dimensional letters that accentuate perspective to give an illusion of increased depth.

Where letterforms meet structures, the professions of architecture and graphic design come face to face. According to Jock Kinneir (1917–1994), there is often a fundamental difference of opinion at this juncture. The graphic designer, as a 'quasi-layman', sees the wording as an integral part of the built environment, while the architect sees signage as something to be added at the end of a project. Kinneir promotes the more holistic approach in this in-depth analysis of the processes and methods involved in public lettering.

Along with his colleague Margaret Calvert, Kinneir designed both the road signage system for the United Kingdom and signage for the British Airport Authority in the late 1950s and early 1960s. However, rather than being a treatise on corporate sign systems, *Words and Buildings* shows a mixture of modern and historical examples of signage from designers and non-professionals alike. The book is illustrated with large black-and-white photographs, arranged for dynamic effect.

An introductory chapter focuses on the permanent nature of signage compared to the ephemerality of so much graphic design, and on the development of the alphabet through public lettering. The second chapter, 'Criteria', studies issues of size, legibility and letter spacing. 'Practice', the third and longest chapter, covers all aspects of sign application and is subdivided into Flush, Relief, Three-Dimensional, Illuminated, Integral and Adjacent Lettering. Each of these is further subdivided into a more detailed analysis of types of manufacture. The next chapter, 'Mise en Scène', deals with lettering as part of the environment, both at street level and at higher elevations, and a final section looks to the future of signage; Kinneir relishes the prospect of a speaking building.

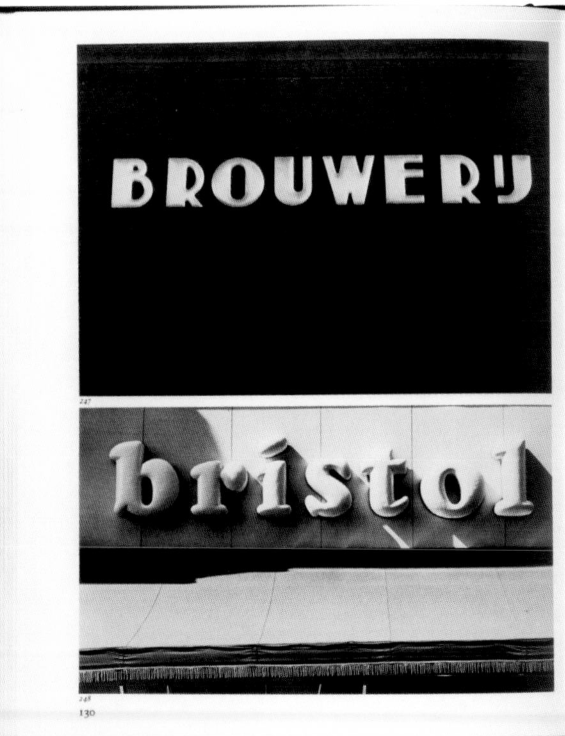

The Dictionary of Visual Language

Philip Thompson, Peter Davenport

Bergstrom & Boyle Books, London, 1980
264 pages
230 × 170 mm (9 × 6.75 in)
Designed by Philip Thompson, Peter Davenport

Originally published in 1975 by the design firm Pentagram as the first in its series of promotional booklets 'Pentagram Papers' under the title *ABC of Graphic Clichés*, Philip Thompson and Peter Davenport's 'dictionary' then ran to only three letters ('a', 'b' and 'c'). In its subsequent book form, the alphabet was completed, with 1200 definitions and 1700 examples of work from designers and artists based largely in Europe and the United States.

The Dictionary of Visual Language is a celebration of the visual cliché. Unlike its overused and banal literary cousin, the graphic counterpart is integral to communication. 'The visual cliché can immediately give life to an idea,' says George Lois in his foreword to the book.

Every definition in the dictionary has a title and is followed by one or more illustrations, each with a caption that includes the image's date, country of origin and designer/artist credits. In a typical example, 'Book on Book' is defined as 'A sophisticated graphic joke, and an example of graphic tautology'. To illustrate this there are three examples of the use of a book as an image: a 'page on a page' by the art director Henry Wolf; an open book as an 'advertisement for a book' from the art director Otto Storch; and a 'double-spread on a double-spread' by designer Roy Carruthers.

As befits a dictionary, the layout does not waver from its three-column grid and the printing is monochrome. Each illustration is enlarged to the column width and each alphabetical section is clearly marked with a large initial Gothic letter. Cross references are used throughout.

The Dictionary of Visual Language *was first published as the first of the 'Pentagram Papers', a series of booklets examined in detail in* The Pentagram Papers, *Thames & Hudson, London, 2007.*

The entry for 'Eye' contains 11 examples by designers such as Tom Eckersley, Erik Nitsche, Paul Rand, William Golden and Henry Wolf.

Ruler. A symbol for any trade that uses a rule but also in a more general sense a symbol for the idea of accuracy or scrupulous honesty.

Ruler as an ergonomic symbol.
France circa 1952 Peter Knapp

Poster for General Dynamics. Ruler as an indication of tidal movement.
USA 1969 George Tscherny

Slide rule as a symbol of statistical analysis.
UK 1970 Mel Calman/Philip Thompson

Rules. Undecorated rules of various lengths and thicknesses are design constraints in many graphic design problems.

A flexible trademark made from rules for a modular furniture manufacturer, Holtzapfel. See also INITIAL LETTER.
Switzerland 1958 Gerstner + Kutter

Illustration (Book 4a 1961).
Iceland 1961 Dieter Rot

Russian Doll. The idea of a large box containing smaller boxes ad infinitum is a fairly obsessive one. Strong childhood associations but the idea persists into adulthood and emerges in colloquial phrases like, 'in every fat person there is a thin one trying to get out'. See also IMAGE ON IMAGE.

Personal Christmas card.
France 1966 Savignac

Drawing.
UK 1969 Mel Calman

Russian Roulette. The game played with a revolver (see GUN) containing one BULLET. A symbol of foolhardiness and risk-taking.

Advertisement. Copy says, 'Don't gamble – call . . .'
USA 1965 Tomi Ungerer

Sachet. The visual characteristics of the modern plastic sachet are the crimped outer edges and the cut off corner. It is a symbol for instant convenience. A naturally condensed and thus potent image.

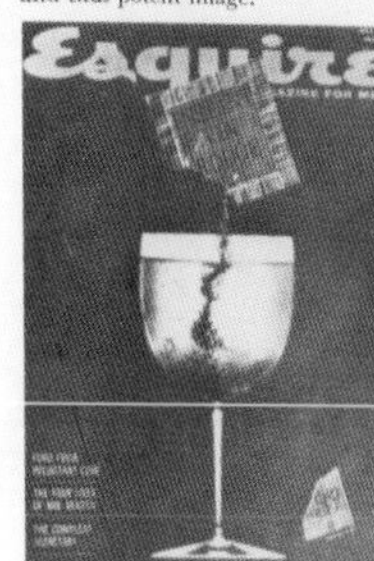

'Instant vin rouge' – an ironic symbol for France. The characteristic snipped end contains the symbol. See also GLASS.
USA 1958 Henry Wolf

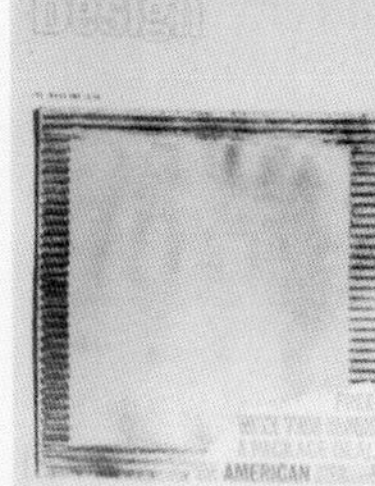

Giant silver sachet on magazine cover supports copy, 'Free with this issue . . .'
UK 1964 Derek Birdsall

Sack. Essentially a crude, tough container. It is associated with portability and heavy-duty use and thus exports. STENCIL LETTERING is the characteristic adjunct. 'The Sack' was a mid-1950s style of dress cut on basic lines.

Big sack equals big mail. See also HYPERBOLE.
UK 1946 Tom Eckersley

Symbol for minimal living. See also BARREL.
UK 1964 Colin Millward/Arthur Parsons

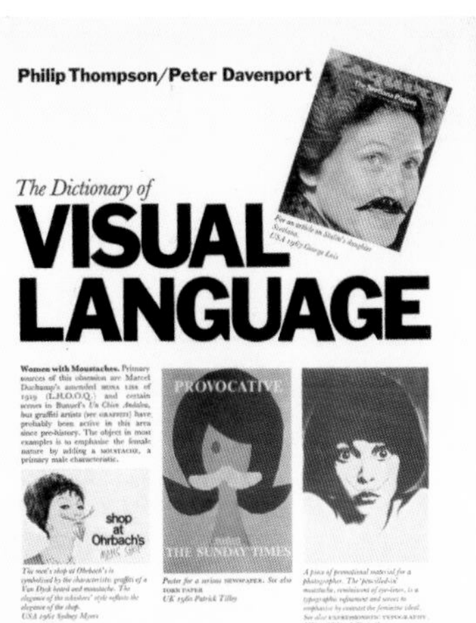
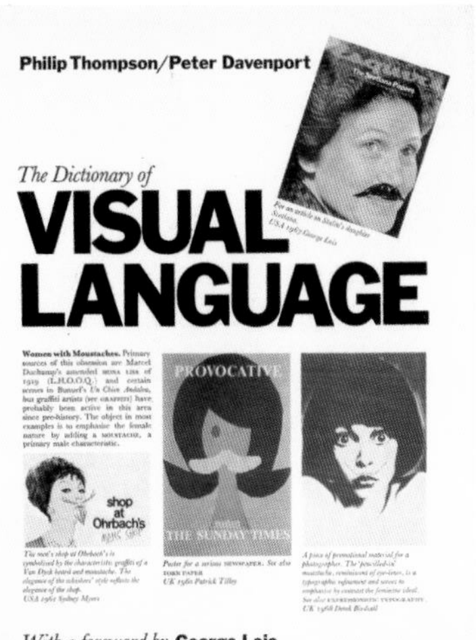

Philip Thompson/Peter Davenport
The Dictionary of
VISUAL
LANGUAGE
PROVOCATIVE
THE SUNDAY TIMES
shop
at
Ohrbach's
With a foreword by George Lois

Women with Moustaches. Primary sources of this obsession are Marcel Duchamp's amended MONA LISA of 1919 (L.H.O.O.Q.) and certain scenes in Bunuel's *Un Chien Andalou*, but graffiti artists (see GRAFFITI) have probably been active in this area since pre-history. The object in most examples is to emphasise the female nature by adding a MOUSTACHE, a primary male characteristic.

Poster for a serious NEWSPAPER. *See also* TORN PAPER
UK 1960 Patrick Tilley

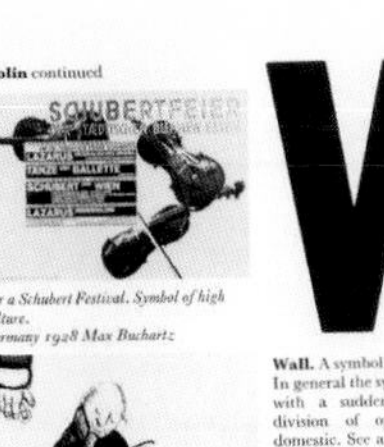

For a Schubert Festival. Symbol of high culture.
Germany 1928 Max Buchartz

The violin also has poverty-stricken associations. See also HAT, ROSE.
UK 1958 André François

Volcano. A symbol for ideas of potency, uncertainty and tension.

W

Wall. A symbol of defence or division. In general the symbolism is associated with a sudden problem or as a division of opinion, political or domestic. See also BRICK WALL.

Wand. The fairy's wand is a symbol of transformation and fulfilled wishes.

Watch. See CLOCK.

Water. Symbol of birth, purification and regeneration. We are born in water and it is our chief constituent. Historically and in modern thought a symbol for life. Like the other elements of air, FIRE and earth, its graphic representation creates technical problems. The Egyptian hieroglyph for water is the WAVY LINE (W) adopted unconsciously by children. See also FOUNTAIN, RAIN.

Wave. WATER in agitation, its graphic representation is explicit. The engulfing wave is a symbol for a disaster. The famous giant wave by Hokusai is often gratuitously used for its decorative value. More imaginatively used as a symbol for Japanese world exports.

R·M·S·P
SOUTH AMERICAN
SERVICE
THE ROYAL MAIL STEAM PACKET CO

Poster for a shipping line.
UK 1921 F.C. Herrick

Pastiche for an article on 'The teeming world of Japanese films'.
USA 1962 Henry Wolf/Gyo Fujikawa

Wavy Line. A kind of structured DOODLE. A natural symbol for WATER or sound waves. See also LINE/LINES.

Trademark for Plessey, telecommunications and electronics firm, using an oscillograph as a basis.
UK 1959 Norbert Dutton

Record sleeve, Sounds from the Alps. *The line suggests the shape of an alpine horn and also sound waves.*
USA 1963 Rudolph de Harak

Weathercock. A symbol of changeability. Sometimes used to support the points of the compass. See also COCK.

Fusion of weathervane with east to west railway line extensions.
UK 1949 Tom Eckersley

Weathercock as a symbol of spring. Advertisement for a department store. Copy reads, 'If it's out of this world it's here' and reference is made to spring collection. See also ARROW, GLOBE.
USA 1949 Paul Rand

Web. Images of formal or organic networks (like spiders' webs) are indicative of inextricable situations. See also SPIDER.

Poster for TV thriller.
USA 1954 George Olden

Wedding Cake. The design of wedding cakes belongs to an immutable tradition (along with biscuit and confectionery design). The tiered CAKE structure is a simple ANALOGY for marriage with a natural propensity for crumbling.

Weight. The image of the weight (that accompanies scales) can be used effectively to convey the idea of the quality of weight.

Advertisment for a typeface demonstrating its range of 'weights' (degrees of boldness).
UK 1963 Herbert Spencer

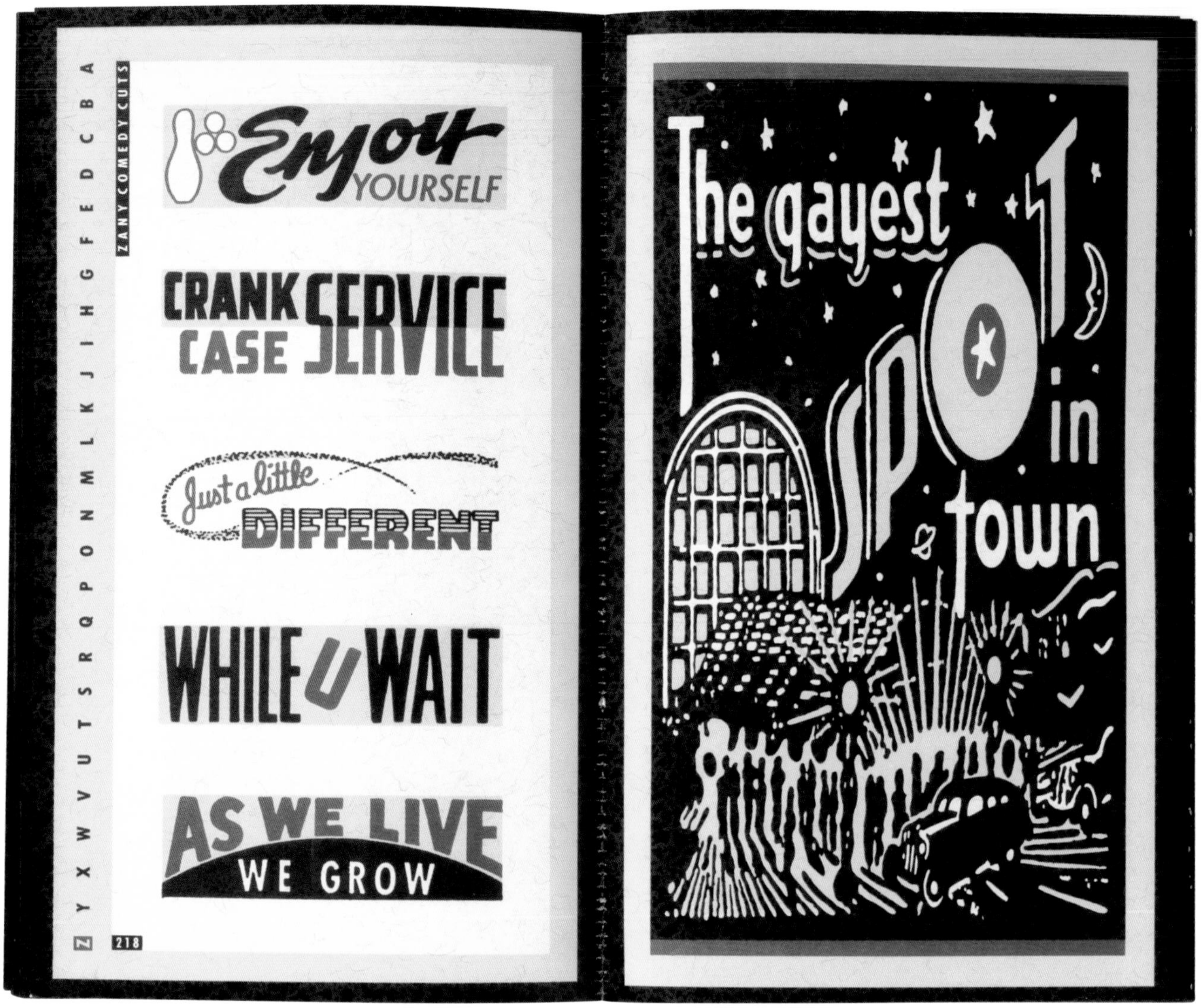

Anderson would later publish the 470-page CSA Archive Volume 1, *CSA Archive Co., Minneapolis, 1995, cataloguing his extensive collection of line drawings and historical illustrations. Original sources of advertising cuts can be found in the matchbook catalogues of companies such as the Superior Match Company of Chicago.*

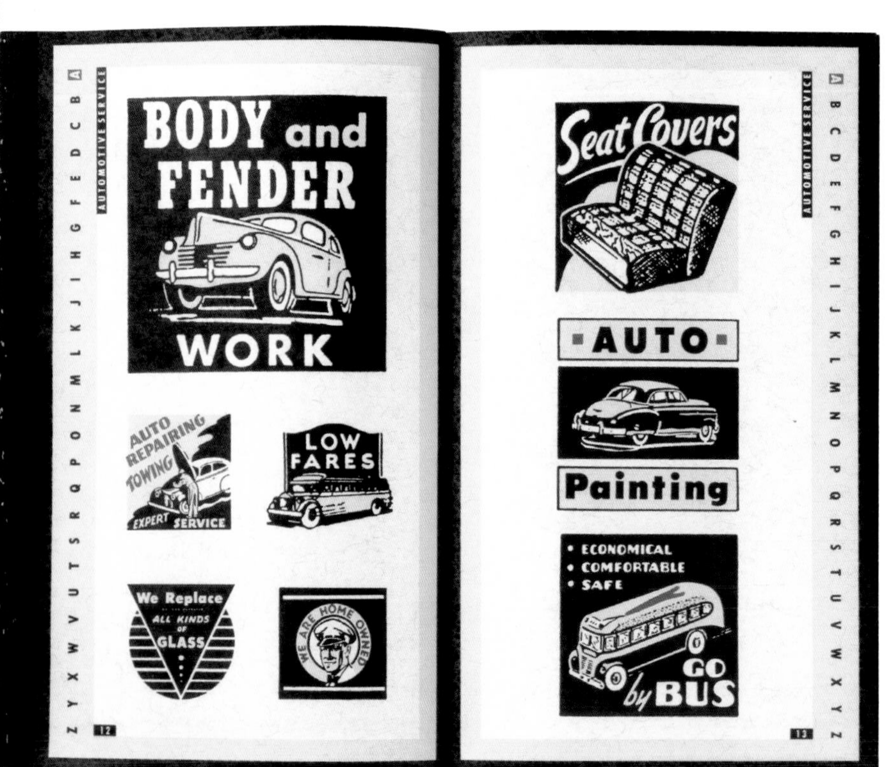

The softcover is printed in a mixture of lithography and thermography.

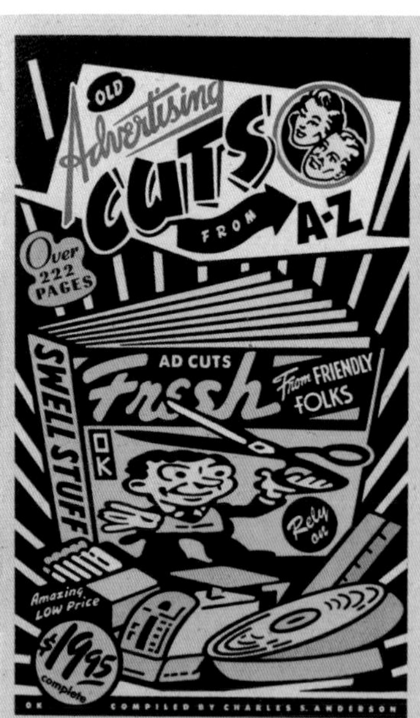

The American advertising cut has been pretty much overlooked by the historians of modern design. Ad cuts represent no formal movement and did not influence the fashion or industrial design of their time – that being the 1930's and 40's. Rather, these decidedly optimistic little renderings mirrored the American values of hard work, good humor and fair play. Stylistically, these cuts evoke the massive qualities of American 40's design. Big cars, buses, and men in baggy suits, all rendered as gutsy, bold images. Heavy blacks, bold typefaces, even the method of printing was massive. Direct impression, ink carried on slabs of metal and smashed onto paper. Steel was king, and its excessive application to everything
Call Us For a
TAXI
AT YOUR SERVICE

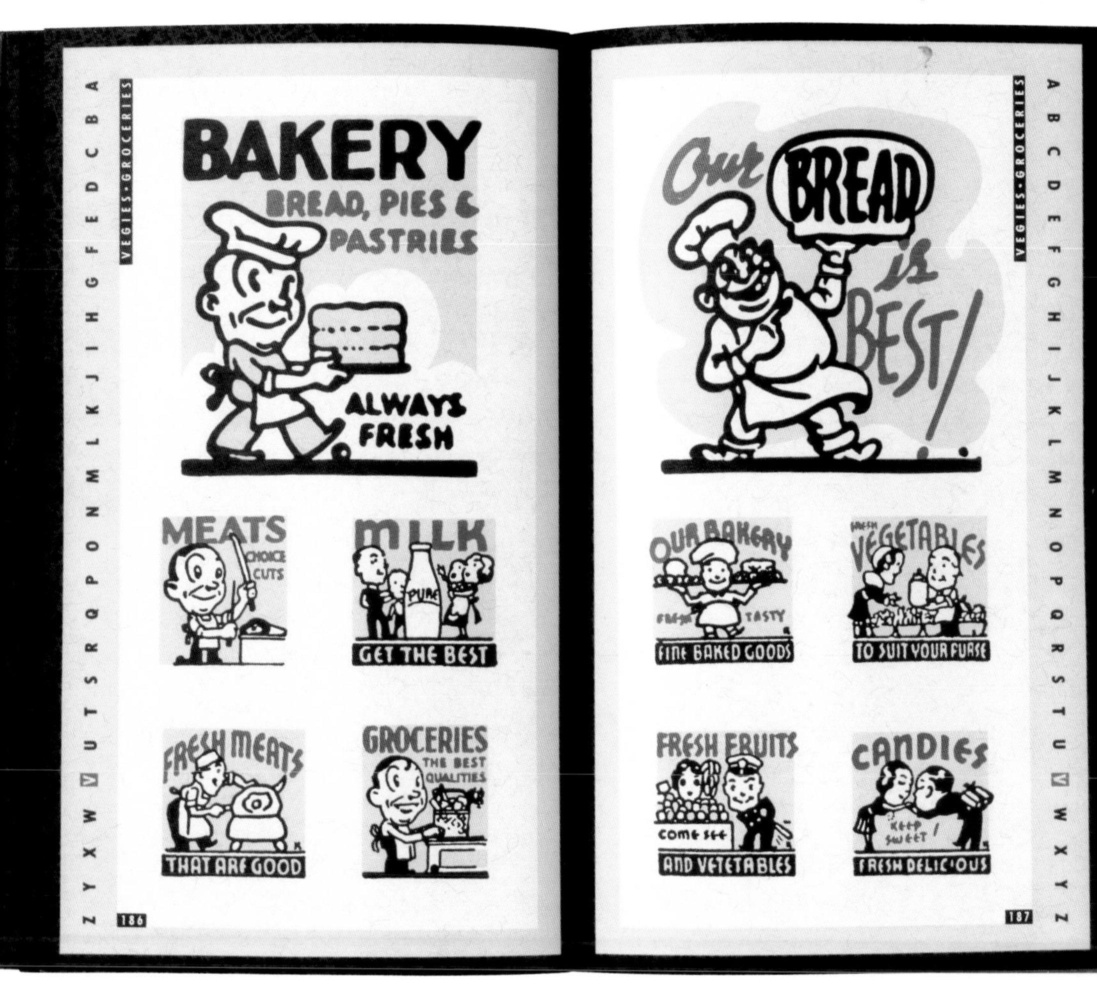

Old Advertising Cuts from A–Z

Charles S. Anderson

French Paper Company, Niles, Michigan, 1989
224 pages
230 × 140 mm (9 × 5.5 in)
Designed by Charles S. Anderson

From an early age, the designer Charles S. Anderson has been obsessed by advertising cuts, the often anonymous drawings found in small ads, matchbooks and other commercial printing. Resolutely American, *Old Advertising Cuts from A–Z* is the first publication to showcase what was then his collection of 800 examples. This later evolved into the massive CSA Images, a stock-image company that currently contains nearly 30,000 items.

Published with the support of Anderson's long-time client, the French Paper Company, the book contains advertising cuts from the heyday of these drawings in the 1930s and 1940s. In some cases they have been altered or tidied up, but there is generally an effort to retain the original designs, which are typified by bold, black linework combined with heavy, muscular lettering. The advertisements were designed to make an impact, and had to be strong to stand up to the often crude letterpress printing of the time.

Laid out thematically from 'A' to 'Z', and mimicking the layouts of the original catalogues, this book is a valuable record of a graphic art that is often ignored in design histories. It is still, however, very much a Charles S. Anderson production, and, with its brash historic graphics and unusual finishing techniques – in this instance the mottled thermography on the cover – a classic example of his distinctive work for the French Paper Company.

Today's Hieroglyphs
Imprints on Packaging for Transport
Hans-Rudolf Lutz
Verlag Hans-Rudolf Lutz, Zurich, 1990
Second edition (pictured), 1996
528 pages
294 × 221 mm (11.625 × 8.75 in)
Designed by Hans-Rudolf Lutz

Seen only by the men and women who fill, transport and unpack cardboard boxes, there may seem to be little need for the graphics adorning these containers to be designed by professionals. *Today's Hieroglyphs* pays homage to the communication skills of the people responsible for these marks. The book's author, the Swiss designer Hans-Rudolf Lutz (1939–1998), calls them 'unsung designers' and contends that the product of their work is a coherent visual language.

Over 15 years of searching Lutz collected 15,000 printed cardboard pieces, which were then edited down to 5000 for this book. They are arranged in 40 unnamed chapters, represented on the contents page by an image. The start of each chapter contains a brief text in German, English, French and Japanese, outlining the rationale for each grouping.

Early chapters explore the way products are depicted, from realistic, stylized or decorative drawings and images of factories and tradesmen to personified representations and graphic characters. The middle chapters start with 948 company logos and then explore the iconography of transport and handling: arrows, umbrellas, stemmed glasses (fragile), stacking, and unpacking. The final chapters show the uses of faces, figures and animals on packaging, often as part of a product's trademarking.

The layout is printed in black only, with the images on each spread arranged in grids, and no attempt has been made to tidy up the illustrations; they are as they were found. They were printed on to the boxes by flexography (etched rubber or polymer plates, sometimes hand-carved), and no apologies are made for the often coarse results.

A chapter opener shows the multilingual introduction and large facing image.

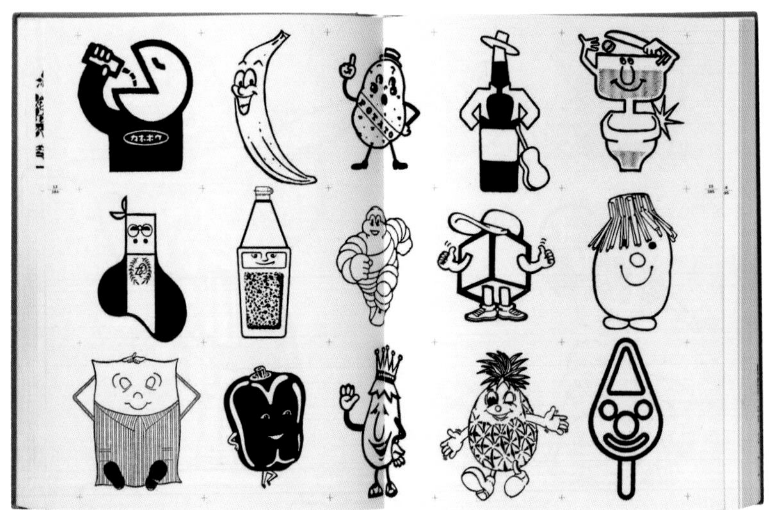

A spread of animated caricatures contrasts with the banal page of filing cabinets above. The pages are laid out in a uniform fashion – each image is given the same amount of space.

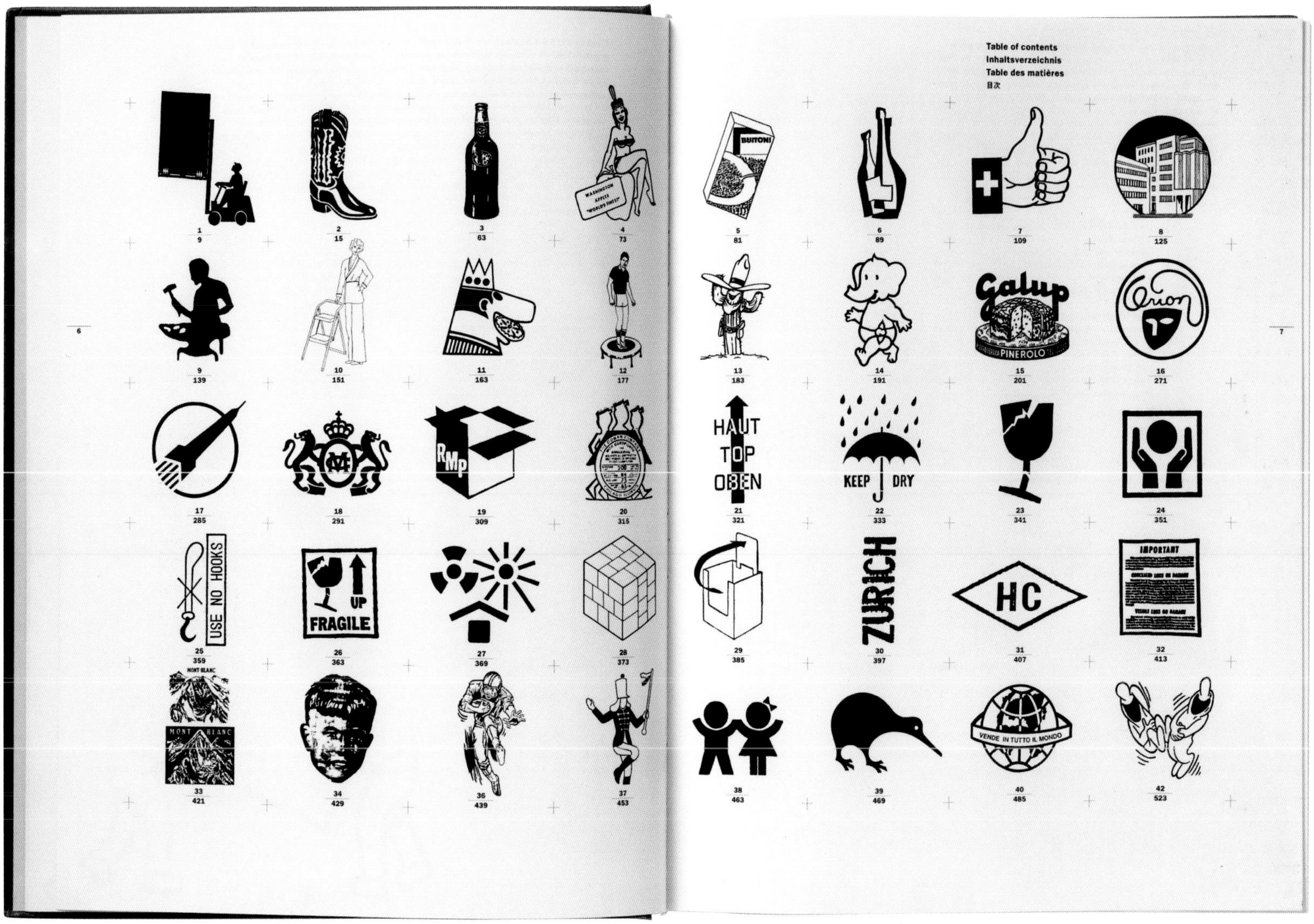

Table of contents
Inhaltsverzeichnis
Table des matières
目次

6

7

The contents page is pictorial – each image represents its respective chapter.

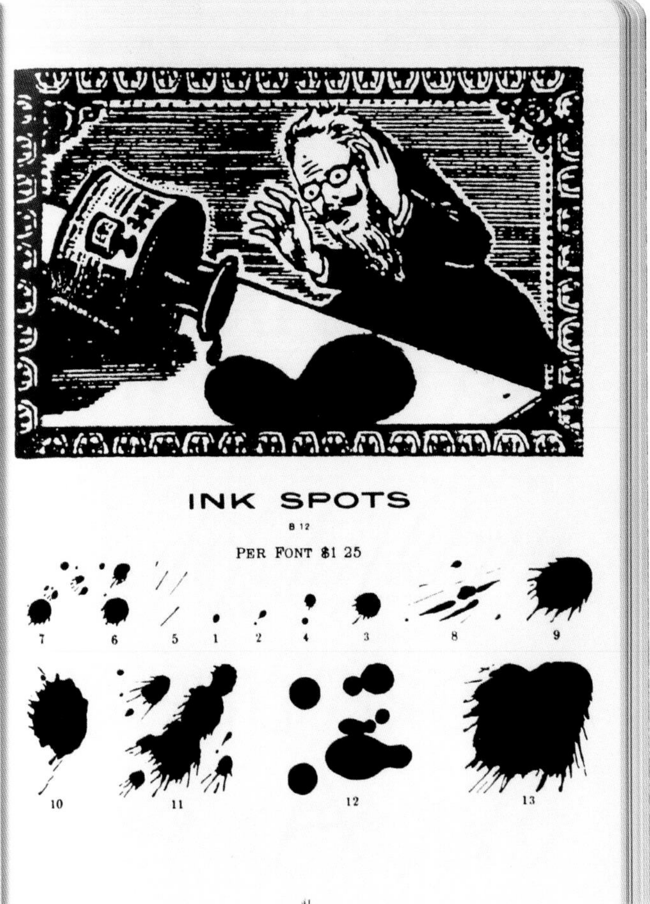

A collection of 132 different printers' hands in a section that includes similar pages of ampersands, arrows and fleurons.

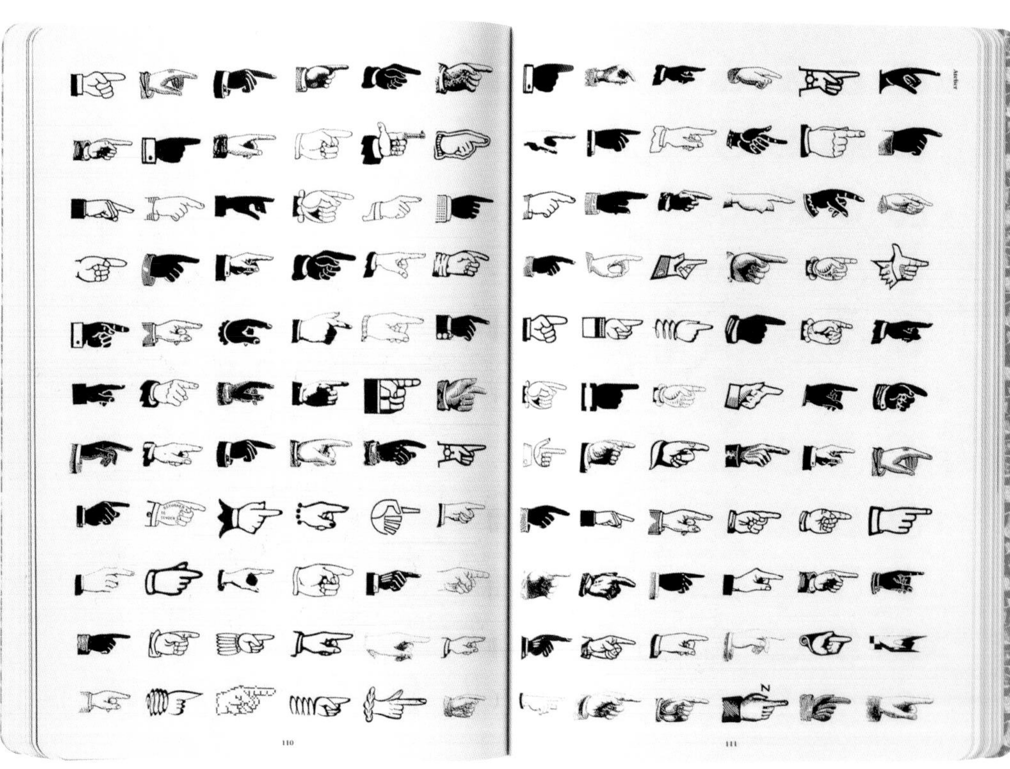

The right-hand page is one of many taken from the French graphic art magazine Arts et Métiers Graphiques *that appear throughout the book.*

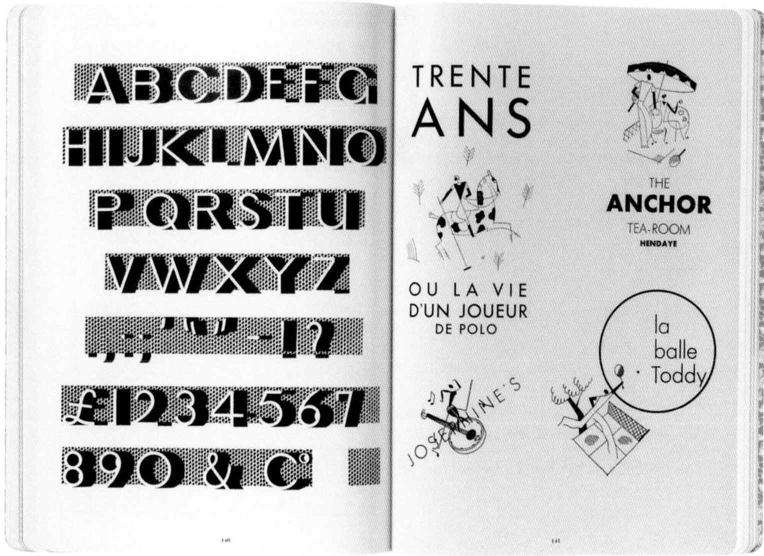

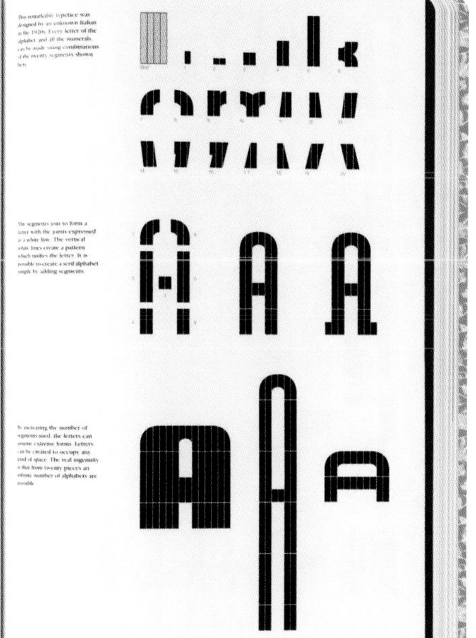

Alphabets & Other Signs

Julian Rothenstein,
Mel Gooding (editors)
Redstone Press, London, 1991
184 pages
297 × 210 mm (11.625 × 8.25 in)
Designed by Julian Rothenstein

In his introduction Mel Gooding sets out the simple aims of *Alphabets & Other Signs*: 'It has no programme. It is intended to be used; it is intended to delight'.

Ignoring the cultured typography of the legibility obsessed book trade and private presses, as well as the asymmetric sans serifs of the New Typography promoted by Jan Tschichold and the Bauhaus, the book looks to present the alphabets and other printers' devices that lived outside this rarified air.

Running through the book are pages from the eclectic French magazine *Arts et Métiers Graphiques*, set up by Charles Peignot, director of the Deberny & Peignot type foundry, and published between 1927 and 1939. Contributor Ruari McLean describes the varied editorial content and the brand of decorative and stylish modernism practised by designers such as A.M. Cassandre, Jean Carlu and Maximilien Vox, which typified its look.

Intertwined with the *Arts et Métiers Graphiques* pages are sections that contain seemingly random selections of pages from various type specimens and printers' devices such as arrows, indicators and even a page of ready-made ink spots. One section displays pages from the 1941 specimen *The Book of American Types*, another reproduces various logos, and the final section shows wood-type pages.

Alphabets & Other Signs is designed to be used for inspiration and for direct copying. It consists of contributions from collectors of printed ephemera, many of whom were practising designers, among them Alan Fletcher, Herbert Spencer, Quentin Newark and Paul Elliman.

A successor to *Alphabets & Other Signs* called *ABZ* was published in 2003 by the same editors and publishers. It features early twentieth-century material from modernist avant-garde publications.

Instructional

lating, the stupefying zone of eternal monotony, world without end. We turn with pleasure to a prospect enlivened by variety because it *promises* something.

Now, mere divisions of space—merely areas in combination, quite apart from any consideration of what they contain, or mean—are stimulating and pleasant, or dull and uninviting. They attract just as variety in a landscape attracts, or repel like the monotony of a desert. How it is possible for mere divisions of space to be stimulating or dull may perhaps be shown by some diagrams in the margin. In (1) the large area is cut into four smaller areas more or less alike. The figure that this makes is all well enough, quiet and unobtrusive. But when you start moving the lines up and down as in (2), you arrive at something which by comparison with (1) is certainly more striking. In (2) you begin to get a pattern that calls attention to itself because it makes A and B different, etc., and there must be some reason for it all—something to be looked into. The effect is increased by adding a set of vertical lines. Obviously (4) has more life and go to it than (3). (3) is regular and settled down and finished, whereas (4) seems to have some notion of *doing* something. It will be noted that the areas in (2) and (4) are emphatically different one from another. They provide a variety and contrast of sizes all done up in one package. Variety and contrast are spicy elements of the "interesting," whereas monotonous uniformity is *not* interesting.

Everything done in typographic design breaks up a major area into smaller areas. The large area is almost always rectangular. The smaller areas are mainly rectangular. Vignettes, flourished lettering, etc., get away from right angles; curved borders make other than rectangular backgrounds; but the main dividing lines are horizontal and perpendicular. In other words,

typographical design on its "pattern" side is a process of designing with divisions of space—mostly rectangular.

Variety in typographic design

We want to prevent these divisions of space from becoming dull; we want to make them diverting and interesting. If I am placing a heading above a body of type and below a limiting boundary I will look out that my heading is not placed after the monotonous fashion of (5), where the spaces above it and below it are the same. I will try to get variety into the spaces by placing the heading as in (6). The same desirable state of affairs can be brought about all over the field by the same process. There are mathematical systems for determining the size of such spaces—*e.g.*, "dynamic symmetry"—but I shall not undertake to discuss them. What I do is to vary the spaces so that they will not all be the same size, and to regulate the variety of their measurements by some feeling I have for a thing called "rhythm." The simple varying of them without any particular consideration for a rhythmical scheme provides a certain degree of spice. The spaces will not be juggled blindly, to be sure; certain headings, or what not, will belong to certain sections of body-matter and will gravitate naturally toward their affinities. There is always the logical arrangement to be looked out for.

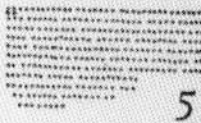

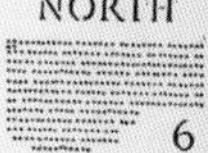

Rhythm

But emphasis must be laid on the word "rhythm." It is a most important part of interesting pattern, graphic or otherwise. It is a part of the charm of poetry and of music. Rhythm is the thing that puts life into a design—keeps it from being dead and mechanical. In graphic space design it may be crudely defined as a living ratio or size-relation among various parts. An instance is the series of ratios of areas in the well-proportioned margins of a book. The rightness or "well-proportion" is all in your eye, but it is a definite and positive thing, nevertheless. There are mathematical formulae for getting these proportions—bottom : fore-

Dwiggins explores the dynamics of layout with a study of 'divisions of space' – an early attempt in the use of grids. Margins are used for thumbnail diagrams and subheadings.

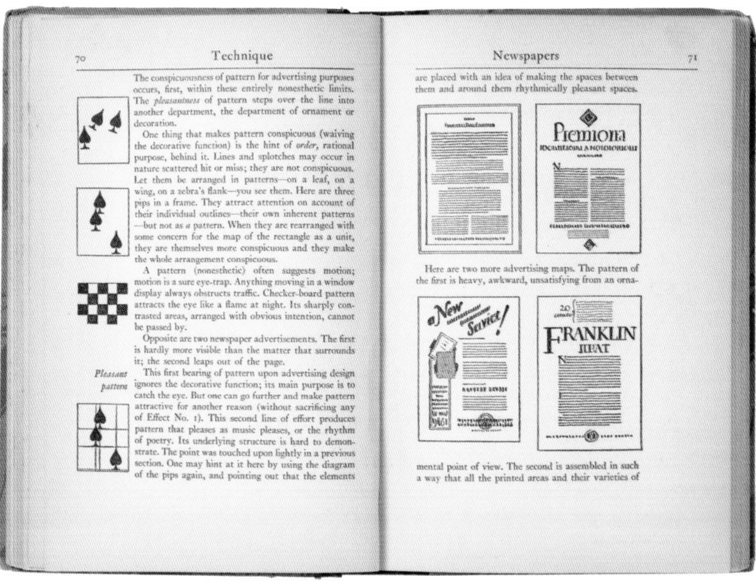

70 Technique

The conspicuousness of pattern for advertising purposes occurs, first, within these entirely nonesthetic limits. The *pleasantness* of pattern steps over the line into another department, the department of ornament or decoration.

One thing that makes pattern conspicuous (waiving the decorative function) is the hint of *order*, rational purpose, behind it. Lines and splotches may occur in nature scattered hit or miss; they are not conspicuous. Let them be arranged in patterns—on a leaf, on a wing, on a zebra's flank—you see them. Here are three pips in a frame. They attract attention on account of their individual outlines—their own inherent patterns—but *not* as *a* pattern. When they are rearranged with some concern for the map of the rectangle as a unit, they are themselves more conspicuous and they make the whole arrangement conspicuous.

A pattern (nonesthetic) often suggests motion; motion is a sure eye-trap. Anything moving in a window display always obstructs traffic. Checker-board pattern attracts the eye like a flame at night. Its sharply contrasted areas, arranged with obvious intention, cannot be passed by.

Opposite are two newspaper advertisements. The first is hardly more visible than the matter that surrounds it; the second leaps out of the page.

Pleasant pattern

This first bearing of pattern upon advertising design ignores the decorative function; its main purpose is to catch the eye. But one can go further and make pattern attractive for another reason (without sacrificing any of Effect No. 1). This second line of effort produces pattern that pleases as music pleases, or the rhythm of poetry. Its underlying structure is hard to demonstrate. The point was touched upon lightly in a previous section. One may hint at it here by using the diagram of the pips again, and pointing out that the elements

Newspapers 71

are placed with an idea of making the spaces between them and around them rhythmically pleasant spaces.

Here are two more advertising maps. The pattern of the first is heavy, awkward, unsatisfying from an ornamental point of view. The second is assembled in such a way that all the printed areas and their varieties of

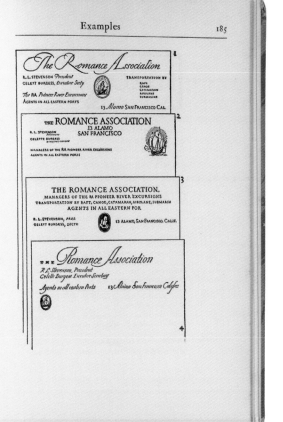

Layout in Advertising
W.A. Dwiggins
Harper and Brothers,
New York, 1928
212 pages
225 × 148 mm (9 × 5.875 in)
Designed by W.A. Dwiggins

Although the American William Addison Dwiggins (1880–1956) is perhaps best known for his work on books, he was a multifaceted designer who turned his talents to type design, calligraphy (he was president and sole member of the Society of Calligraphers) and commercial design. He worked in the tradition of the craftsman fine printer that had been shaped by William Morris and the Arts and Crafts Movement in the nineteenth century, but he was a modernist in outlook and, in a 1922 article in the *Boston Globe*, was the first person to use the term 'graphic designer' to describe his newly forming profession.

Layout in Advertising is Dwiggins's articulate description of this new vocation. Writing very much in the first person, he airs his views on the art of successful layout and is careful to remind the reader 'to build up his own structure of judgments and standards, based upon the exercise of his own faculty of criticism'.

Part I, 'Apparatus', looks at the raw materials of the trade: paper, type, lettering, ornament and pictures. Part II, 'Technique', studies the actual layout process across a variety of printed media. Dwiggins invents designs from fictitious projects for his practical examples, which are shown as sketches. The margins of the text are filled with thumbnails, and there are many, often cryptic, subheads such as 'Boredom fatal' and 'The bizarre' to draw in the reader.

Dwiggins touches on the issue of trademarks but did not foresee the advent of corporate identity. However, while styles and technology may have moved on since *Layout in Advertising* was published, much of what he has to say about the basic structure of a graphic designer's day-to-day existence and the design choices that have to be made is still applicable today.

176 Technique

placed according to a sense of balance of the three objects. A blank space to the left of the word "soap" helps to make that word stand out. The shape of the right-hand margin of the lettering is contrived, not accidental. The beginnings of the three small lines of text make a slanting line and a triangular area of blue that emphasizes the circular cake of soap. All this, of course, is *pattern*—arranging areas of space and color so that they play into each other's hands instead of cancel each other out. The lettering is made as simple as possible, so that it can be read.

Window card The window card was set down in a rough pencil sketch practically in its final form. It is predicated upon the assumption that the strange and rather awkward gestures of the broad gold bands will catch the pedestrian's eye; and that once his eye is caught, the design may proceed to announce its short admonition in positive tones. If the admonitory phrase arouses a desire for further information, the information is there.

The advertising effectiveness of the card will depend upon the oddity of the "map." If the pattern is indeed unlike the patterns of other window cards, then the

Examples 177

design should succeed. The straps around the top and sides are gold; they serve (in addition to their function as pattern) to cut the field away from other articles in the window. The background is white. The line "Color," etc., is gold. The silhouette and the remainder of the lettering, black. The three smaller rectangular pictures are in full color; the triangular disposition of these three areas of color is to be noted; it helps to settle the eye upon the word "Vividol." The small type matter at the sides is not rigidly balanced; it is given a little play up and down. The two regions of

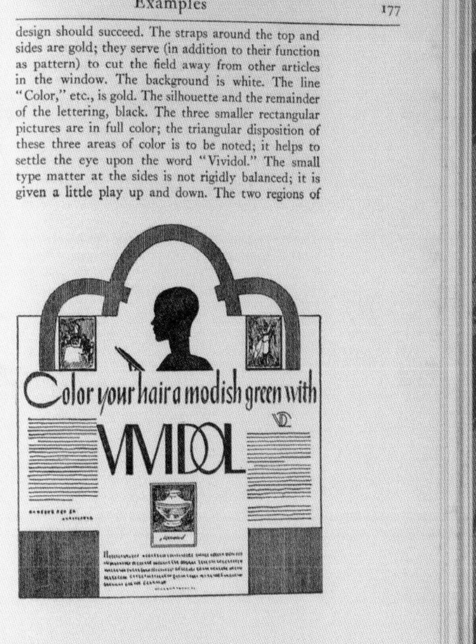

Layout in Advertising *gives detailed descriptions of the many formats of publicity with which the modern commercial artist would need to be acquainted – this spread highlights the 'Street-car card' and the 'Window card'.*

Layouts for confectionery packaging and letterheads have been mocked up by Dwiggins for imaginary products and companies.

184 Technique

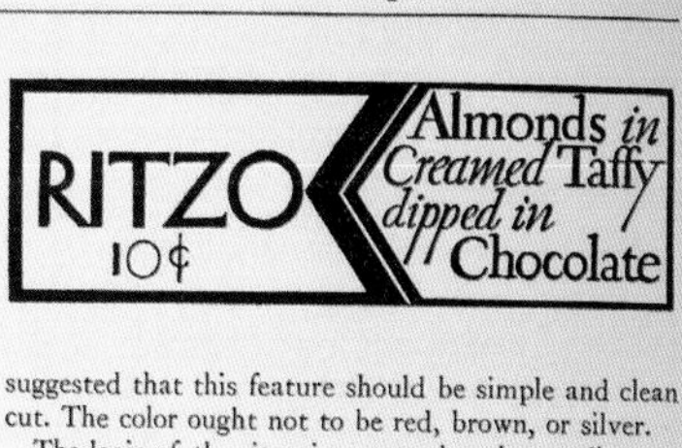

suggested that this feature should be simple and clean cut. The color ought not to be red, brown, or silver.

The logic of the situation seemed to be to dispense with cajolery in the form of purple and fine linen, and to put the proposition straight at the customer, telling him as plainly as possible what the candy was made of, what was its name, and how much it cost. The plain statement of the ingredients was more appetizing than any picture or symbol of fine flavor could be. This statement had to be big enough to be legible on the stand; it was the "sales talk" to new customers. These considerations converged in the above design.

Layout points (in addition to the foregoing analysis) are: The chevron, name, and edging lines are gold; the price and description, black; the paper is cream white. Several packages lie packed together on the tray, competing packages packed on either side; hence the blank spaces above and below the name, to set off this word on a white ground. The price, in black, is provided with blank spaces before and behind to make it conspicuous. The design appears on the four long faces; the manufacturer's name is printed on the end-flaps. The lettering is made sharp and simple.

Letter-heads The letter-head examples show four ways in which a characteristic group of letter-head material may be

Examples 185

1
The Romance Association
R. L. STEVENSON President
CELETT BURGESS, Executive Secty
The RA Pioneer River Excursions
AGENTS IN ALL EASTERN PORTS
TRANSPORTATION BY RAFT CANOE CATAMARAN AIRPLANE SUBMARINE
13 Alamo SAN FRANCISCO CAL.

2
THE ROMANCE ASSOCIATION
13 ALAMO
SAN FRANCISCO
R. L. STEVENSON
CELETTE BURGESS
MANAGERS OF THE RA PIONEER RIVER EXCURSIONS
AGENTS IN ALL EASTERN PORTS

3
THE ROMANCE ASSOCIATION.
MANAGERS OF THE RA PIONEER RIVER EXCURSIONS
TRANSPORTATION BY RAFT, CANOE, CATAMARAN, AIRPLANE, SUBMARIN
AGENTS IN ALL EASTERN POR
R. L. STEVENSON, PRES.
CELETT BURGESS, SECTY.
13 ALAMO, SAN FRANCISCO, CALIF.

THE Romance Association
R. L. Stevenson, President
Celett Burgess Executive Secretary
Agents in all eastern Ports
13 Alamo San Francisco Calif.
4

Mise en Page
The Theory and Practice of Lay-out
Alfred Tolmer
The Studio, London, 1931
118 pages
260 × 210 mm (10.25 × 8.25 in)
Designed by M. Louis Caillaud

Mise en Page is an impressive piece of production. Printed in blue and black, it contains numerous tipped-in pages with some outrageous pieces of finishing. Foils, embossing, hand-painting, different stocks (including wood veneer) and enamelling are just some of the arsenal of devices on display. That the book was produced by a printer is no surprise.

Alfred Tolmer (1876–1957) was a French printer who also ran his own design studio, a not uncommon practice in 1920s Paris. This book on the art of layout was a highly influential publication, which promoted the *moderne* style of design – a seductive blend of curvilinear forms that ignored the intellectual tendencies of the avant-garde.

Mise en Page, or 'layout', demonstrated to designers the possibilities inherent in the 'free use of process' afforded by the use of photo-reproduction. This liberation from the constraints of traditional print forms meant they could effectively cut and paste layouts, photographs could be cut out and juxtaposed, and image, line and text could be overlaid.

Tolmer reached back into the history of art, and delighted in the contrast between antiquity and the modern. A sarcophagus and a cocktail shaker stand side by side, an ancient female torso mirrors the hull of a yacht, and Josephine Baker poses with a statue of Saint Anthony. As much as it represented the decadence of the age, this playful mélange of elements opened the way for new forms of advertising and design.

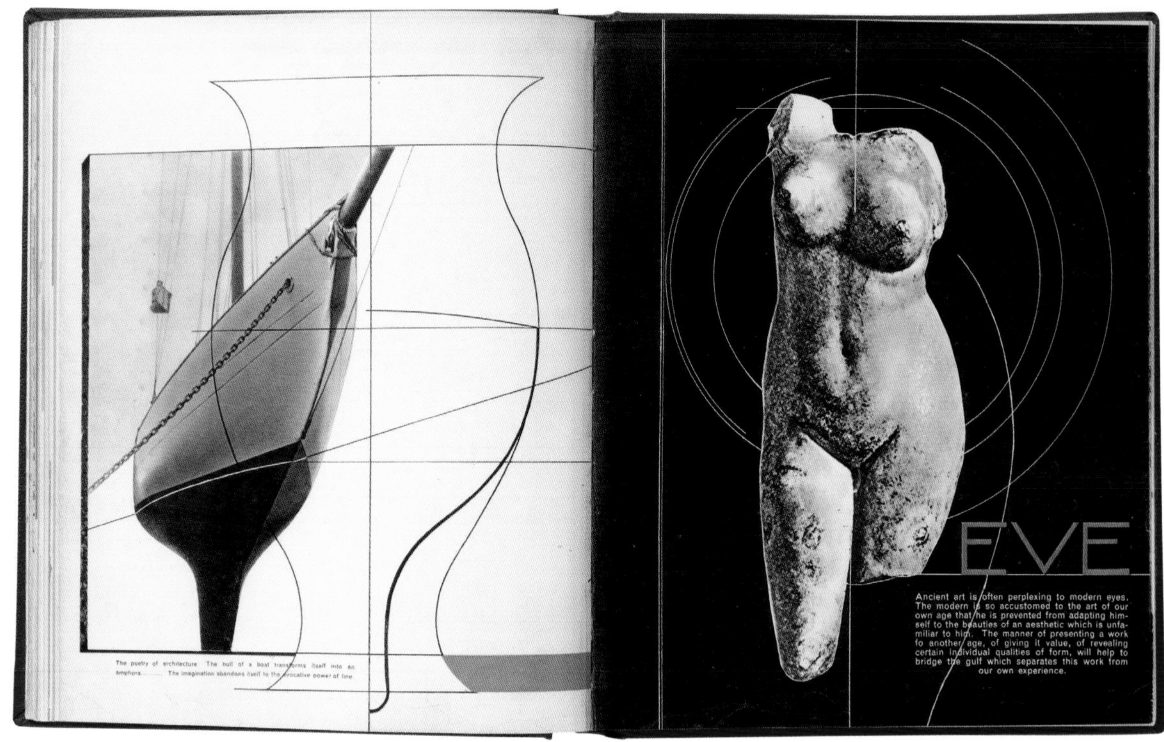

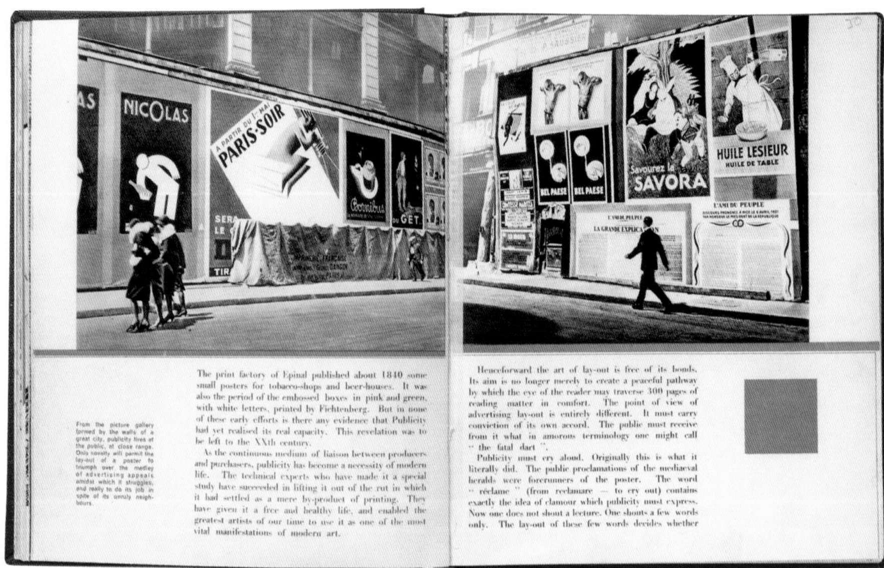

Mise en Page contains a number of tipped-in pages that are often flamboyant pieces of production. This example is printed by silkscreen on a sheet of wooden veneer. Note should also be made of the use of diagonally placed type on the left-hand page.

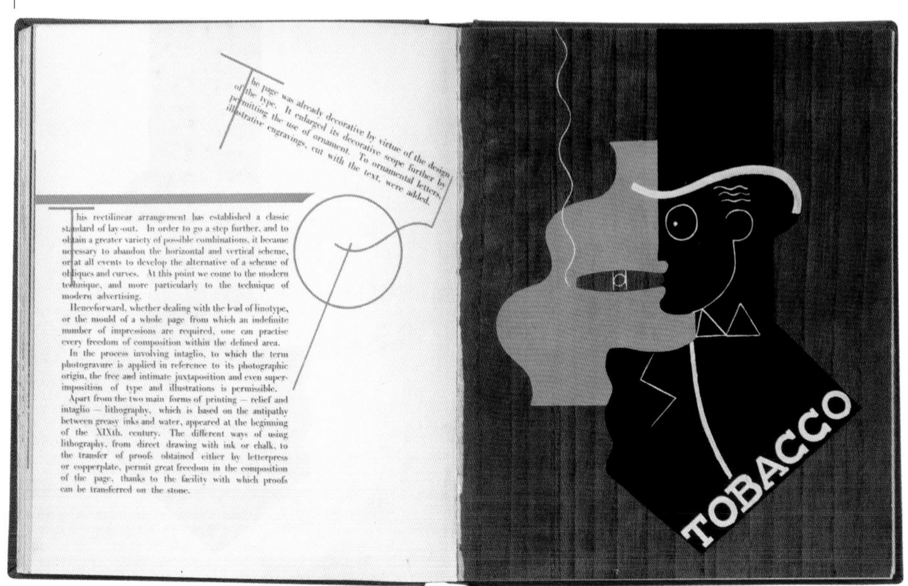

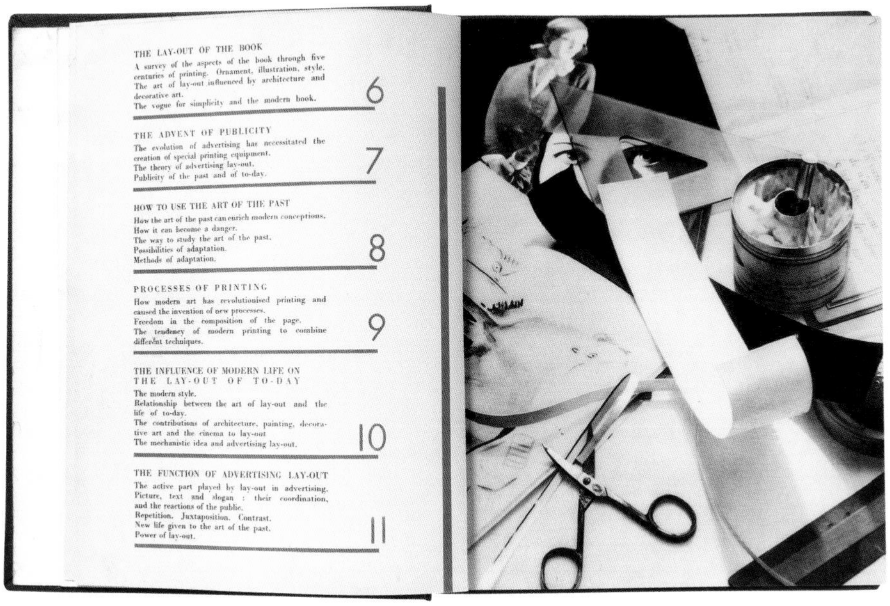

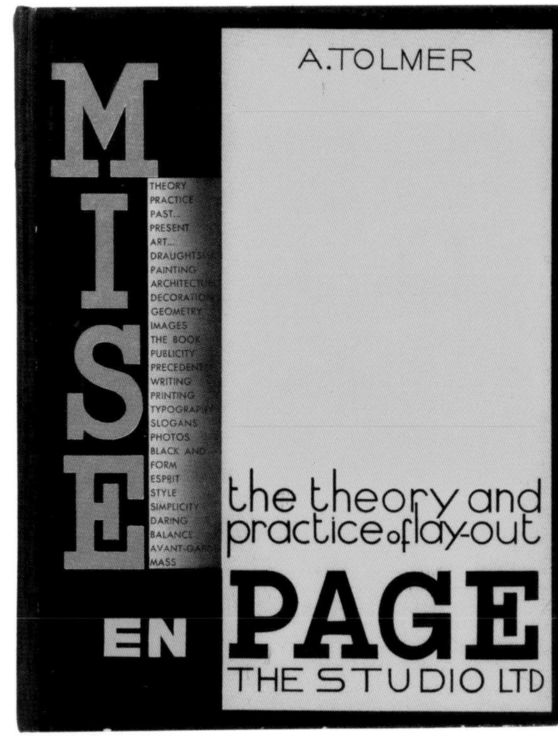

The photograph facing the contents illustrates the new tools of the commercial artist – the scissors and paste that would liberate the design process.

Tolmer saw that the advent of photography would radically change the graphic arts. Images could be juxtaposed to great effect and new forms of image-making were possible through the use of photograms.

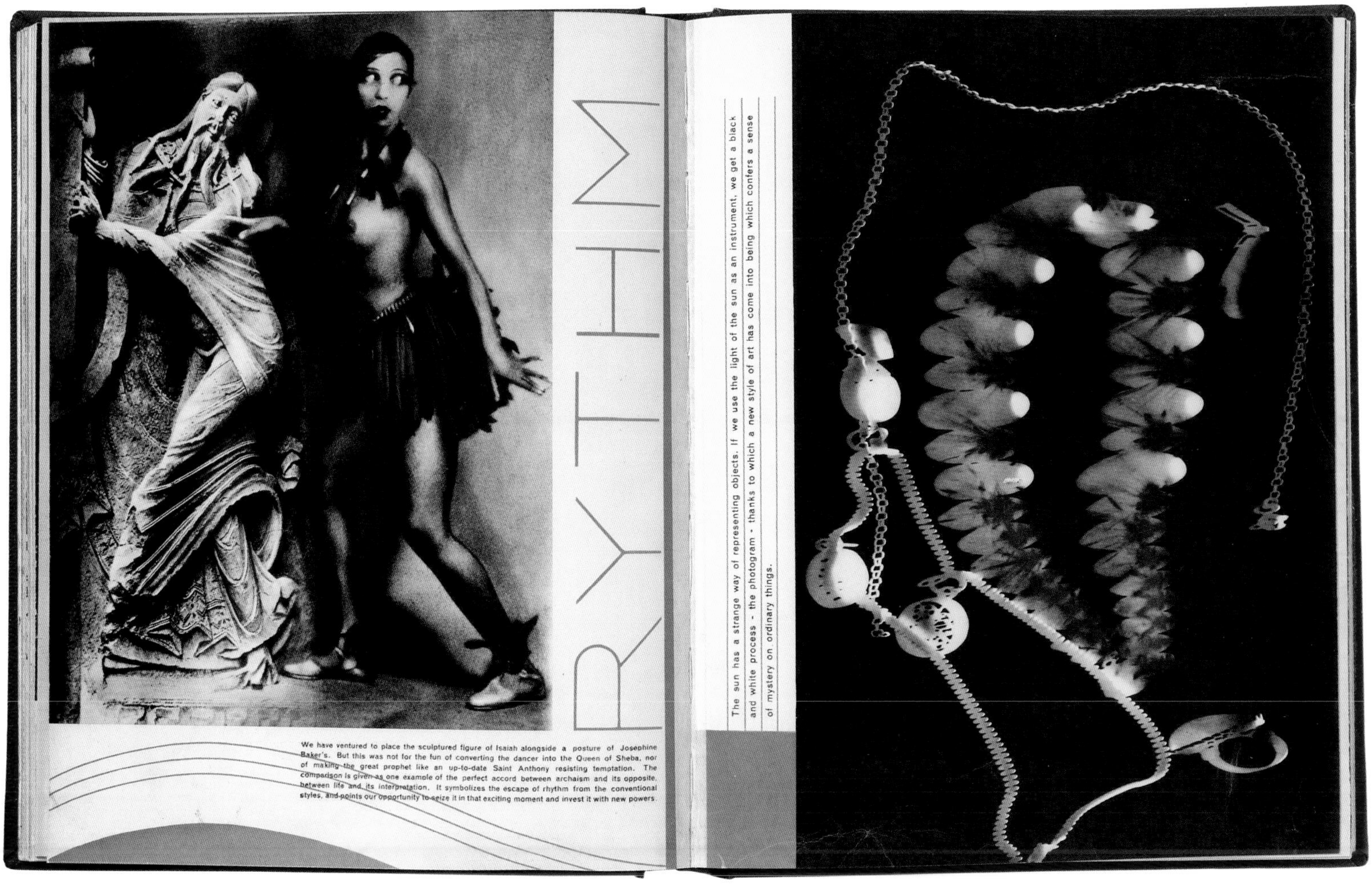

RYTHM

We have ventured to place the sculptured figure of Isaiah alongside a posture of Josephine Baker's. But this was not for the fun of converting the dancer into the Queen of Sheba, nor of making the great prophet like an up-to-date Saint Anthony resisting temptation. The comparison is given as one example of the perfect accord between archaism and its opposite, between life and its interpretation. It symbolizes the escape of rhythm from the conventional styles, and points our opportunity to seize it in that exciting moment and invest it with new powers.

The sun has a strange way of representing objects. If we use the light of the sun as an instrument, we get a black and white process - the photogram - thanks to which a new style of art has come into being which confers a sense of mystery on ordinary things.

A visual timeline for the history of commercial art, beginning with prehistoric cave painting.

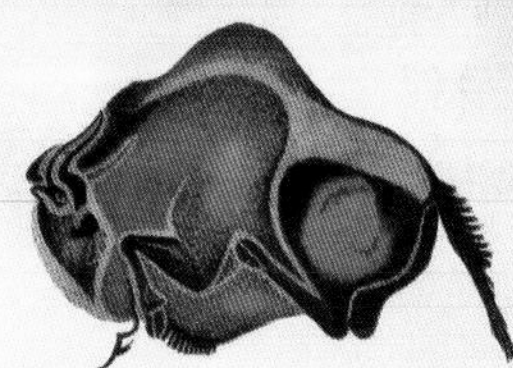

Prehistoric Cave Drawing

Greek Vase

Manuscript

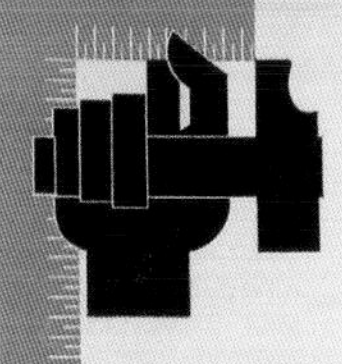

Advertising Design by Joseph Binder

contact with the colour-circle. The mixing of the single colours with black or white determines their brightness or their darkness respectively. The brightness or darkness of colours is the simplest means of representing space plastically. For black and white correspond to the phenomena of light and shade, that is to say to modelling. Impressionism for the first time consciously introduced these optical laws into art. Manet, and even more his successor Monet, made use of the harmony of coloured contrasts, in order to give a direct impression of natural light (open air). For that reason, impressionism renounces modelling in light and shade to a very large degree, and replaces it by a mosaic of complementary colours. The co-operation of the contrasting colours stimulates the imagination of the contemplator to create for himself the illusion of space.

STIMULATING THE EYE

We pause consciously at the word stimulation. Because from here we have an easy and direct connection with the poster. A poster must stimulate and it must occupy the eye ; consequently, it is an obvious idea to make use of the principle of impressionism for posters. The history of art shows that men have unconsciously gone in this direction. The connections under consideration go beyond the mere achievements of art. For, simultaneously with the development of optics as a natural science, the development of modern life led to those forms of intercommunication in large towns which are well known to us all. Advertisement expanded suddenly, from modest beginnings. Posters were created, and that in the town where the modern life of a capital received its first universally valid stamp—in Paris. Here it was Jules Chéret, who developed the poster-style directly from impressionistic painting. He simplified the complicated system of small blobs and strokes of the brush—which in the paintings of impressionists were placed side by side like a mosaic—down to a clearly arranged ornament in the flat, comprehensible for every unprejudiced contemplator. A few systems of contrasting colours formed the basis of his composition. As a matter of fact, he did not go to the logical extreme, for, in the details, he kept to the drawings. It was his pupil and successor, Toulouse-Lautrec, who first found the courage to complete the conventionalisation of the surface consistently so as not to disturb the long-distance effect by petty details. Historically it was the discovery of Asiatic art which gave him the impetus for this. In the woodcuts of Hokusai he discovered the simple language of line and colour, which he then transferred to lithography. In England Nicholson and the Beggarstaff brothers almost reached the modern poster in their progress.

14

15

CREATING ATMOSPHERE

It is very hot, but here is comfort and cool shade. These are people who take a pride in themselves and their home and have a social status and a standard of taste. All of this is said by colour : the predominance of red also calls attention to the important part which " Summer Home Furnishings " play in the scheme of things.

The sunny effect of this design is obtained by the yellow, the colour of the sun. A very light green is used as a complementary colour to this very light yellow, which enhances the friendly character of the whole " atmosphere." The shadows are also light and the red, which strikes one most, has its brilliance increased by yellow. The plastic effect which is endangered by the lack of dark tones for the shadows, is achieved by a very skilful diagonal composition with interlacing of these single elements of the picture.

Colour in Advertising

Joseph Binder

The Studio, London, 1934
130 pages
284 × 220 mm (11 × 8.5 in)
Designed by Joseph Binder

EFFECT GAINED BY DECORATIVE LETTERING ON BANDS OF COLOUR

Three-colour poster with white letters on coloured and black surfaces. The arrangement is strictly linear. A maximum of coloured effect is obtained by variations between black and white. All representation is left out. The whole attention is drawn to the conception of the book. Only a laurel leaf appears as a symbol of literature.

An economical but effective result can be obtained by the use of lettering only, as is shown in this three-colour poster.

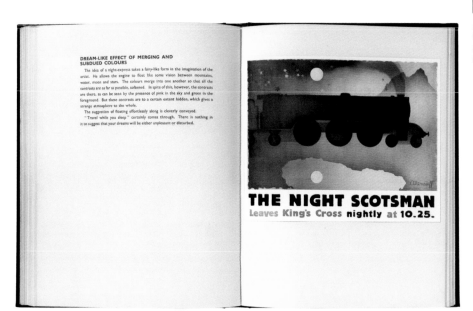

One of Binder's own posters, Give Books *(1929), a typographic layout using bands of colour, is reproduced in the plate section.*

DREAM-LIKE EFFECT OF MERGING AND SUBDUED COLOURS

The idea of a night-express takes a fairy-like form in the imagination of the artist. He allows the engine to float like some vision between mountains, water, moon and stars. The colours merge into one another so that all the contrasts are as far as possible, softened. In spite of this, however, the contrasts are there, as can be seen by the presence of pink in the sky and green in the foreground. But these contrasts are to a certain extent hidden, which gives a strange atmosphere to the whole.

The suggestion of floating effortlessly along is cleverly conveyed.

"Travel while you sleep" certainly comes through. There is nothing in it to suggest that your dreams will be either unpleasant or disturbed.

THE NIGHT SCOTSMAN
Leaves King's Cross nightly at 10.25.

'Economy in poster-painting, as in everything else, is a sign of perfection.' These are the words of Joseph Binder (1898–1972), the Viennese poster designer, in his book on the use and effects of colour in publicity. His own style, based on Art Deco-inspired shapes in simple colour combinations, followed this article of faith. He also saw a clear distinction between the techniques and goals of the fine artist and those of the commercial counterpart, and *Colour in Advertising* is in large part a definition of working practices in the relatively new profession of the graphic artist.

The first part looks at the practice and theory of colour in advertising. Binder promotes the use of a prismatic colour wheel for working out harmonious combinations through sympathetic and complementary colours, and goes on to study the symbolism and psychology of colour.

Through the use of an imaginary client, a grocer, he guides readers step by step through the design of a trademark, the accompanying typography, stationery and promotional booklet, and finally the poster. He stresses the need for colour and type to be consistent across the various applications.

The second part of the book is a plate section showing 24 examples of the use of colour in commercial art, from booklets and showcards to fashion drawings and posters. The book is letterpress printed and uses sans serif type; colour illustrations are tipped-in for the plate section.

Binder was well travelled (he settled permanently in New York City in 1935) and his selection of works from a wide variety of modern graphic artists in Europe and America reflects this. The majority of examples, however, are from artists based in Britain, such as Edward McKnight Kauffer, Tom Purvis and Eric Fraser.

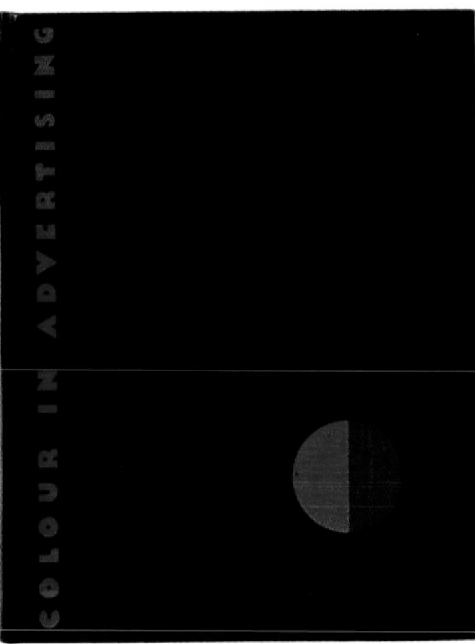

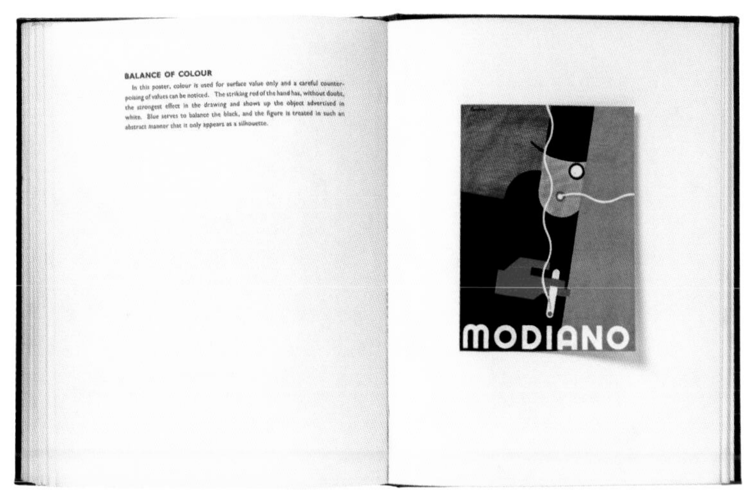

BALANCE OF COLOUR

In this poster, colour is used for surface value only and a careful counter-poising of values can be noticed. The striking red of the hand has, without doubt, the strongest effect in the drawing and shows up the object advertised in white. Blue serves to balance the black, and the figure is treated in such an abstract manner that it only appears as a silhouette.

Language of Vision

György Kepes

Paul Theobald, Chicago, 1944

228 pages

277 × 213 mm (11 × 8.375 in)

Designed by György Kepes

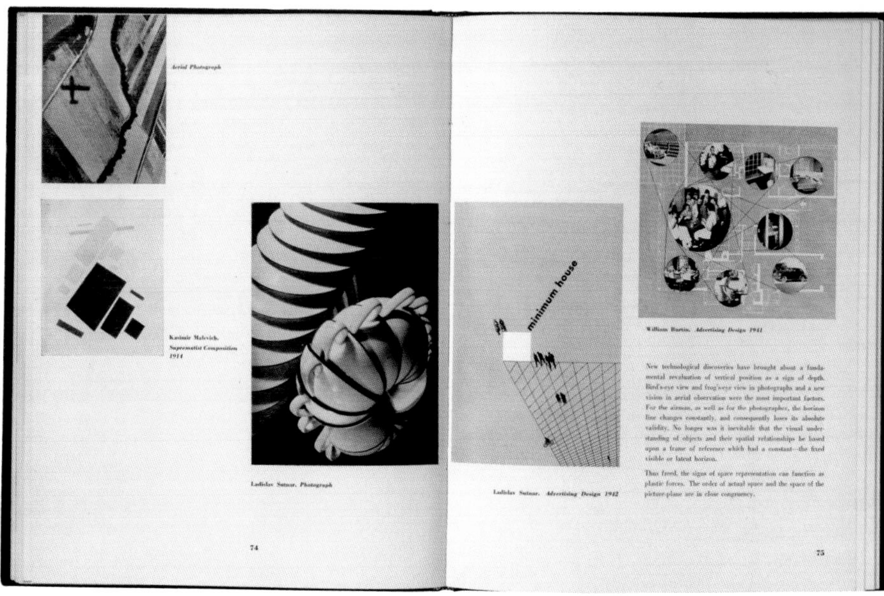

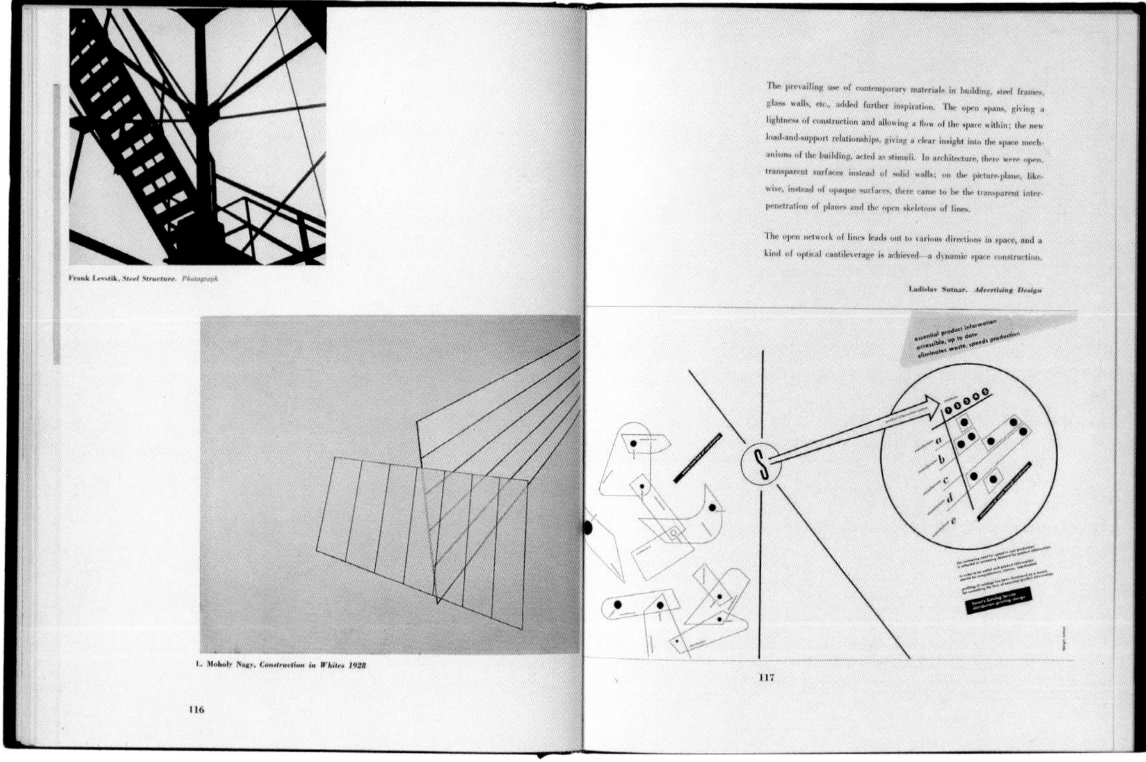

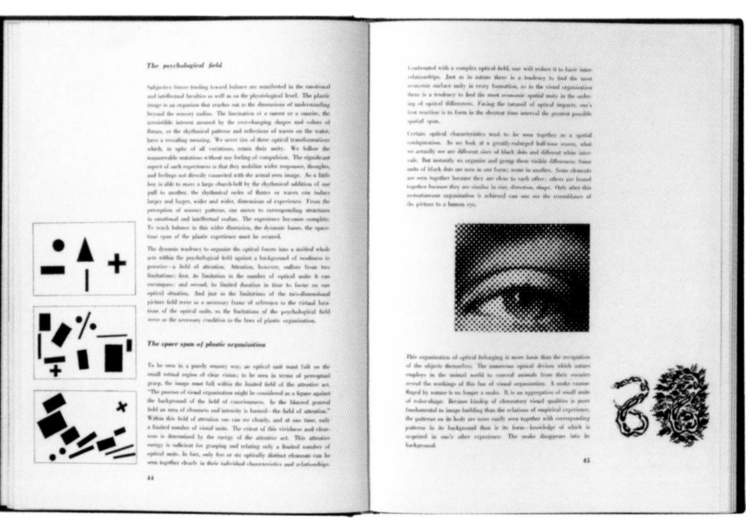

Kepes drew uncaptioned abstract diagrammatic compositions in the margins to accompany the text.

A Hungarian who emigrated to the United States, György Kepes (1906–2001) worked with his compatriot László Moholy-Nagy in an effort to set up a new Bauhaus, which became the Institute of Design in Chicago. *Language of Vision* embodies the ethos of his teaching and is illustrated with work from contemporary designers and artists and from the students on his own course.

Kepes's aim was to develop a new visual language for a contemporary age, based on the advances in twentieth-century modern art and the need to incorporate the dynamic potential and dominance of photography as a visual medium. He was a disciple of gestalt psychology, which posits that an object has a balance and wholeness that is worth more than the sum of its parts.

The first of three chapters, 'Plastic Organization', studies the arrangement and interaction of elements that go to make up an image. The second chapter, 'Visual Representation', looks at the idioms of spacial dynamics. The third chapter, 'Toward a Dynamic Iconography', is a call to artists, and especially the advertising profession, to use these concepts in the making of a new language of representation.

Kepes saw designers, and their need to speak to a contemporary audience, as being in the vanguard of the effort to forge a new iconography. The book contains images by many designers working at the time in the United States, such as the Czech Ladislav Sutnar and the German William Burtin, and also displays the home-grown talents of Lester Beall and Paul Rand.

As a practising designer, Kepes included some of his own work for clients, and was also responsible for the many abstract visual diagrams that litter the book. The design of *Language of Vision*, with its asymmetric layout, integration of text and image, and bold use of white space, was as significant as Kepes's theories in influencing visual language and its teaching.

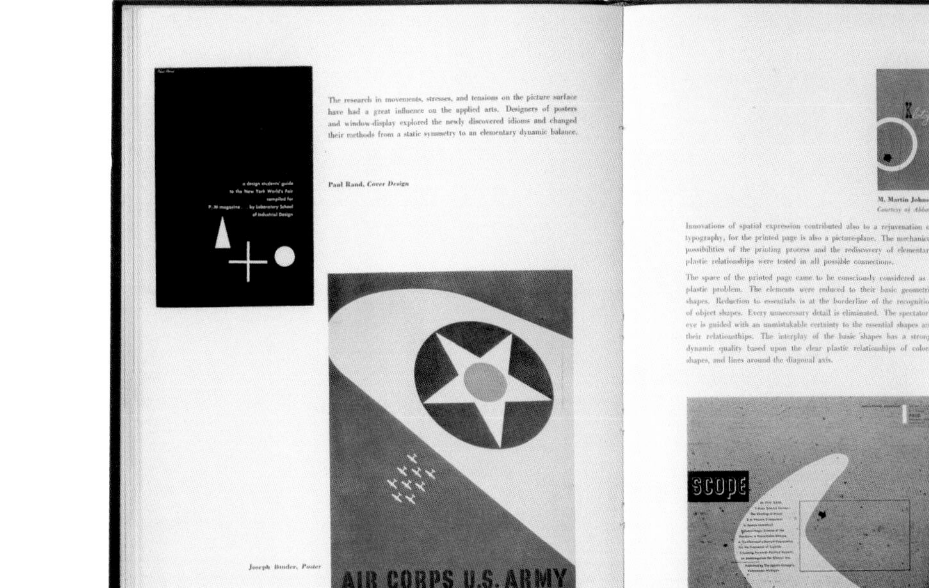

The research in movements, stresses, and tensions on the picture surface have had a great influence on the applied arts. Designers of posters and window-display explored the newly discovered idioms and changed their methods from a static symmetry to an elementary dynamic balance.

Paul Rand, *Cover Design*

Joseph Binder, *Poster*

112

M. Martin Johnson, *Four Advertising Designs*
Courtesy of Abbott Laboratories

Innovations of spatial expression contributed also to a rejuvenation of typography, for the printed page is also a picture-plane. The mechanical possibilities of the printing process and the rediscovery of elementary plastic relationships were tested in all possible connections.

The space of the printed page came to be consciously considered as a plastic problem. The elements were reduced to their basic geometric shapes. Reduction to essentials is at the borderline of the recognition of object shapes. Every unnecessary detail is eliminated. The spectator's eye is guided with an unmistakable certainty to the essential shapes and their relationships. The interplay of the basic shapes has a strong, dynamic quality based upon the clear plastic relationships of colors, shapes, and lines around the diagonal axis.

W. Burtin, *Advertising Design*

113

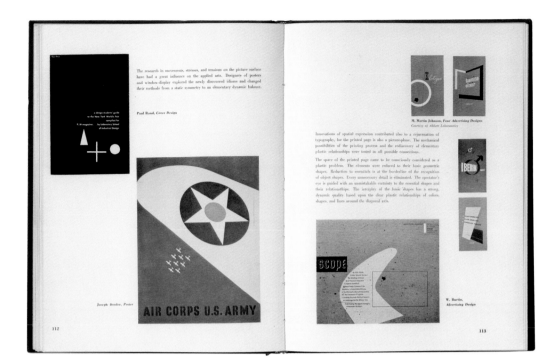

A spread of photograms in commercial use by Lester Beall, Harold Walter and Kepes. The asymmetric layout and use of white space as a design element proved influential in book design.

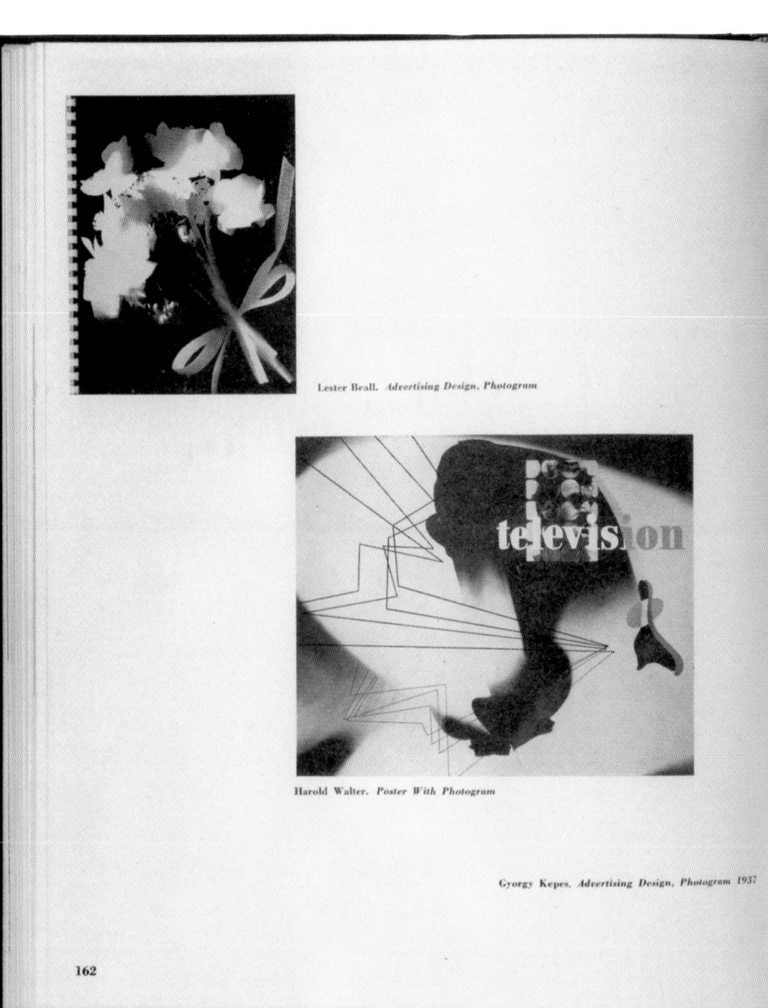

Lester Beall. *Advertising Design, Photogram*

Harold Walter. *Poster With Photogram*

Gyorgy Kepes. *Advertising Design, Photogram* 1937

162

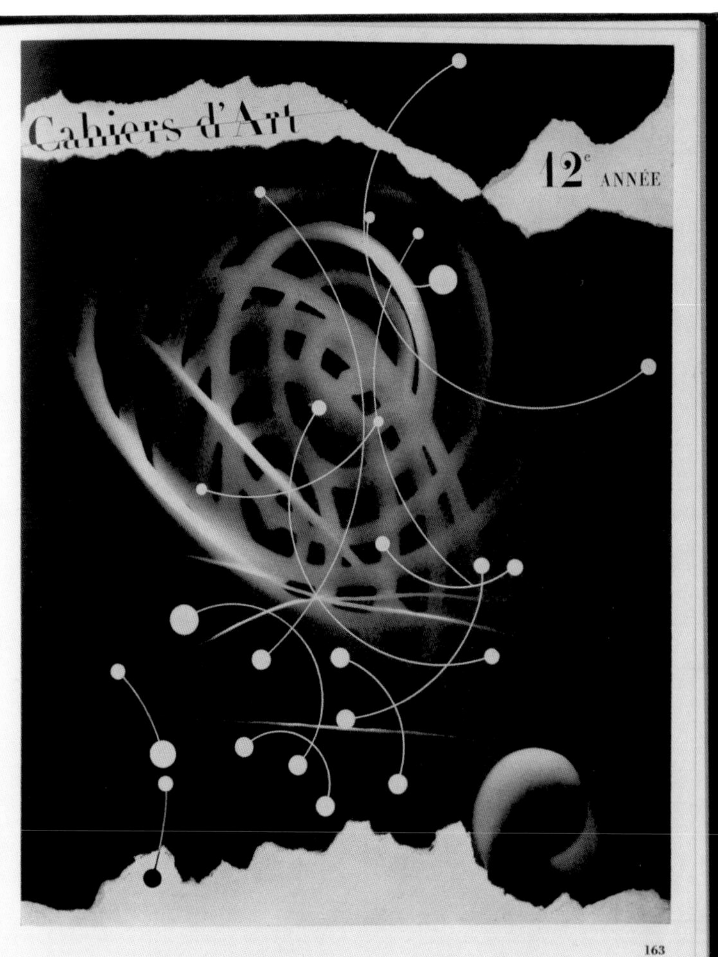

163

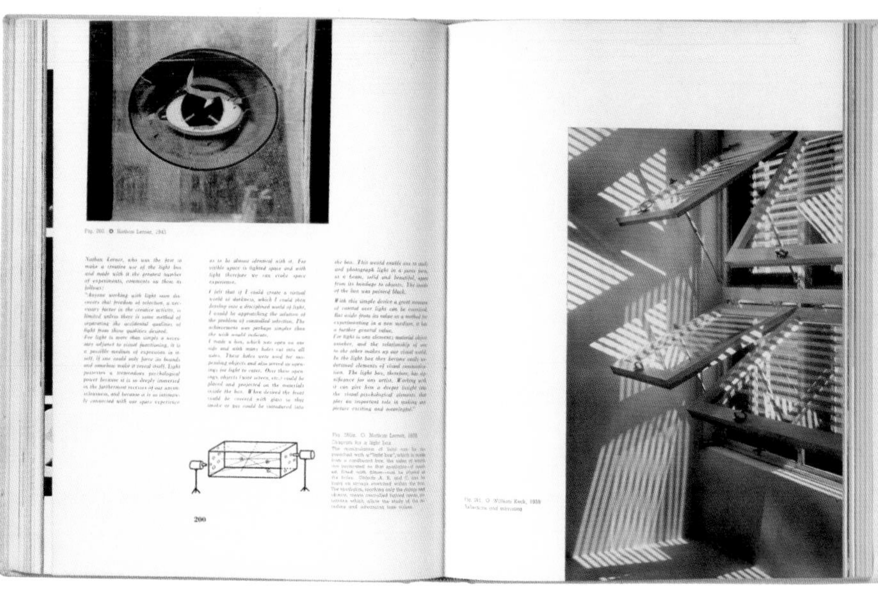

The role of photograhy as a modern communication tool is given great prominence by Moholy-Nagy – this spread shows one of his own photograms and a photograph by Lester Beall.

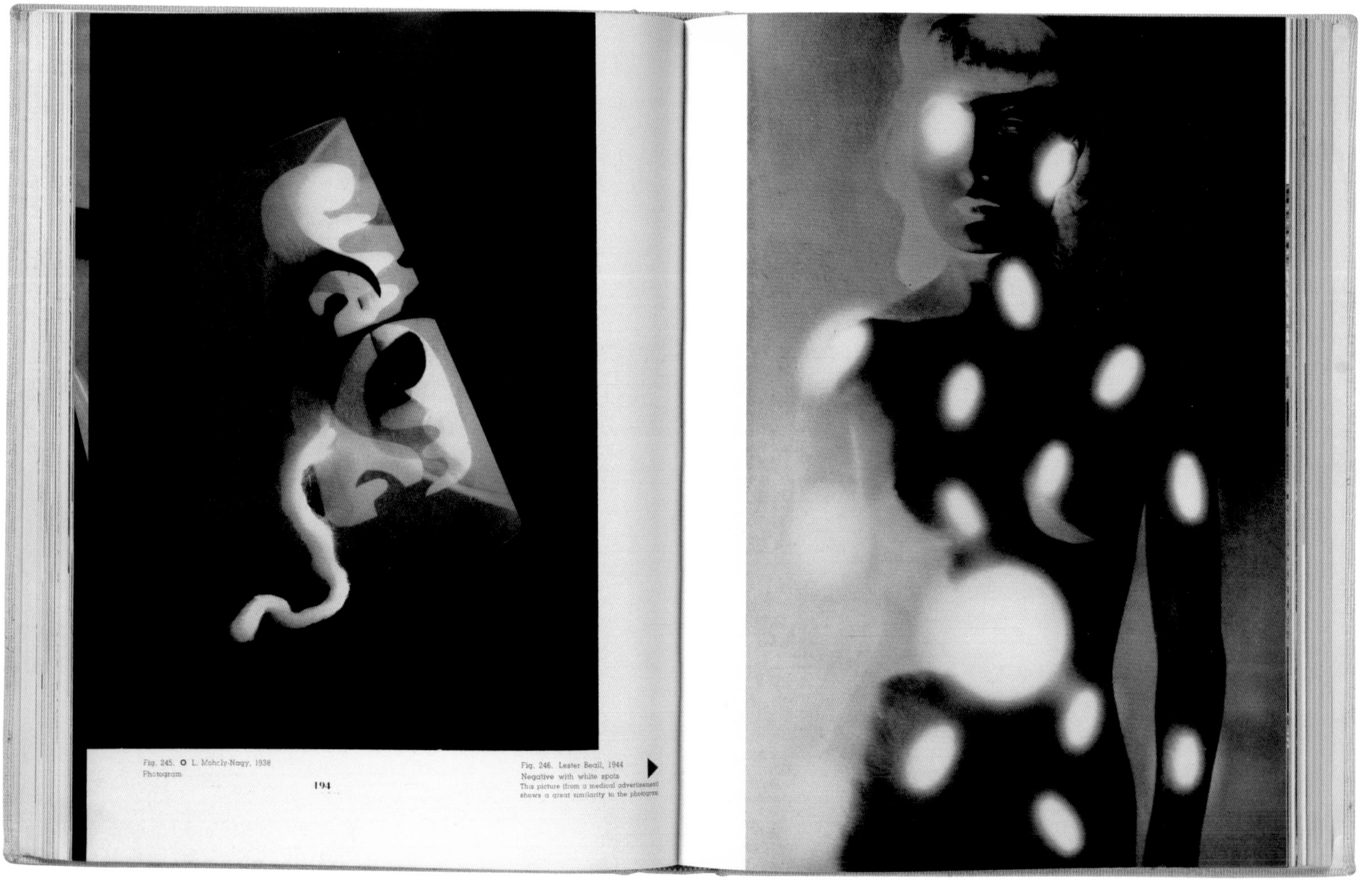

Fig. 245. L. Moholy-Nagy, 1938
Photogram

194

Fig. 246. Lester Beall, 1944
Negative with white spots
This picture (from a medical advertisement) shows a great similarity to the photogram

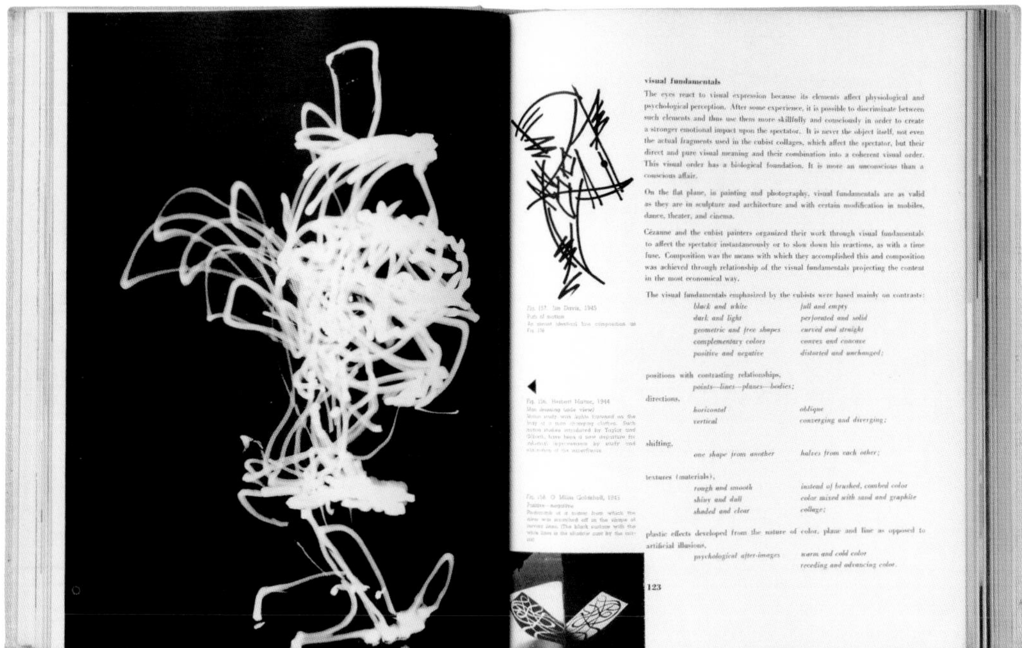

Vision in Motion *broke new ground in book design – the use of extended captions and sidebar information gave illustrated books a new dynamic.*

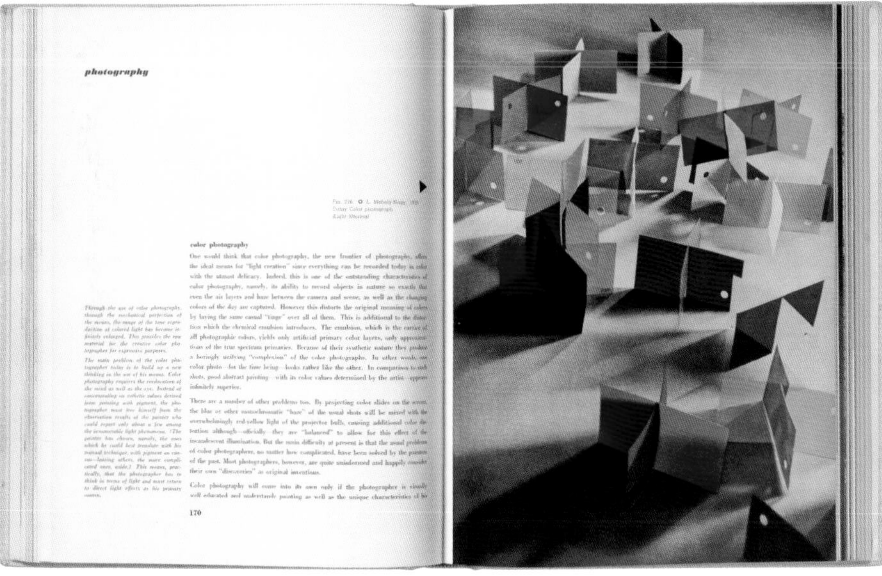

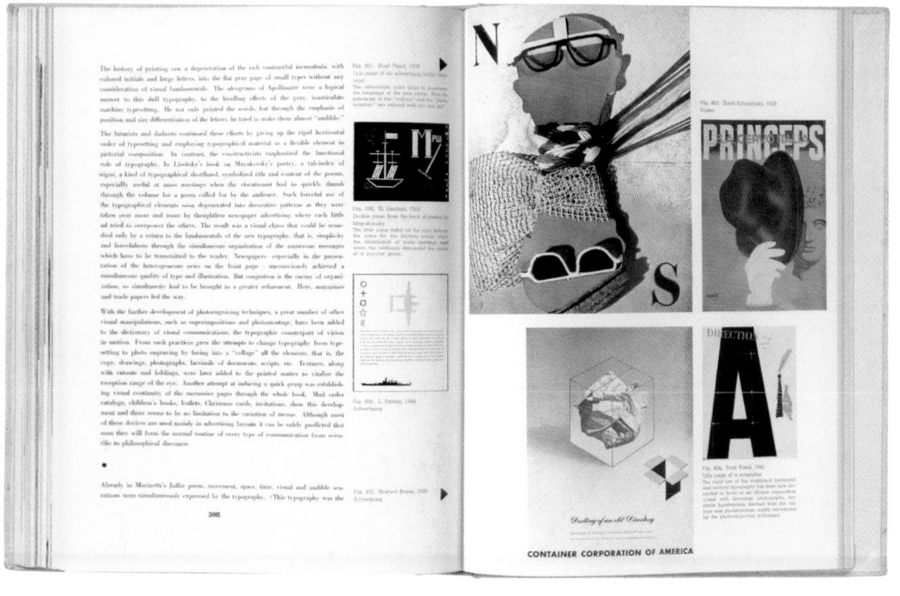

Vision in Motion
László Moholy-Nagy
Paul Theobald, Chicago, 1947
Third reprint (pictured), 1947
376 pages
302 × 250 mm (11.875 × 10 in)
Designed by László Moholy-Nagy

This is not a graphic design book, but has had far more influence on the profession and how it is taught than many books dedicated to the subject. The Hungarian artist and educator László Moholy-Nagy (1895–1946), a central figure in the Bauhaus, emigrated to the United States in order to establish a new Bauhaus with his colleague György Kepes. This led to the establishment of the Institute of Design in Chicago, the educational programme of which is central to the book's message.

Vision in Motion puts art and design at the centre of modern life, and makes the case for a synthesis of technological advance and the emotional well-being of society through the discovery of new ideas in all facets of the visual arts. In simpler but cryptic terms, Moholy-Nagy says the premise is 'seeing while moving'.

The works of relatively few graphic designers, among others Lester Beall, Paul Rand and Xanti Schawinsky, are shown alongside examples by artists, students (including a young Robert Brownjohn), photographers, writers and architects. These are offset by lessons in the advances in visual interpretation and perception, particularly in the field of photography, as well as contemporary ways of displaying text that offered new forms of typographic expression.

Moholy-Nagy broke new ground in book design, integrating text and image on a page without the need for separate plate sections for illustrations. He also provided extended captions and images in margins so readers could skip through a book, a format that has remained in common use.

Education takes up a great portion of *Vision in Motion*. At its root is a basic course (or foundation) in which students are introduced to the building blocks of the arts through the study of elementary forms, shapes, textures, materials and visual dynamics. This is applied across all forms of media to give students a rounded view of the arts that helps them to select areas for further study. The system became the blueprint for art education for decades.

The Graphic Artist and His Design Problems

Josef Müller-Brockmann

Arthur Niggli, Teufen, 1961
Third edition (pictured), Hastings House, New York, 1968
186 pages
224 × 256 mm (8.875 × 10 in)
Designed by Josef Müller-Brockmann

The first book by the Swiss designer Josef Müller-Brockmann (1914–1996), who taught graphic design at the Zurich Kunstgewerbeschule from 1957 to 1960, *The Graphic Artist and His Design Problems* was published shortly after his tenure ended. Based on his systematic teaching philosophy and guidelines for graphic design in advertising, it is illustrated with his own work and that of his students.

The book is divided into three sections: 'Illustration and Subjectivity', 'Graphic Art and Objectivity' and 'Training of the Graphic Artist'. The first two provide a portfolio of Müller-Brockmann's considerable body of work up until 1960. Examples from his early career as a competent illustrator, with which he soon became dissatisfied, are shown as a prelude to the more objective and constructed graphic art in which he excelled, displayed in the second section. Here Müller-Brockmann's graphic design work is split into themes such as typography, photography, drawing and colour. Each is introduced with an often forthright text that describes his design theory for the subject area. The texts, in German, English and French, include lists of criteria for graphic artists to follow. On typography, for instance, he lists nine 'rules of thumb' including 'Never combine different type families' and 'Never use different forms of the same family'.

The third section describes the format of his design class in Zurich and shows the work of the students he taught. The formal exercises in solving graphic problems and the rigid simulation of professional practice are in marked contrast to the teachings of Armin Hofmann and Emil Ruder in Basel.

Well illustrated, the book is printed in black apart from two small colour sections, and contains some of Müller-Brockmann's best-known pieces. A series of safety posters for the Automobil-Club der Schweiz and identity work for clients such as L+C are included, as well as the collection of concert posters he designed for the Tonhalle-Gesellschaft in Zurich from 1950 onwards.

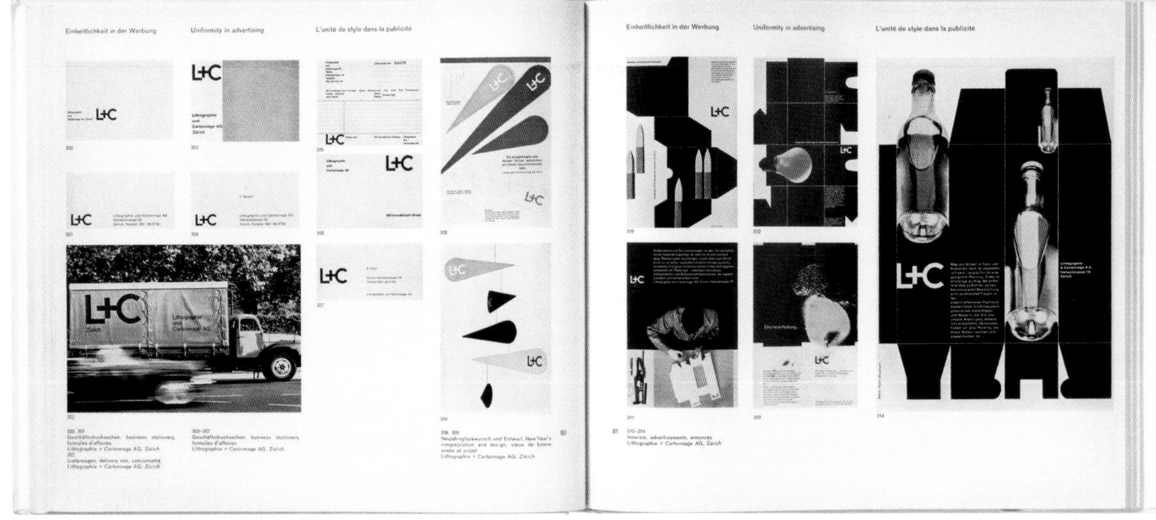

Students on Müller-Brockmann's design course in Zurich were encouraged to work on structured design briefs. Their work is displayed in the last section of the book.

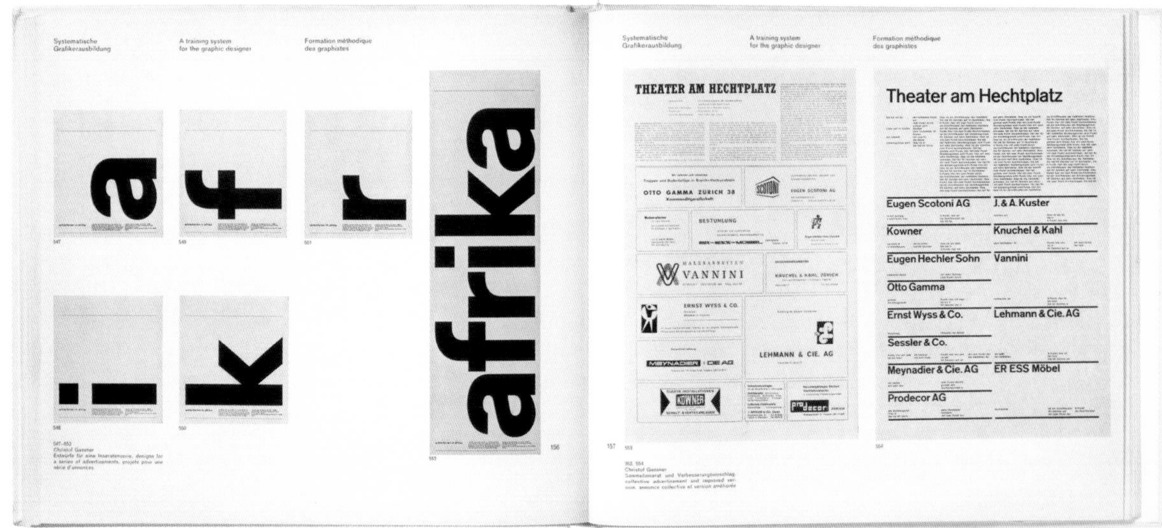

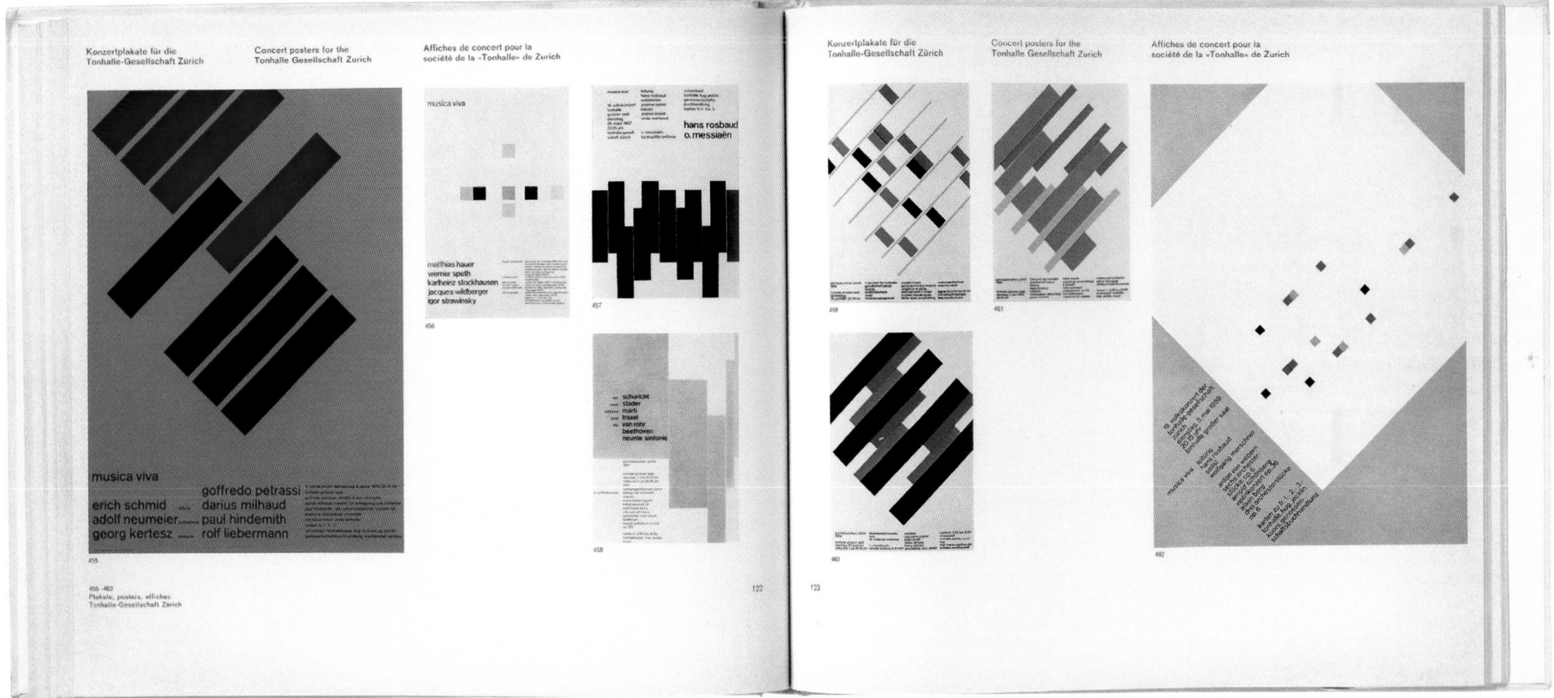

Printed here are Müller-Brockmann's posters for the Tonhalle-Gesellschaft in Zurich in one of the two small colour sections. An in-depth study of Müller-Brockmann's career can be found in Lars Müller (ed.), Josef Müller-Brockmann: Pioneer of Swiss Graphic Design, *fourth edition, Lars Müller Publishers, Baden, 2001.*

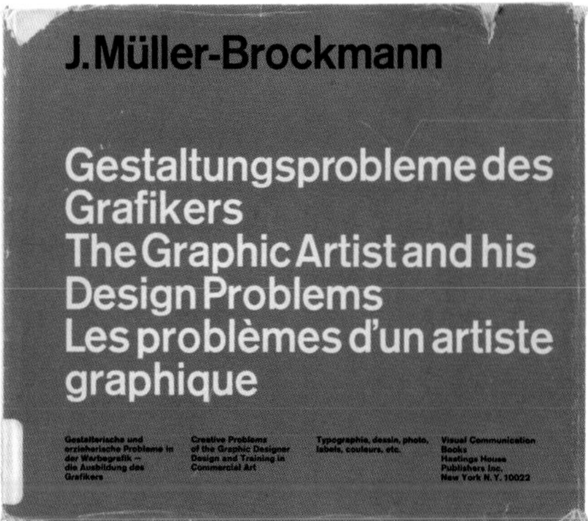

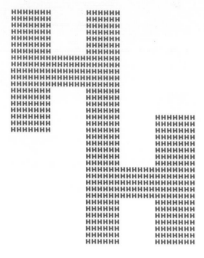

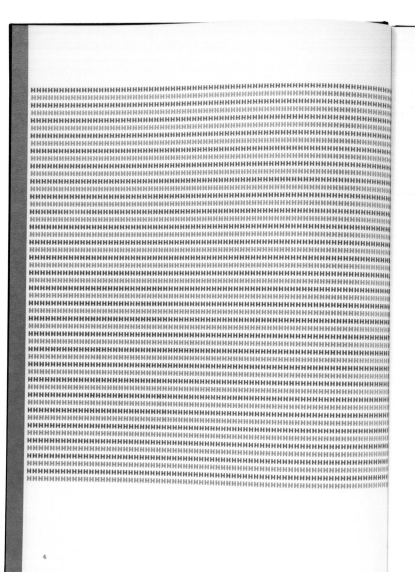

The typographic examples have been stripped of their context and page margins, and represent the type as viewed when received from the typesetter.

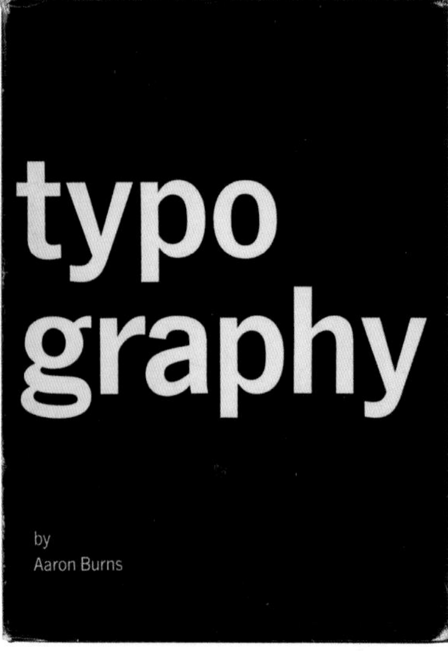

"What's
the good
word from
Madison
Avenue?"

"Indefectible! That's the good
word. Incredible creativity.
Perspicacious! Ideas that are
ornaments of intellect...
layouts, merely consummate.
Sudler & Hennessey, obviously.
The observed of all observers,
the cynosure of all eyes, S & H
casually create incomparable
comprehensives, meticulous
mechanicals & fastidious
finishes. To say nothing of
apt art, felicitous photography
& resplendent retouching.
Typographic knowledge?
Encyclopaedic! Lettering?
Legendary! What's more their
reputation rests on reason,
practicality & pragmatism.
The good words from
Madison
Avenue?
Sudler &
Hennessey!"

"Who told you?"
"Father"*

THAT'S WHAT HE SAID, WHEN ASKED

IN A GREENWICH VILLAGE NIGHT CLUB, FATS WALLER HAD JUST FINISHED PLAYING AND SINGING HIS WAY THROUGH A STUNNING TWENTY-MINUTE SET WHICH INCLUDED HONEYSUCKLE ROSE, SWEET GEORGIA BROWN, I'M JUST WILD ABOUT HARRY, BASIN STREET BLUES, BODY AND SOUL, SOMEBODY LOVES ME AND BLUE TURNING GRAY OVER YOU. PERSPIRING, LAUGHING, LOVING THE APPLAUSE, FATS LEFT HIS PIANO AND WALKED OVER TO THE BAR WHERE HE ENCOUNTERED A FASHIONABLY-DRESSED WOMAN. "OH," SHE SAID, "JUST THE MAN I WANT TO SEE. I'M SURE YOU CAN ANSWER MY QUESTION. TELL ME, MR. WALLER, WHAT IS SWING?" FATS REACHED FOR HIS DRINK WITH ONE HAND, MOPPED HIS FACE WITH THE OTHER, LOOKED AT THE WOMAN SQUARELY AND REPLIED, "LADY, IF YOU GOTTA ASK, YOU AINT GOT IT!" RELAXING BETWEEN SETS, ART TATUM SAT AT A TABLE IN A FIFTY-SECOND STREET BISTRO, DRINKING BEER FROM A BOTTLE. "BUT FAITH IS YOUR SALVATION," SAID THE BROWNSKIN GIRL. AND ART TOOK A SWIG OF HIS BEER. "WITHOUT IT YOU ARE LOST," SAID THE BROWNSKIN GIRL, AS BLIND ART TATUM SADLY SIPPED HIS BEER. "ALL GOD'S CHILDREN ARE LOST," SAID ART, "BUT ONLY A FEW CAN PLAY THE PIANO."

ART TATUM, 1910-1957 (LOST MAN PLAYED FINE PIANO)

44

boldness and beauty
are brilliantly balanced
in new fall fabrics
by Milliken!

45

A small front section printed with colour shows some expressive examples of typography. This spread features the work of Herbert Matter and Paul Rand.

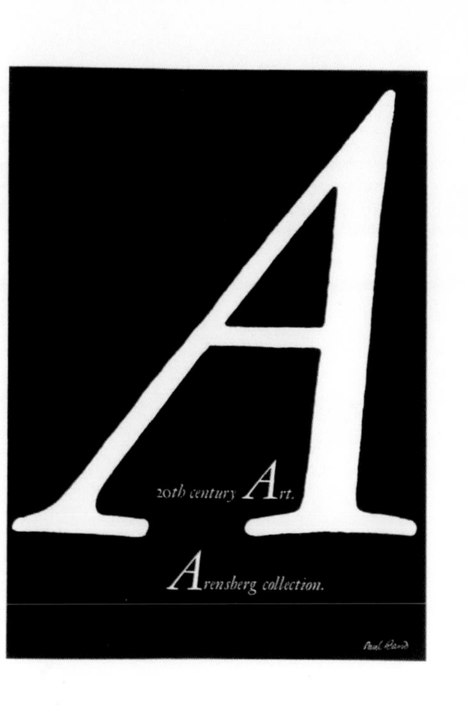

14

15

Typography

Aaron Burns

Reinhold Publishing Corporation, New York, 1961

112 pages

335 × 253 mm (13.25 × 10 in)

Designed by Aaron Burns

Context and layout have been stripped from the examples shown in *Typography*. All that is left are the raw black-and-white proofs as the designer or art director would have received them from the typographer, ready to be pasted on to the mechanicals or marked up and returned for amendments. The type arrangements sit on the pages surrounded by acres of white space, made available by the book's large format. There are no captions, which gives the book the appearance of a collection of concrete poetry.

Compiled by the American designer Aaron Burns (1922–1991), the book features typography by prominent designers, particularly those working in New York in the late 1950s and early 1960s, such as Herb Lubalin, Lou Dorfsman, Bob Gill, Gene Federico and the design group Brownjohn, Chermayeff & Geismar Associates. Burns had commissioned some of them when he was director of the typesetting firm the Composing Room, where he produced a series of typographic booklets, samples of which make up a number of the examples shown in the book. He also ventured further afield with the inclusion of European designers such as Karl Gerstner, Willem Sandberg and Herbert Matter.

The book's table of contents is at the back of the book, as are the index of designers and a list of featured typefaces. Also contained in this rear section are a practical guide to typographic usage and a critique by Burns of the type arrangements featured in the front of the book.

Typography: Basic Principles

Influences and Trends since the 19th Century

John Lewis

Reinhold Publishing Corporation, New York, 1964

96 pages

196 × 165 mm (7.75 × 6.5 in)

Designed by John Lewis

'Typographic design is as fluid as language and as changing as modern life.' This is the conclusion the designer and writer John Lewis reaches at the end of *Typography: Basic Principles*. It is a theme he pursues eloquently in this guidebook to type usage and practice, originally produced by London-based publisher Studio Books in 1963.

His opening chapter is a concise study of the historical influences on typography and considers the part that art movements such as Cubism, Constructivism, Dada, De Stijl and Art Nouveau played in opening up creative avenues for designers to explore. It is well illustrated with work from Joost Schmidt, Jan Tschichold, Kurt Schwitters, Edward McKnight Kauffer and others. Lewis pays particular attention to William Morris and the Arts and Crafts Movement as a precursor to the Bauhaus through a shared interest in industrial design.

Modern typographic form is considered in the second chapter, with a debate on the use of sans serif typefaces and asymmetric layouts in creating a modern form of book design. Lewis offers some of his own educated opinions but leaves the subject open-ended as a challenge to his readers.

The three, more practical chapters that follow give readers an idea of the design process in the 1960s; there are a couple of immaculate hand-drawn pencil layouts by the noted English designer Anthony Froshaug, traced from type-specimen pages. Notes on typographic styling are illustrated with practical examples.

Typography: Basic Principles was part of a series of small-format paperbacks on graphic design, of which Lewis was the editor. Other titles included *Graphic Design: Visual Comparisons* (see page 130) by Fletcher/Forbes/Gill and *Graphics Handbook* by Ken Garland. They were accessible, cheap and by all accounts sold very well.

Crucial to Typography: Basic Principles *was an understanding of the historical factors that shaped the form of modern typographic design. These examples are by Théo van Doesburg and Joost Schmidt.*

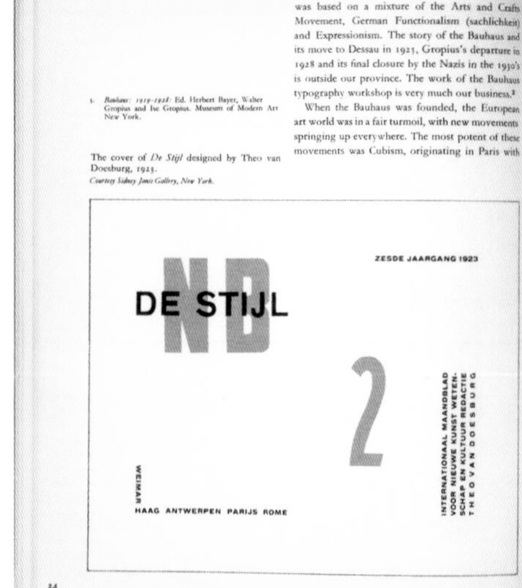

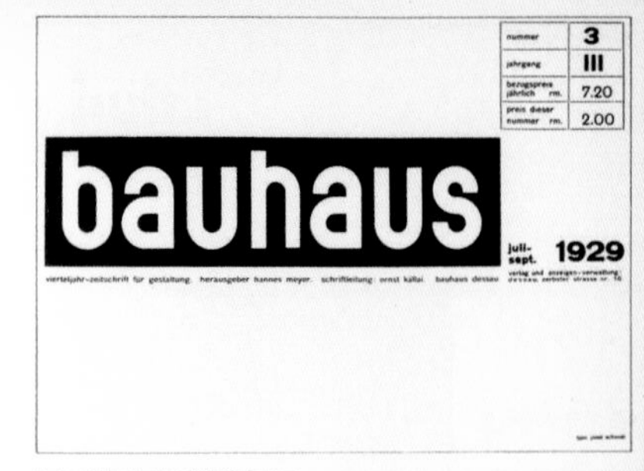

The right-hand page displays a hand-drawn layout of accounts by Anthony Froshaug. Lewis gives practical guidance for designers recommending different pencils for drawing varying type sizes: H for 6 point, HB for 12 point and 2B for display-sized characters.

Setting punctuation marks outside the measure may cause the compositor some trouble, but can on occasions greatly improve the appearance of a piece of displayed setting.

'I pray God,' said Lord Hawke, 'that no professional will ever captain England.' Poor Lord Hawke!

Even in free setting, the single quotation mark looks better if thrown into the left margin.

There are endless refinements in the arrangement and spacing and placing of punctuation marks in displayed setting. For further information on spacing, consult Geoffrey Dowding's book *Finer Points in the Spacing and Arrangement of Type* (Wace). NARROW MEASURES: Practically the only method of achieving even spacing in narrow columns of type of less than 30 characters is by free setting, that is with a straight left hand edge and a ragged right hand edge, as results when typewriting. This is rather more difficult to set because the lines as far as possible should be broken as the sense dictates. For narrow measures always use a small setting. The wider the measure the larger the type. LETTER-SPACING IN DISPLAY: Any capitals larger than 8 point look better with letter-spacing, with the sole exception of condensed capitals, which are designed as space-savers and if spaced at all widely, not only lose their purpose but also tend to look like a row of fencing posts and become unreadable.

Condensed type should be set solid, whether the words are set in capitals or small letters.

PRINTED Ephemera

P R I N T E D
E p h e m e r a

L A N D I N G - S T A G E   LANDING-STAGE

Too great a letter-spacing (left) makes copy more difficult to read. The juxtaposition of the capital letters 'L' and 'A' governs the letter-spacing through the rest of the copy.

80

LANDING STAGE
WOODBRIDGE

LANDING STAGE
WOODBRIDGE

Top: Too much space between the words LANDING and STAGE and too little space between the lines. Below: a reasonable spacing.

The amount of letter-spacing used for capital letters should be about the same as the space between the verticals of a capital letter 'H' of the fount. Letters must be visually, not mechanically spaced.

Never letter-space or word-space for that matter, to more than the space between the lines. Trust your eye more than any mechanical method of positioning your spacing.

In display, though lower case letters are used very widely there are still certain occasions when capitals look better. For instance in headlines on title pages of books or for very short words which, when set in lower case, may make an awkward shape; words such as bag BAG, pal PAL, ape APE.

bag BAG pal PAL ape APE

ALIGNMENT When displaying capital letters, where more than one line has to line up vertically with another, the letters A C G J O G Q S T V W X Y should be lined up optically; that is, they should over run the measure. The most difficult capital letter to begin or end a line with is T with its over hanging cross bar. The word 'THE' is one of the most difficult words to space and position.

Vertical alignment of difficult letters. The 'N' of Normandy ranges with the left margin, the 'A' and 'T' are thrown out slightly.

THE
ARCHITECTURE OF
NORMANDY

PUNCTUATION With punctuation marks, a more even effect can be achieved if certain marks such as hyphens, full points, commas and quotes are also thrown out beyond the

81

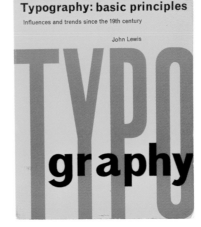

Pages on typographical styling are clearly illustrated with straightforward examples.

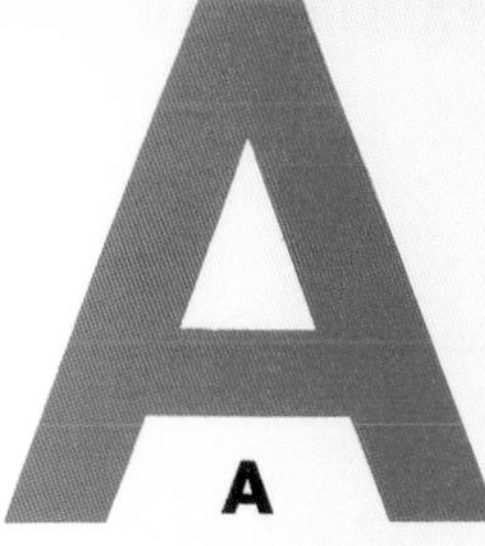

'Monophoto' HEADLINE BOLD

The same matrices that were used to set the line in 24 point above were used here for *this paragraph in ten point*. This same 'B' set of film matrices can be used for any size from 8 up to 22 and 24 point.

FOR THE 7 AND 6 POINT SIZES, USE THE 'A' SET OF MATRICES Here is a specimen of Series 595 in the six point size, produced with the 'A' set of matrices which can also be used for 7 pt.

'Monophoto' GARAMOND

The same matrices that were used to set the line in 24 point above were used here for *this paragraph in* TEN POINT. This same 'B' set of film matrices can be used for any size from 8 up to 22 and 24 point.

FOR THE 7 AND 6 POINT SIZES, USE THE 'A' SET OF MATRICES Here is a specimen of Series 156 in the six point size, produced with the 'A' set of matrices which can also be used for 7 pt. **The related Bold is Series 202.**

For Monophoto filmsetting there are three basic film matrices; the A set is for 6 and 7 point, though it can be used for smaller sizes; the B set is for from 8 to 12 point and the C set is for sizes from 14 to 24 point.

stereo

This word could have been made from a C Monophoto matrix.

unlimited flexibility in letter size, in leading and spacing. This means he can set in 14½ point with ½ point leading if he so wishes. With an accurate lay-out the bulk of the make-up can be done on the filmsetter. As a result instead of having to assemble a number of separate strips of letters, a whole page can be exposed on one piece of film. The availability of typefaces varies from one typesetting house to another. In theory it would seem that any typeface that is cast in hot metal could be used for photo-typesetting.

A very real advantage of photo-typesetting is that sizes larger than 14 point (the normal maximum for Monotype keyboard setting) can be set as easily as small text sizes. The advantages of this method for children's books hardly needs emphasising.

68

A
A

Most filmsetters can set up to 24 point; some can set up to 4 inches high.

stereo

SLANT

On the photosetter letters can be reversed, can have a screen over them, can be made to slope backwards or forwards, be elongated or contracted.

Author's corrections in hot metal are time-wasting, usually unnecessary or the result of incompetence and are inevitably costly. They are even more time-wasting and costly in photo-typesetting. It is important to send 'clean' copy to the printer and layouts should be accurate – really ACCURATE.

Modern typesetting machines produce a typewritten proof which can be corrected before the film is made. Layouts for filmsetting should differ in one important particular from layouts for hot metal setting. There must be one line of reference, a base line, from which all measurements will be taken. For leading, indicate a measurement from the body line of one line of type to the body line of the next line.

Point Sizes
X-HEIGHT
INTERLINEAR CHANNEL
X-HEIGHT

Display: Filmsetting offers various additional factors that are useful for design purposes. It is possible to lay a half-tone screen over letters to reduce their tone.

There are different types of filmsetters and it is advisable for the typographer to check with the printer for any peculiarities or limitations which he should follow. For display uses, some filmsetting machines can produce a letter 4" high; most can set to 24 points.

Letters can be distorted.

There have been many articles in trade papers about photo-typesetting, but by far the simplest description that I have seen is in a little booklet called *Film Setting* issued by the Westerham Press in 1963, from which some of these illustrations have been reproduced.

69

Printed Ephemera, John Lewis, W.S. Cowell, Ipswich, Suffolk, 1962
Magazine Design, Ruari McLean, Oxford University Press, London, 1969
Typography: Basic Principles, John Lewis, Studio Books, London, 1963
Pioneers of Modern Typography, Herbert Spencer, Lund Humphries, London, 1969
The Visual Display of Quantitative Information, Edward R. Tufte, Graphics Press, Cheshire, Connecticut, 1983
Anthony Froshaug, Robin Kinross, Hyphen Press, London, 2000
Typographica, Rick Poynor, Laurence King Publishing, London, 2001
Notes on Book Design, Derek Birdsall, Yale University Press, New Haven and London, 2004
Swiss Graphic Design, Richard Hollis, Laurence King Publishing, London, 2006
Active Literature: Jan Tschichold and New Typography, Christopher Burke, Hyphen Press, London, 2007

Graphic Design Manual

Principles and Practice

Armin Hofmann

Arthur Niggli, Teufen, 1965

Fourth edition (pictured), 1988

200 pages

244 × 210 mm (9.625 × 8.25 in)

Designed by Armin Hofmann

The designer and educator Armin Hofmann (1920–) taught at the Basel Allgemeine Gewerbeschule from 1947 to 1987. Aided by fellow teacher Emil Ruder, he was highly influential on a generation of Swiss graphic designers who went on to use his programme of systematic design exercises in the development of an identifiable Swiss style of graphic design based on constructed geometric grids and sans serif typography. Hofmann's teaching posts at Yale and Philadelphia universities, as well his many lectures and seminars at other colleges, spread his impact even wider.

A distillation of his core teachings, *Graphic Design Manual: Principles and Practice* was first printed in 1965 with text in German, French and English, and is still a standard title on many student reading lists. Its four chapters explore what for Hofmann were the basic building blocks of graphic design. The first chapter, 'The dot', is followed by 'The line', both vital elements in composition and reproduction. The third chapter, 'Confrontation', explores how multiple elements can be combined within a design, and finally 'Letters and signs' addresses typographic concerns.

The chapters are prefaced by short introductory essays, all of which are grouped at the front of the book. The illustrations are examples of work completed by students on the graphics course in Basel, and are a mixture of formal exercises (sometimes very dry) and applied projects such as posters and packaging design.

A critical appraisal of Armin Hofmann's career can be found in *Armin Hofmann: His Work, Quest and Philosophy*, Hans Wichmann (ed.), Birkhäuser, Basel, 1989.

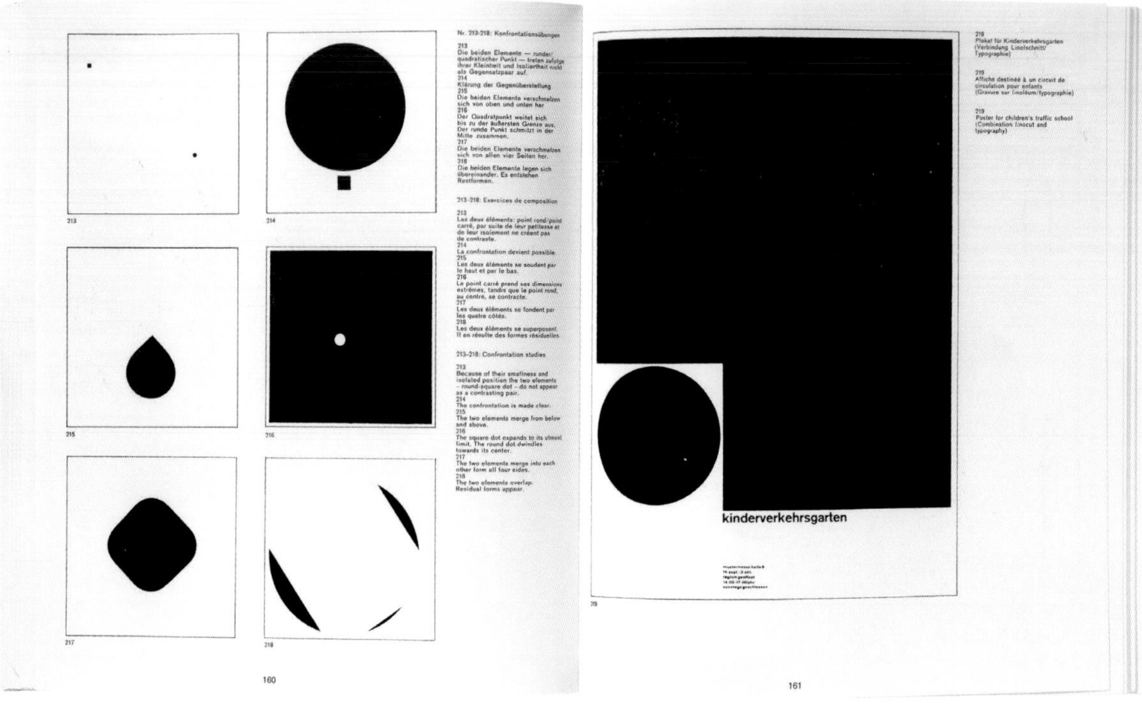

Nr. 213-218: Konfrontationsübungen

213
Die beiden Elemente — runder/quadratischer Punkt — treten zufolge ihrer Kleinheit und Isoliertheit nicht als Gegensatzpaar auf.
214
Klärung der Gegenüberstellung
215
Die beiden Elemente verschmelzen sich von oben und unten her
216
Der Quadratpunkt weitet sich bis zu der äußersten Grenze aus. Der runde Punkt schmilzt in der Mitte zusammen.
217
Die beiden Elemente verschmelzen sich von allen vier Seiten her.
218
Die beiden Elemente legen sich übereinander. Es entstehen Restformen.

213-218: Exercices de composition

213
Les deux éléments: point rond/point carré, par suite de leur petitesse et de leur isolement ne créent pas de contraste.
214
La confrontation devient possible.
215
Les deux éléments se soudent par le haut et par le bas.
216
Le point carré prend ses dimensions extrêmes, tandis que le point rond, au centre, se contracte.
217
Les deux éléments se fondent par les quatre côtés.
218
Les deux éléments se superposent. Il en résulte des formes résiduelles.

213-218: Confrontation studies

213
Because of their smallness and isolated position the two elements – round-square dot – do not appear as a contrasting pair.
214
The confrontation is made clear.
215
The two elements merge from below and above.
216
The square dot expands to its utmost limit. The round dot dwindles towards its center.
217
The two elements merge into each other form all four sides.
218
The two elements overlap. Residual forms appear.

219
Plakat für Kinderverkehrsgarten (Verbindung Linolschnitt/Typographie)

219
Affiche destinée à un circuit de circulation pour enfants (Gravure sur linoléum/typographie)

219
Poster for children's traffic school (Combination linocut and typography)

160

161

Printed in black only, Graphic Design Manual *reinforces the purity of its contents. Exercises at the Basel Allgemeine Gewerbeschule under Hofmann dealt with the essential building blocks of visual communication – this spread studies 'the square dot'.*

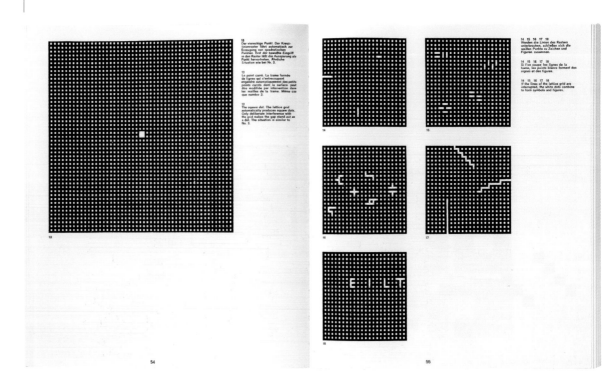

13
Der viereckige Punkt. Der Kreuzlinienraster führt automatisch zur Erzeugung von quadratischen Punkten. Erst der bewußte Eingriff in den Raster läßt die Aussparung als Punkt hervortreten. Ähnliche Situation wie bei Nr. 3.

13
Le point carré. La trame formée de lignes qui s'entrecoupent engendre automatiquement des petits points carrés dont la surface peut être modifiée par intervention dans les mailles de la trame. Même cas que numéro 3.

13
The square dot. The lattice grid automatically produces square dots. Only deliberate interference with the grid makes the gap stand out as a dot. The situation is similar to No. 3.

54

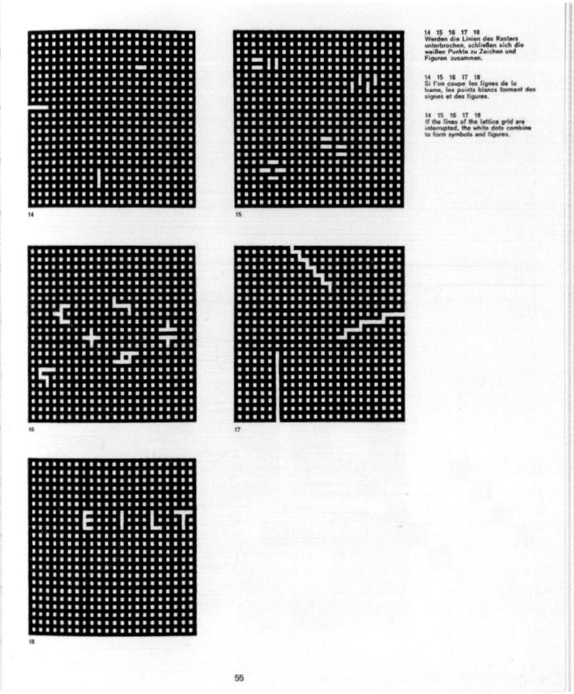

14 15 16 17 18
Werden die Linien des Rasters unterbrochen, schließen sich die weißen Punkte zu Zeichen und Figuren zusammen.

14 15 16 17 18
Si l'on coupe les lignes de la trame, les points blancs forment des signes et des figures.

14 15 16 17 18
If the lines of the lattice grid are interrupted, the white dots combine to form symbols and figures.

55

256
Senkrechte und waagrechte Linien stoßen zusammen und kreuzen sich. Durch die Differenzierung der Liniendicke entsteht ein neuer weißer Linienwert.
257
Drei Buchstaben H, auf das äußerste differenziert

256
Les lignes verticales et horizontales se rejoignent et se croisent. Les différentes épaisseurs des lignes transforment les intervalles blancs en de nouvelles lignes.
257
Trois lettres H extrêmement différenciées

256
Vertical and horizontal lines meet and intersect. Differences in the thickness of the line produce a new white linear value.
257
Three letter H's showing extreme variations of form

256

257

178

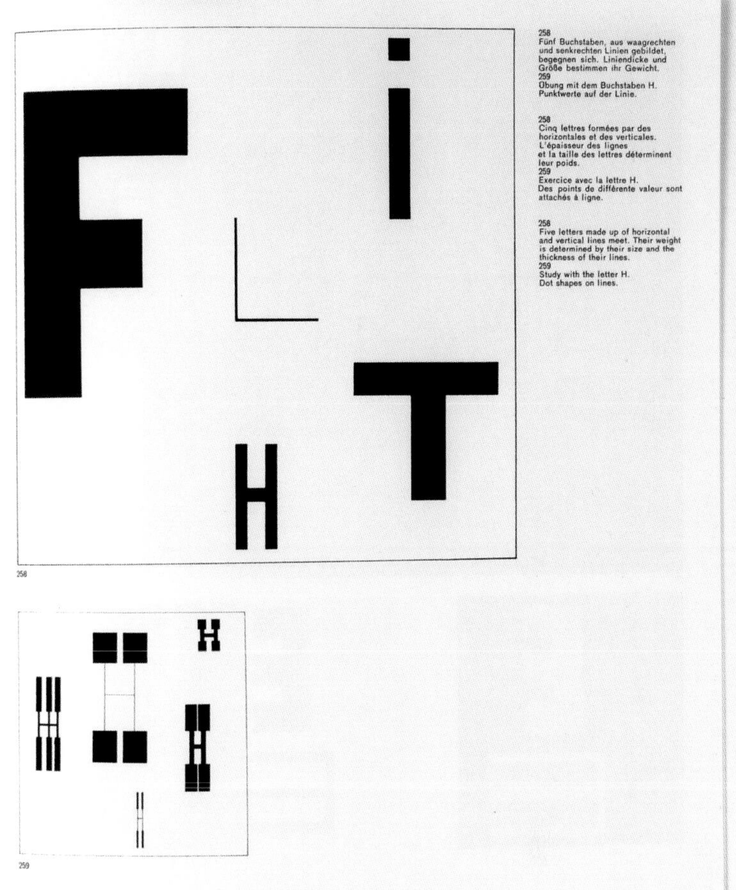

258
Fünf Buchstaben, aus waagrechten und senkrechten Linien gebildet, begegnen sich. Liniendicke und Größe bestimmen ihr Gewicht.
259
Übung mit dem Buchstaben H. Punktwerte auf der Linie.

258
Cinq lettres formées par des horizontales et des verticales. L'épaisseur des lignes et la taille des lettres déterminent leur poids.
259
Exercice avec la lettre H. Des points de différente valeur sont attachés à ligne.

258
Five letters made up of horizontal and vertical lines meet. Their weight is determined by their size and the thickness of their lines.
259
Study with the letter H. Dot shapes on lines.

258

259

179

METHODIK
DER FORM- UND
BILDGESTALTUNG
Aufbau
Synthese
Anwendung
MANUEL
DE CRÉATION
GRAPHIQUE
Forme
Synthèse
Application
GRAPHIC
DESIGN
MANUAL
Principles
and
Practice
Armin
Hofmann

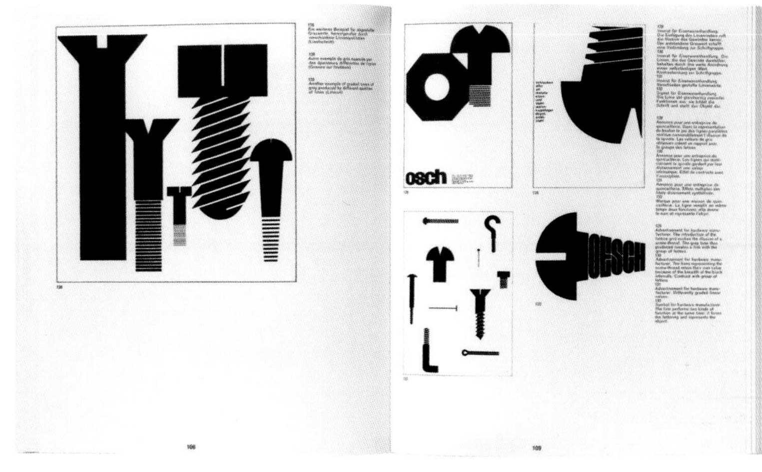

Students would use their formal training in applied projects – in this case a hardware manufacturer. The page layout still retains the abstract qualities of the more basic themes explored earlier in the book.

Wir sind von Strahlen umgeben, aber nur wenige Strahlungsarten werden mittelbar sichtbar. Alle anderen bleiben unsichtbar. Am Telefon, vor dem Radio oder Fernsehgerät denken wir gewiss nicht an die Ströme und Strahlungen, die zwischen Sendern und Empfängern vermitteln. Der Grafiker versucht, diese Vorgänge bewusst zu machen. Die dynamische Anordnung von Linien macht sie sinnfällig und teilt die Empfindung der Vibration mit.

We are surrounded by radiations but only a few of them are of the directly visible kind. All the others remain invisible. On the telephone or listening to the radio or watching TV we certainly do not think of the currents and radiations forming the link between transmitters and receivers. The designer attempts to bring these processes home to the beholder. A dynamic arrangement of lines gives them striking expression and conveys the sense of vibration.

Nous sommes environnés de rayons, mais la plupart nous restent cachés. Certains d'entre eux seulement sont indirectement visibles. Au téléphone, devant la radio et l'appareil de télévision, nous ne pensons guère aux trains d'ondes reliant émetteurs et récepteurs. Le graphiste tente de concrétiser ces phénomènes. Une ordonnance dynamique des lignes les rend évidents et transmet la sensation de vibration.

1

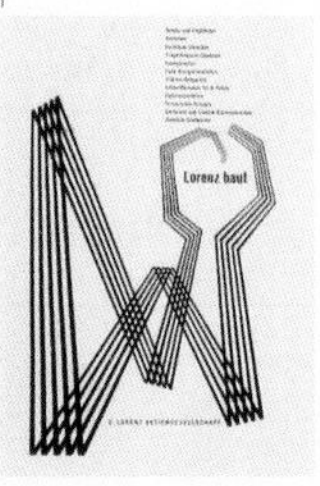

2

3

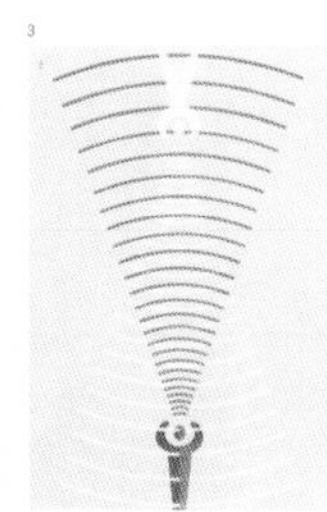

4a

1
Thema: raumdurchdringende Wirkung des Rundfunks. Inserat, 1953. Firma SEL.
2
Thema: Die ganze Nachrichtentechnik, Wellen und Strahlen. Broschürentitel, 1961. Firma SEL.
3
Thema: Zwei Partner richten einander Mitteilungen oder Kommandos aus. Kalenderblatt, 1957. Firma SEL.
4 (rechte Seite)
Thema: Senden, Ausstrahlen, Vibration. Kalenderblatt, 1957. Firma SEL.
4a
Aussenansicht eines Sendeturms.

1
Theme: radio waves permeating space. Press ad., 1953, for SEL.
2
Theme: Telecommunications, waves and radiations. Front page of brochure, 1961, for SEL.
3
Theme: two partners give each other information or commands. Calendar, 1957, for SEL.
4 (right page)
Theme: transmission, radiation, vibration. Calendar, 1957, for SEL.
4a
External view of radio tower.

1
Sujet: La radiodiffusion à travers l'espace. Annonce, 1953. Firme SEL.
2
Sujet: Technique d'information, ondes et rayons. Titre de brochure, 1961. Firme SEL.
3
Sujet: Deux partenaires se transmettent des informations ou des ordres. Feuille de calendrier, 1957. Firme SEL.
4 (page droite)
Sujet: Emission, radiation, vibration. Feuille de calendrier, 1957. Firme SEL.
4a
Tour d'émission. Vue extérieure.

80

A spread on television and radio waves is laid out in a typical format for the book. A large graphic on the right-hand page illustrates the theme with practical examples of usage on the left.

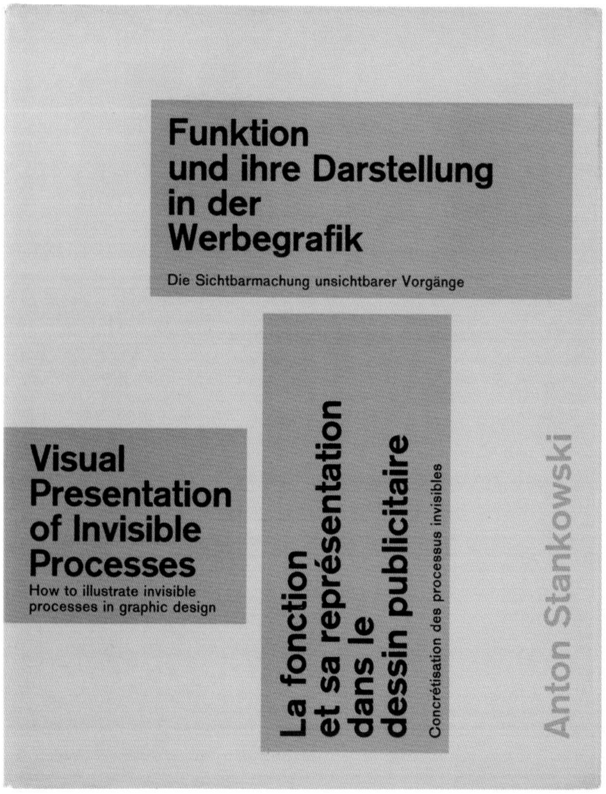

Funktion und ihre Darstellung in der Werbegrafik

Die Sichtbarmachung unsichtbarer Vorgänge

Visual Presentation of Invisible Processes

How to illustrate invisible processes in graphic design

La fonction et sa représentation dans le dessin publicitaire

Concrétisation des processus invisibles

Anton Stankowski

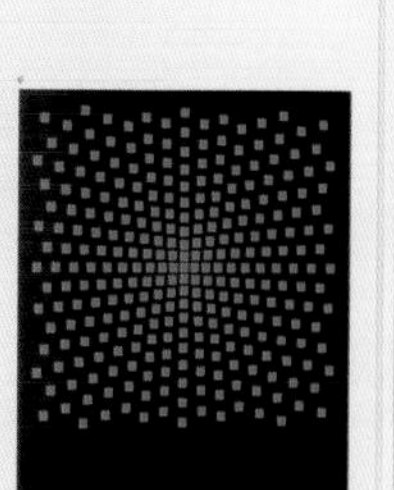

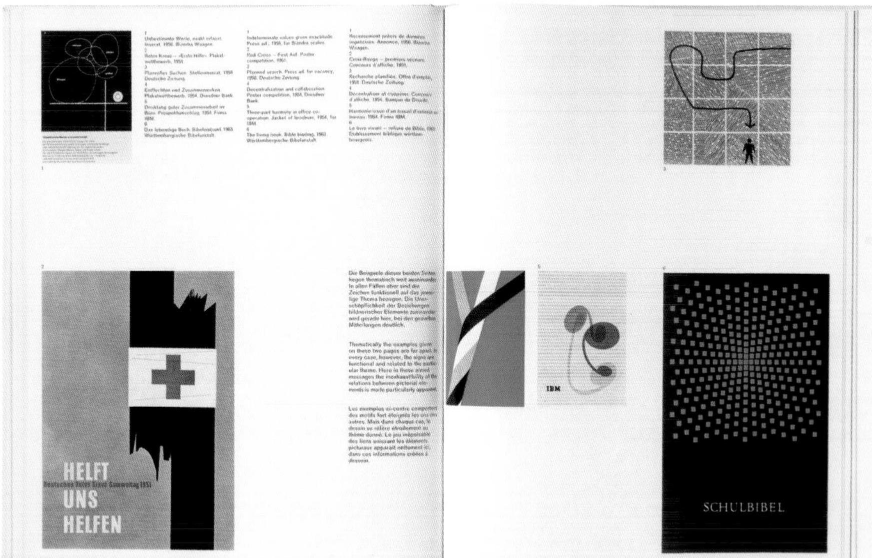

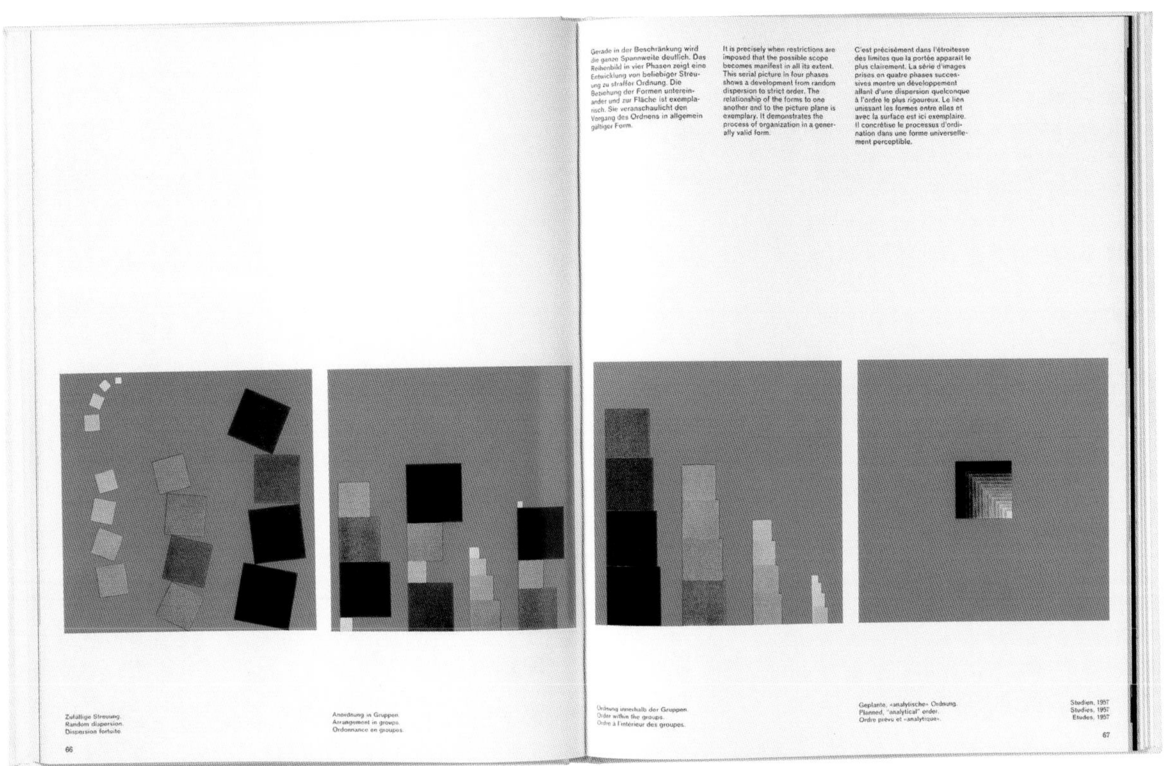

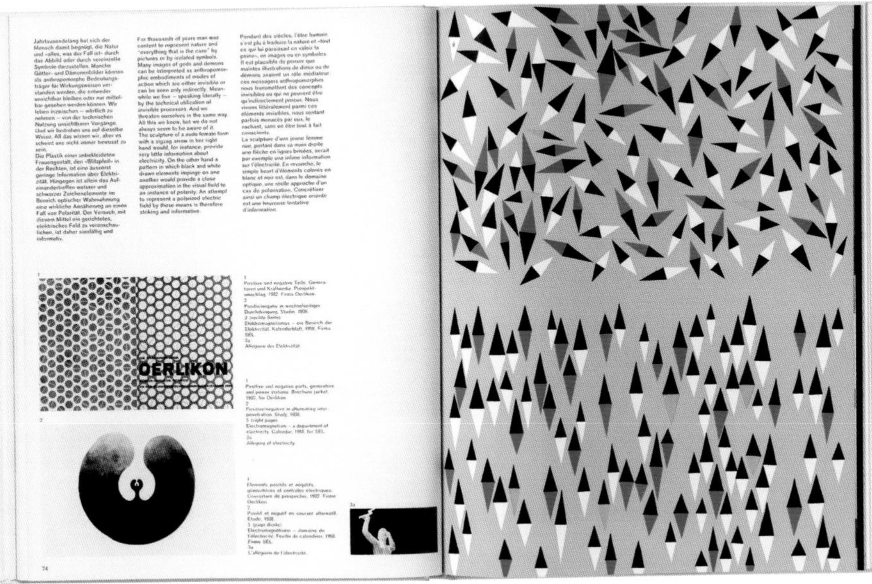

Formal studies by Stankowski to show 'a development from random dispersion to strict order'.

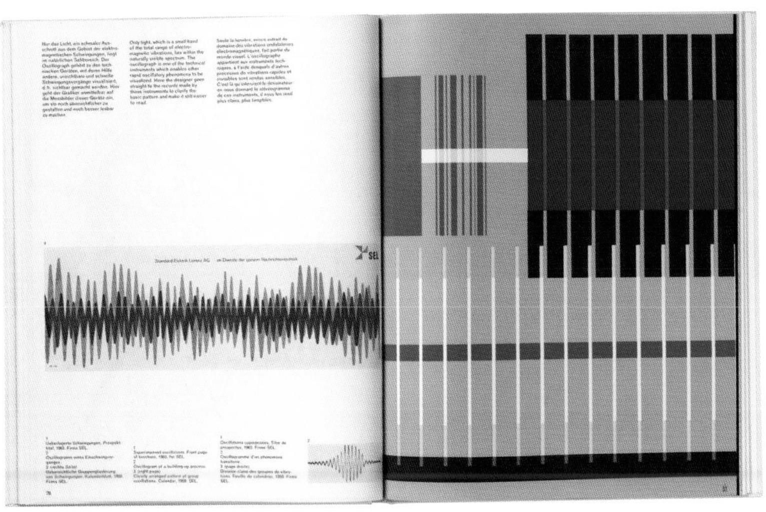

Visual Presentation of Invisible Processes

How to Illustrate Invisible Processes in Graphic Design

Anton Stankowski

Arthur Niggli, Teufen, c.1967

128 pages

297 × 235 mm (11.75 × 9.25 in)

Designed by Anton Stankowski

Visual Presentation of Invisible Processes has no chapters or sections; it is a series of spreads, each of which addresses a different concept or theme. With text in German, English and French, it is an organized scrapbook of visual experiments. Invariably the applications deal with complex scientific and industrial processes that are often abstract in nature and difficult to illustrate with traditional representations.

The German designer Anton Stankowski (1906–1998) devoted his career to the study of such problems and elaborates on them in detail in this book. He was at the vanguard of the graphic design profession and became one of its most established practitioners, excelling in the use of geometric graphic elements for visual problem-solving.

This book covers his career up to the mid-1960s. In the early 1930s he worked in Switzerland, where he incorporated the new constructive typography and use of photography in work for his industrial clients. He influenced many designers, such as Herbert Matter, Max Bill and Richard Paul Lohse, who went on to establish the foundations of the Swiss style. Stankowski returned to Germany and, after captivity in Russia during the Second World War, he established himself as the designer of choice for many German corporations.

In *Visual Presentation of Invisible Processes* Stankowski deals almost exclusively with aesthetic issues, rarely detailing problems relating to a particular client. His rigorous research, kept in organized sketchbooks, provided a library of ideas that were frequently saved for upcoming projects. Featured towards the end of the book is a spread of studies for the Standard Elektrik Lorenz logo (1953) that demonstrates the depth of scrutiny Stankowski brought to projects.

Other books of interest include *Visuelle Kommunikation. Ein Design-Handbuch* by Anton Stankowski and Karl Duschek (Reimer, Berlin, 1989) and the more recent *Stankowski 06* (Ulrike Gauss (ed.), Hatje Cantz, Ostfildern-Ruit, 2006), which covers his whole career.

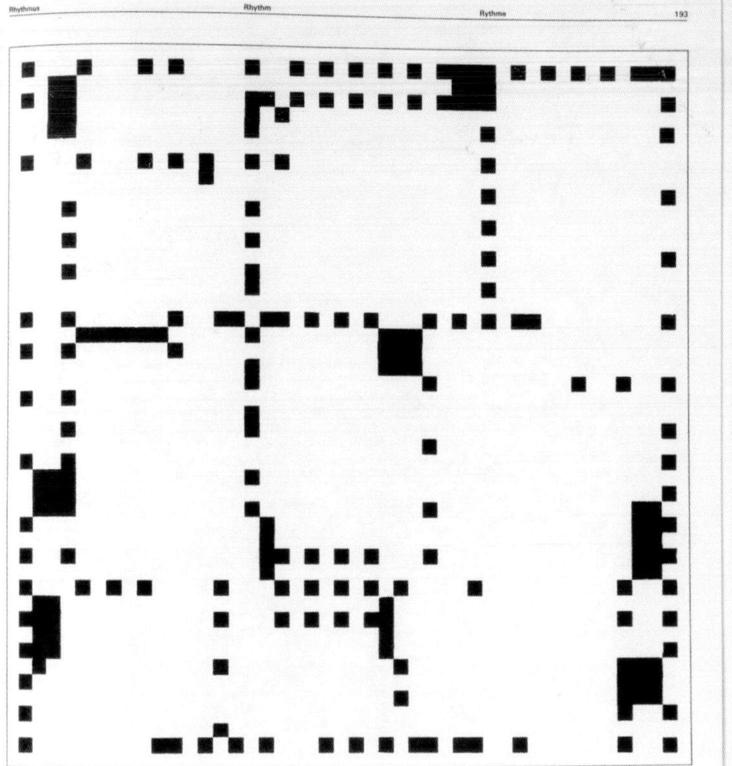

Many of the graphic exercises are similar to those used by Armin Hofmann in his Graphic Design Manual *(see page 88).*

Farbe | Colour | Couleur | 158

Das typographische Material, Typen, Linien, Schmuck, verhält sich der Farbe gegenüber eher spröde. Die wesentliche typographische Farbe ist Schwarz, mit einer unübersehbar reichen Grauskala, verursacht durch unterschiedliche Typengrößen und -fetten, durch verschiedene Abstände und Sperrungen. Zu diesem Schwarz können leuchtende Farben in Beziehung gebracht werden, vor allem Rot. Kein dumpfes oder bläuliches Rot, sondern ein gebliches, helles, leuchtendes Rot. Es ist das Rot der Wiegendrucke, in kleiner Menge als Initiale oder Alineazeichen einer größeren Schwarz- oder Graufläche gegenübergestellt. Die starke Farbwirkung wird nur durch große und fette Typen ermöglicht; kleine und magere Typen hemmen die Farbwirkung: Rot verblaßt zu Rosa, Gelb läuft auf der weißen Fläche aus, Blau kann nicht mehr von Schwarz unterschieden werden. Rot ist die eigentliche typographische Buntfarbe schon während Jahrhunderten, und die folgenden Beispiele befassen sich mit dem Einsetzen von Rot in ein Druckwerk. Die Dosierung von Rot darf nicht dem Zufall überlassen werden.

Gerade hier, wie in allen Gebieten der Typographie, soll auf klare Proportionen geachtet werden. Eine bunte Farbe soll zu Schwarz in einem Spannungsverhältnis stehen, in einem Verhältnis, das schon im ersten Entwurf eines Druckwerks klar in Erscheinung tritt. Rot kann dominieren, das heißt in großer Menge zu einer kleinen Menge Schwarz stehen, was dieser Farbe, die sich andern Farben nicht gerne unterordnet und herrschsüchtig ist, im innersten Wesen entspricht. Eine kleine Menge Rot aber, zu viel Schwarz und in größte Nähe von Schwarz gestellt, gewinnt an Kostbarkeit und Leuchtkraft. Sie ist, wie Augusto Giacometti treffend sagt: der Sonntag in der Reihe der grauen Alltage, das Fest. Man vermeide das Zusammenführen zweier Farben in gleicher Menge, wodurch eine unangenehme Rivalität zwischen den zwei Farben entsteht. Das Kräfteverhältnis ist nicht geklärt, und das Auge kann den dominierenden Farbton nicht ermitteln.

Zu den Beispielen auf Seite 159:

1 bis 9 Überleitung einer kleinen Menge Rot zum dominierenden Rot.
1 Gutes Spannungsverhältnis Schwarz-Rot. Rot ist durch die kleine Menge kostbar geworden.
2 Schon etwas unklares Verhältnis Schwarz-Rot. Rot steht zu Schwarz wohl noch in kleinerer Menge, springt aber über seine Grenzen und beansprucht mehr Wirkung, als ihm zukommt.
3 Gleichgewicht Schwarz-Rot durch die Aggressivität des Rots leicht gestört. Das Auge empfindet die Rivalität der beiden Farben als unangenehm.
4 Das umgekehrte Mengenverhältnis von 2, aber durch die Überstrahlung von Rot im klareren Spannungsverhältnis.
5 Eindeutiges Dominieren von Rot.
6 Klare Schwarzwirkung und klare Rotwirkung.
7 Schwächung der Schwarzwirkung durch lineare Form, Verstärkung von Rotwirkung durch Einbau in Schwarz.
8 bis 11 Schwächung von Schwarz- und Rotwirkung durch Aufsplitterung.
8 Eindeutige Farbwirkungen
9 Beginn der Schwächung von Rot und Schwarz.
10 Weitere Aufsplitterung von Rot und Schwarz.
11 Die Aufsplitterung läßt keine eindeutige Farbwirkung mehr zu. Das Auge vermischt Rot und Schwarz in der Richtung zu Braun.
12 Rotwirkung bedroht durch die zu kleine Menge Rot; die zu große Schwarzmenge erstickt das Rot.
13 Verstärkung der Rotwirkung.
14 Gutes Spannungsverhältnis Schwarz-Rot. Die Rotmenge kann sich gegenüber dem dominierenden Schwarz behaupten.
15 und 16 Schwächung der Rotmenge von 14 durch Auflösung. Die Rotwirkung ist gestört, und auch die Schwarzwirkung ist leicht geschwächt.
17 Dominierendes Rot zu einer klaren Schwarzwirkung gestellt.
18 Die Schwarzmenge von 17 aufgelöst, dadurch Verzicht auf klare Farbwirkungen.
19 Dominierendes Rot zu einer kleinen Schwarzmenge gestellt, die sich noch knapp behaupten kann.
20 Schwächung der Schwarzwirkung von 19 durch lineare Anordnung.
21 Weitere Schwächung der Schwarzwirkung durch Auflösung.

The typographer's material – type, lines, ornamentation – does not take readily to colour. Black is the paramount colour in typography, and there is an almost infinite scale of grey tones derived from the different sizes and thicknesses of the type, and from the different spaces and gaps. This black goes very well with brilliant colours, red in particular. Not a dull, bluish red, but a bright, gleaming, yellowish red. It is the red of the incunabula, used sparingly in initial letters or paragraph marks and contrasting with the larger area of black or grey. But colour can only be used to effect if the type is large and bold; small and light type works against colour: red pales to pink, yellow seeps out of the white surface, blue becomes indistinguishable from black. Red is the really bright colour in typography, and has been for centuries, and the following examples are concerned with the use of red in a printed work. But the amount of red to be used cannot be left to chance.

Here again, as in every department of typography, proportions must be clearly thought out. There should be tension between a bright colour and black, and this tension should be clearly apparent in the first draft of a printed work. Red can dominate, i.e. a large amount of it can be juxtaposed to a small quantity of black, and this lies very much in the nature of red, which is not a colour that likes to truckle to others but is imperious by disposition. But a small amount of red, placed near too much black, gains in richness and luminosity. As Augusto Giacometti says so pertinently: it is the Sunday in a row of grey weekdays; it is the festival. The juxtaposition of two colours in equal quantities is something to be avoided; it sets up an uncomfortable rivalry. It is not clear what the pattern of forces is between the colours, and the eye cannot decide which colour tone is the dominant one.

Notes on examples on page 159:

1 to 9 Transition from a small quantity of red to red as the dominant colour.
1 The tension between black and red is good. Being small in quantity, the value of the red is enhanced.
2 The relationship between black and red is already a little equivocal. True, there is less red than black, but it bursts its bounds and makes a greater impact than it should.
3 The equilibrium between black and red is slightly upset by the aggressive nature of the red. The rivalry between the two colours conveys an impression of unease to the eye.
4 The same quantities as 2 but reversed. But the red outshines the black and creates a clear pattern of tension.
5 Red definitely in the ascendancy.
6 Black creates a definite effect; so does red.
7 The black effect is weakened by linear form; the red effect is intensified by being boxed in the black.
8 to 11 Attenuation of black and red effect by fragmentation.
8 Unequivocal colour effects.
9 Incipient attenuation of red and black.
10 Further fragmentation of red and black.
11 The fragmentation is no longer compatible with an unequivocal colour effect. The eye mixes red and black and tends to make brown of them.
12 The red effect is compromised by too small a quantity; the excessive quantity of black overwhelms the red.
13 Intensification of the red effect.
14 Good pattern of tension between black and red. The red can more than hold its own against the dominant black.
15 and 16 The quantity of red in 14 is attenuated by diffusion. The red effect is destroyed and the black effect is slightly weakened.
17 Dominant red opposed to an unequivocal black effect.
18 The quantity of black of 17 diffused, thereby forfeiting unequivocal colour effects.
19 Dominant red opposed to a small quantity of black, which can still just hold its own.
20 Weakening of the black effect of 19 by linear arrangement.
21 Further weakening of the black effect by diffusion.

Le matériel typographique, caractères, lignes, ornements, sont des moyens plutôt timides auprès de la couleur. Le colorant typographique fondamental est le noir avec, presque inépuisable dans sa richesse, toute la gamme des gris qu'engendrent les multiples corps des caractères et les divers espacements. Des couleurs lumineuses peuvent être mises en contact avec ce noir. Le rouge, par exemple, occupe une place privilégiée dans cette confrontation: non pas un rouge bleuté, étouffé, mais un rouge jaunâtre, clair, éclatant. Le rouge des incunables en petites touches dans les initiales ou les signes-alinéas opposé aux grandes surfaces noires ou grises. La violence de l'effet chromatique est donnée par les caractères grands et gras; les caractères petits et maigres paralysent cette action de la couleur. Ainsi le rouge pâlira jusqu'au rose, le jaune se diluera dans la surface blanche, le bleu ne se distinguera plus du noir. Dans la chromotypie typographique, le rouge est depuis des siècles la couleur par excellence. Les exemples suivants traitent de cette mise en place du rouge dans une œuvre typographique et montrent que le dosage de cette couleur ne doit pas être laissé au hasard.

Là encore, comme dans tous les domaines de la typographie, de justes proportions doivent être gardées. Une couleur doit s'opposer au noir dans un certain rapport de tension, dans un rapport qui apparaisse évident dès la première maquette. Le rouge peut régner, c'est-à-dire être en plus grand apport que le noir, ce qui correspond à son caractère dominateur qui ne se laisse pas facilement assujettir. Mais une touche de rouge, auprès d'un grand aplat noir, gagne en valeur et en luminosité. Elle devient, comme le disait si pertinemment Augusto Giacometti: ‹Un dimanche dans la grisaille quotidienne, une fête.› Que l'on évite cette rivalité déplaisante qu'engendre l'affrontement de couleurs en quantité égale. Le rapport des forces ne serait pas résolu et l'œil ne saurait à quelle nuance accorder la prédominance.

Exemples page 159:

1 à 9 Passage d'une touche de rouge à un rouge dominant.
1 Juste rapport de tension entre le noir et le rouge. Par sa petite quantité, le rouge est rendu précieux.
2 Un rapport plus confus entre le noir et le rouge. Le rouge est inférieur en quantité au noir, mais outrepasse déjà ses limites et revendique un effet qui lui est dénié.
3 Equilibre noir-rouge légèrement perturbé par l'agressivité du rouge. La rivalité des deux couleurs est déplaisante à l'œil.
4 Rapport de quantité inversé en référence au 2, mais cependant dans un lien de tension plus clair dû à la surintensité du rouge.
5 Le rouge domine clairement.
6 Effet du rouge et du noir bien déterminé.
7 Faiblesse du noir due à la forme linéaire. L'effet du rouge est renforcé par son incorporation au noir.
8 à 11 Rouge et noir affaiblis par le morcellement des couleurs.
8 Effet bien déterminé des couleurs.
9 Début d'affaiblissement du rouge et du noir.
10 Autre morcellement du rouge et du noir.
11 Le morcellement entrave l'effet des coloris. Pour l'œil, le rouge et le noir s'acheminent vers le brun.
12 Effet du rouge menacé, étouffé par un trop grand aplat noir.
13 Renforcement du rouge.
14 Bon rapport de tension entre le noir et le rouge. Le rouge s'affirme dans une juste proportion face au noir dominant.
15 et 16 Le même rouge qu'à la fig. 14 est ici affaibli, parce que dilué. L'effet de coloris s'en trouve ralenti. Le noir, de même, est légèrement affaibli.
17 Rouge dominant un noir clairement défini.
18 Dans une même proportion qu'à la fig. 17, le noir est ici dilué et renonce à une définition claire.
19 Rouge dominant confronté à un peu de noir, qui parvient de justesse à s'affirmer.
20 Même noir qu'à la fig. 19, mais affaibli par une division linéaire.
21 Faiblesse du noir encore accentuée par dilution.

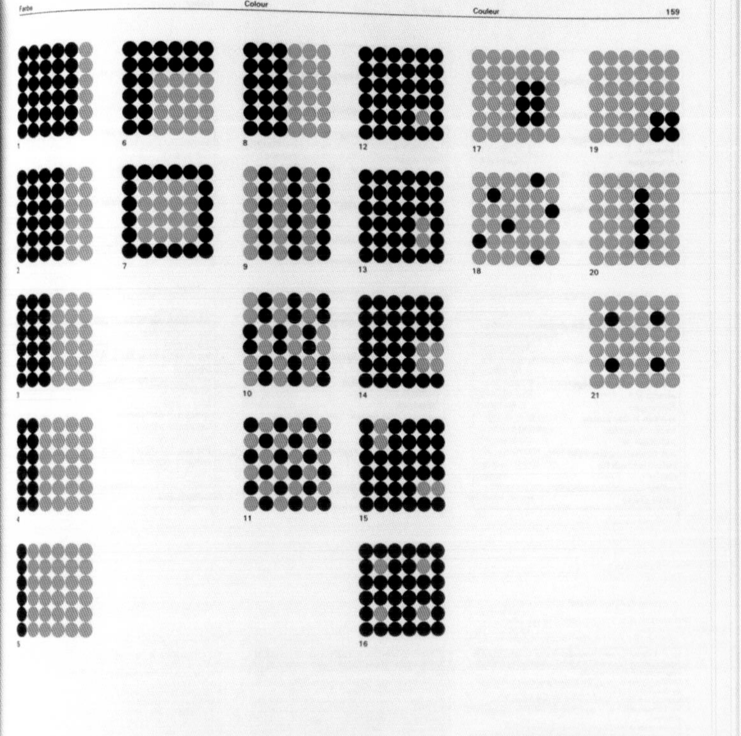

Typography
Emil Ruder
Arthur Niggli, Teufen, 1967
Third edition (pictured), 1977
274 pages
235 × 225 mm (9.25 × 8.875 in)
Designed by Emil Ruder

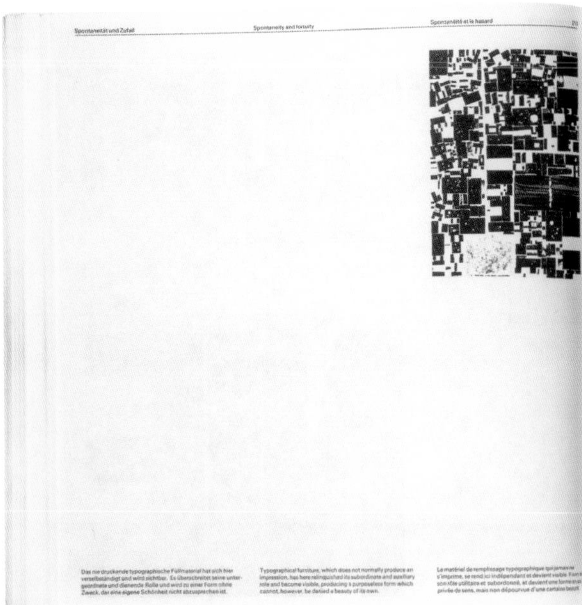

Ruder's typographic teaching was rooted in the practice of letterpress printing, exposed here in the use of typographic furniture for a spread on tonality.

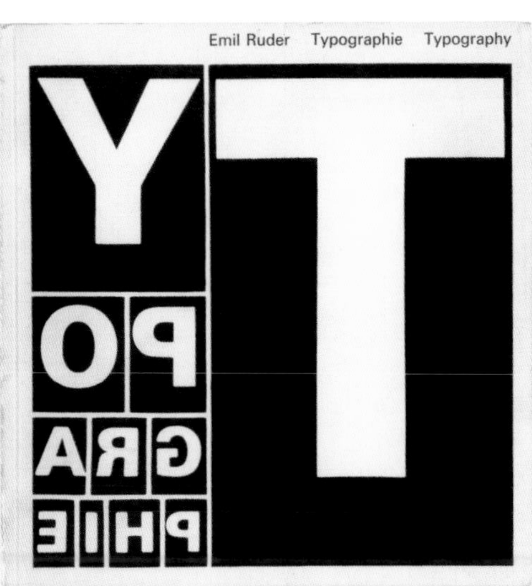

Emil Ruder (1914–1970) specialized in teaching typography at the Allgemeine Gewerbeschule in Basel, Switzerland. Alongside Armin Hofmann, he was responsible for the school's international reputation for producing students who had a thorough grounding in graphic design through the methodical study of basic dynamic elements.

Typography is a large and detailed textbook that takes readers on a point-by-point journey through all the facets of typographical design. In common with Hofmann's *Graphic Design Manual* of 1965 (see page 88), there are many lessons in abstract composition. Where Ruder's book differs from Hofmann's is in its more practical application of typographic forms and ideas. This was forged in part by his devotion to the tradition and practice of letterpress printing, which formed the basis of his design and teaching.

The idea of contrast in typography was particularly important to Ruder, and one of the nine chapters is devoted to the subject. Others concentrate on the classic foundations of the Gewerbeschule's teaching methods, such as 'Point, Line, Surface' and 'Rhythm'. References to broader areas of subject matter than typography, such as architecture, art and nature, elaborate on themes in the book and extend its coverage. The illustrations are largely by Ruder himself, but include work by students on his course as well as contributions from other practising designers.

The text is in German, English and French, and the book is printed largely in black with a small section of colour and some pages using red as a second colour. Univers is used in the design and in many of the examples shown. Ruder was an avid supporter of this typeface, designed by his friend, the Swiss typographer Adrian Frutiger. Its many complementing type styles, all cut with the same x-height, allowed for varied typographic arrangements that were impossible to create with previous metal typefaces.

A Sign Systems Manual

Crosby/Fletcher/Forbes

Praeger Publishers,
New York, 1970
76 pages
265 × 217 mm (10.5 × 8.5 in)
Designed by
Crosby/Fletcher/Forbes

In response to queries about its work in devising the sign system for the ocean liner *Queen Elizabeth 2*, Crosby/Fletcher/Forbes, the British company that would later form the nucleus of the design group Pentagram, decided to produce a book describing the processes involved in such a project. *A Sign Systems Manual*, published by Studio Vista in London and Praeger in New York, is essentially a blueprint for a generic system of signs, and is aimed at informing a readership of design students, clients considering signage implementation and practising designers. It also confirmed the company's own expertise in such systems.

The book is simply and clearly laid out, beginning with a primer on lettering and typography. This is followed by a detailed description of Airport, a typeface Colin Forbes and Matthew Carter adapted from Akzidenz Standard for London's Heathrow Airport in the early 1960s. Further sections examine all the facets of a successful signage system: measuring systems, spacing (including a full kerning chart), sizing, layout, use of symbols, project management and production. A final section shows the work of other designers: among them Paul Rand for IBM, Kinneir Calvert Associates for British Rail and Total Design for Schiphol Airport, Amsterdam.

Well printed on uncoated stock, *A Sign Systems Manual* is monotone throughout except for the pages that illustrate the use of colour. It also contains two pull-out sections; one shows differing letter sizes and the other compares the signage symbol systems for three different Olympic Games, by Masaru Katsumie (Toyko 1964), Otl Aicher (Munich 1972) and Manuel Villazón and Mathais Goeritz (Mexico 1968).

Terminology

Correct use of this manual will require an understanding of the terminology of printing.

As with other crafts, printing has had to come to terms with technical innovations and new commercial processes, with the result that the traditionally rich and evocative vocabulary of printers' terms has diminished, although a few still remain to confound those who are unfamiliar with the industry.

These unavoidable technical words and expressions needed to explain or identify a process or description are those normally used by typographers and designers, as well as printers, and a brief glossary has been included to guide the reader.

The terms used to describe the common physical characteristics of various letterfaces are illustrated below – giving some idea of the significant if sometimes narrow range of differences between alphabets, which are explained in some detail on the following few pages.

The historical reasons for many of the names, characteristics and peculiarities of alphabets and typefaces used in this book are either fairly clear, or are well explained elsewhere in a number of specialist books and publications on typography.

Glossary

Artwork or mechanical: The design in a state from which the manufacturer can reproduce.

Ascender: The part of the lower case letter that extends to the height of a capital letter, for example bdfhkl.

Cap height: The height of a capital letter.

Cicero: Continental equivalent of the Anglo-American pica; a Cicero is subdivided into 12 points.

Counter: An area enclosed by the face of a letter.

Descender: The part of the lower case letter that extends below the base of the x-height, for example gipqy. In the case of a 'y' it is more commonly referred to as a tail.

Didot: Continental point system for measuring type; Didot point is slightly larger than the Anglo American point (0.376mm against 0.351mm).

Face: The part of the letter that is reproduced, the printing surface.

Fount: The complete typeface (upper case, lower case, punctuation, figures, spaces) in one size only.

Line space: The same number of units normally occupied by a line of type.

Module: Standard unit used for measuring and expressing proportions.

Pica: English and American method of measuring type; a pica is subdivided into 12 points.

Point: A point is the basic unit of measurement in printing. There are approximately 72 points to the inch.

Sans serif (Sanserif): Type family without serifs.

Serif: Cross-line finishing off a stroke of a letter.

Stroke: The stem and curves of the letter.

Typeface: The printing surface of a type; the style of the printed letter.

Typography: The means whereby printed letters and sentences are arranged into a legible and aesthetic order.

Weight: The boldness of a typeface determined by the way it is constructed – its thickness, the contrast of strokes and the proportion between face and counter.

x-height: The height of the main body of a piece of type without ascenders or descenders.

Cap height

Ascender

A bracketed serif

Counter

A hairline serif

x-height

A slab serif

Descender

Abpx

Futura, a sanserif (i.e. without serifs) typeface designed by Paul Renner. An even width of strokes is a characteristic of most sanserif typefaces.

Plantin, an alphabet named after the famous sixteenth-century printer Christophe Plantin, was designed by F. H. Pierpont. Known as an Old face the letters have bracketed serifs.

Bodoni, named after Giambattista Bodoni, is adapted from the type designer's original designs. This letter shows the characteristics of a Modern face, the contrasting weight of the strokes, the typical flat unbracketed hairline serifs.

Antique No. 6 taken from the foundry of Vincent Figgens and issued by Stevens Shanks, this mid-Victorian face has the slab serif characteristic of so-called Egyptian typefaces.

6

7

An introduction to letter-spacing was followed later in the book by a full letter-spacing chart. The system Crosby/Fletcher/Forbes promotes uses Airport, a typeface developed by Colin Forbes and Matthew Carter.

Letter, word and line spacing

When assembling letters into words careful consideration must be given to the spaces between each character. As the forms of the letters are variable so are the spaces – and a badly spaced word not only hinders legibility but is also visually irritating.

The principle of letter spacing is that words have to look visually correct and, therefore, the proportional relationship between the face, counter and actual spaces is critical.

The illustrations show the basic letter constructions of curves, vertical and angled strokes and demonstrate that the interfaces between one form of letter and another can produce quite different shapes of space depending on the combination. The permutations of letter combinations likely to be encountered are numerous and the skill required to optically arrange the elements quite considerable.

There is a minimum and a maximum amount of space considered sufficient to separate one letter from another. If the inter-letter spaces are too great they will cease to hold the characters together as a word.

Back illuminated letters, translucent white letters on opaque black or colour and vice versa, will in most cases require the addition of two extra unit spaces to those recommended in order to compensate for light diffusion.

The aesthetic perception of the human eye coupled with design experience can never be equalled by any mechanical device. Nevertheless for mass assembly of words it is necessary to have a standard method.

The unit measurement scale proposed for letter heights also serves the spaces between letters when constructing words and sets of figures. A chart is provided on pages 50 and 51 to give a comprehensive and easy method of establishing inter-letter and word spaces in all the permutations for the alphabet Airport.

As with letters the spaces between words should be the minimum necessary in order to separate them from one another, but at the same time should be sufficient to prevent them from merging together. The space between lines must be more than that between words to ensure that the eye can travel easily along each horizontal line of type and absorb the phrases in the sequential order.

When the inter-word spaces exceed the linear spaces the eye finds it difficult to follow messages line by line and in the case of blocks of copy the vertical white rivulets of space tend to produce dazzle.

Word spaces can be determined as precisely as those between letters. The method of arriving at the correct measure is by an addition of a constant 9 units to the letterspace unit which would be used if the last letter of the preceding word and the first letter of the following word happened to be adjacent. See diagrammatic explanation on chart page.

The linear spaces are keyed in proportion to the height of the capitals and this fixed difference, should be observed throughout the system to ensure uniformity of layout.

Atque ut odia etiam
sunt luptam propte

24

25

A sign systems manual

Crosby/Fletcher/Forbes

A Sign Systems Manual *is an adaptable template for creating a unified signage system; this spread covers the use of colour.*

Colour coding

Colour is often necessary to help differentiate one category of information from another; that is to say it can provide an easily identifiable mode for routing traffic, can distinguish floors or areas, properties and services, act as an emphasis within a typographic layout or even be applied for decorative reasons to lend colour to the environment.

The following basic colours and their combinations are keyed to the proposed sign classification – even if they are not followed they can be of some guidance when deciding on an alternative scheme.

Red to be used for direction.

Blue to be used for information.

Green to be used for identification.

The purpose and function of a colour code will to some extent indicate the way in which it is introduced into the sign system.

Generally it will either be used as a separate form of identification such as plain colour panels, strips or squares or be incorporated within the sign by colour type, symbol and background.

Again as with panel sizes, the freedom of choice should be restricted to manageable and effective permutations.

The disadvantage of mixing colour type combinations in close proximity, such as multiple sign assemblies, with the typeface reversed out of black or a colour together with colour type on white, is the optical effect which gives a difference of letter weight.

Comparing the bolder appearance of the white type on black with its positive couterpart, both letters actually are identical in size. This descrepancy is even more accentuated in internally illuminated signs as the light tends to produce a halo.

Having established the theoretical colour designations for coding, it is essential to match the selected colour range to an accepted standard specification for suitable paints and/or silkscreen inks.

When signs are produced by a variety of reproduction techniques on differing materials there are bound to be degrees of colour discrepancy, but it is wiser to know what these are before commitment than at a later date when the programme is already being implemented.

Certain colours have accepted connotations when associated with danger and emergency and should, therefore, be observed and not forced into a code. For example a red cross does not have the same significance if rendered in black or yellow.

Red should always be used for fire protection and safety devices (e.g. fire engines, alarm boxes, fire extinguishers, hydrants, exit signs, etc.). This means that to a certain extent the use of red for this specific area of information may cut across the recommended categories. Local byelaws and government regulations often stipulate red for obvious reasons.

A range of different colours, combinations of panel ground, type and symbols.

Assuming that the signs have been divided into three categories according to their function, the variations using colour, black and white, should prove adequate for subdividing any one category.

Prop tera

Prop tera

Prop tera

Propte

Propte

Propte

Prop tera

Prop tera

Prop tera

Propte

Propte

Propte

Prop tera

Prop tera

Prop tera

Propte

Propte

Propte

46

47

Ex Libris
Henk van Assen

Dutch Type, Jan Middendorp, Uitgeverij 010, Rotterdam, 2004
Pioneers of Modern Typography, Herbert Spencer, revised edition, Lund Humphries, London, 1983
About Face: Reviving the Rules of Typography, David Jury, Rotovision, East Sussex, 2002
The Alphabetic Labyrinth: The Letters in History and Imagination, Johanna Drucker, Thames & Hudson, London, 1995
The Story of Writing: Alphabets, Hieroglyphs & Pictograms, Andrew Robinson, Thames & Hudson, London, 1995
Typography, Emil Ruder, Hastings House, New York, 1981
Grid Systems in Graphic Design, Josef Müller-Brockmann, Arthur Niggli, Niederteufen, 1981
Type & Typography, Phil Baines, Andrew Haslam, Laurence King Publishing, London, 2002
Design Writing Research: Writing on Graphic Design, Ellen Lupton, J. Abbott Miller, Princeton Architectural Press, New York, 1996
Printed Matter, Robin Kinross, Jaap van Triest, Karel Martens (editors), Hyphen Press, London, 1996

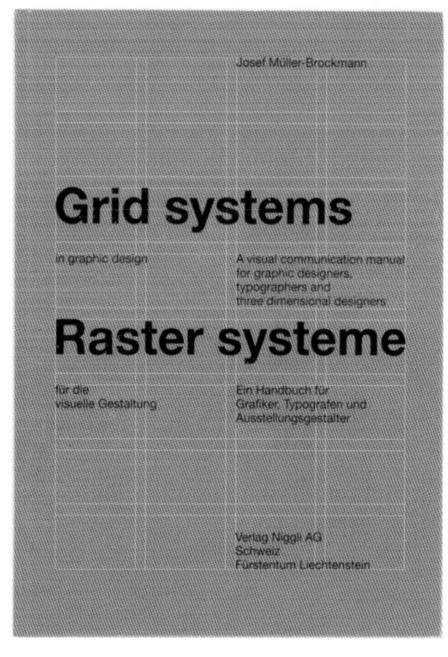

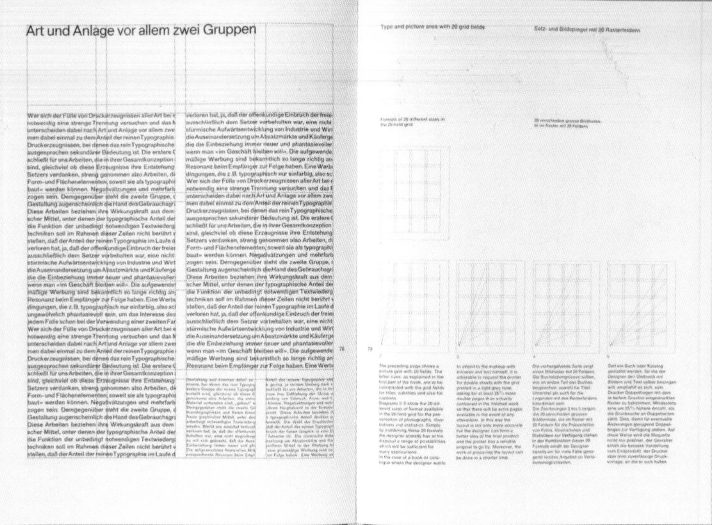

For added clarity, red is used to draw the underlying grids in the book. The text is in English and German.

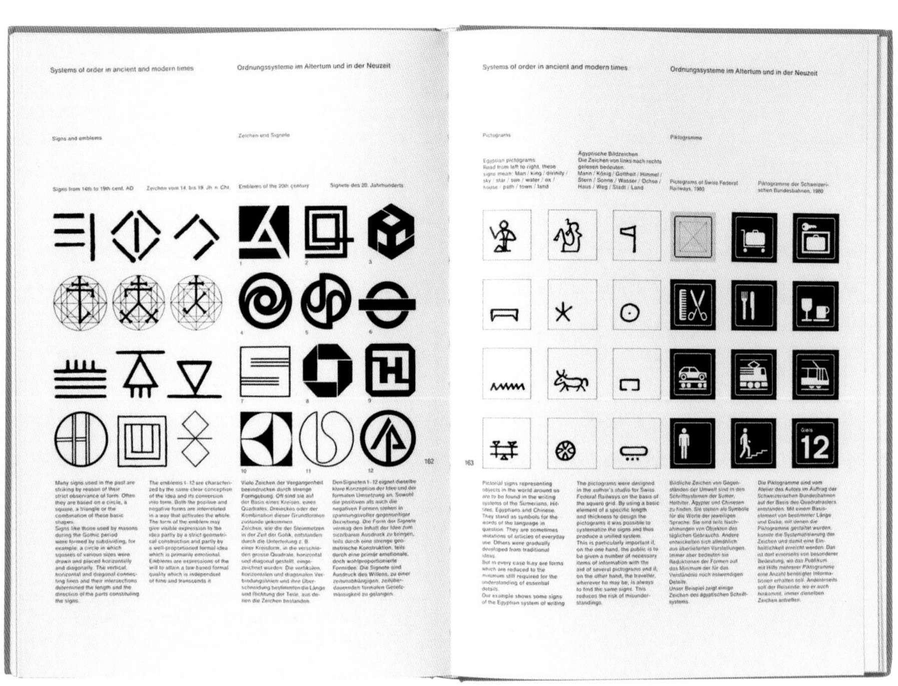

Part of the section 'Systems of Order in Ancient and Modern Times'. Müller-Brockmann had earlier written a fine history of graphic design, A History of Visual Communication *(Arthur Niggli, Teufen, 1971).*

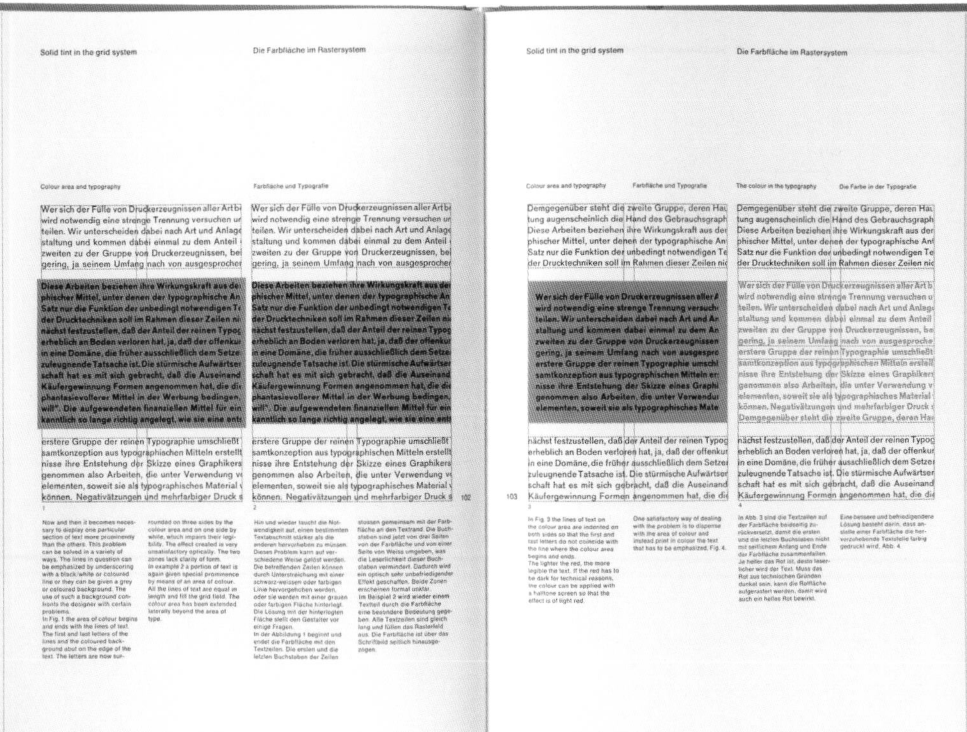

A section showing practical examples of design by Müller-Brockmann and other selected designers sitting side by side with their respective grids.

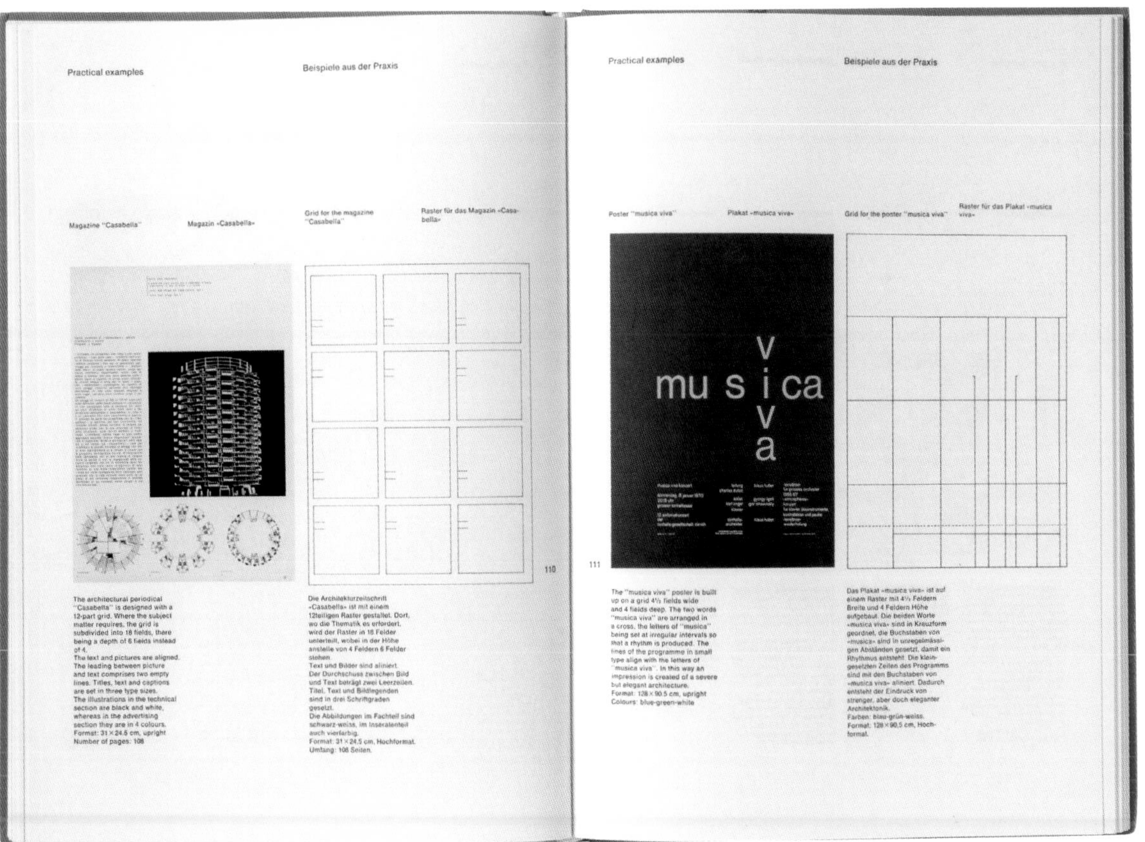

Grid Systems in Graphic Design

A Visual Communication Manual for Graphic Designers, Typographers and Three Dimensional Designers

Josef Müller-Brockmann

Arthur Niggli, Niederteufen, 1981
Fourth edition (pictured), Verlag Niggli, Sulgen, 1996
176 pages
296 × 206 mm (11.625 × 8.125 in)
Designed by Josef Müller-Brockmann

In *The Graphic Artist and His Design Problems* (see page 82), published in 1961, Josef Müller-Brockmann was the first person to write at any length about grids. They were an integral part of the Swiss movement in objective typography and design, and it is surprising that it was a further 20 years before they were the subject of a separate book – but no surprise that *Grid Systems in Graphic Design* has been regularly reprinted ever since.

It is a rigorous study that deals with all facets of the working of grids. Primarily an instructional tool for designers and students, it begins with an introductory section studying the philosophy and purpose of the grid before moving on to a step-by-step guide to their construction. The size of paper, selection of typeface, column widths, leading, margins and pagination are all discussed before Müller-Brockmann deals directly with the finer points of the grid.

Samples of grids and methods of construction are introduced in increasing complexity, from eight grid fields to 32. The use of red as a second colour to highlight the underlying grids and allow the clear presentation of accompanying drawings provides layouts of great clarity. Further sections tackle the use of photography and illustration within the grid system.

An international field of designers contributed their work to a section that displays practical examples of the system. Page layouts by Wim Crouwel, Paul Rand, Otl Aicher and Massimo Vignelli, among others, are shown next to drawings of the relevant grids.

For Müller-Brockmann, however, the grid was not simply a means of organization. It was at the heart of his design philosophy, part of a system of order that could extend through the page layout on to corporate identity systems, and could, moreover, 'be a contribution to general culture and itself form part of it'.

The Visual Display of Quantitative Information

Edward R. Tufte

Graphics Press, Cheshire, Connecticut, 1983

Eleventh reprint (pictured), 1991

200 pages

266 × 217 mm (10.5 × 8.5 in)

Designed by Howard Gralla, Edward R. Tufte

Edward R. Tufte (1942–) took out a second mortgage on his house to self-publish this 'celebration of data graphics', and *The Visual Display of Quantitative Information* became the first in a successful series of books that established him as a world authority on information graphics. All of them carry the same trademarks; they are incisive, educational, immaculately researched, elegantly designed and very finely printed.

Tufte sets out his stall by introducing readers to three of his statistical heroes, whom he uses as yardsticks of 'graphic excellence' throughout the book. They are William Playfair (1759–1823), the English political economist who invented the bar chart; Charles Joseph Minard (1781–1870), the French engineer who plotted a map showing the progress of Napoleon's army in Russia from six variable data sources – and produced what Tufte says 'may well be the best statistical graphic ever drawn'; and E.J. Marey (1830–1904), whose graphical schedule for trains from Paris to Lyon provides the cover for the book.

In contrast to the elegance of these pinnacles of information design, the next section details the graphical lies, deceptions and graphic confusion so prevalent in printed communication.

The second half of the book is a study in developing a theory and language of quantitative graphics. In it a wide-ranging selection of illustrations and practical solutions is explored, and Tufte explains, with passion, his new vocabulary of information graphics including terms such as data-ink ratios, chartjunk, data-ink maximization, multifunctioning and data density.

Tufte has subsequently written and published *Envisioning Information* (1990), *Visual Explanations* (1997) and *Beautiful Evidence* (2006).

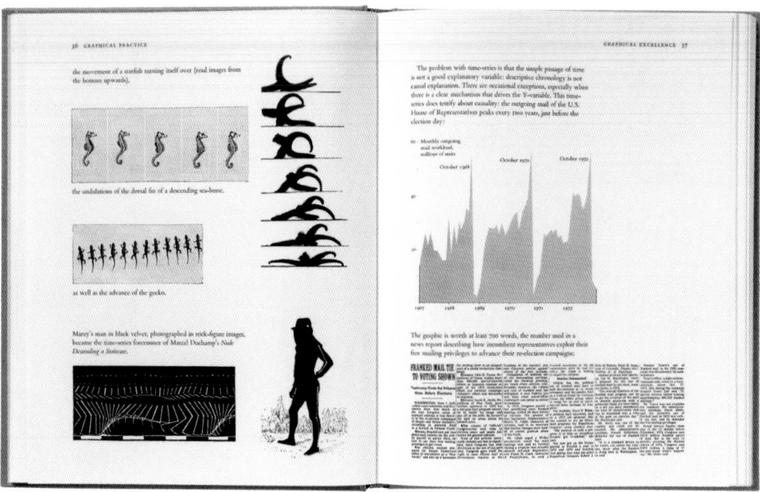

36 GRAPHICAL PRACTICE

the movement of a starfish turning itself over (read images from the bottom upwards).

the undulations of the dorsal fin of a descending sea-horse.

as well as the advance of the gecko.

Marey's man in black velvet, photographed in stick-figure images, became the time-series forerunner of Marcel Duchamp's *Nude Descending a Staircase.*

GRAPHICAL EXCELLENCE 37

The problem with time-series is that the simple passage of time is not a good explanatory variable: descriptive chronology is not causal explanation. There are occasional exceptions, especially when there is a clear mechanism that drives the Y-variable. This time-series does testify about causality: the outgoing mail of the U.S. House of Representatives peaks every two years, just before the election day:

The graphic is worth at least 700 words, the number used in a news report describing how incumbent representatives exploit their free mailing privileges to advance their re-election campaigns:

FRANKED MAIL TIE TO VOTING SHOWN

The clean and uncluttered design by Tufte and Howard Gralla, with its large margins, has defined the series of books produced by Graphics Press. This spread shows Minard's 1869 map of Napoleon's advance and retreat from Moscow, held by Tufte as an exemplar of graphic design.

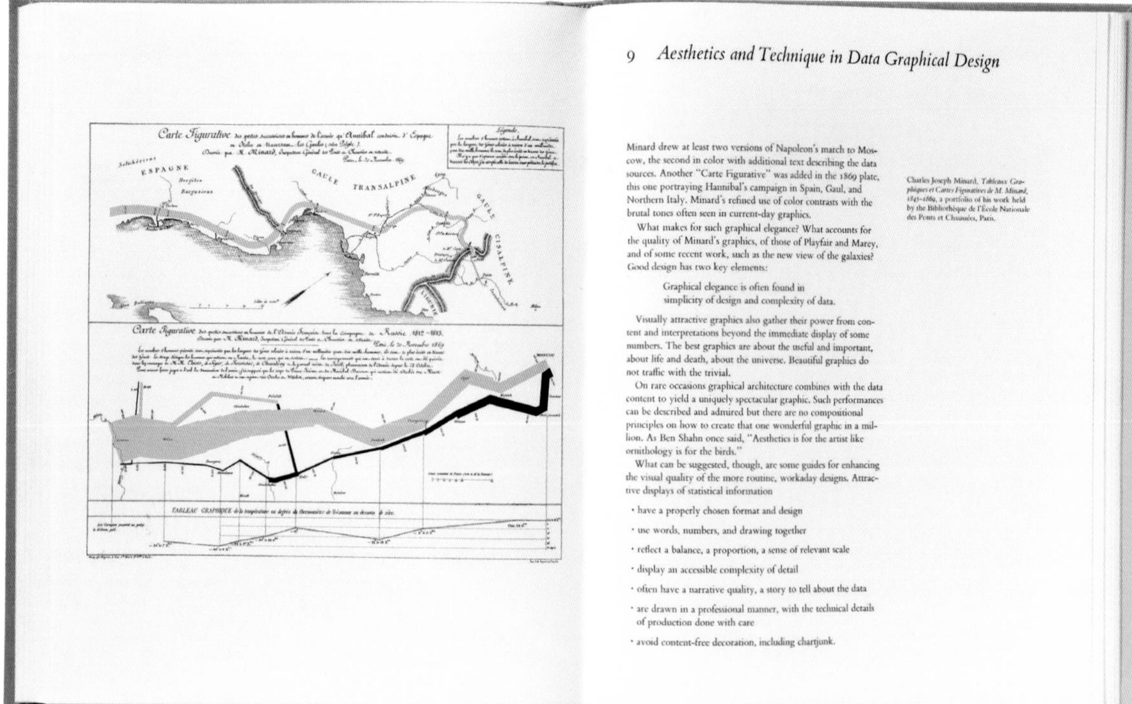

9 *Aesthetics and Technique in Data Graphical Design*

Minard drew at least two versions of Napoleon's march to Moscow, the second in color with additional text describing the data sources. Another "Carte Figurative" was added in the 1869 plate, this one portraying Hannibal's campaign in Spain, Gaul, and Northern Italy. Minard's refined use of color contrasts with the brutal tones often seen in current-day graphics.

What makes for such graphical elegance? What accounts for the quality of Minard's graphics, of those of Playfair and Marey, and of some recent work, such as the new view of the galaxies? Good design has two key elements:

> Graphical elegance is often found in simplicity of design and complexity of data.

Visually attractive graphics also gather their power from content and interpretations beyond the immediate display of some numbers. The best graphics are about the useful and important, about life and death, about the universe. Beautiful graphics do not traffic with the trivial.

On rare occasions graphical architecture combines with the data content to yield a uniquely spectacular graphic. Such performances can be described and admired but there are no compositional principles on how to create that one wonderful graphic in a million. As Ben Shahn once said, "Aesthetics is for the artist like ornithology is for the birds."

What can be suggested, though, are some guides for enhancing the visual quality of the more routine, workaday designs. Attractive displays of statistical information

- have a properly chosen format and design
- use words, numbers, and drawing together
- reflect a balance, a proportion, a sense of relevant scale
- display an accessible complexity of detail
- often have a narrative quality, a story to tell about the data
- are drawn in a professional manner, with the technical details of production done with care
- avoid content-free decoration, including chartjunk.

Charles Joseph Minard, *Tableaux Graphiques et Cartes Figuratives de M. Minard*, 1845–1869, a portfolio of his work held by the Bibliothèque de l'École Nationale des Ponts et Chaussées, Paris.

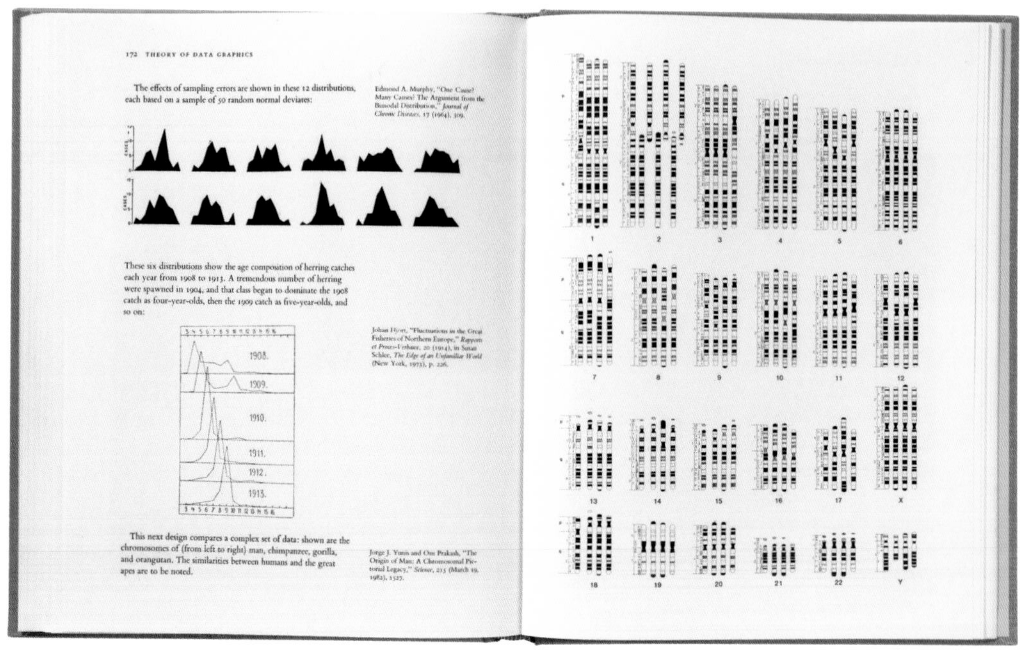

172 THEORY OF DATA GRAPHICS

The effects of sampling errors are shown in these 12 distributions, each based on a sample of 50 random normal deviates:

Edmond A. Murphy, "One Cause? Many Causes? The Argument from the Bimodal Distribution," *Journal of Chronic Diseases*, 17 (1964), 309.

These six distributions show the age composition of herring catches each year from 1908 to 1913. A tremendous number of herring were spawned in 1904, and that class began to dominate the 1908 catch as four-year-olds, then the 1909 catch as five-year-olds, and so on:

Johan Hjort, "Fluctuations in the Great Fisheries of Northern Europe," *Rapports et Procès-Verbaux*, 20 (1914), in Susan Schlee, *The Edge of an Unfamiliar World* (New York, 1973), p. 226.

This next design compares a complex set of data: shown are the chromosomes of (from left to right) man, chimpanzee, gorilla, and orangutan. The similarities between humans and the great apes are to be noted.

Jorge J. Yunis and Om Prakash, "The Origin of Man: A Chromosomal Pictorial Legacy," *Science*, 215 (March 19, 1982), 1527.

The Elements of Typographic Style, Version 3.0, Robert Bringhurst, Hartley & Marks, Vancouver, 2004
Fuel, Three Thousand, Miles Murray Sorrell, Laurence King Publishing, London, 2000
Designing Programmes, Karl Gerstner, third edition, Lars Müller Publishers, Baden, 2007
Designing Books: Practice and Theory, Jost Hochuli, Hyphen Press, London, 2003
Envisioning Information, Edward Tufte, Graphics Press, Cheshire, Connecticut, 1990
The Stroke: Theory of Writing, Gerrit Noordzij, Hyphen Press, London, 2005
The Typographic Grid, Hans Rudolf Bosshard, Verlag Niggli, Sulgen, 2000
Schriftgestalten, Tino Graß, Verlag Niggli, Sulgen, 2008
2d Visuelle Wahrnehmung, Moritz Zwimpfer, Verlag Niggli, Sulgen, 1994
Schriftanalysen 1+2, Max Caflisch, Typotron, St Gallen, 2003

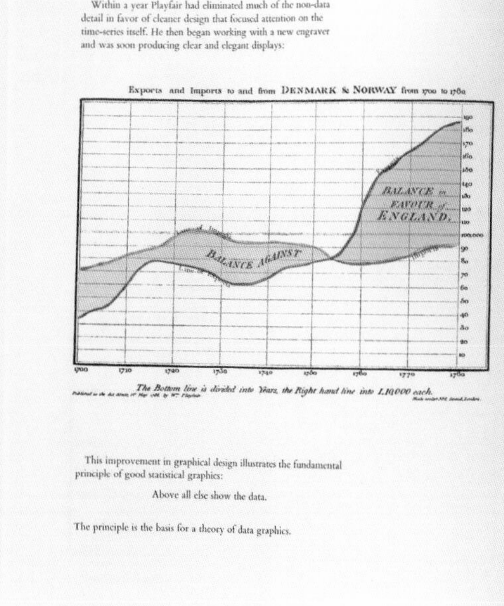

Tufte is unafraid to show what he considers to be poor examples of information graphics. Here a strong and simple line graph is contrasted with a confusing map of death rates in the USA.

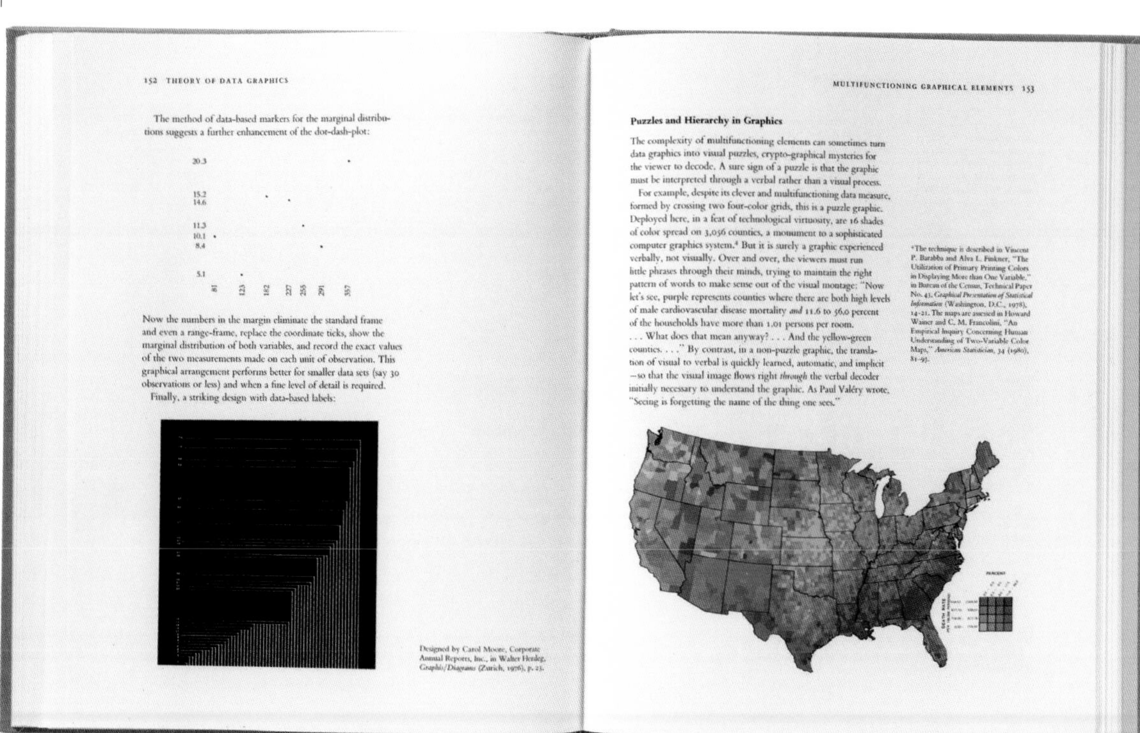

Ex Libris
Mario Eskenazi

Typography, Emil Ruder, Arthur Niggli, Teufen, 1967
Pioneers of Modern Typography, Herbert Spencer, Lund Humphries, London, 1969
Letter and Image, Robert Massin, Studio Vista, London, 1970
Identity Kits: A Pictorial Survey of Visual Signals, Germano Facetti, Alan Fletcher, Studio Vista, London, 1971
Grid Systems in Graphic Design, Joseph Müller-Brockmann, Arthur Niggli, Niederteufen, 1981
Paul Rand: A Designer's Art, Paul Rand, Yale University Press, New Haven and London, 1985
Modern Typography: An Essay in Critical History, Robin Kinross, Hyphen Press, London, 1992
Printed Matter, Robin Kinross, Jaap van Triest, Karel Martens (editors), Hyphen Press, London, 1996
The Art of Looking Sideways, Alan Fletcher, Phaidon Press, London, 2001
Notes on Book Design, Derek Birdsall, Yale University Press, New Haven and London, 2004

front cover

notes on
book design
by
Derek Birdsall

endpapers
half title
frontispiece
title page
dedication
imprint/colophon
contents
acknowledgements
foreword
preface
introduction
note to the reader
chapter openings
text
quotations
captions
pictures
plates
gate-folds
figures
diagrams
graphs
reconstructions
charts
tables
maps
catalogue entries
recto/verso
obverse/reverse
folios
running heads/feet
footnotes
appendices
glossary
abbreviations
concordances
collation
biographies
bibliographies
exhibitions
index
picture sources
formats/paper
typefaces
grids

deadlines

The cover lists the component parts of a book's make-up. All the items are referred to in the book, either in the text or in the form of labels, as seen here in the 'front cover' on the top left.

Notes on Book Design

Derek Birdsall

Yale University Press,
New Haven and London, 2004
236 pages
297 × 246 mm (11.75 × 9.625 in)
Designed by Derek Birdsall

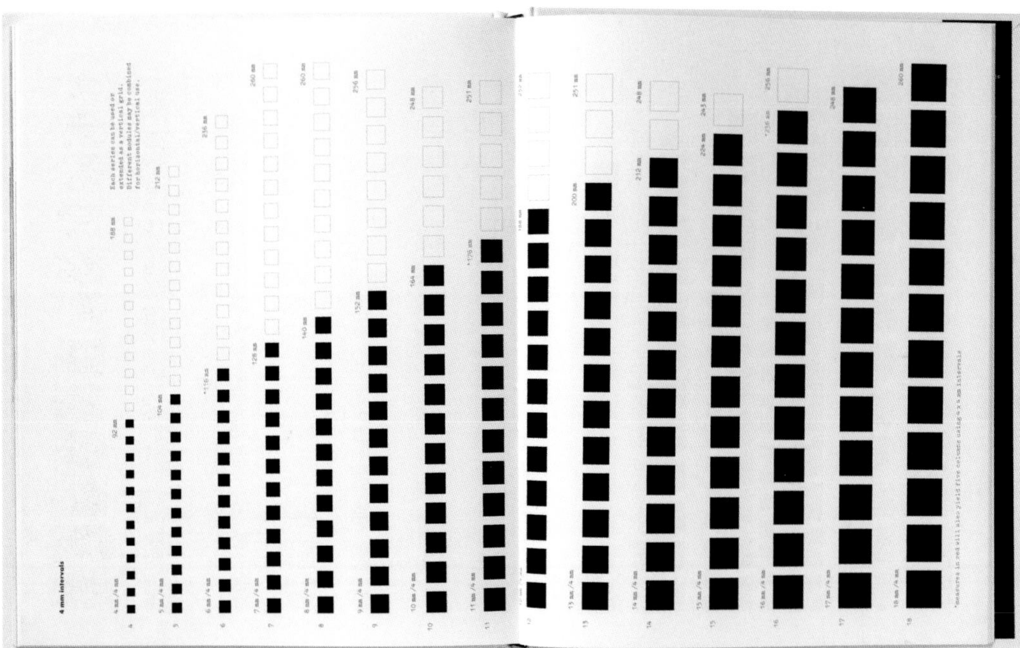

The appendix includes valuable pages on grid systems designed to leave column widths and inter-column spaces in whole millimetre units. These measures define the book's margins.

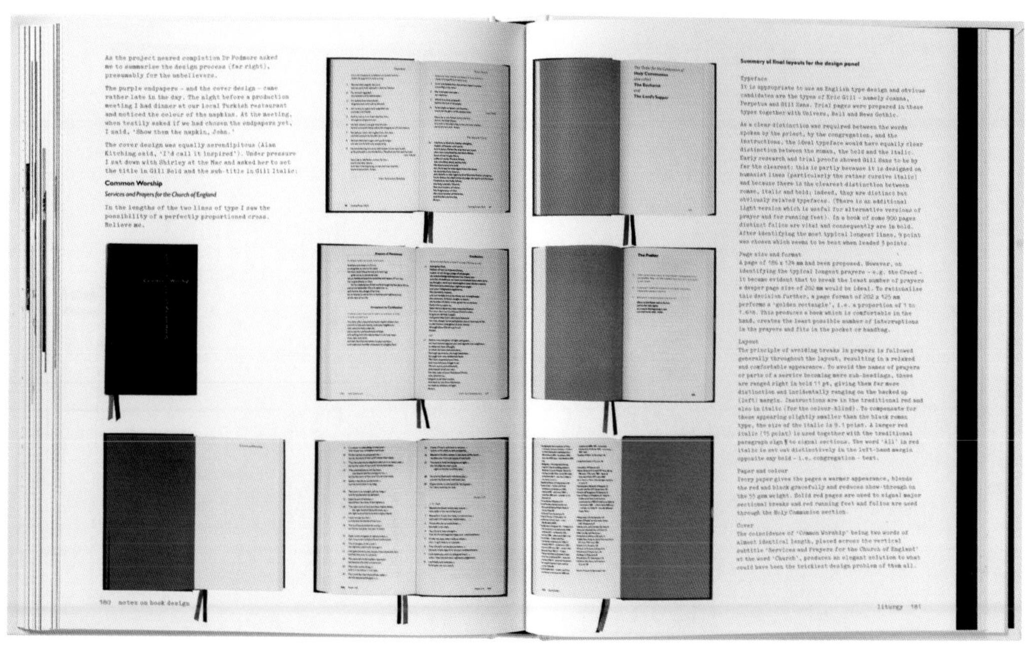

The genesis of *Notes on Book Design* was the large collection of notes and cuttings Derek Birdsall (1934–) gathered during his distinguished career. Using his second-hand Olivetti Lettera 35 typewriter he transposed them onto A6 index cards, placed them in a box and finally arranged them into the sections for this book.

Derek Birdsall emerged from the burgeoning British design industry in the late 1950s and early 1960s. His book design is exemplary; he describes his ethos as 'quite simply the decent setting of type and the intelligent layout of text and pictures based on a rigorous study of content'.

The first part of the book looks at the processes and methods of book design through detailed examples of Birdsall's work. A large proportion of his book designs are shown in the second part, including the recent *Common Worship* (2000); earlier Penguin covers; the huge *catalogue raisonné* of Mark Rothko (1998); the smaller scale *Shaker Design* (1986); *The Technology of Man* (1978), which he co-authored with Carlo M. Cipolla; and the catalogue *Images of an Era: The American Poster 1945–75* (see page 110).

An extensive appendix includes a selection of typeface specimens, a glossary of book design terms and a practical guide to grids, based on a millimetre system. An illustrated biography gives a taste of Birdsall's extensive and varied design life outside the world of books.

Birdsall has designed *Notes on Book Design* so that it deconstructs itself as a book: 'endpapers', 'imprint', 'section opener' and other essential book elements are labelled for the reader to better understand its organization.

Histories

The three-column grid is occasionally broken to feature full-page illustrations – their captions are laid at 90 degrees to the page. This spreads shows the striking images by Paul Peter Piech for W. & T. Avery Ltd (1955).

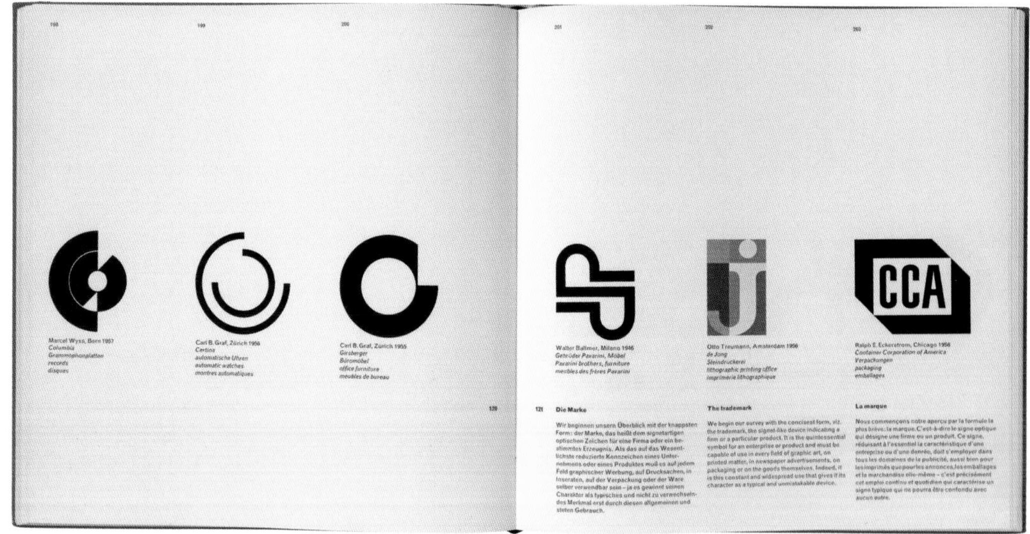

The New Graphic Art

Karl Gerstner, Markus Kutter

Arthur Niggli, Teufen, 1959
248 pages
230 × 230 mm (9 × 9 in)
Designed by Karl Gerstner

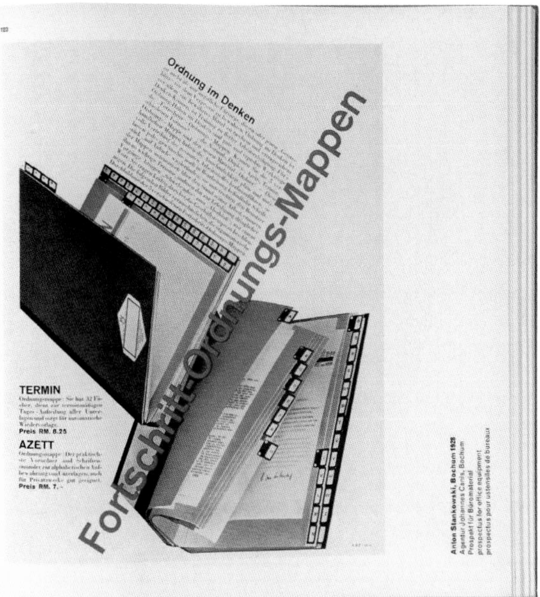

Spreads from the first sections of Gerstner and Kutter's history of graphic design – this is told in large part through the illustrations.

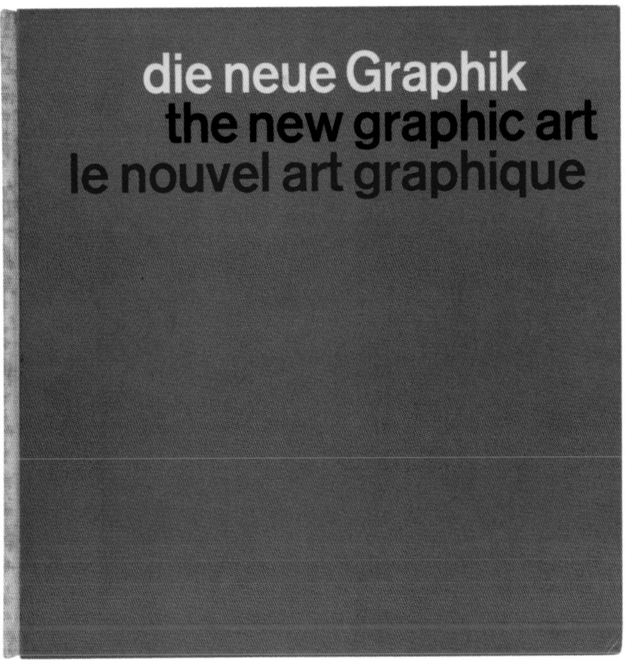

die neue Graphik
the new graphic art
le nouvel art graphique

The New Graphic Art is a history of graphic design, 'its origins, its evolution, its peculiarities, its tasks, its problems, its manifestations and its future prospects'. No small task, but one to which its authors, the Swiss designer Karl Gerstner (1930–) and colleague Markus Kutter (1925–2005) were equal. This was the first book to place modern concepts of the grid and the constructed page at the apex of design history.

The text is in German, English and French, and the first section, 'Beginnings', looks at nineteenth-century graphic arts from the ephemeral to polished Art Nouveau posters. The second, 'Breakthrough', shows the work of avant-garde-inspired designers in the first half of the twentieth century and their crucial rejection of centred, symmetrical typography. The last two sections, 'Present' and 'Future', concentrate on the period after the Second World War and the development of a more systematic form of layout and design. Many of the illustrations, which are numerous but very high in standard, had not previously been published. The authors clearly saw this modern approach to design as an international trend, and works from America and many European nations are included.

Made in Switzerland, the book is printed on a thin paper stock, mostly in black but with occasional colour pages, and lacks little in reproduction quality. Exceptionally well laid out and methodically ordered, the three-column grid is visible but not domineering. The cover does not give the contents away and sets an often-repeated standard for Swiss books on graphic design: sans serif type with the title in the three languages used within.

Gerstner would write other critically acclaimed books on graphic design, including *Designing Programmes* (Arthur Niggli, Teufen, 1964) on his systematic approach to graphic problem-solving and *Kompendium für Alphabeten* (Arthur Niggli, Teufen, 1972), a textbook of typographic usage translated as *Compendium for Literates* (MIT Press, Cambridge, Mass., 1974).

Functional Graphic Design in the 20's
Eckhard Neumann
Reinhold Publishing Corporation, New York, 1967
96 pages
202 × 202 mm (8 × 8 in)

Eckhard Neumann's preparations for the 1963 exhibition 'Werbegrafik 1920–1930' ('Graphic Design 1920–1930') in Frankfurt, and the production of its catalogue, provided a ready-made outline for this subsequent book. However, *Functional Graphic Design in the 20's* benefits from a more detailed study of the subject area and the addition of more visual material. It concentrates on Europe, with an emphasis on German designers, and its 113 illustrations include many previously unpublished examples of works from the 1920s.

The decade was an important point of transition in graphic design. Neumann was particularly interested in how it was influenced by early twentieth-century art movements and in the later development of a modern style within commercial design. Typographic standards were being thrown out the window, and Neumann devotes two early chapters to the study of the Futurist and Dada experimentation with design in their manifestos, poetry and posters. There are excellent examples of work by Ardengo Soffici, Raoul Hausmann and Kurt Schwitters.

The advent of the Bauhaus is given its own chapter, while the subsequent focus on design practice, and the increasing use of photography in advertising, is explored in the chapter 'New Art – New Advertising'. An illustrated reprint of Walter Dexel's 1927 article 'What is New Typography?' follows. El Lissitzky's work for Pelikan Ink, Herbert Bayer's paper money and kiosk designs, and photomontages by John Heartfield are just some of the outstanding works reproduced in these chapters.

Functional Graphic Design in the 20's is in a small square format. It is printed in black on uncoated stock with the economical addition of red and yellow spot colours.

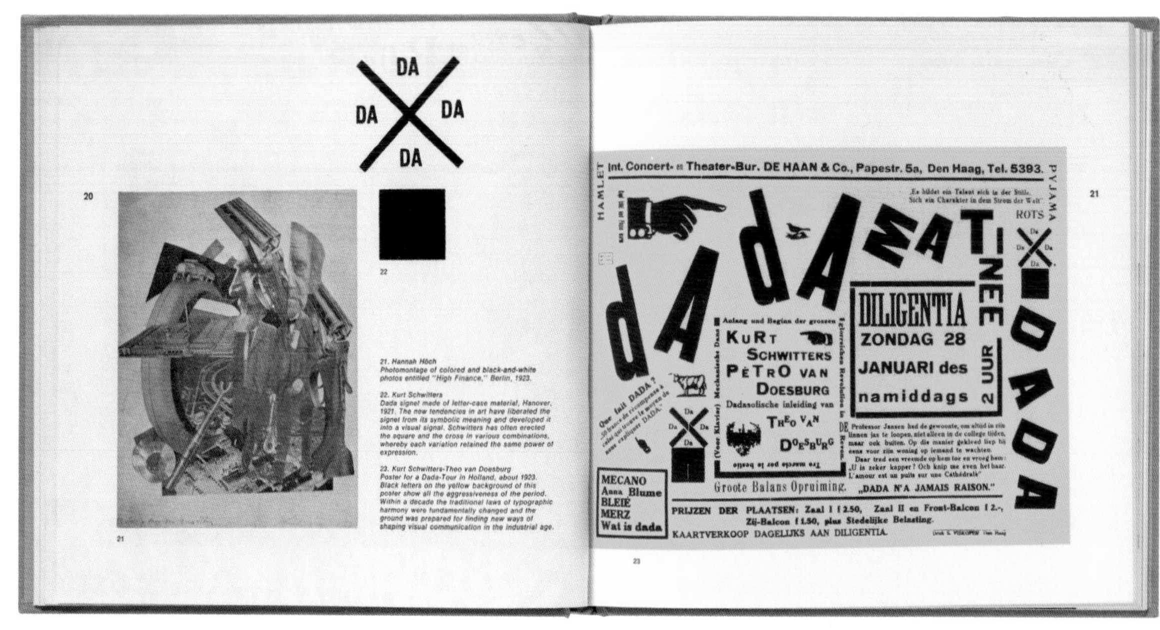

DA
DA
DA
DA
20
21
22
21. Hannah Höch
Photomontage of colored and black-and-white photos entitled "High Finance," Berlin, 1923.
22. Kurt Schwitters
Dada signet made of letter-case material, Hanover, 1921. The new tendencies in art have liberated the signet from its symbolic meaning and developed it into a visual signal. Schwitters has often erected the square and the cross in various combinations, whereby each variation retained the same power of expression.
23. Kurt Schwitters-Theo van Doesburg
Poster for a Dada-Tour in Holland, about 1923. Black letters on the yellow background of this poster show all the aggressiveness of the period. Within a decade the traditional laws of typographic harmony were fundamentally changed and the ground was prepared for finding new ways of shaping visual communication in the industrial age.
Int. Concert- en Theater-Bur. DE HAAN & Co., Papestr. 5a, Den Haag, Tel. 5393.
dAdA
MATINEE
DADA
DILIGENTIA
ZONDAG 28
JANUARI des
namiddags
2 UUR
KURT SCHWITTERS
PETRO VAN DOESBURG
THEO VAN DOESBURG
MECANO
Anna Blume
BLEIE
MERZ
Wat is dada
Groote Balans Opruiming.
„DADA N'A JAMAIS RAISON."
PRIJZEN DER PLAATSEN: Zaal f 2.50, Zaal II en Front-Balcon f 2.-, Zij-Balcon f 1.50, plus Stedelijke Belasting.
KAARTVERKOOP DAGELIJKS AAN DILIGENTIA.
23

81. Willi Baumeister
Advertisement of department store in a daily paper, Stuttgart, 1926. Development of a typographic system which could be used for a variety of tasks in department store promotion. Baumeister's principal aim was to design forms that would signify the corporate image.
82. Anonymous
Poster for Schocken department store, Stuttgart, about 1928. The unison of architecture and graphic art is the outstanding factor in this poster. (Architect Erich Mendelsohn, Berlin.)
70
71
ZUM WOCHENENDE
TIETZ
Schaarschmidt
VOLKSVERBAND DER BÜCHERFREUNDE
81
BLICK VON DER KÖNIGSTRASSE SCHOCKEN

103, 104. *Robert Michel*
Advertising surfaces for proprietary articles, Frankfurt, 1926-1927. The principles of the new form applied to a large surface.

88

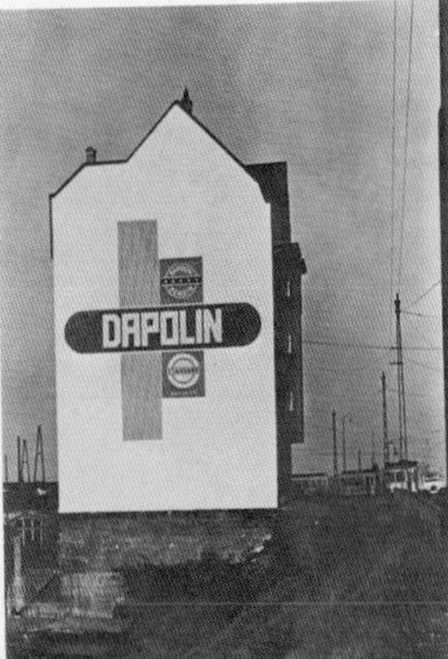

103

104

105

tant works was the design of a corporate image for *Kahl*, from the building of stores to designing publicity. For large firms in the brand article industry, Robert Michel designed big advertisements that were placed on rooftops. In the same sense the graphic artist Hans Leistikow also worked for the city. Leistikow had a studio in City Hall as advisor for printing designs, assuming responsibility for all typographical problems from the simplest to posters and bookcovers. For the municipal offices the use of this service was obligatory. Working with the municipal board of buildings enabled him to exercise his influence regarding the color schemes of settlements. The city tried to achieve a unified look and did everything to attain this desirable ideal.

A special service at Frankfurt was the *Frankfurter Register*, a supplement to the magazine *Das Neue Frankfurt* which advertised products of good quality and good design and appearance which were chosen by a jury. Johannes Canis was responsible for the typography of this paper.

In 1933 this promising development came to an end. The magazine died and its staff dispersed. But the pioneers, wherever they had worked, had created patterns and set standards which survived. Today's artists have taken up their ideas and applied them to new problems. The great inventiveness of the first half of our century secured a sound foundation for the future.

105. Karl Peter Röhl
Design for a system of signs for the medical profession, Frankfurt, 1926: Hospital, Doctor, Gynecologist, Obstetrician, Eye doctor

89

106. Johannes Canis
Supplement Das Frankfurter Register *to the periodical* Das Neue Frankfurt, *Frankfurt, 1926 to 1933. The desire for good design was not limited to packaging but led to a demand for quality of design within industrial production.* Das *Frankfurt, 1926: Hospital, Doctor, Gynecologist, Obstetrician, Eye doctor.*

106

A plain book in design terms is enlivened by the breadth of images and the careful use of second colours.

12. "New York Dada," around 1920 (in the original positive).

13. Title page for Dada Almanach, *Berlin, 1920.*

14. Title page for En avant Dada, *Hanover, 1920.*

15. Cover of the periodical Der blutige Ernst, *Berlin, 1919, with a drawing by George Grosz.*

16. Page from the periodical Merz, *Hanover.*

17. Cover Der dada, *volume 2, Berlin, 1919.*

16

18. Cover Dada, *volumes 4-5, Zurich, 1919.*

12

17

13

14

15

16

17

18

Pioneers of Modern Typography, Herbert Spencer, Lund Humphries, London, 1969

Tokyo Type Directors Club Annuals

Dada: Zurich, Berlin, Hannover, Cologne, New York, Paris, Leah Dickerman (editor), National Gallery of Art, Washington, 2005

The Russian Avant-Garde Book: 1910–1934, Margit Rowell, Deborah Wye (editors), Museum of Modern Art, New York, 2002

Ed Ruscha, Richard D. Marshall (editor), Phaidon Press, London, 2003

Weingart: Typography, Wolfgang Weingart, Lars Müller Publishers, Baden, 2000

Come Alive! The Spirited Art of Sister Corita, Julie Ault, Four Corners Books, London, 2007

Today's Hieroglyphs, Hans-Rudolf Lutz, Verlag Hans-Rudolf Lutz, Zurich, 1990

Lawrence Weiner, Phaidon Press, London, 1998

Merz to Emigre and Beyond: Avant-Garde Magazine Design of the Twentieth Century, Steven Heller, Phaidon Press, London, 2003

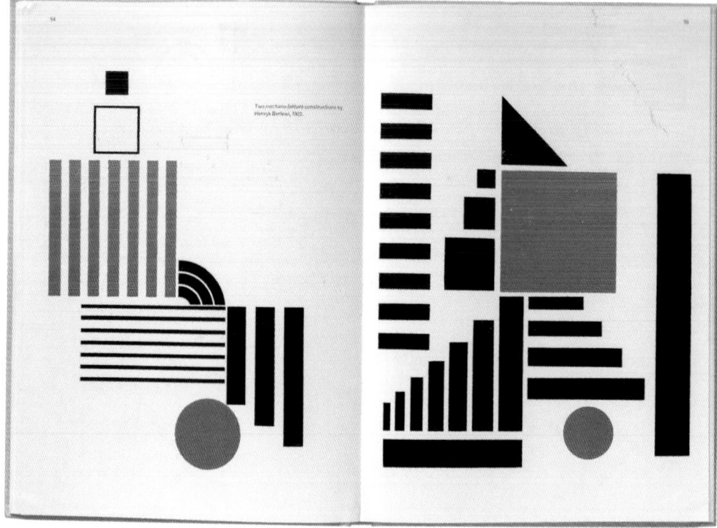

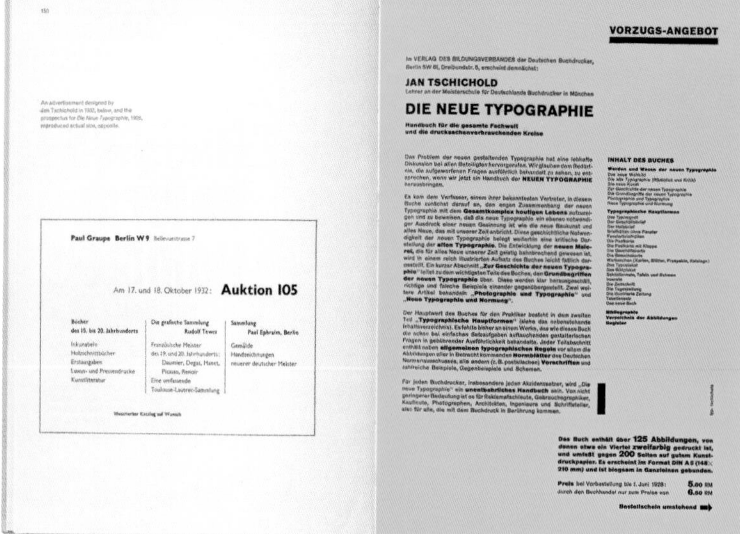

Spencer's considered layout, with its effective use of white space and colour, contributed to the book's success.

Pioneers of Modern Typography
Herbert Spencer
Lund Humphries, London, 1969
160 pages
297 × 210 mm (11.75 × 8.25 in)
Designed by Herbert Spencer

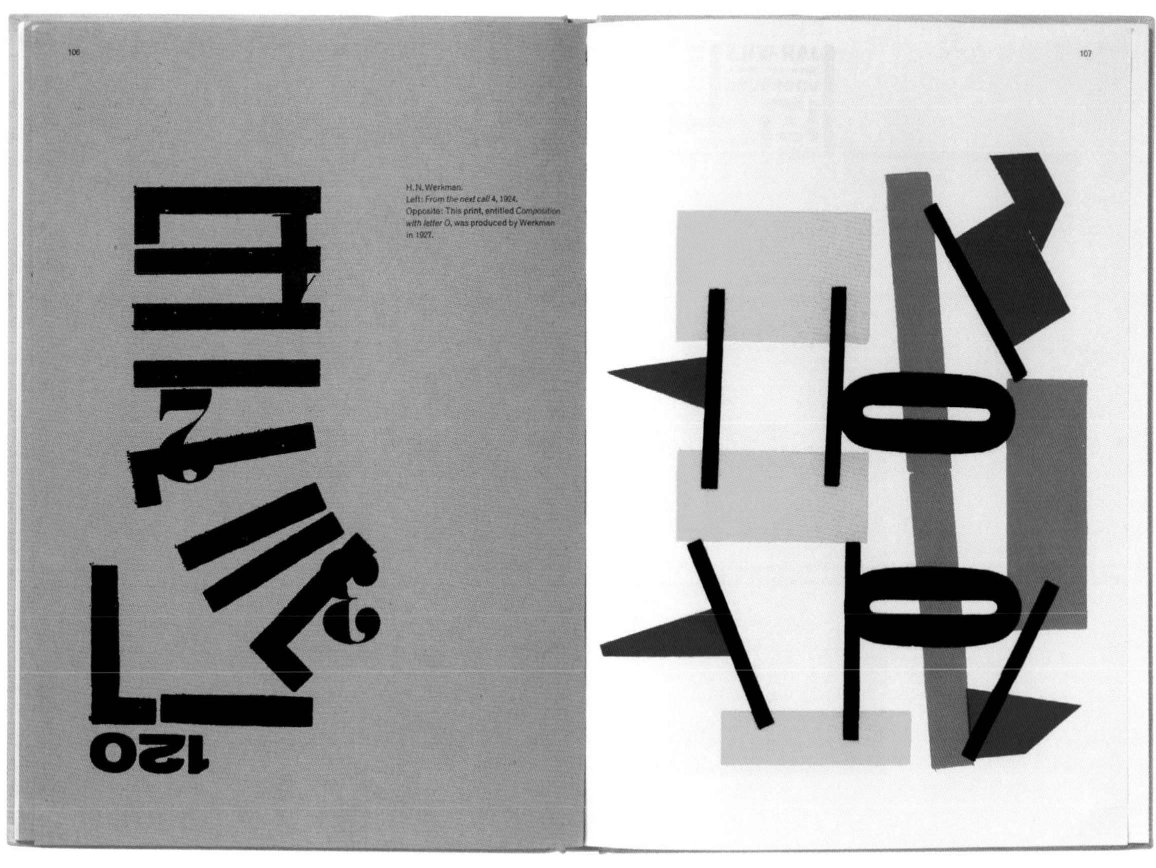

The first edition of Pioneers of Modern Typography *features pages of different stock – here the work of H.N. Werkman is printed on kraft paper.*

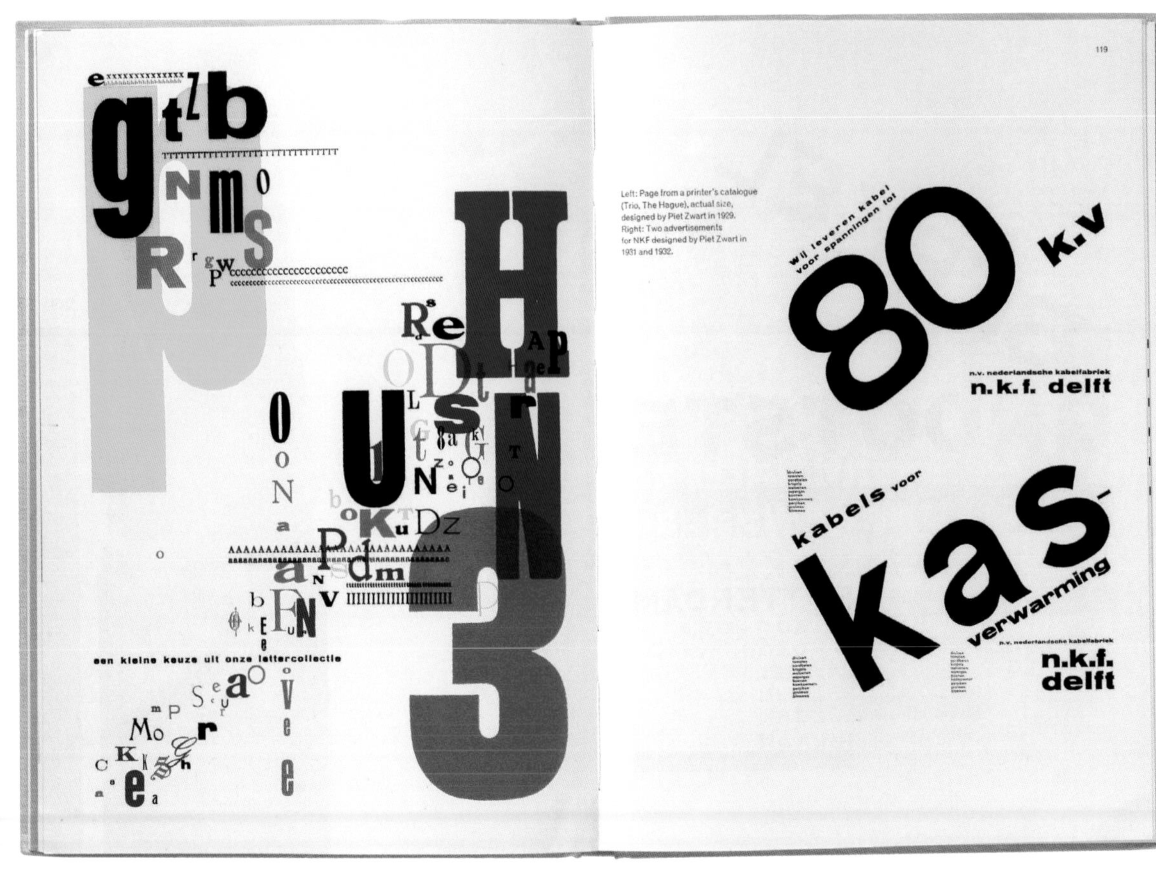

Since its publication in 1969, this book by Herbert Spencer (1924–2002) has inspired many students of graphic design. In it, Spencer tells the story of the birth of modern typography in the first half of the twentieth century through the study of ten key figures associated with avant-garde art movements such as Futurism, Dadaism, Constructivism, Suprematism, De Stijl and the Bauhaus. The beginning of this extraordinary period of typographic experimentation, he writes, started on 20 February 1909 with the publication in *Le Figaro* of Filippo Tommaso Marinetti's manifesto of Futurism and peaked in the early 1920s, by which time the modern style of 'asymmetry and contrast' in typographic forms had been firmly established.

After the lengthy introduction, each of the ten designers is given their own chapter. The accompanying illustrations show clearly how the traditional letterpress medium was pushed to its limits by the likes of Piet Zwart and Kurt Schwitters, which, in turn, led to the design of the modern geometric sans serif alphabets beloved of Herbert Bayer and Jan Tschichold.

Pioneers of Modern Typography has been republished many times since 1969. The first edition was taller in format than the later square editions, and was printed on a mix of different paper stocks. It also used a bigger range of colours including a yellow and blue. Later editions had the benefit of further research, and extra illustrations were added. The iconic cover, presumably designed by Spencer himself, has only recently been replaced.

Images of an Era
The American Poster 1945–75
John Garrigan, Margaret Cogswell, Milton Glaser, Dore Ashton, Alan Gowans
National Collection of Fine Arts, Smithsonian Institution, Washington D.C., 1975
292 pages
248 × 243 mm (9.75 × 9.5 in)
Designed by Derek Birdsall

Condensing 30 years of post-war poster design in the United States, *Images of an Era* reflects the passion and hope of a key period in America's political and cultural history. Brought together for the exhibition of the same name at the Smithsonian Institution in Washington D.C., the posters are broad-ranging and include examples by graphic designers, artists and many anonymous or amateur designers.

Designed by Derek Birdsall, the book is covered by Andy Warhol's silkscreened poster for the Fifth New York Film Festival at the Lincoln Center. Only the type on the book's spine gives its contents away. The plate section comes after the introductory essays and is sandwiched between an oversized '1945' and '75'; the laid paper of the front and back of the book gives way to coated stock for the illustrations.

In his introduction, Milton Glaser bemoans the lack of commercial posters, offering the view that corporations seemed to be unable to summon the vigour displayed in other areas of American life. Posters for the civil rights movement and anti-Vietnam protests are among the most powerful images in the book, and these are often by non-designers. The growing ecology movement is represented with works from Jacqueline S. Casey and Henry Wolf.

There are also many contributions from artists of the time – Claes Oldenburg, Roy Lichtenstein and Saul Steinberg among others; the psychedelic era of the mid-1960s is well covered, with posters by Wes Wilson and Victor Moscoso prominent. Designers represented include Paul Rand, Milton Glaser, Seymour Chwast and Paul Davis.

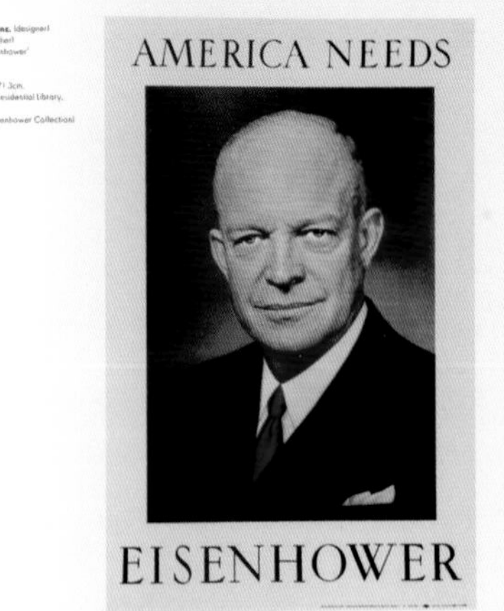

This poster by Jacqueline S. Casey, on the right-hand page below, is also featured in the book of her work for MIT – Posters, *The MIT Museum, Cambridge, Mass., 1992.*

104
Seymour Chwast
'Elektra'
1969,
offset lithography,
24 × 36in, 61 × 91.5cm,
Push Pin Studios, New York, N.Y.
ELEKTRA

105
Lee Conklin
'Procol Harum and Santana'
1969
offset lithography,
54.5 × 35.5cm,
The Museum of Modern Art, New York, N.Y.

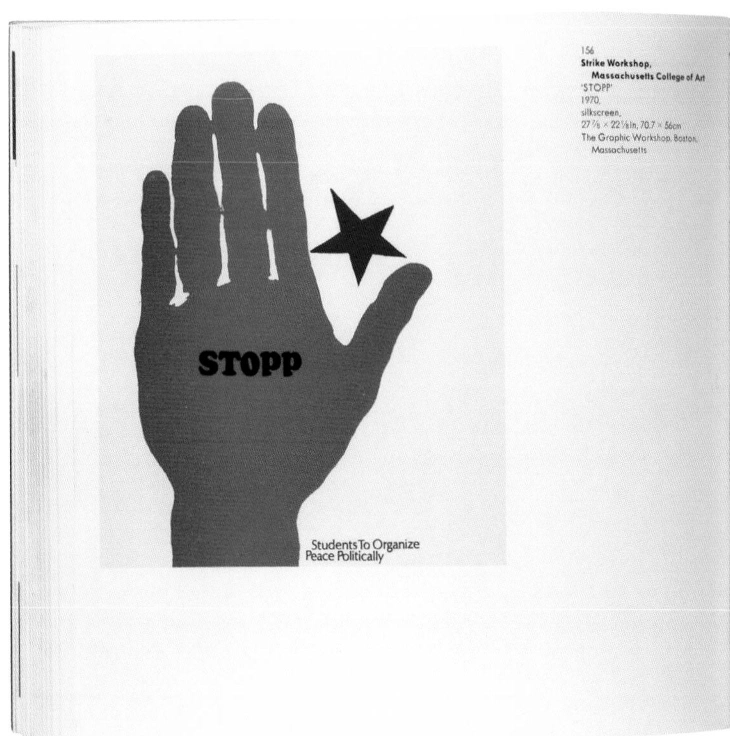

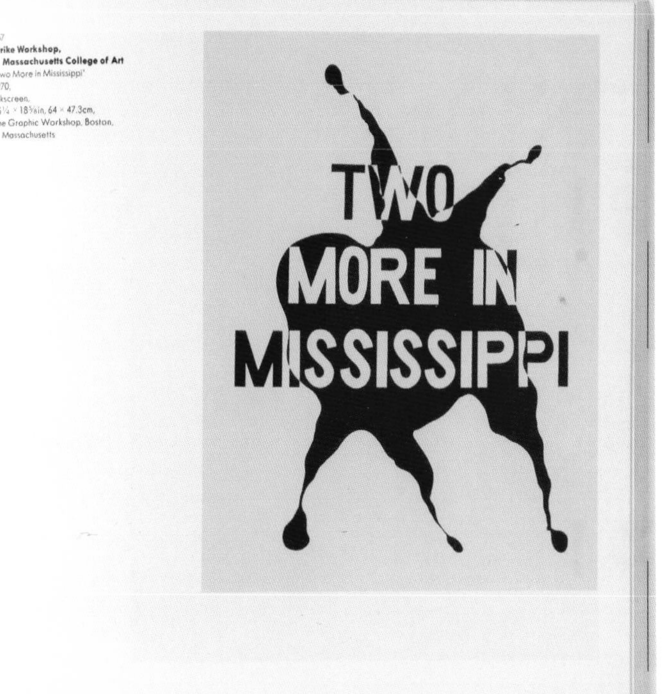

The book's cover is a reproduction of Andy Warhol's poster for the Fifth New York Film Festival. Printed on stiff card, it wraps round the softcover of the book.

Arranged thematically, The Language of Graphics *has spreads with images drawn from across the graphic design spectrum. Here, 'The Cultural Poster in Show Business' places posters by Roman Cieslewicz, Max Bill, Shigeo Fukuda, Saul Steinberg, Ryuichi Yamashiro, Wojciech Zamecznik, Tadanori Yokoo and Kohei Sugiura all on the same spread.*

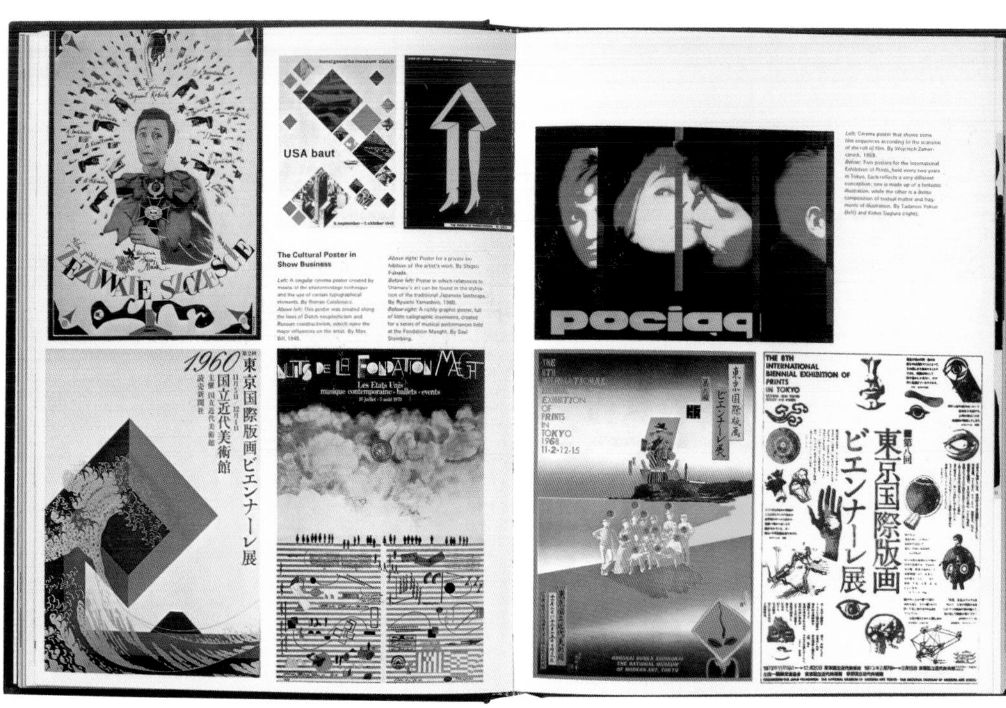

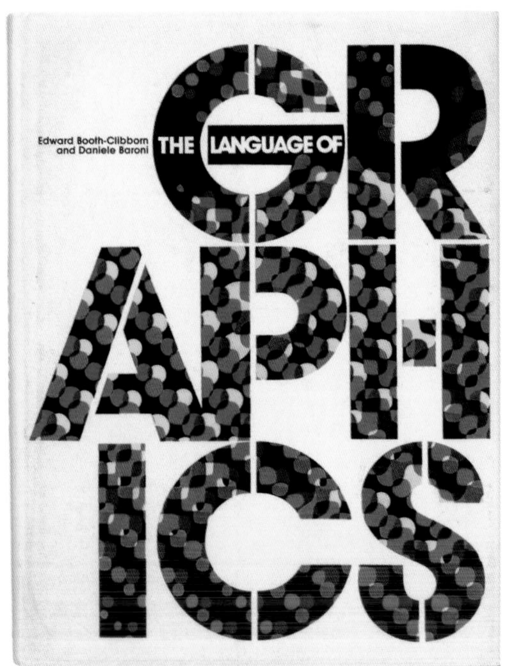

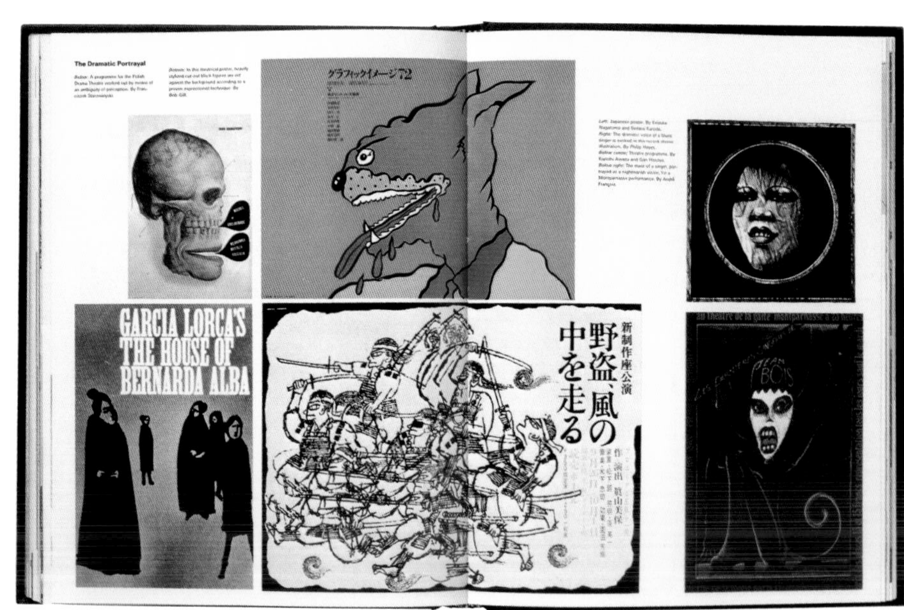

The Language of Graphics

Edward Booth-Clibborn, Daniele Baroni

Harry N. Abrams, New York, 1980
320 pages
272 × 210 mm (10.75 × 8.25 in)
Designed by Gabriele Marinazzi

The dense layout crams as many illustrations on to the page as possible – here 11 images fight for space on one spread.

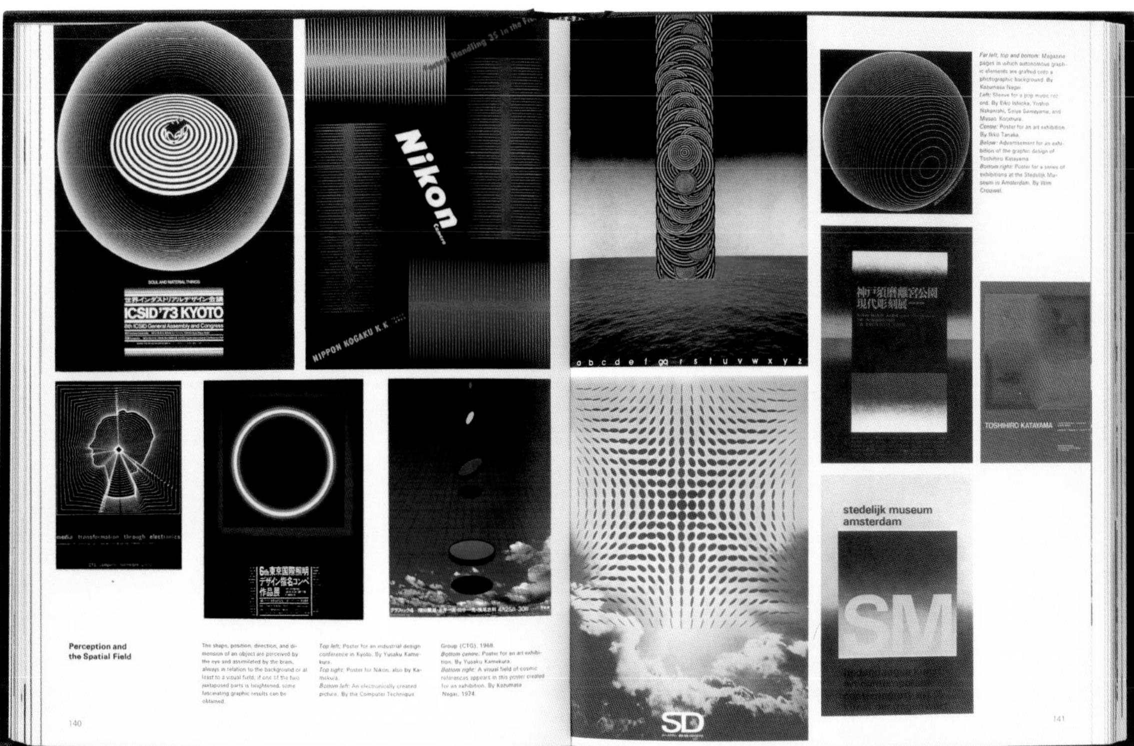

Compiled by Edward Booth-Clibborn, ex adman turned writer (and soon to be publisher), and Daniele Baroni, the Italian designer and writer, *The Language of Graphics* is a visual treat, packed with over 1000 illustrations and printed in sumptuous, supersaturated full colour.

Its strength is the breadth and wealth of imagery that it contains, taken from all periods of graphic design history and from across the globe. This imagery was originally published in a seven-volume series, *Graphic Design of the World*, produced by the Japanese company Kodansha between 1974 and 1976, and then repackaged as *Il Linguaggio della Grafica* by Italian publishers Arnoldo Mondadori in 1979.

The layout of the book appears haphazard: the images are placed and viewed in much the same way that people are exposed to the juxtaposition of graphic images in everyday life. Little space is wasted and, although the illustrations are grouped under themes, there seems to be a conscious effort not to make the layouts too tidy. Advertising and design sit side by side. Old and new share the same page.

Often neglected in design histories, illustration gets its own chapter, as do packaging and environmental graphics. Also touched upon for one of the first times is the then-emerging field of computer-generated imagery. A chapter at the beginning of the book is devoted to the origins of signs and symbols, and further chapters explore the role of the graphic image within sociology, strategy and psychology. The final chapter is a chronological history of graphic art from the Industrial Revolution to the mid-1970s.

A History of Graphic Design

Philip B. Meggs

Allen Lane,
Harmondsworth, 1983
514 pages
275 × 210 mm (10.75 × 8.25 in)
Designed by Paul Chevannes
Jacket designed by
Gerald Cinamon

'This chronicle of graphic design was written in the belief that if we understand the past, we will be better able to continue a cultural legacy of beautiful form and effective communication.' So writes the American designer Philip Meggs in the foreword to *A History of Graphic Design*.

When Meggs began teaching at the Virginia Commonwealth University in Richmond, Virginia, in 1968 it became obvious to him that graphic design students had no knowledge of the most basic history of what they were studying. Devising a series of lectures to fill this gap in their learning led in 1983 to the eventual publication by Van Nostrand Reinhold in the USA and by Penguin's hardback imprint, Allen Lane, in the UK of this landmark book. The first linear history of graphic design, it remains the pre-eminent work on the subject and is often the first title on a student's reading list.

The scope of *A History of Graphic Design* is impressive. The prologue starts in 15,000–10,000 BC with the Lascaux Caves in France and ends with the invention of movable type by Gutenberg in the fifteenth century. The next section, on printing and typography in Europe, leads up to one on the Industrial Revolution and nineteenth-century graphics. The final and largest section deals with the twentieth century and the evolution of modern graphic design.

Originally printed in black only, the book's success led to three subsequent revisions, in which colour reproductions were added and welcome wholesale changes were made to the layout. These editions also addressed Meggs's prophetic epilogue, which pointed to the advent of the computer and the inevitable effect it would have on graphic design.

The basic layout, black-and-white printing and thin, uncoated paper of this first edition give it the feel of a school textbook.

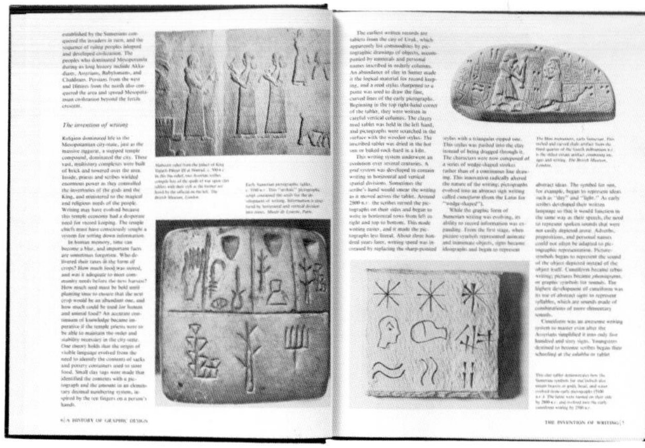

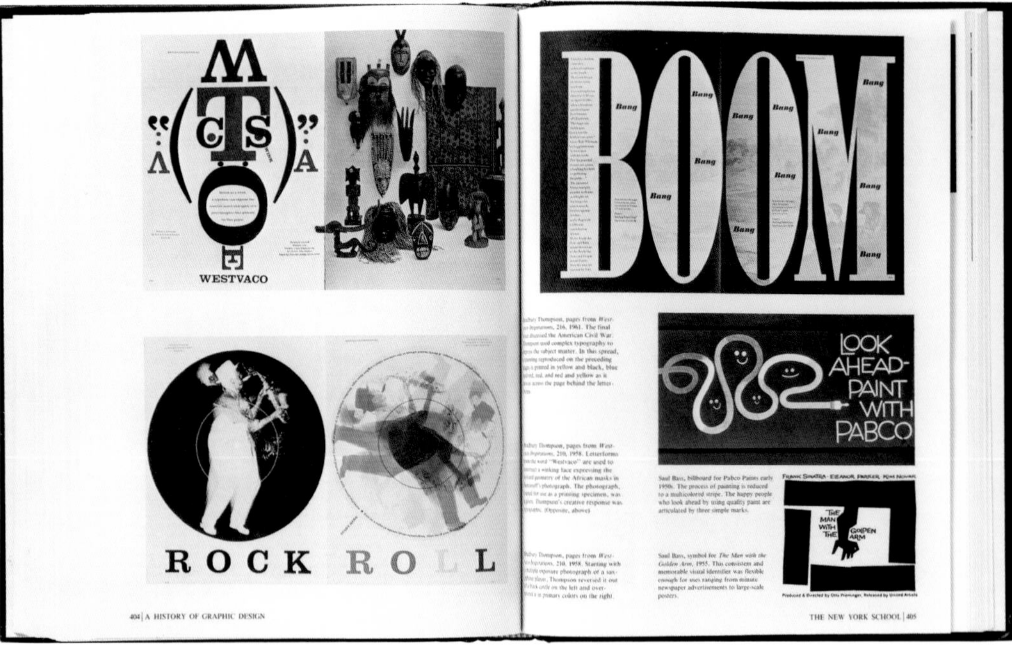

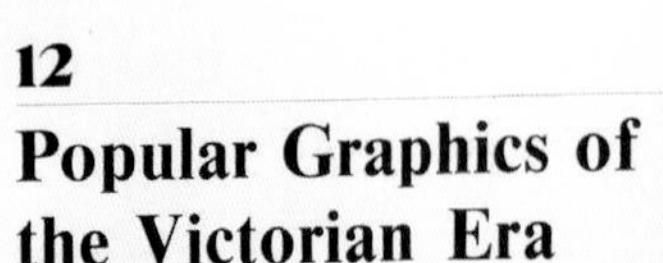

12

Popular Graphics of the Victorian Era

THE LONG REIGN OF VICTORIA (1819-1901), who became Queen of the United Kingdom of Great Britain and Ireland in 1837, spanned two-thirds of the nineteenth century and is called the Victorian Era. This was a time of strong moral and religious beliefs, proper social conventions, and optimism. "God's in his heaven, all's right with the world" was a popular motto. The Victorian period was an era in search of a style. Aesthetic confusion led to a number of often contradictory design styles and philosophies mixed together in a helter-skelter fashion. A taste for the Gothic, which suited the pious Victorians, was fostered by the English architect A. W. N. Pugin (1812-1852), who designed the ornamental details of the British House of Parliament. The first nineteenth-century designer to articulate a philosophy, Pugin defined design as a moral act which achieved the status of art through the designer's ideals and attitudes. Although he said that he looked to earlier periods—particularly Gothic—not for *style*, but for a *principle*, the net result of Pugin's influence was a wide mimicking of Gothic architecture, ornament, and letterforms.

Popular narrative and romantic painting of the Victorian Era was closely linked with the graphic pictorialism of chromolithographers including Louis Prang (1824-1909). Prang often commissioned art and held competitions to acquire subjects for use in his printed images. The English designer, author, and authority on color, Owen Jones (1809-1874) became a major design influence at mid-century. During his mid-twenties, Jones traveled to Spain and the Near East and made a systematic study of

180

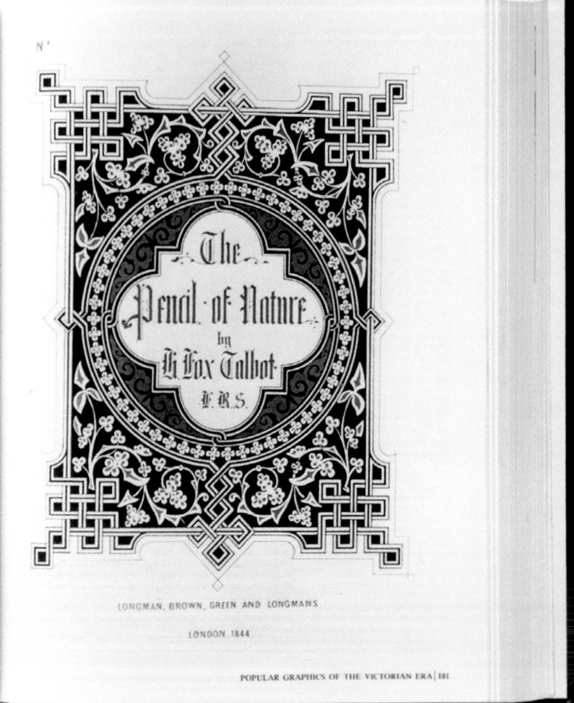

Title page, 1844. This title page demonstrates the eclectic confusion of the Victorian era. Medieval letterforms, Baroque plant forms, and geometric interlaces are combined into a dense symmetrical design.

POPULAR GRAPHICS OF THE VICTORIAN ERA | 181

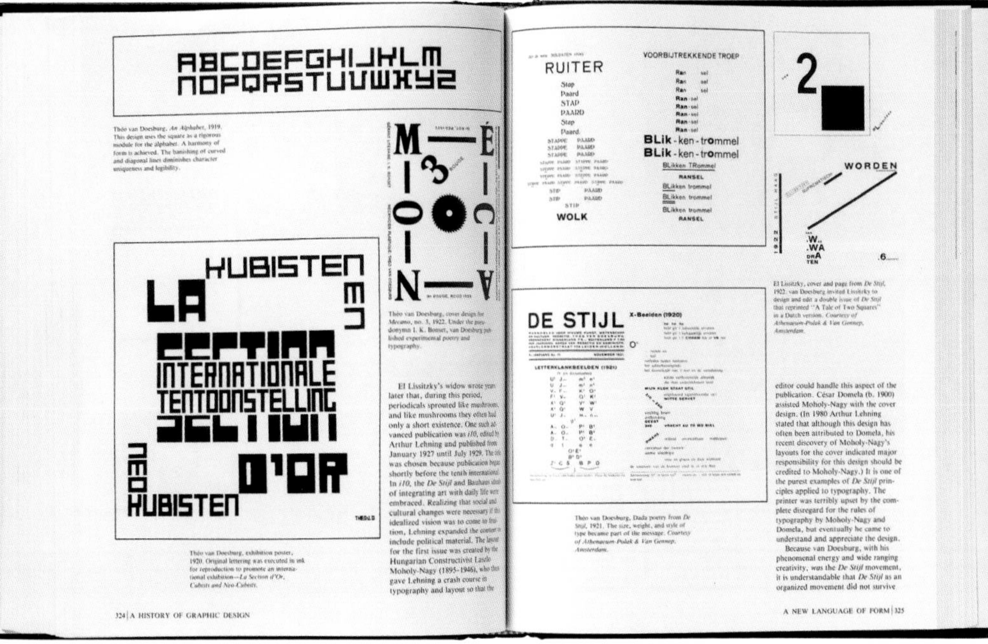

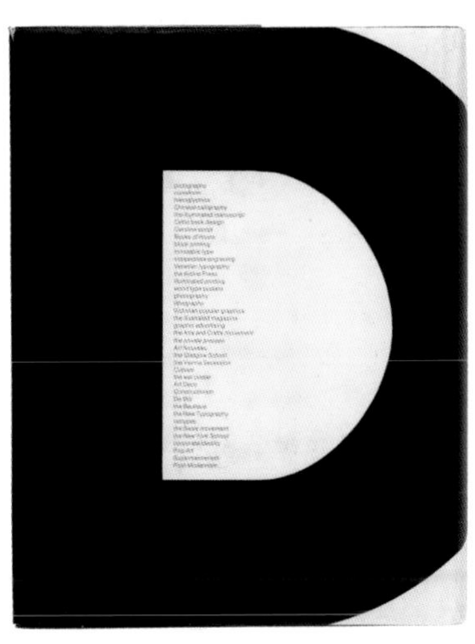

This cover of the UK edition has a bold cover with an extra large 'G' and 'D' placed on the front and back of the jacket respectively. It was designed by Gerald Cinamon at Penguin Books.

A History of Graphic Design, Philip B. Meggs, Allen Lane, Harmondsworth, 1983
Graphic Design: A Concise History, Richard Hollis, Thames & Hudson, London, 1994
Graphic Design in the Mechanical Age, Deborah Rothschild, Ellen Lupton, Darra Goldstein, Yale University Press, New Haven and London, 1998
Decoding Advertisements, Judith Williamson, Marion Boyars Publishers, London, 1994
Design Writing Research: Writing on Graphic Design, Ellen Lupton, J. Abbott Miller, Princeton Architectural Press, New York, 1996
Design Literacy: Understanding Graphic Design, Stephen Heller, Karen Pomeroy, Allworth Press, New York, 1997
Tibor Kalman: Perverse Optimist, Peter Hall, Michael Bierut (editors), Booth-Clibborn Editions, London, 1998
Paul Rand: A Designer's Art, Paul Rand, Yale University Press, New Haven and London, 1985
Sagmeister: Made You Look, Peter Hall, Booth-Clibborn Editions, London, 2001
The Art of Looking Sideways, Alan Fletcher, Phaidon Press, London, 2001

AULA IM BAUHAUS DESSAU

DAS NEUE MÖBEL

FÜR
WOHNUNGEN
BÜROS
SCHULEN
KINOS
KRANKENHÄUS
LÄDEN
THEATER
KAFFEES
RESTAURANTS

210

211

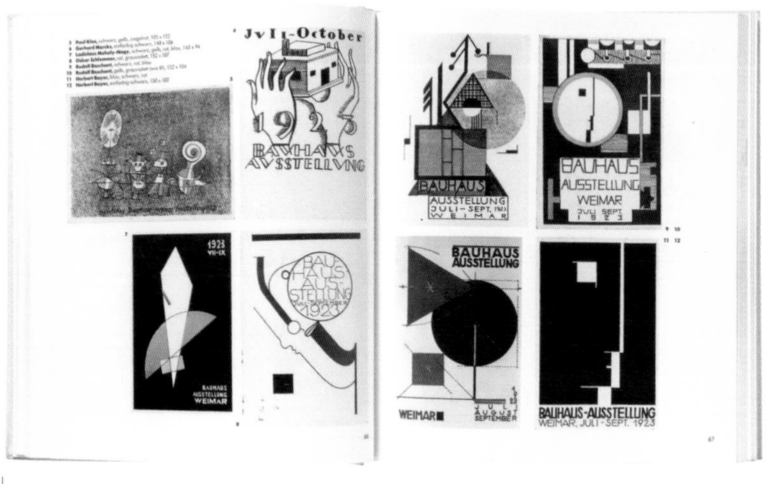

Early examples of Bauhaus typography and poster design.

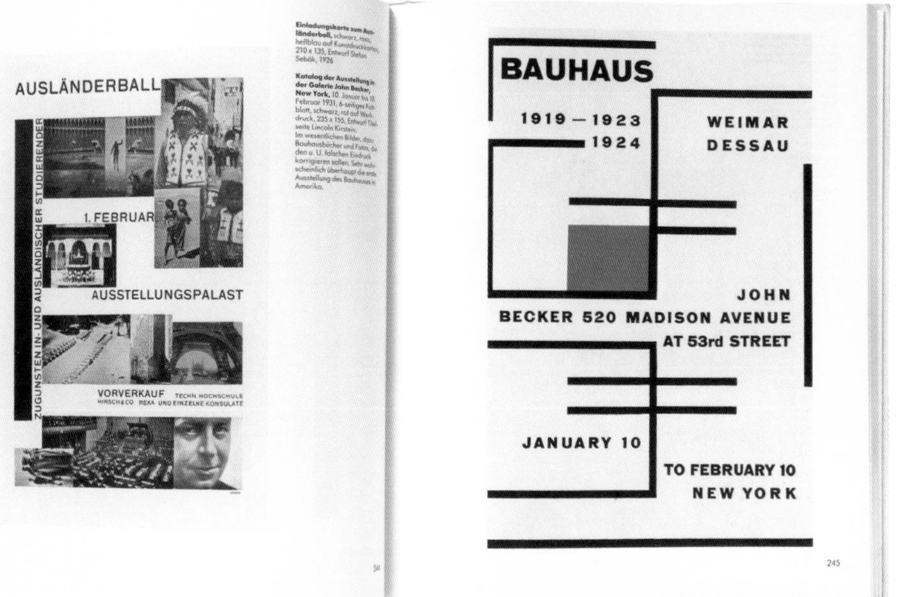

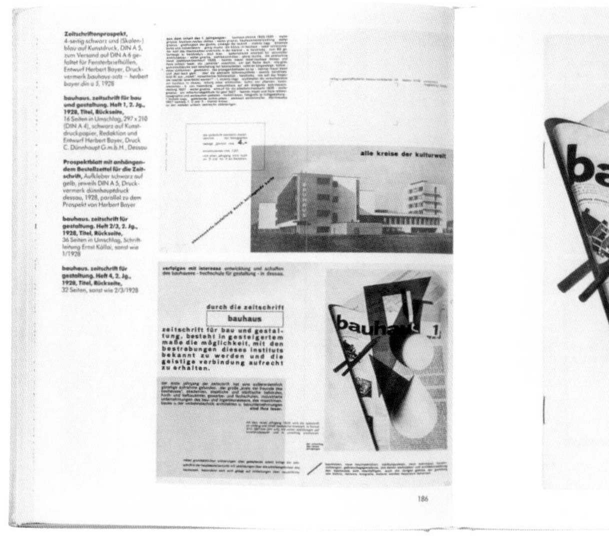

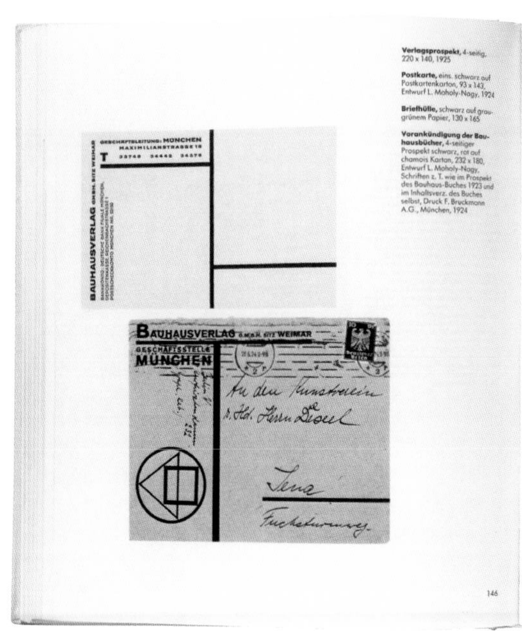

Bauhaus: Drucksachen, Typografie, Reklame

Gerd Fleischmann

Edition Marzona,
Dusseldorf, 1984
360 pages
280 × 235 mm (11 × 9.25 in)

The classic text on the Bauhaus is Hans Wingler's mighty book of the same name. Its slipcase with a large 'BAUHAUS' on the spine has pride of place on many a designer's bookshelf, often as confirmation of the owner's modernist credentials. This book by typographer Gerd Fleischmann (1939–) is smaller in scale, and highlights only one area of the famous design school's output, but is perhaps more relevant to the readers of this book. *Bauhaus: Drucksachen, Typografie, Reklame* translates as 'Bauhaus: Printed Matter, Typography, Advertising' and is an extensive study of the graphic design produced by the students and staff at the Bauhaus.

The many illustrations range from posters, books, magazines, prospectuses and catalogues to more mundane items such as internal forms and letterheads. They are arranged in a trio of sections that cover the Bauhaus in Weimar (1919–25), Dessau (1925–32) and Berlin (1932–33), largely showcasing the classic characteristics of Bauhaus typography, defined by the use of lower-case sans serif type in geometric layouts, emphasized by printed rules and contrasting sizes of letters.

A final section then divides into studies of the work of individual designers at the Bauhaus, such as Max Bill, László Moholy-Nagy, Xanti Schawinsky, Joost Schmidt and Studio Z. It includes both designs made at the Bauhaus and works that date from after the school's closure in 1933, when many of the designers had emigrated to other European countries or America.

The text is in German only, and there are contemporary essays at the beginning of the book. These include writings by Josef Albers, Herbert Bayer and others. An appendix includes more written source material. All the illustrations are captioned in detail to provide information on size, material, colour and, where possible, the designer.

Typography: When Who How
Friedrich Friedl, Nicolaus Ott, Bernard Stein
Könemann Verlagsgesellschaft, Cologne, 1998
592 pages
300 × 240 mm (11.75 × 9.5 in)
Designed by Ott + Stein

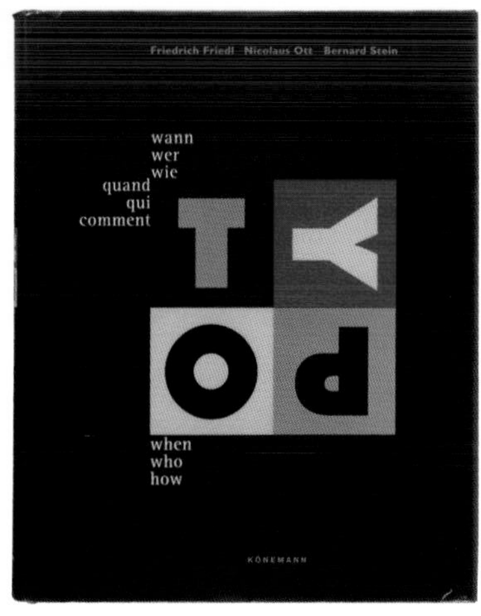

Described in the sleeve notes as a 'dictionary of the designed word', this is a mighty piece of reference. Despite its size and its 2000 illustrations, the authors view it as only a 'beginning' – the start of the task of cataloguing the history of typography from the first written forms to modern-day digital designs.

There are three main chapters. 'When' works back from the present day to 3000 BC, and each spread describes different eras in typographic history. 'Who' is an alphabetical listing of practitioners: designers, typographers, type designers, letterers and artists. Biographical details and information on any publications are supported by illustrations of their work. 'How' sets out the evolution of the technology and tools that have shaped the display of letters and words.

A consistent layout throughout the book, with a central area for illustrative material, allows for the trilingual text to be displayed: German on the top, English at the bottom and French to the left and right. The visual elements are exceptionally well sourced, and provide unique juxtapositions in the alphabetically arranged 'Who' chapter.

Of the editors, Nicolaus Ott and Bernard Stein run their own Berlin-based studio, Ott + Stein, and Friedrich Friedl is professor of typography at the Hochschule für Gestaltung in Offenbach am Main.

A spread from the 'Who' section featuring the work of the Cuban designer Félix Beltrán, German typographer Georg Belwe and American type designer Ed Benguiat. Examples of their work are contained in the central panel. Where the designers are responsible for typefaces, these are shown in a standard format grid.

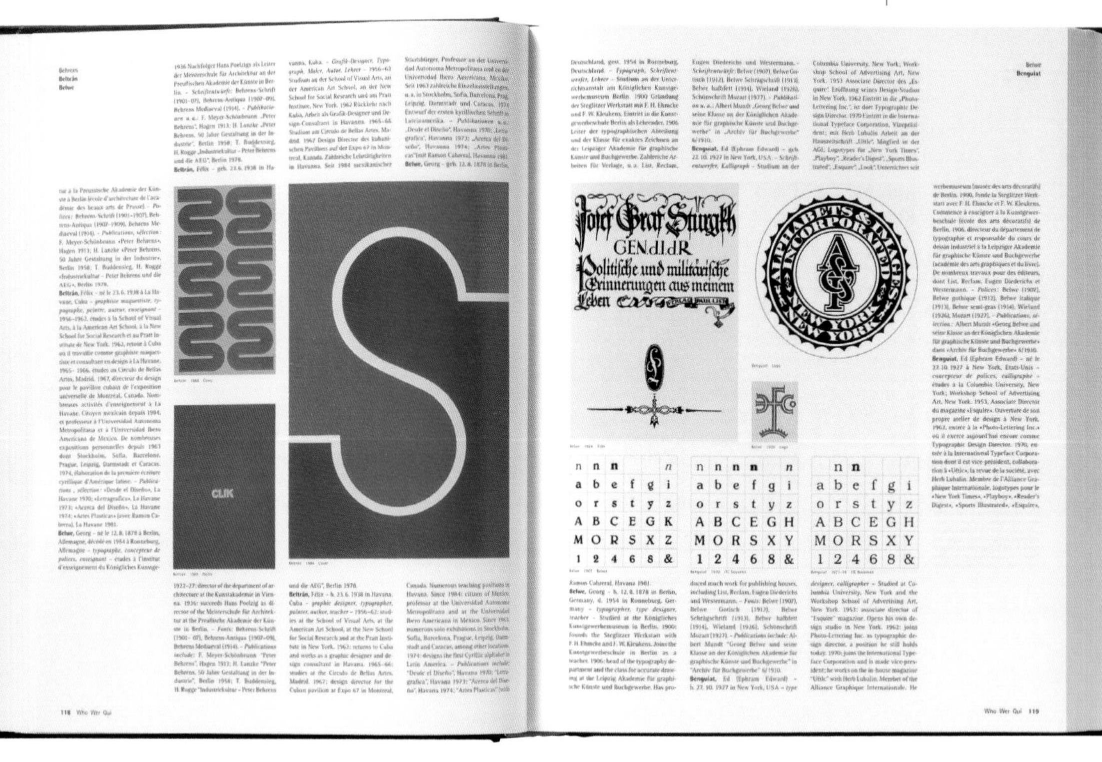

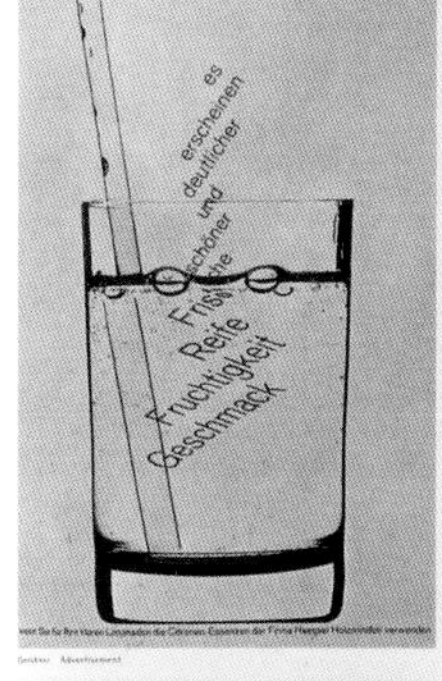

A spread from the 'When' section on the 'International Typographic Style'. Text in German (top), French (left and right) and English (bottom) surrounds the central area of illustrations.

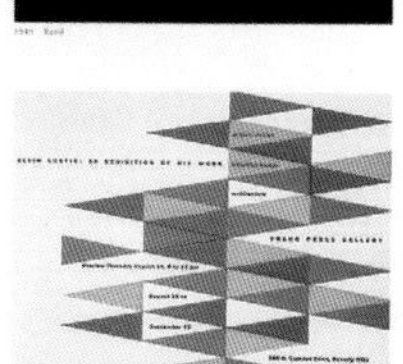

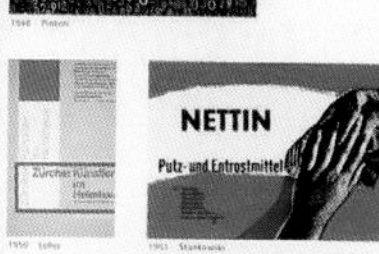

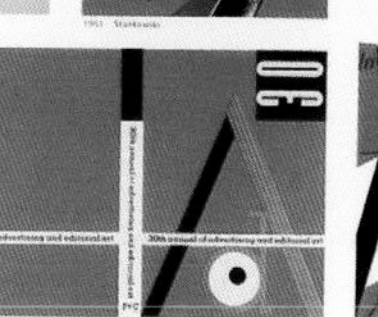

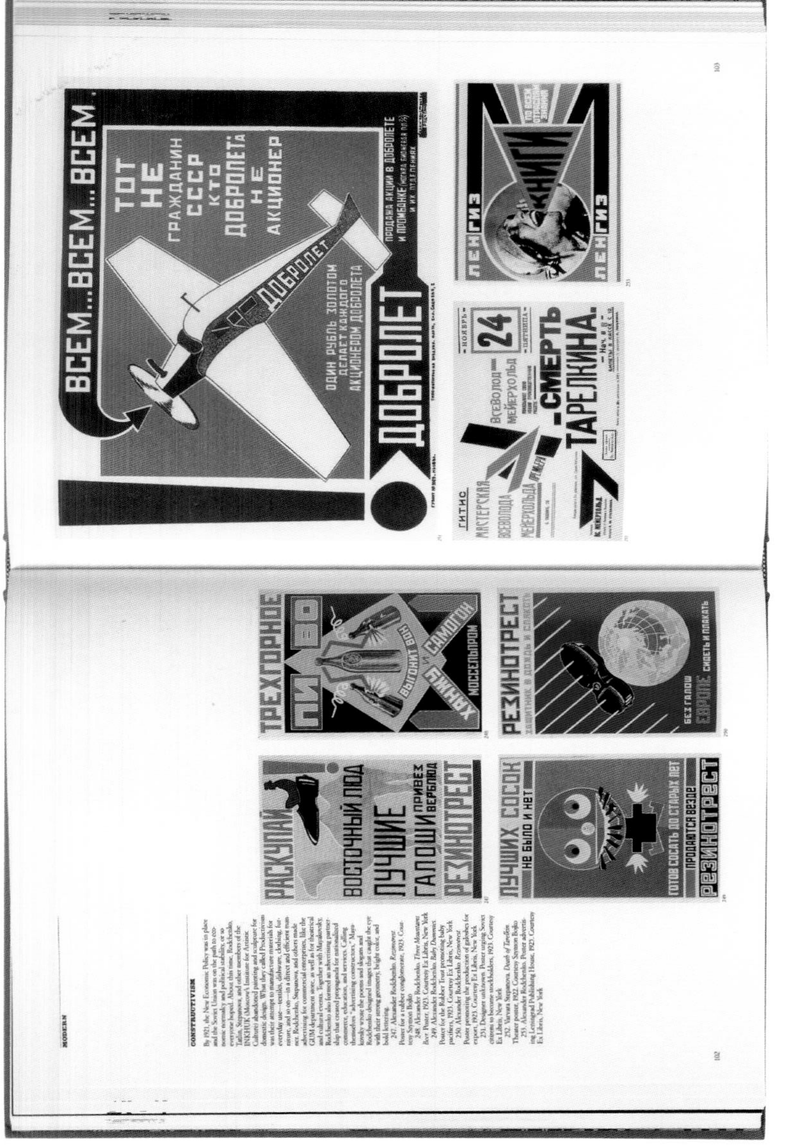

A spread on psychedelia in the 'Late Modern' chapter. In the top left corner is an archetypal piece of decoration and a capital 'A'. The concise text and captions are contained in one column, leaving space for the illustrations.

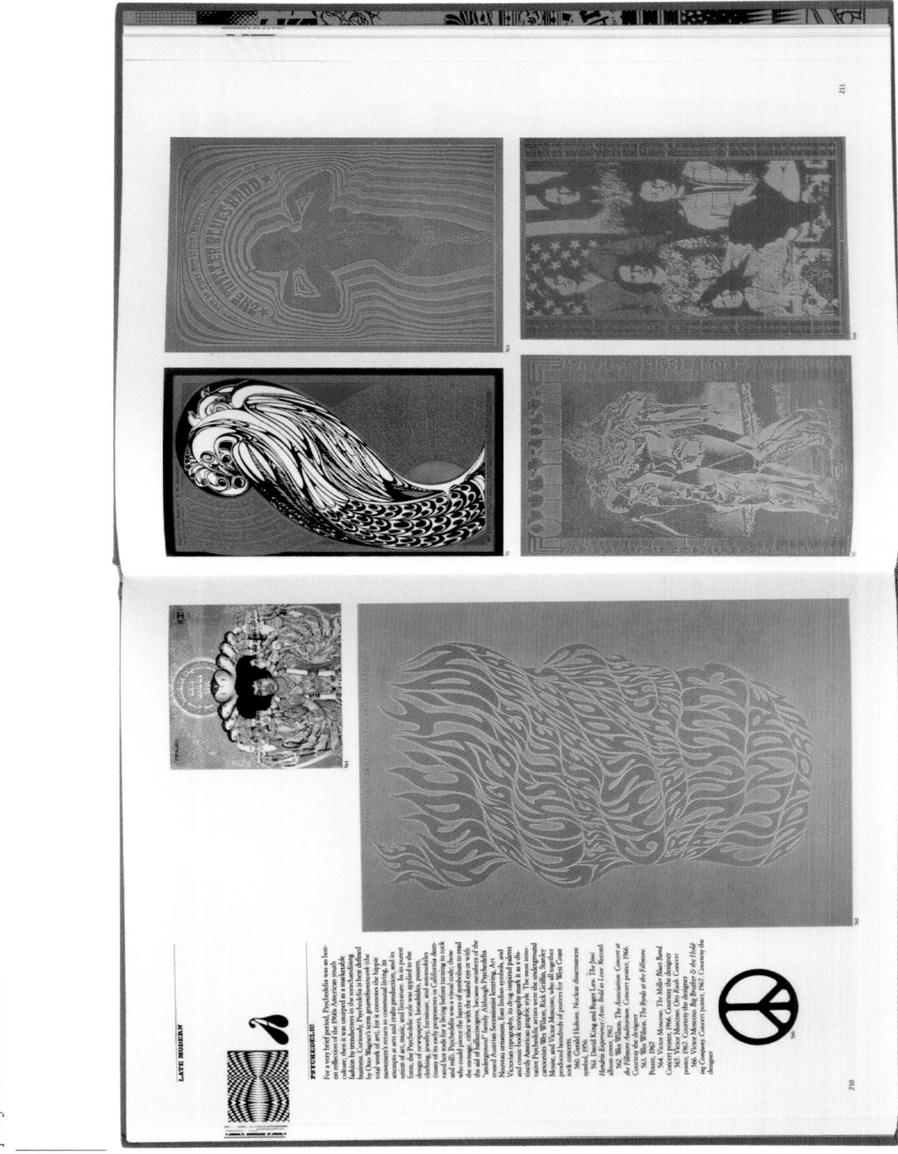

Ex Libris
Gabriele Wilson

By its Cover: Modern American Book Cover Design, Ned Drew, Princeton Architectural Press, New York, 2005
Front Cover: Great Book Jacket and Cover Design, Alan Powers, Mitchell Beazley, London, 2001
Classic Book Jackets: The Design Legacy of George Salter, Milton Glaser, Thomas Hansen, Princeton Architectural Press, New York, 2005
Penguin by Design: A Cover Story 1935–2005, Phil Baines, Allen Lane, Harmondsworth, 2005
Graphic Styles, Steven Heller, Seymour Chwast, Harry N. Abrams, New York, 1988
A Smile in the Mind, Beryl McAlhone, David Stuart, Phaidon Press, London, 1996
Typography: When Who How, Friedrich Friedl, Nicolaus Ott, Bernard Stein, Könemann Verlagsgesellschaf, Cologne, 1998
Alexey Brodovitch, Gabriel Bauret, Assouline, Paris, 1998
Printed Matter, Robin Kinross, Jaap van Triest, Karel Martens (editors), Hyphen Press, London, 1996
Paul Rand: A Designer's Art, Paul Rand, Yale University Press, New Haven and London, 1985

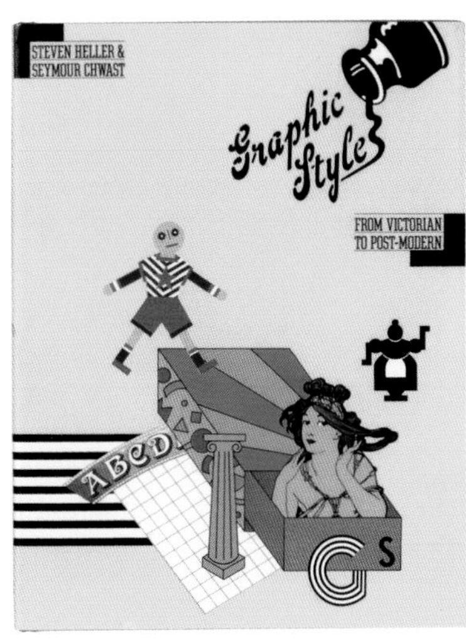

Graphic Styles
From Victorian to Post-Modern
Steven Heller, Seymour Chwast
Harry N. Abrams, New York, 1988
240 pages
292 × 220 mm (11.5 × 8.5 in)
Designed by Seymour Chwast

Graphic Styles is a history not of individuals but of surface. Its interest is in the graphic traits and mannerisms that define particular stylistic movements in the history of printed communications. Although this approach is used regularly in the history of art, this was the first time an attempt had be made to apply it to graphic design.

The book runs in chronological order and is divided into 11 chapters, beginning with the Victorian era and finishing with postmodernism. Each of these chapters is subdivided into sections that allow for more detailed analysis of 48 identifiable styles, highlighting different national trends and artistic movements. The chapters include 'Art Nouveau', 'Modern' (which includes many twentieth-century avant-garde styles), 'Art Deco' and 'Late Modern'. A chapter on 'Heroic Realism' demonstrates how the Soviet Union and National Socialist Germany used graphic design in their propaganda. A useful timeline at the beginning of the book shows the periods of each graphic style and their relationships to other styles over time, as well as important historical and cultural dates.

Graphic Styles has been thoroughly researched and contains over 700 images culled from private and public collections. There is an effort to look beyond design icons and concentrate on examples that typify an era. Many illustrations are ephemera by anonymous designers: magazine covers, packaging, propaganda and advertising.

The designer (and co-author) Seymour Chwast (1931–) has added a representative cap 'A' with an example of decoration as an introduction to each style. His simple layout maximizes the space available for the rich grouping of images on each spread.

Steven Heller co-authored a series with Louise Fili on Art Deco graphics, which has been published as the single volume Euro Deco *(Chronicle, San Francisco, 2004; Thames & Hudson, London, 2004).*

Graphic Design: A Concise History

Richard Hollis

Thames & Hudson, London, 1994
Revised edition, 2001
Reprint (pictured), 2005
224 pages
210 × 148 mm (8.25 × 5.75 in)
Designed by Richard Hollis

Graphic Design: A Concise History is small enough to be carried around all day. That it is so small does not mean its author, the designer and writer Richard Hollis (1934–), left anything out of his history. Quite the opposite: the book is a thorough examination of its subject area.

Hollis begins with a chapter on 'The Art Poster' at the end of the nineteenth century, when printers handed over the design of layouts to artists, then maps out avant-garde developments in the early twentieth century, and the emergence of modernism in both Europe and the United States, before studying post-Second World War design across the globe. Many chapters are divided geographically, acknowledging the distinct regional differences that have defined the evolution of graphic design.

The text is annotated with hundreds of black-and-white thumbnail illustrations placed in the margins or sandwiched in the text. Designed for reference only, these work in the same way as a slide presentation, encouraging further study. Captioning is minimal, listing project name, item description, year and designer. The only colour reproductions are in one 16-page section inserted at the end of the first chapter, which describes important facets in the history of graphic design.

Hollis's writing is taut and his interest infectious; important figures, pivotal moments, connections and key pieces are clearly described, and his design, integrating text and small images, engages the reader's attention. Later editions have been expanded to reflect the significant changes that have taken place in graphic design since the book was first published. Hollis has since written the definitive guide to the development of the 'International Style' originating in Switzerland from 1920 to 1965, *Swiss Graphic Design* (Laurence King Publishing, London, 2006).

Designed for reference, the layouts incorporate images embedded in the text and in the margins.

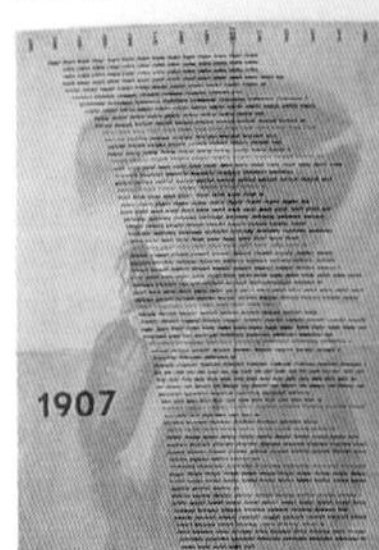

Graphic Design: A Concise History *is part of the 'World of Art' series. Of note for graphic designers is* Art Without Boundaries: 1950–1970 *by Gerald Woods, Philip Thompson and John Williams (Thames & Hudson, London, 1972) on the blurred line between art and design.*

Variants of Modernism in Europe

an imaginative use of graphic elements. His career shows stages of development like that of an artist. He trained as an architect, was a Futurist painter in the 1920s and became a graphic designer in the 1930s, making the most advanced use of both photography and technical drawing, the two means he employed to extend the scope of graphic expression. He was an early user of photograms. These provided abstract images that evoked chemical and physical processes. By laying objects like syringes or phials on photographic paper, Grignani gave the ordinary paraphernalia of medical treatment an unexpected elegance. As art director of the Dompé company magazine, *Bellezza d'Italia*, he showed that sophistication need not consist of the obvious delicacy of Bodoni: he gave it a robust mid-twentieth-century *Bd'I* for its symbol (see p.198).

Grignani also designed a logotype of initials for Alfieri and Lacroix. The firm gave Grignani the opportunity to experiment in a series of advertisements in the printing trade press. Addressed to his fellow designers, the message was, month after month, 'Watch me. See what I can do.' He advertised aspects of graphic design and linked them to Alfieri and Lacroix with didactic statements like

speed alters graphics
speed alters colour
speed alters vv ii ss ii oo nn

and

where does a sign live?
Not within the arc of space granted it
nor in its own architecture
cut off by the conventions of graphics.

It lives through its ability to bring energy
to the scene of dialectical play
which is a performance, a vivid dialogue . . .

After exhausting the conventional techniques of cut-out half-tones, flat colour and type reversed out of solid colour or black to show white, which he did in the most dramatic manner, Grignani began his improvisations. At first, he used lettering abstractly, as shapes and not as signs. Often he distorted them through water or irregularly patterned glass, an

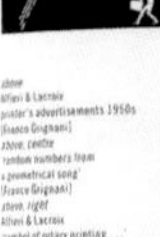

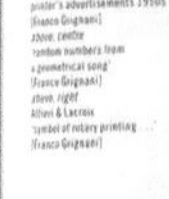

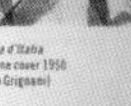

144

idea that Huber had used in the lettering of a book cover in 1945. Grignani's work often anticipates Optical Art of the 1960s, but another precedent is the advertising for a family engineering concern designed by its vice-president, Antonio Pellizzari. Grignani made photographic images flat by 'posterization'; that is, he knocked out the middle tones so that the images were either light or shadow, and the shadows decoration, a process that became one of the most over-used techniques of the following decade. Photographing striped and chequered material allowed Grignani to play with spatial illusion. He later experimented with lettering and images projected onto three-dimensional objects and conjured with space by distortions in complex geometrical perspectives.

Grignani believed that the creative person in Italy, unlike in America, 'is often his own art director, as well as designer, photographer, technical draughtsman and retoucher.' He thought that working as part of a team could inhibit the designer's inventiveness. It was more usual in Italy than elsewhere for designers to work in more than one field. Some made important contributions in several specializations. Marcello Nizzoli, for example, had become art director for Olivetti in 1938; and after the war the typewriters he designed for the company had an international success. Typically versatile, too, were Bruno Munari (see p.43) and Enzo Mari, both of them interested in three-dimensional design. Munari's 1960 poster, which brought together more than thirty printed versions of the Campari name on a red background, was almost unique in its use of collage for consumer advertising. In the 1960s Munari also worked with Huber in designing books for the publishers Einaudi, emphasizing

Italy and the Milanese Style

145

The Designer and the Art Director

The Man with the Golden Arm poster and title sequence 1955 [Saul Bass]

Anatomy of a Murder 1959 *Exodus* 1960 film logotypes [Saul Bass]

techniques. From the simplest paper cut-out to the most sophisticated studio photography, he interpreted the essence of each film in an arresting emblem.

Working on advertisements for *The Man with the Golden Arm*, he and Preminger asked each other, 'Why not make it move?' So, as well as advertisements, Bass moved on to designing title sequences, using the same techniques of visual metaphor. This was a new, hybrid medium. Graphics were transformed when in movement and reinforced by sound. The credit titles of *The Man with the Golden Arm* are a straightforward animation of the publicity graphics, but by the time he made the sequence for *Walk on the Wild Side* in 1962, the metaphor was entirely conceived as live-action film. Charles Eames, too, moved towards film, but by another route. In 1953 he used a full range of graphics in a twenty-minute film that explained communications theory.

A Communications Primer film 1953 [Charles Eames]

Called *A Communications Primer*, its technique was a development of the methods that Eames had experimented with in multiple-screen slide shows, combining diagrams, animation, still photographs and live action with a voice-over by Eames himself. It was the forerunner of a series of films and multi-media presentations that Eames produced during the following twenty-five years. Mostly popularizing scientific ideas and history, they often accompanied exhibitions. American ideas were having a significant impact outside the United States. Eames's successor to the *Communications Primer* was *The Information Machine*, an animated film sponsored by IBM for the Brussels World Fair in 1958, where the display

122

in the American pavilion was designed by a newly formed partnership, Brownjohn, Chermayeff & Geismar. It comprised fragments of the American environment, including parts of a giant Pepsi-Cola sign and pedestrian traffic signals.

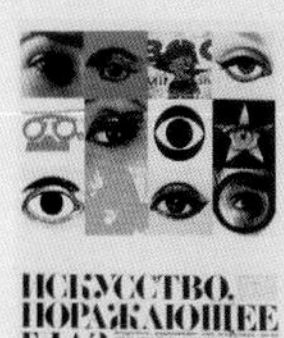

Graphic signs became the way in which the United States communicated its character to the outside world during the period of the Cold War. In 1959, the Russian-language magazine *Amerika*, distributed by the United States Information Agency in the Soviet Union, devoted an issue to the American graphic arts, because 'so much of the vitality and spirit of this country is expressed in graphics'. As designer and writer of the issue called 'Carnival of the Eye' the New York advertising designer Herb Lubalin provided a useful summary: 'At the heart of American graphics is the idea, the concept. All else – photography, typography, illustration, design – is its handmaiden.' Lubalin's career exemplifies a particularly American type of graphic design and its development.

Like many of the designers whose careers began before the Second World War, Lubalin had worked for the 1939 World's Fair. He worked in advertising agencies, since 1945 at Sudler & Hennessey, who specialized in pharmaceutical products. Here, Lubalin's first contribution was in using words as images. He stretched the limits of metal typesetting by cutting proofs, re-spacing, and by an attention to details in a way described in a book called simply *typography*, published in 1961. Its author was Aaron Burns, a designer who was a director of The Composing Room, a typesetting firm which, apart from its exhibition space, published the pre-war *PM* magazine and its successor *A-D*. The enthusiastic Burns introduced designers to new typefaces and in 1960 he produced four small booklets: with Lester Beall (on cars), with Brownjohn, Chermayeff & Geismar (on New York), with Gene Federico (on apples) and with Lubalin (on jazz). These were the mature expression of modern graphic design in the United States. (They aroused much excitement in Europe when reprinted in the German print trade magazine *Der Druckspiegel*.) By now a vernacular of words and images was used with wit and assurance, serviced by a graphic arts industry that supplied photography, typography and printing of expert craftsmanship.

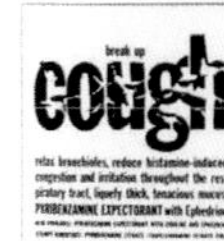

The United States 1945 to the 1960s

123

Anthologies

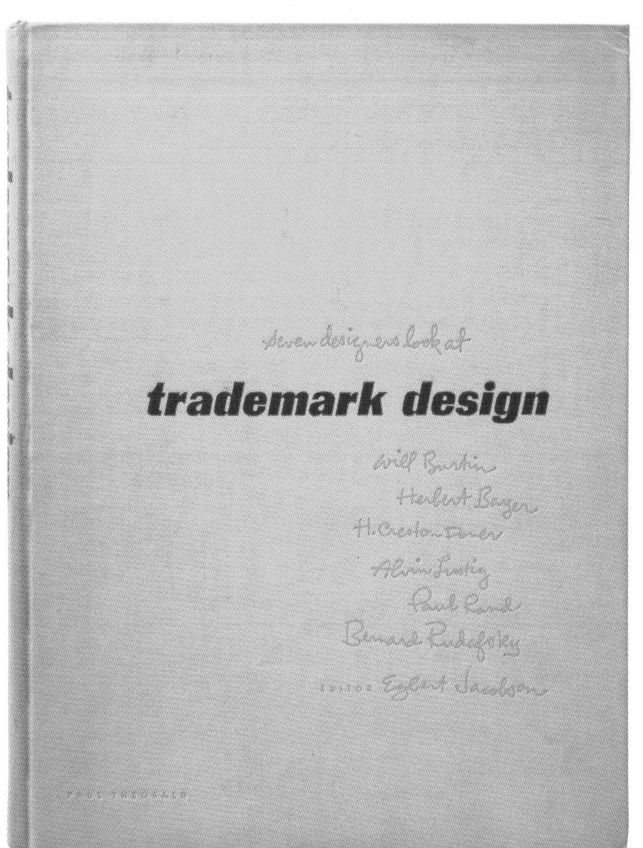

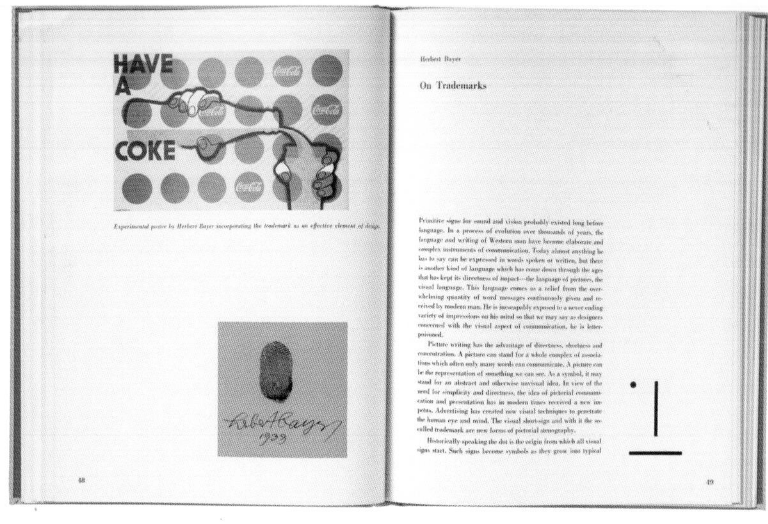

Experimental poster by Herbert Bayer incorporating the trademark as an effective element of design.

Herbert Bayer 1939

Herbert Bayer

On Trademarks

Primitive signs for sound and vision probably existed long before language. In a process of evolution over thousands of years, the language and writing of Western man have become elaborate and complex instruments of communication. Today almost anything he has to say can be expressed in words spoken or written, but there is another kind of language which has come down through the ages that has kept its directness of impact—the language of pictures, the visual language. This language comes as a relief from the overwhelming quantity of word messages continuously given and received by modern man. He is inescapably exposed to a never ending variety of impressions on his mind so that we may say as designers concerned with the visual aspect of communication, he is letter-poisoned.

Picture writing has the advantage of directness, shortness and concentration. A picture can stand for a whole complex of associations which often only many words can communicate. A picture can be the representation of something we can see. As a symbol, it may stand for an abstract and otherwise unvisual idea. In view of the need for simplicity and directness, the idea of pictorial communication and presentation has in modern times received a new impetus. Advertising has created new visual techniques to penetrate the human eye and mind. The visual short-sign and with it the so-called trademark are new forms of pictorial stenography.

Historically speaking the dot is the origin from which all visual signs start. Such signs become symbols as they grow into typical

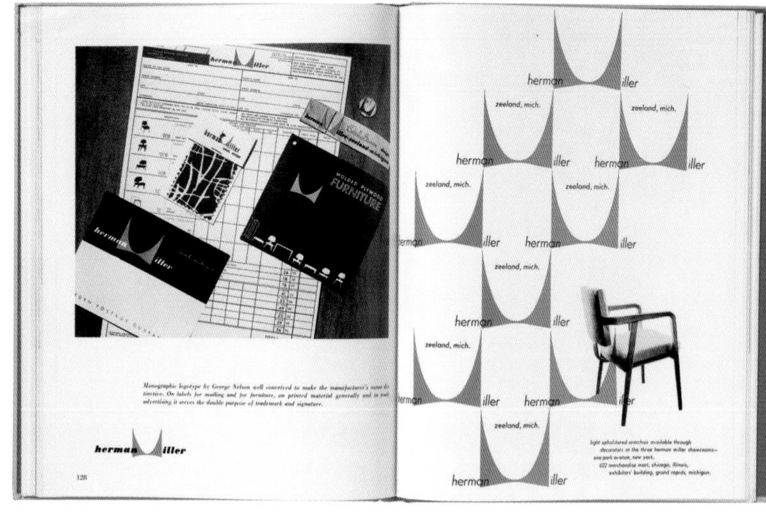

Monographic logotype by George Nelson well conceived to make the manufacturer's name distinctive. On labels for mailing and for furniture, on printed material generally and in [illegible] advertising it serves the double purpose of trademark and signature.

herman miller

128

light upholstered armchair available through decorators at the three herman miller showrooms— one park avenue, new york, 622 merchandise mart, chicago, illinois, exhibitors' building, grand rapids, michigan.

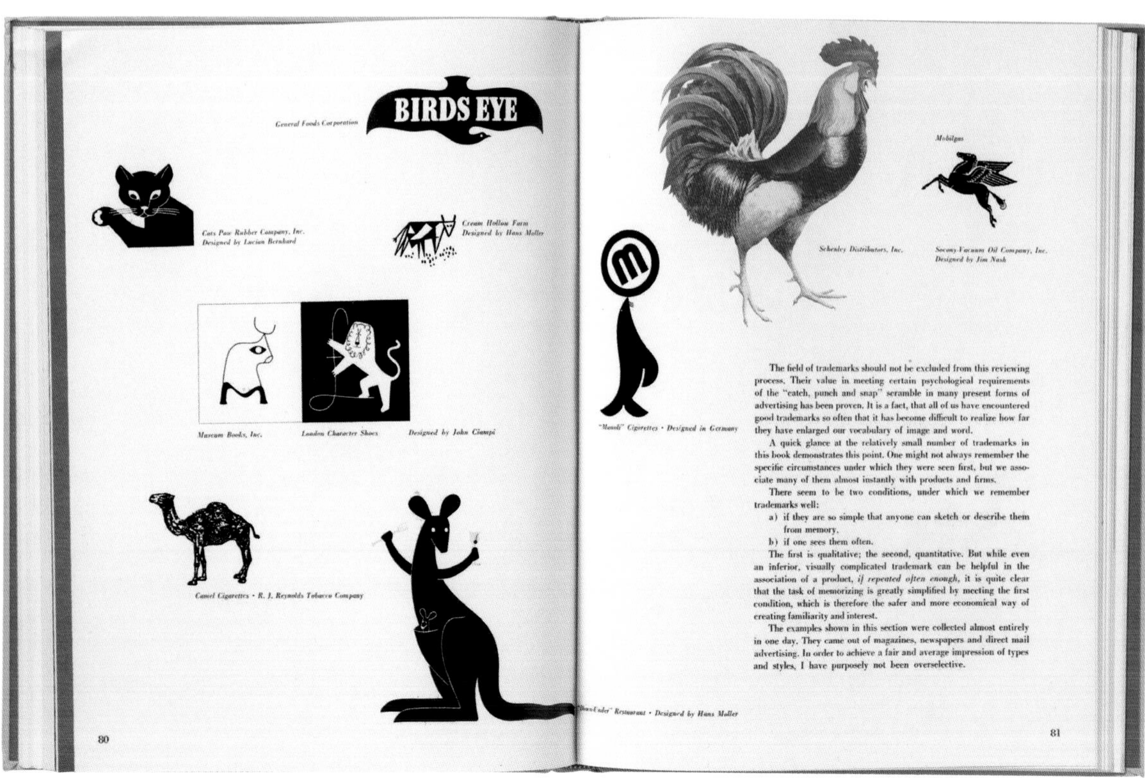

General Foods Corporation

Cats Paw Rubber Company, Inc.
Designed by Lucian Bernhard

Cream Hollow Farm
Designed by Hans Moller

Museum Books, Inc. London Character Shoes Designed by John Ciampi

Camel Cigarettes • R. J. Reynolds Tobacco Company

"Down Under" Restaurant • Designed by Hans Moller

80

Mobilgas

Schenley Distributors, Inc.

Socony-Vacuum Oil Company, Inc.
Designed by Jim Nash

"Manoli" Cigarettes • Designed in Germany

The field of trademarks should not be excluded from this reviewing process. Their value in meeting certain psychological requirements of the "catch, punch and snap" scramble in many present forms of advertising has been proven. It is a fact, that all of us have encountered good trademarks so often that it has become difficult to realize how far they have enlarged our vocabulary of image and word.

A quick glance at the relatively small number of trademarks in this book demonstrates this point. One might not always remember the specific circumstances under which they were seen first, but we associate many of them almost instantly with products and firms.

There seem to be two conditions, under which we remember trademarks well:

a) if they are so simple that anyone can sketch or describe them from memory.

b) if one sees them often.

The first is qualitative; the second, quantitative. But while even an inferior, visually complicated trademark can be helpful in the association of a product, *if repeated often enough,* it is quite clear that the task of memorizing is greatly simplified by meeting the first condition, which is therefore the safer and more economical way of creating familiarity and interest.

The examples shown in this section were collected almost entirely in one day. They came out of magazines, newspapers and direct mail advertising. In order to achieve a fair and average impression of types and styles, I have purposely not been overselective.

81

Pages from Will Burtin's study of trademarks. The work of Burtin and other American modernists can be found in R. Roger Remington and Barbara J. Hodik's Nine Pioneers in American Graphic Design, *MIT Press, Cambridge, Mass., 1989.*

Seven Designers Look at Trademark Design

Egbert Jacobson (editor)
Paul Theobald, Chicago, 1952
186 pages
280 × 213 mm (11 × 8.375 in)

A spread of signatures of French kings in an essay by Bernard Rudofsky on the early forms of trademarks. Also included in this chapter are cattle earmarks in Madagascar, masons' marks from ancient Greece up to the seventeenth century, and fifteenth-century French watermarks.

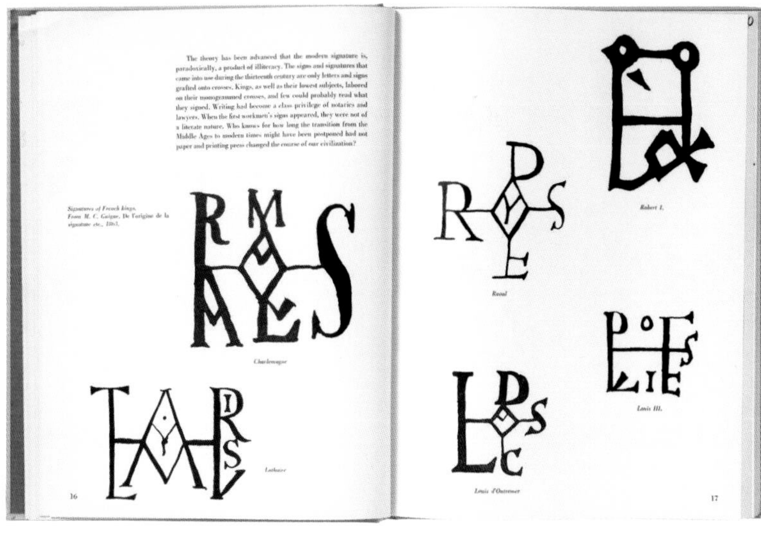

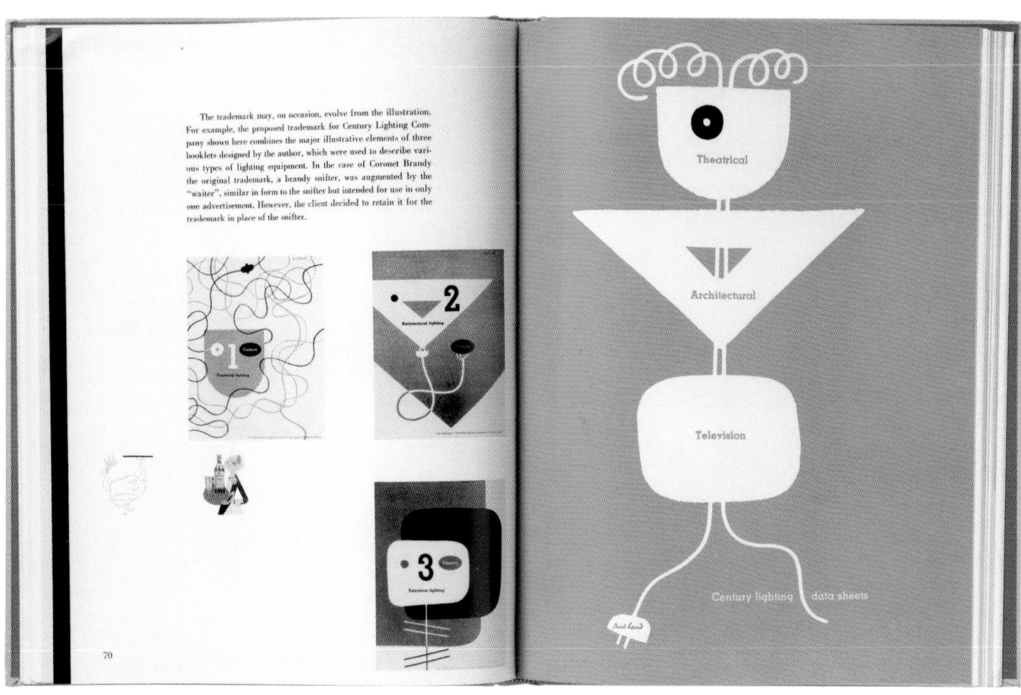

The essays in this anthology are by important creative figures in post-Second World War America. They range from historical and critical studies on trademark design to more practical lessons about form and application, as well as a chapter with samples of contemporary usage.

Seven Designers Look at Trademark Design starts with a study of the origins of trademarks by the Austrian émigré Bernard Rudofsky, a designer, architect, fashion designer and exhibition curator. Another Austrian, Herbert Bayer, the consummate designer, examines types of trademark, and notes that any 'design element' can eventually become one – even 'a badly designed mark can become valuable through proper use, and a good mark can fail by insufficient exploitation'.

Two American modernists, Alvin Lustig and Paul Rand, look at the design of trademarks. Lustig shows a small selection of his own work, from geometrically inspired to figurative forms. In 'The Trademark as an Illustrative Device' Rand uses his own designs for Disney Hatmaker and Century Lighting Company to show how to develop a visual language around a trademark.

Will Burtin, a German émigré, analyzes trademarks through methodical research, with particular reference to the pharmaceutical firm The Upjohn Company, for whom he created graphics and exhibition designs. H. Creston Doner, an industrial designer, writes about how the L-O-F Glass Company used its trademark across its product line.

Egbert Jacobson, the art director at the Container Corporation and the editor of this anthology, contributes an essay on the psychology of graphic forms. He also assembled the chapter showcasing the best of American trademark design, which is notable for the work of Herbert Matter at Knoll, George Nelson at Herman Miller and the variable trademarks of publishers Random House and Knopf – the latter's famous borzoi device is taken to its extreme by Paul Rand with his simplification of the mark to a couple of lines.

Polski Plakat Filmowy

Tadeusz Kowalski (editor)

Filmowa Agencja Wydawnicza, Warsaw, 1957
150 pages
285 × 200 mm (11.25 × 7.875 in)
Designed by Tadeusz Kowalski

The Polish poster stands almost in isolation as a graphic art form. Fenced off from the Western world, the tradition of the poster or graphic artist remained intact after the Second World War, and was fostered by Poland's state publishing agency, Wydawnictwo Artystyczno-Graficzne. The posters were widely distributed and promoted as a form of contemporary art, part of a programme of artistic education for the masses; over 200 were commissioned each year.

Distinguished by their illustrative and figurative approach, with predominantly hand-drawn lettering, the posters gave their creators the opportunity to develop distinctive individualistic styles. *Polski Plakat Filmowy* ('The Polish Film Poster') – here with a German jacket – was published by the Polish Film Agency, with text in Polish, French, Russian, English and German, and shows the work of 49 artists from 1946 to 1957. The book's lively layout and many colour reproductions make for a striking display of poster art. The artists are in alphabetical order and include all the foremost proponents of Polish film poster art, among others Mieczyslaw Berman, Roman Cieslewicz, Jan Lenica, Eryk Lipinski, Henryk Tomaszewski and Tadeusz Trepkowski.

While most of the posters are for Polish films, there are many designed for films made in other communist bloc countries and some from the West, which are very different to the posters for their original release. Many avoided the trappings of commercialism; in his introduction the designer Jan Lenica claimed the posters had 'completely done away with the "sentimental" and "potboiler" style, creating at once … a new poetry of the film poster'.

There is a mixture of colour and black-and-white images on the pages. The reproduction quality is good but the paper stock is poor.

A spread of posters by Roman Cieslewicz, who would later live and work in France. His career is documented in Roman Cieslewicz *by Margo Rouard-Snowman, Thames & Hudson, London, 1993.*

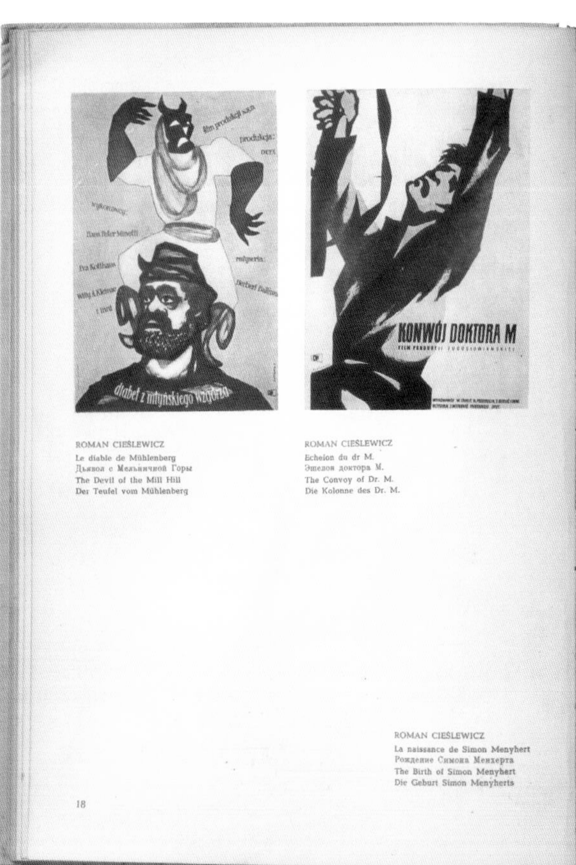

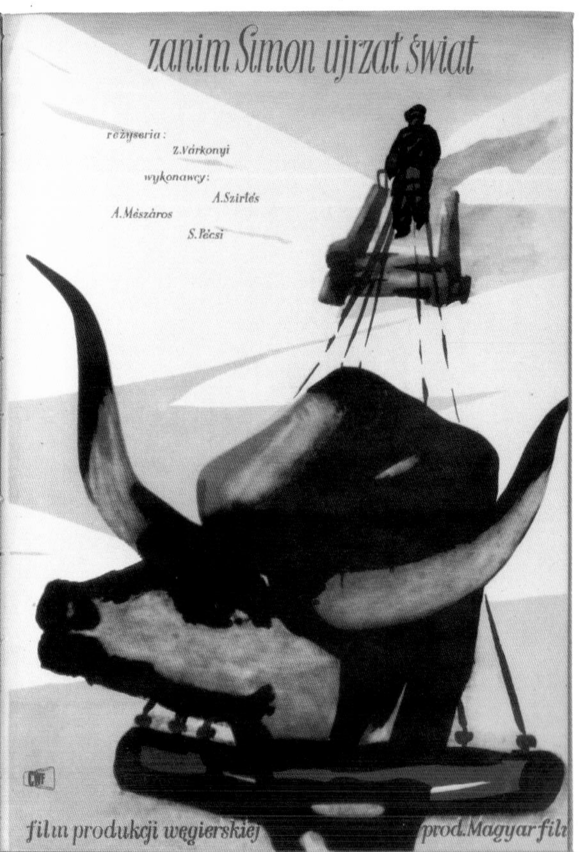

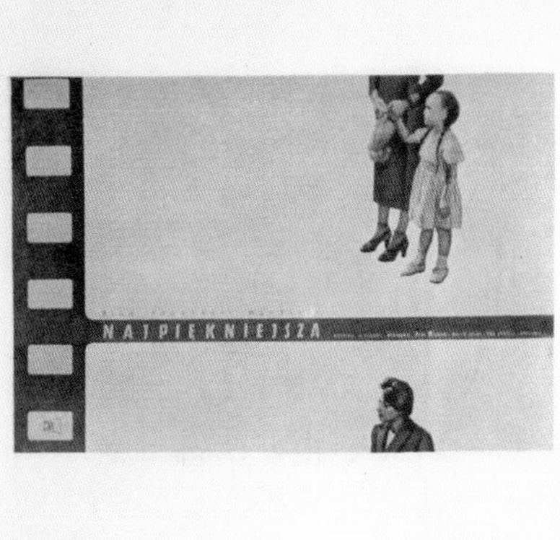

HENRYK TOMASZEWSKI
Bellissima
Прелестница
Bellissima
Bellissima

HENRYK TOMASZEWSKI
Maître après Dieu
Хозяин после Бога
First After God
Der erste nach Gott

HENRYK TOMASZEWSKI
Le Réviseur
Ревизор
The Revisor
Der Revisor

ERYK LIPIŃSKI
Nos coeurs
Наши сердца
Our Hearts
Unsere Herzen

ERYK LIPIŃSKI
La vérité n'a pas de frontières
Граничная улица
Border Street
Die Grenzstrasse

ERYK LIPIŃSKI
La dernière nuit
Последняя ночь
The Last Night
Die letzte Nacht

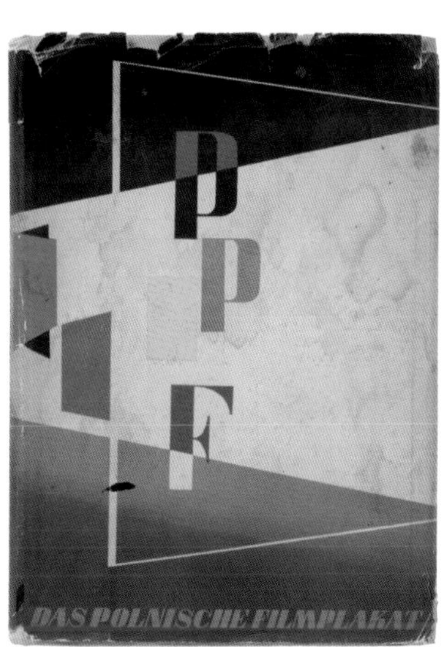

62

HYP NO TISM

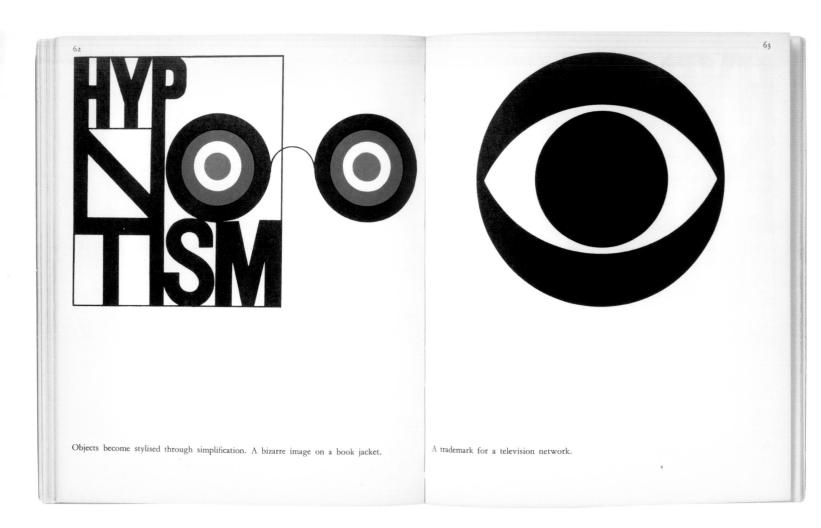

Objects become stylised through simplification. A bizarre image on a book jacket.

63

A trademark for a television network.

Two approaches to trademarks using an 'H', on the left by Gerstner+Kutter for a furniture manufacturer and on the right by Norman Ives for a hotel chain.

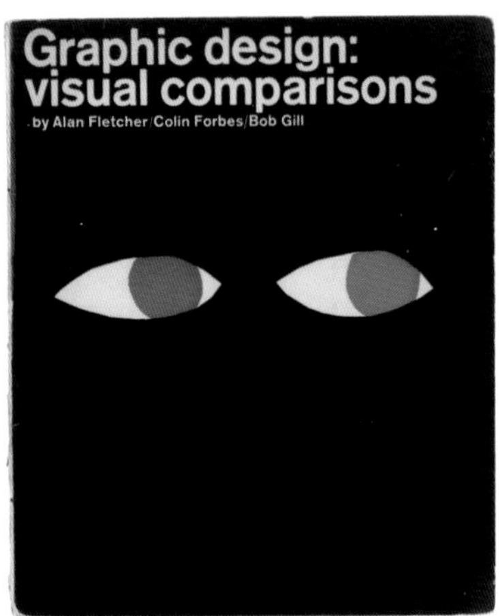

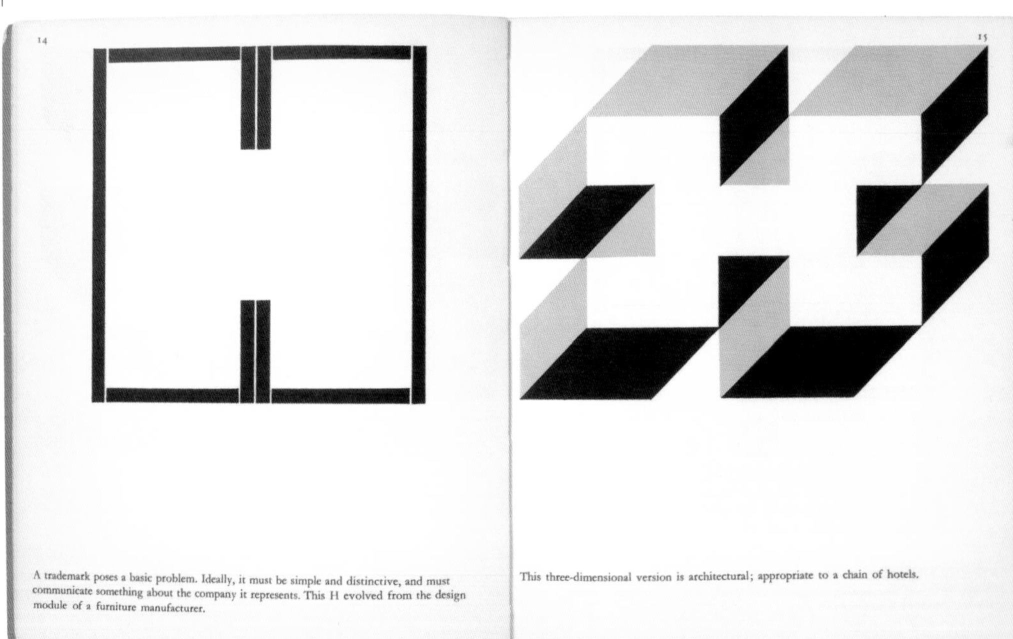

14
15
A trademark poses a basic problem. Ideally, it must be simple and distinctive, and must communicate something about the company it represents. This H evolved from the design module of a furniture manufacturer.
This three-dimensional version is architectural; appropriate to a chain of hotels.

Graphic Design: Visual Comparisons

Alan Fletcher, Colin Forbes, Bob Gill

Studio Books, London, 1963
96 pages
196 × 165 mm (7.75 × 6.5 in)
Designed by Fletcher/Forbes/Gill

Graphic Design: Visual Comparisons was the first book written by the fledgling designers Alan Fletcher (1931–2006), Colin Forbes (1928–) and Bob Gill (1931–). They wanted to produce a work that was of its time and they offered a clear statement of intent: 'Our thesis is that any one visual problem has an infinite number of solutions; that many of them are valid; that solutions ought to derive from the subject matter; that the designer should therefore have no preconceived graphic style.'

The authors set out to prove their thesis by pairing similar graphic problems on each spread to compare how the final outcomes differed. They chose to exhibit some of their own work but most of the examples are by fellow designers in Europe and the United States. The comparisons are striking. A transfixed pair of eyes on a book jacket by Milton Glaser meets the focused CBS eye of William Golden. A lyrical and rounded piece of experimental typography by Brownjohn, Chermayeff & Geismar Associates meets the hard-edged logo for the German steel company Friederichs Heyking by Anton Stankowski. Both use the same play of positive and negative space within letterforms.

Published as part of a series of student guides, the format is small. The reproduction is simple, printed on uncoated stock with some impositions in black and warm grey and the others in black, red and blue. Artwork that did not conform to the colour scheme was rejected.

The book is a succession of double-page spreads with pairs of designs. The layout is uncomplicated, with only an illustration and small descriptive caption on each page. This gives the book a singular point of view and considerable graphic punch. The credits for the designers are all contained in an index at the end of the book.

80
81
Negative as well as positive space can be dynamic. A page from an experimental booklet on typography.
A trademark for a steel company.

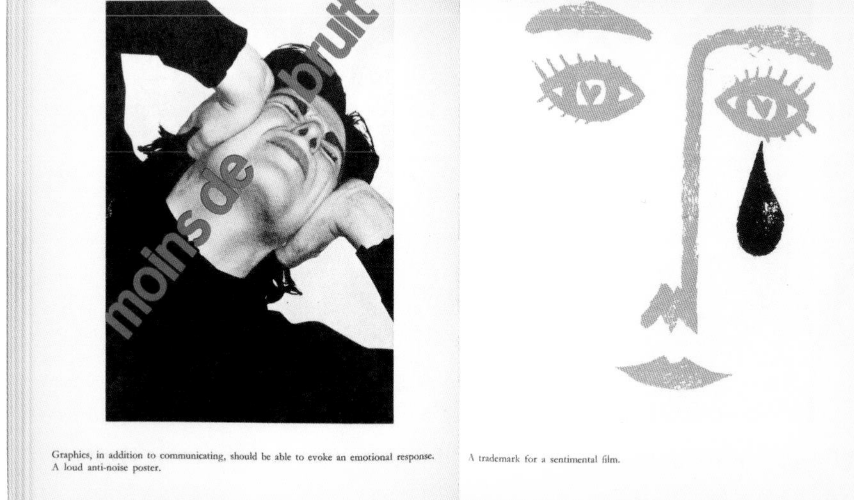

68
69
moins de bruit
Graphics, in addition to communicating, should be able to evoke an emotional response. A loud anti-noise poster.
A trademark for a sentimental film.

The simple layout and large reproduction of work makes a bold statement. This spread shows design as solution to a problem as seen through the work of Giovanni Pintori for an Olivetti ad and a catalogue cover for the Museum of Modern Art by Chermayeff & Geismar Inc.

32
Design, in addition to solving specific problems, occasionally, like painting, justifies itself. A variation of a trademark becomes the illustration in this advertisement.

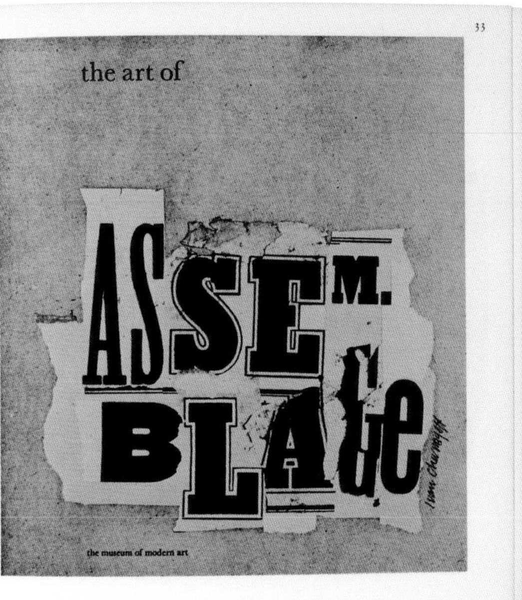

33
the art of
ASSEM.
BLAGE
the museum of modern art
An exhibition of collage is illustrated on its catalogue cover.

Publicity and Graphic Design in the Chemical Industry

Hans Neuburg

ABC Verlag, Zurich, 1967
240 pages
250 × 250 mm (9.875 × 9.875 in)
Designed by Hans Neuburg, Walter Bangerter

Publicity and Graphic Design in the Chemical Industry by Hans Neuburg (1904–1983) was the fourth and last in a series of books highlighting the Swiss graphic design industry published by ABC Verlag. The previous titles were *Graphic Art of a Swiss Town*, *Official Graphic Art in Switzerland* and *Graphic Design in Swiss Industry*.

At the time of the book's publication in 1967, Switzerland was home to some of the world's major chemical and pharmaceutical companies: Geigy, Ciba, Roche and Sandoz. Based largely in Basel, they benefited from the production line of talent generated by Armin Hofmann's instruction at the Allgemeine Gewerbeschule.

A large proportion of the book is taken up by the prodigious output of Geigy, which was one of the first companies to utilize the 'Swiss style' of geometric-based layout and exclusive use of the typeface Berthold Akzidenz Grotesk.

Neuburg was interested in the fact that the chemical industry offered a unique problem: with no physical product to promote beyond a pill, bottle or liquid, designers had to rely on objective graphic solutions to create successful promotional material. A more subjective viewpoint or abstract treatment was frowned upon as 'Americanization'. In his introduction to the book, the designer Josef Müller-Brockmann warns that he has seen examples of this in some recent Swiss work. He begrudgingly agrees 'in principle' to the examples exhibited in the book.

A study in all facets of pharmaceutical marketing, the book is split into sections such as publicity, announcements and packaging. Printing quality is very high and spot colour is used throughout the book to great effect. Thanks to the trilingual text in English, German and French, which allowed for an international distribution, many readers were able to experience Swiss graphic design (and high production values) for the first time.

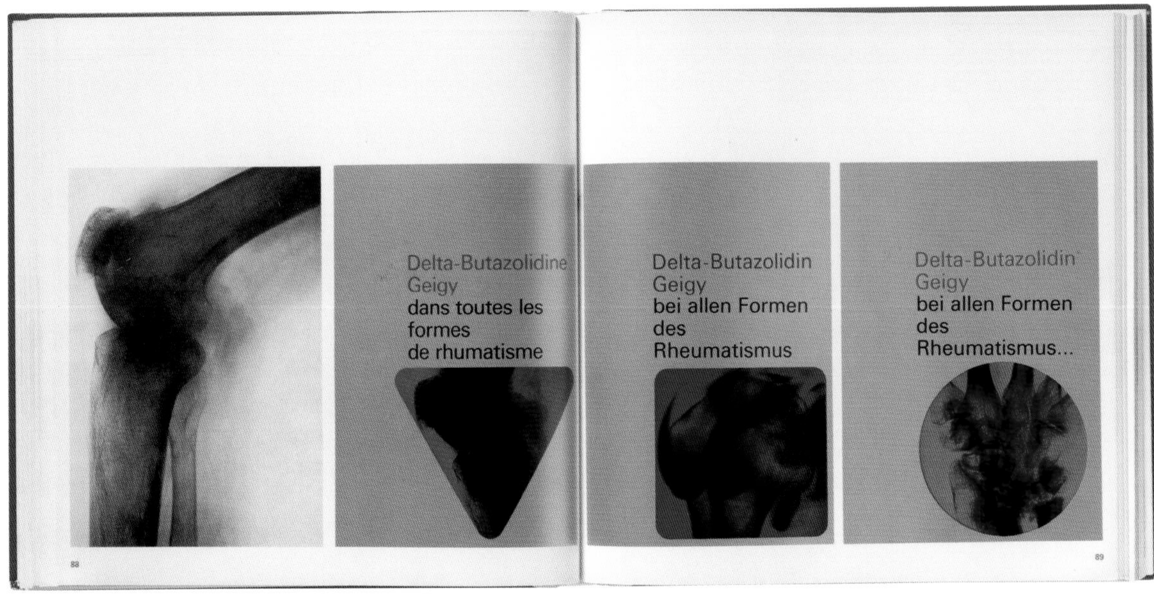

A special silver is used for these striking Geigy promotional brochures for an arthritis medication designed by Fritz Schrag.

Detailed captions provide information on the products and the graphic solutions employed. The designers' credits are relegated to an index at the back of the book.

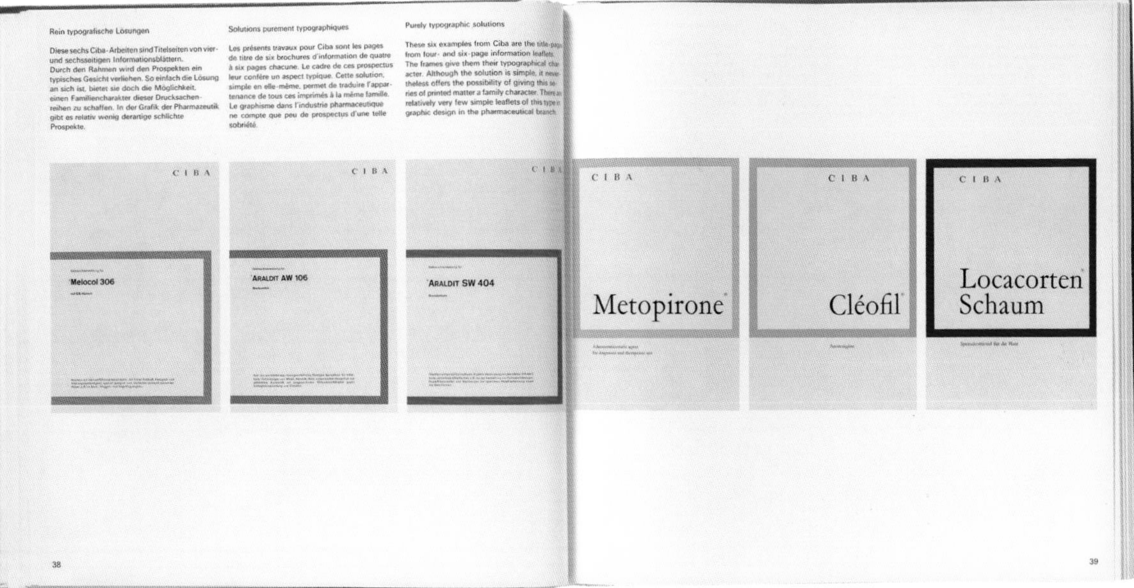

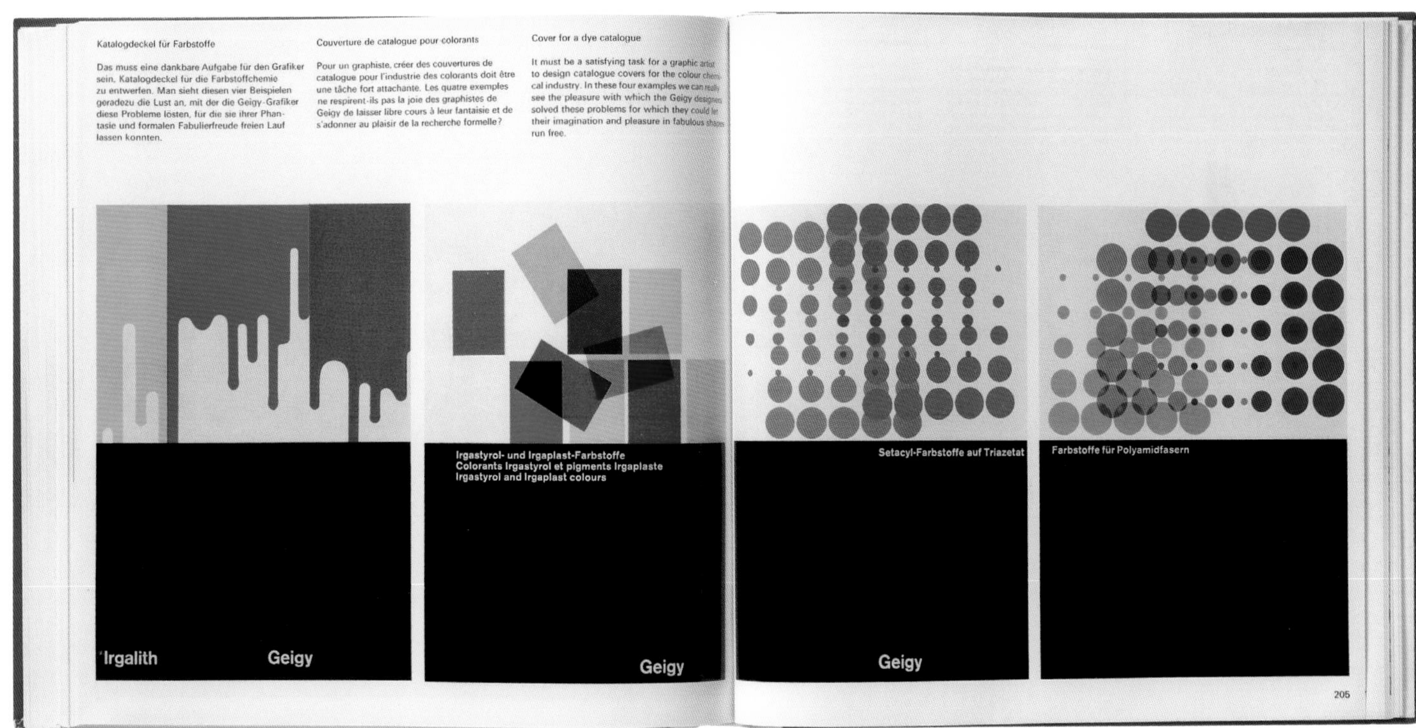

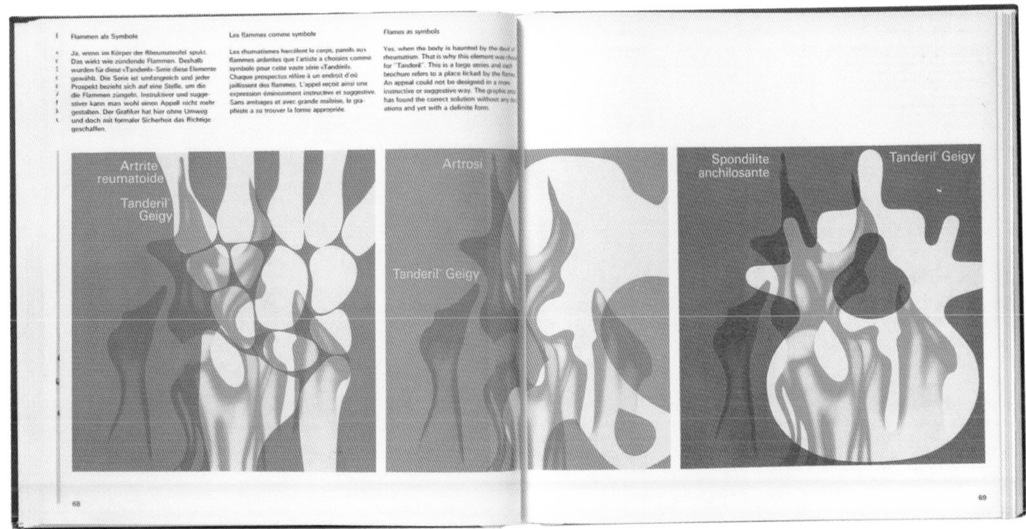

Ex Libris
Tony Brook

Wim Crouwel: Mode en Module, Frederike Huygen, Hugues C. Boekraad, Uitgeverij 010, Rotterdam, 1997
Design of a Lifetime: Ben Bos, Dirk van Ginkel, Paul Hefting, BIS Publishers, Amsterdam, 2000
The New Graphic Art, Karl Gerstner, Markus Kutter, Arthur Niggli, Teufen, 1959
The World as Design, Otl Aicher, Ernst & Sohn, Berlin, 1994
Design Coordination and Corporate Image, F.H.K. Henrion, Alan Parkin, Studio Vista, London, 1967
8vo: On the Outside, Mark Holt, Hamish Muir, Lars Müller Publishers, Baden, 2005
79 Short Essays on Design, Michael Bierut, Princeton Architectural Press, New York, 2007
Jan Van Toorn: Critical Practice, Rick Poyner, Uitgeverij 010, Rotterdam, 2008
Printed Matter, Robin Kinross, Jaap van Triest, Karel Martens (editors), Hyphen Press, London, 1996
Designing Design, Kenya Hara, Lars Müller Publishers, Baden, 2007

The unique metallic cover is described as having been printed in 'four colours by letterpress using the DUFEX process. The material is wax-laminated aluminium foil and it should not be subjected to high temperatures.'

Spreads showing, on top, Eliot Noyes and Paul Rand's Westinghouse logo and, below, British traffic signs by Kinneir Associates.

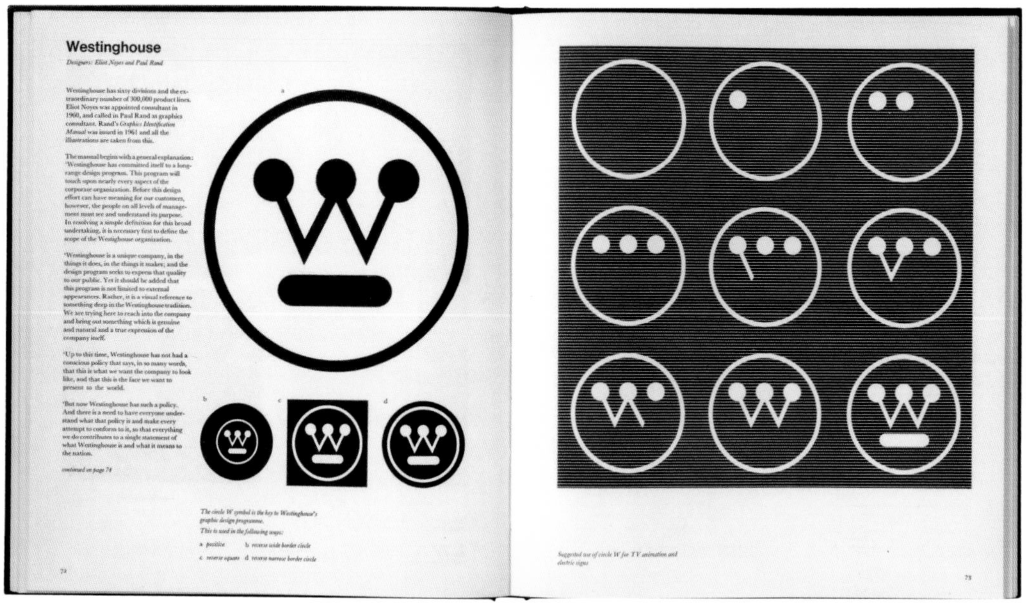

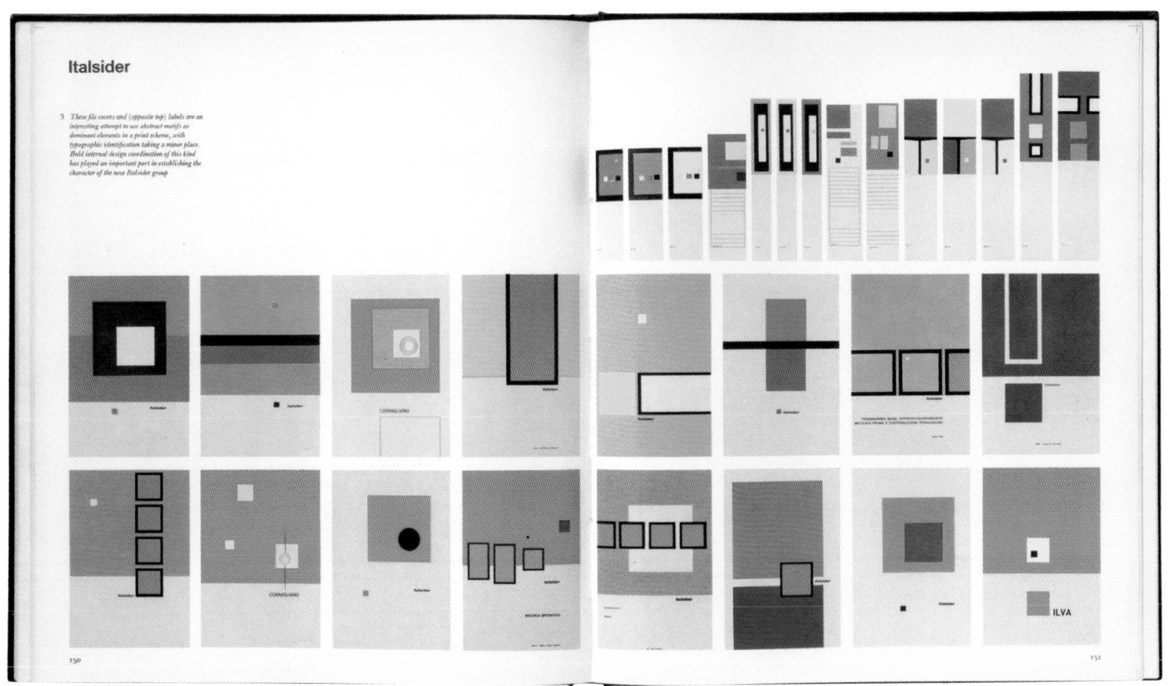

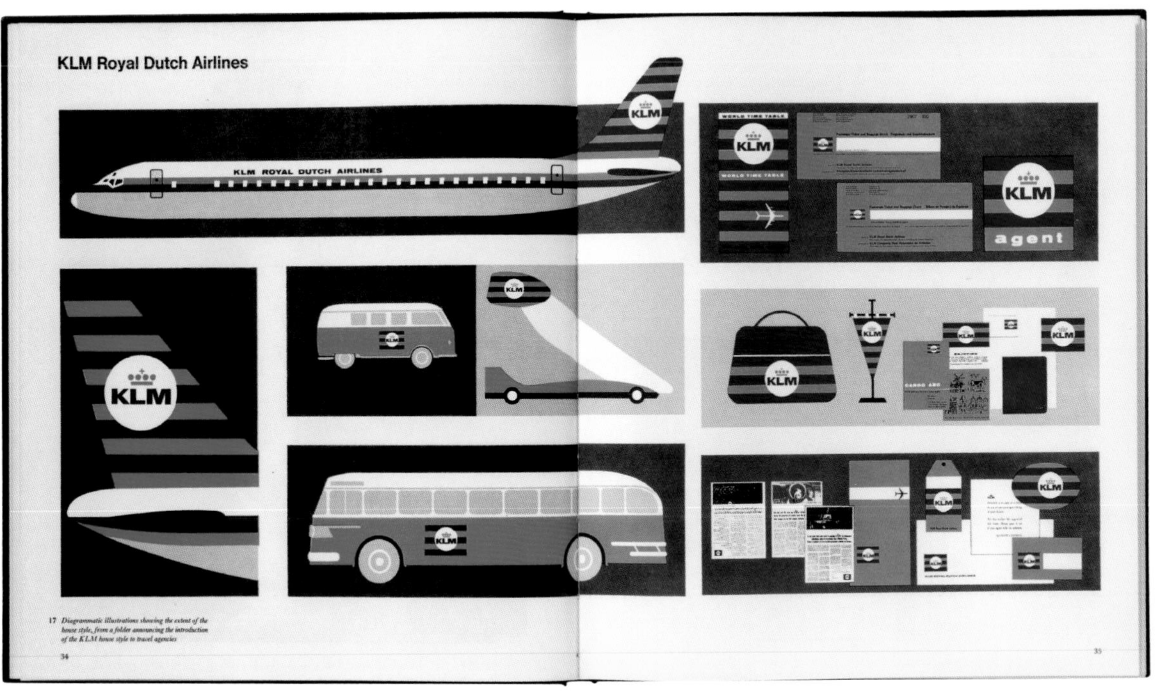

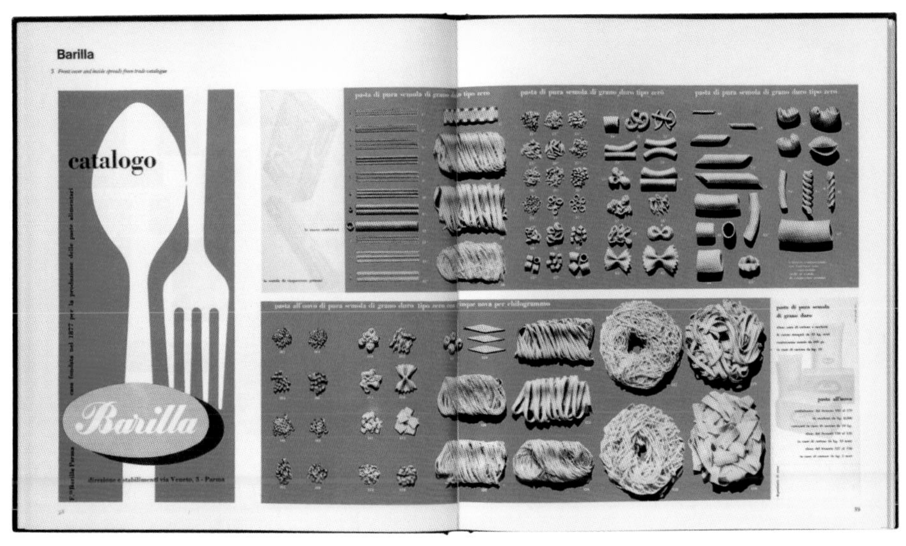

Design Coordination and Corporate Image

F.H.K. Henrion,
Alan Parkin

Studio Vista, London,
and Reinhold Publishing Corporation, New York, 1967
208 pages
265 × 235 mm (10.5 × 9.25 in)
Designed by F.H.K. Henrion

F.H.K. Herion (1914–1990) was born in Germany and emigrated to the United Kingdom in 1939. In 1951, he founded Henrion Design Associates (HDA), one of the first European firms to pioneer the emerging discipline of 'corporate identity'. The co-author of *Design Coordination and Corporate Image* Alan Parkin joined HDA in 1961.

The book showcases 27 projects from around the world, ranging from large multinational companies such as IBM, Olivetti and Pirelli to Dick Merricks, a small apple farmer in Kent, UK, and special projects such as the 1964 Tokyo Olympic Games and British traffic signs. Henrion also includes two of his own clients, KLM Royal Dutch Airlines and Metra International.

The introduction is a formal in-depth analysis of design coordination. It reflects Henrion's belief that scientific procedures and quantifiable criteria should be utilized in successful corporate design, and promotes involvement at board level as an essential prerequisite for successful projects.

Each project has a short introduction and is spread over a number of pages; a generous amount of space is devoted to visual elements. Henrion felt that too much emphasis was placed on logo development in its own right, and the layouts reflect this. There is an effort to show the breadth of work produced for each client, from stationery to packaging, signage and architecture.

Included among the projects is Eugenio Carmi's rarely seen work for the Italian steel group Italsider. Created while the artist was the company's design director from 1958 to 1965, it uses bold colour schemes in abstract arrangements to create a striking range of corporate literature.

Most of *Design Coordination and Corporate Image* is printed in black and white, eight pages are in full colour and good use is made of two-colour sections: cyan with black at the front of the book and red with black at the back.

Graphis Diagrams

The Graphic Visualization of Abstract Data

Walter Herdeg (editor)

Graphis Press, Zurich, 1974
Fifth edition (pictured), 1983
208 pages
240 × 235 mm (9.5 × 9.25 in)
Designed by Walter Herdeg
Cover designed by Dietmar R. Winkler

There is an inherent abstract beauty in a well-conceived and executed diagram, a fact made manifest throughout the pages of *Graphis Diagrams*. A good diagram has a function to perform and a message to convey, and the more clearly these objectives are achieved the better – and the more elegant – the outcome. This holds true for every example in the book, whether it is from a product price list for Knoll by Massimo Vignelli or a highly illustrated encyclopaedia from the publishers Kodansha in Japan.

The book's editor and designer, Walter Herdeg (1908–1995), was the co-founder and editor of the highly influential graphic design magazine *Graphis*. Unsurprisingly, the selection of work he assembled from designers around the world is impressive. Massimo Vignelli, Otl Aicher, Saul Bass, Herbert Bayer, Wim Crouwel, Odermatt & Tissi and Pentagram, among others, contributed examples of their diagrammatic work.

Set out as a showcase, the book has no running text but there are extended captions in German, French and English and detailed designer credits. It is split into six chapters covering specialist subject areas: 'Comparative Statistical Diagrams', 'Flow Diagrams, Organizational Charts, etc.', 'Diagrams Visualizing Functions, Processes', 'Tabulations, Timetables, etc.', 'Cartographic Diagrams, Decorative Maps', and 'Diagrams Used as Design Elements'. Later editions included a supplement of work produced after the publication of the first edition.

As is to be expected from a Swiss publication, *Graphis Diagrams* is impeccably printed in a mixture of full colour and black and white. The Graphis Press produced a series of square-formatted books of which *Graphis Diagrams* was the first. Of note was the compilation also edited by Herdeg of international environmental graphics *Archigraphics* (1978).

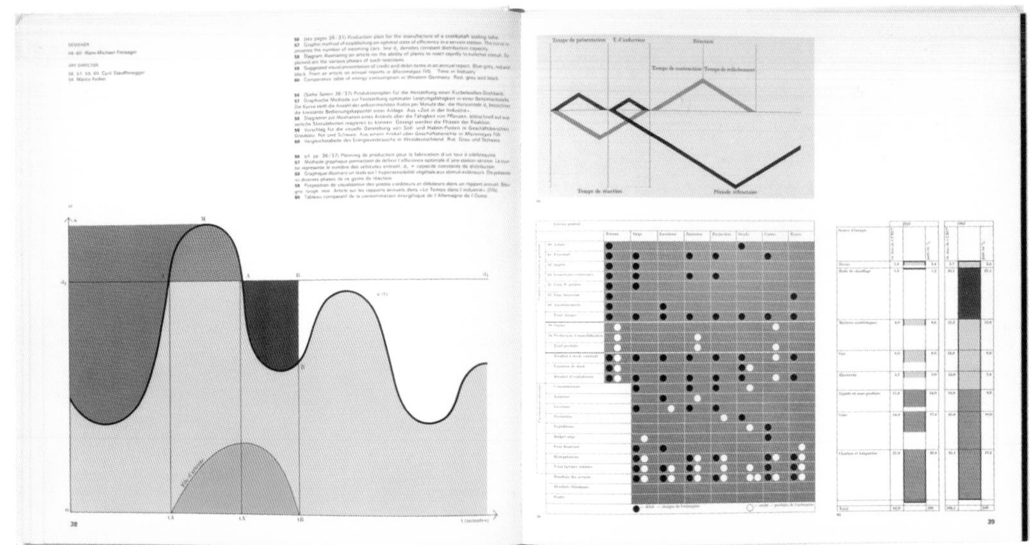

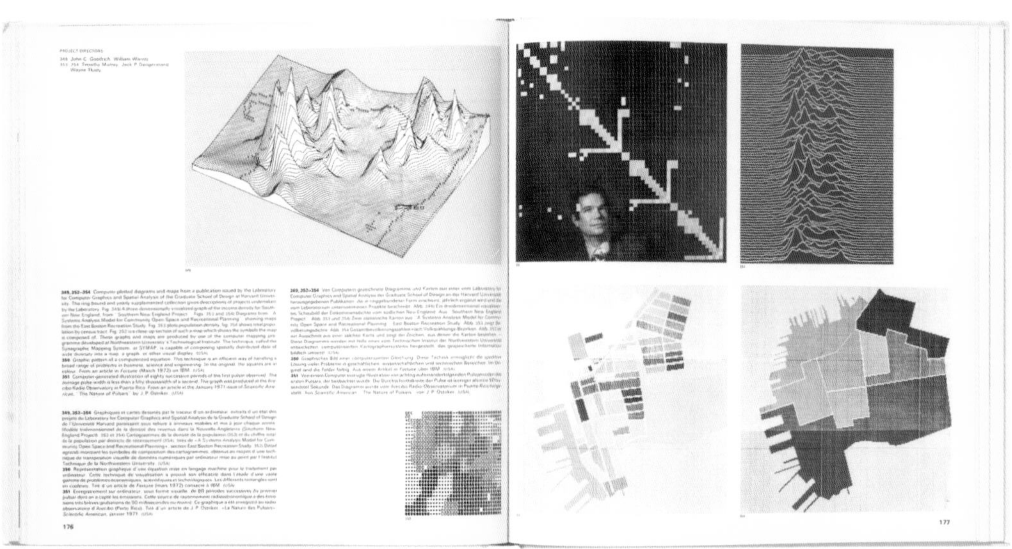

Diagrams from The Modern World Encyclopedia *published by Kodansha in Japan in 1972.*

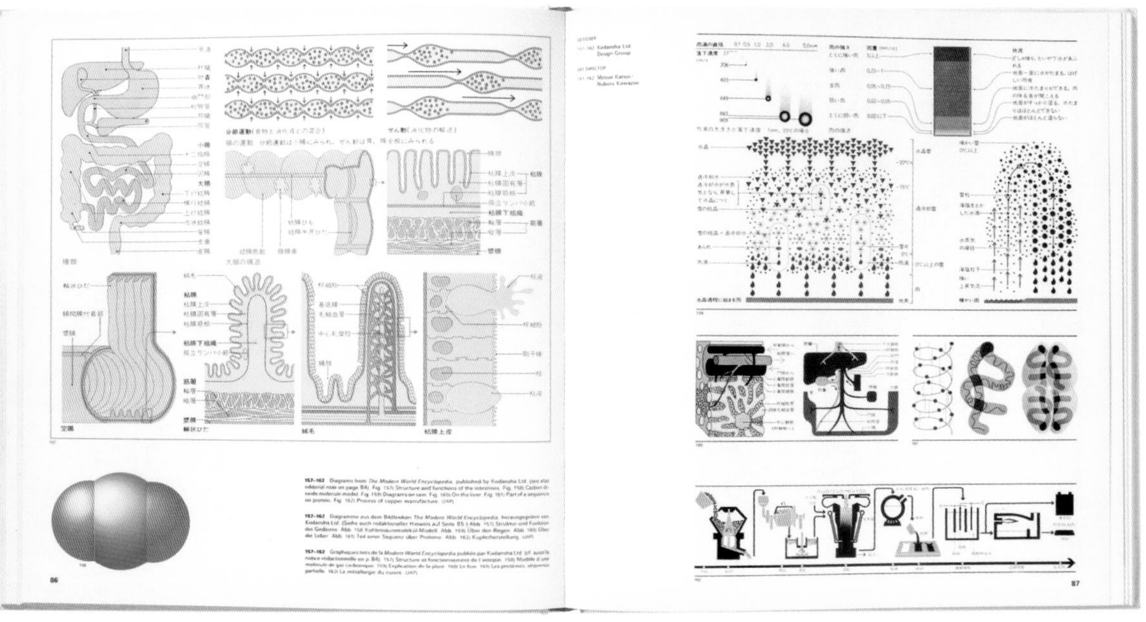

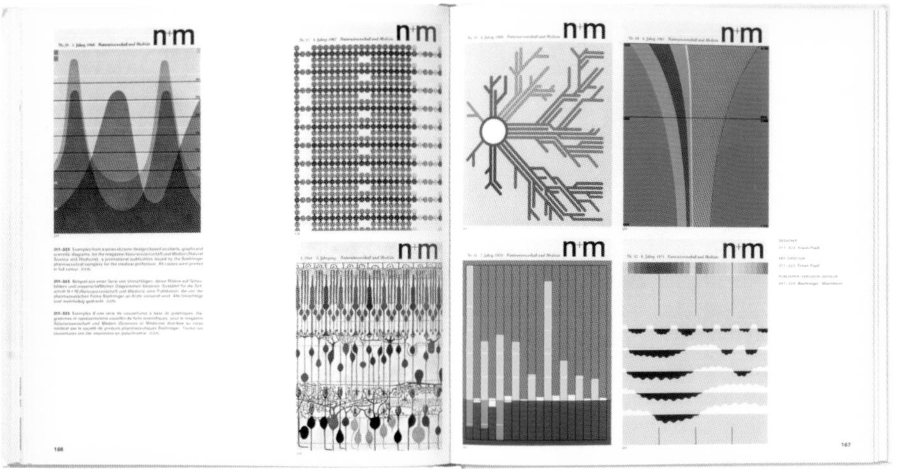

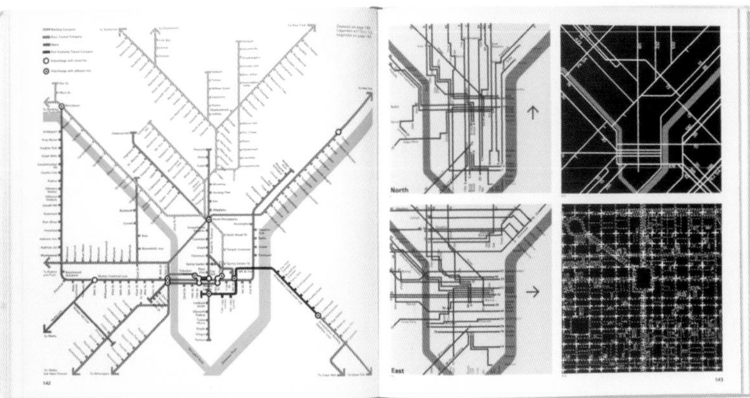

Some projects are covered in detail across a number of examples, as here with work by the designer Richard Saul Wurman for the brochure Man-Made Philadelphia: A Guide to its Physical and Cultural Environment *(1972). The image on the bottom right is by the architect Louis I. Kahn.*

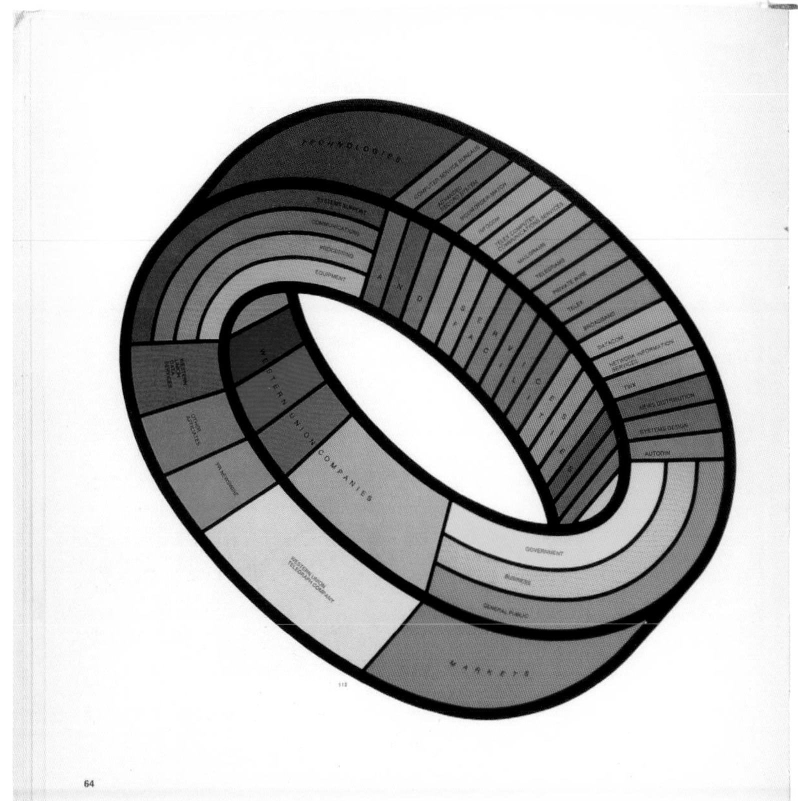

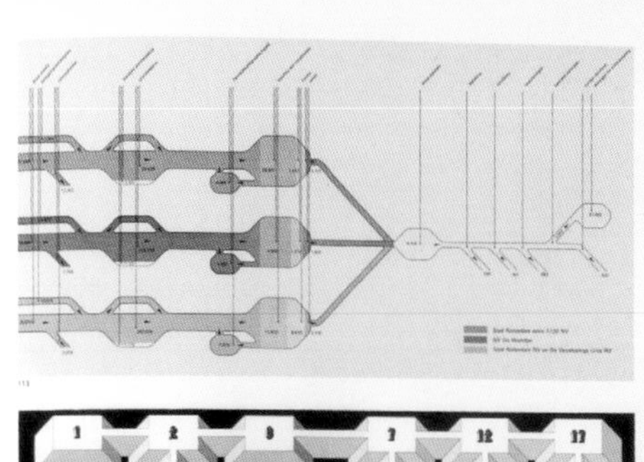

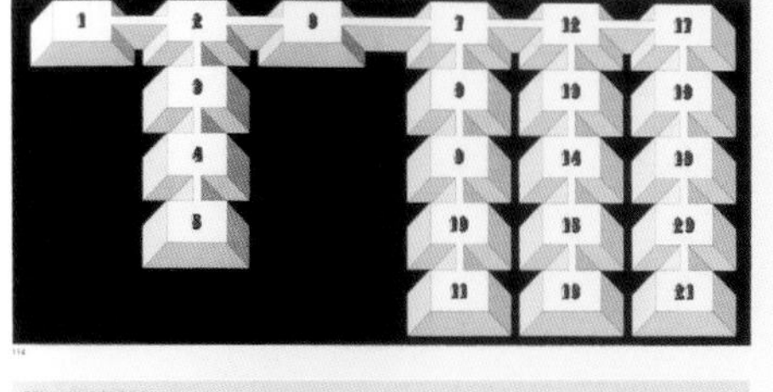

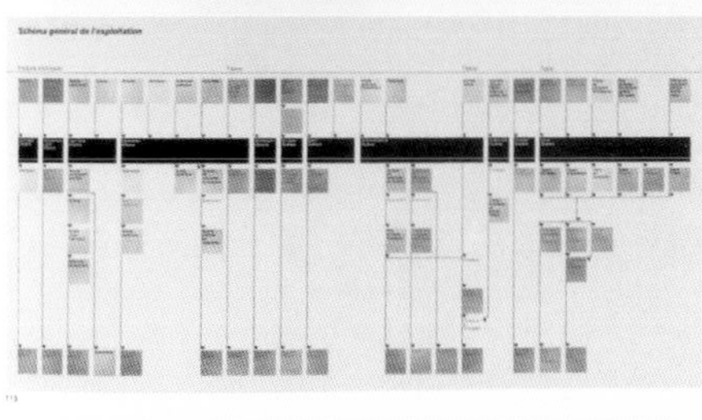

112 Diagram in Moebius band form from an annual report of Western Union, giving in one composite picture a listing of this corporation's affiliated companies, its markets, various services and the areas of its technological contributions. (USA)
113 Flow chart showing the use and distribution of incoming money in three divisions of an insurance company. From an annual report of the Assurantieconcern Stad Rotterdam anno 1720 NV. Blue, orange, grey and black on white. (NLD)
114 Double-page chart from an annual report of The Commercial Bank of Australia Limited. The numbered blocks represent the banks wholly owned, partly owned and associated subsidiaries and other interests. The colours are light blue, yellow and ochre on a black ground. (AUL)
115 Organization chart used in an annual report of Celanese Canada Limited. It provides a survey of the flow of products into and out of the various plants. Multi-coloured. (CAN)

112 Diagramm in der Form eines Möbius-Bandes aus einem Geschäftsbericht der Western Union. Das Bild gibt einen Überblick über die Zweiggesellschaften, die Marktgebiete, die Dienstzweige und technologischen Beiträge dieser Firma. (USA)
113 Diagrammatische Darstellung der Anwendung und Verteilung des einkommenden Geldes in den drei Tochtergesellschaften eines Versicherungskonzerns. Aus einem Geschäftsbericht des Assurantieconcerns Stad Rotterdam anno 1720 NV. (NLD)
114 Doppelseitige Tabelle aus einem Jahresbericht der Commercial Bank of Australia Limited. Die numerierten Blöcke stellen die Hauptbank, deren angeschlossene Mitgliederbanken und andere mit der Bank verbundene Interessengemeinschaften dar. Hellblau, Gelb und Ocker auf Schwarz. (AUL)
115 Übersichtstabelle der Produkte, die in den Fabrikanlagen der Celanese Canada Limited verarbeitet und produziert werden. Aus einem Geschäftsbericht. Mehrfarbig. (CAN)

112 Graphique en forme de bande de Moebius présentant de façon intégrée les sociétés affiliées, les marches, les divers services et les domaines d'activité techniques du groupe Western Union. Extrait d'un rapport annuel. (USA)
113 Schéma montrant la destination et répartition des recettes dans trois divisions d'une société d'assurances. Tiré d'un rapport annuel de l'Assurantieconcern Stad Rotterdam anno 1720 NV. Bleu, orange, gris, noir sur blanc. (NLD)
114 Tableau double page figurant dans un rapport annuel de la Commercial Bank of Australia Ltd. Les blocs numérotés représentent les banques du groupe ainsi que les intérêts que ce dernier possède dans d'autres banques et des secteurs extra-bancaires. Bleu clair, jaune, ocre sur fond noir. (AUL)
115 Schéma général de l'exploitation de la Celanese Canada Ltd. donnant un aperçu des produits transformés dans les diverses usines du groupe. En polychromie. (CAN)

DESIGNER

112 Richard Hess / Hiroshi Morishima
113 Eelco Bos
114 Barrie Tucker / Ernie James
115 Gazette Creative Services

ART DIRECTOR

113 Eelco Bos
114 Tucker & James
115 Frank A. Lipari

AGENCY-STUDIO

113 Eelco Bos & Partners
114 Jackson Wain (Victoria) Pty. Ltd.
115 Gazette Creative Services

65

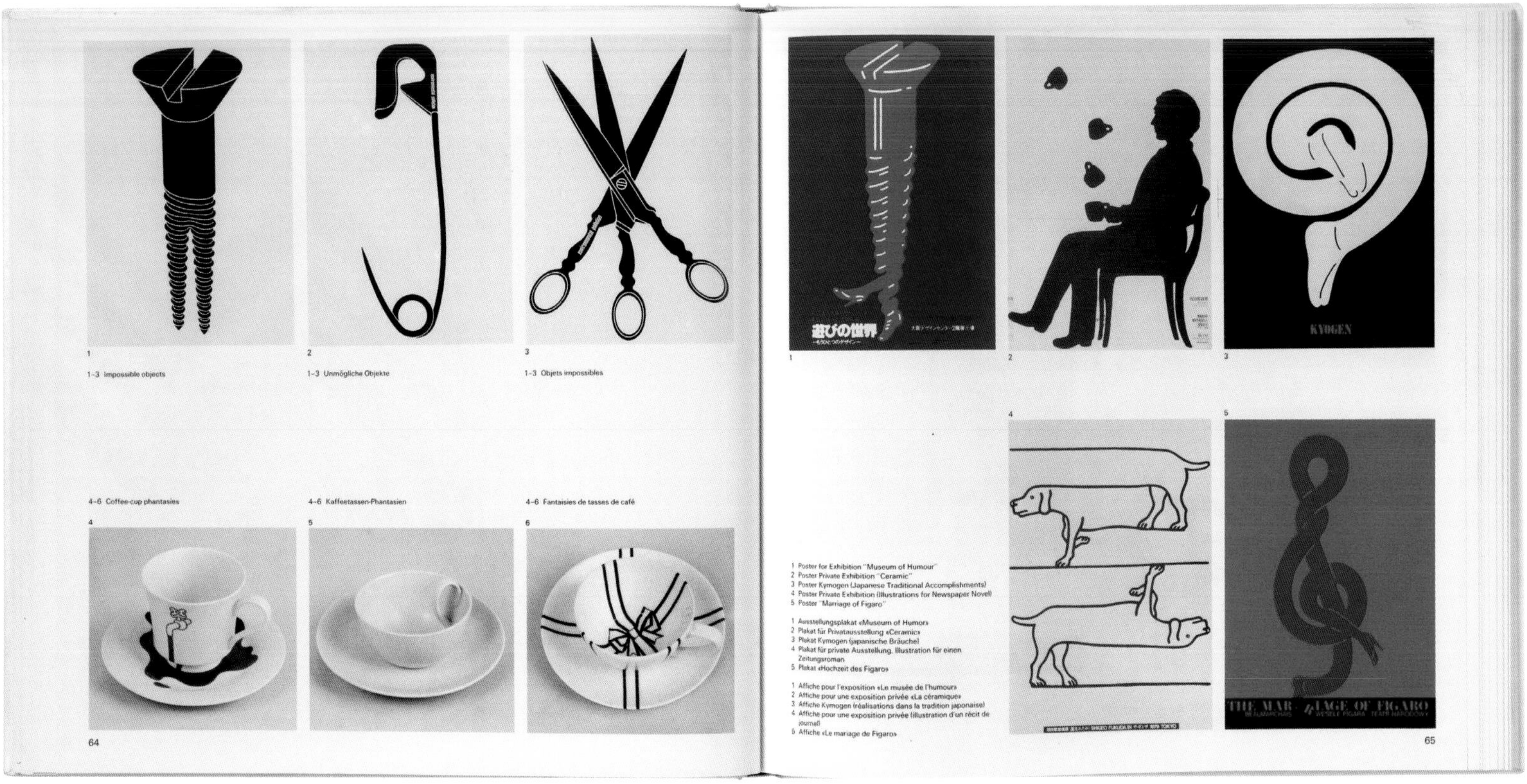

1 2 3

1–3 Impossible objects

1–3 Unmögliche Objekte

1–3 Objets impossibles

4–6 Coffee-cup phantasies

4–6 Kaffeetassen-Phantasien

4–6 Fantaisies de tasses de café

4 5 6

64

1 2 3 4 5

1 Poster for Exhibition "Museum of Humour"
2 Poster Private Exhibition "Ceramic"
3 Poster Kymogen (Japanese Traditional Accomplishments)
4 Poster Private Exhibition (Illustrations for Newspaper Novel)
5 Poster "Marriage of Figaro"

1 Ausstellungsplakat «Museum of Humor»
2 Plakat für Privatausstellung «Ceramic»
3 Plakat Kymogen (japanische Bräuche)
4 Plakat für private Ausstellung, Illustration für einen Zeitungsroman
5 Plakat «Hochzeit des Figaro»

1 Affiche pour l'exposition «Le musée de l'humour»
2 Affiche pour une exposition privée «La céramique»
3 Affiche Kymogen (réalisations dans la tradition japonaise)
4 Affiche pour une exposition privée (illustration d'un récit de journal)
5 Affiche «Le mariage de Figaro»

65

There are between three and five spreads dedicated to each of the 18 designers featured in Top Graphic Design. *Shown here is work by the Japanese designer Shigeo Fukuda.*

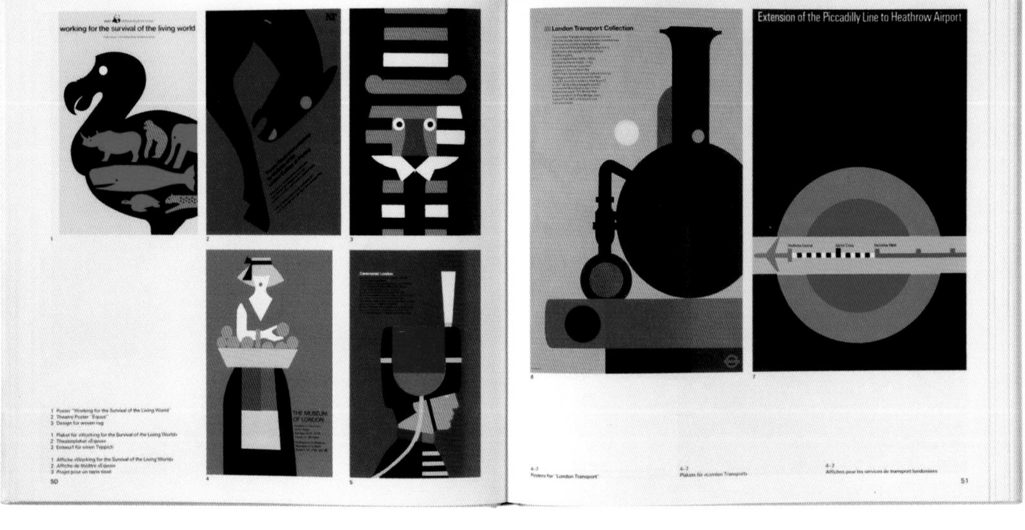

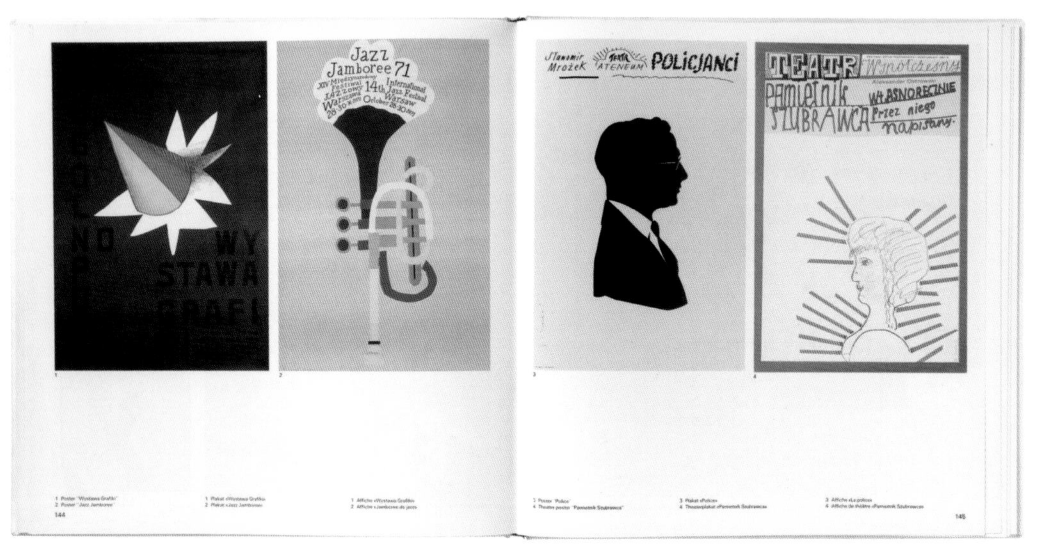

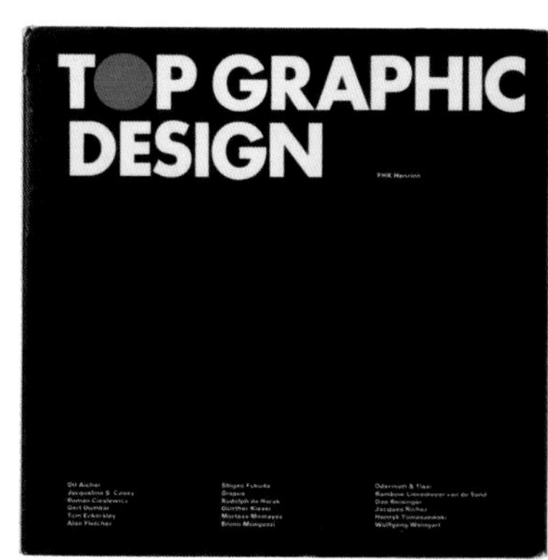

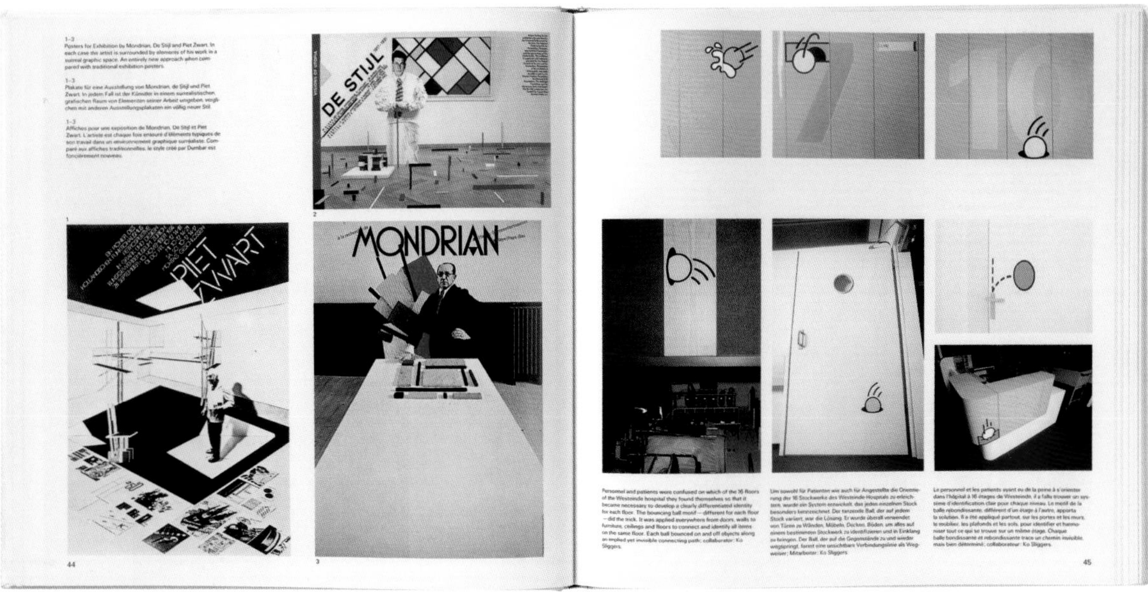

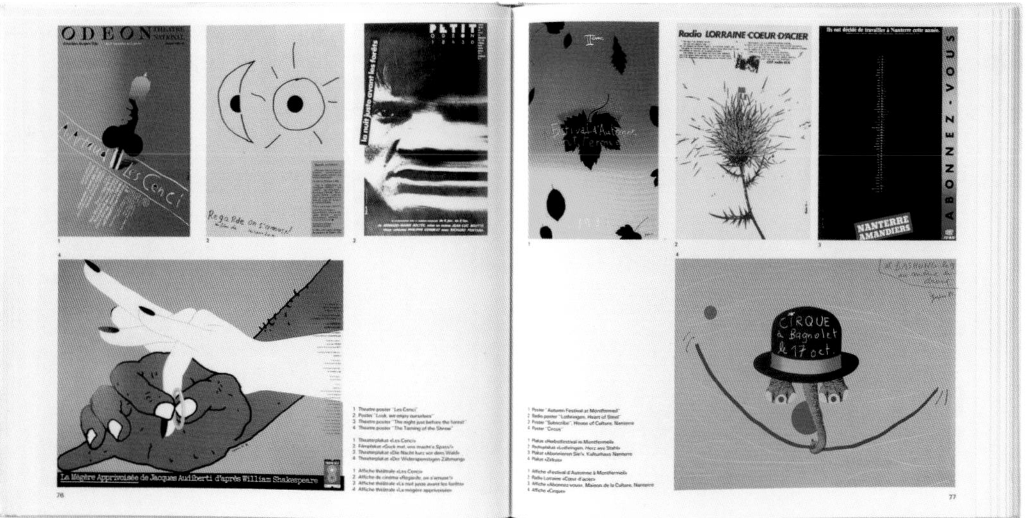

This work by Otl Aicher for the German town of Isny is the subject of its own book, Das Allgäu (Bei Isny) *by Otl Aicher and Katharina Adler (Isny, 1981).*

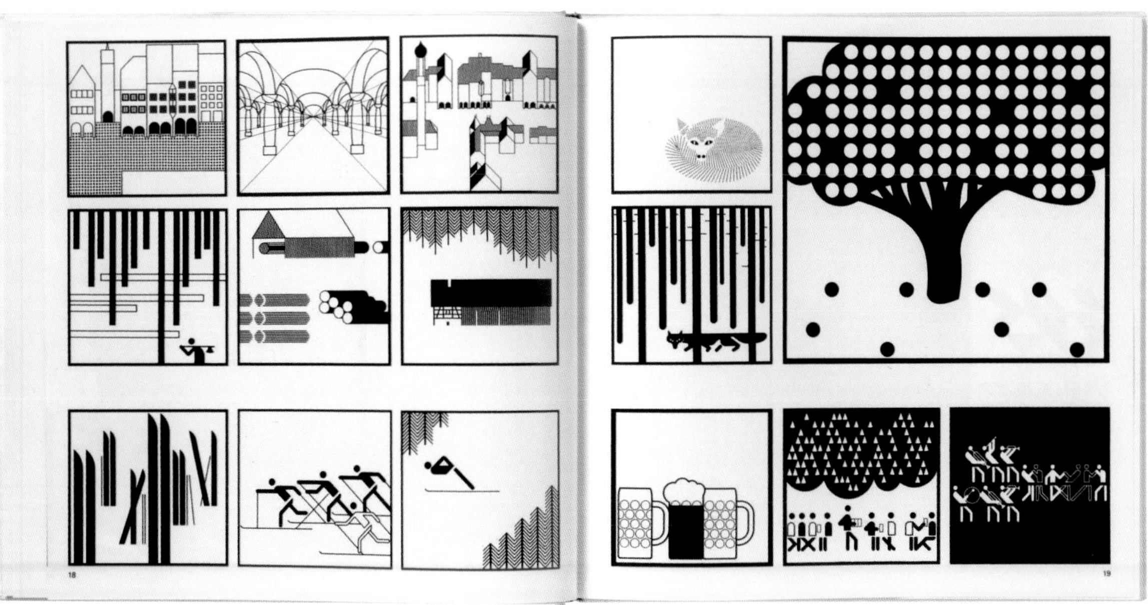

Top Graphic Design

F.H.K. Henrion

ABC Verlag, Zurich, 1983

160 pages

250 × 255 mm (9.875 × 10 in)

Designed by Hans Rudolf Ziegler

Top Graphic Design looks at the work of 18 designers and design agencies carefully selected by its author, F.H.K. Henrion, to give the book geographical variety and demonstrate the possibilities offered by different approaches to design solutions and management. All bar two were members of the Alliance Graphique Internationale (AGI), an elite club of graphic designers elected by their peers in the countries where they work.

Henrion chose designers who had not previously been given significant exposure in the design press and other publications. All of them display a distinctive and often innovative attitude to design. Their work is first-rate and the high standard of the illustrations helps to elevate the book above its slightly staid layout – by the 1980s the square format with a three-column grid had been adopted in many of ABC Verlag's publications.

Highlights include experimental work by the Dutch designer Gert Dumbar, with his use of papier mâché figures, illustrations that are perforated then backlit, and a signage system that utilizes graphics of different bouncing balls to signpost the floors of a hospital. The Swiss typographer Wolfgang Weingart and the French collective Grapus push the boundaries of their craft and the sensibilities of their audience, the former with dynamic typographic assemblages, the latter with posters of childlike abandon. The visual illusions of the Japanese designer Shigeo Fukuda and the surreal photographic montages of the German partnership Rambow Lienemeyer van de Sand provide a contrast in conceptual styles.

There are also surprises. Otl Aicher, famed for his work in ruthlessly organizing the graphic design for the 1972 Munich Olympic Games, is represented by his touching graphic landscapes and illustrations for the German town of Isny.

The Liberated Page

An Anthology of Major Typographic Experiments of this Century as Recorded in 'Typographica' Magazine

Herbert Spencer (editor)

Lund Humphries, London, 1987

232 pages

273 × 208 mm (10.75 × 8 in)

Designed by Herbert Spencer

The Liberated Page contains 17 articles from *Typographica*, a journal that devoted itself to publishing critical essays on milestones in twentieth-century typography. It ran for a total of 32 issues from 1949 to 1967, and was edited by the English designer Herbert Spencer, who, as is hinted in the title of this book, was an ardent supporter of asymmetric typography.

The articles are taken from the second series of *Typographica*, which ran from 1959 to 1967 in a smaller format than the previous 16 editions. They are facsimile reproductions from the original journal and suffer in quality as a consequence. This is more than compensated for by the calibre and breadth of the book's content.

Typographica was decidedly international in outlook. The French designer Massin and the Americans Brownjohn, Chermayeff & Geismar Associates are typical of the contemporary designers it featured. Typographic history was well covered, and authors such as Eckhard Neumann and Camilla Grey contributed pieces exploring the major transformations brought about by the avant-garde in the 1920s. *The Liberated Page* includes essays on John Heartfield, Alexander Rodchenko and Henryk Berlewi and his 'Mechano-faktura'. Artists who worked with type, such as the concrete poet Dieter Roth and Pop artist Richard Hamilton, are prominently featured – a reminder that the foundations of twentieth-century typographic innovation were largely forged by artists.

A highly visual journal, *Typographica* was inspirational to designers in the years after the Second World War. The publication of *The Liberated Page* 20 years after it folded provided a new generation with a taste of its original impact.

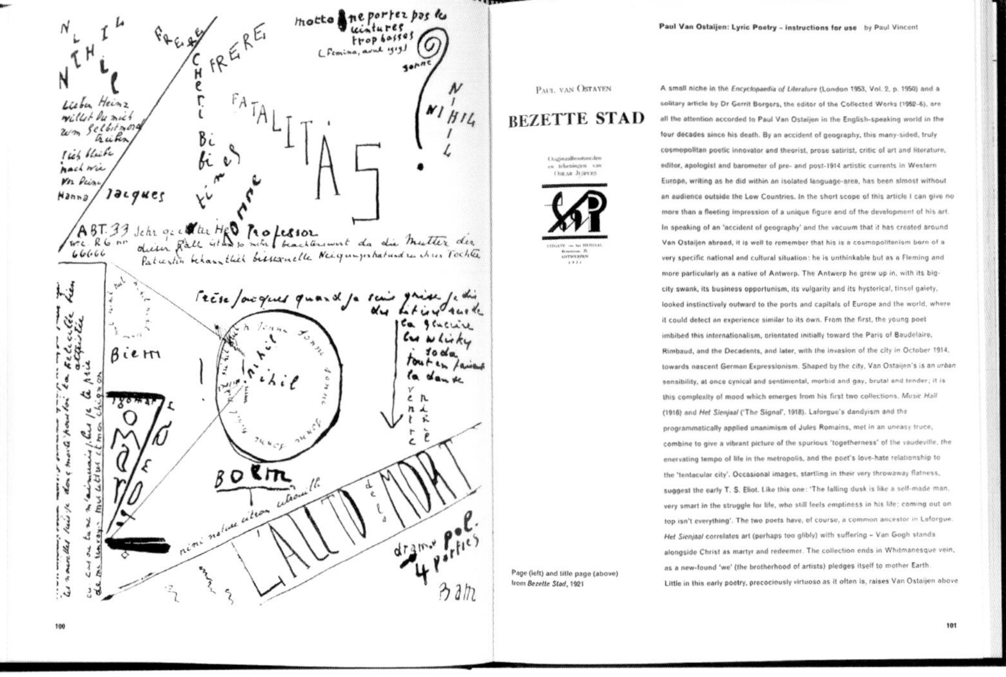

PAUL VAN OSTAYEN

BEZETTE STAD

Page (left) and title page (above) from *Bezette Stad*, 1921

Paul Van Ostaijen: Lyric Poetry – instructions for use by Paul Vincent

A small niche in the *Encyclopaedia of Literature* (London 1953, Vol. 2, p. 1950) and a solitary article by Dr Gerrit Borgers, the editor of the Collected Works (1952–6), are all the attention accorded to Paul Van Ostaijen in the English-speaking world in the four decades since his death. By an accident of geography, this many-sided, truly cosmopolitan poetic innovator and theorist, prose satirist, critic of art and literature, editor, apologist and barometer of pre- and post-1914 artistic currents in Western Europe, writing as he did within an isolated language-area, has been almost without an audience outside the Low Countries. In the short scope of this article I can give no more than a fleeting impression of a unique figure and of the development of his art. In speaking of an 'accident of geography' and the vacuum that it has created around Van Ostaijen abroad, it is well to remember that his is a cosmopolitanism born of a very specific national and cultural situation: he is unthinkable but as a Fleming and more particularly as a native of Antwerp. The Antwerp he grew up in, with its big-city swank, its business opportunism, its vulgarity and its hysterical, tinsel gaiety, looked instinctively outward to the ports and capitals of Europe and the world, where it could detect an experience similar to its own. From the first, the young poet imbibed this internationalism, orientated initially toward the Paris of Baudelaire, Rimbaud, and the Decadents, and later, with the invasion of the city in October 1914, towards nascent German Expressionism. Shaped by the city, Van Ostaijen's is an *urban* sensibility, at once cynical and sentimental, morbid and gay, brutal and tender; it is this complexity of mood which emerges from his first two collections, *Music Hall* (1916) and *Het Sienjaal* ('The Signal', 1918). Laforgue's dandyism and the programmatically applied unanimism of Jules Romains, met in an uneasy truce, combine to give a vibrant picture of the spurious 'togetherness' of the vaudeville, the enervating tempo of life in the metropolis, and the poet's love-hate relationship to the 'tentacular city'. Occasional images, startling in their very throwaway flatness, suggest the early T. S. Eliot. Like this one: 'The falling dusk is like a self-made man, very smart in the struggle for life, who still feels emptiness in his life: coming out on top isn't everything'. The two poets have, of course, a common ancestor in Laforgue. *Het Sienjaal* correlates art (perhaps too glibly) with suffering – Van Gogh stands alongside Christ as martyr and redeemer. The collection ends in Whitmanesque vein, as a new-found 'we' (the brotherhood of artists) pledges itself to mother Earth. Little in this early poetry, precociously virtuoso as it often is, raises Van Ostaijen above

100 101

The spreads of The Liberated Page *are direct facsimiles of the influential typographic journal* Typographica.

Pages of the work of the Dutch designer Paul Schuitema show the occasional use of a second colour in a book predominantly printed in black and white.

These designs for Berkel were produced by Paul Schuitema during the late 1920's.

162

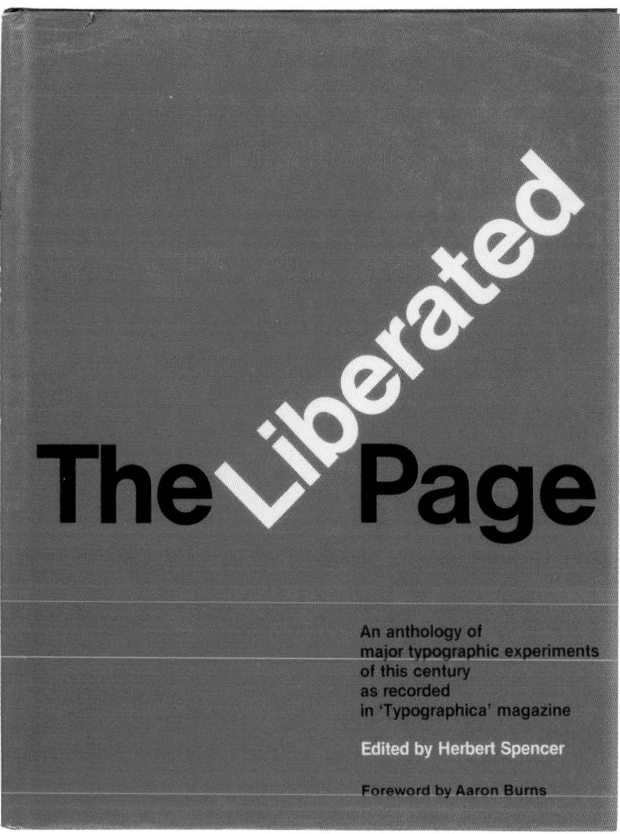
The Liberated Page
An anthology of major typographic experiments of this century as recorded in 'Typographica' magazine
Edited by Herbert Spencer
Foreword by Aaron Burns

Herbert Bayer's photographic experiments by Eckhard Neumann

At the Bauhaus in Weimar Herbert Bayer developed into a designer of wide ability. The experiments he carried out at that time were of great importance to his creative evolution and they have continued to influence his subsequent typographic and graphic design work, including even his most recent projects in the United States – projects which can no longer be categorized but which, grouped together under the title of 'environment design', reflect the universal design problems of our present-day society.

It was in 1922 during Herbert Bayer's period as a student at Weimar that the Bauhaus embarked upon the great departure from the handicraft-orientated ideology of the initial years and moved towards the new conception expressed by Walter Gropius in the slogan 'Art and Technology – A New Unity'. The Bauhaus Exhibition in the summer of 1923 was characteristic of this new concept. At that time many different forces were beginning to influence the teachings of the Bauhaus and Theo van Doesburg, from outside, and Laszlo Moholy-Nagy, from inside, were among those who sought to remould the school. The individual currents of power in Weimar did not directly drive the young Herbert Bayer in any particular direction, but they did provide the creative climate in which he was able to evolve his own logical and personal style.

In his handling of typography Herbert Bayer preserved a direct, functional, almost

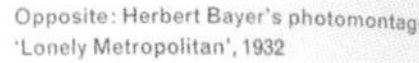
Opposite: Herbert Bayer's photomontage 'Lonely Metropolitan', 1932

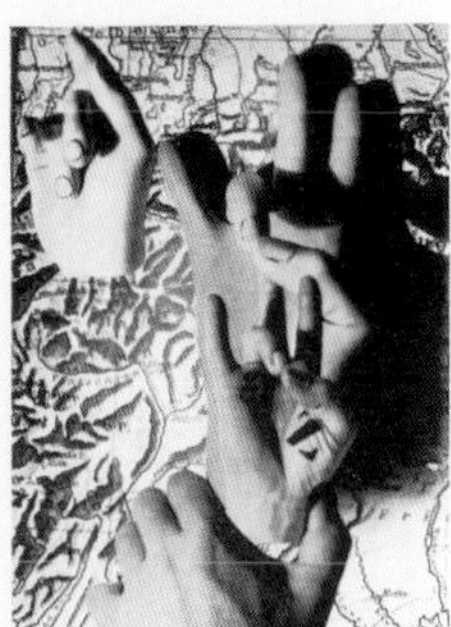
Herbert Bayer
'Hand-lung' (hand-acting), 1932

Herbert Bayer
'Monument', 1932

Herbert Bayer
'Bone Breaker', 1931

198

199

as a designer i realized there is no escaping being post-modern, since the typefaces available are very old or are based on very old models. Even when you try to do something contemporary, you rely on these old typefaces and conventions

Jeffery Keedy
Application of Keedy typeface
Emigre magazine, 1990

¶For Keedy, Deck, Emigre Graphics and colleagues such as NEVILLE BRODY and JONATHAN BARNBROOK in Britain, and MAX KISMAN in The Netherlands, designing typefaces for personal use is a way of ensuring that graphic design projects carry their own specific

identity

and tone of voice. The pre-digital typefaces that Brody drew for *The Face* emphasised the new perspectives on contemporary culture embodied in the magazine's editorial. They also functioned as a medium through which Brody could develop a socio-cultural

commentary

of his own. Typeface Two, designed in 1984, was deliberately authoritarian in mood, in order, Brody said, to draw a parallel between the social climate of the 1930s and 1980s. The typeface's geometric rigidity was persistently undermined by the light-hearted manner in which it was applied. Other designers take an even more idiosyncratic approach. For Barry Deck, the starting point for a type design is not traditional notions of legibility or elegance, but a highly subjective and seemingly arbitrary

narrative

founded on the supposed correlation between sexuality and letterforms.

Neville Brody
12" single cover
1984

Neville Brody
Typeface Two
1984

Neville Brody
Application of Typeface Two
The Face magazine, 1984

5. Designer's statement.

"With this in mind, I began imposing narratives of sexual angst, deviation and perversion on the design of my type. Because the F is a particularly important letter in the language of sexuality, it came to be a major point of activation in all of the alphabets."[5]

¶In this polymorphous **digital realm,** typefaces can cross-fertilise each other or merge to form strange new **hybrids.** Kisman's Fudoni Bold Remix mixes Futura and Bodini; Barnbrook's Prototype is collaged together from the parts of ten other typefaces, among them Bembo, Perpetua and Gill; and Deck's Canicopulus Script is Gill Sans Serif with the satirical addition of puppy-dog tails. Other typeface designs are more polemical than practical in their acknowledgement of the contingency, impermanence and potential for chaos which is a basic condition of the **digital medium.** ERIK VAN BLOKLAND and JUST VAN ROSSUM's Beowolf is a family of unpredictable **random fonts** programmed for three levels of randomness whose broken, antique outlines shift and reform every time a letter is produced so that no character is ever the same twice. Van Blokland and van Rossum, mavericks with a semi-serious message about the shortcomings of computerised perfection, speculate on the possibility of developing fonts that will cause characters to drop out at random, or to print upside down, and typefaces that will slowly decay until they eventually become illegible in a **digital parody** of hot-metal type. Jonathan Barnbrook goes a step further by extending this nihilistic randomising principle to the text itself. His typeface Burroughs (named after the novelist with a penchant for textual "cut-ups") replaces whatever is typeset with a **stream of gibberish** generated at random by the software.

Rick Poynor's text and the design by Why Not Associates are in close sync throughout the book.

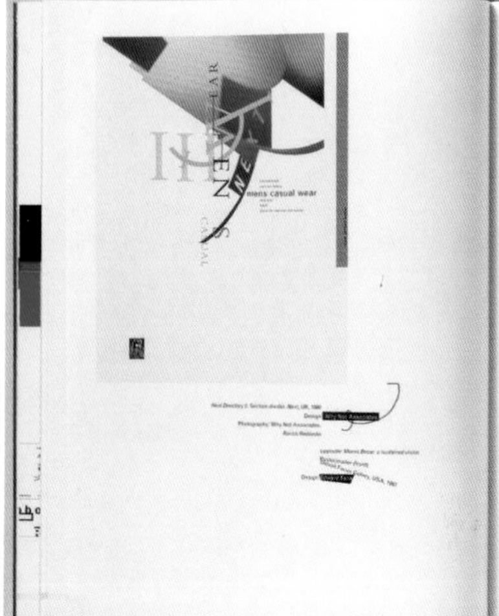

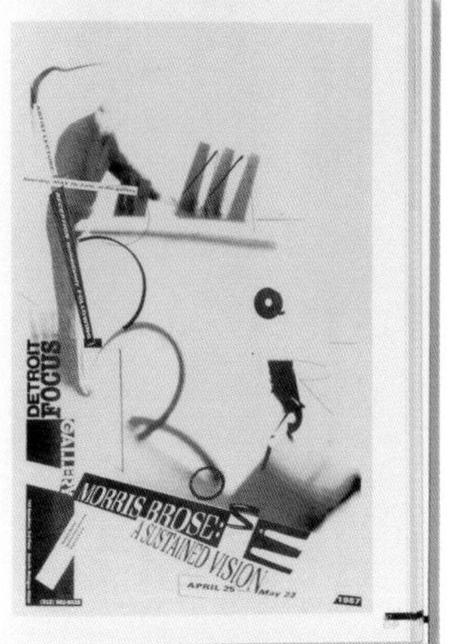

Typography Now
The Next Wave
Edward Booth-Clibborn, Why Not Associates, Rick Poynor
Booth-Clibborn Editions, London, 1991
224 pages
273 × 215 mm (10.75 × 8.5 in)
Designed by Why Not Associates

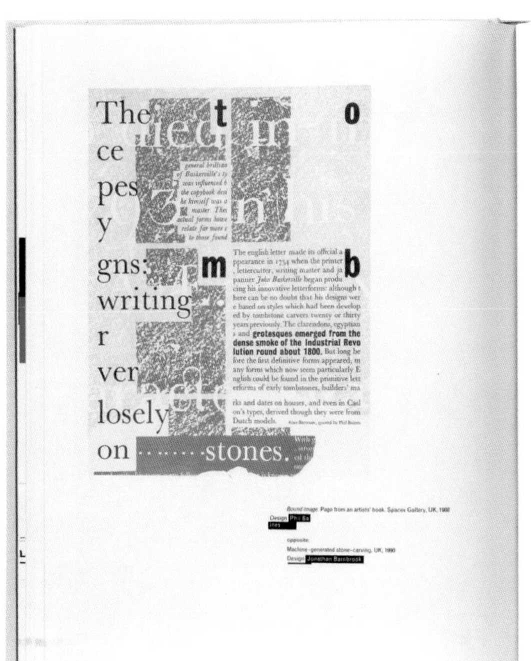

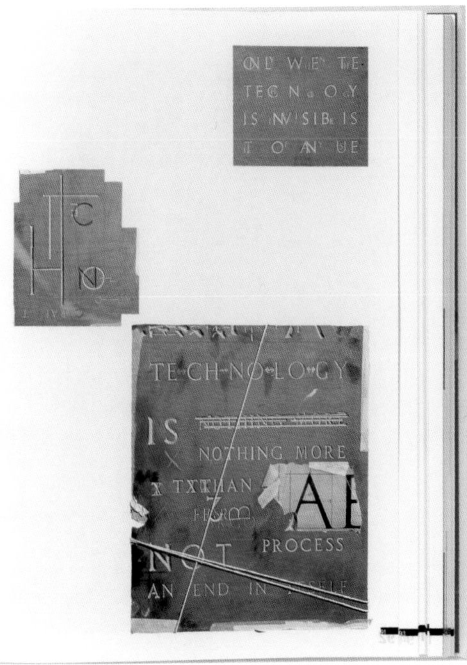

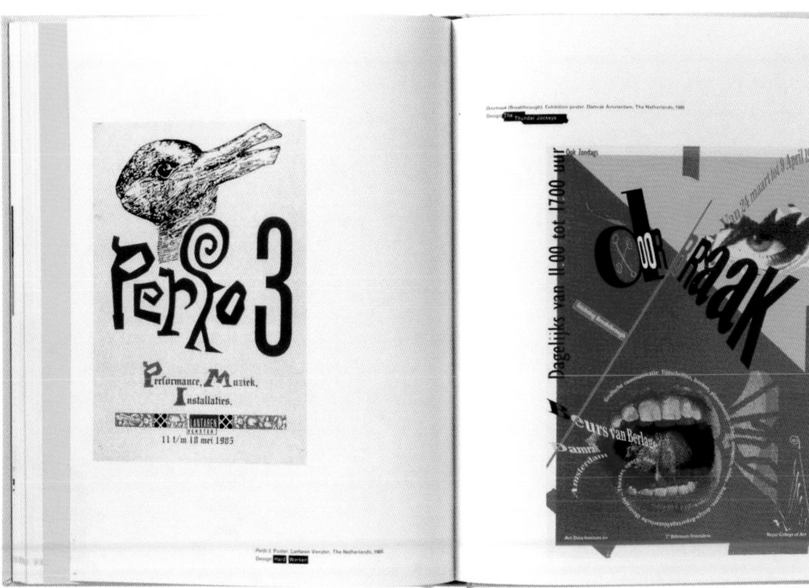

In contrast to the introduction and section openers, the spreads are restrained, with minimal captioning. Seen here are the work of Phil Baines (left) and Jonathan Barnbrook (right).

Before 1991, an art bookshop would have contained a very slim selection of books on graphic design: some annuals, the occasional monograph and perhaps the ubiquitous *The Graphic Language of Neville Brody*. Into this near-vacuum stepped *Typography Now*, by publisher Edward Booth-Clibborn, writer Rick Poynor and British designers Why Not Associates.

The book showcased a revolution in graphic design. It brought together an international selection of typographic mavericks who had tired of the Swiss-inspired orthodoxy that was still prevalent in much of the design industry at the time, and who were simultaneously exploring the freedoms afforded by the advent of digitized page layout and type design.

Describing *Typography Now* as only 'an interim report' on this nascent movement, the text by Rick Poynor pulls the disparate collection of designers together under a common cause. Packaged by Why Not Associates in their flamboyant deconstructionist style, the way the book looks is as much an exhibit as its contents.

The selections vary from the gung-ho spirit of the Thunder Jockeys to the theoretical work of Cranbrook Academy of Art disciples Katherine McCoy, Allen Hori and P. Scott Makela, and the craft-based designs of Phil Baines and Jonathan Barnbrook. Cultural events, the music industry and magazines dominate. Well represented are designers such as Neville Brody, David Carson, Studio Dumbar, 8vo and Ed Fella.

Many pages are devoted to Rudy VanderLans and Zuzana Licko, and their pioneering type foundry, Emigre, and the magazine of the same name, which proved new markets existed for graphic design products. *Typography Now* changed book publishing in a similar fashion: its success paved the way for the myriad graphic design books that followed.

Carouschka's Tickets

Carouschka Streijffert, Peter Kihlgard

Testadora, Stockholm, 1998

394 pages

220 × 338 mm (8.625 × 13.25 in)

Designed by Pia Högberg, Clara von Zweigbergk

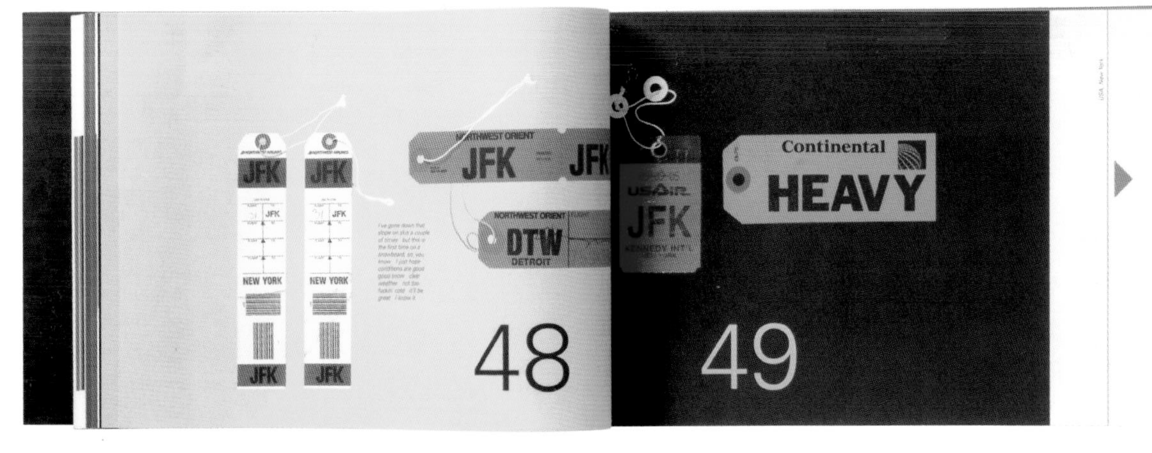

'Soon tickets will be gone,' warns the artist and designer Carouschka Streijffert (1955–) in the introduction to *Carouschka's Tickets*, foreseeing the advent of plastic metro cards and e-tickets. Her disappointment is tangible – 30 years of avid collection, meticulous cataloguing and eager anticipation of the next discovery have instilled in her a zealot's passion for printed tickets. For Streijffert, 'a find on the shining surface of a wet street can take my breath away, make me fall to my knees'.

Arranged according to the 70 countries from which they were gathered, all the tickets are somewhat haphazard in their design yet at the same time they bear witness to the order we have created in our world. Invariably they are designed anonymously and printed economically, the reason for their constant appeal to graphic designers.

However, Streijffert was less interested in the tickets as ephemera than she was in the stories they tell, and they appear with text of thoughts and overheard speech created in collaboration with the writer Peter Kihlgard. Whether these are real or imagined is unclear; nonetheless they give the pages the lyricism that takes the book beyond a mere collection.

At nearly 3 kilograms (6.5 pounds), *Tickets* is hefty. Its pages are French-folded and bound by a couple of long binding posts. The design by Pia Högberg and Clara von Zweigbergk uses clever enlargement and a bold colour scheme of rectangular elements to enhance the rather threadbare and tattered appearance of the tickets. The extra-large pagination makes it difficult to lose your place in the book.

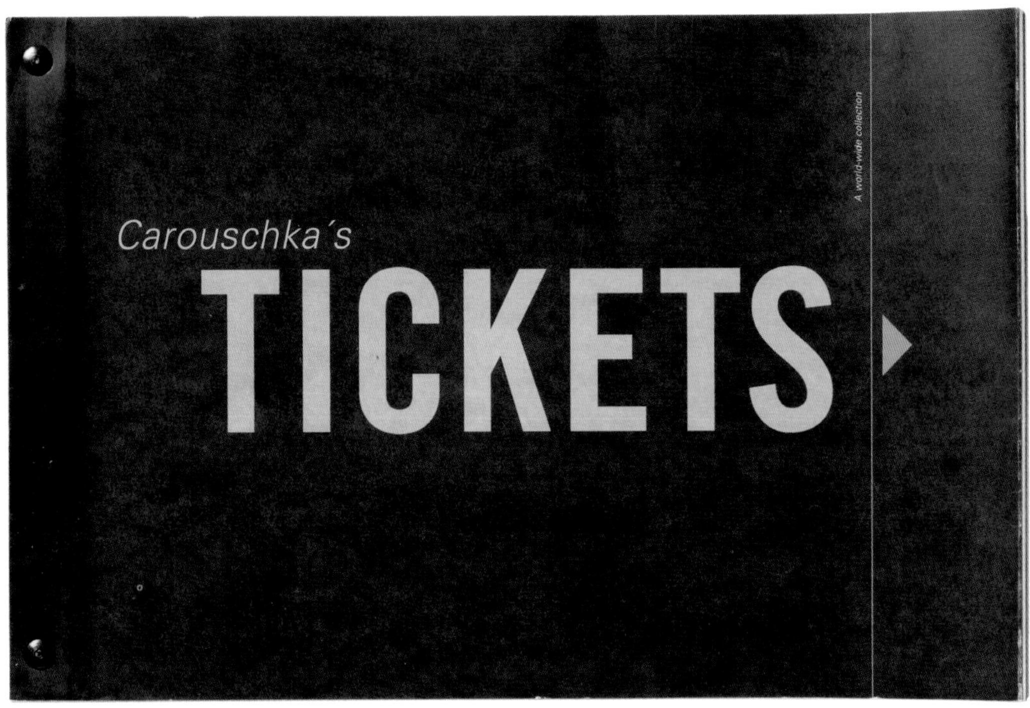

Carouschka's Tickets *is self-covered, 50 mm (2 in) thick and bound by the binding posts, seen on the left.*

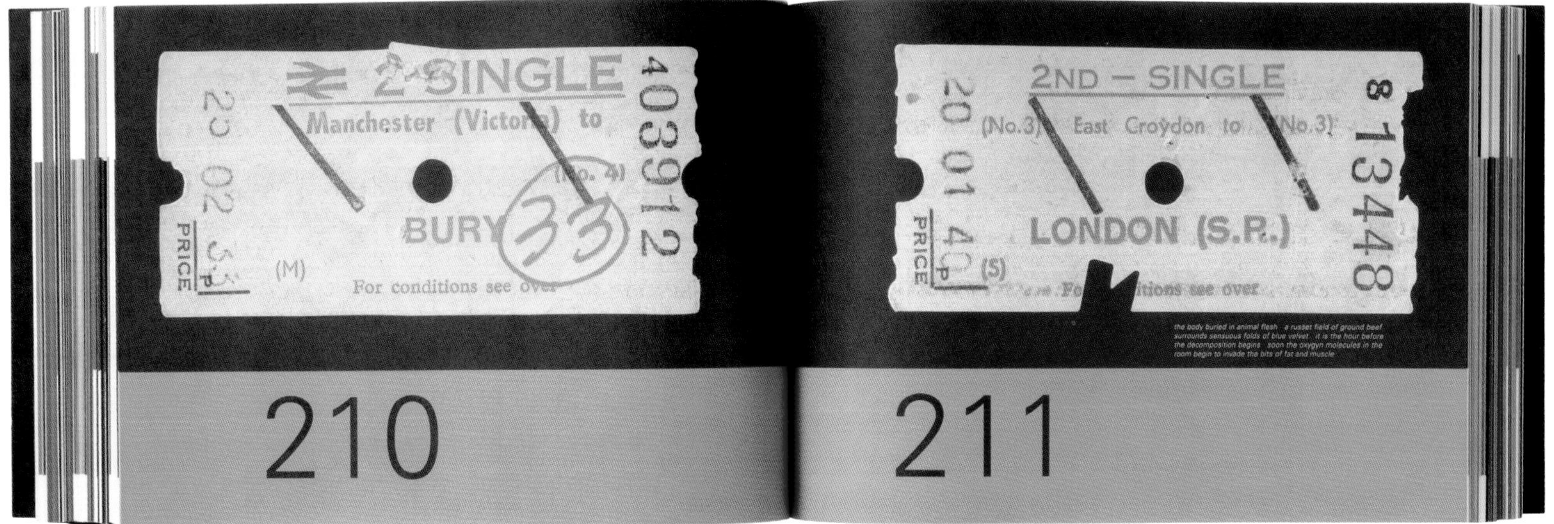

The design of the layouts is bold: the tickets are placed on varying coloured backgrounds, the tickets change size from spread to spread and the supersized pagination mimics numerals on the tickets.

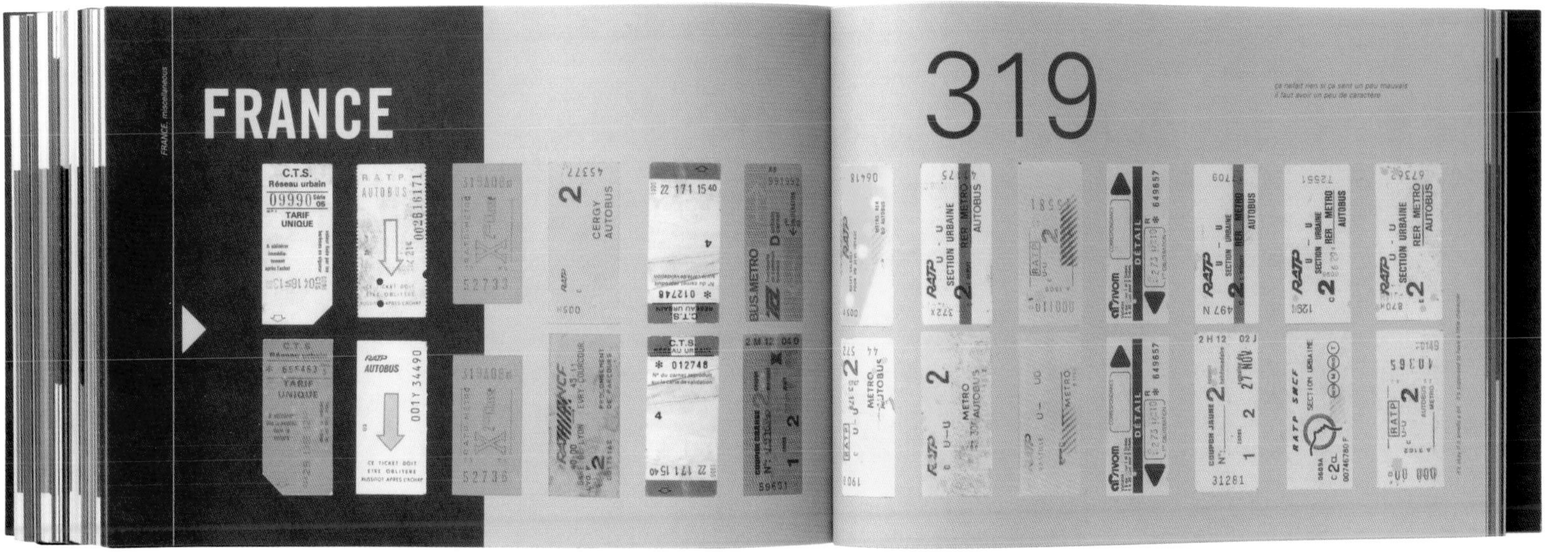

Monographs

Rand was afforded few full-colour pages. Here he uses full-bleed for the cover of *Jazzways* magazine (1946).*

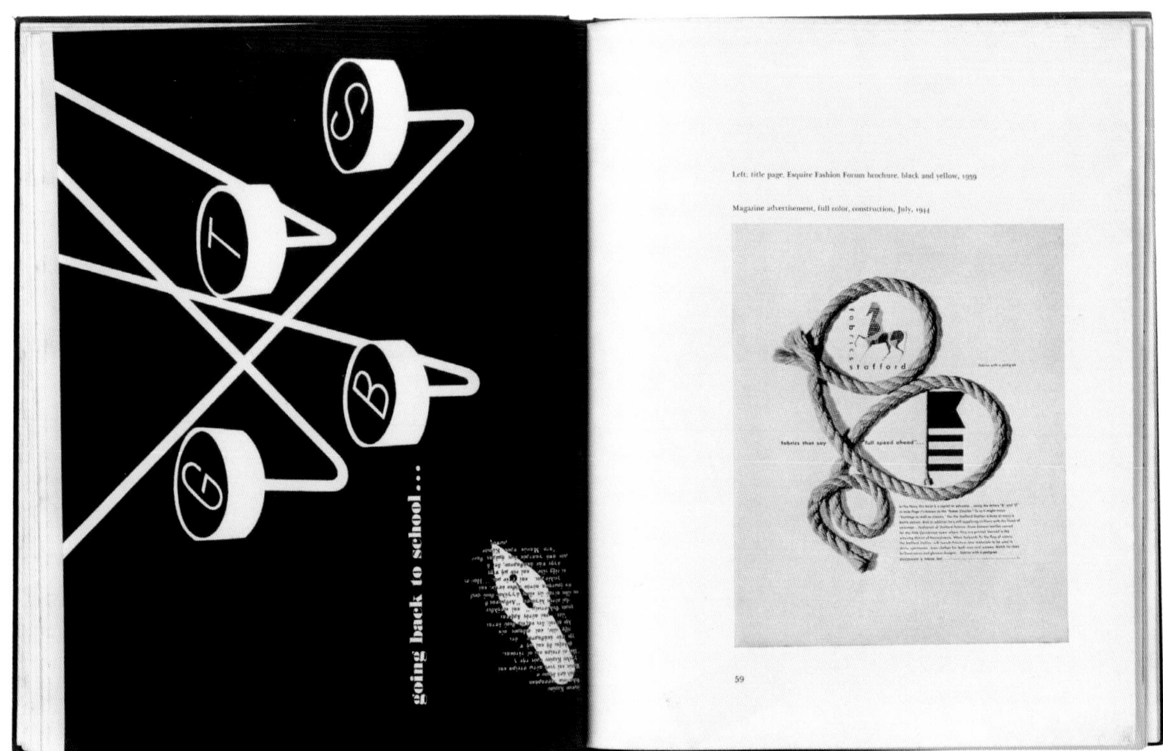

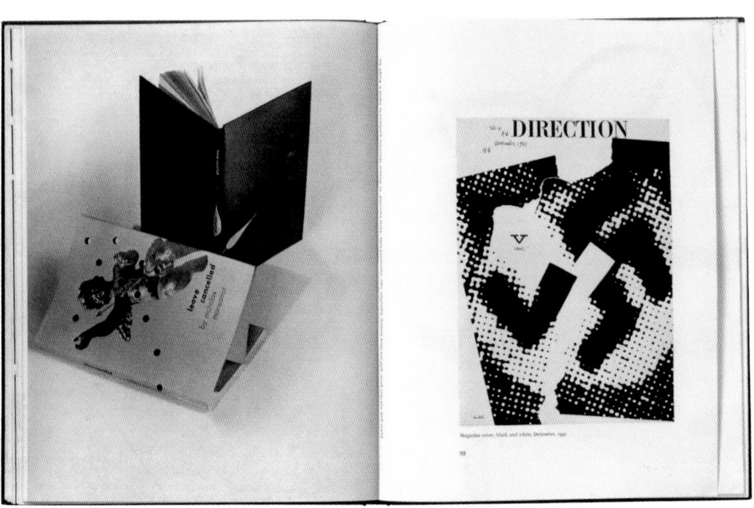

Thoughts on Design

Paul Rand

Wittenborn, New York, 1947
172 pages
267 × 213 mm (10.5 × 8.375 in)
Designed by Paul Rand

Thoughts on Design by Paul Rand (1914–1996) was a seminal text that defined modern graphic design and influenced a generation or more of designers (it was three decades before Rand's next book was published). Only 32 at the time of its publication, Rand had refined his beguilingly simple blend of art and advertising through his own practice and a stint working as art director to the famed copywriter William Bernbach at the Weintraub Agency in New York City.

As the book's enticing title suggests, Rand offers readers his views on the art of a designer. His essays are succinct and deal with a range of subjects, including the role of symbols, the importance of humour, and the use of collage and typographic expression – French and Spanish texts are available at the end of the book. Rand's ability to clearly articulate his ideas undoubtedly set him apart from his contemporaries and added greatly to the legacy of his graphic design.

The book's open design and large margins provide ample space to display Rand's portfolio of work. Playful advertising work for Coronet Brandy is balanced by the graphic strength of his collage covers for *Direction* magazine. Other clients who are well represented are Stafford Fabrics and Jacqueline Cochran Cosmetics. The cover, with its photogram of an abacus, became a design icon.

Although Rand touched on the subject of symbols, *Thoughts on Design* predates the advent of corporate identity and many of Rand's more famous pieces of work. Some of these designs are included in a re-edited and redesigned edition published in 1970 (Studio Vista, London; Van Nostrand Reinhold Company, New York), and, more notably, in *A Designer's Art*, a complete update of the original book (see page 174).

Notable books on Rand's career include Steven Heller's comprehensive survey *Paul Rand* (Phaidon Press, London, 1999) and *Paul Rand: Modernist Design* edited by Franco Nunoo-Quarcoo (Center for Art and Visual Culture, University of Maryland, Baltimore, 2003).

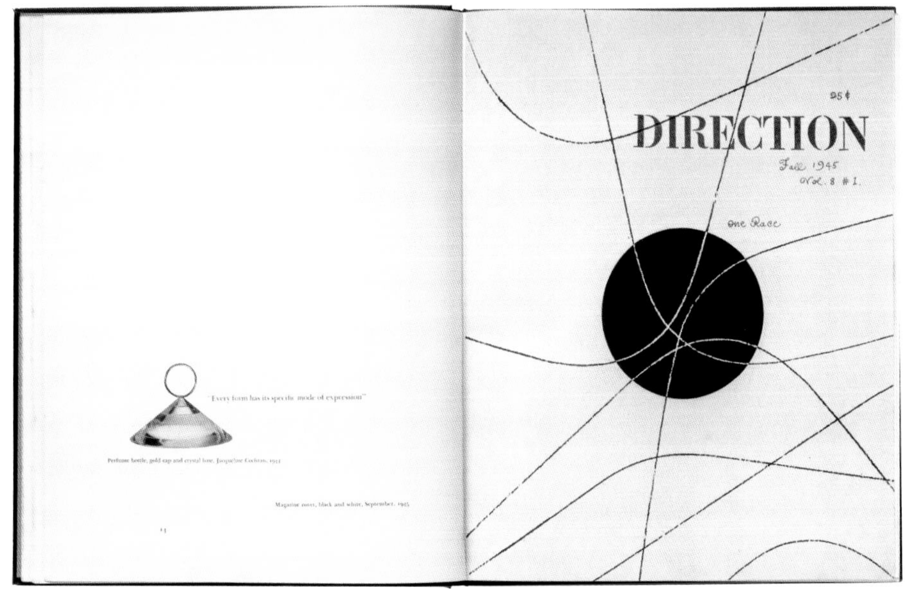

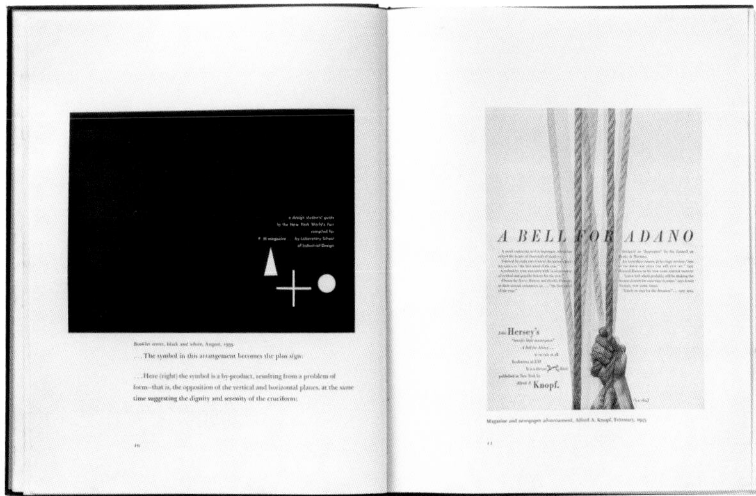

Rand's skill at the art of placement is evident in the featured work and in his considered page layouts.

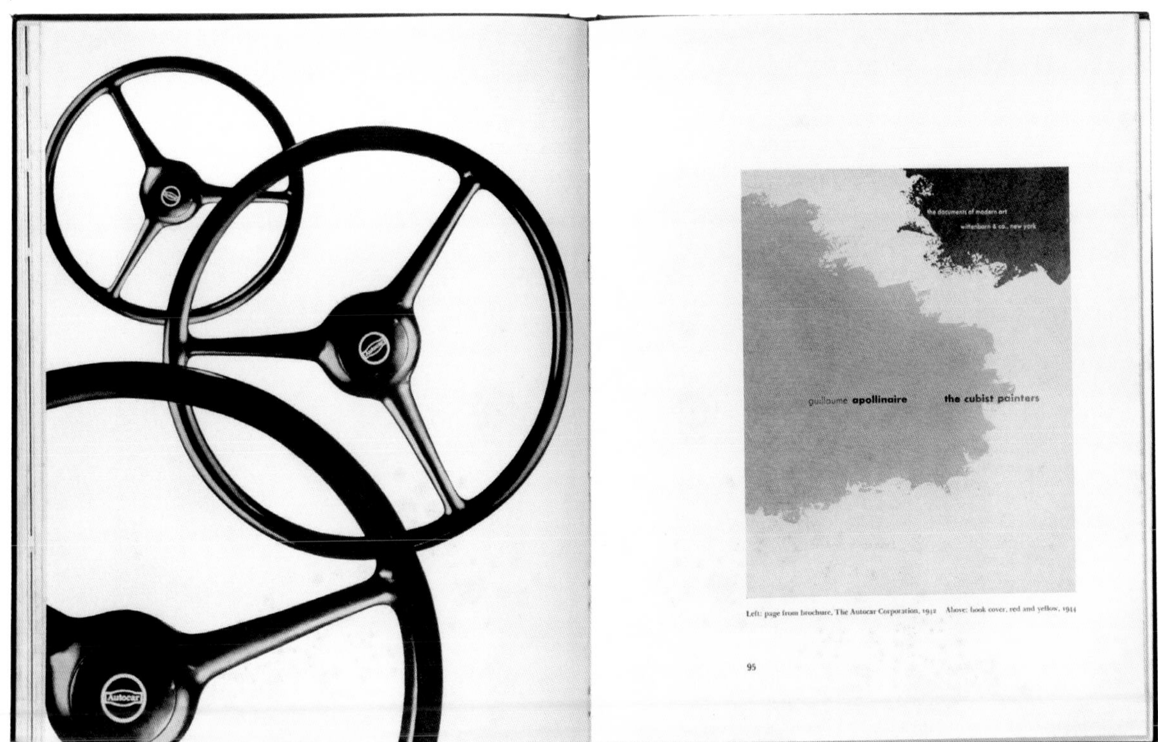

Esposizioni e Mostre

Erberto Carboni
Silvana, Milan, 1957
218 pages
288 × 215 mm (11.375 × 8.5 in)
Designed by Erberto Carboni

The Italian designer Erberto Carboni (1899–1984) originally studied architecture but moved to a career in the graphic arts. An associate of Studio Boggeri in Milan, which dominated much of Italian graphic design and advertising in the middle of the twentieth century, Carboni went on to develop his own impressive list of clients including major corporations such as Agip, Pirelli and Barilla.

An aspect of his work that made full use of all his talents as a designer was exhibition design. The trade fairs and expositions that had developed from the Great Exhibition, London (1851), required the design of temporary structures that could easily be moved and relocated. They had to incorporate three-dimensional elements, images, text, sound and vision, and the flow of people around them had to be controlled. Carboni's sculptural sense, illustrative ability and modern typographical style created a unique set of environments for this discipline.

Esposizioni e Mostre ('Exhibitions and Displays') represents Carboni's prodigious output of exhibition design from 1934 to 1955. In his introduction Herbert Bayer calls it 'a document of an amazingly productive mind in the service of our times'. The book begins with a note of congratulation from Walter Gropius for Carboni's work on the Italian Aeronautical Exhibition in Milan (1934), and the hundreds of photographs that follow look at his designs in chronological order. Printed mostly in black and white, with some colour images that give a better idea of the impact of his work, it includes notable projects such as the Industrial Chemicals Hall in Milan (1950) with its apparatus-like forms, and his space age, television-shaped tunnel for RAI, the Italian broadcaster (1954). English, German and French translations are provided.

In the late 1950s and early 1960s Carboni published a number of books on different aspects of his work, including *Radio and Television Publicity* (New York Graphic Society, Greenwich, 1959) and *25 Publicity Campaigns* (New York Graphic Society, Greenwich, 1961).

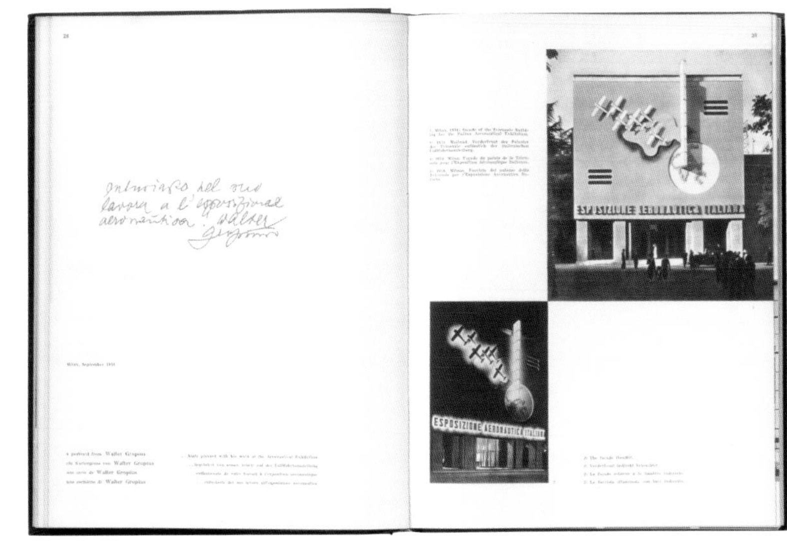

Carboni made an extensive record of his exhibition spaces, with many images of each featured project, from general photographs to details of the artwork and typography.

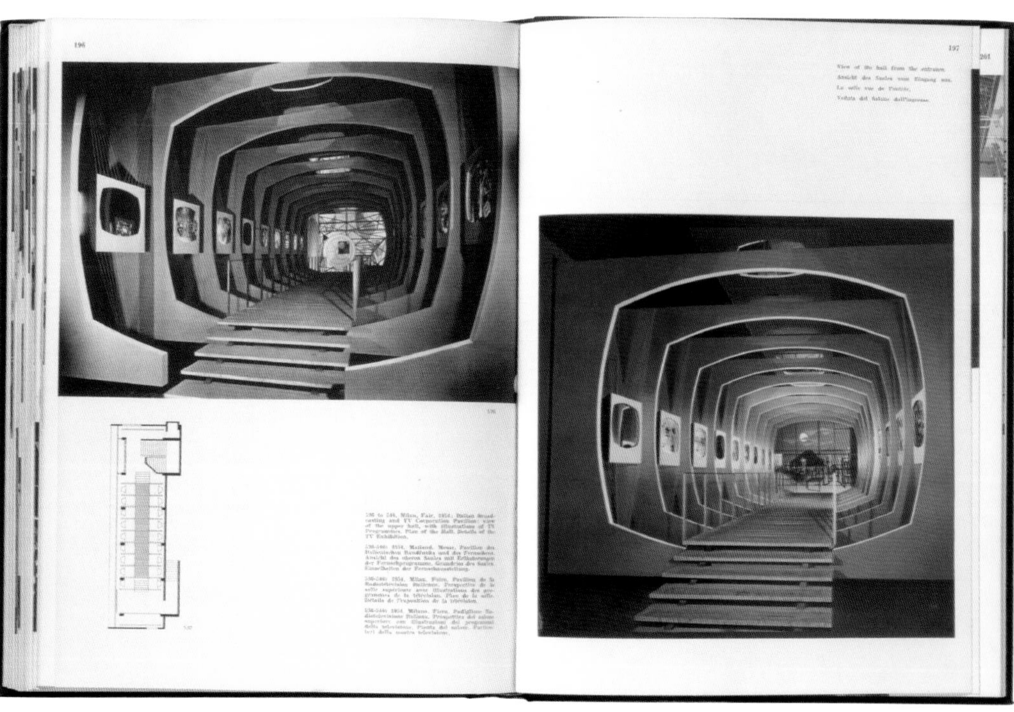

Carboni employs available colour plates for maximum visual impact, as here for the sculptural forms in his design for the Industrial Chemicals Hall in Milan (1950).

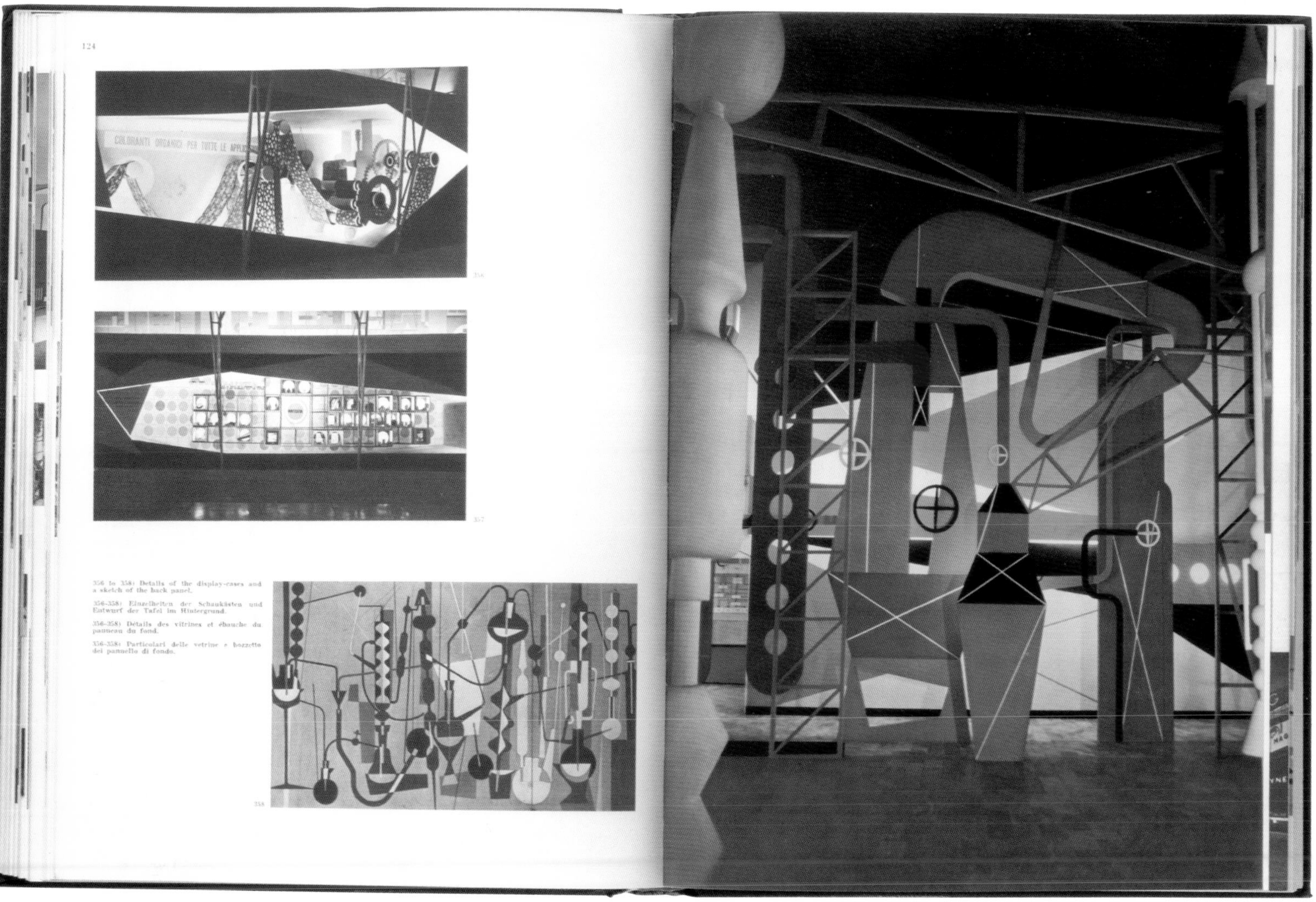

124

COLORANTI ORGANICI PER TUTTE LE APPLI

356 to 358) Details of the display-cases and a sketch of the back panel.

356-358) Einzelheiten der Schaukästen und Entwurf der Tafel im Hintergrund.

356-358) Détails des vitrines et ébauche du panneau du fond.

356-358) Particolari delle vetrine e bozzetto del pannello di fondo.

c/3 — new typography — new visual interest with photographs

New techniques for utilizing photographs and photomontages were introduced to create attention-commanding effects on posters and book jackets. As a new design element, the photograph lent itself to many imaginative innovations. Possibly for the first time, a detail from a photograph was selected and blown up to "poster" size to increase impact. Another device was to incorporate a photograph in a geometrical or abstract design, for a feeling of reality. — (Examples from Sutnar's book jackets, 1929–1938) — Some of the early design ideas of photograph applications are here illustrated. Poster-type book jacket, with a blown-up cropped photograph, (below, right). Montages incorporated in a simple geometrical design for a set of books, (below, left). Jacket design which was developed organically out of the photographed subject, (opposite page, top), and photograph superimposed on abstract map design, (opposite page, bottom), for immediate appeal of a dramatic symbol. — Such was the forerunner of today's practice.

A spread from one of the four 'colour portfolios' found in the book. These were printed on uncoated stocks. This portfolio was entitled 'An interval of design freedom' and features Sutnar's powerful abstract compositions.

Visual Design in Action
Principles, Purposes
Ladislav Sutnar
Hastings House, New York, 1961
188 pages
310 × 210 mm (12.25 × 8.25 in)
Designed by Ladislav Sutnar

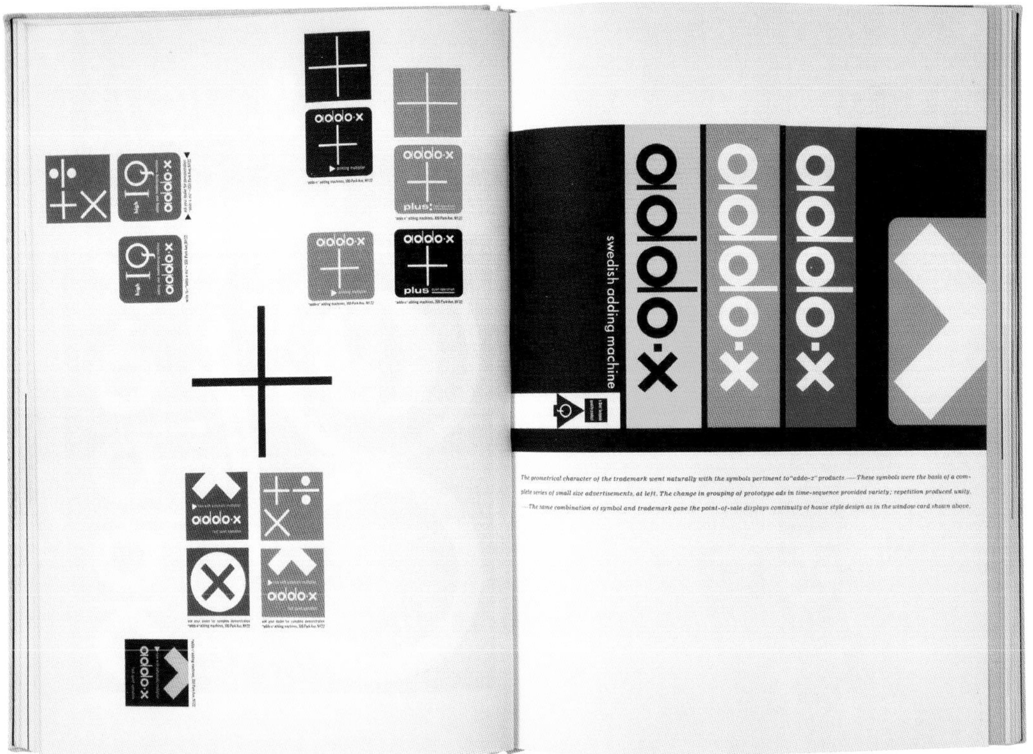

Pages from another 'colour portfolio' – 'Adventures with a logotype', a study of Sutnar's work on the development of the identity for Addo-x business machines.

The career of the Czech designer Ladislav Sutnar (1896–1976) spanned major eras in the history of modern graphic design. Always an innovator, he was one of the pioneers of modernism in Europe in the vital period of the late 1920s and early 1930s, and, after emigrating to the United States in 1939, he greatly influenced the development of an American graphic design.

Visual Design in Action is an overview of Sutnar's best work, unique talent and typographic principles. In the first section he proclaims his belief in a functional and rational dynamic modernism that is not underpinned by any system of stylistic rules. The layout of the book exemplifies his way of thinking: designs are boldly arranged on spreads and mixed with restrained typography, both expertly paced from page to page.

A major section in the book is given over to Sutnar's work in America. It contains subsections that look at numerous elements of graphic design, including symbols, direct mail, magazines and alphabets, and shows examples of his work for his major clients: Addo-x, Scarves by Vera, Sweet's Catalog Service and Carr's department store.

Visual Design in Action is mostly black and white on glossy Champion Kromekote, with interjections called 'colour portfolios', often on different stocks, that show Sutnar's dynamic graphic skills. The last, and most impressive, of these is 'An interval of design freedom', which exhibits abstract compositions unshackled by commercial constraints.

A final section looks back at Sutnar's work during the first half of his career as a disciple of the New Typography in Czechoslovakia; among other items, it displays the striking book jackets he designed from 1928 to 1938, including the much-reproduced *Nejmenší Dům* ('Minimum House') of 1931.

Love and Joy about Letters

Ben Shahn

Cory, Adams & Mackay,
London, 1964
80 pages
254 × 343 mm (10 × 13.5 in)

As a schoolboy Ben Shahn (1898–1969) relished the laborious task of copying Hebrew letters. It was the start of a lifelong love of lettering for this American artist, which he recounts in this book. His family's emigration from Lithuania to the United States and his subsequent exposure to the Roman alphabet only increased his interest in letterforms. Apprenticeship to a commercial lithographer at the age of 14 forced him to focus on the typographic nuances of letter drawing and spacing, and fostered a belief in himself as a craftsman.

Printed in Switzerland in a mixture of colour and black and white on substantial uncoated paper, and first published by Grossman Publishers in New York in 1963, *Love and Joy about Letters* is an extension of this craftsman's ethos. The running autobiographical text is interlaced with illustrations of Shahn's lettering in paintings, posters, graphic art and illustrations.

Mixed with these are examples of work that influenced and interested him. He admired the rawness and direct nature of graffiti, handwriting and amateur lettering, and specimens of these are included alongside Chinese and Japanese calligraphy, which, for Shahn, could simultaneously encompass both artistic discipline and expression. This joy in lettering is clearly seen in the many religious commissions he undertook in both the Hebrew and the Roman alphabets.

Socially aware, Shahn was drawn to subjects that dealt with injustice, including, in the 1920s, the trial for murder of the political radicals Nicola Sacco and Bartolomeo Vanzetti, who were subsequently executed even though another man confessed to the crime. Inspired to illustrate Vanzetti's words before execution, he developed an alphabet with the wrong stress on letters, common to many amateur efforts at lettering. He continued to use these letterforms, and the angular, thick and thin alphabet became synonymous with his work and was much mimicked by other graphic artists.

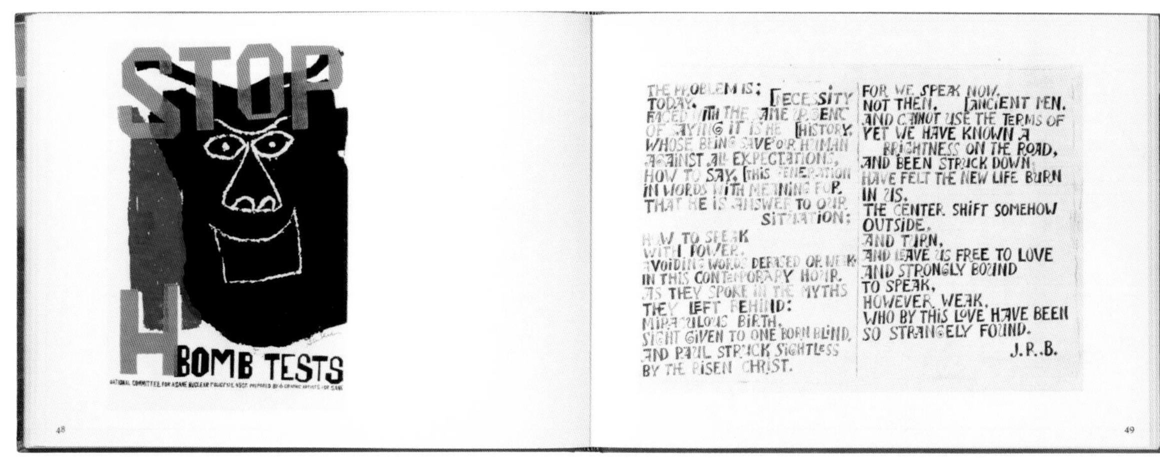

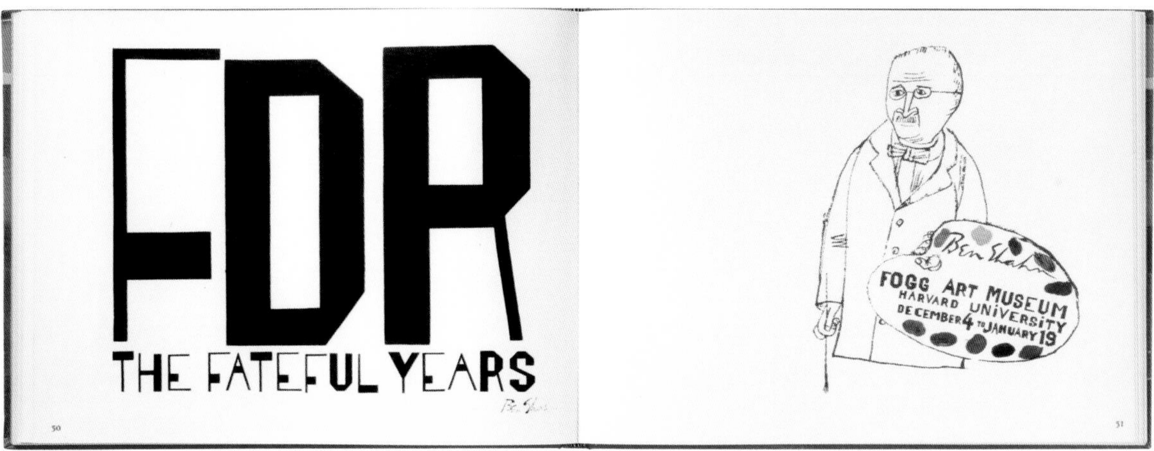

IF IT HAD NOT BEEN FOR THESE THING, I MIGHT HAVE LIVE OUT MY LIFE TALKING AT STREET CORNERS TO SCORNING MEN. I MIGHT HAVE DIE, UNMARKED, UNKNOWN A FAILURE. NOW WE ARE NOT A FAILURE. THIS IS OUR CAREER AND OUR TRIUMPH. NEVER IN OUR FULL LIFE COULD WE HOPE TO DO SUCH WORK FOR TOLERANCE, FOR JOOSTICE, FOR MAN'S ONDERSTANDING OF MAN AS NOW WE DO BY ACCIDENT. OUR WORDS - OUR LIVES - OUR PAINS NOTHING! THE TAKING OF OUR LIVES - LIVES OF A GOOD SHOEMAKER AND A POOR FISH PEDDLER - ALL! THAT LAST MOMENT BELONGS TO US - THAT AGONY IS OUR TRIUMPH.

40

THEN UP SPOKE OUR LORD JESUS

HE SPAKE FROM MARY'S HEART

I'LL MAKE THAT CHERRY TREE BOW DOWN

I'LL TAKE MY MAMMY'S PART

41

A spread showing on the left the alphabet that would define Shahn's lettering style, designed for artwork on the Sacco and Vanzetti case.

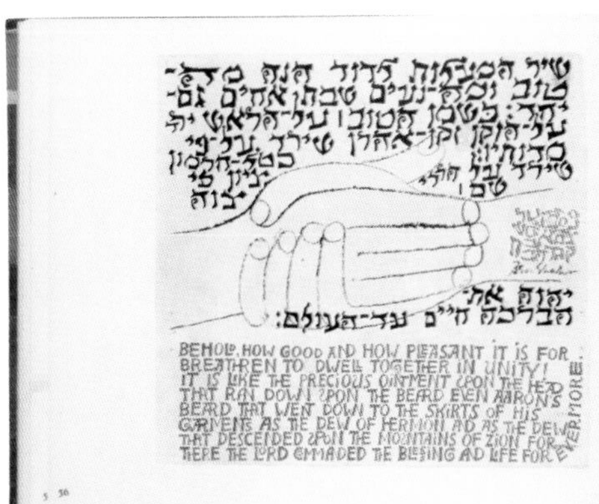

An unusual layout with two posters placed on their side and facing each other.

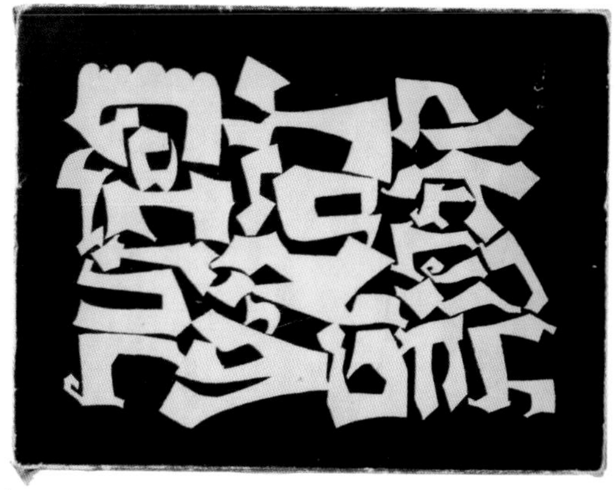

The slipcase for Love and Joy about Letters *with its Hebrew lettering.*

60

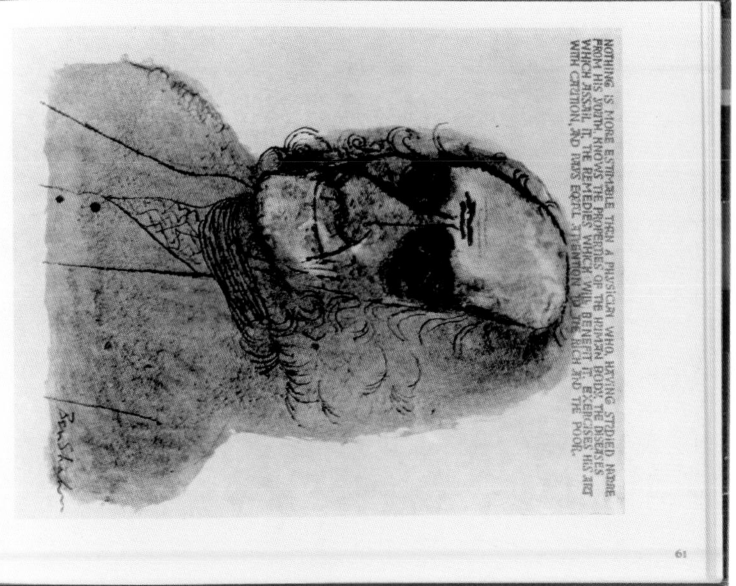

61

Glaser's famous Big Nudes *poster (1968) is run across the book's gutter, accentuating the drawing's conceit of the nude not fitting on its own paper.*

The Visual Craft of William Golden, Cipe Pineles Golden, Kurt Weihs, Robert Strunsky (editors), Braziller, New York, 1962
Graphic Design Manual, Armin Hofmann, Van Nostrand Reinhold Company, New York, 1965
The Medium is the Massage, Marshall McLuhan, Quentin Fiore, Random House, New York, 1967
American Wood Type: 1828–1900, Rob Roy Kelly, Van Nostrand Reinhold Company, New York, 1969
Aim for a Job in Graphic Design / Art, S. Neil Fujita, Richards Rosen Press, New York, 1968
Milton Glaser: Graphic Design, Milton Glaser, The Overlook Press, Woodstock, 1973
The Art of Advertising, George Lois, Bill Pitts, Harry N. Abrams, New York, 1977
Fellow Readers: Notes on Multiplied Language, Robin Kinross, Hyphen Press, London, 1994
Design Writing Research: Writing on Graphic Design, Ellen Lupton, J. Abbott Miller, Princeton Architectural Press, New York, 1996
Make it Bigger, Paula Scher, Princeton Architectural Press, New York, 2002

Milton Glaser: Graphic Design
Milton Glaser
The Overlook Press,
Woodstock, 1973
Third reprint (pictured), 1983
242 pages
259 × 259 mm (10.125 × 10.125 in)
Designed by Milton Glaser

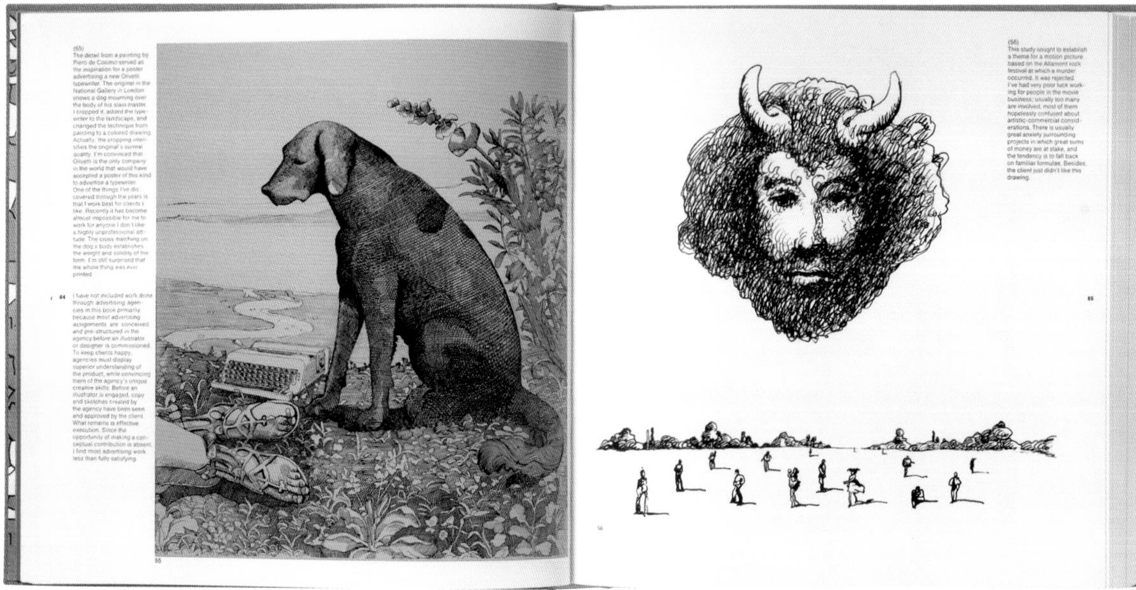

Milton Glaser: Graphic Design *is printed in a combination of full-colour sections and two-colour ones. Here a spread using black and beige shows Glaser's skill as a draughtsman. The illustration for Olivetti on the left references Piero de Cosimo's* Satyr Mourning over a Nymph *(c.1495).*

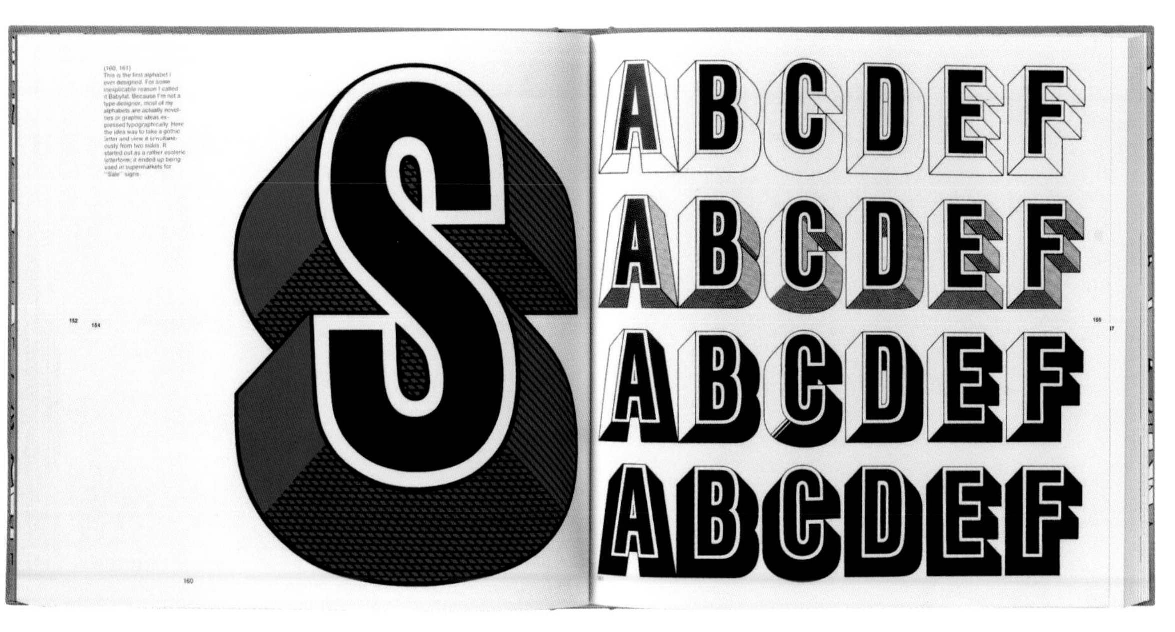

This was the first blockbuster graphic design book, an artist's monograph in disguise that has set the standard for design publishing ever since. It details the work of one of the most important American graphic designers, Milton Glaser (1939–), who, as co-founder of the influential Push Pin Studio, helped to shape the visual landscape of much of cultural America from the late 1950s through his posters, book jackets, LP sleeves, editorial illustrations and magazine design.

Glaser's range of work and sources of inspiration were far reaching. Each new problem afforded him new ways of interpretation, whether it was the diagonal lines on Jean-Michel Folon's letterhead to match the Belgian illustrator's slanted writing, or the decorative possibilities afforded by various combinations of his concert poster for Mahalia Jackson (1967).

The book is short of the design rhetoric common to many publications. It has no chapters; instead there is a rolling sequence of works, each one annotated with informative captions by Glaser that deal with the intricacies of graphic problem-solving and designer–client relationships.

As a skilled artist, who had studied drawing under the painter Giorgio Morandi in Italy, Glaser's virtuoso pen and brush skills were undoubtedly part of the reason for his popularity beyond a graphic design audience. His cross-hatching and his brushwork in watercolour are highlighted in the designs at the start of the book.

Glaser's iconic 1966 portrait of Bob Dylan is on the book's cover. When questioned in the introduction by his interviewer (and publisher) Peter Mayer about what makes the image so 'American', Glaser links it to the work's believability in the 'cultural moment' – his original inspirations were a Marcel Duchamp silhouette and patterning in Turkish painting. He considered the whole world of art as his resource, and the many styles in which he worked as by-products of the 'boredom' of being confined too narrowly in any artistic direction.

The Graphic Design of Yusaku Kamekura

Yusaku Kamekura

Weatherhill/Bijutsu Shuppan-Sha, New York and Tokyo, 1973
188 pages
244 × 259 mm (9.625 × 10.25 in)
Designed by Yusaku Kamekura

The Graphic Design of Yusaku Kamekura begins with a foreword by Herbert Bayer and an unillustrated introduction, which are followed by the dazzling colour section of work. Here the first illustrations are the vivid posters Yusaku Kamekura (1915–1997) created for the camera company Nikon. Their bold geometric layout, sharp optical effects and heightened colour palette make reference to traditional Japanese graphic arts but clearly reflect a contemporary Japan – one whose flourishing camera industry meant the country was at the forefront of reprographic techniques.

Kamekura is best known for his work for the 1964 Olympic Games in Toyko. He designed the powerful symbol for the event, a large rising sun sitting above the famous five rings. A set of posters for the games is reproduced in the book; they feature carefully cropped, freeze-frame photographs of athletes in mid-action.

Pages with logo designs, printed in black only and often without lettering, provide a calming break in the book's progression. Kamekura's love of optical tricks and devices is evident in many of them, and his reworking of the Shell logo, which is featured across a number of spreads, is no exception. It was designed for an unsuccessful pitch to the petroleum company, and Kamekura accentuates the converging lines on the back of the shell, borrowing from traditional Japanese drawings of chrysanthemums.

His designs for packaging, book jackets and magazine covers come at the end of the section of work and are well illustrated. All the captions are in the appendix. Written by Kamekura, they provide a lively and often candid accompaniment to the many projects featured.

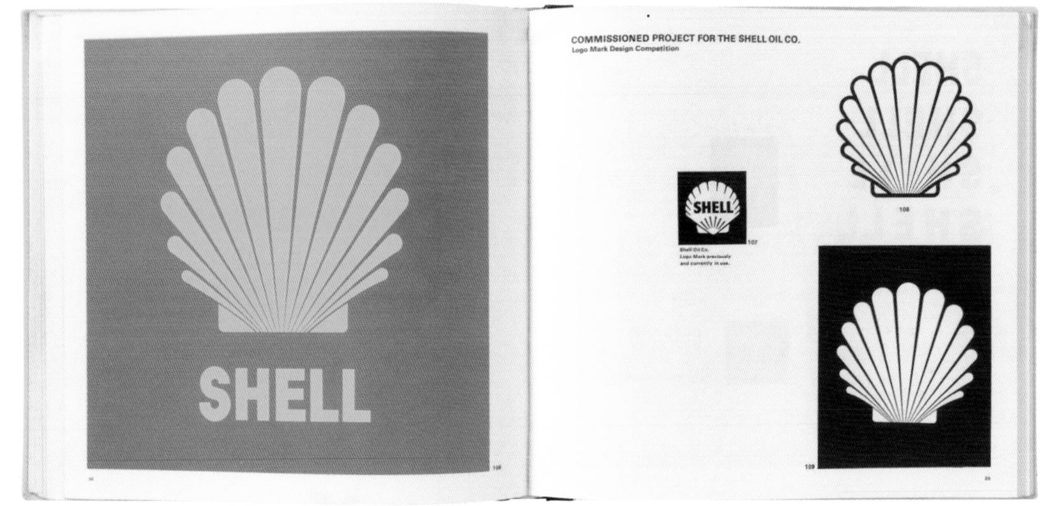

Pages showing an unused proposal commissioned by Shell, a detailed account of which is contained in the outspoken captions in the book's appendix.

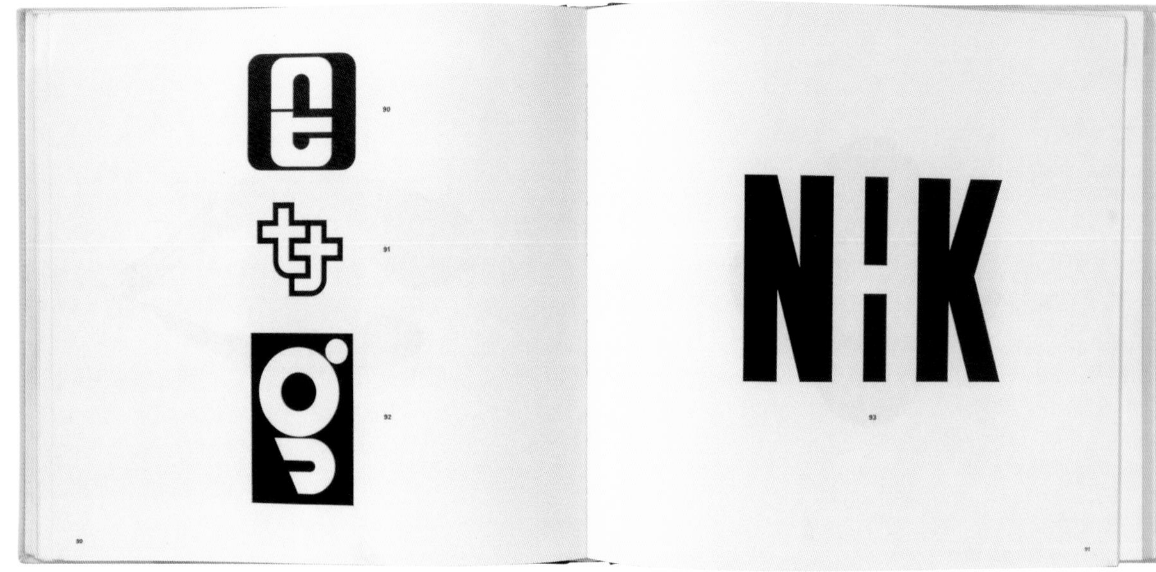

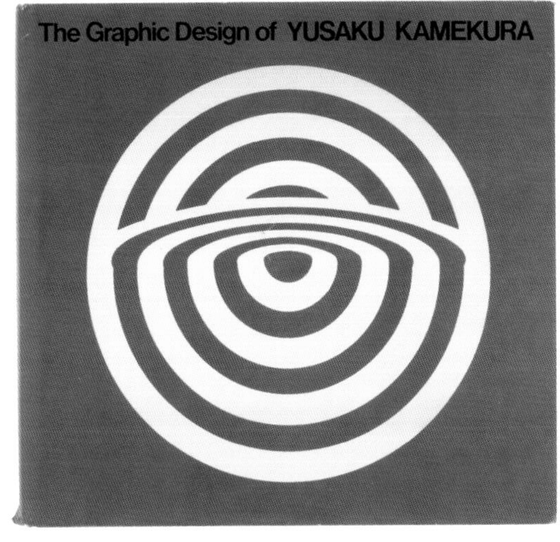

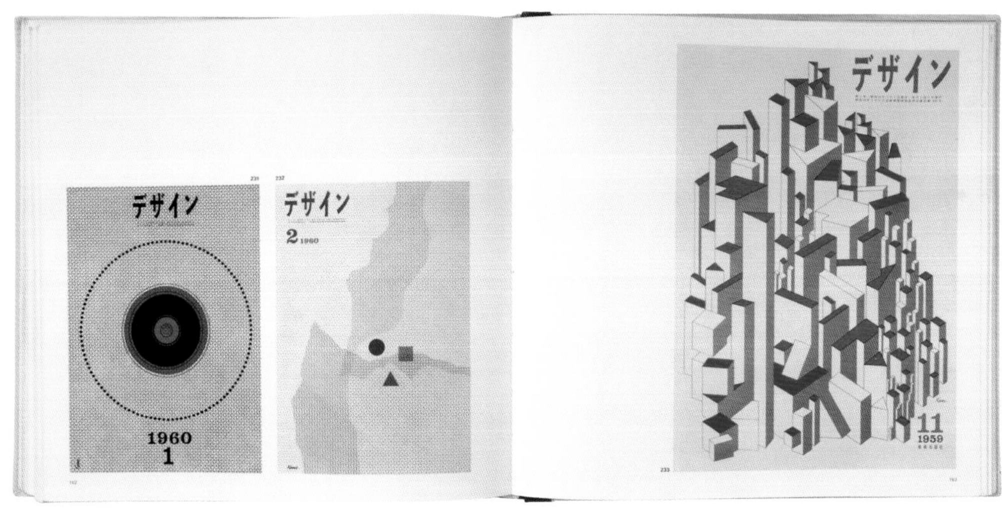

The vibrant posters for Nikon by Kamekura are well represented in the book, and benefit from the full-colour printing.

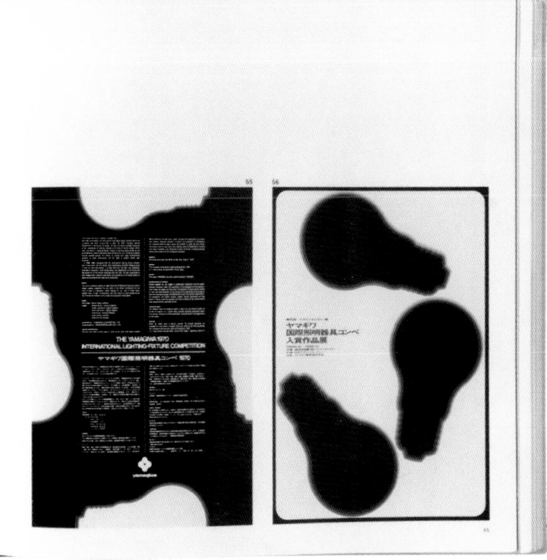

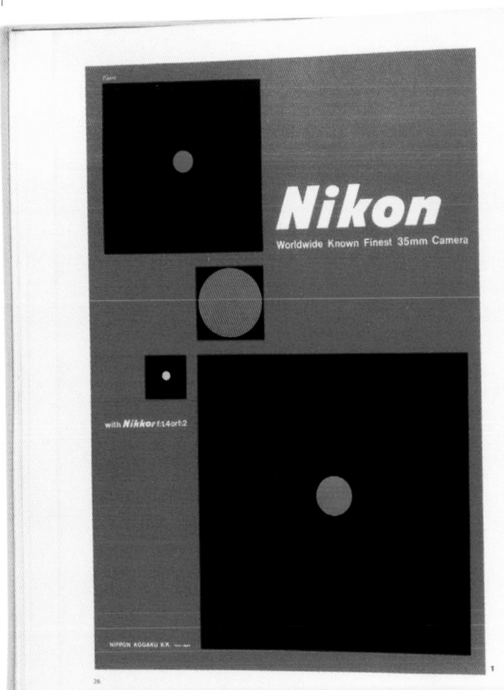

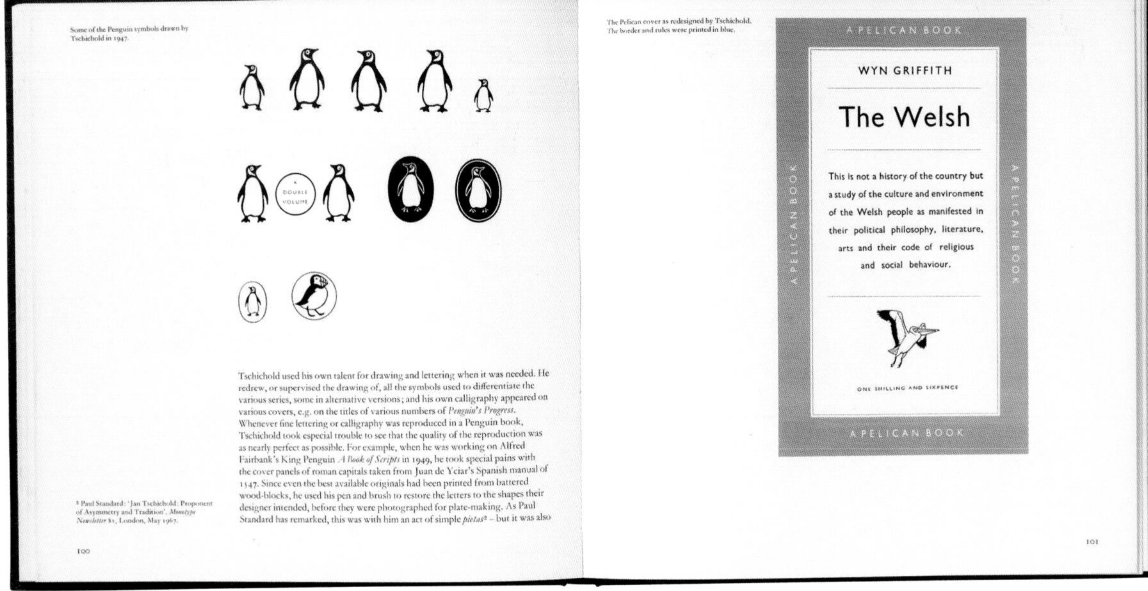

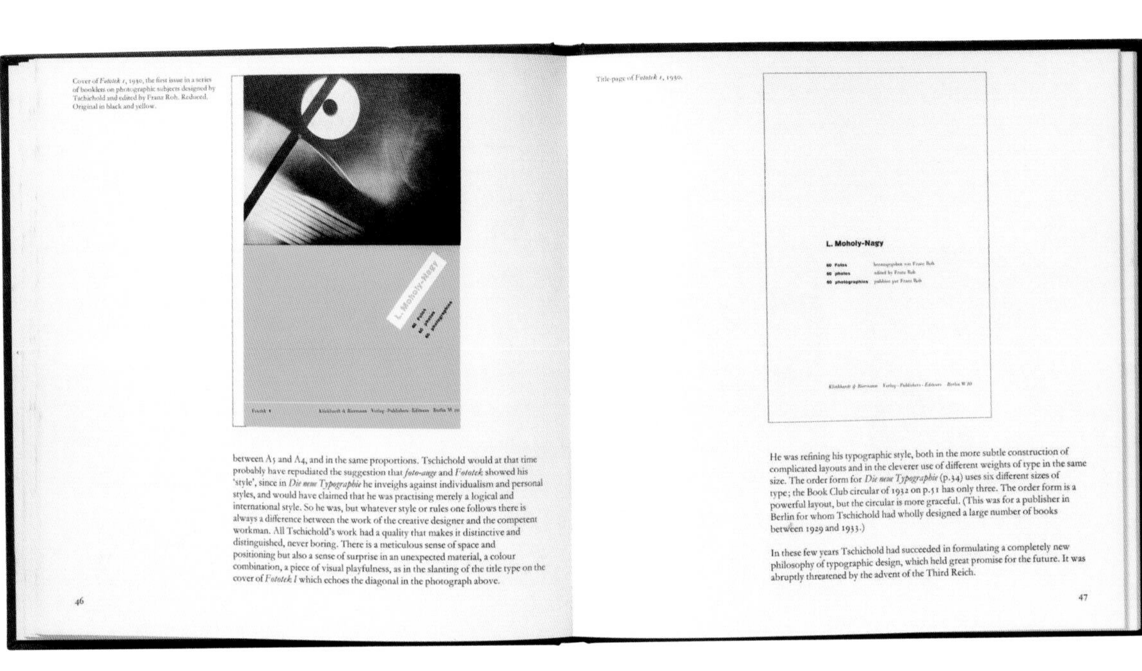

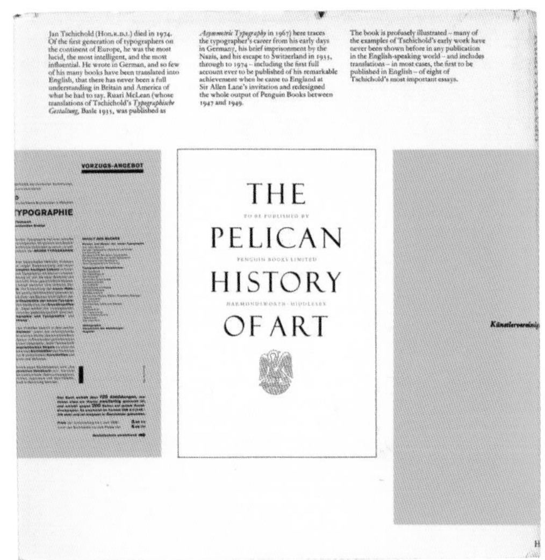

The back of the jacket extends the frieze of work from the front. Tschichold's design for a cover for an exhibition catalogue from 1933 folds around the spine.

Joseph Beuys: Posters, Isabel Siben, Prestel, Munich, 2004
Rauschenberg: Posters, Marc Gundel, Prestel, Munich, 2001
Tàpies' Posters and the Public Sphere, Nuria Enguita Mayo, Fundació Antoni Tàpies, Barcelona, 2006
Tom Phillips: Works, Texts to 1974, Tom Phillips, Edition Hansjörg Mayer, Stuttgart, 1975
Photography and Painting in the Work of Gerhard Richter: Four Essays on Atlas, Gerhard Richter, Actar, Barcelona, 2000
Swiss Graphic Design, Richard Hollis, Laurence King Publishing, London, 2006
Alle Radici della Communicazione Visiva Italiana, Heinz Waibl, Centro di Cultura Grafica, Como, 1988
Jan Tschichold: Typographer, Ruari McLean, Lund Humphries, London, 1975
Robert Brownjohn: Sex and Typography, Emily King, Laurence King Publishing, London, 2005
The Dictionary of Visual Language, Philip Thompson, Peter Davenport, Bergstrom & Boyle Books, London, 1980

Jan Tschichold: Typographer

Ruari McLean

Lund Humphries, London, 1975
160 pages
239 × 239 mm (9.375 × 9.375 in)
Designed by Herbert Spencer, Christine Charlton

In 1939, impressed with the typographic work of Jan Tschichold (1902–1974), a young Ruari McLean, then working for a printing works in Bradford, UK, used his holiday time to visit Tschichold in Basel, Switzerland. This resulted in a friendship that lasted until Tschichold's death a year before this biography was published.

Tschichold was the father of New Typography, and the early chapters in *Jan Tschichold: Typographer* show his progression from his earlier calligraphic design to one based on the clarity of asymmetric layouts and sans serif fonts. His first writings, a 1925 article, 'Elementare Typographie' ('The Principles of Typography') in the Leipzig *Typographische Mitteilungen*, followed in 1928 by *Die Neue Typographie* (see page 14), both advocated the application of these new typographic ideals and were highly influential. One of the most lucid of designers, he continued to write throughout his career. The appendix contains translations of some of his essays, available in English for the first time.

Persecution by the Nazis led Tschichold to leave his native Germany for Switzerland in 1933. His experience in book design had led him to realize that there were instances when symmetrical layouts and serif fonts were advantageous, and the well-illustrated chapter on his work for the Swiss publisher Birkhäuser shows how he excelled in this adaptation.

In 1947, after the Second World War, Tschichold moved to London at the invitation of Penguin Books. A detailed chapter describes his meticulous transformation of all the printed matter produced by this famous publisher. On returning to Switzerland he continued to design and write; his last major contribution was creating the Sabon typeface.

Jan Tschichold: Typographer is an elegant tribute to the man. The restrained layout and clever use of three colours (black, red and yellow) across a wide selection of images give nuance and balance to Tschichold's work.

Tschichold's affinity for book design is seen in the many covers for the Swiss publisher Birkhäuser. Here are examples from 1944 (left) and 1945 (right). The illustrations sometimes had to fit with the book's colour scheme – the right-hand jacket was originally printed black and green on ochre.

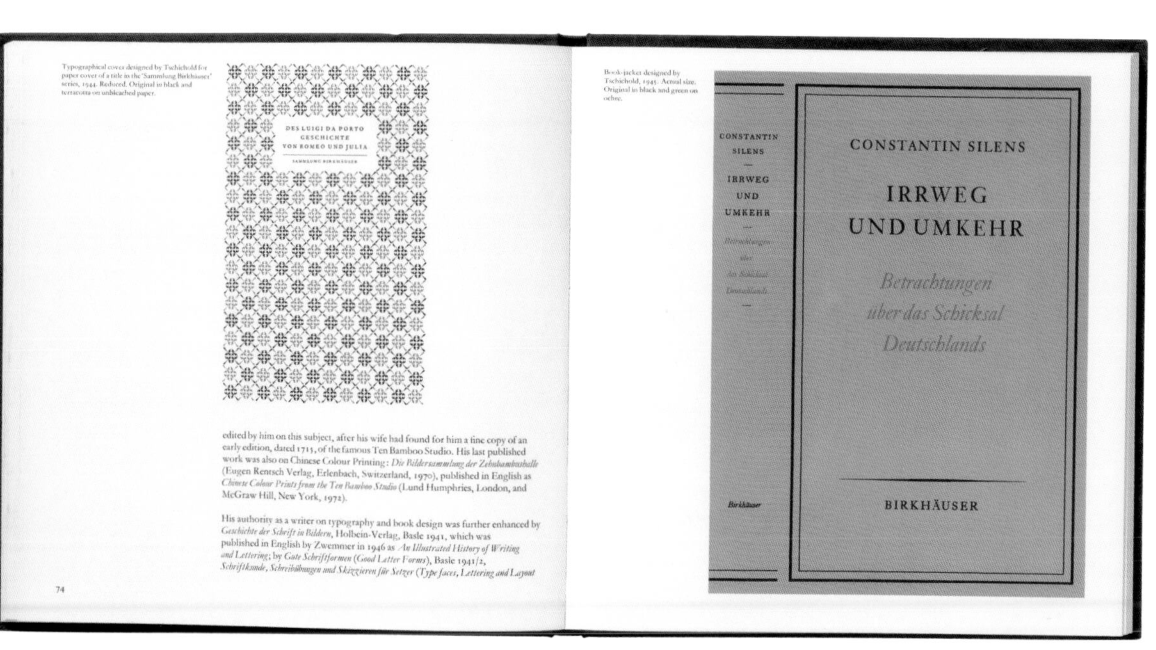

The Art of Advertising
George Lois on Mass Communication
George Lois, Bill Pitts
Harry N. Abrams, New York, 1977
332 pages
301 × 301 mm (11.875 × 11.875 in)

The Art of Advertising is a big book. It contains some of the most iconic works of the 1960s and early 1970s, all produced by the 'Madison Avenue maverick' George Lois (1931–). The most outspoken of a new generation of American admen in the years after the Second World War, Lois believed passionately that creative thinking had the power to move a mass audience. He boasted that he could 'out-design any one alive' and you wouldn't want to argue with him.

The book is divided into 18 themed chapters, such as 'New York', 'Eating', 'Drinking', 'Song' and 'Politicians', and the work it displays ranges from the Stevens '25¢ a leg' stockings ('Anyone who pays more ought to have her knees examined') to Lois's portrayal of Muhammad Ali as the martyred Saint Sebastian.

Lois's talent for shaping an idea through a combination of words and images is represented in his classic covers for *Esquire* magazine, to which one of the chapters is devoted. Also prominent is the 'When you got it – flaunt it' campaign created for Braniff Airways in 1967. This starred the chance meeting of artist Andy Warhol and boxer Sonny Liston and received the ultimate accolade when the headline became a saying in everyday use.

The insightful and entertaining narration throughout the book reflects Lois's enthusiasm and dedication. His story about the campaign for Goodman's Matzos is typical: he tells how he secured approval for a poster by threatening to throw himself off the client's window shouting 'You make the matzoh, I'll make the ads!'.

Profusely illustrated, mostly in full colour, with two pull-out pages, *The Art of Advertising* lacks for nothing in production values.

Lois's work for Esquire *would later become the subject of its own book,* Covering the 60s: George Lois – The Esquire Era, *Monacelli Press, New York, 1996.*

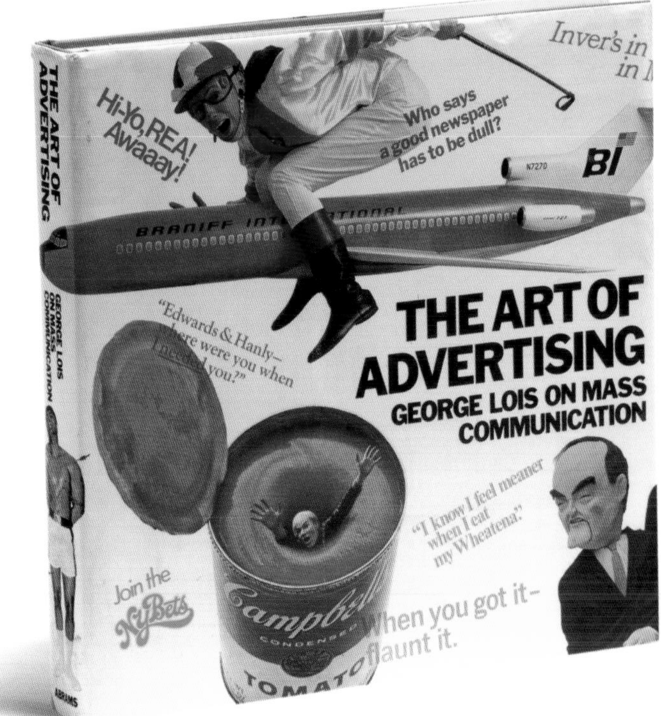

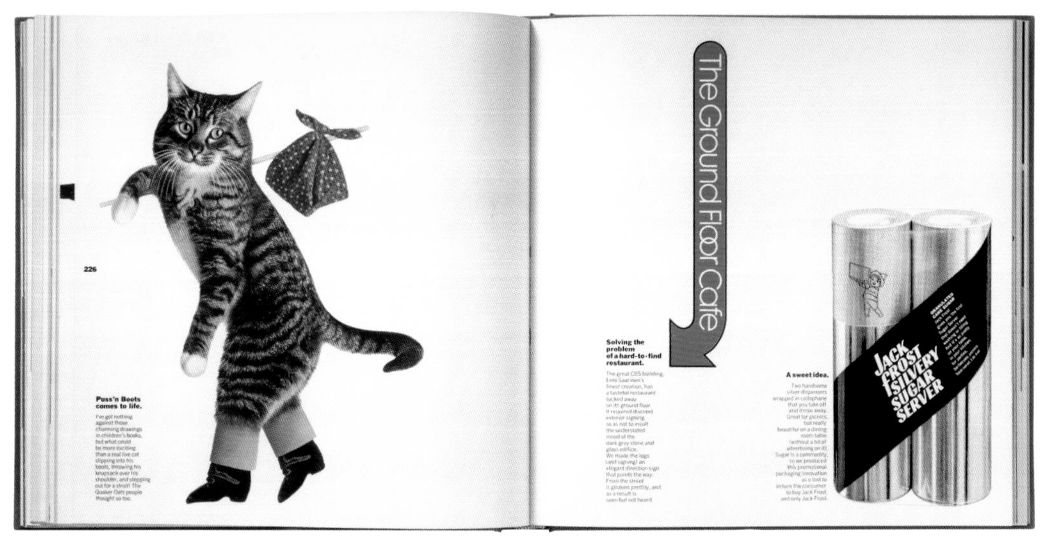

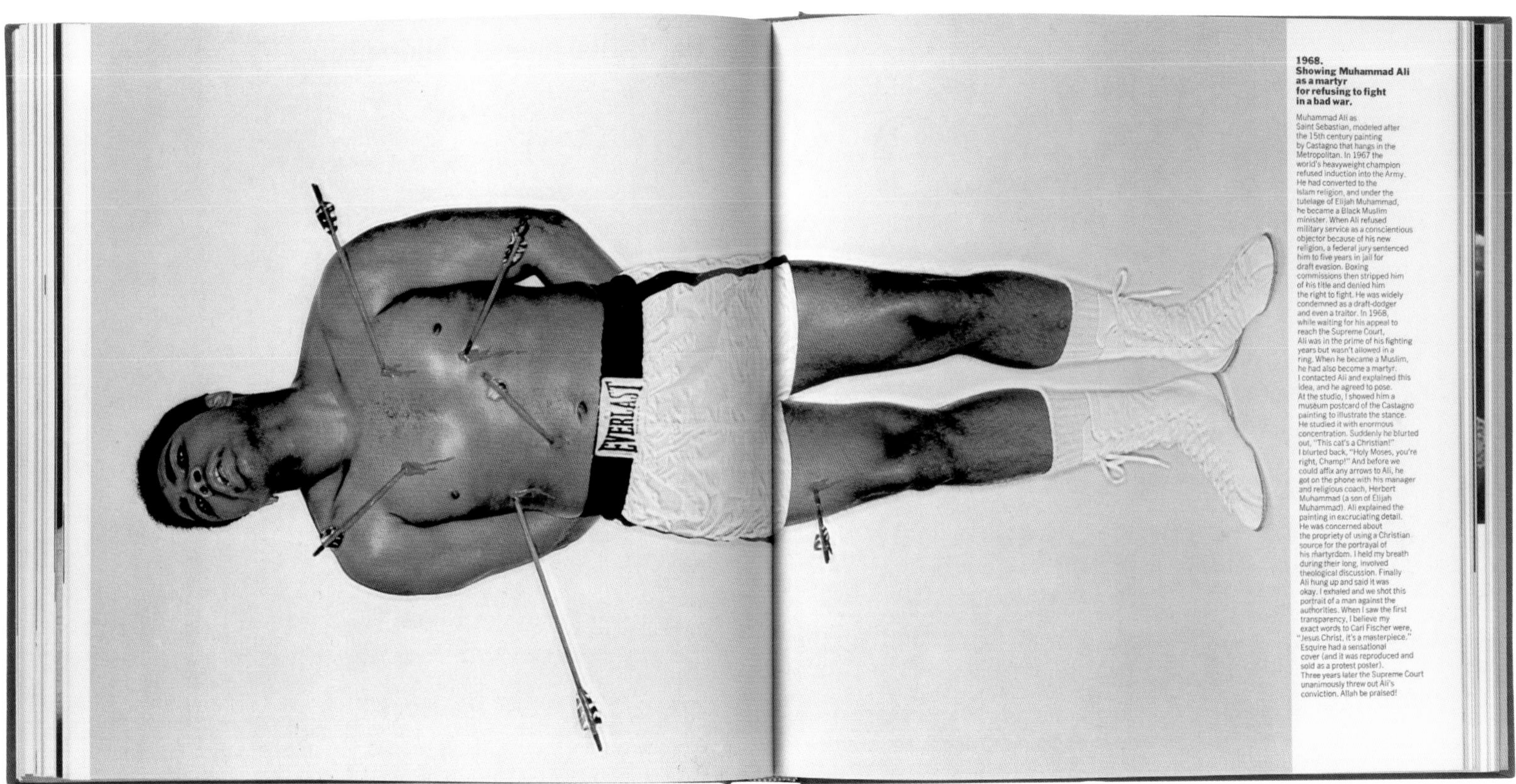

1968. Showing Muhammad Ali as a martyr for refusing to fight in a bad war.

Muhammad Ali as Saint Sebastian, modeled after the 15th century painting by Castagno that hangs in the Metropolitan. In 1967 the world's heavyweight champion refused induction into the Army. He had converted to the Islam religion, and under the tutelage of Elijah Muhammad, he became a Black Muslim minister. When Ali refused military service as a conscientious objector because of his new religion, a federal jury sentenced him to five years in jail for draft evasion. Boxing commissions then stripped him of his title and denied him the right to fight. He was widely condemned as a draft-dodger and even a traitor. In 1968, while waiting for his appeal to reach the Supreme Court, Ali was in the prime of his fighting years but wasn't allowed in a ring. When he became a Muslim, he had also become a martyr. I contacted Ali and explained this idea, and he agreed to pose. At the studio, I showed him a museum postcard of the Castagno painting to illustrate the stance. He studied it with enormous concentration. Suddenly he blurted out, "This cat's a Christian!" I blurted back, "Holy Moses, you're right, Champ!" And before we could affix any arrows to Ali, he got on the phone with his manager and religious coach, Herbert Muhammad (a son of Elijah Muhammad). Ali explained the painting in excruciating detail. He was concerned about the propriety of using a Christian source for the portrayal of his martyrdom. I held my breath during their long, involved theological discussion. Finally Ali hung up and said it was okay. I exhaled and we shot this portrait of a man against the authorities. When I saw the first transparency, I believe my exact words to Carl Fischer were, "Jesus Christ, it's a masterpiece." Esquire had a sensational cover (and it was reproduced and sold as a protest poster). Three years later the Supreme Court unanimously threw out Ali's conviction. Allah be praised!

Muhammad Ali as Saint Sebastian for an Esquire *cover (1968), placed on its side to allow the image to be reproduced as large as possible.*

The face of a hero.
"John, is that Billy coughing?"
"Get up and give him some Coldene."
No product, no ingredients, no diagrams, no logo.
283

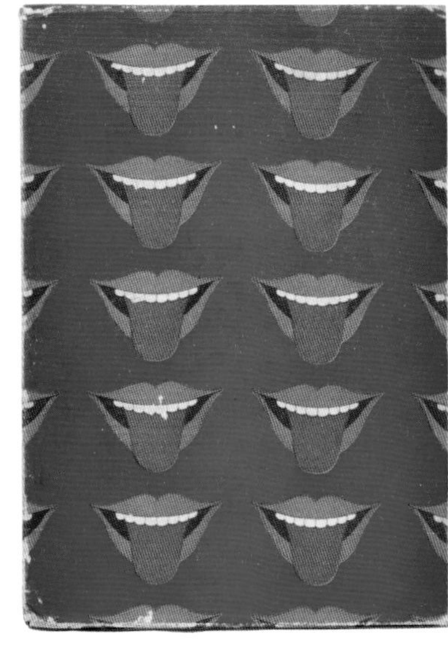

The slipcase (top) and the cover (bottom) both contain elements from work for the exhibition 'Word and Image' at the Museum of Modern Art, New York (1967).

Photographs of Yokoo attest to his own celebrity. This spread shows the meeting of a black-and-magenta-printed signature with a black-and-red one.

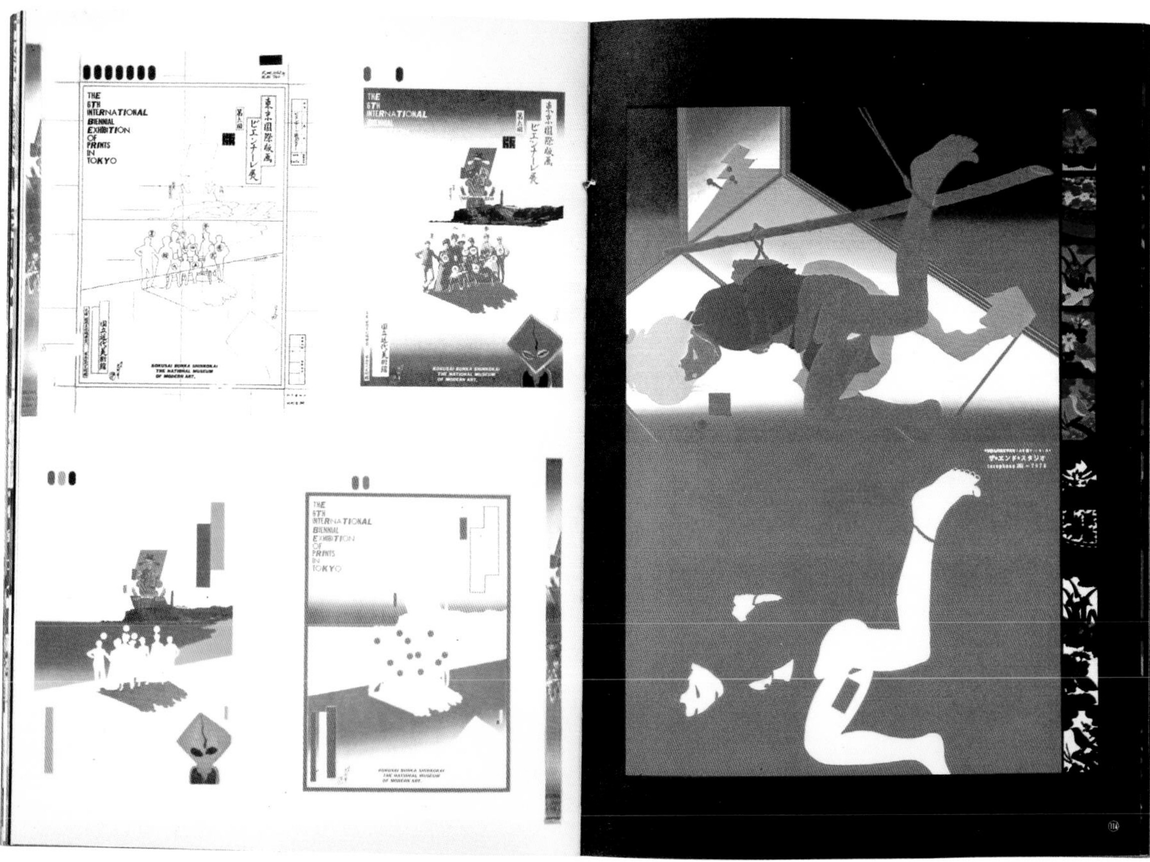

Yokoo's poster designs often involved complicated printing techniques – examples of marked-up mechanicals and interim proofs appear frequently in the book.

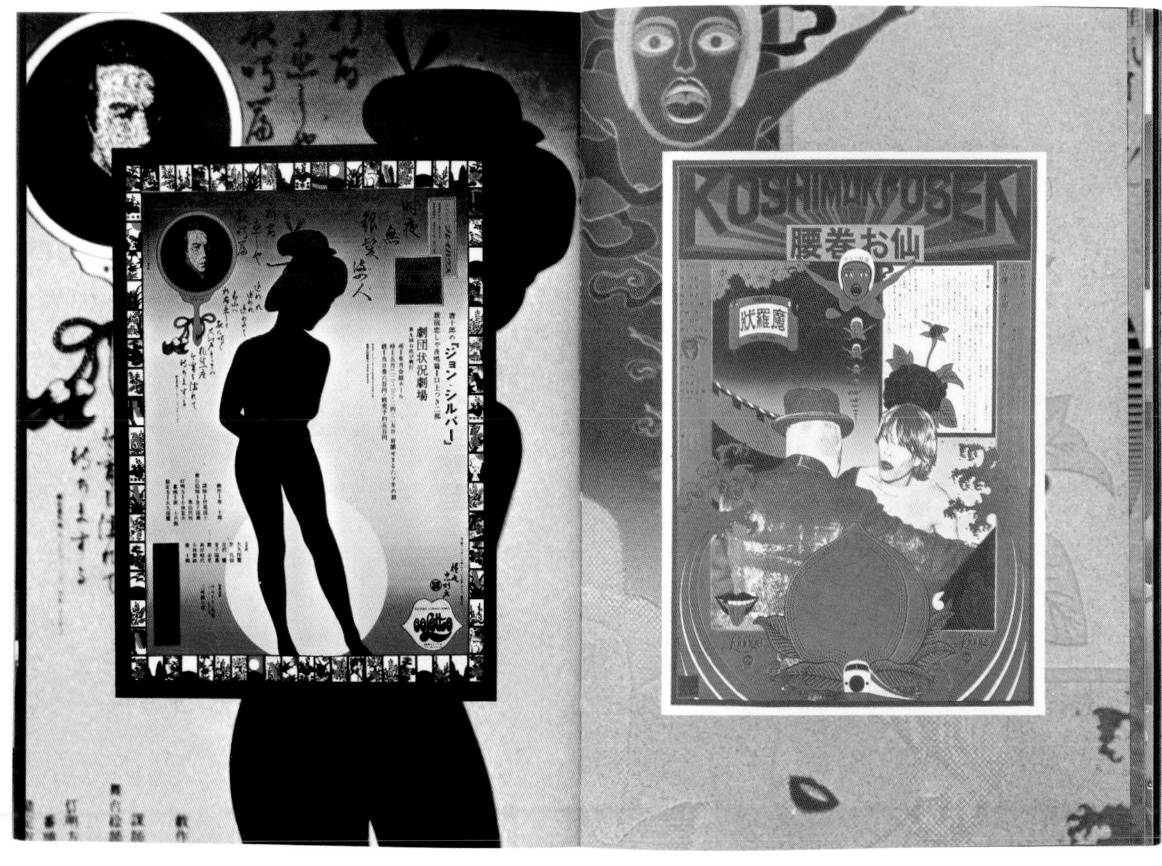

The Complete Tadanori Yokoo

Tadanori Yokoo

Kodansha, Tokyo, 1971
328 pages
210 × 148 mm (8.25 × 5.75 in)
Designed by Tadanori Yokoo

Milton Glaser described the Japanese designer and poster artist Tadanori Yokoo (1936–) as having an 'almost total eclecticism'. His work draws on an endless supply of influences: the Pop artists who reconditioned commercial art, graphic designers such as those at Push Pin Studio who reconditioned previous artistic styles, traditional Japanese woodcuts, naive painting, psychedelic poster art; the list goes on.

While he frequently repeats motifs such as the rising sun, his work is in a constant state of reinvention. According to Yokoo, *The Complete Tadanori Yokoo* represented a 'cemetery' for his most recent designs and artworks, which allowed him to be 'free for a moment from Death's shadow'. Such morbid thoughts are reflected in many of his posters, as are his obsessions with celebrity and sex. The images of exhibition openings, happenings and his work in cinema give a clue to Yokoo's fame at the time of the book's publication.

The small-format paperback is in a slipcase adorned with the open-mouth device conceived for the poster for the 'Word and Image' exhibition at New York's Museum of Modern Art in 1967. The book has no internal structure, and contains a gallimaufry of posters, magazine pages, drawings, books and photographs – an expression of Yokoo's prodigious creative output from the mid- to late 1960s. The anarchic layout was ahead of its time for a graphic design publication and was a deliberate counterpoint to modernist design thinking.

Pages with elaborate marked-up artwork and overlays show how far Yokoo pushed his printers with graduated backgrounds and multiple colour reproductions. The book is printed in 41 full-colour or varying two-colour eight-page signatures. It includes occasional writings and a biography in Japanese, and a one-page introduction in English.

Yokoo's posters are the subject of many books including *100 Posters of Tadanori Yokoo* (Kodansha, Toyko, 1978) and *Selected Posters 116* (Amus Arts Press, Kyoto, 2002).

'Walk Away René'
An ABC of the Work of Hipgnosis
George Hardie, Storm Thorgerson
Dragon's World, Limpsfield, Surrey, and A&W Visual Library, New York, 1978
160 pages
304 × 235 mm (12 × 9.5 in)
Designed by George Hardie, Storm Thorgerson

The blurb on the back cover of *'Walk Away René'* states: 'A book of designs and photographs for rock'n'roll bands.' This is, of course, only part of the truth; in reality the book is a lesson in the power of the art-directed image in pop iconography. And Hipgnosis's clients were not merely rock'n'roll bands: Pink Floyd, Led Zeppelin, 10CC, Genesis and Wings were worldwide supergroups. This was the heyday of the album cover, when the 12-inch square sleeve was king and Hipgnosis was the undoubted master of its design.

The company was led principally by Storm Thorgerson with his partners Aubrey Powell and Peter Christopherson. Its work was typified by photographic fantasies that often used surreal, lateral or obtuse ideas inspired by an album's title or lyrics. It had on call a collective of freelance specialists: art directors, designers and photographic specialists, including talents such as the designer Geoff Halpin, illustrator Colin Elgie and photo-retoucher Richard Manning. The appendix gives full credits to album covers shown in the book, confirming the amount of teamwork involved in the conception and delivery of each piece of work.

The book is an A to Z tour of album covers, which are loosely grouped under arbitrary subject headings. Thorgerson's text details the production of images and the often fraught dealings with superstar clients and record companies. Each subject is introduced with the relevant letter of the alphabet, delightfully illustrated by the book's co-designer George Hardie of NTA Studios, who frequently collaborated with Hipgnosis. *'Walk Away René'* is printed in full colour throughout, with a changing palette of subtle pastel-shaded backgrounds.

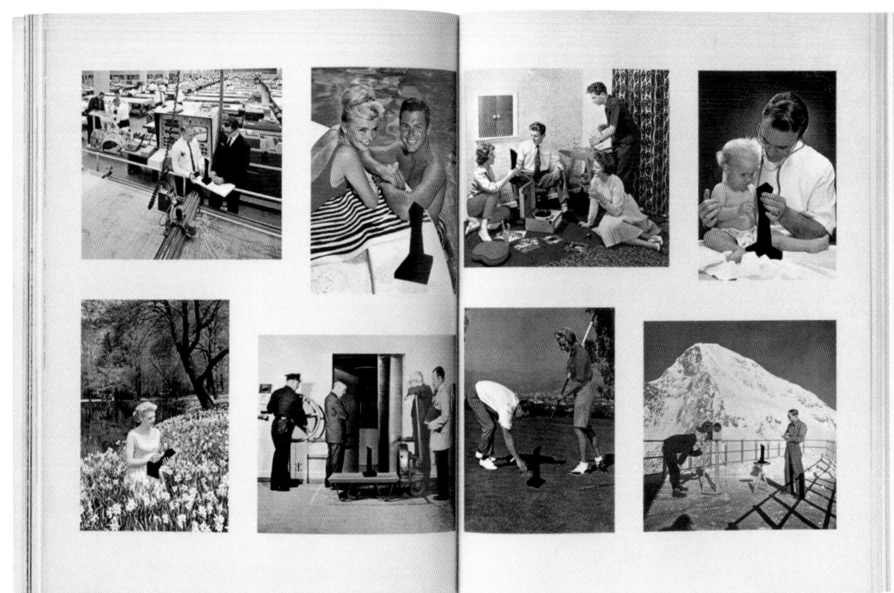

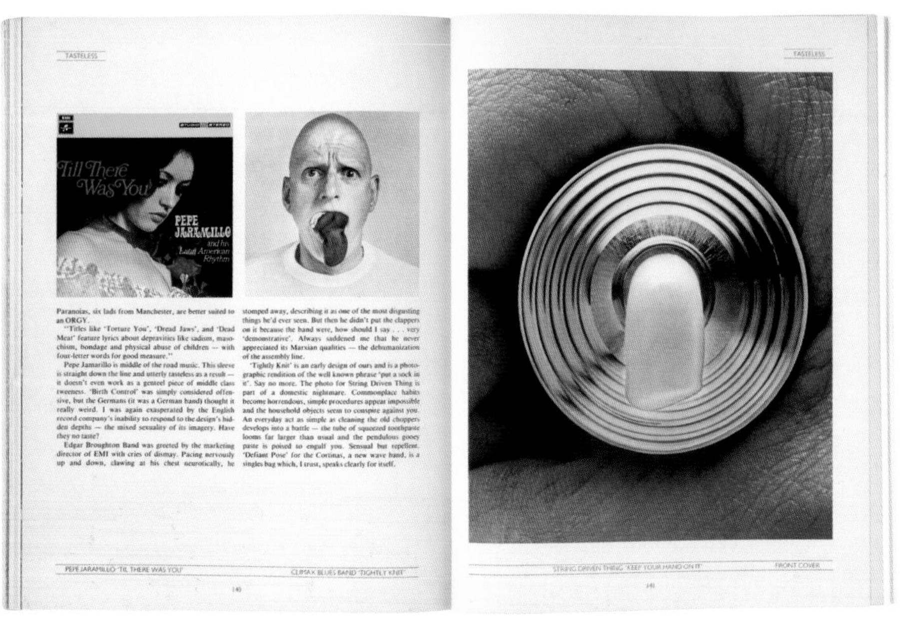

A frequent partner of Hipgnosis, the designer and illustrator George Hardie helped to compile and design 'Walk Away René'. *This spread shows his illustration for the Black Sabbath* Technical Ecstasy *album (1976) and one of the caps he devised for each of the chapters – in this case 'F' for 'Fiasco'.*

FIASCOS

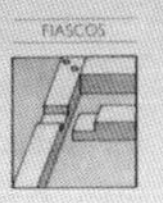

One of the more distressing events in our past took place when we worked for the Rolling Stones on 'Goatshead Soup' about four years ago. They decided to go with an idea about satyrs, in which the heads and chests of the band would be vignetted photographically onto the bodies of horses and goats. (On reflection, I don't think it was a great idea; David Bowie and Roger Daltrey have tried it on sleeves in the years that followed but it still hasn't been worth it.) The design entailed shooting the Stones themselves dressed in leotards. We hired a big studio thinking ours was a bit small and scruffy for the 'greatest rock and roll band' in the world. We stocked up with crates of beer and soft drinks for the band, and Jack Daniels scotch for Keith. We set up the lights and waited.

And we waited. Getting more and more nervous by the minute. Po was in a world of his own, rushing about furiously, fussing over details, trying to get everything just right. Not one of us felt relaxed. Three hours later the Stones finally arrived. Already our time was running out. And then to our horror Keith refused to be photographed in a leotard; he thought it silly. Now, I think he's very entitled to his opinion but why hadn't anyone told him earlier what we were going to do? So there was Keith arguing with Mick in the dressing room doorway, looking as black as night and as though he hadn't slept in a week. An hour of embarrassing inactivity passed — it felt terrible, all our worst paranoid fears come true. Finally Keith agreed and posed, actually with more enthusiasm than the others, but the moment had gone. Needless to say they later rejected the idea; nor did they like any of the publicity shots that they had asked us to take. Not surprising, but deeply disappointing.

Allan Clarke's second solo album was an artistic blunder of our own making. He stressed the need to convey the idea of co-operation on his album — of the musicians all helping each other, trying to build a single successful entity. We suggested a gymnastic sculpture like the human pyramid. Allan wasn't exactly bowled over by this idea but went along with our enthusiasm. We shot the thing twice, once with girls and once with boys. We reckoned that the gymnasium itself would be pretty striking, and then when one thinks of all those lovely young girls (or boys) in gym slips and aertex . . . it fairly takes the breath away. Well, we were wrong; very wrong. The whole thing looked charmless. Cap in hand we had to tell Allan that it was crummy. And we were the ones who had told him that it was going to be great.

I once shot a studio photosession of the Pretty Things and omitted to check the flash setting on the camera lens. It was on manual, not on flash and thus the shutter wasn't synchronized with the light. No illumination, no exposure. Two hours hard endeavour and absolutely nothing on the film. Blank, blank. You should've seen the group's faces. But of course you couldn't, because nothing came out. The burning man on 'Wish You Were Here' (see W) wore an asbestos suit under his ordinary suit. The asbestos stretched over his head and he wore a wig. He was literally set on fire, but the first time we did it the wind was blowing the wrong way, and so the flames licked round the front and burnt his moustache. Yikes!

For Wishbone Ash 'Argus' (pg. 42) we told the band and manager how we wished to shoot a picture of this timeless warrior at the mouth of a magnificent gorge, waiting patiently for the arrival of the space visitors. We described in breathtaking terms the Gorge du Verdun in Provence, Europe's answer to the Grand Canyon, and how the warrior, motionless as a sentinel, would look remarkable in relation to the vista around him, the jagged rocks, the rising cliffs and the floor of the plain behind, stretching magically into the distance. (We envisaged the warrior in medium long shot.) Don't sound so bad, does it? Well, the Gorge du Verdun *is* incredible. The trouble was that it was too incredible. A sheer knife cut two thousand feet deep, straight through the floor of an alpine valley. Hills rise above it and then suddenly it drops, miles and miles down to a tumbling river. We drove from

DEEP GOAT

49

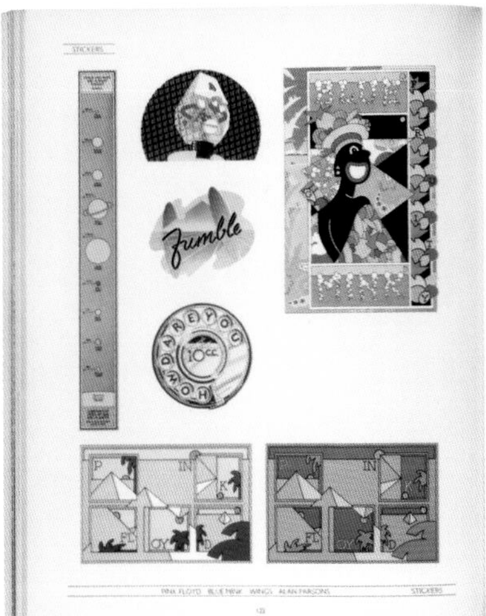

The enigmatic cover for Living by Design *– the book's title is on the spine.*

Books designed by the partners of Pentagram. This was one of the few spreads in the book to benefit from colour reproduction.

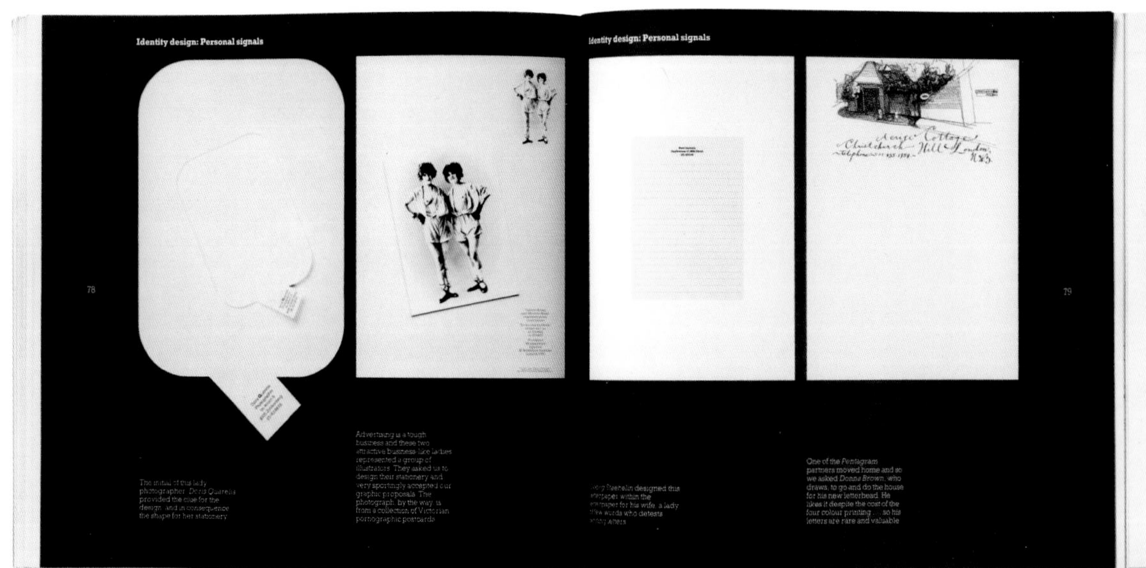

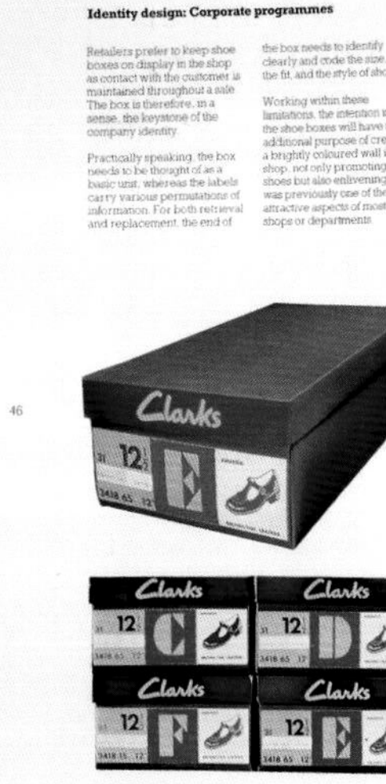
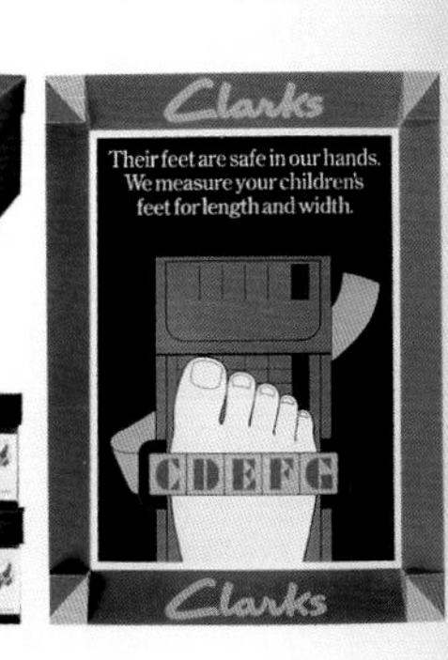

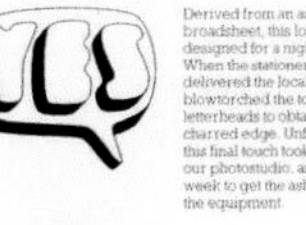
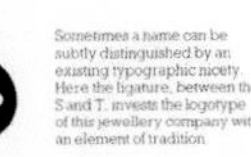

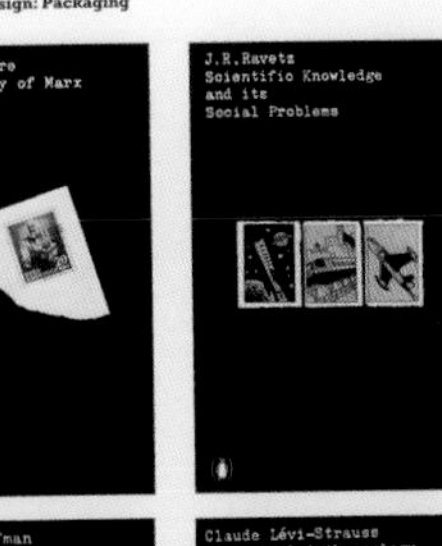

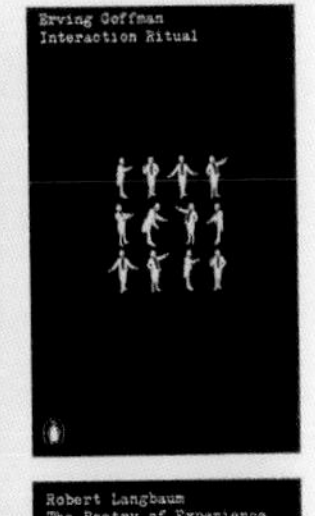

Living by Design

The Partners of Pentagram
Peter Gorb (editor)
Lund Humphries, London, and Whitney Library of Design, New York, 1978
300 pages
198 × 210 mm (7.75 × 8.25 in)
Designed by Pentagram

Living by Design is about design. Not about Pentagram. Which is, of course, quintessential Pentagram. It *was* design, and this book is perhaps the most succinct expression of its philosophy.

It was also a defining point for this partnership of designers, which, by 1978, had nine members (Theo Crosby, Alan Fletcher, Colin Forbes, Kenneth Grange, Peter Harrison, Ron Herron, David Hillman, Mervyn Kurlansky and John McConnell) and had just opened an office in New York City. Design was a way of life and clarifying what this meant was the objective of this book. It could be read as both an introduction to design and a manifesto of Pentagram's beliefs.

The striking, abstract, glossy, split-fountain cover makes *Living by Design* as much a piece of product design as it is a book. Inside there are 800 illustrations printed in a mixture of black and white and full colour, accompanied by engaging essays on design theory and practice.

The book is divided into four main sections. 'Identity Design' deals with large corporate programmes for BP and Reuters as well as more playful work for Clarks Shoes and witty personal letterheads. 'Information Design' shows posters, packaging (including some outstanding book jackets for Penguin) and Pentagram's own famed self-promotion output. The last two sections are 'Environmental Design' and 'Product Design'.

'How Pentagram Works', a small section at the back of the book, is the only place where the designers talk about themselves and their practice freely. It includes photographs of day-to-day work in the studio and extended biographies of the Pentagram partners.

Pentagram has been a prolific publisher of its own work. Books of note include *Pentagram: The Work of Five Designers* (Lund Humphries, London, and Whitney Library of Design, New York, 1972), *Pentagram: The Compendium* (Phaidon Press, London, 1993) and *Profile: Pentagram Design* (Phaidon Press, London, 2004).

Forget All the Rules You Ever Learned about Graphic Design. Including the Ones in this Book.

Bob Gill

Watson-Guptill Publications, New York, 1981
168 pages
280 × 210 mm (11 × 8.25 in)
Designed by Bob Gill

On the half-title page of *Forget All the Rules …* the American designer Bob Gill (1931–) writes: 'If this book helps only one designer get only one original idea, then all the months I spent putting it together will not have been worth it.' It is to be hoped that, rather than being defeatist, this reflected Gill's wish that many designers would benefit from his writings.

He takes pains to express his desire that any preconceived ideas about what constitutes 'good design' (including his own) are to be rejected. The cover, inside flaps and endpapers, boldly laid out in black and white, are devoted to this premise: the extended title leads to a subtitle that deliberately breaks mid-sentence to entice readers to turn the cover.

Bob Gill was a successful designer in New York before he became part of a wave of American designers who moved to London in the early 1960s. He teamed up with Alan Fletcher and Colin Forbes to set up the successful and highly influential Fletcher/Forbes/Gill in 1962. He left the company five years later to continue his own work in illustration, teaching, film-making and design. He returned to New York in 1975.

Forget All the Rules … shows Gill's work over a span of 30 years and emphasizes his belief that an original solution to any graphic problem lies not in the initial brief but in its redefinition. He made this discovery in 1954 when he was having problems with the titles for a CBS television comedy, *Private Secretary,* about a 'stupid' secretary. He realized that a unique solution lay in the combination of an image of a secretary and of her stupidity but 'without *actually* saying it'. The titles he devised looked as though a secretary had done them, complete with corrections and mistakes.

The book contains eight chapters, all with snappy titles such as 'The problem *is* the problem', 'Stealing is good', and 'I was only following orders'.

Forget all the rules you ever learned about graphic design.

Including the ones in this book.

Forget how good design is *supposed* to look. What you think is good design, is what other

designers think is good design, too.

That's why design is in a rut. And that's not good. That's boring.

This book is about how to get out of the rut; how to take an ordinary graphic problem and turn it into an original graphic solution.

Text from the cover is continued on to the inside flaps and endpapers.

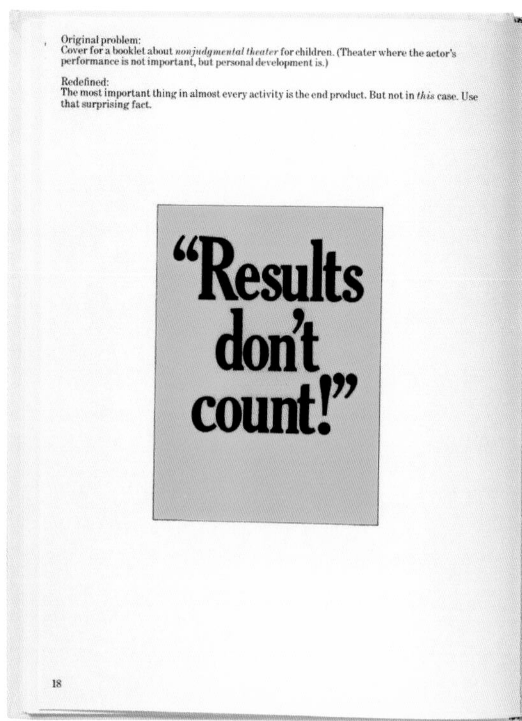

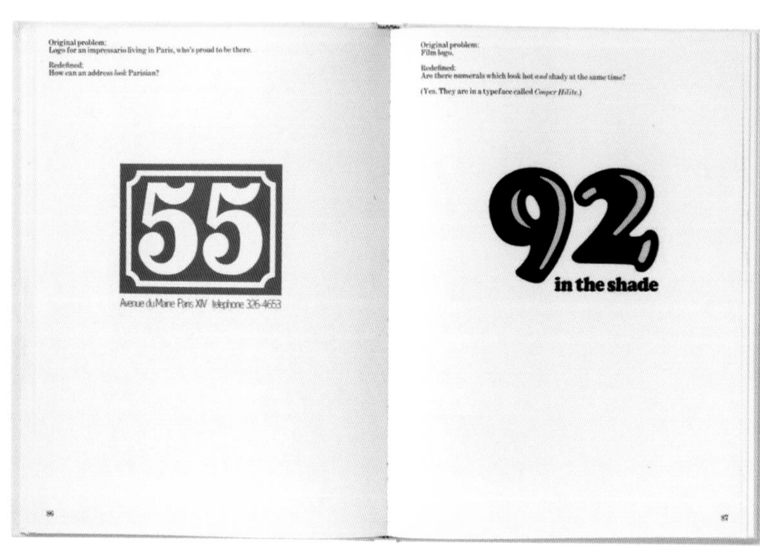

The layout follows a simple formula, with one illustration per page and a caption at the top containing the original brief and Gill's redefinition.

I redefined the problem, emphasizing that part of the problem which communicated something that was unique:

How can an image which says one thing (private secretary) *also* say something else (that she is stupid) without *actually* saying it?

I did some research. I visited offices. I watched secretaries.

I decided that the most appropriate way to say *private secretary* was to type it.

private

secretary

The next thing was to suggest that the secretary was stupid. I discovered how to do that by watching secretaries make mistakes. And then correct them.

private

secretary

8

The last thing was to put the rest of the information on the title card.

I tried to make it look like a *secretary's* solution. (A layout done by a secretary who hadn't studied layout.)

private

secretary

....

CBS television

9

Original problem:
Moving announcement for a display studio.

Redefined:
Make a relationship between moving *and* display.

(I wish I hadn't used all caps for the address lines. The typography looks dated to me now.)

102

Original problem:
Cover for a magazine with a lead article about badly designed signs.

Redefined:
Make a relationship between the magazine's sign (its logo) *and* a badly designed sign.

103

Deberny & Peignot 1933 1 Marchio per lo Studio Boggeri
Antonio Boggeri 1933 2 Copertina per opuscolo promozionale dello Studio Boggeri 15,5x20,5
1934 3 Fotografia sperimentale per la rivista Campo grafico di Attilio Rossi 22,8x16,3
L'UOVO DI COLOMBO

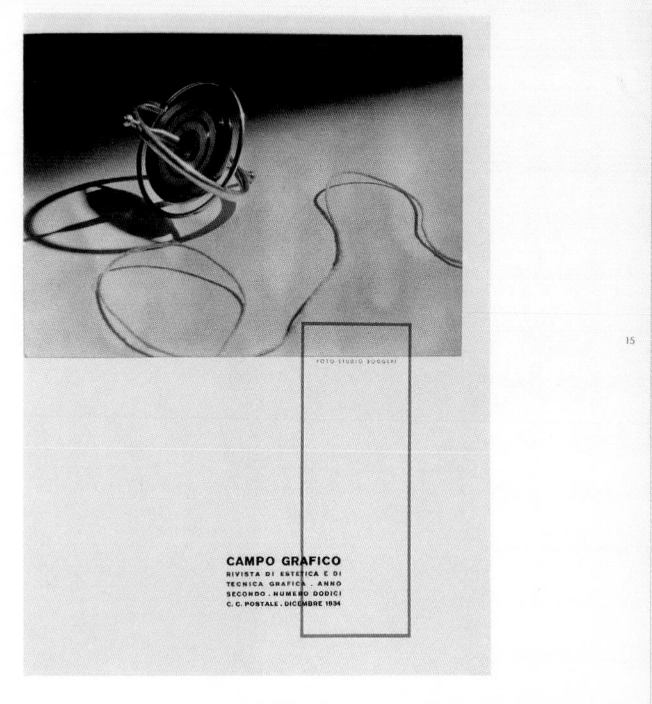

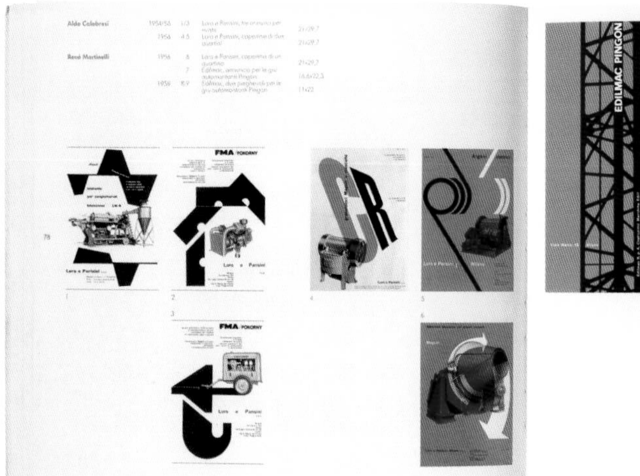

The printed slipcase for Lo Studio Boggeri: 1933–1981 *and the cover (below) reproduce a promotional brochure for the company designed by Max Huber in 1945.*

Lo Studio Boggeri: 1933–1981

Bruno Monguzzi (editor)

Electa Editrice, Milan, 1981
120 pages
222 × 237 mm (8.75 × 9.25 in)
Designed by Bruno Monguzzi

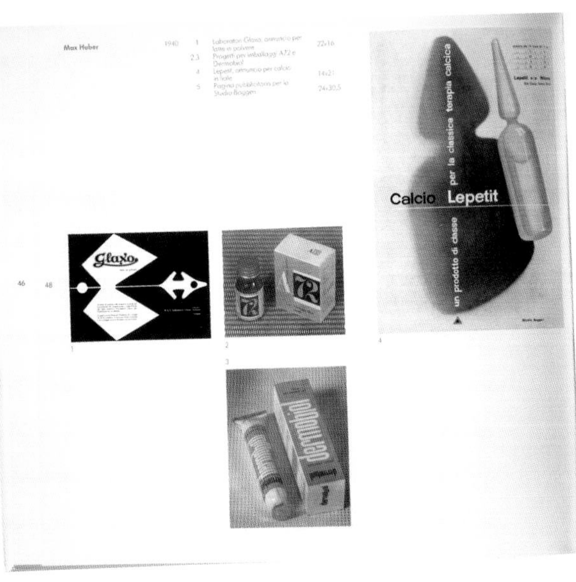

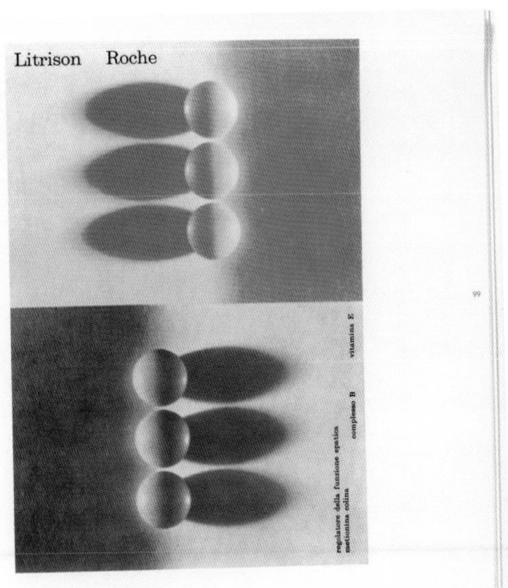

Each spread has numbered illustrations; the captions placed together on the page give the designer, date, description and original size of the artwork. Seen here is the work of Aldo Calabresi for the pharmaceutical company Roche.

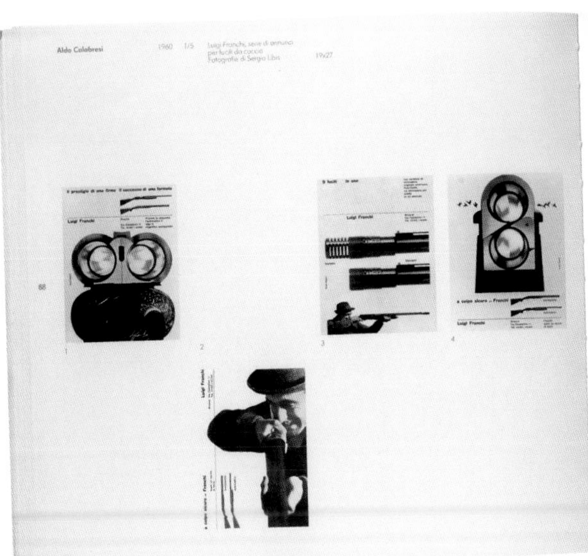

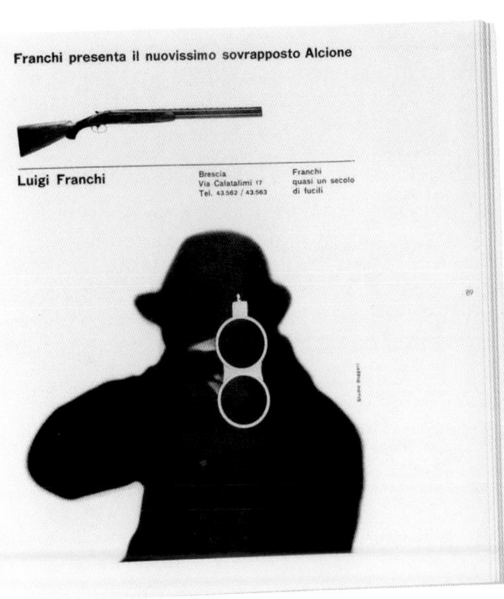

Studio Boggeri dominated Italian graphic design for much of the twentieth century. It was established in 1933 by the one-time violinist Antonio Boggeri (1900–1989), who had come into contact with the work of progressive designers such as Jan Tschichold, László Moholy-Nagy and El Lissitzky while he was working for a printer in Milan. The studio became a revolving door for both Italian and international talent, and retained the spirit of its avant-garde inspiration for the next 50 years.

Lo Studio Boggeri: 1933–1981 was part of an excellent series on Italian graphic design published by Electa. This included *Campo Grafico: 1933–1939* (1983), a look at the influential Italian design magazine, and *Max Huber: Progetti Grafici, 1936–1981* (1982), a study of the work of the émigré Swiss designer who worked at Studio Boggeri and played a large part in the studio's output and in defining Italian graphic design after the Second World War. All the books were paperbacks, in the same square format and boxed in slip cases. They were Italian language only.

Designed and edited by studio member Bruno Monguzzi (1941–), who also wrote the introduction, *Lo Studio Boggeri: 1933–1981* is printed in black and red throughout, with the addition of a few full-colour pages. The book is a portfolio of work produced by the studio in chronological order. The early examples are dominated by Xanti Schawinsky and other former Bauhaus students, such as Imre Reiner and Kate Bernhardt, who brought with them advanced photographic techniques and clarity of layout. The advent of a new generation of designers in the early 1940s and after the war – chiefly Max Huber but including Bruno Munari, Erberto Carboni and Albe Steiner – is typified by a more dynamic use of photography, multiple overlays and elastic typography. Later work from designers such as Monguzzi and Aldo Calabresi shows the influence of Swiss typographic rigidity while retaining Studio Boggeri's trademark exuberance.

Paul Rand: A Designer's Art

Paul Rand

Yale University Press,
New Haven and London, 1985
240 pages
254 × 188 mm (10 × 7.75 in)
Designed by Paul Rand

Paul Rand: A Designer's Art was published nearly 40 years after Rand's seminal *Thoughts on Design* (see page 148). At its core it is a complete reworking of the 1947 original, with rewritten text, redesigned layouts and new essays. Modern illustrations from the considerable body of work Rand produced in the intervening years are combined with his original vintage work. A new generation of designers familiar with his reputation as America's foremost graphic modernist, and often unable to source the book's long out-of-print predecessor, found it inspiring: the quintessential lesson in the art of good design.

Rand's text is concise and his essays are short, often advantages when writing for designers. The 27 chapters explore subjects ranging from 'Versatility of the Symbol' and 'The Role of Humor' to 'Collage and Montage'. His work speaks for itself, from the exemplary corporate programmes for clients such as IBM, Westinghouse and UPS to his playful collaged book jackets and magazine covers.

Rand was present when *Paul Rand: A Designer's Art* was on press and reportedly changed up to 50 per cent of the book at this late stage. The end result is a superbly printed volume, near faultless in its production; its thin covers bound in black cloth give it the feel of a notebook.

Rand would write two more books that were less critically acclaimed but noteworthy nonetheless – *Design, Form, and Chaos* (Yale University Press, New Haven and London, 1993) and *From Lascaux to Brooklyn* (Yale University Press, New Haven and London, 1996).

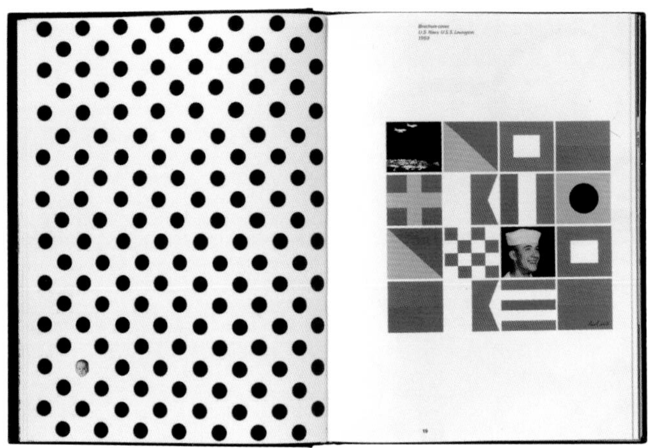

Themed chapters provide a mixture and contrast of artwork on the spreads, here between the new, a poster for IBM (1981), and the old, an advertisement for the El Producto cigar (1952), in 'The Rebus and the Visual Pun' chapter.

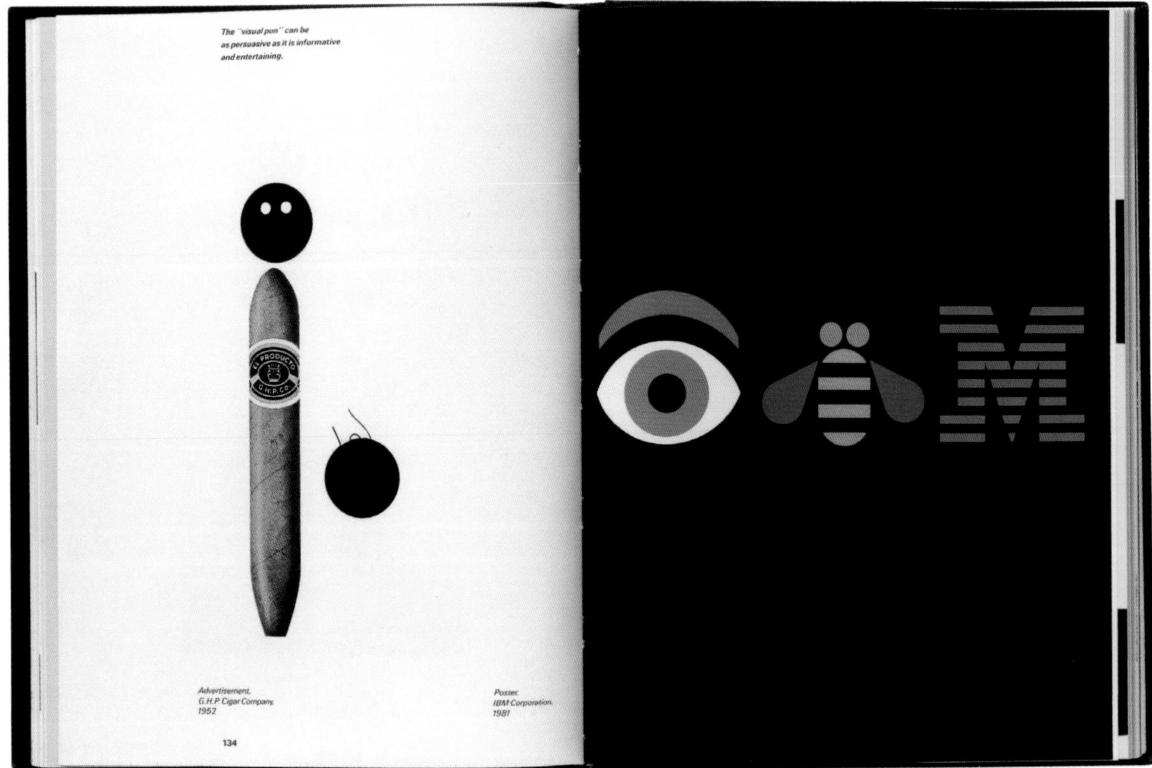

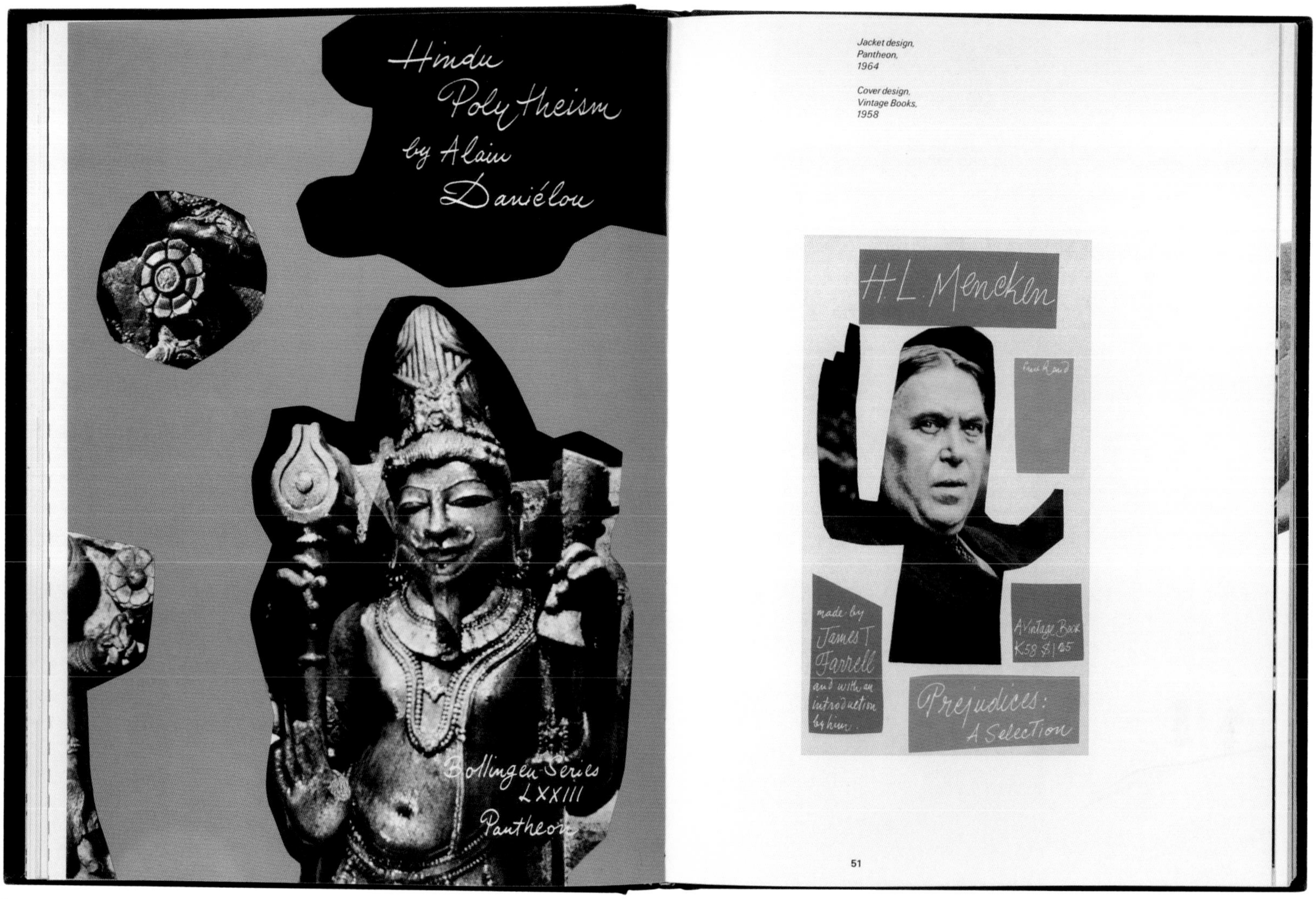

Jacket design,
Pantheon,
1964

Cover design,
Vintage Books,
1958

51

Paul Rand: A Designer's Art *is printed in a seamless mixture of full-colour and two-colour (black and warm grey) pages.*

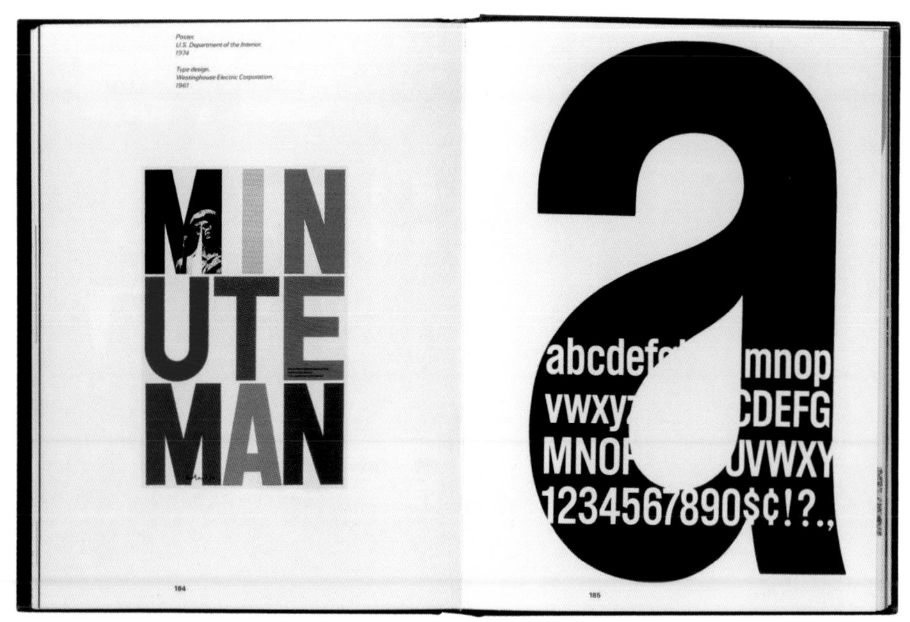

AVANT GARDE 13

PORTRAITS OF THE AMERICAN PEOPLE A MONUMENTAL PORTFOLIO OF PHOTOGRAPHS

20.

68

Avant Garde, another Ginzburg publication, came after the demise of Fact. It was more ambitious in design and production.

20. Cover from Avant Garde showing a good use of the Avant Garde typeface.

21.-35. Spreads and single pages from Avant Garde.

21.

22.

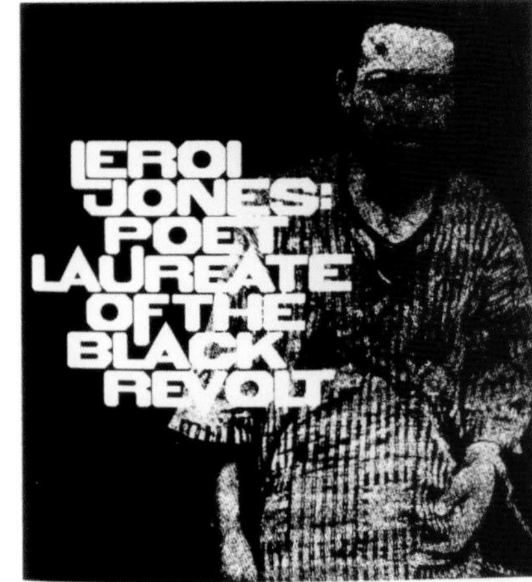

23.

69

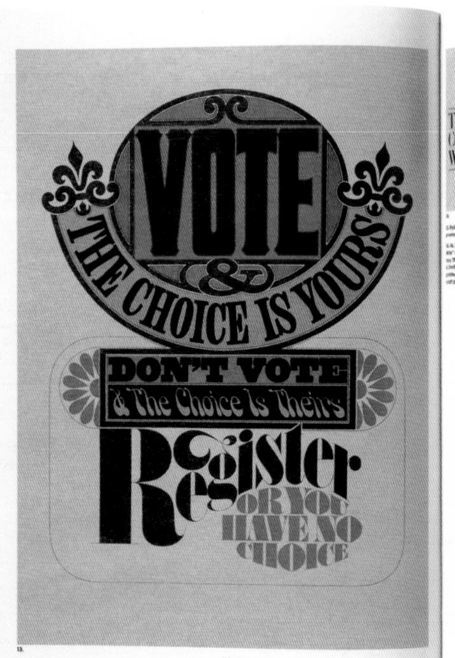

Pages from a two-colour section with images from the magazine Avant Garde.

Herb Lubalin: Art Director, Graphic Designer and Typographer

Gertrude Snyder, Alan Peckolick

American Showcase, New York, 1985
Paperback edition (pictured), 1985
184 pages
302 × 228 mm (12 × 9 in)
Designed by Alan Peckolick

Herb Lubalin (1918–1981) was a designer of words: wonderfully constructed, his designs could take on any shape or form and were often highly expressive. Devoted to his layout pad, he made rough sketches of his ideas and his team of assistants then turned these into artwork. The endpapers of *Herb Lubalin*, with roughs on one page and completed artwork on the other, show just how close his first sketches were to the finished designs.

The book is divided into subject areas such as logos, editorial, advertising and typeface design, and Lubalin's work across these many fields is covered by numerous illustrations. The introduction describes his working practices in detail and outlines his career.

Herb Lubalin influenced a whole generation of American designers and his legacy cannot be understated. As creative director at the advertising agency Sudler & Hennessey in the 1950s and early 1960s, he helped to pioneer the use of the word as image, and continued to do so with renewed vigour after he opened his own design company in 1964. His designs as art director of the magazines *Eros*, *Fact*, *Avant Garde* and *U&lc* broke new ground in page layout. *Avant Garde* spawned the multi-ligatured, angled typeface of the same name, which would become one of the most popular (and abused) fonts of its time. *U&lc* was the mouthpiece for the International Typeface Corporation (ITC); founded by Aaron Burns with Lubalin's help, the company provided a new outlet for aspiring type designers.

Designed by Alan Peckolick, a partner in Lubalin's firm, *Herb Lubalin* has authenticity as well as sympathy with its subject. Two-colour sections give the chapters on logos and typeface design added depth and neatly offset the remaining sections, all of which are in colour.

Part of the total design for a never-published magazine. This logo has won numerous awards, and is in the permanent collection of the Museum of Modern Art. Typographically, the logo not only states the name but graphically interprets the message. Lubalin felt that the suggestion of the fetus in the logo was one of his finest typography designs.

9a. In 1965, Lubalin's assistant, Alan Peckolick, developed this logo from tissues Lubalin had given him.

9b. Filling O's in words was a Lubalin specialty. Obligingly, Peckolick put the words "and child" in the O of Mother, and returned the tissue to Lubalin.

9c. This was the final logo developed by Lubalin and Tom Carnase.

50

The endpapers, with Lubalin's loose sketch of logos on the left and the resulting composition on the right.

Cassandre
Henri Mouron
Schirmer/Mosel, Munich, 1985
Thames & Hudson, London, 1985 (pictured)
318 pages
272 × 242 mm (10.75 × 9.5 in)

There is a certain irony in the fact that Adolphe Mouron (1901–1968) originally used A.M. Cassandre as a pseudonym so that his real name could be kept for his career as a painter – *Cassandre* is the type of monograph normally reserved for pre-eminent fine artists. The book, published in German by Schirmer/Mosel, Munich, in French by Skira, Geneva, and English by both Thames & Hudson, London, and Rizzoli, New York, is a large-format hardback with a weighty introductory main text followed by a large section of colour plates. As perhaps the finest graphic artist of the twentieth century, Cassandre undoubtedly deserved such status.

Written by his son, Henri Mouron, the monograph benefits from the author's first-hand knowledge of his subject and his efforts to compile as complete a visual record as possible of his father's work. Mouron's text covers four chapters and is well illustrated, with over 300 images of poster designs, magazine covers, typographic specimens and photographs. There are a handful of colour reproductions but this section is largely printed in black and white.

The colour plate section, which follows the main text, begins with a double spread of the large (4-metre/13-foot wide) poster, *Au Bucheron*, that Cassandre produced in 1923 for a Parisian furniture store. His first notable work, this exhibits his trademark use of geometric layout and synthesis of image and typography. In all there is a total of 70 colour plates, including all his major posters, such as *L'Intransigeant* (1925), *Nord Express* (1927), *Etoile du Nord* (1927), *Normandie* (1935) and the famous Dubonnet drinking man (1932).

Cassandre's typographic work is described in considerable detail in the first chapters of the book. His friendship with Charles Peignot, proprietor of Deberny & Peignot, the French type company, led to the design of the sans serif headline font Bifur (1929), Acier (1930) and later Peignot (1937).

The plate section is formatted with posters on the right-hand page and captions on the left. This first plate, Au Bucheron, *is one of the few exceptions to this rule.*

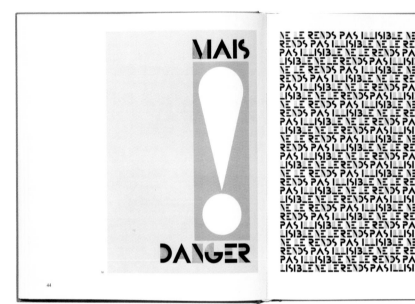

37 DUBO DUBON DUBONNET, TRIPTYCH, 1932

Lithographic poster
240 × 320 cm (94½ × 126 in), all three panels
Alliance Graphique, Paris

Collection Philip Williams Posters, New York

Also published (by Alliance Graphique) in different rectangular formats grouping the three panels in a single poster. The background of the second panel reproduced here has been modified to respect the artist's original intention

Many of the posters reproduced in Cassandre *can also be found in the book by Maximilien Vox,* A.M. Cassandre: Peintre d'Affiches *(Les Editions Parallèles, Paris, 1948).*

209. *LE PEIGNOT, from the cover of the Peignot specimen, Deberny & Peignot, 1937.*

LE PEIGNOT

earliest typographical posters, though they belong to his first period as a poster artist, will now be discussed in conjunction with his later, purely textual designs, to show the evolution of his experiments in this field. In the curved 1925 *Huilor* composition, which is a typographical reminder of the illustrated *Huilor* of the same year (itself derived from a design for *Croix Verte* cooking oils), Cassandre uses dramatic lighting to transform the letters virtually into the object. More interesting, however, is the 1926 design *A La Maison Dorée*—a particularly successful example of a modular composition based on a 6:8 relationship. It inevitably recalls the work of the Bauhaus graphic artists. The German influence is apparent in the way the text is organized on the page and in the geometrical treatment of the letters connected by 45° diagonal lines and constructed, like the letters in Albers's stencil alphabet, with three basic figures—a square, an isoceles right-angle triangle and a half-circle.

With a monumental typographical composition designed in 1928, *J'Achète Tout Aux Galeries Lafayette*, Cassandre inaugurated a radically new approach to the typographical poster, one that was to be special to him for several years. The geometrical structure—far subtler than in *A La Maison Dorée*—is based on a rythmical cascade of squares. It is further enriched by a distinctly pictorial treatment which endows the image-word with a surreal quality that transmutes it into an optically riveting poetic object.

Continuing his researches in this field, Cassandre designed a superb poster for *Deberny & Peignot* the following year. Unfortunately, it was displayed only on the company's delivery trucks. The geometrical element is almost forgotten in the celebration of the dense objective nature of the typographical material. The "eyes" of the noble Elzevir display letters, tracing a handsome graphic architecture on the ambiguous picture plane, fill the two squares of an improbable, Escher-like construction in which imagined reality appears more substantial than reality itself. The poster is a splendid stylistic exercise on one of Cassandre's favorite themes.

Paris Films (1931), with its bright electric lights and vibrating straight lines, is a remarkable anticipation of Op Art and kinetic art.

210. *Cover of the black-and-gray Acier specimen, Deberny & Peignot, 1930.*

92

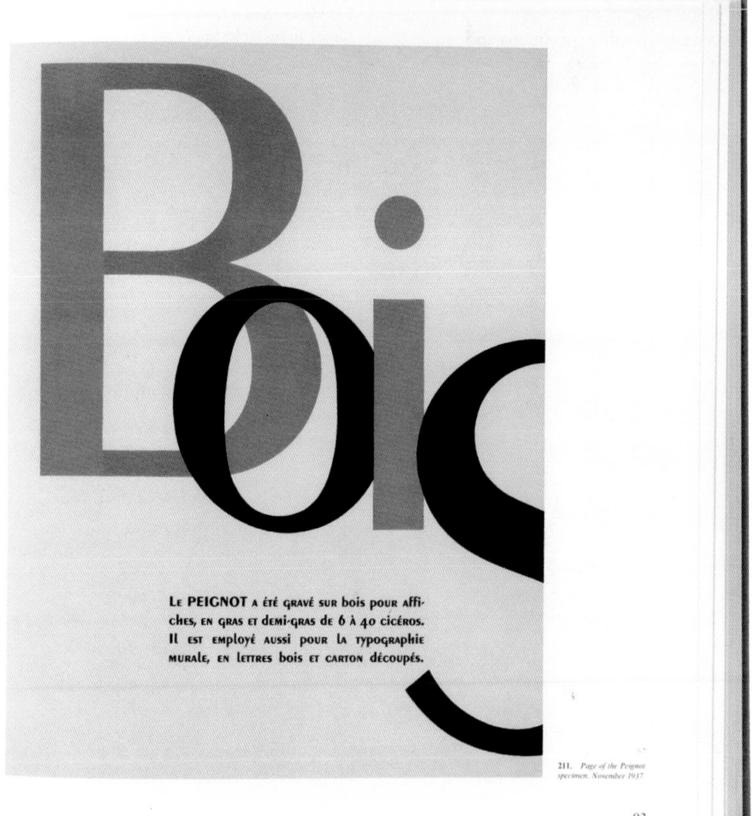

Bois
LE PEIGNOT A ÉTÉ GRAVÉ SUR BOIS POUR AFFICHES, EN GRAS ET DEMI-GRAS DE 6 À 40 CICÉROS.
IL EST EMPLOYÉ AUSSI POUR LA TYPOGRAPHIE MURALE, EN LETTRES BOIS ET CARTON DÉCOUPÉS.

211. *Page of the Peignot specimen, November 1937.*

93

28

[15] For a cover of *New York* Magazine on European terrorism, I wanted to show the banality of terror: an embroidered ski mask, usually an accessory of innocent recreation, becomes the menacing silhouette of a terrorist.

The broadside and the poster are traditional media of protest. I am simply continuing the practice. [16] I designed *End Bad Breath* to protest the bombing of Hanoi during the Vietnam War. I took a mundane advertising slogan, married it to our most recognizable national symbol, and pushed the message home with an absurd but true idea. The blue plate is a woodcut; the flat colors were printed offset. [17] *War Is Good Business: Invest Your Son* was a common slogan printed on buttons during the Vietnam War. My version is a turn-of-the-century call to arms. [18] *March for Peace and Justice* was an assignment for the Peace March Committee—an announcement of the June 12, 1982 anti-nuke rally. The group asked me to do a positive image of peace, rather than a negative one of war, generally an easier approach. I rendered the dove, a timeworn but effective symbol, to suggest the notion that the marchers will come from different walks of life.

15

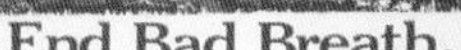

16

29

17

18

A spread showing pages from issue 54 of The Push Pin Graphic. *A facsimile of this issue, 'The South', is bound into the excellent review written by Chwast of this famous periodical,* The Push Pin Graphic *(Chronicle Books, San Francisco, 2004).*

120

[142] This issue of the *Push Pin Graphic* was done in 1969 as a response to a period of civil rights activism in the south. My idea in designing this was to contrast popular images of Dixie with current events. Each color piece represented the old, and was rendered in a different style in order to approximate the look of the found pieces of art I borrowed from. A black-and-white newspicture showing the current reality was imposed over each mythic image and a bullet hole was die-cut through every page. The photographs showed Mrs. Viola Liuzzo, housewife, shot to death for giving a ride to civil rights workers; Emmitt Till, age 15, shot for allegedly whistling at a white girl; Harry Moore, leader of the Florida NAACP, killed by a bomb blast; Medgar Evers, civil rights leader, murdered by a sniper; Goodman, Chaney, and Schwerner, activists, beaten and killed; Martin Luther King, Jr., assassinated. With the final image of the March on Washington, the situation was reversed; the news photograph was blown to full page and inset was an old Southern dame shot through the head, signifying the emergence of a new consciousness.

The South

121

142

The jacket folds out in the front and rear to display six different applications of left hands in the process of drawing.

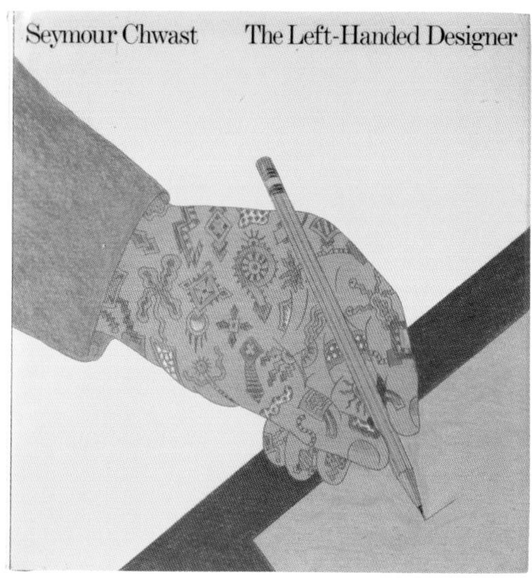

The Left-Handed Designer

Seymour Chwast

Booth-Clibborn Editions, London and Paris, 1985
144 pages
257 × 246 mm (10.125 × 9.625 in)
Designed by Seymour Chwast

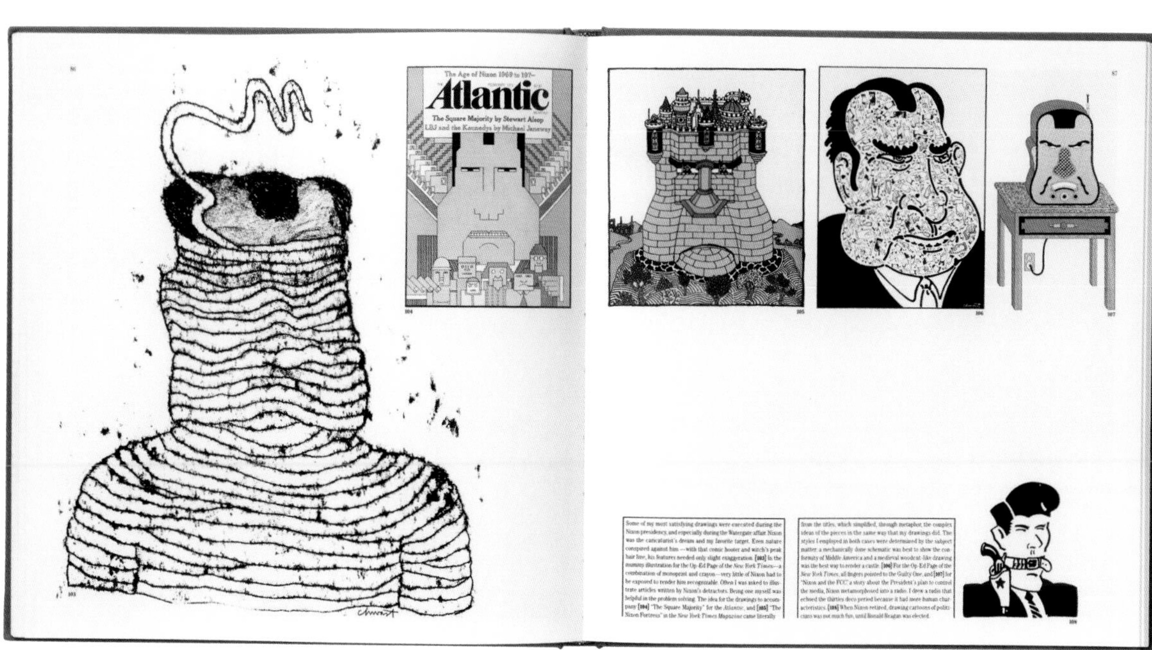

The cover for *The Left-Handed Designer* folds out to reveal six distinctly different variations on the same theme: a left hand creating a work of art. Stylistically and conceptually they differ from one another, typifying the approach of the American designer Seymour Chwast (1931–), who uses illustration almost exclusively in the realization of his graphic ideas, but is not confined to any one style. Style, though, is often an integral part of his concepts.

With ex-Cooper Union classmates Milton Glaser and Ed Sorel, Chwast was a co-founder in 1954 of the highly influential Push Pin Studio. They created a new visual language through the rediscovery and appropriation of artistic styles from the past, and promoted themselves through the *Push Pin Graphic*, a publication that changed its theme with each edition. Early issues show Chwast experimenting with woodcut techniques quite different from the simple line drawings for which he is well known.

The Left-Handed Designer, published as a Push Pin Editions title by Abrams in New York and by Booth-Clibborn in London and Paris, begins with an interview by Steven Heller, followed by a brief chapter 'The Process of Idea and Style', which is an illustrated guide to the progression of a commissioned job – the design of a poster for the production of *Nicholas Nickleby* for Mobil's Masterpiece Theater. The final five chapters cover the breadth of graphic work conceived by Chwast: his posters, book jackets, book designs, LP sleeves, children's books, *The Push Pin Graphic* and editorial illustrations.

Chwast's use of wit as a mainstay of his work is clearly evident, applied to light-hearted projects like the 300 drawings of Johann Sebastian Bach to celebrate the composer's 300th birthday, and also in pieces that champion political causes such as anti-war posters from the Vietnam era and a 1969 issue of *The Push Pin Graphic* devoted to the American South during the civil rights movement.

Dorfsman & CBS

Dick Hess, Marion Muller

American Showcase,
New York, 1987
216 pages
302 × 228 mm (11.875 × 9 in)
Designed by Dick Hess
Cover designed by Lou Dorfsman, David Suh

Lou Dorfsman (1918–2008) pioneered a form of total design. CBS, the American broadcasting company, was his employer for 40 years, and was one of the first organizations to fully control its visual output. Dorfsman led an in-house team that was in charge of all advertising, design, signage and on-air promotions. The depth of his commitment and the consistent excellence of the work is clearly in evidence in the pages of *Dorfsman & CBS*, a rare design study in microcosm of one person, one company, one career.

Hired by CBS in 1946, Dorfsman worked as assistant to the famed art director William Golden, originator of the company's iconic eye logo and the CBS Didot typeface (for more information on his work see *The Visual Craft of William Golden*, Cipe Pineles Golden, Kurt Weihs and Robert Strunsky (eds.), Braziller, New York, 1962). On Golden's untimely death in 1959 Dorfsman succeeded him as art director. The high standards and all-encompassing reach continued. Pages dense with advertisements (printed here in black on a special varnish) are an indication of the department's prodigious output, which mirrored Dorfsman's contemporaries Herb Lubalin and George Lois in inventive use of type and image.

The book has two main sections. The first, 'The Man and the Company', records Dorfsman's career; the second, 'The Work', is a portfolio of his prodigious output of design. The hundreds of illustrations include promotional brochures, advertising, books, annual reports, signage and stationery. Highlights include the environmental graphics for CBS's new headquarters in the 1960s, which involved a complete head-to-toe corporate make-over, with unrivalled attention to detail. Fire exits, lift buttons and clock numerals were all changed to CBS livery. Matchbook covers were designed for a restaurant on the ground floor, with still-life photography commissioned from Irving Penn.

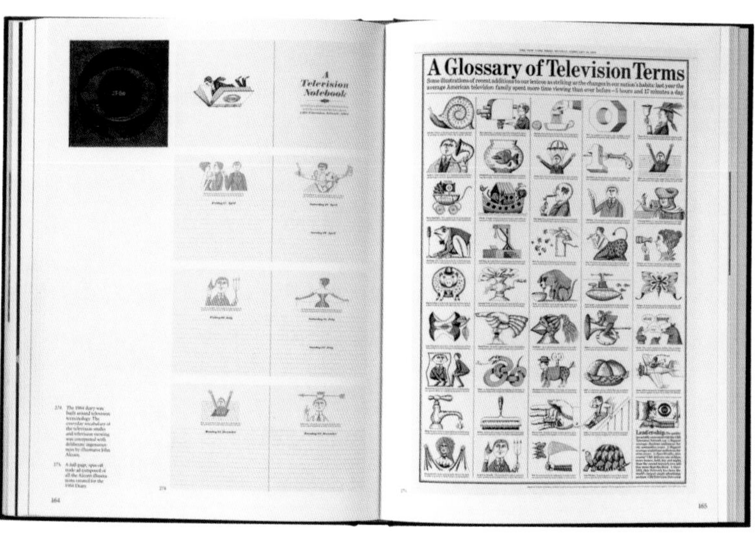

Dorfsman's extensive and thorough corporate branding for CBS's new offices in the 1960s is represented in this block of photographs.

The purchase of a double page in Variety *magazine to run a one-third column ad for CBS is perhaps Dorfsman's most famous ad, and is effectively reproduced over a complete spread in the book.*

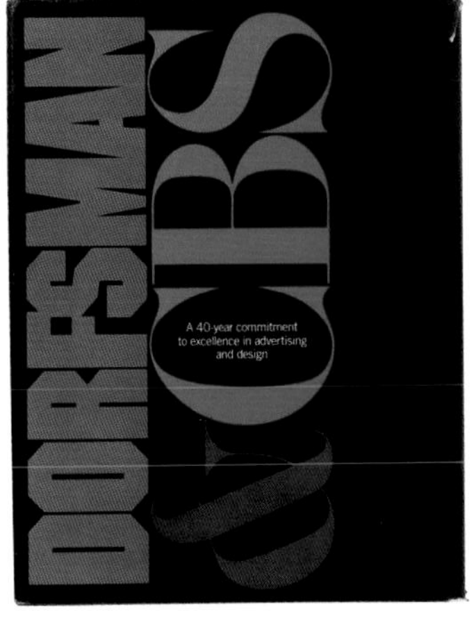

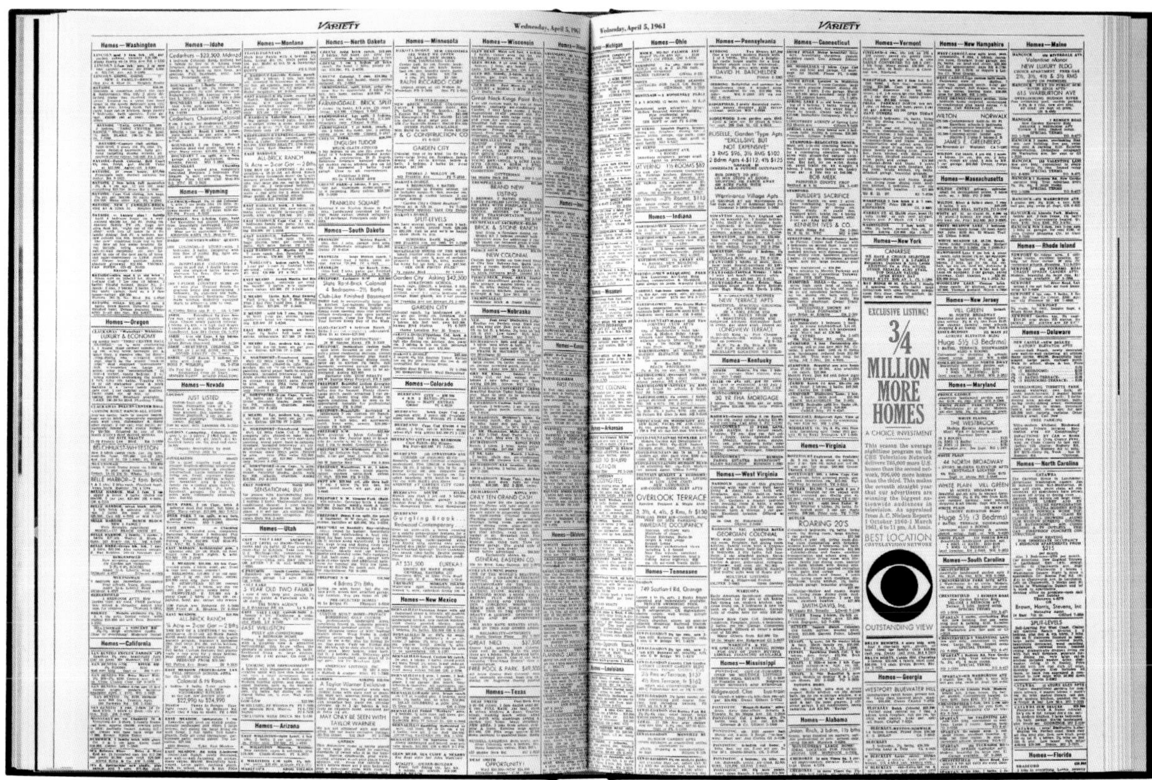

VARIETY — Wednesday, April 5, 1961

EXCLUSIVE LISTING!

3/4 MILLION MORE HOMES

A CHOICE INVESTMENT

This season the average nighttime program on the CBS Television Network delivers 786,000 more U.S. homes than the second network, 996,000 more homes than the third. This makes the seventh straight year that our advertisers are winning the biggest nationwide audiences in television. As appraised from A.C. Nielsen Reports 1 October 1960-1 March 1961, 6 to 11 pm, AA basis.

BEST LOCATION

CBS TELEVISION NETWORK

OUTSTANDING VIEW

A spread of typographic advertisements – a faint varnish is used to define the layouts.

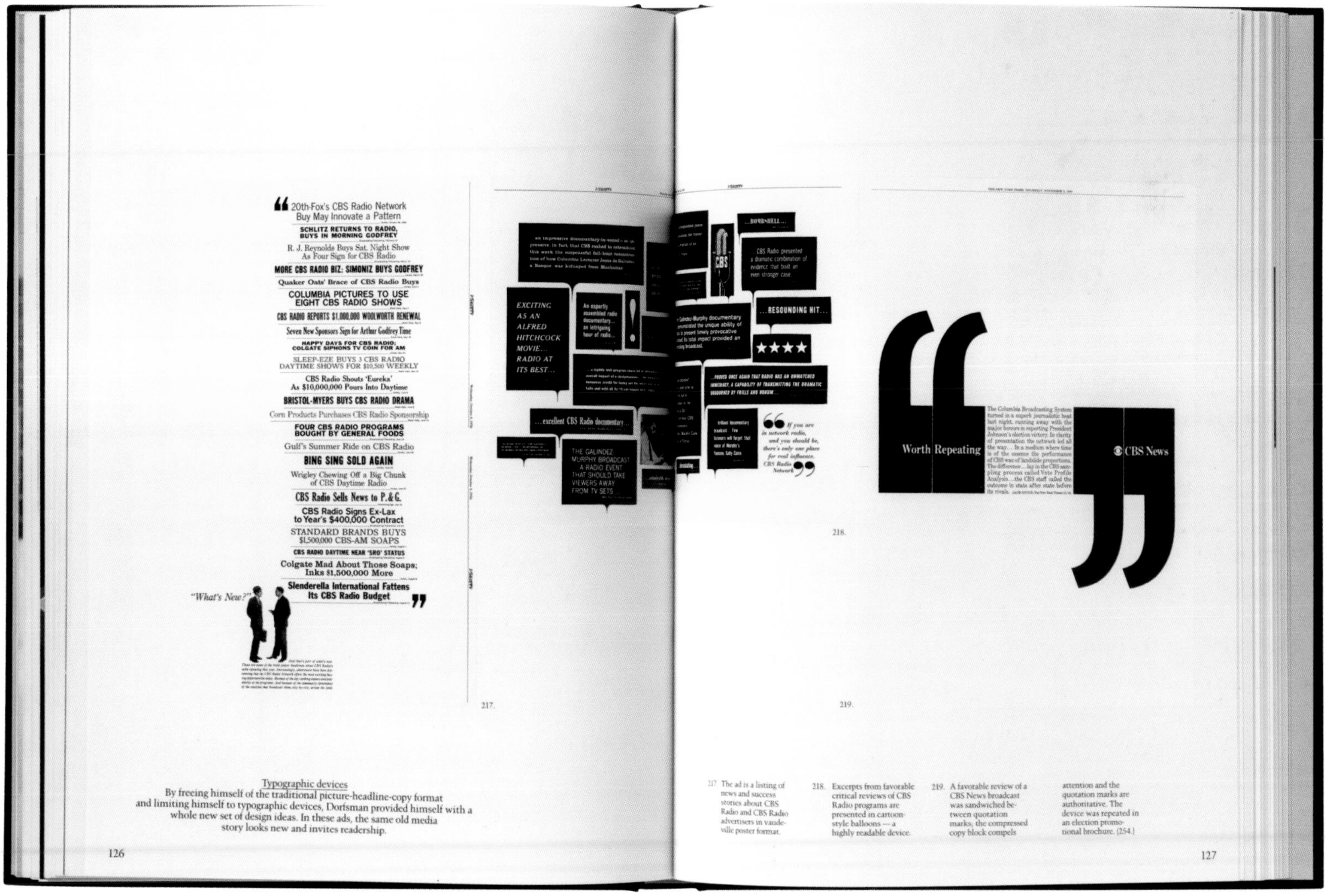

"20th-Fox's CBS Radio Network Buy May Innovate a Pattern
SCHLITZ RETURNS TO RADIO, BUYS IN MORNING GODFREY
R. J. Reynolds Buys Sat. Night Show As Four Sign for CBS Radio
MORE CBS RADIO BIZ: SIMONIZ BUYS GODFREY
Quaker Oats' Brace of CBS Radio Buys
COLUMBIA PICTURES TO USE EIGHT CBS RADIO SHOWS
CBS RADIO REPORTS $1,000,000 WOOLWORTH RENEWAL
Seven New Sponsors Sign for Arthur Godfrey Time
HAPPY DAYS FOR CBS RADIO; COLGATE SIPHONS TV COIN FOR AM
SLEEP-EZE BUYS 3 CBS RADIO DAYTIME SHOWS FOR $10,500 WEEKLY
CBS Radio Shouts 'Eureka' As $10,000,000 Pours Into Daytime
BRISTOL-MYERS BUYS CBS RADIO DRAMA
Corn Products Purchases CBS Radio Sponsorship
FOUR CBS RADIO PROGRAMS BOUGHT BY GENERAL FOODS
Gulf's Summer Ride on CBS Radio
BING SING SOLD AGAIN
Wrigley Chewing Off a Big Chunk of CBS Daytime Radio
CBS Radio Sells News to P.&G.
CBS Radio Signs Ex-Lax to Year's $400,000 Contract
STANDARD BRANDS BUYS $1,500,000 CBS-AM SOAPS
CBS RADIO DAYTIME NEAR 'SRO' STATUS
Colgate Mad About Those Soaps; Inks $1,500,000 More
Slenderella International Fattens Its CBS Radio Budget"

"What's New?"

217.

EXCITING AS AN ALFRED HITCHCOCK MOVIE... RADIO AT ITS BEST...

An expertly assembled radio documentary... an intriguing hour of radio...

...excellent CBS Radio documentary...

THE GALINDEZ-MURPHY BROADCAST A RADIO EVENT THAT SHOULD TAKE VIEWERS AWAY FROM TV SETS

...BOMBSHELL...

CBS Radio presented a dramatic combination of evidence that built an even stronger case.

...RESOUNDING HIT...

★★★★

"If you are in network radio, and you should be, there's only one place for real influence. CBS Radio Network"

218.

Worth Repeating

CBS News

219.

Typographic devices

By freeing himself of the traditional picture-headline-copy format and limiting himself to typographic devices, Dorfsman provided himself with a whole new set of design ideas. In these ads, the same old media story looks new and invites readership.

217. The ad is a listing of news and success stories about CBS Radio and CBS Radio advertisers in vaudeville poster format.

218. Excerpts from favorable critical reviews of CBS Radio programs are presented in cartoon-style balloons — a highly readable device.

219. A favorable review of a CBS News broadcast was sandwiched between quotation marks; the compressed copy block compels attention and the quotation marks are authoritative. The device was repeated in an election promotional brochure. (254.)

126

127

112 *R Stands for Righteous.* Here the letter R is used in normal position, reverse position, upside-down position, upside-down reverse position, and in color.

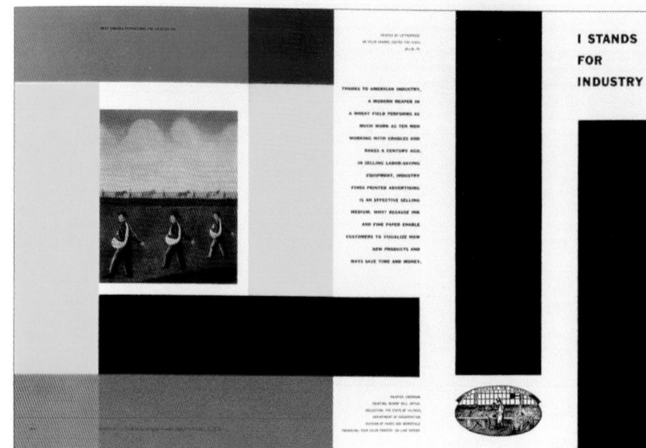

113 *I Stands for Industry.* The simplest letter in the alphabet can provide dynamic asymmetrical design, and with black printing only available on one of the pages.

114 *C Stands for Constitution.* The letter C has many unexplored, intriguing possibilities in design, with overlapping colors, tones, and spatial relationships.

115 *A Stands for Abundance.* Unlike the vital design in motion on page 94, the same letter A provides a symmetrical design in a colorful but stolid tranquility.

100

101

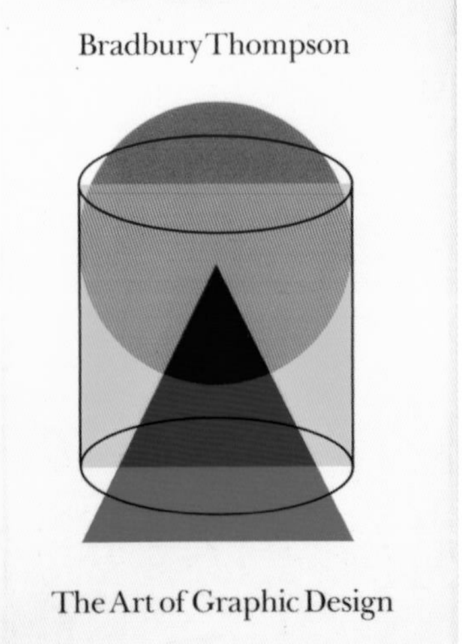

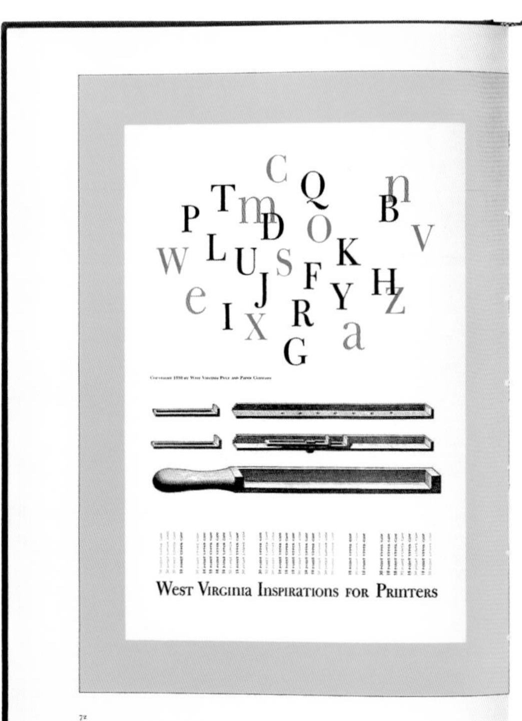

6

Alphabet 26

Experiments provide a readable and practical simplified alphabet, 1950

The plan for simplifying and improving our alphabet, entitled *Alphabet 26*, was first presented in *Westvaco Inspirations 180* in 1950. It recommended the use of only one symbol, upper- and lowercase, for each of the 26 letters. Our conventional alphabet contains 19 letters having dissimilar symbols (such as A and 'a') and 7 letters (c-o-s-v-w-x-z) having symbols that are identical.

The plan pointed out how misleading it is for a letter, or for any graphic symbol, to have two different designs [page 74]. It illustrated the confusion that might set in when school children are taught to recognize words even before they have learned to recognize different symbols for the same letter [page 74]. To remedy this, *Alphabet 26*, a plan based upon the logic of consistency, made this recommendation for the 19 letters that have dissimilar symbols: 15 letters should use the uppercase designs (black letters opposite) and 4 letters should use the lowercase designs (red letters). The other 7 letters already have identical symbols (blue letters).

Only 6 lowercase letters (a-e-m-n-r-u) could be used in typesetting because all others have ascenders or descenders that would protrude above or below the type body if enlarged for uppercase usage. The uppercase R design was preferred because enlargement of the lowercase 'r' would make an awkward fit next to lowercase letters. The uppercase U and the lowercase 'u' are almost identical, the former design having been selected for its simplicity.

The lowercase letter symbols a-e-m-n have key characteristics that will contribute to the *Alphabet 26* plan. They do not have the severely angular appearance of the A-E-M-N and the majority of the other uppercase letters. Because of this and their relatively frequent use in the language, they contribute variety and individuality to the shapes of words.

Alphabet 26 provides the necessary large letters for emphasis at the beginning of the sentence and for denoting proper nouns, an advantage over the exclusive use of an all lowercase alphabet, as recommended at the Bauhaus.

The original showing of *Alphabet 26* in 1950 [pages 72–79] by necessity employed a combination of capitals, small capitals, and lowercase letters [see specifications, opposite below]. Because the lowercase a-e-m-n were not yet redesigned to fit so harmoniously in the same words with capitals, small capitals, and lowercase letters, a degree of aesthetic harmony was lacking in the original version. However, for *Inspirations 213* in 1960 [page 81] and *Inspirations 217* in 1962 [page 82] the large a-e-m-n letters were redesigned to fit with the uppercase fonts, and the small a-e-m-n letters were redesigned to fit with the small-cap fonts.

These first special characters for *Alphabet 26* in text sizes were cast by Lanston Monotype Machine Company and were at one time available in all text sizes of *Baskerville* type. The first special characters for larger sizes were produced by Photo-Lettering, Inc. Both were manufactured from drawings by the author.

Although only *Baskerville* letters were employed for text setting in these pages, the *Alphabet 26* plan is applicable to all type families. The choice of *Baskerville* to introduce *Alphabet 26*

93 *Alphabet 26*, opposite. This was the title page of *Westvaco Inspirations 180*. It illustrates the plan as well as the way in which to specify it with two sizes of type. The composing stick recalls the old world of metal type. 1950

72

73

The Art of Graphic Design

Bradbury Thompson

Yale University Press,
New Haven and London, 1988
220 pages
340 × 242 mm (13.375 × 9.5 in)
Designed by
Bradbury Thompson

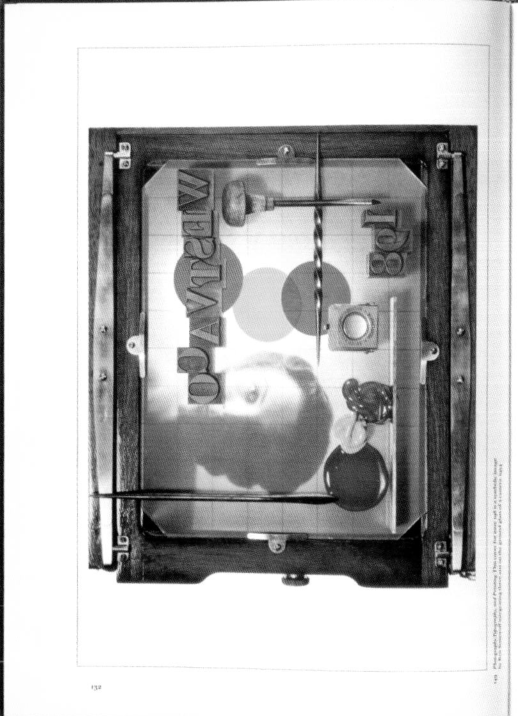

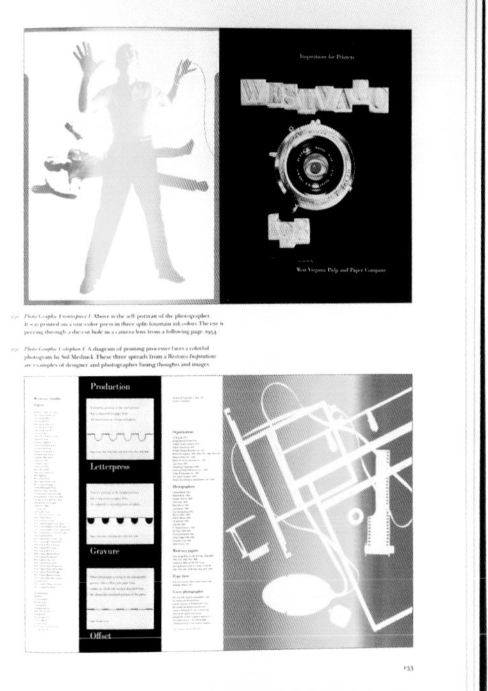

Bradbury Thompson (1911–1995) was just 27 when he was asked to design *Westvaco Inspirations*, a periodical published for the printing trade, graphic arts industry and cultural institutions by the paper company Westvaco Corporation. It was a relationship that lasted for 24 years and included the design of over 60 issues, alongside many other design projects sponsored by Westvaco. As Thompson notes in his introduction to *The Art of Graphic Design*, this was 'a rare opportunity for experimentation', and, as the book itself shows, it was fully exploited.

Of the monograph's 16 chapters, the first 12 are devoted to Thompson's work for *Inspirations* – unsurprisingly, as the book was sponsored in part by Westvaco. His trademark use of process colours, necessitated by small commissioning budgets, brought life and motion to spreads and is explored in a number of chapters. Alphabet 26, his development of a simplified monalphabet with no separation of upper and lower case, was the subject of a number of issues of the periodical and is studied in detail in the book. Experimental and playful layouts labelled 'Type as a Toy' illustrate Thompson's prowess with typographical elements.

In common with Westvaco's output, *The Art of Graphic Design* is exceedingly well produced and printed. The care taken is mirrored in the 'Homage to the Book' portfolio and also in the American Classic Book Series. The corporation produced these every year as seasonal gifts, for which Thompson repackaged famous literary texts.

The rest of Thompson's career is restricted to the four chapters at the back of the book. One of these is devoted to the many United States postage stamps he designed, a discipline he described as 'visual haiku' – a reference to the 17-syllable Japanese verse form. He art-directed many publications other than *Inspirations*, most importantly *ARTnews* for 27 years and the fashion magazine *Mademoiselle* for 15 years.

Three quarters of The Art of Graphic Design *recounts Bradbury Thompson's famous involvement with the Westvaco Corporation. The paper company helped to fund the book's publication. Below is a classic example of Thompson's overprinting of process colours for* Westvaco Inspirations *(1958).*

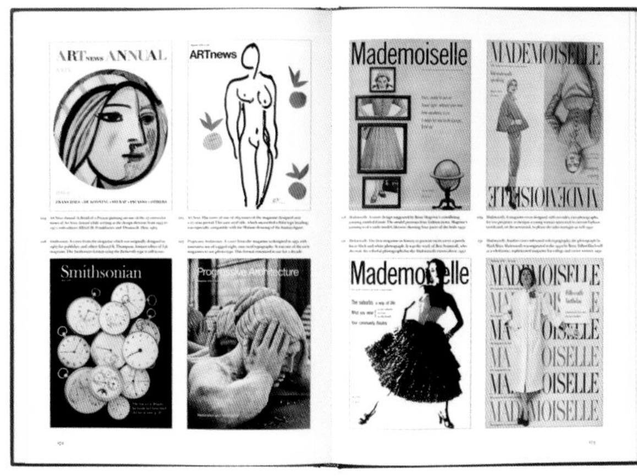

The Graphic Language of Neville Brody
Neville Brody, Jon Wozencroft
Thames & Hudson, London, 1988
Reprint (pictured), 1995
160 pages
302 × 250 mm (11.875 × 9.875 in)
Designed by Neville Brody

Neville Brody (1957–) left art college in 1979 knowing that designing for the music industry was his chosen vocation. He admired designers such as Barney Bubbles (Colin Fulcher) and the Rocking Russian studio, who were part of England's post-punk music scene at the time, and decided to follow their path. He worked at Stiff Records and then at Fetish Records, and also struck up long-term relationships with the bands Cabaret Voltaire and 23 Skidoo. In 1981 he became art director of the definitive style magazine of the time, *The Face*, and shaped its trendsetting agenda with his brand of constructed typography. His success there, and his own notoriety, quickly led to work on more magazines: *New Socialist, City Limits* and *Arena*.

In 1988, when he was not even ten years out of college, *The Graphic Language of Neville Brody,* a review of his short and highly productive career to date, was published. A collaboration between Brody and the writer Jon Wozencroft, such a combination of youthful vigour and serious design discourse had not been seen before. It was tailor-made for a readership brought up on the style culture of the time, and its popularity was helped by Brody's high profile.

The introduction sets out Brody's influences: the Dada artists, avant-garde designers of the 1920s and books such as Herbert Spencer's *Pioneers of Modern Typography* (see page 108) had showed him the value of experimentation. The text and captions reveal his meticulous design reasoning and attention to detail, as well as his commitment to left-wing politics in Margaret Thatcher's Britain. Dominating the book is his fabricated type, drawn largely by hand or constructed from mixed Letraset letterforms. The pages show an art form that is constantly evolving through Brody's need to push boundaries and his distrust of imitators.

The Graphic Language of Neville Brody 2 (Thames & Hudson, London, 1994), written by Jon Wozencroft, explored his change to a more computer-based aesthetic. *G1* (Laurence King Publishing, London, 1996), an eclectic mix of found and contemporary graphics written with Lewis Blackwell, was published two years later.

A colour spread showing Brody's work for the band Cabaret Voltaire. The book is printed in a mixture of black-and-white, full-colour and two-colour sections in black and red, examples of which are seen to the right and below.

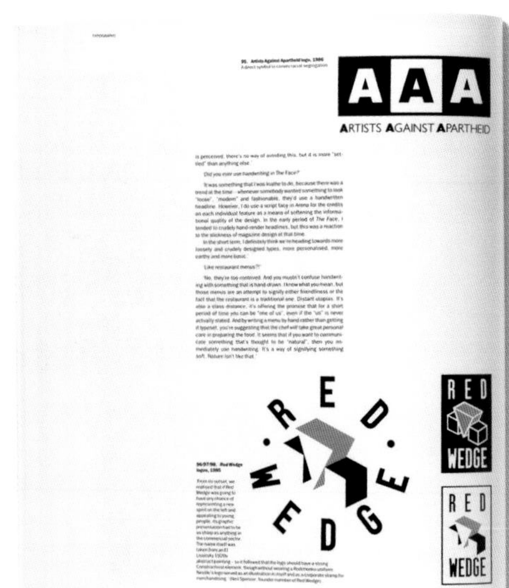

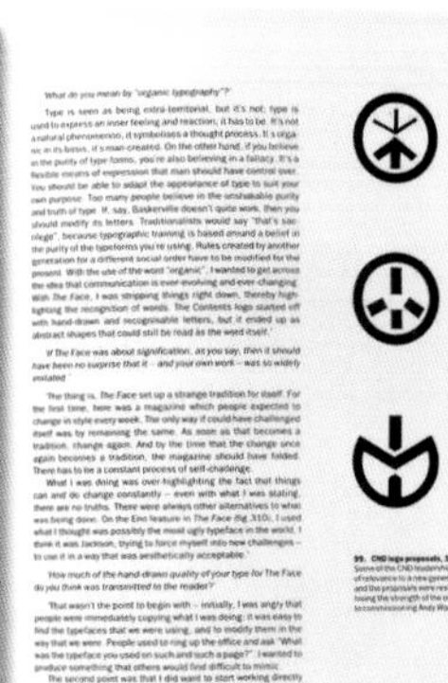

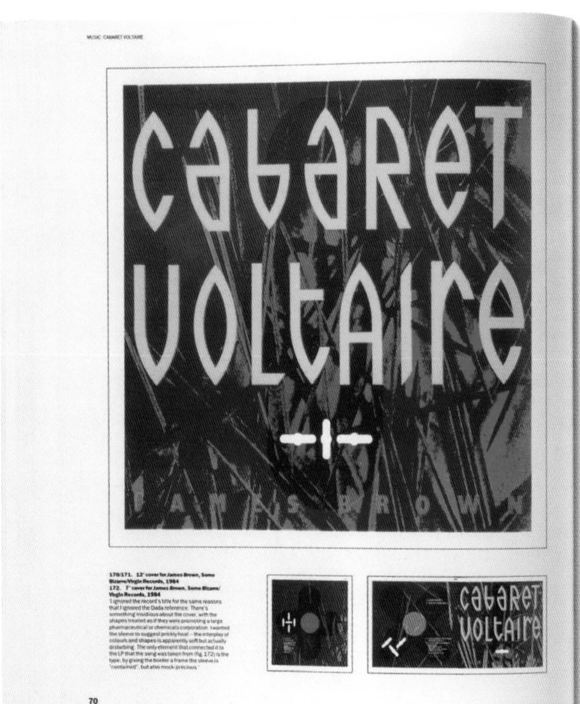

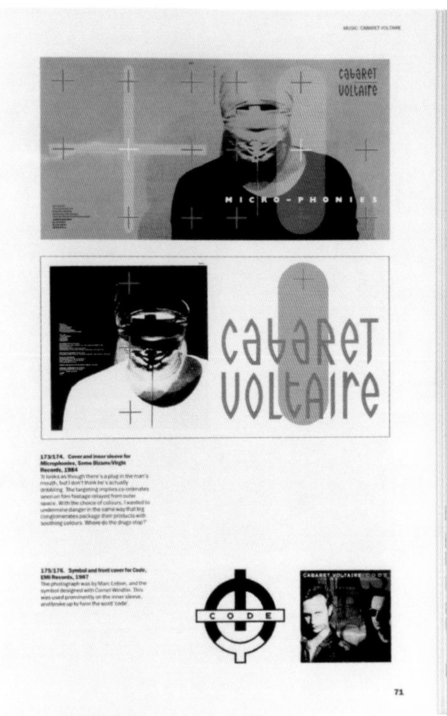

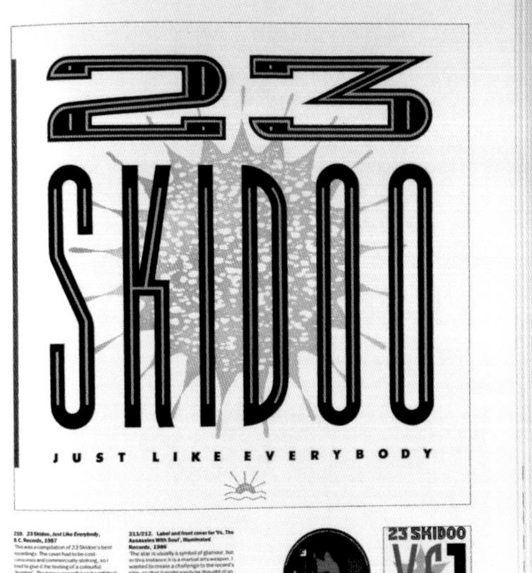

23 SKIDOO
JUST LIKE EVERYBODY
23 SKIDOO
VS 1

THE GRAPHIC LANGUAGE OF
NEVILLE BRODY

BRODY

Brody's blend of youth culture, music, politics and typography proved a potent and popular mix – his role as art director of style magazine The Face *cemented his reputation and is given its own chapter.*

THE FACE

Neville Brody's work for *The Face* questioned the traditional structure of magazine design.

'Everything in *The Face* was reasoned, every single mark on the page was either an emotive response or a logical extension of the ideas. If I was bleeding type off the edge of the page, it wasn't a case of "Oh, let's bleed type off the page". I was wanting to suggest three things. Firstly, how much of a headline do you need to be able to recognise it? Secondly, I wanted to give the idea that with each spread of *The Face* there was an infinite choice, and what we had done was to section out *one small part of that*; and lastly, I wanted to use the three-dimensional space of a magazine. Magazines are 3D items in space and time – there's a connection between page 5 and pages 56 and 57, a continuum. A magazine doesn't have to divide up space on a page like a newspaper, and the information it carries has more time to make connections between the different ideas that might be present. Why be inhibited by the edge of the page?

'There was a built-in order to what I was doing, and a relationship to all the elements, a balance and a rhythm. If Classicism represents the 'ideal' of a constant tradition and Romanticism a desire for change, I chose to work between the two. Within magazine bounds, I think *The Face* was very classical, because it still performed the basic functions that a magazine should work with. People missed that completely. To their credit, *New Sounds New Styles* and *iD*, two of *The Face*'s competitors, went much further in challenging the actual body text, rendering it unreadable in many places, but it was a main priority in *The Face* that you should read it. Editorial and design worked hand in hand – it was never a case of copy being handed over and that was that.

'The text itself wasn't presented emotively. What was surrounding the writing would affect and colour your appreciation, but if you isolated the writing itself, you should be able to judge it purely on what it was saying. *The Face* had two narratives, the writing and the design. We wanted people to be their own editors.'

'The grid was based on a simple system that could be adapted when necessary. The magazine started off with a four-column grid, was then firmly established as a three-column grid, and became a three and a two once the four-column had been abandoned completely. Exceptions were 'Intro' and the review-based 'Monitor' section, which needed the flexibility of allowing small pictures to be dropped in. The whole thing allowed you to centre design elements on the page very easily, and allowed for the inclusion of good medium-sized photographs.

'*The Face* had a very distinctive and quite unusual policy of allowing photographers a free hand – apart from briefing them beforehand, if necessary, rather than heavily adapting their work later. We felt that this would achieve a much better and more adventurous result. We did not want the photographs to become subservient to the identity of the magazine. We did not want to pursue the punk quality of photomontage, or to make the photographs graphic. The very act of giving photographers a free hand meant that they were already stepping out of the accepted norm. Montage was used in other ways. Design was working alongside the photography – again 'the third mind'. I felt that if I started to interfere with the photos, the design would be overstepping its mark when it didn't need to.

231. Logo for 'Expo', *The Face*, No. 58, February 1985
'Neville came in with his portfolio in the very early days of *Smash Hits*. I thought it was really good, but not for *Smash Hits*. I made a mental note, however – I knew I wasn't going to be doing *Smash Hits* forever. In the meantime, I thought that maybe I'd turn Neville into a writer, but that didn't turn out so well.' (Nick Logan, July 1987).

232. 'Hard Times' spread, *The Face*, No. 29, September 1982
Giving this amount of weight to the headline was unusual at the time, recalling 'tabloid' newspapers, but also the mood of the story – a blend of social documentation and dress codes.

96

233/234. 'Killer' cover, *The Face*, No.59, March 1985
This cover typifies the conviction of *The Face*'s tag-line, 'The World's Best Dressed Magazine'. It featured the new omnipresent Felix for the first time, and shows the strong influence that Buffalo had on the magazine – stylist Ray Petri with, in this case, photographer Jamie Morgan.

97

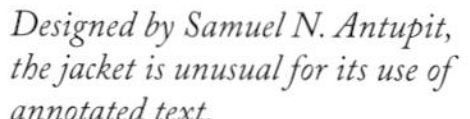

Designed by Samuel N. Antupit, the jacket is unusual for its use of annotated text.

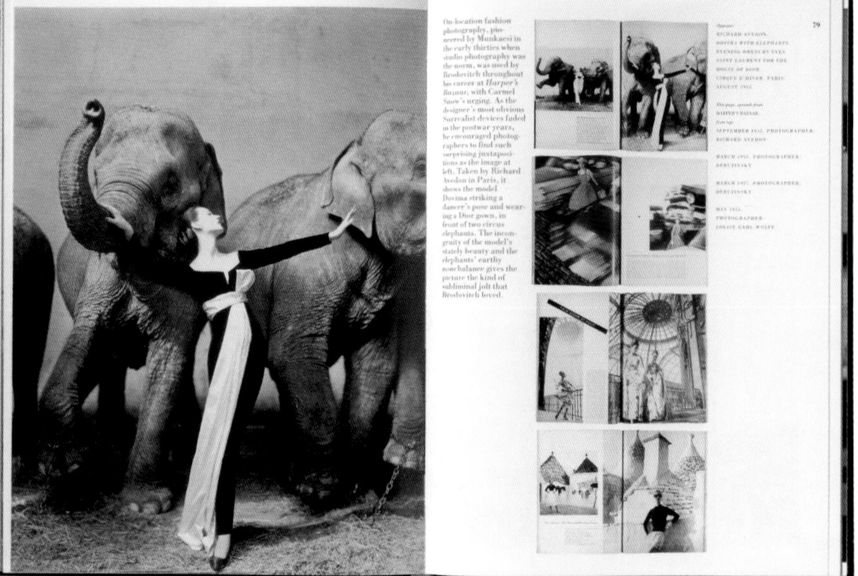

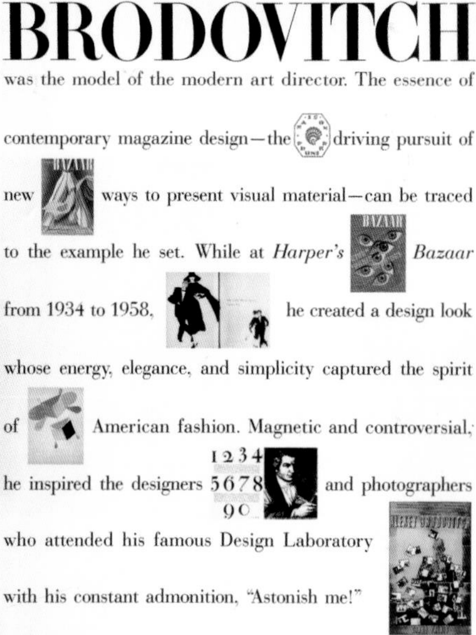

BRODOVITCH
was the model of the modern art director. The essence of contemporary magazine design—the driving pursuit of new ways to present visual material—can be traced to the example he set. While at *Harper's Bazaar* from 1934 to 1958, he created a design look whose energy, elegance, and simplicity captured the spirit of American fashion. Magnetic and controversial, he inspired the designers and photographers who attended his famous Design Laboratory with his constant admonition, "Astonish me!"
ANDY GRUNDBERG
MASTERS OF AMERICAN DESIGN

A fifth colour, grey, is printed throughout. All the black-and-white imagery is reproduced as duotones, and some of the text also uses this special colour, adding a depth and richness to the spreads.

Brodovitch

Andy Grundberg
Harry N. Abrams, New York, 1989
166 pages
304 × 228 mm (12 × 9 in)
Designed by Ray Komai
Jacket designed by
Samuel N. Antupit

The Russian émigré Alexey Brodovitch (1898–1971) left a profound legacy to American design. This sumptuous book, written by the photographic critic Andy Grundberg, is a testament to his achievements as an art director, designer and educator. *Brodovitch* contains 340 illustrations of work from all periods of his career and some excellent portraits, all knitted together by Ray Komai's elegant layout. The addition of introductory text in the form of a cover by Samuel N. Antupit (art director at Abrams at the time of the book's publication) makes for a near-perfect graphic design monograph.

The book has six chapters, many of which are devoted to Brodovitch's defining work as art director at *Harper's Bazaar* from 1934 to 1958. His dramatic use of photography counterpointed by contrasting Bodoni type is clearly shown in the many spreads displayed throughout. The photographic talent he employed was of the highest order: Brassaï, Walker Evans, Henri Cartier-Bresson, Man Ray and Cecil Beaton were all commissioned. Cassandre frequently provided cover illustrations.

Nurtured by Brodovitch, Richard Avedon became the photographer most identified with *Bazaar*. His *Observations* (Simon & Schuster, New York, 1959) was designed by Brodovitch and is highlighted in one of the book's eight 'In Focus' sections that look at important projects Brodovitch undertook beyond *Bazaar*. Among these are the short-lived graphic arts quarterly *Portfolio*, and his masterpiece of book design, *Ballet* (J.J. Augustin, New York, 1945), which features his photographs of the Ballets Russes in the late 1930s.

A chapter is devoted to the Design Laboratory, a challenging and often confrontational workshop for students set up by Brodovitch, which provided inspiration for many aspiring designers and photographers.

Brodovitch was the first title in the Masters of American Design series, produced by Documents of American Design, and was followed by *Frederic Goudy* by D.J.R. Bruckner (Harry N. Abrams, New York, 1990). Unfortunately, planned books on Saul Bass and Will Burtin failed to materialize.

Siegfried Odermatt & Rosmarie Tissi: Graphic Design
Odermatt & Tissi
Jack Waser, Werner M. Wolf (editors)
Waser Verlag, Zurich, 1993
184 pages
229 × 229 mm (9 × 9 in)
Designed by Siegfried Odermatt

Design duo Siegfried Odermatt (1926–) and Rosmarie Tissi (1937–) are not really a duo; they each work on their own projects and with their own clients, but it is reported that they occasionally share their thoughts about each other's work. They have done this since 1968, in their shared studio space in Zurich.

Siegfried Odermatt & Rosmarie Tissi: Graphic Design provides very little first-hand information about working practices or philosophy. This has been left to the writers of the four essays that are interspersed between the five chapters on their work – these cover general design, trademarks, advertising campaigns, corporate identity and posters. All text is in both German and English.

Some of the illustrations predate their partnership – the earliest is from 1947. With 45 years worth of work on display, the book provides a unique oversight of two designers who not only contributed to the development of the international style in Switzerland in the 1950s and early 1960s, but used this as a foundation to help forge a new identity for Swiss graphic design in the 1980s.

Odermatt's insurance company brochures (1960–61), with large headlines suffering various typographic accidents, and his identity, with its cropped logo, for Grammo Studio (1957) – a record and turntable store – are typical of this classic period of Swiss graphic design. Tissi's commissioned line drawings feature in the Grammo Studio work, and are the first evidence in the book of the designers appearing together.

In the chapter devoted to Odermatt & Tissi's poster work, there is an emphasis on the many outstanding examples designed in the 1980s. These are typified by lines of cut-out text and the bold use of geometric shapes and colour, freed from the confines of a rigid grid.

Siegfried Odermatt & Rosmarie Tissi: Graphic Design uses a simple layout designed by Odermatt. An 'O' or 'T' in the captions indicates the designer responsible for each work. A sense of scale between reproductions is maintained within each chapter.

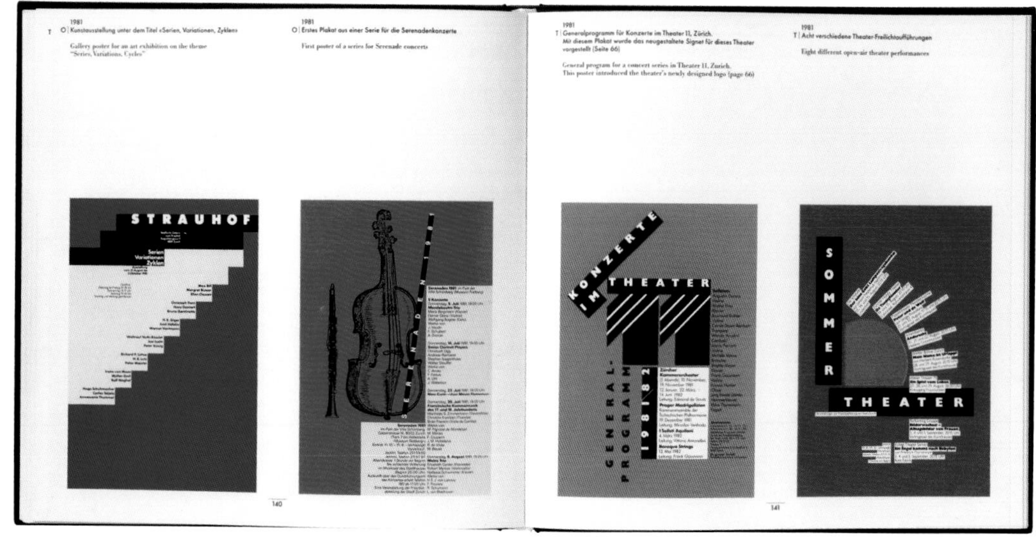

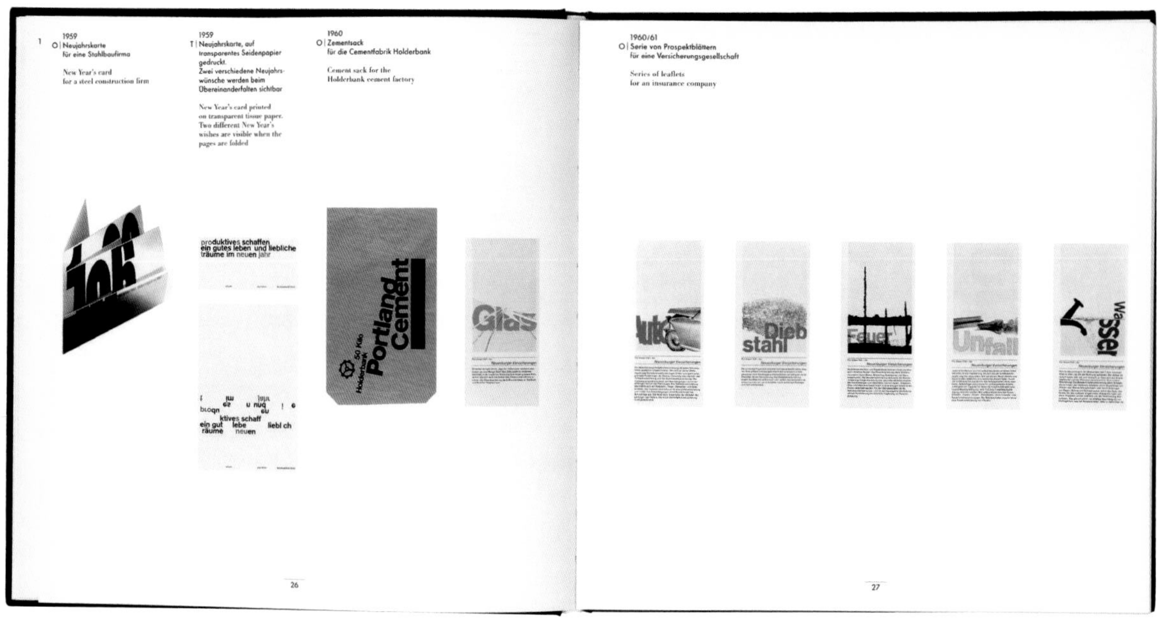

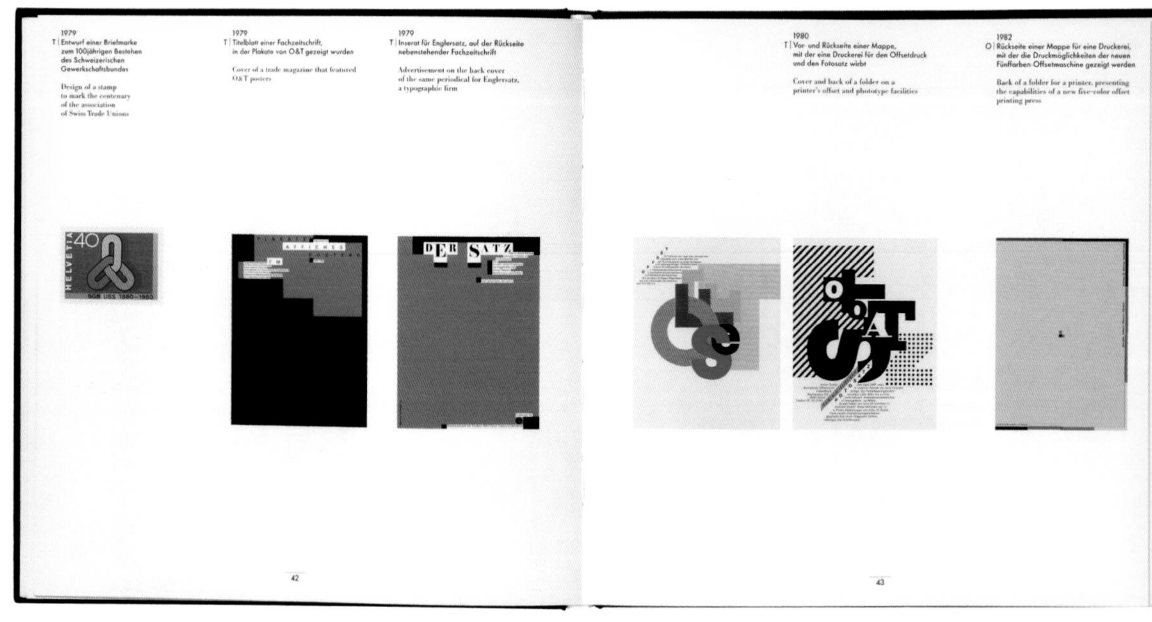

1988
O | Entwurf für den Wettbewerb der Migros-Klubschulen

Entry in a poster competition for the Migros Club Schools

1988
O | Entwurf für eine Farbenfabrik

Poster project for a paint manufacturer

1988
T | Eines der sechs preisgekrönten Plakate aus dem Wettbewerb für die Migros-Klubschulen.
- Henri-de-Toulouse-Lautrec-Medaille in Silber und bestes Plakat in der Kategorie «Plakate zur Wirtschaftsförderung» an der 6. Plakat-Triennale in Essen, 1990.
- Unter den besten Schweizer Plakaten des Jahres 1989

One of the prizewinners in the competition for a poster on educational courses offered by Migros Club Schools.
- Won the Henri de Toulouse-Lautrec silver medal and was chosen as best poster in the category "Posters for the promotion of trade" at the 6th Poster Triennial in Essen, 1990.
- Was also among the Best Swiss Posters of the Year 1989

1988
T | Internationale Kieler Segelwoche 1990.
- 1. Preis in einem eingeladenen Wettbewerb.
Das Plakat ist Teil eines ganzen Design-Programms: von der Anstecknadel über Krawatte, T-Shirt, Foulard, Bierkrug sowie Prospekte usw. bis zum Schwarzweiss-Kleininserat

International Sailing Week at Kiel, Germany, 1990.
- Won 1st prize in a competition among invited designers.
The poster is part of a complete design program, from lapel pins, ties, T-shirts, shawls, beer steins, folders, etc., to small black-and-white advertisements

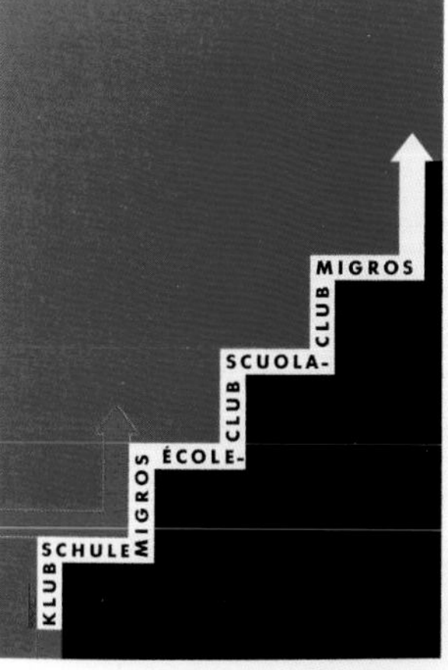

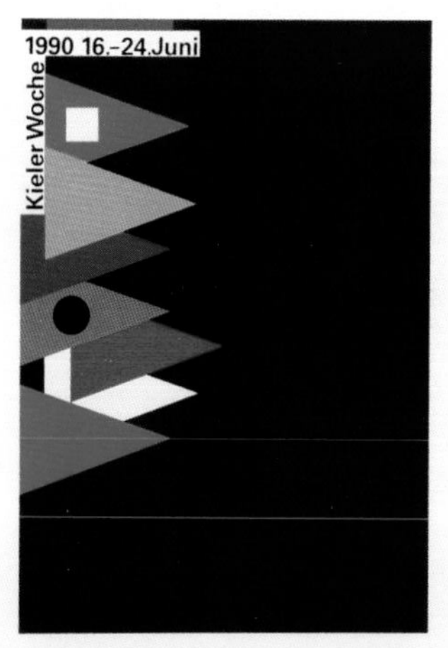

156

157

Posters designed in 1988 – the layout shows the book's use of Futura for text in German and Bodoni for text in English.

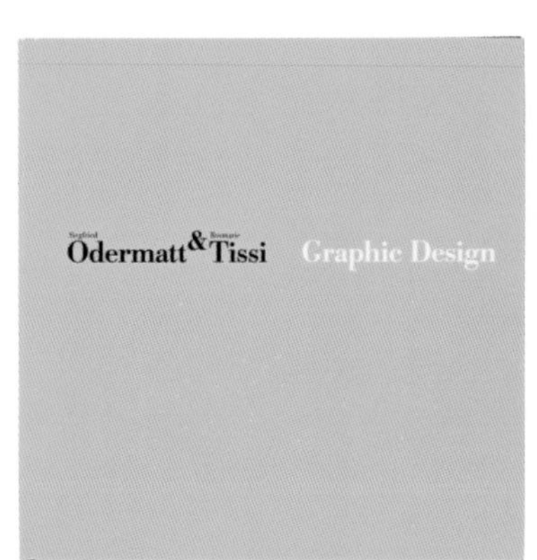

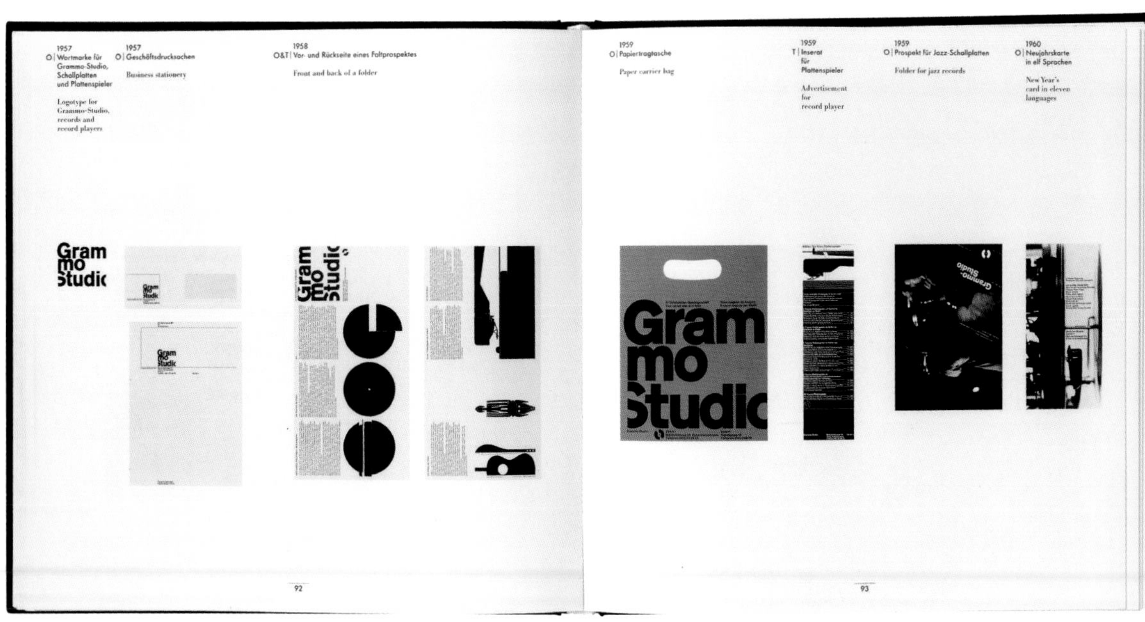

1957
O | Wortmarke für Grammo-Studio, Schallplatten und Plattenspieler

Logotype for Grammo-Studio, records and record players

1957
O | Geschäftsdrucksachen

Business stationery

1958
O&T | Vor- und Rückseite eines Faltprospektes

Front and back of a folder

1959
O | Papiertragtasche

Paper carrier bag

1959
T | Inserat für Plattenspieler

Advertisement for record player

1959
O | Prospekt für Jazz-Schallplatten

Folder for jazz records

1960
O | Neujahrskarte in elf Sprachen

New Year's card in eleven languages

92

93

In the simple layout by Odermatt, all the visual material hangs from a line across the page, with all the caption material hanging from another line above.

1966

The year
Everyone cheered and laughed as Bobby Moore's England beat Germany in the World Cup final at Wembley. Everyone grieved and cried over the Aberfan disaster which buried a school and 144 children under a coal slag slip. The prisons continued to leak, this time spy George Blake escaped from Wormwood Scrubbs. Having trouble with its slim Commons majority from 1964, Labour improved its position in another general election. Further away the Soviet's *Venus III* spacecraft was the first to land (crash, in fact) on another planet. Indira Ghandi became Prime Minister of India. The Red Guards ran amok in China purging revisionists. At the cinema Michael Caine kissed the girls and made them cry in *Alfie*. A year of classics in the charts had *Yellow Submarine* and *Eleanor Rigby* from the Beatles, *River Deep, Mountain High* from Ike and Tina Turner and *Good Vibrations* from the Beach Boys. The Monkees arrived on TV from Hollywood doing a Beatles rip-off every week, and doing it pretty well too. Also new on the small screen were Johnny Speight's beguiling bigot Alf Garnett in *Till Death Us Do Part*, and just the right mix of actors, graphics and tongue-in-cheek in *Batman*. *Cathy Come Home* continued the BBC's first-class reputation for working-class television drama. Carnaby Street vied with the King's Road as London's centre of pop fashion. And Twiggy became Woman of the Year although not obviously qualifying yet.

Subsections containing the highlights of each year of Nova's *publication begin with a brief description of cultural and political events.*

September 1966

Nova: 1965–1975*'s large format allows for impressive, sizeable reproduction of original photography and illustration. Seen here are photographs by Jeanloup Sieff from 1966.*

1966

March 1966
Jeanloup Sieff photographed the startling Paris creations of Cardin, Ungaro and Paco Rabanne, picked as the year's stars by fashion editor Molly Parkin.

Nova: 1965–1975
David Hillman,
Harri Peccinotti
David Gibbs (editor)
Pavilion Books, London, 1993
224 pages
333 × 256 mm (13 × 10.125 in)
Designed by David Hillman,
Karin Beck

The oversized, provocative cover of *Nova: 1965–1975*, with large red lips at 90 degrees, mirrors the impact of this women's magazine during its brief and exhilarating 11 years of publication. It was prepared to push boundaries both editorially and creatively. *Nova* was published during a period in the late 1960s when Britain was a centre of the world's attention in fashion, music and the arts. As such *Nova* was a reflection of the atmosphere and creativity of its time.

Compiled by two of *Nova*'s art directors, David Hillman and Harri Peccinotti, this book is the visual story of the magazine's evolution told largely through its covers and spreads. A chronological journey through all the covers is followed by an opening chapter giving an overview of pioneering magazines of the late 1950s and early 1960s, most notably Willy Fleckhaus's uncompromising *Twen,* the subject of *Twen 1959–1971: Revision einer Legende* (Umschau, Frankfurt am Main, 1995). Highlights of *Nova's* contents are displayed over the next three chapters, which contain subsections covering each individual year of publication. Detailed captions describe the contents of articles, and writers, photographers and illustrators are credited. Each yearly subsection is prefaced with a summary of important events and cultural milestones.

Tightly cropped and often overtly erotic photography, coupled with an unashamed use of illustration, typifies the spreads. This imagery gave the magazine its edge and was commissioned from some of the best talent available: a highlight was Celestino Valenti's 4.25-metre (14-foot) nude printed over eight spreads. Regular photographic contributors shown in *Nova: 1965–1975* include Helmut Newton, Terence Donovan, Diane Arbus, Tony Evans and Sarah Moon. Illustrators and artists such as Jean-Paul Goude, Peter Blake, Alan Aldridge, Roger Law and Philippe Weissbecker were also an integral part of *Nova*'s visual identity.

The End of Print

The Graphic Design of David Carson

Lewis Blackwell, David Carson

Laurence King Publishing, London, 1995

160 pages

287 × 243 mm (11.25 × 9.5 in)

Designed by David Carson

A graphic iconoclast, the American designer and one-time professional surfer David Carson (1957–) practises a design that challenges many typographical conventions head-on. Type is deliberately obscured, cropped and overlaid; emphases and hierarchies are turned upside down.

Borrowed from a comment about Carson's work by Neville Brody, *The End of Print* is an evocative but fitting title for this book, published by Chronicle Books in the USA and Laurence King Publishing in the the UK. Brody's judgement on Carson's attack on graphic design norms was also a nod to the changes wrought by the computer and the advance of the Internet as the new form of communication. It guaranteed attention from both Carson's critics and his admirers, and undoubtedly contributed to the book's popularity.

It is no surprise that *The End of Print* looks very much like a magazine: Carson's brand of disintegrating layouts and indecipherable text was formed when he was art director at a succession of magazines. A long chapter looks at his trailblazing work at *Transworld Skateboarding*, *Beach Culture* and *Surfer*, and, from 1992, at the new music monthly *Ray Gun*. Scattered throughout the book are numerous commissions that illustrate the book's title, by artists including Brad Holland, Marshall Arisman and Gary Baseman.

Success led to commissions in the advertising world, and the chapter labelled 'Selling Out' shows work done for major corporations such as Pepsi, Nike and Levi Strauss. An interview with Carson gives an insight into his views on contemporary design and his working practices.

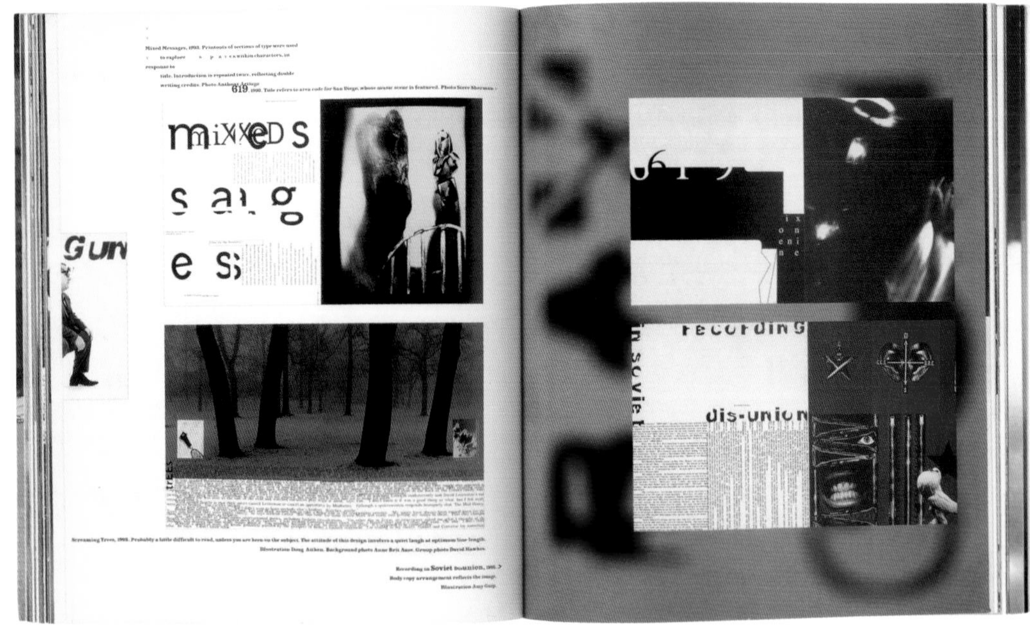

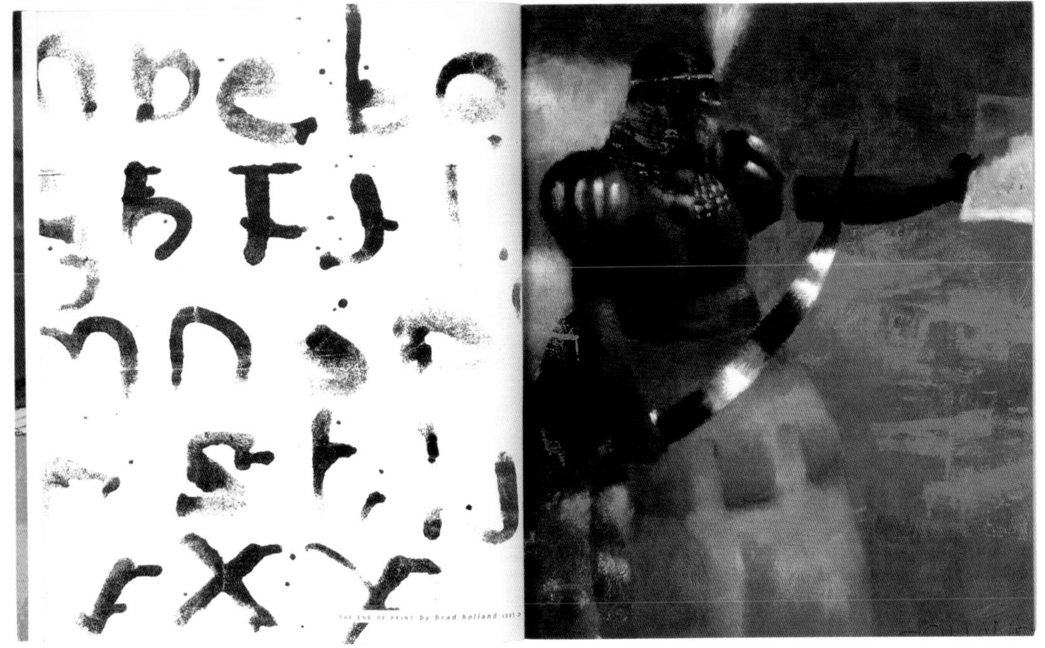

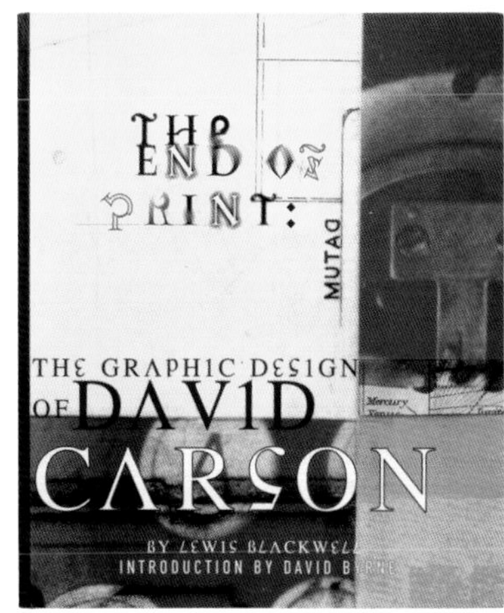

Illustrations entitled 'End of Prints' are placed throughout the book – on the right-hand page above is one by Brad Holland.

A spread of layouts from Beach Culture *magazine, packed full of layered imagery.*

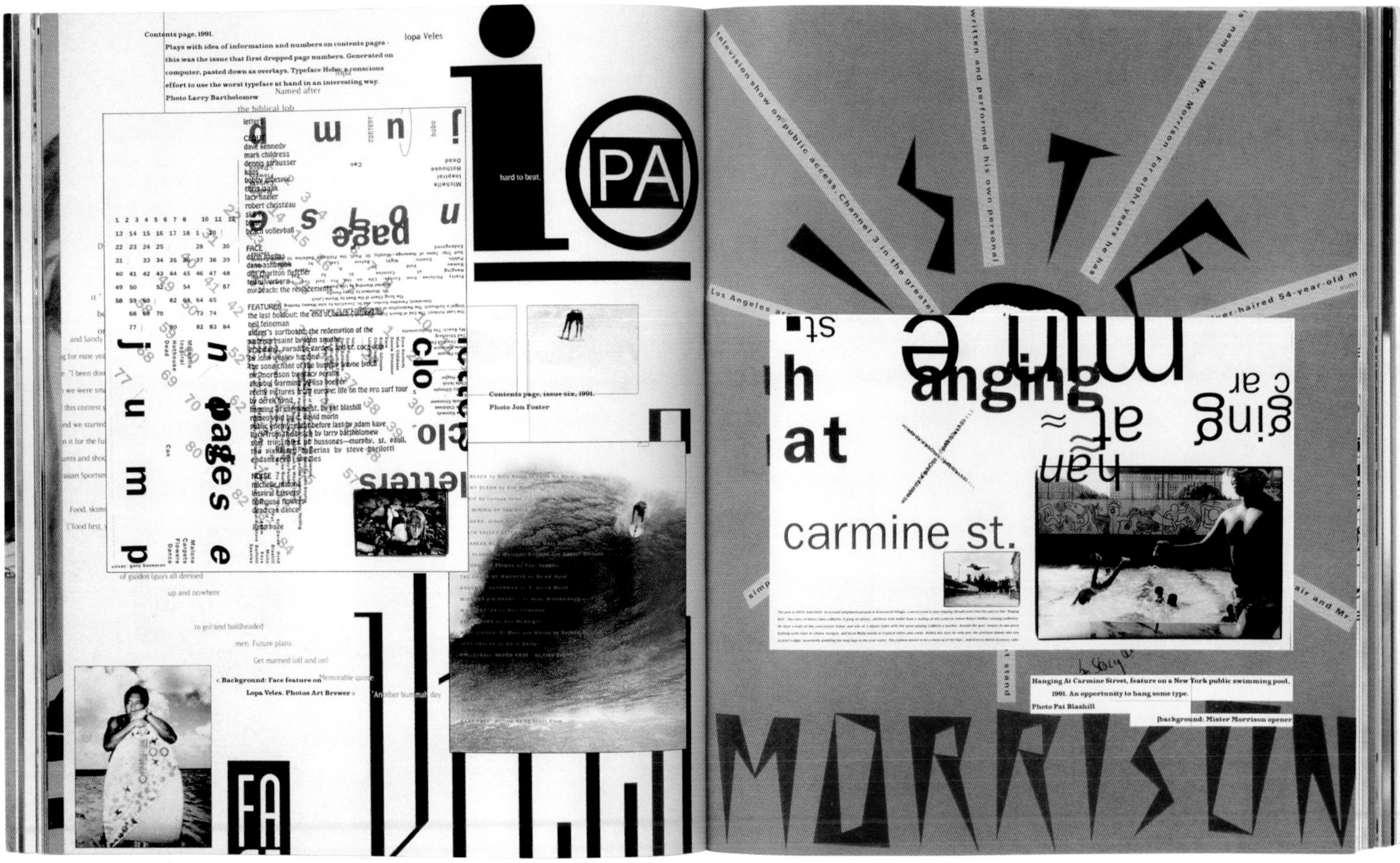

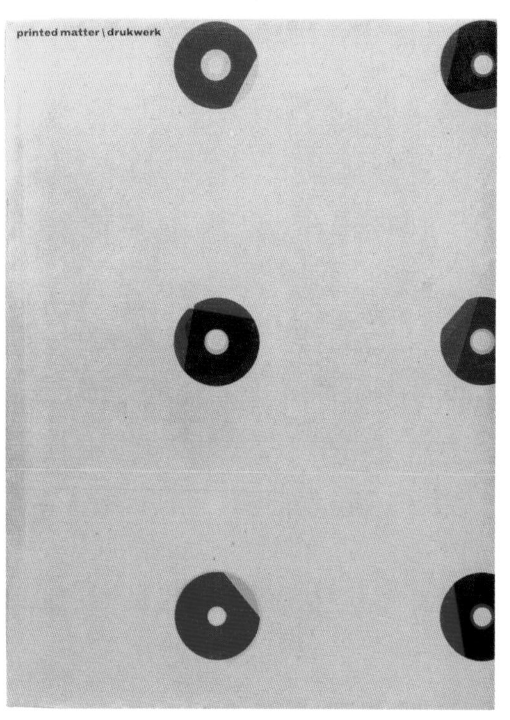

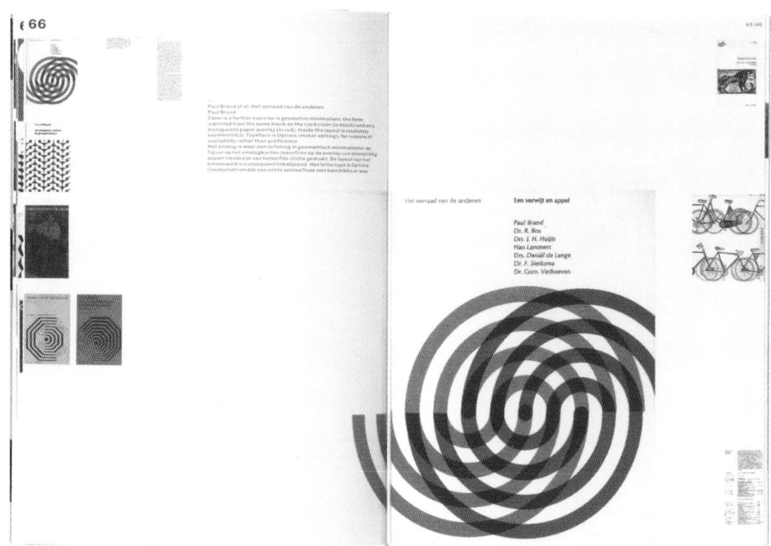

The second edition of Printed Matter *was expanded to include work since 1996. This spread shows some of Martens's experimental printmaking.*

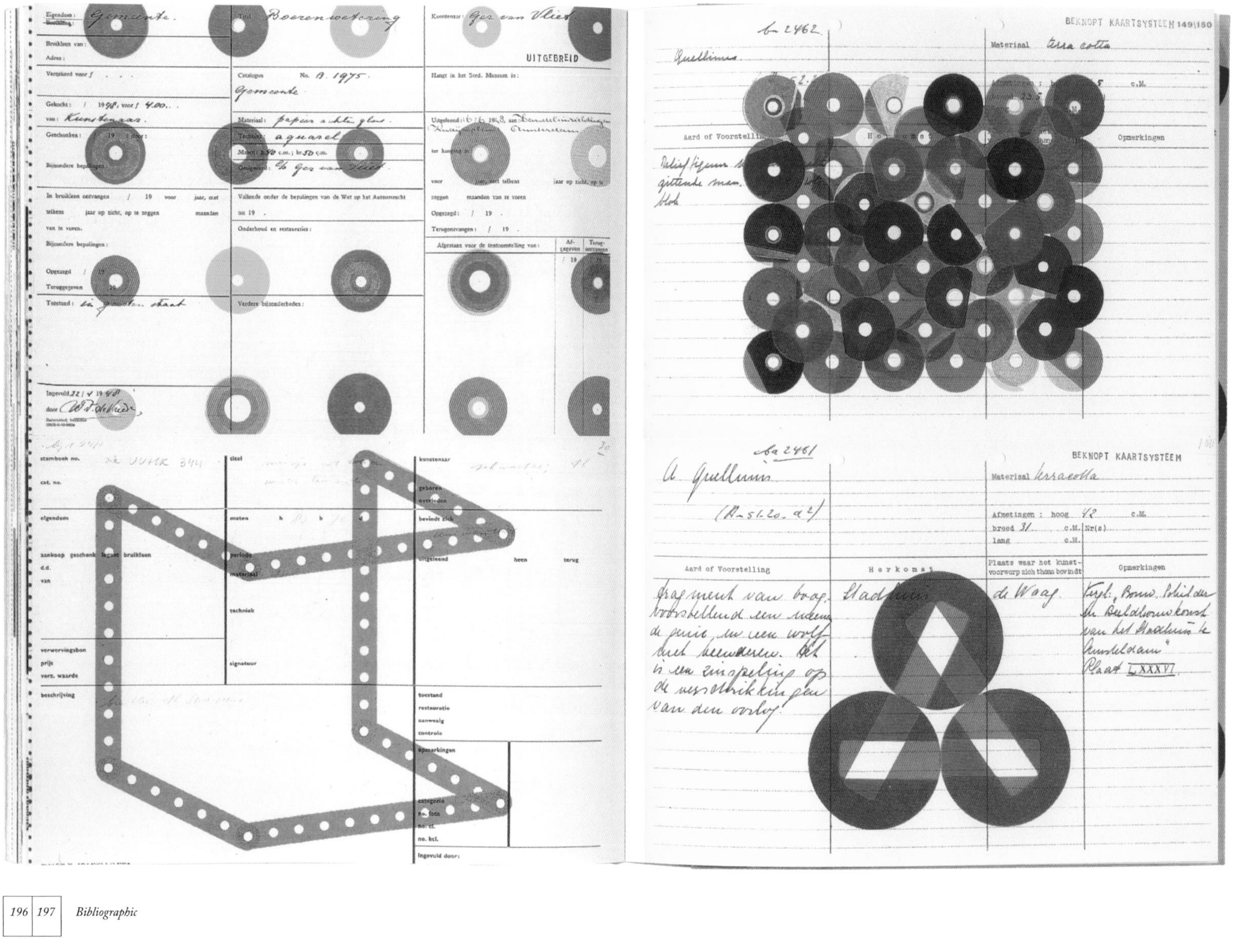

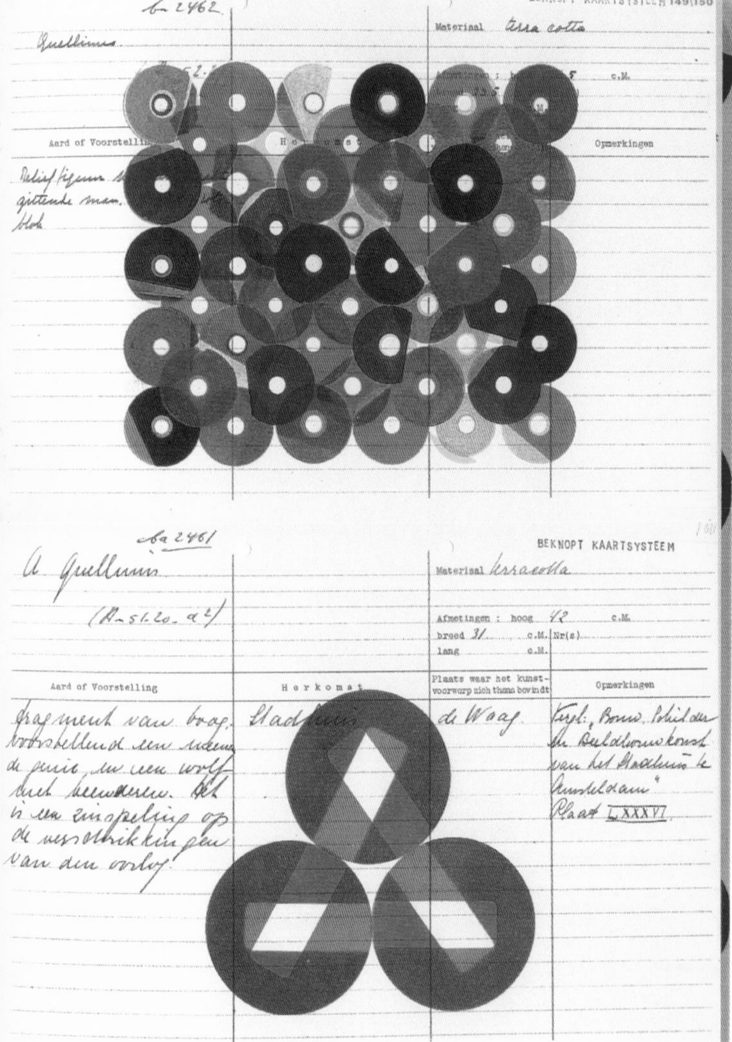

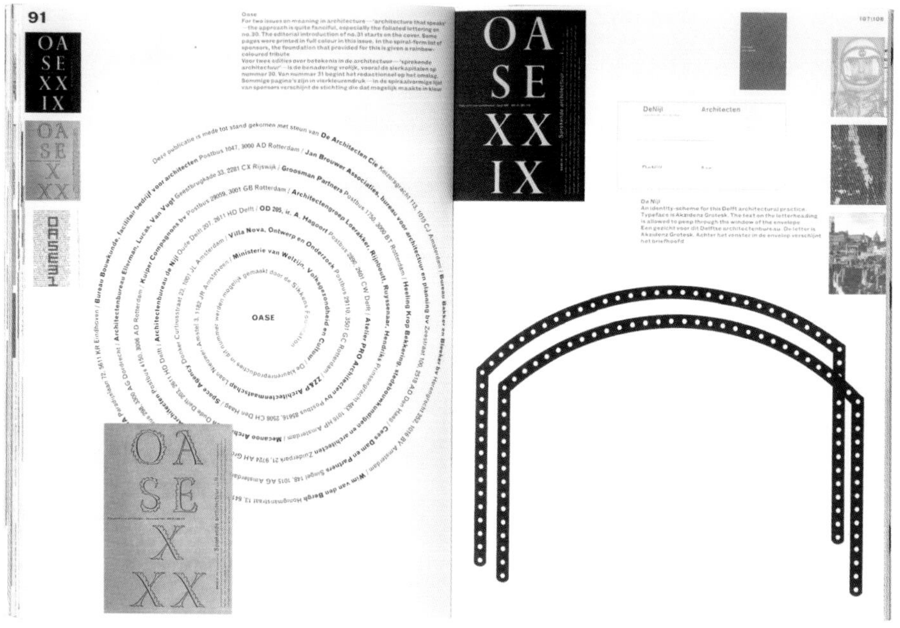

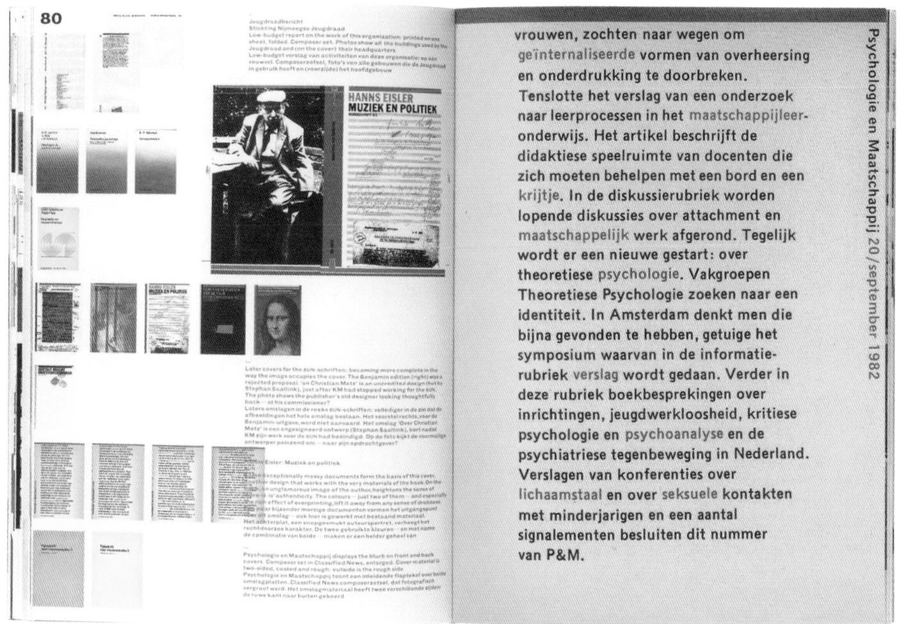

Printed Matter
Robin Kinross, Jaap van Triest, Karel Martens (editors)
Hyphen Press, London, 1996
Second edition (pictured), 2001
144 pages
231 × 170 mm (9.125 × 6.75 in)
Designed by Jaap van Triest, Karel Martens

Karel Martens (1939–) is the kind of designer who reaffirms the nature of the graphic artist. His work constantly reminds viewers that it comes from a printing press or is the result of a reproductive process. *Printed Matter* is no different; designed by Martens and Jaap van Triest (who also designed the Wim Crouwel monograph *Mode en Module* – see page 198), it experiments within its format. Overprinting, French folds, non-existent margins and overlapping images all contribute to a unique book.

Published to mark Martens being awarded the Heineken Prize for Art in 1996, the book is a retrospective of his work. Printed in English and Dutch, the two texts are stacked on top of each other. A second edition, published in 2001, includes an extra section to bring it up to date.

The book begins with an image of two envelopes that Martens printed with Lego bricks while on national service. An illustrated essay by the design historian and publisher of Hyphen Press, Robin Kinross, follows. Martens's work is then displayed year by year from 1960 to 1996.

Printed with a French fold, the work is displayed on two levels: small one-eighth-size reproductions butt up to the edge of the paper fold and often continue on to the next page; feature items, such as book designs, jackets, stamps and coins fill the middle of the spreads. Martens's work with the socialist publisher SUN, particularly on its architectural journal *OASE*, stands out, as do his telephone card designs for PTT Telecom, with their patterns of overprinted numerals at different sizes signifying various values.

Martens's prints from widgets and pieces of Meccano-type construction sets became an integral part of many of his designs from the late 1980s, and provide the cover image for the book.

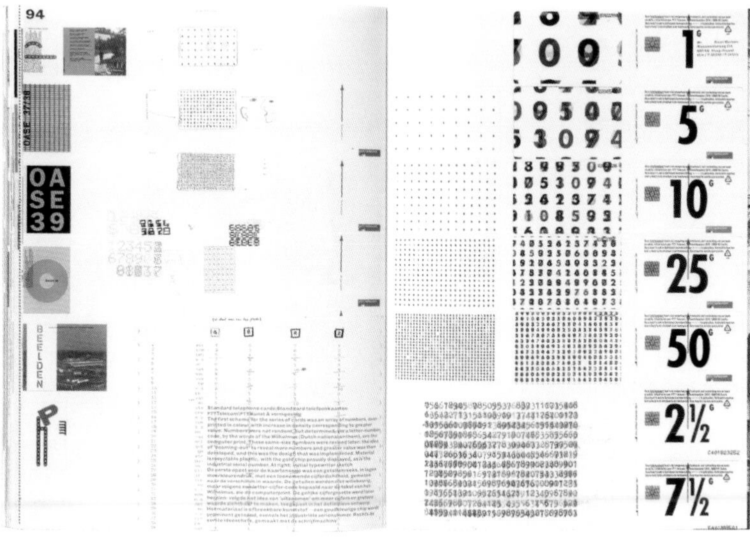

Spreads from the work section of the book with the featured year displayed in the top left-hand corner and captions printed in cyan. These pages show studies and finished designs for PTT Telecom phone cards in 1994.

Wim Crouwel: Mode en Module

Frederike Huygen, Hugues C. Boekraad

Uitgeverij 010, Rotterdam, 1997

432 pages

230 × 175 mm (9 × 6.875 in)

Designed by Karel Martens, Jaap van Triest

This book gives a near complete picture of the famed Dutch graphic designer Wim Crouwel (1928–). Effectively a *catalogue raisonné*, it contains numerous essays and a comprehensive biography, chronology and bibliography. Most importantly (especially for those who cannot read Dutch) there is also a visual library of almost all of Crouwel's work, laid out in strict chronological order.

There are nine chapters. The front of the book is printed in black and white only, and includes seven chapters that study, among other things, Crouwel's exhibition design with Total Design (the influential Dutch design group Crouwel co-founded in 1963) and his defining clients, the Van Abbemuseum, Eindhoven, and the Stedelijk Museum, Amsterdam. Displayed in these chapters are photographs of family and working life, press cuttings, records of exhibition spaces, and sketches and correspondence that Crouwel had managed to archive.

Crouwel's systematic and organized approach to design becomes evident through the work displayed in the eighth chapter, printed in full colour, which catalogues his entire output of work. Each item is captioned with description, title, date, format, size, client and designer's credit. His work for the Van Abbemuseum and the Stedelijk is prominent, as is his development of the New Alphabet typeface in 1967, which married Crouwel's interest in constructed letterforms with the fast approaching digital world. The angular lower-case-only font proclaimed a new – if hard to read – age of typographic innovation.

A final chapter printed in blue only is a biographical timeline listing Crouwel's book and periodical entries, judging assignments, lectures, quotes, teaching commitments and conferences.

The designers of *Wim Crouwel: Mode en Module*, Karel Martens and Jaap van Triest, used the small format to maximum effect, creating a book that is a testament to a highly productive career.

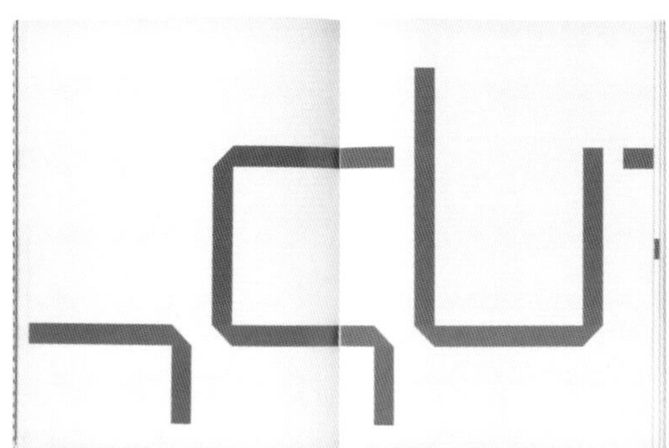

The opening spread for chapter six. Each of the openers uses their corresponding number from Crouwel's notoriously illegible New Alphabet typeface.

A bow-tie-wearing Wim Crouwel can just be made out from the dot matrix on the cover.

Medewerkers TD, jaren '70, van links naar rechts, boven: Wim Verboven, Zdena Srncova, stagiaire, Wiet Wetaling, Wim Miltenberg, Ernst Hellemink, Wim van der Weerd, Tineke Starreveld-van de Wijer, Wim Crouwel, Jolijn van de Wouw, Daphne Duijvelshoff, Ben Bos, Gerda Snels, Jurriaan Schrofer, vooraan: Wim Vermeer, Bram Engelse, Regina Overwater, Romana Gardeslen, Tjeerd Frederikse

wellicht omdat het Crouwel-stempel de TD-vormgeving al te zeer had bepaald. Mogelijk ook liet hij zich teveel leiden door de rationele aanpak van de aankomende nieuwe partners. Hoe dan ook, tegen het einde van de jaren zeventig was dat inhoudelijke aspect binnen TD zwaar verwaarloosd met alle gevolgen vandien. Alle energie was opgebrand aan interne perikelen en bedrijfstechnische kwesties. Ook Blacks tweede punt was Crouwel op het lijf geschreven. Toen hij als aangenomen leider wegviel en daarvoor in de plaats aangewezen directieleden de vlag overnamen, werd TD steeds meer een hiërarchisch bedrijf met employé's die zich moesten houden aan strikte uren en andere formaliteiten. Het individuele eerbetoon heeft Crouwel nooit iemand onthouden. Wèl werd hij, tegen wil en dank of bewust, de personificatie van het bureau. Kennelijk was er na 1972 niemand meer sterk genoeg om naast hem te kunnen staan. En ook jongeren als Anthon Beeke en Van der Toorn Vrijthoff konden hem niet zomaar opvolgen.

Het bureau TD waar Crouwel bij betrokken was, kan op basis van bovenstaande worden ingedeeld in grofweg drie fasen. De eerste tot 1972 waarin er een goed inhoudelijk evenwicht bestond tussen de partners en werk tot stand kwam dat baanbrekend, inventief en intelligent was. De algehele welvaart en het gebrek aan concurrentie droegen ertoe bij dat TD zich een reputatie verwierf. De tweede fase duurde tot 1980. Daarin was Crouwel aanvankelijk het gezicht van TD, maar gaandeweg trad hij meer op de achtergrond. Na de crisis van 1972 maakte hij een bewuste keuze voor het voortbestaan en dus voor het compromis tussen inhoud en economie. De gevolgen waren dat het bureau heen en weer zwenkte omdat een duidelijke lijn ontbrak. Het werk dat TD verliet, ging sporen van routine vertonen en de organisatie was niet

Jelle van der Toorn-Vrijthoff

Rechts en volgende pagina's: wervingsaffiche Total Design met werk van 1977 tot 1982

Vergadering op Total Design, van links naar rechts Paul Mijksenaar, Loek van der Sande, Ben Bos en Esther Verdonk

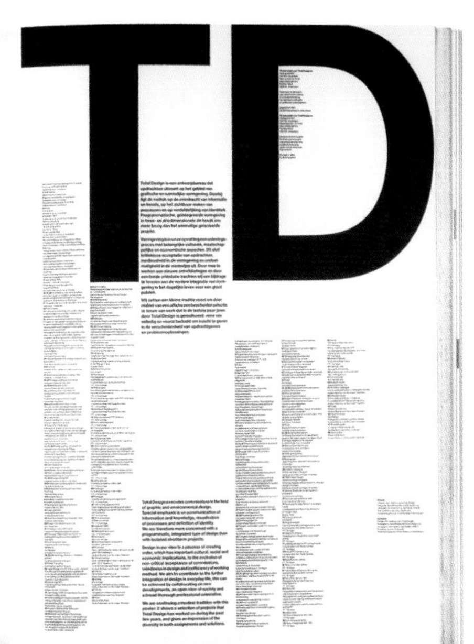

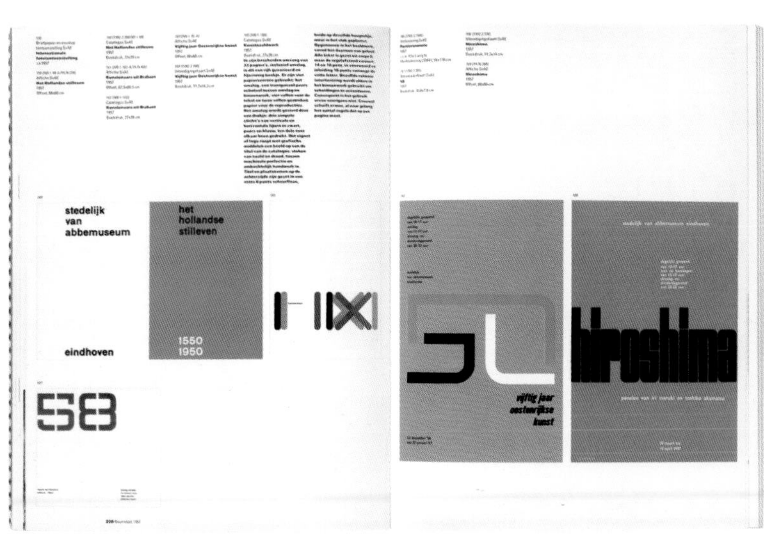

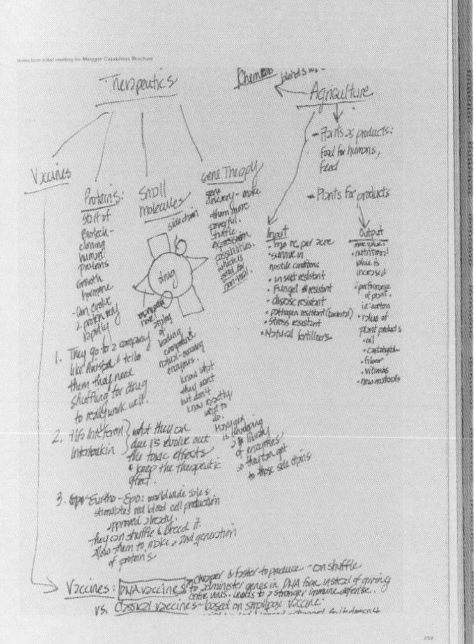

Exposing the creative process – a photograph of a brick wall is used to signify dead ends, while a page of meeting notes signals the genesis of future ideas.

Spreads with examples of work include brief descriptions and often outspoken comments from both clients and employees of Cahan & Associates.

9641-A

Geron 1996 Annual Report Companion

This pocket-sized book is an extension of a theme in the larger book that asked the question: "What Does Getting Old Mean to You?" People's responses are handwritten next to their photos. This brochure was used by itself and as a supplement to the annual report. It has a quick, accessible message that functions as a reminder of what Geron's science is all about.

William Mercer McLeod (Photographer): "Most of the people were family or friends or neighbors. Just people. The guy who repairs my cameras. The guy at the corner store. I would shoot someone, go in, and then talk to them. The thing about Cahan is it's the kind of place where you're part of the process. I don't just shoot pictures. I can help. I can lobby for stuff that I like."

Bob Dinetz (Designer): "I think the only part of Bill's life that he didn't shoot for this book was his cat."

192

9060

Cahan & Associates Lecture Poster

This poster physically demonstrates the power of shifting one's perspective in order to find simple solutions to complex problems. Seen straight on, the poster is indecipherable. Seen from two different angles, the poster delivers two different phrases that add up to one message.

Sharrie Brooks (Designer): "It's hard to design for your own company. You get bogged down in all the different things you want to say. Then all of a sudden you find the bigger picture again. That's what happens with this poster. It's just random letters at first, then all of a sudden it's an exact expression of what we do."

Bill Cahan: "This poster was a good metaphor for what it feels like working with some of our clients. You hit a wall of incomprehensible material, and slowly find a path that tells a story about the company that makes sense to the reader. Sometimes we get background materials that weigh hundreds of pounds—you never know where to start."

193

I Am Almost Always Hungry
Cahan & Associates
Princeton Architectural Press, New York, 1999
262 pages
280 × 215 mm (11 × 8.5 in)
Designed by Bill Cahan, Bob Dinetz

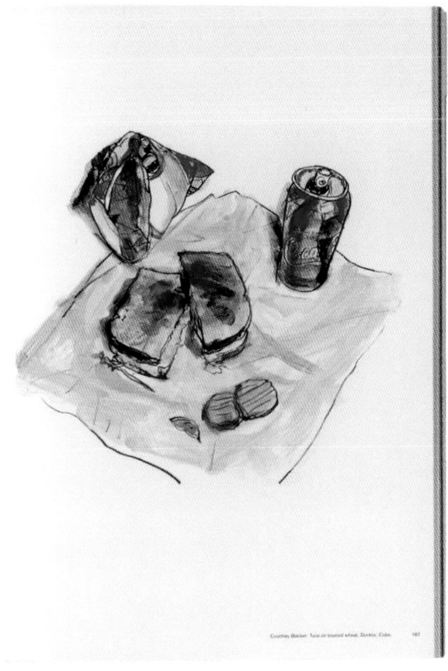

"THIS APPROACH USES A CLEAN TYPEFACE IN A BRIGHT COLOR. SIMPLE BLACK-AND-WHITE PICTURES PROVIDE A DRAMATIC LOOK IN A SQUARE FORMAT AND SUGGEST A PHOTO-JOURNALISTIC STYLE. MAGAZINE-QUALITY PAPER IS USED FOR THE EDITORIAL SECTION."

"THIS APPROACH FEATURES PATIENTS WHO ARE SUFFERING FROM LIFE-THREATENING DISEASES. BY REVEALING THE HUMAN SIDE OF THE STORY, SUGEN IS ELEVATED FROM A COMPANY DOING RESEARCH IN A LAB TO ONE SOLVING THE WORLD'S DEADLIEST DISEASES."

I Am Almost Always Hungry is a book by and about Cahan & Associates, San Francisco-based designers who specialize in the design of corporate communications, often for pharmaceutical and technology companies. By applying to themselves the kind of research criteria they apply to their clients' projects, they explore their own business and expose in a highly visual manner the processes involved in their brand of design.

Getting to the root of what a company stands for and what its objectives are is key to their approach. Words are essential in achieving this goal; they are explored throughout the book, juxtaposed and often with double meanings; they are used to find the language that best represents the culture and aims of a company.

I Am Almost Always Hungry, published by Booth-Clibborn Editions in London and Princeton Architectural Press in New York, is a visual representation of the journey taken to produce a corporate brochure. It begins with spreads of photographs of the faceless world of cubicled offices and empty corridors that is often the first place of contact with new clients, and ends with a portfolio of finished work. In between are pages that epitomize this creative process and others that are more esoteric: examples of impenetrable corporate literature, sketchy notes, photographs of objects picked up on the journey to work and illustrations of office lunches.

The section of finished work is accompanied by frank comments from both clients and designers. There are successful jobs, such as the 1996 Adaptec annual report in the format of a children's book and the 1998 Klein Bicycle brochure – as well as the 1999 version, which was pulled at the last moment. When deciphered, a poster for a lecture by Cahan & Associates reads 'complex problems, simple solutions'.

Printed with a French fold and with numerous changes in paper stock for the different sections, *I Am Almost Always Hungry* is a feat of production. Designed by Bill Cahan and Bob Dinetz, it is clearly laid out and tells its story effectively, often with abstract imagery.

Tibor Kalman: Perverse Optimist
Peter Hall, Michael Bierut (editors)
Booth-Clibborn Editions, London, 1998
420 pages
240 × 202 mm (9.5 × 8 in)
Designed by Michael Bierut, Michael English

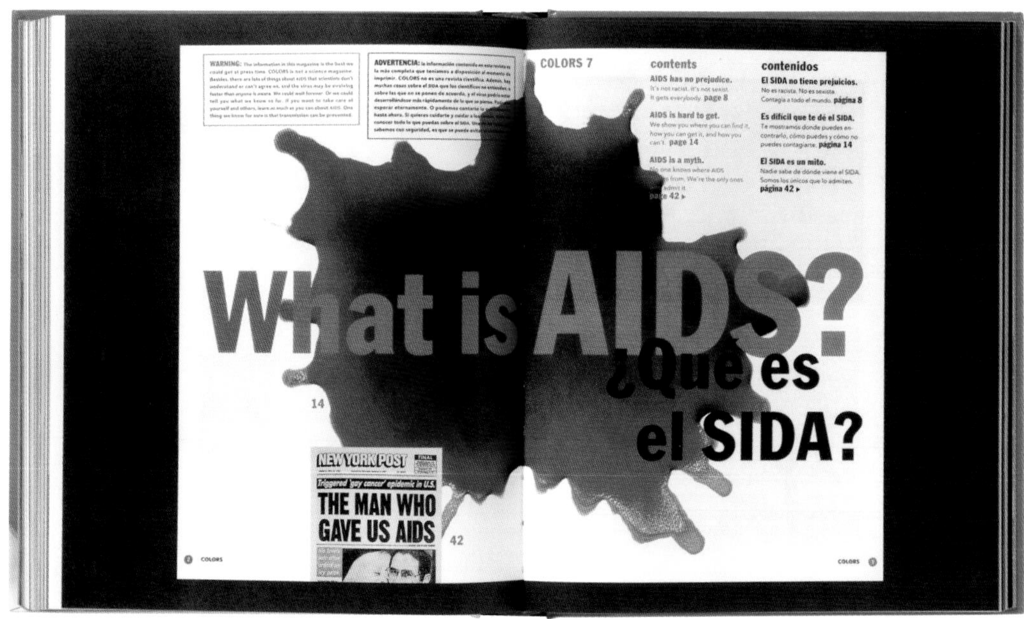

Untrained as a designer, Tibor Kalman (1949–1999) ventured into the graphic design industry via dressing windows for the fledgling bookshop Barnes & Noble. His career (and this monograph) are a lesson in how to learn on the job, constantly challenging oneself creatively and setting meaningful ideals of social awareness through design. As the smiling portrait on the cover shows, it is also a lesson in how to enjoy yourself in the process – a balance Tibor Kalman and his company, M&Co, carried off in spades.

Edited by the critic Peter Hall (who also contributes an essay) and the designer Michael Bierut (who designed the book with Michael English), *Tibor Kalman: Perverse Optimist* was published by Princeton Architectural Press in the USA and Booth-Clibborn in the UK. It includes essays by Steven Heller, Kurt Anderson and Rick Poynor. Around these are fitted examples of Kalman's work and numerous articles by clients and associates, as well as quotes from the array of talented designers Kalman amassed at M&Co.

A 26-page proclamation designed and written by Kalman begins the book; it is a call to arms for graphic designers to engage themselves in the ethical dilemmas of the time. The message is coupled with layouts of found photographs and simple, bold type, the design concept that had been so successful in his work as editor of *Colors* magazine for the Benetton clothing empire, which is extensively covered in the book.

Further pages chart the story of M&Co, from its shaky but profitable start in 1979 to its ground-breaking, witty, low-tech work for the Florent restaurant in New York City – which led to a succession of jobs for high-profile clients such as the band Talking Heads, *Interview* magazine and the Times Square regeneration project.

Also noteworthy are the pages on M&Co's pioneering self-promotion through designed gifts. Its playful watches, clocks, rulers and paperweights helped to forge a new creative avenue, and its regular Christmas gifts to clients and friends became a design event.

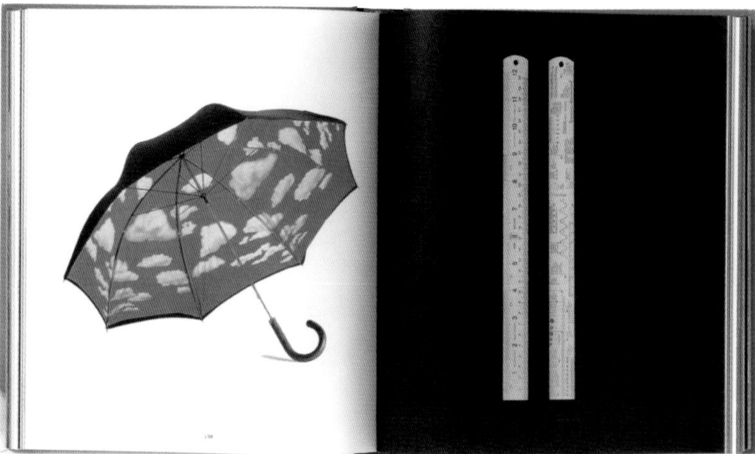

The cover shows a portrait of Tibor Kalman painted by the Vanguard Studios in Bombay (c.1992).

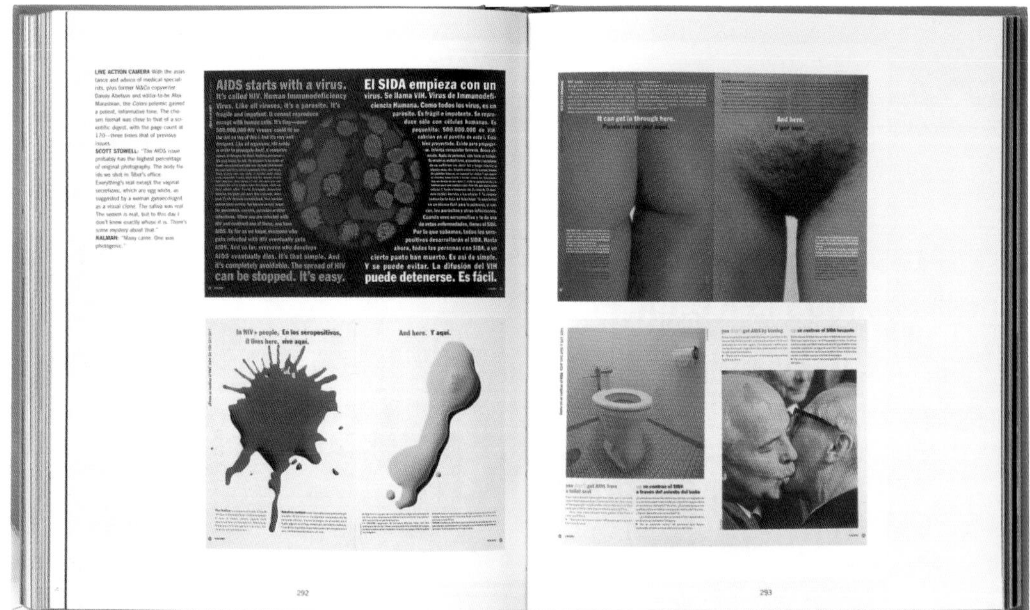

A Critic Writes: Essays by Reyner Banham, Reyner Banham, University of California Press, Berkeley, 1999
Looking Closer 3, Michael Bierut, Steven Heller, Jessica Helfand, Rick Poynor (editors), Allworth Press, New York, 1999
The Elements of Typographical Style, Robert Bringhurst, Hartley & Marks, Vancouver, 1992
8vo: On the Outside, Mark Holt, Hamish Muir, Lars Müller Publishers, Baden, 2005
Tibor Kalman: Perverse Optimist, Peter Hall, Michael Bierut (editors), Princeton Architectural Press, New York, 2000
Unjustified Texts: Perspectives on Typography, Robin Kinross, Hyphen Press, London, 2008
Josef Müller-Brockmann: Pioneer of Swiss Graphic Design, Lars Müller, fourth edition, Lars Müller Publishers, Baden, 2001
Jan Van Toorn: Critical Practice, Rick Poynor, Uitgeverij 010, Rotterdam, 2006
Things I Have Learned in My Life So Far, Stefan Sagmeister, Harry N. Abrams, New York, 2008
Art Without Boundaries: 1950–1970, Gerald Woods, Philip Thompson, John Williams, Thames & Hudson, London, 1972

The book's extensive page count allows space for bold graphic spreads. Kalman was not afraid to court controversy – his image of a black Queen Elizabeth II for Colors *magazine in 1993 caught international media attention.*

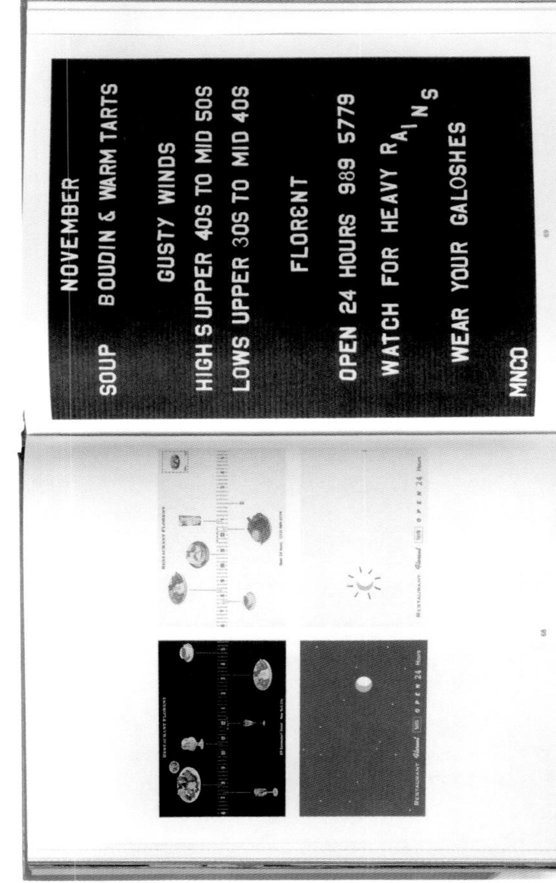

Ample room is provided in the book's 520 pages to exhibit the many personal projects that helped shape Weingart's career. Below are two spreads from the sections 'The letter M' (top) and 'Typography as Endless Repetition' (bottom).

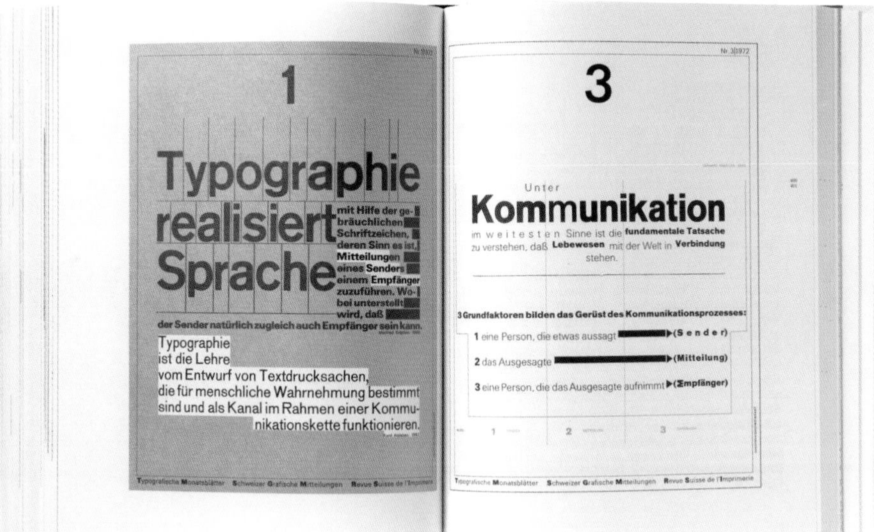

Printed mostly in black, the book includes small sections of colour. The 14 noteworthy covers for the journal Typographische Monatsblätter, *produced in 1972 and 1973, which were, as Weingart notes, 'received by readers with outrage, bewilderment or highest praise', are printed with a special silver.*

Weingart: Typography
Wolfgang Weingart
Lars Müller Publishers,
Baden, 2000
520 pages
274 × 222 mm (10.75 × 8.75 in)
Designed by Wolfgang Weingart

Childhood memories and recollections of travelling in the Near East dominate much of the work of Wolfgang Weingart (1941–). His design is often highly personal, and *Weingart: Typography* is in large part a visual biography of his professional life. Facets of his work are inspired by memories and events – photographs taken on his journeys become points of departure for ideas.

Weingart trained as a typesetter, but in 1964 an interest in typographic design led him to enrol at the famous Allgemeine Gewerbeschule in Basel, Switzerland, where he was taught by Armin Hofmann and Emil Ruder. As a student Weingart exhibited a rebelliousness that would continue throughout his career, shunning the preferred Univers typeface in favour of the 'ruggedness' of Akzidenz Grotesk. However, a talent had been recognized and Weingart was asked to teach at the school from 1968.

Coinciding with his early years as a teacher was a new-found interest in the materials and process of photolithography and type on film. By layering and cutting items, employing mixed-dot screens and the inventive use of a repro camera, Weingart created collages made up of graphic elements gleaned from his own experiences, and developed an entirely original and personal design form. The collages heralded a new direction for Swiss design and had a profound influence on typography worldwide.

With text in both German and English, the book is divided into ten sections. The first three study Weingart's life and artistic development. The next six are devoted to his many independent projects; among these are his early 'Round Compositions', his studies of the letter 'M' and his experiments with repeated elements. A last section details Weingart's professional design work, reproducing magazine, catalogue and book designs alongside a selection of posters.

Maeda @ Media
John Maeda
Thames & Hudson, London, 2000
464 pages
223 × 202 mm (8.75 × 8 in)
Designed by John Maeda

John Maeda (1966–) reached two decisions while he was working on *Maeda @ Media*. The first was that trying to write a computer program to aid in the book's layout would be a futile effort (a relief to book designers everywhere); the second was that this would be the last time he would present his ideas on the graphic arts and digital media, allowing him to move into new areas of exploration.

Obsessed with programming from a young age, Maeda studied computer science at the Massachusetts Institute of Technology until a chance reading of Paul Rand's seminal *Thoughts on Design* (see page 148) changed his career. He left M.I.T. to study art and design in Japan.

Maeda is never without a pen. In *Maeda @ Media* his copious handwritten notes and thumbnails are shown side by side with the results of his endeavours. His unique perspective on computing transcends the realm of standard software packages and their formulated solutions – experiments and exercises in digital environments and image-making and interaction are spread throughout the book.

The book, published by Rizzoli in New York and Thames & Hudson in London, charts how Maeda evolved as a designer and the key points in this evolution, from the landmark advent of online technologies that 'overnight made digital culture creative' to his realization that ditching the Swiss-inspired grid did not mean that he would automatically be struck by lightning.

Books on the digital media rarely succeed in translating luminosity, interactivity and multidimensionality. *Maeda @ Media* proves it is possible to do this. A mixture of paper stocks contributes to its success, along with varied presentation and concise bite-sized blocks of text that give a nod to Maeda's idol, Paul Rand.

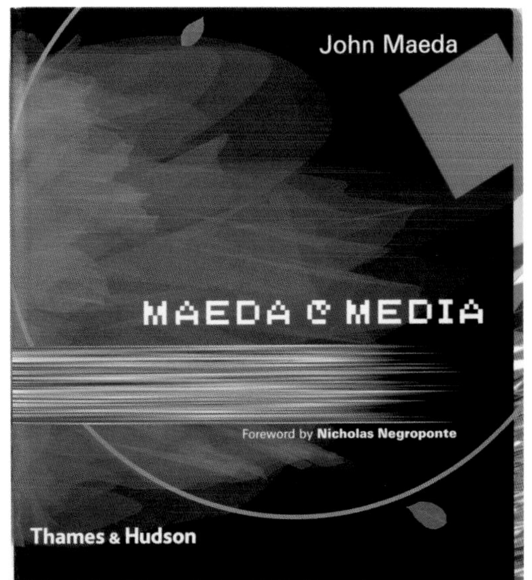

As a devotee of Paul Rand's brand of art and design, Maeda shows occasional references to the layout of Rand's A Designer's Art *(see page 174), for instance in his use of full-bleed images to counterpoint silhouetted objects on the opposite page and in the similar typographic stylings.*

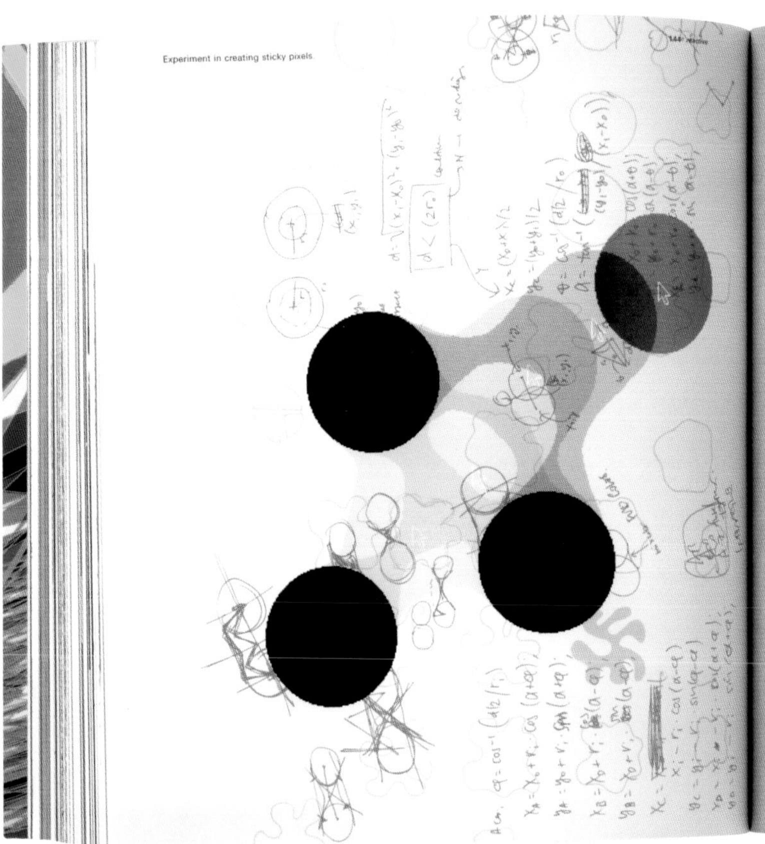

145

5 ***paper*** I would like to say that I never leave the house in the morning without a pen, but sometimes I do make this disastrous mistake. Once I realize my error, the feeling I get is not unlike what a drug addiction must be like. "Must have pen!" is all that runs through my mind as I check my pockets over and over, hoping it might appear by sheer will. The second I satisfy my fix with pen in hand, another fundamental need wells up with equal force, "Must have paper!" However, I find that the paper addiction is much easier to satisfy than the pen addiction because in the worst case I can write on a scrap piece of paper from my wallet or the interior of my car, on a napkin or placemat, or, as a last resort, my hands (although recently I have discovered that, depending upon the season, the abdomen can be a flatter surface). To most of us, paper is more a state of mind than an object—it is a place outside our minds to think and reflect. It is unfortunate that the display technology of the computer we use has been designed around the flat, rectangular metaphor of machine-cut paper, instead of the unflat, unrectangular, and infinitely multidimensional space of pure computation.

In designing Maeda @ Media, *the author uses the 'interactive' potential of the book format, including changes in paper stock and the use of the edge of the page to reveal text.*

198
Relationship in shape and color as five nodes.
Tomoe 3

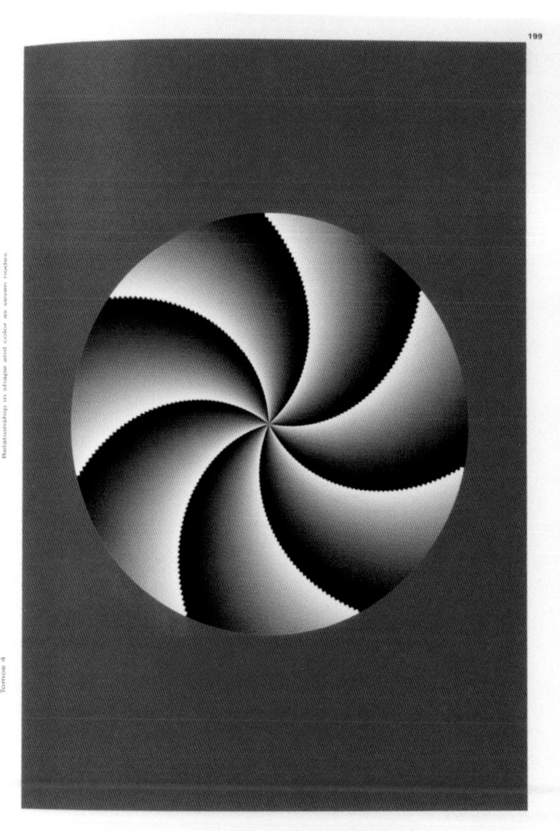

Ex Libris
George Hardie

Simple Heraldry, Iain Moncreiffe, Don Pottinger, Thomas Nelson & Sons, London, 1953
Printing Types, London County Council, 1965
Letter and Image, Robert Massin, Studio Vista, London, 1970
Edward Bawden, Douglas Percy Bliss, Pendomer Press, Godalming, 1979
Pioneers of Modern Typography, Herbert Spencer, revised edition, Lund Humphries, London, 1990
Understanding Comics: The Invisible Art, Scott McCloud, Harper Perennial, New York, 1994
A Smile in the Mind, Beryl McAlhone, David Stuart, Phaidon Press, London, 1996
Thinking Aloud, Richard Wentworth, Hayward Gallery, London, 1998
The Art of Looking Sideways, Alan Fletcher, Phaidon Press, London, 2001
A.B.C / A.R.K, Jan Middendorp, René Knip, Atelier René Knip, Amsterdam, 2004

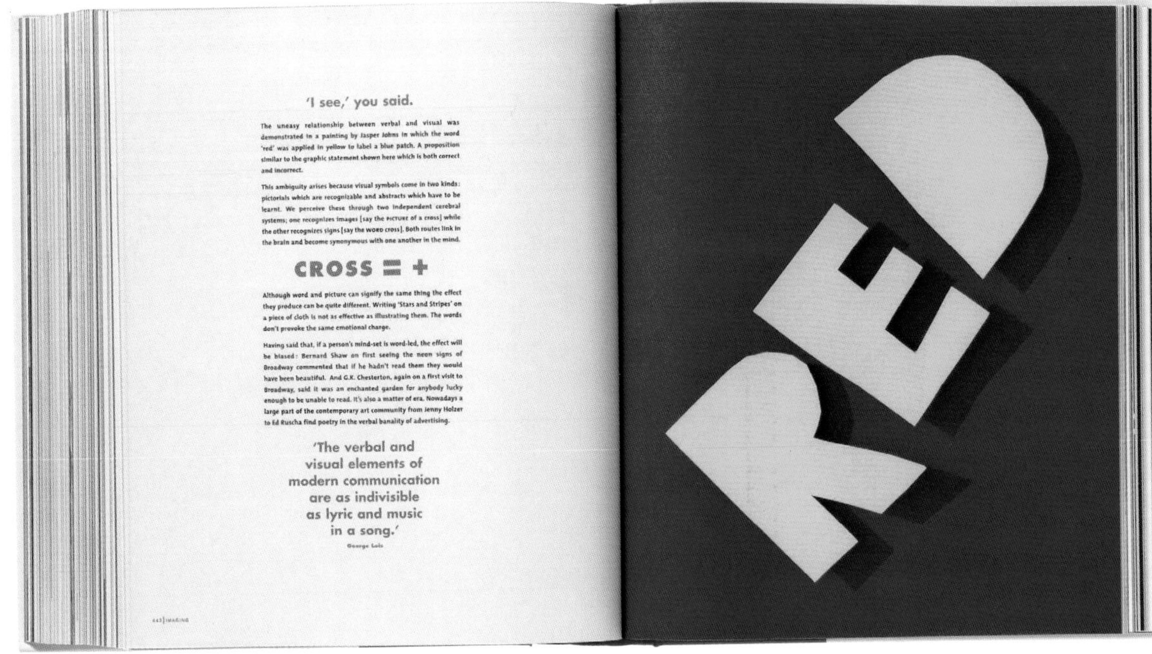

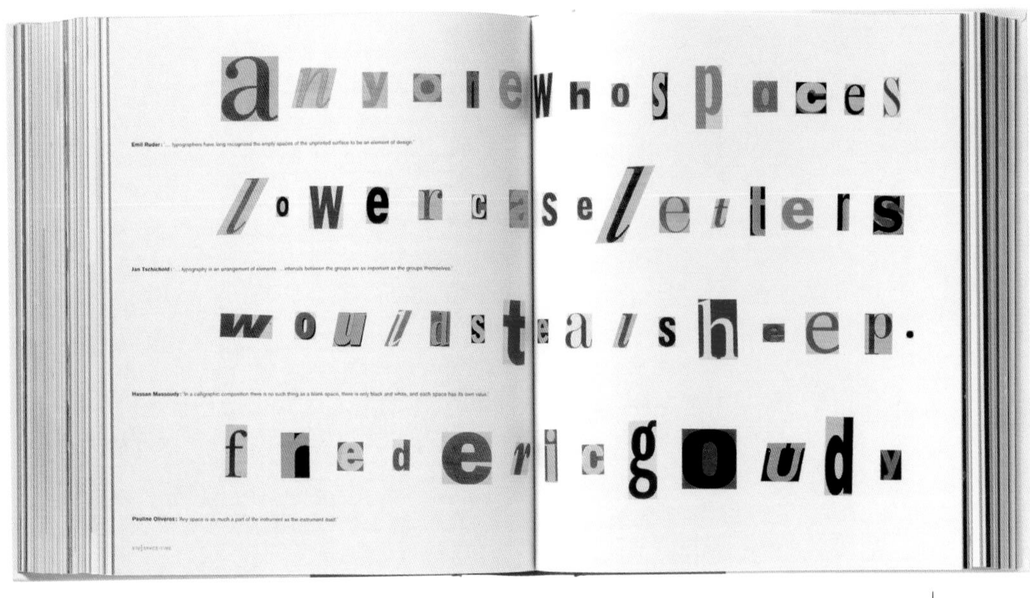

The typography of each spread in The Art of Looking Sideways *is treated differently, apart from the chapter openers (see left), which remain constant. Above the famous quote by Frederic Goudy is made from collaged letters.*

The Art of Looking Sideways

Alan Fletcher
Phaidon Press, London, 2001
1064 pages
245 × 210 mm (9.625 × 8.25 in)
Designed by Alan Fletcher

Held together only by its sturdy binding, *The Art of Looking Sideways* is a collection of 'stuff' acquired by Alan Fletcher (1931–2006) throughout his career. The 72 chapter headings help readers to catch their breath as they move through the assembled thoughts and quotes concerning all matters visual. Perhaps Fletcher described it best – as 'a journey without a destination'. At more than 1000 pages, this is quite a voyage.

In 1992 Fletcher had left the design firm Pentagram. Free from the confines of large corporate clients he embarked on a productive period of artistic exploration. Fletcher's playful nature is in evidence throughout the book. Many of his drawings, sketches and collages, as well as texts in his distinctive handwriting, litter the pages. Artefacts gathered on his extensive travels, clips from newspapers and memorable ephemera are displayed with recollections of what made each one attract his attention. Informal typographic styling and a multitude of different typefaces are masterfully laid out, animating each new thought.

Apart from Fletcher's own work there are many visual examples from fellow graphic designers such as Milton Glaser, Paul Rand, Willem Sandberg, Shigeo Fukuda and Tibor Kalman. Artists he admires, particularly the Surrealists René Magritte, Man Ray and Salvador Dalí, are regularly quoted. There are frequent anthropological references, and also many of the brain-teasers and visual illusions of which Fletcher was particularly fond.

The Art of Looking Sideways is very colourful, and printed mainly on thin uncoated stock. A section exploring colour is printed on gloss paper, and small inserts of coloured paper printed in one colour are scattered throughout the book.

An earlier book which shows Fletcher's interest in unusual and sometimes obtuse design references is *Identity Kits: A Pictorial Survey of Visual Signals* (Studio Vista, London, 1971) written with Germano Facetti, then art director of Penguin Books.

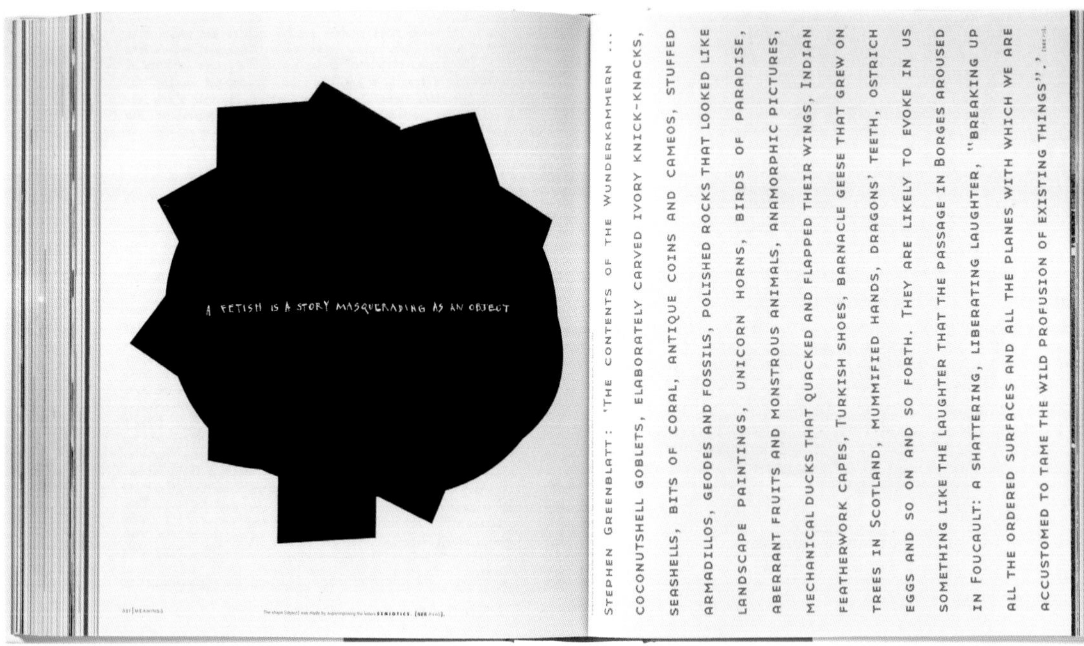

Fletcher frequently includes his distinctive hand-drawn lettering. This spread shows the landscape of the Maltese island Gozo made up from the names of the villages on the island.

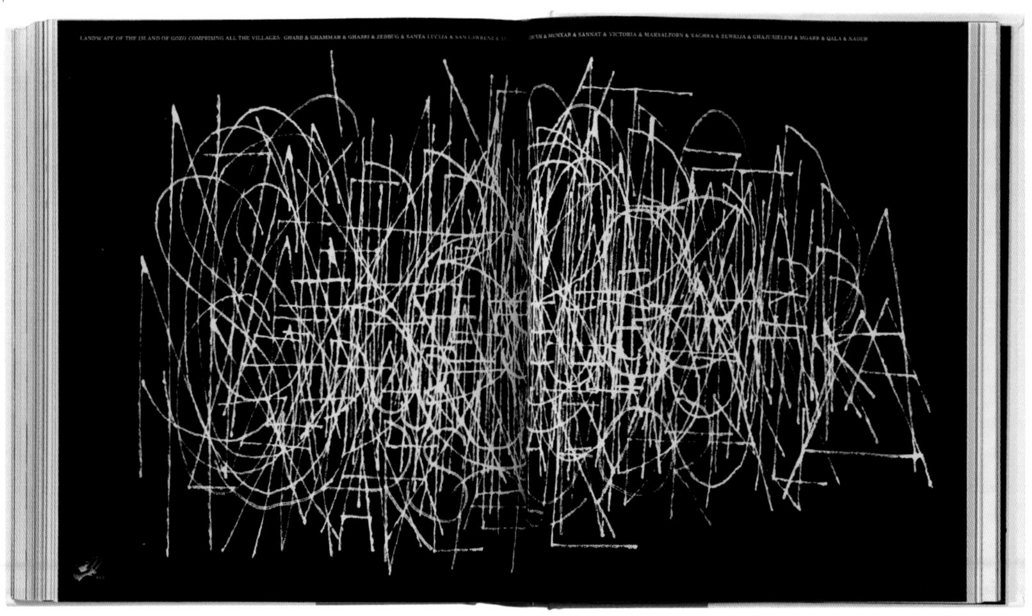

Sagmeister: Made You Look
Peter Hall
Booth-Clibborn Editions, London, 2001
292 pages
248 × 171 mm (9.75 × 6.75 in)
Designed by Sagmeister Inc.

Visible through the transparent red slipcase of this book is a picture of a docile guard dog; when the book is removed the hidden image of an angry attack dog is revealed. This is the kind of visual trick of which Stefan Sagmeister (1962–), the New York-based Austrian designer, is fond.

Sagmeister: Made You Look is a chronological narrative of his career. It is an uncensored and candid study of all his work and the day-to-day frustrations (and successes) in a graphic designer's life. Sagmeister has kept a diary since he was 14, and extracts from this provide an engaging counterpoint to Peter Hall's main text. Although Sagmeister is often highly self-critical, his passion to improve and to push boundaries is an ever-present driving force.

His story starts in Austria, moves to New York, goes back to Vienna, then continues in Hong Kong. It ends in New York where, after a brief spell at M&Co, he set up his own studio. One of his few goals in this new business was to 'design good CD covers'. Examples of work for artists such as David Byrne, Lou Reed, Pat Metheny and the Rolling Stones take up a large portion of the book, and show how Sagmeister's love for interactive three-dimensional graphic solutions is ideally suited to CD packaging. An arsenal of devices, including coloured plastic, various slipcases, die cuts and undersized booklets, displays his inventiveness.

His two most identifiable projects are posters for the American Institute of Graphic Arts (AIGA) – the first for a 1997 conference in New Orleans and the second for a talk Sagmeister gave in Detroit in 1999. These are given top marks in the studio's ruthless scoring system in the book's appendix. Both were hand-drawn, the latter with a razor blade on Sagmeister's torso, the former over an image of a headless chicken. Their power to shock created debate and, perhaps more importantly, resulted in high attendances.

Encased in a transparent red slipcase, the guard dog on the cover dramatically changes when pulled out (see bottom right), revealing the hidden red print.

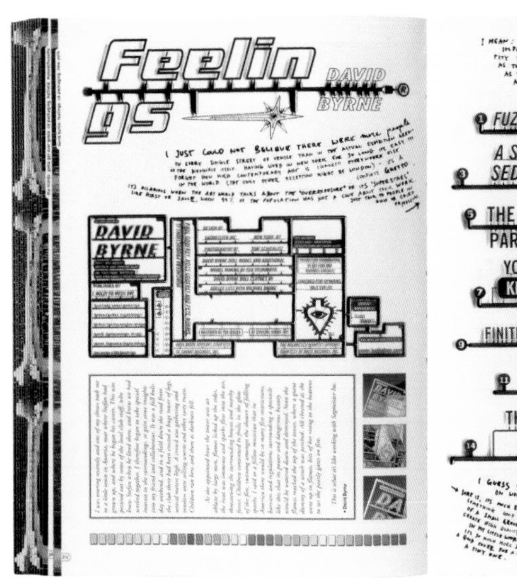

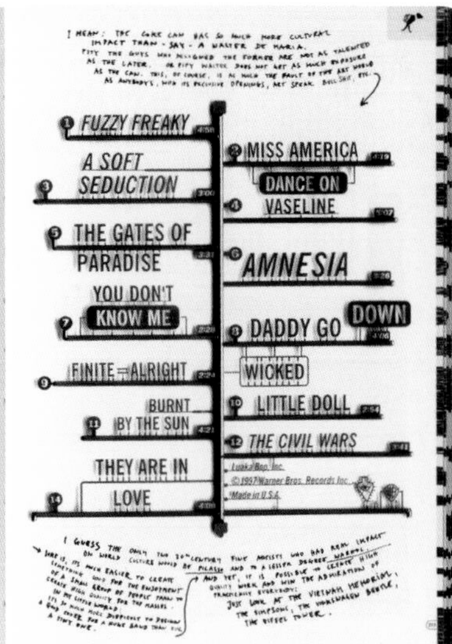

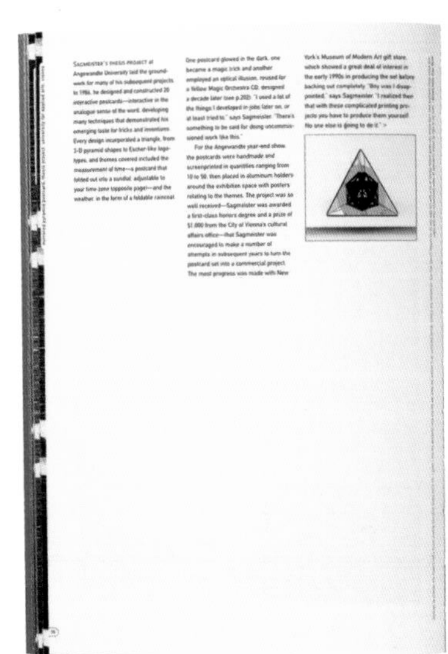

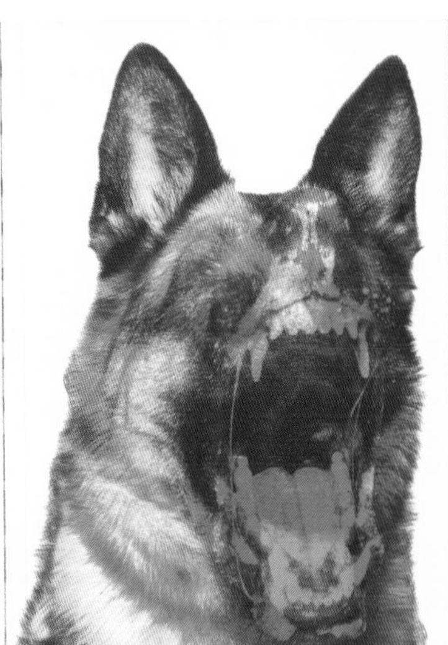

Brodovitch, Andy Grundberg, Harry N. Abrams, New York, 1989
A Smile in the Mind, Beryl McAlhone, David Stuart, Phaidon Press, London, 1996
Graphis Annuals, Graphis Press, Zurich, 1952–
Sagmeister: Made You Look, Peter Hall, Booth-Clibborn Editions, London, 2001
Points of View, Felice Varini, Lars Müller Publishers, Baden, 2004
Tokyo Type Directors Club Annuals
Evidence 1944–1994, Richard Avedon, Random House, New York, 1994
Beware Wet Paint: Designs by Alan Fletcher, Jeremy Myerson, Rick Poynor, David Gibbs, Phaidon Press, London, 1996
Postage Paid: The Story of the First Dutch Postage Stamp, J.J. Havelaar, Walburg Pers, Zutphen, 2002
Eric Gill: The Engravings, Christopher Skelton, The Herbert Press, London, 1990

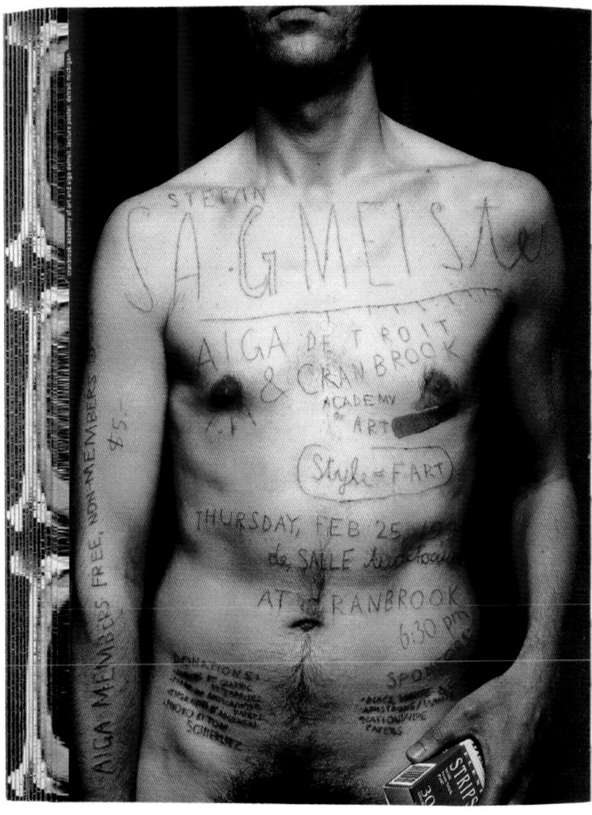

PROBABLY THE MOST NOTORIOUS poster to have emerged from Sagmeister's studio, the advertisement for a talk hosted by the Detroit chapter of the AIGA in 1999, was intended to reflect the ordeals of the design profession. Or, as Sagmeister put it, "the anxious periods, the fighting and the pain." Having experimented with cutting a small amount of text into his skin for the *Whereishere* project (p.176), Sagmeister reasoned that doing it again on a larger scale would be relatively painless.

He was wrong. Sagmeister stood in front of the mirror with a blade at 9:00 am on the day of the photoshoot, and found himself unable to make a single incision. Part of the problem was cutting in reverse, part of the problem was cutting accurately and part of the problem was cutting. He emerged, humbled, from the bathroom, blade in hand, in search of a willing surgeon. Sagmeister's normally loyal accomplice Hjalti Karlsson looked at the amount of copy and bluntly refused. Karlsson gestured to the studio intern, the Swiss designer Martin Woodtli. Being something of a precision-obsessed engineer (with a background in silk-screened fliers with tiny type sizes), Woodtli obliged.

"Eight hours of cutting," recalls Woodtli calmly, "it was very strange." The process began slowly and got slower, Woodtli having to ensure that the incisions were minimal, but deep enough for the letters to be legible. Half way through, the initially irritating scratches began to accumulate into recognizable pain. "I began to have serious doubts," Sagmeister says, "but there was no going back—I had no other ideas." The worst hour was the last, when Woodtli began carving the "stupid" tiny credits around the pelvis.

The poster did its job, and the talk in Detroit was well-attended, though whether Sagmeister lived up to its publicity is in some doubt. "Probably some people were disappointed at what a tame guy I am," he says. The scars, which took a month or so to disappear, had an unexpected resurgence one summer's afternoon when Sagmeister was lying on a beach. As the sun's rays triggered the skin's melanin, Sagmeister noticed the faint, but irrefutable trace of his name, rising in pink to the surface of his chest.

The poster, like the AIGA chicken piece (pp.160-165), signalled a turning point for the design profession, away from aspirations of digital perfection toward a higher appreciation for a designer's personal mark. Twelve years of computer-driven design had initiated a backlash in favor of the tactile and hand-hewn—anything that showed physical evidence of a creator and evoked an equally physical response, even repulsion. That it was related to a parallel movement in architecture was subsequently documented in the 2000 Triennial exhibition at the Cooper Hewitt National Design Museum, where Sagmeister's poster was juxtaposed with architect Steven Holl's sponge-like MIT residence in a section titled "Physical."

FEB 10 1999
THE FIRST THING I SHOULD BE THINKING ABOUT IS DESIGN THAT TOUCHES. THAT COULD ALSO INCLUDE PURELY FORMAL SOLUTIONS. THE WHOLE THING HAS to be BEAUTIFUL. BEAUTIFUL.

Sagmeister's famous poster for an AIGA talk in Detroit, 1999. The opposite page has Hall's text as well as Sagmeister's hand-drawn diary entry.

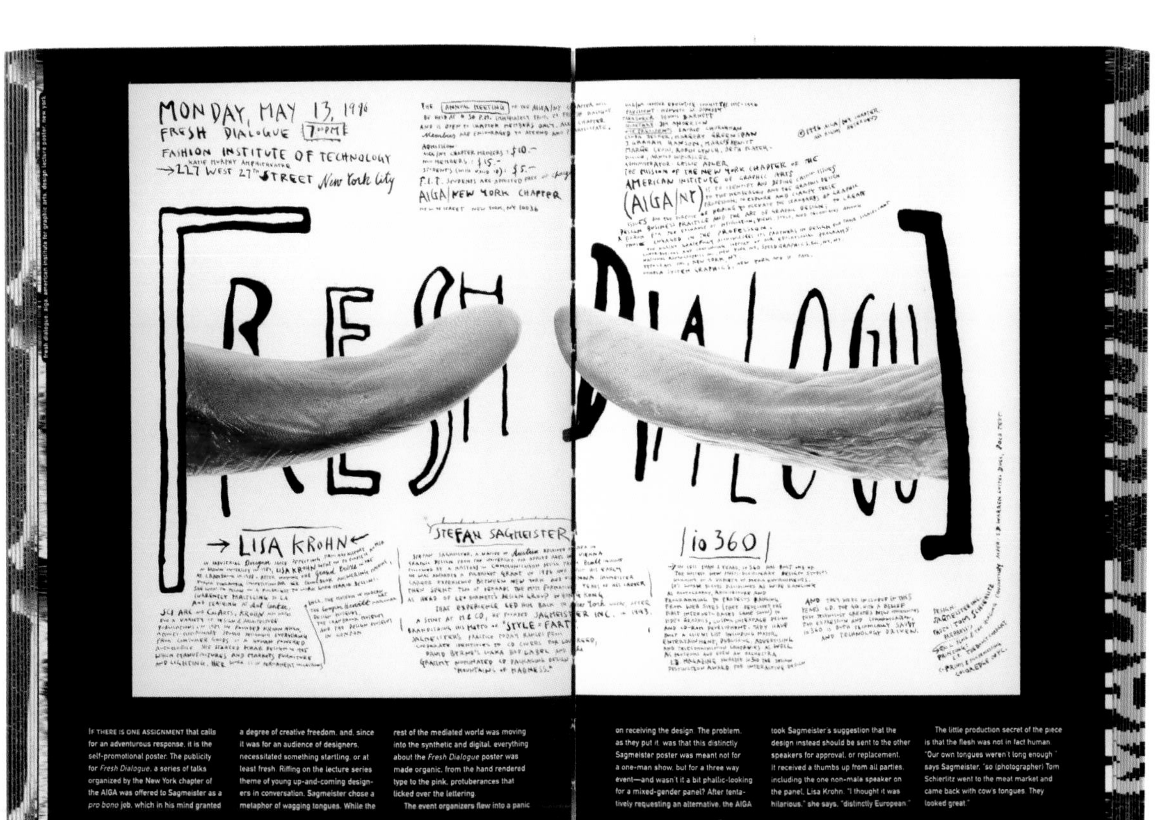

IF THERE IS ONE ASSIGNMENT that calls for an adventurous response, it is the self-promotional poster. The publicity for *Fresh Dialogue*, a series of talks organized by the New York chapter of the AIGA was offered to Sagmeister as a *pro bono* job, which in his mind granted a degree of creative freedom, and, since it was for an audience of designers, necessitated something startling, or at least fresh. Riffing on the lecture series theme of young up-and-coming designers in conversation, Sagmeister chose a metaphor of wagging tongues. While the rest of the mediated world was moving into the synthetic and digital, everything about the *Fresh Dialogue* poster was made organic, from the hand rendered type to the pink, protuberances that licked over the lettering.

The event organizers flew into a panic on receiving the design. The problem, as they put it, was that this distinctly Sagmeister poster was meant not for a one-man show, but for a three way event—and wasn't it a bit phallic-looking for a mixed-gender panel? After tentatively requesting an alternative, the AIGA took Sagmeister's suggestion that the design instead should be sent to the other speakers for approval, or replacement. It received a thumbs up from all parties, including the one non-male speaker on the panel, Lisa Krohn. "I thought it was hilarious," she says, "distinctly European."

The little production secret of the piece is that the flesh was not in fact human. "Our own tongues weren't long enough," says Sagmeister, "so (photographer) Tom Schierlitz went to the meat market and came back with cow's tongues. They looked great."

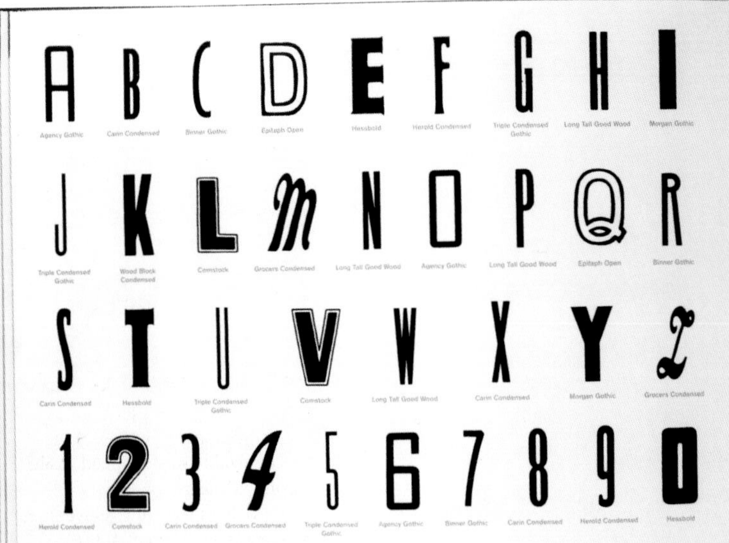

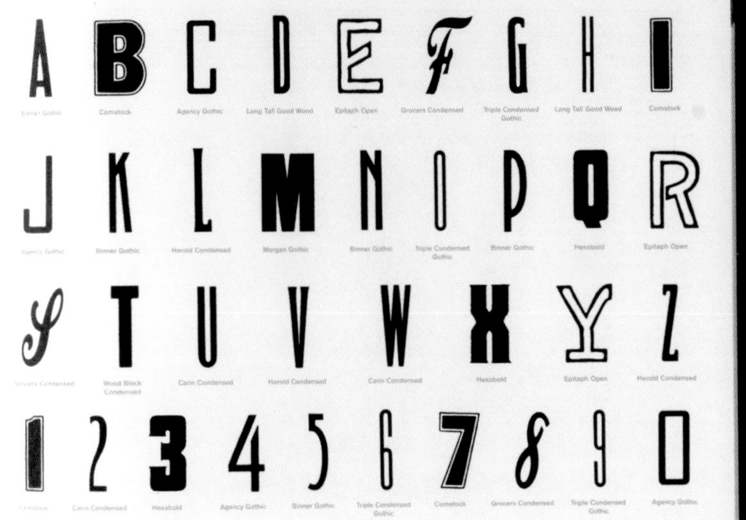

Scher's use of a landscape format for a graphic design monograph is unusual.

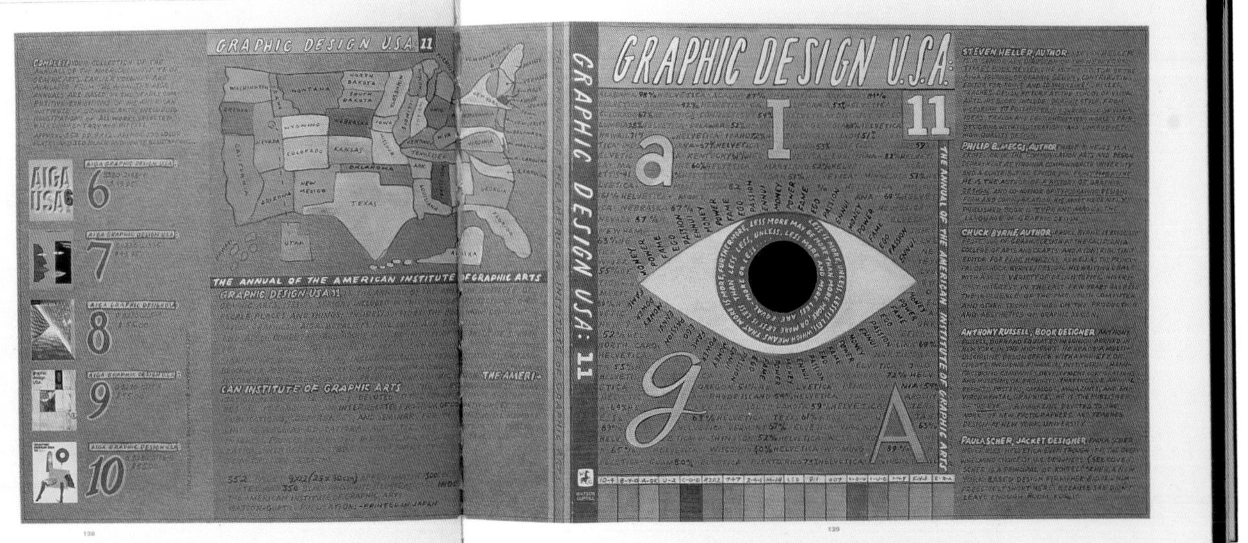

STYLE WARS

AIGA

In 1990 Caroline Hightower, then director of the American Institute of Graphic Arts, asked me to design the cover for the coming annual, *Graphic Design USA II*, which was a compendium of all the exhibits and competitions the AIGA had held in 1989. She told me there was no design fee, but that the AIGA would contribute $1000 for "design expenses." I asked what design expenses were, and Hightower replied that they could be the purchase of photography, retouching, necessary typography. I asked what would happen if I didn't have any expenses, and she told me I'd get to keep the money anyway. I vowed then and there not to incur any expenses.

The 1990 AIGA cover was a spoof on graphic design in America, not dissimilar to the *Print* parody cover. I painted the information instead of typesetting it. It was writing as design. The cover simply took the words *Graphic Design USA* literally and then dished out some completely useless, nonsensical information. The front cover featured an eye whose lashes listed all the emotions and desires that might be attributed to ambitious designers: fame, power, money, ego, and ennui. The eyeball carried an absurd dissertation about whether or not less is more. The background of the painting had a listing of every state in the United States, and the percentage of people in each state who used Helvetica. I made up the statistics, but I decided to base them loosely on the 1986 Reagan-Mondale presidential election. I reasoned that if Reagan carried a state the local designers were probably inclined to use a lot of Helvetica. The back cover had a map of the United Stated that I had painted from memory (I inadvertently left out Utah). I painted all the flap-copy information simply to ensure that I could keep the entire thousand dollars.

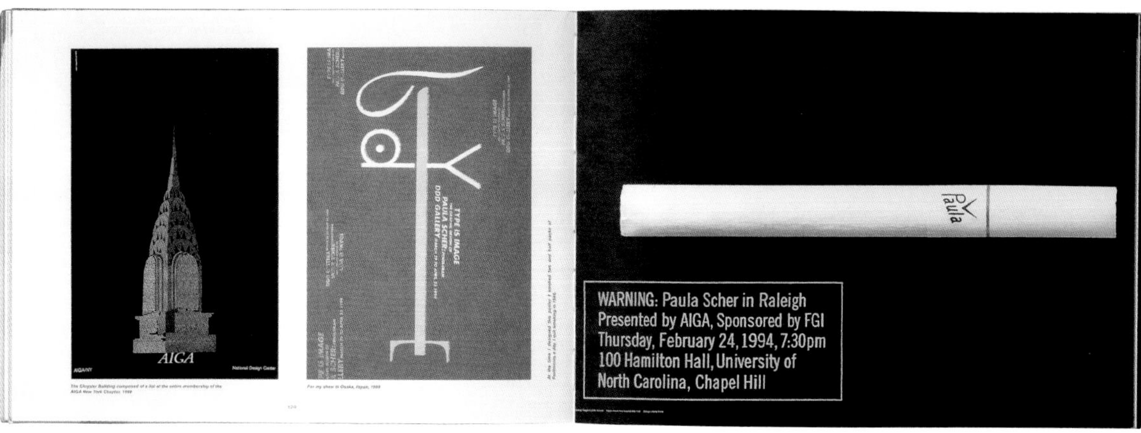

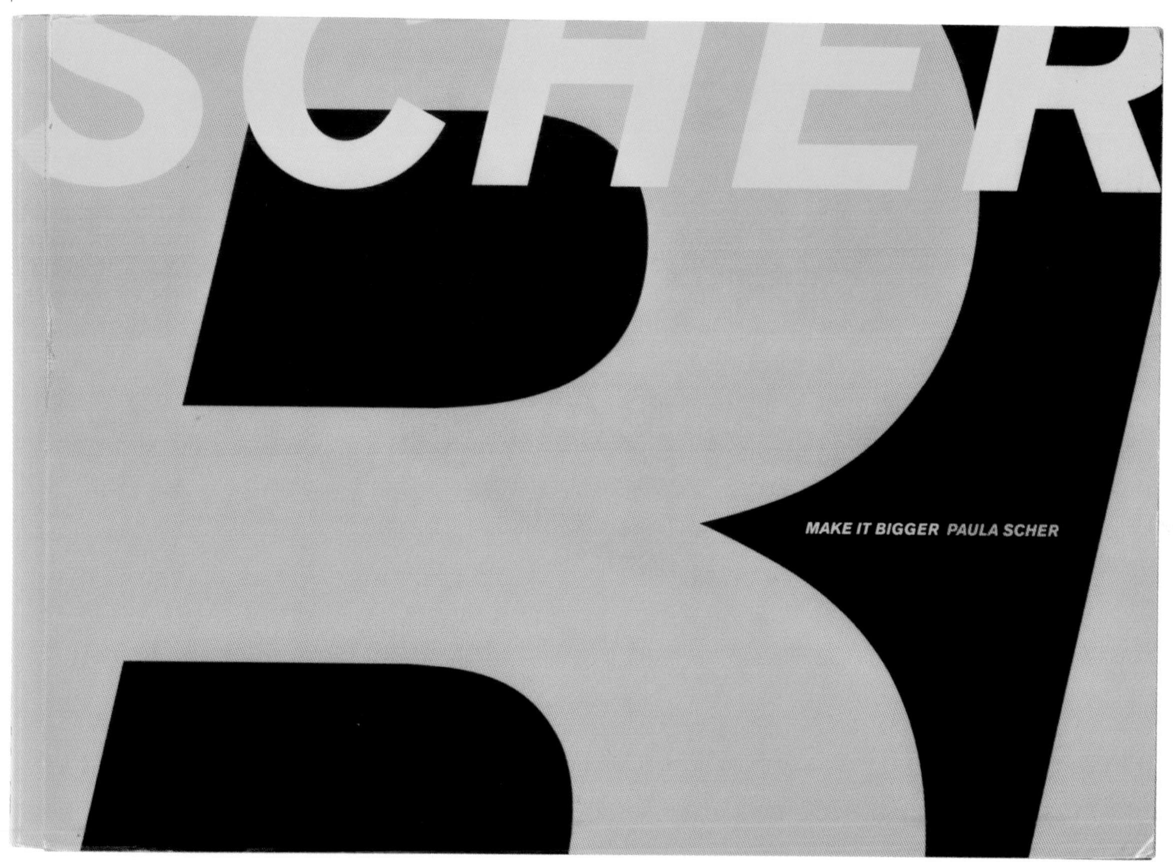

The cover is mounted on thick card and encased in 'bigger type', which bleeds off the cover and continues on the sides and spine of the book.

Make it Bigger

Paula Scher

Princeton Architectural Press, New York, 2002

332 pages

163 × 233 mm (6.5 × 9.125 in)

Designed by Paula Scher

Make it Bigger is a reference to the clarion call of clients wanting to make sure type sizes are maximized on a layout. In Paula Scher's (1948–) case, her client, Swatch, was insisting on this for the headline on her infamous *Swatch* poster of 1985 – a light-hearted homage to the 1936 classic modernist travel poster, *Schweiz*, by Herbert Matter – which became notorious for its perceived plundering of a graphic icon.

Borrowing from past graphic styles is a stock-in-trade for Scher. From the start of her career, when she designed numerous LP sleeves for CBS, to her current membership of Pentagram, *Make it Bigger* catalogues her eclectic tastes and references. The logo for the Public Theater in New York (1994), made up of progressively condensing Gothic letters, drew inspiration from type weights displayed in Rob Roy Kelly's *American Wood Type* (see page 30). The striking 'no-nonsense' layout of its posters, her most recognizable work, looked to old London theatre posters.

Scher's recurring reinvention as a designer is a central theme in *Make it Bigger* – whether the result of economic necessity, creative malaise or luck, she celebrates the need for such changes. A commission to design the cover for the *AIGA 11* annual with an expenses-only budget led to her using solely hand-painted text – the success of this added a new dimension to her work, with ever more intricate and laborious pieces of hand-drawn information and maps.

Diagrams and charts litter the book, among them ones representing the chains of command in the design department at CBS, the evolution of Pentagram and the timeline of a client meeting. These complement the entertaining text, which recounts the many collaborations involved in fostering a career in design.

Designed by Peter Saville
Emily King (editor)
Frieze, London, 2003
192 pages
280 × 228 mm (11 × 9 in)
Designed by Christopher Wilson

It is apt that *Designed by Peter Saville* is based on a series of essays, all with a different view of the man. Peter Saville (1957–) has always been difficult to pin down. He's a bit of an enigma: a perfectionist with unorthodox practices, a designer with artistic sensibilities best described by Peter York as 'deliciously haphazard'. This is perhaps the reason why writers love to write about him.

In this book, published by Frieze in London and Princeton Architectural Press in New York, essays by Emily King, Paul Morley, Rick Poynor, Peter Hall, Miranda Sawyer, Peter York and Christopher Wilson (the book's designer, who also contributes an insightful interview with Saville) are interspersed with examples of Saville's works. These range from the seminal period of Manchester's Factory Records in the late 1970s and 1980s – notably covers for Joy Division, OMD and New Order – to designs for more recent clients, in particular various catalogues for Yohji Yamamoto and artwork for the bands Pulp and Suede in the 1990s. His collaborations with the photographers Nick Knight and Trevor Key are also given prominence.

The book's cover is a modern reappraisal of the 1979 cover of Joy Division's *Unknown Pleasures* LP sleeve, Saville's most famous piece of work. The original is a carefully placed line graph (showing successive pulses from the first pulsar discovered) on a black background; the version for the cover is a modern rendering on a white background. As with the original album cover there is no type on the jacket; the title is printed on a bright red band that wraps around the book.

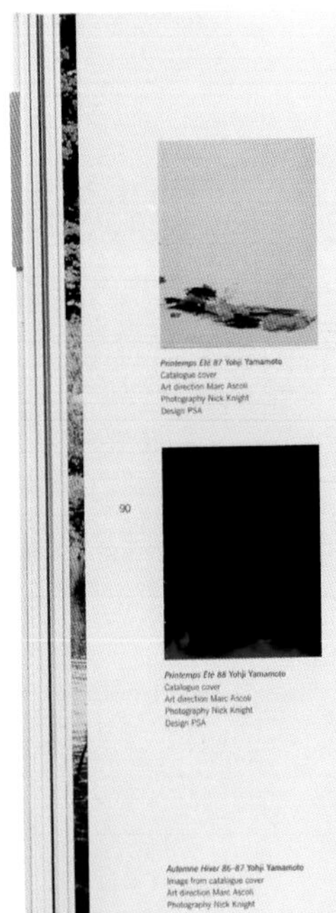

layouts sprinkled with idiosyncratic and historicist motifs. If its motive, to upturn the monumental authority of modernism, was valid, Saville considered its means tiresome. 'I was tired of meaningless reference,' he says. 'I wanted something essential.'

The first Saville/Knight/Ascoli catalogues for Yohji Yamamoto were shot in black and white, with one splash of colour – on the cover of the women's catalogue – in a bright red bustle. The black silhouettes and stripped out white backgrounds made a stark contrast to the tropes at work in mainstream fashion photography: a comparable *Vogue* shoot by Patrick Demarchelier finds his models *en plein air*, their slick, shiny flesh set against the scenery of the Moroccan desert, or gazing across the ocean. But sexually-charged atmospherics were strikingly absent from Knight's shots, which had more in common with David Bailey's vibrant portraits of the swinging sixties. They made no attempt at the pretence of a setting, nor an appeal to some fantasy narrative. Saville's pacing and arrangement of the images further emphasised the strangeness of the shapes made by the dressed bodies. This was bare bones image-making, in which the model became a malleable graphic form.

The challenging caveat of the Yamamoto account was that Knight was required to think anew each season. Yamamoto maintained a distance from the process, offering only minimal maxims like 'surprise me' (according to Saville) and 'show me my dreams' (according to Knight), while Ascoli would 'goad' Knight into challenging his own preconceptions. Knight's response was to strenuously experiment with shooting and processing techniques. The camera, film and processing became, in Knight's hands, less tools than paints. With the summer 1987 catalogue, he and London lab BDI introduced the strangely blown-out 'cross-processed' colour that quickly became *de rigeur* in editorial and subsequently advertising for the duration of the decade. Achieved by running transparency film through a bath of negative developing fluid, it had an effect reminiscent of a television screen with the colour contrast on full; mid-tones disappeared leaving highly saturated, glowing colours.

For Saville, Yamamoto's hands-off creative direction and spare-no-expense approach to craftsmanship provided a unique opportunity to indulge his creative instincts. The women's catalogue from spring/summer 1988 gave a slight nod in the direction of Kubrick's *2001: A Space Odyssey*, with white Yamamoto hats floating like spacecraft across a smooth surface of smooth, deep, black ink. The black cover featured no type, forming an impassive monolith alleviated only by the hint of deep red solar flares, bleeding off the edge and spilling into the exaggerated colours of the models – who floated, like the hats, on blackness. 'The catalogue production was exemplary,' says Saville, who adds that Yamamoto's organisation only questioned his design specifications once, when Saville called for black thread-sewn pages in the outer space catalogue. 'I received a fax from the head of production,' he says. 'It said: "Black thread not possible".' Instead they sought out black staples.

Throughout the five seasons in which Knight, Ascoli and Saville worked together, the catalogues had a consistently reductive, pared-down appearance – conveying Yamamoto's sense of refinement, almost to the point of aloofness. The sensibilities contributing to the task seemed particularly well matched: Knight's photographs, which frequently explored and tested visual extremes, were presented in Saville's quietly lyrical settings. Design became present only in the absence of design.

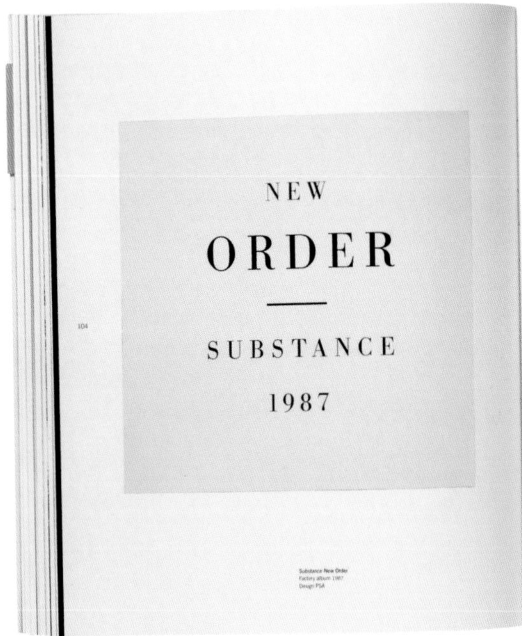

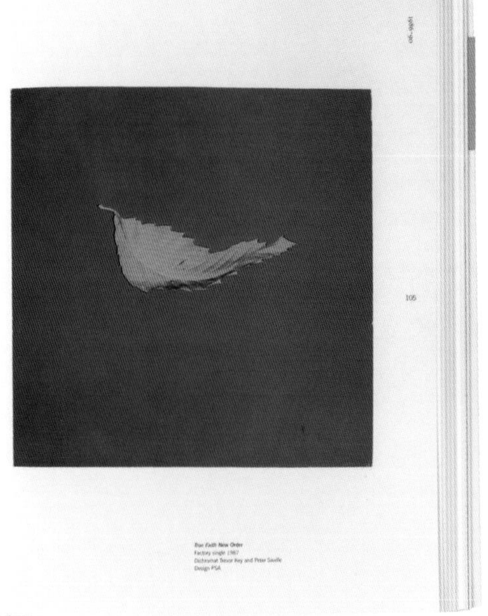

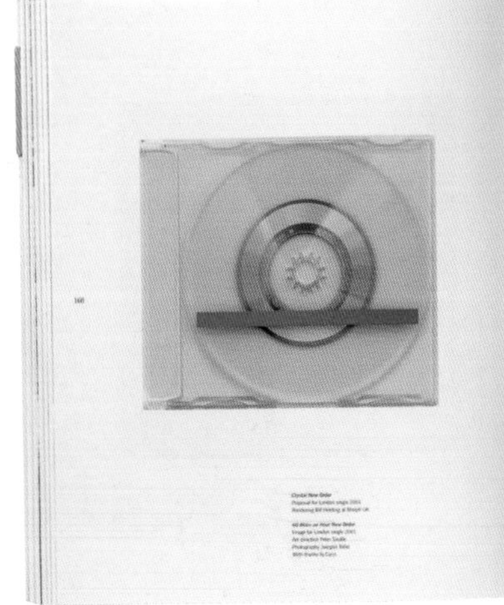

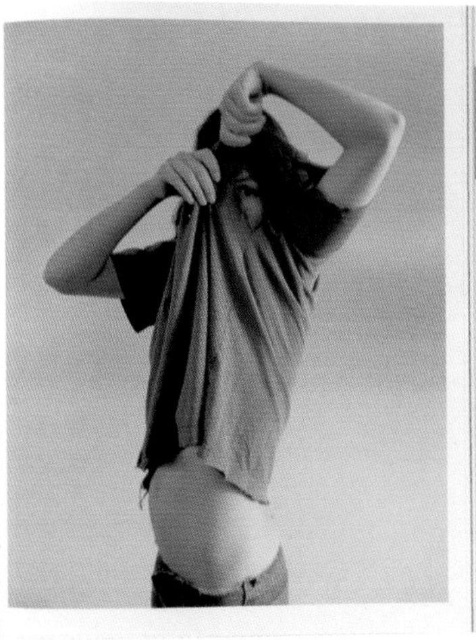

Saville's work for the band New Order is also covered in Factory Records: The Complete Graphic Album *(Thames & Hudson, London, 2006) by Matthew Robertson.*

but as soon as you saw it, it was absolutely the only sleeve possible. It was visual sound, processed memory, static movement, collapsed space, smooth friction, tuned time, detailed nothing, and it helped create the reality whereby the group could be perceived as truly great.

6 Saville never really worked well with groups or products that began with 'the'. He worked best when there was a space where 'the' might have been, in a time before and after 'the', in a way that avoided 'the', for reasons that have something to do with a sentence that begins with 'the.'

7 Only time will tell if Saville will ever actually finish what he started. The Factory list, the collection he inspired, the order he made happen, the art and the numbers, were like his *Citizen Kane*; he did so much so early, and along the way, obviously, there has been his *F for Fake*, and his *Macbeth*, and his *Touch Of Evil*, and there have been voice overs, hack work and ad work, but you tend to wonder if he'll ever get a chance to produce his *Don Quixote*, if he'll ever get to finish his history, or did he finish it when no-one was looking, and after all that appearance, that manipulation of appearance, the thing he has achieved is a disappearance, as part of his history, his imaginative history of design history. He changed everything to such an extent there was no room left for anything else. He changed the look of things so that he could find somewhere to hide.

8 a/ The art of seeing things that are invisible.
b/ The art of seeing that rescues the existence of things.

9 For Saville there is only one I in the Universe, and it is his I, the I of the form, the I in the ego, the I for an I, the I which everything revolves around, the I of Saville, the I in his smile, which is an I for a story, the story of I, the designing of a designed world he wants his I to occupy and patrol.

10 I'm not sure if Wham had Saville or if Saville had Wham, but either way this sentence finishes with a !

11 On reflection, it is a shame that Benetton or Nike or Mercedes-Benz didn't turn out to be the Factory of Saville's later life.

12 My feeling is that Saville found ways to work for other people and create something that was all about him, whilst also being representative of his client, so that he created a series of portraits that capture both the illusion of the subject, their different stages, as well as the illusion of his own personality, his own shifting moods, emotional needs and changing skills. There are also various grades and shades of reality connecting him to the illusion of his work, a lot of them to do with his sense of history, his sense of humour, his nerve, and basically his taste, which controls him.

13 In fact, I don't usually like having art on my walls, and at the moment, I have no art on my walls. They are bare. They are waiting for Godot. But once upon a time, I had some Saville-designed posters on my wall, and as far as I was concerned, they

The book's layout is restrained; this spread from the interview by Christopher Wilson (also the book's designer) shows the extensive use of marginalia.

Untitled Blue Monochrome (IKB 175)
Yves Klein
Dry pigment in synthetic resin on fabric on wood 1957
©Yves Klein, ADAGP Paris

Peter Saville and Richard Thomas in Lyon with *Titaanzink* and *Aluchrome* 1987
See p.99–101

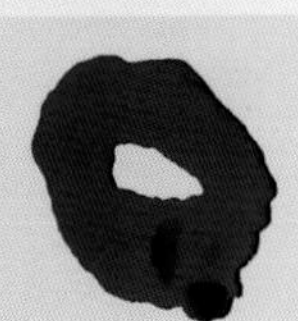

First dichromat test 1987
Trevor Key and Peter Saville

Peony 1987
Dichromat Trevor Key and Peter Saville

at my girlfriend's flat, thinking 'Maybe that's something to look at now ...' Talk about essentialism – I was *obsessed* with Klein in '85/'86 – the blue, the gold, the manifestation of nothing, the show called *The Void* – fantastic.

After engaging with a cultural reference on that level, do you file it away in your own past – 'Klein was my 1985 – end of story' – or does it continue to have resonance for you?
You keep it. Unfortunately things do get devalued by people like me, so we'll find pseudo-Klein postcards and bubblebath in shops in Notting Hill, and it all gets trashed. But the essence of Klein is timeless.

If you were to lay out the designs chronologically, would there be a 'before and after *Low-life*' split?
You can see it distinctly. It's still retrievalist, but what happens in '85 is that I pick up the last modern moment. A fifteen-year retrospective period runs from '70 to '85. In '85 I still look back, because I don't know how to go forward, but I look back to the last modern moment of the twentieth century. So instead of de Chirico it's Klein. Instead of early experimental photography it's Bailey's sixties. Instead of romantic nineteenth-century flower painting it's Andy's flowers. In '85 I start playing sixties.

That is still referentialism.
Yes, because that was the only way I knew how to work. But I *felt* that I was being modern. *Low-life* is the manifestation of it. That having been done, you see the little seeds being sown – *Brotherhood* being the first. Not sure what to grow, but I'll just deal with something that *is*. So my Klein colour fields are the sheets of Aluchrome and Titaanzink that Trevor found in the builders merchant's yard. Aluchrome cost £2 a sheet, and seemed more real than Klein's gold leaf. The notion to do something fresh was pushing me. 'Is it a straight reproduction of ... ? Then what's the point?' All I've done is go back to a period that I lived through. I didn't partake in it, but I could feel it. Every other period that I'd raided, I didn't have any feeling of. They were all removed. But I knew something of the spirit of the sixties – I knew who the Beatles and Andy Warhol were. Having experienced it 'real time', I couldn't see the point in copying it exactly. So when we start to do stripes in '87, they're like Bridget Riley, but the end result is different. The *Substance* peony is like a Warhol flower, but it's not a Warhol flower. Aluchrome is like Klein, but it's not Klein.

Is it really so significant that now you were making the marks, rather than taking verbatim the marks of someone else?
Yes, because you bring something new to the visual wealth of the world. The peony's still great. All you can say about *Thieves Like Us* is that it's a fabulously clever reassemblage of a painting in photographic form. As a conceit, it's interesting that it's a record cover in 1984. But it's not important. Whereas for me the peony is an important new thing – the world had never had a flower like that before.

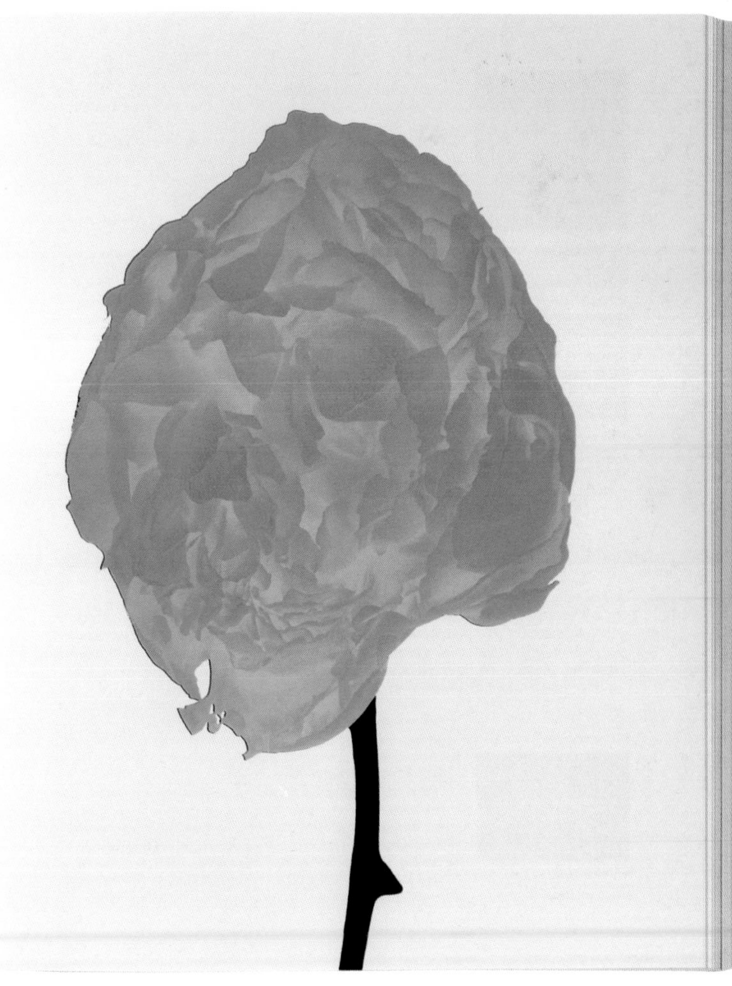

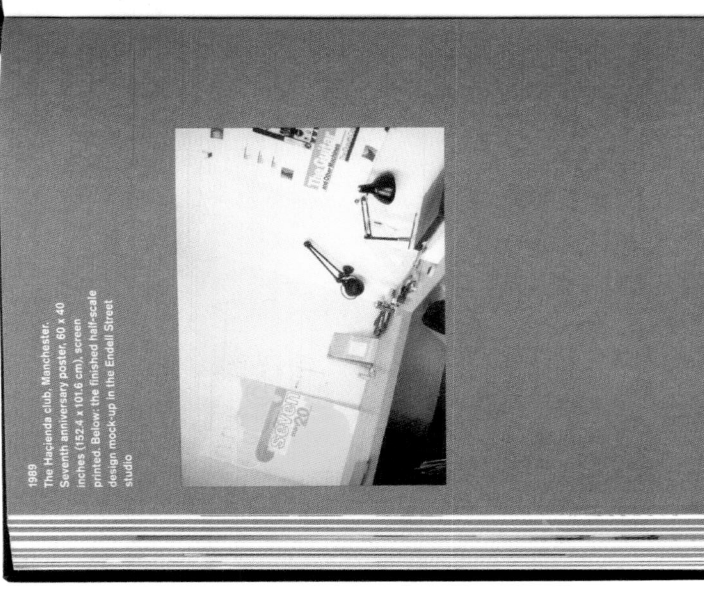

1989
The Haçienda club, Manchester.
Seventh anniversary poster, 60 x 40 inches (152.4 x 101.6 cm), screen printed. Below: the finished half-scale design mock-up in the Endell Street studio
184

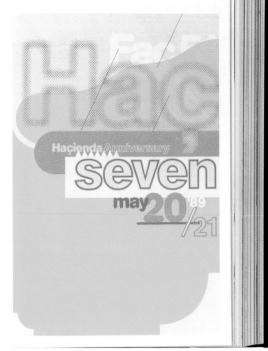

Ex Libris
Wim Crouwel

A History of Graphic Design, Philip B. Meggs, Alston W. Purvis, fourth edition, John Wiley & Sons, Hoboken, New Jersey, 2006
Modern Typography: An Essay in Critical History, Robin Kinross, second edition, Hyphen Press, London, 2004
Anthony Froshaug, Robin Kinross, Hyphen Press, London, 2000
Jan Tschichold: Typographer, Ruari McLean, Lund Humphries, London, 1975
A History of Visual Communication, Josef Müller-Brockmann, Arthur Niggli, Teufen, 1971
Compendium for Literates: A System of Writing, Karl Gerstner, MIT Press, Cambridge, Massachusetts, 1974
Review of 5x10 Years of Graphic Design, Karl Gerstner, Hatje Cantz, Ostfildern-Ruit, 2001
Paul Renner: The Art of Typography, Christopher Burke, Hyphen Press, London, 1998
The Designer and the Grid, Lucienne Roberts, Julia Thrift, Rotovision, East Sussex, 2002
8vo: On The Outside, Mark Holt, Hamish Muir, Lars Müller Publishers, Baden, 2005

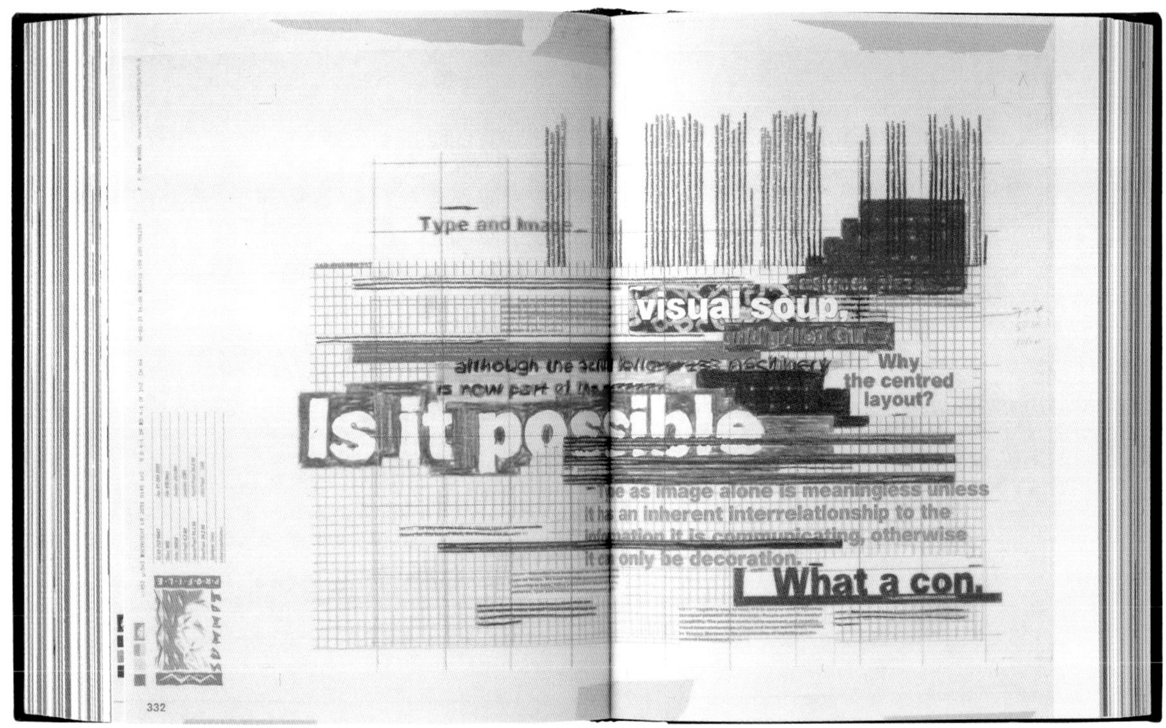

Proof corrections for Octavo 90.7, *an example of how each stage of the production process was an important and integral part of any job.* 8vo: On the Outside *shows as many examples of mock-ups and proofs as of finished pieces.*

8vo: On the Outside

Mark Holt,
Hamish Muir
Lars Müller Publishers,
Baden, 2005
536 pages
160 × 120 mm (6.25 × 8.5 in)
Designed by Mark Holt,
Hamish Muir

In his contribution to *8vo: On the Outside*, the designer Wolfgang Weingart aptly refers to it as a 'workbook'. This small-format book contains the workings of the London-based design group 8vo, which practised from 1984 to 2001. It is not a portfolio of finished pieces, but a detailed illustration of the firm's philosophy: its graphic design process was shaped by a job's contents, both in the construction of layouts and the choices made in the project's mechanical and reproductive stages.

The book's authors, Mark Holt and Hamish Muir, members of 8vo, describe the group's beginnings designing for the band the Durutti Column and the Manchester club the Haçienda, and also tell the story of *Octavo*, the ground-breaking typographical magazine. Self-published by 8vo and other contributors, there were eight issues, between 1986 and 1992, and *Octavo* found an audience ready for serious typographic commentary. The magazine was radical in its layout and at the forefront of production techniques. *8vo: On the Outside* shows the meticulous mock-ups and complicated artwork involved in its design.

There are detailed descriptions of work 8vo did for the Museum Boijmans Van Beuningen in Rotterdam (undertaken at the invitation of Wim Crouwel) and the group's information graphics for the automated billing of American Express, Orange and Powergen.

8vo straddled the world of design before and after the introduction of the computer. The profound change computerized design brought about in working practices in the industry was perhaps particularly pronounced for 8vo. The move from drawing board to screen, and the increased responsibility of designers in pre-press matters, are intertwined in their story.

For a time the group described themselves as 'visual engineers', distancing themselves from a design culture and profession they had always been unwilling to join. The description was also a reflection of their need to push themselves into new areas creatively and remain 'on the outside'.

A diagram showing the structure and use of colour in an exhibition catalogue for the Design Museum, London. The grey background is a special used for all the text in the book.

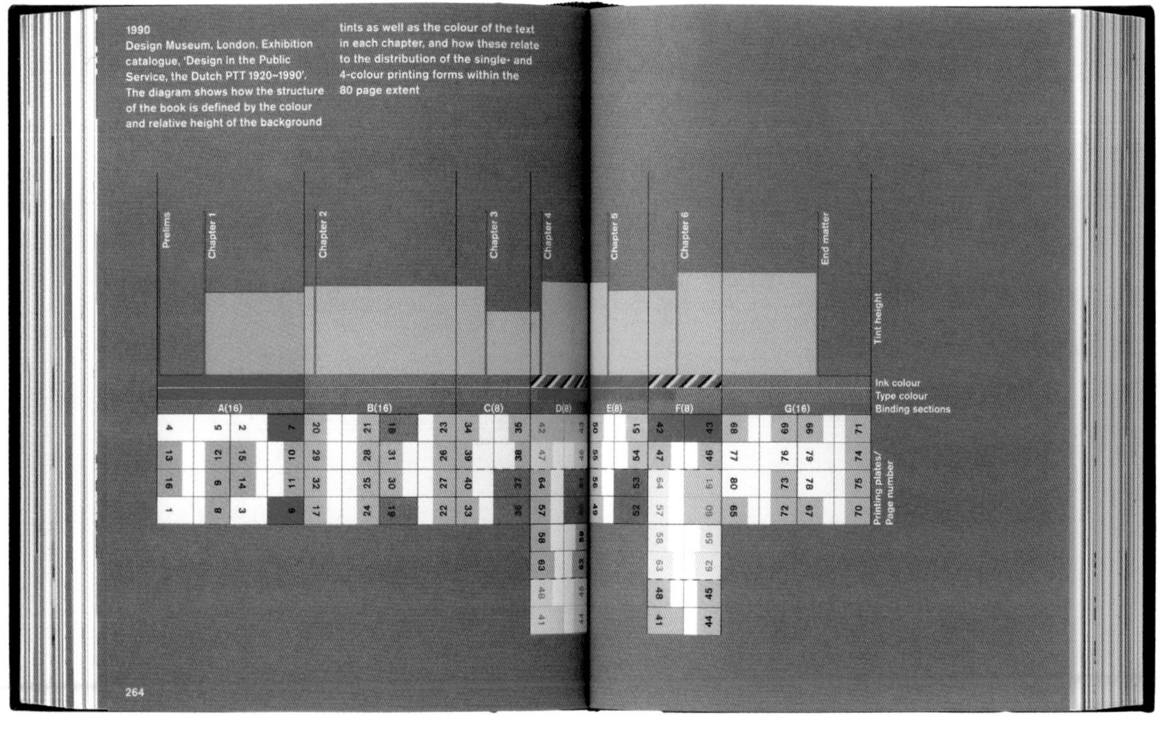

Robert Brownjohn: Sex and Typography
Emily King
Laurence King Publishing, London, 2005
240 pages
230 × 190 mm (9 × 7.5 in)
Designed by Atelier Works

Printed on gold-covered boards, the cover of *Robert Brownjohn: Sex and Typography* shows a photograph taken by Herbert Spencer of the model Margaret Nolan and the designer Robert Brownjohn (1925–1970) during the shoot for Brownjohn's most famous piece of work: the title sequence for the Bond film *Goldfinger* (1964). The book's title comes from an article of the same name that Brownjohn wrote for Spencer's *Typographica* magazine.

Sex and Typography reads more like the biography of a jazz musician than that of a graphic designer. An American who moved to London in 1960, Robert Brownjohn was supremely talented, with an ego to match. He lived life to the full, hanging out with the in-crowd, but had to deal with addictions that never ceased to haunt him.

The first part of the book, published by Laurence King Publishing in London and Princeton Architectural Press in New York, is the story of his career, told through quotes and anecdotes provided by friends and colleagues. Skilfully edited by the book's author, Emily King, it not only paints a picture of Brownjohn's tumultuous life but also provides a rare record of the design and advertising scene in New York in the late 1950s and in London during the 1960s. Accompanying artefacts add interest to the story. Photographs of Brownjohn and his family enjoying themselves on their roof terrace in the company of Miles Davis are contrasted with his letters from hospital to his wife Donna about his hopes of tackling his drug addiction.

Brownjohn's work is studied in more detail in the second half of the book. Highlights range from projects for Pepsi at Brownjohn, Chermayeff & Geismar Associates and their brilliant *Watching Words Move* booklet (1962) to his famous title designs for the Bond movies *From Russia with Love* (1963) and *Goldfinger* (1964). The book has been sympathetically designed by Atelier Works.

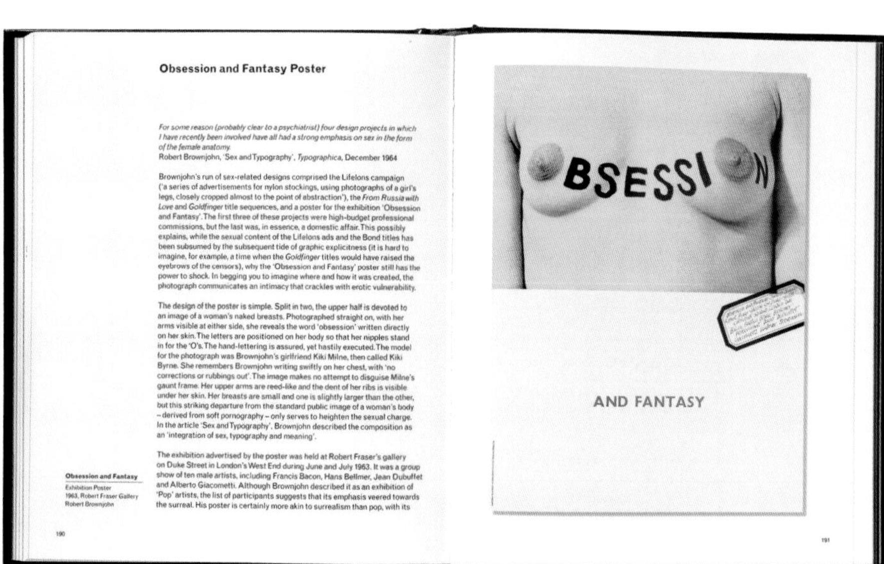
Obsession and Fantasy Poster

For some reason (probably clear to a psychiatrist) four design projects in which I have recently been involved have all had a strong emphasis on sex in the form of the female anatomy.
Robert Brownjohn, 'Sex and Typography', *Typographica*, December 1964

Brownjohn's run of sex-related designs comprised the Lifelons campaign ('a series of advertisements for nylon stockings, using photographs of a girl's legs, closely cropped almost to the point of abstraction'), the *From Russia with Love* and *Goldfinger* title sequences, and a poster for the exhibition 'Obsession and Fantasy'. The first three of these projects were high-budget professional commissions, but the last was, in essence, a domestic affair. This possibly explains, while the sexual content of the Lifelons ads and the Bond titles has been subsumed by the subsequent tide of graphic explicitness (it is hard to imagine, for example, a time when the *Goldfinger* titles would have raised the eyebrows of the censors), why the 'Obsession and Fantasy' poster still has the power to shock. In begging you to imagine where and how it was created, the photograph communicates an intimacy that crackles with erotic vulnerability.

The design of the poster is simple. Split in two, the upper half is devoted to an image of a woman's naked breasts. Photographed straight on, with her arms visible at either side, she reveals the word 'obsession' written directly on her skin. The letters are positioned on her body so that her nipples stand in for the 'O's. The hand-lettering is assured, yet hastily executed. The model for the photograph was Brownjohn's girlfriend Kiki Milne, then called Kiki Byrne. She remembers Brownjohn writing swiftly on her chest, with 'no corrections or rubbings out'. The image makes no attempt to disguise Milne's gaunt frame. Her upper arms are reed-like and the dent of her ribs is visible under her skin. Her breasts are small and one is slightly larger than the other, but this striking departure from the standard public image of a woman's body – derived from soft pornography – only serves to heighten the sexual charge. In the article 'Sex and Typography', Brownjohn described the composition as an 'integration of sex, typography and meaning'.

The exhibition advertised by the poster was held at Robert Fraser's gallery on Duke Street in London's West End during June and July 1963. It was a group show of ten male artists, including Francis Bacon, Hans Bellmer, Jean Dubuffet and Alberto Giacometti. Although Brownjohn described it as an exhibition of 'Pop' artists, the list of participants suggests that its emphasis veered towards the surreal. His poster is certainly more akin to surrealism than pop, with its

Obsession and Fantasy
Exhibition Poster
1963, Robert Fraser Gallery
Robert Brownjohn

190

191

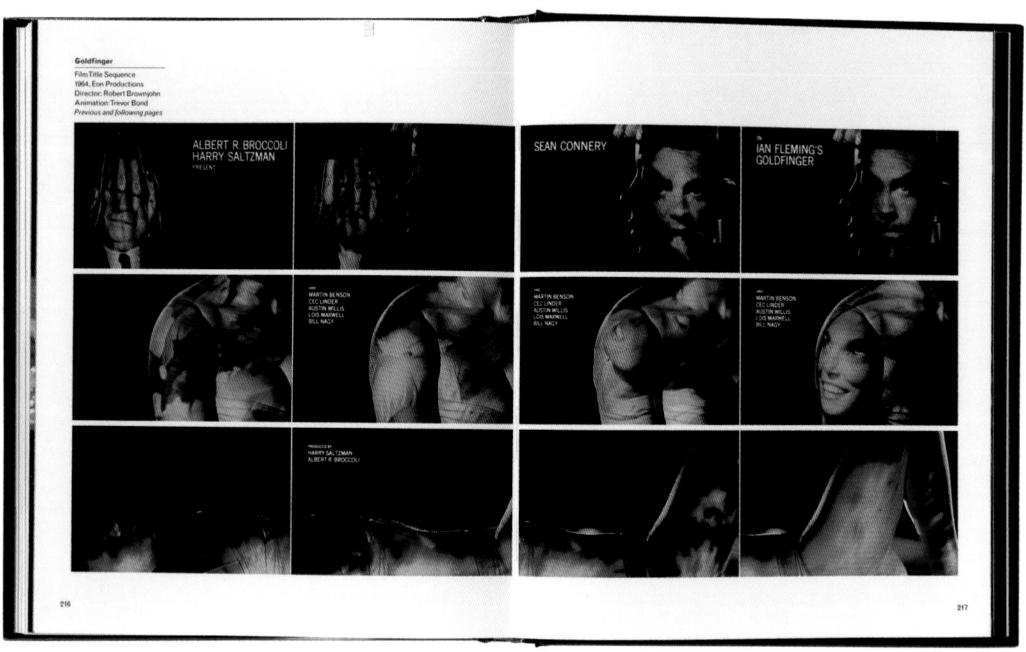
Goldfinger
Film Title Sequence
1964, Eon Productions
Director: Robert Brownjohn
Animation: Trevor Bond
Previous and following pages

216

217

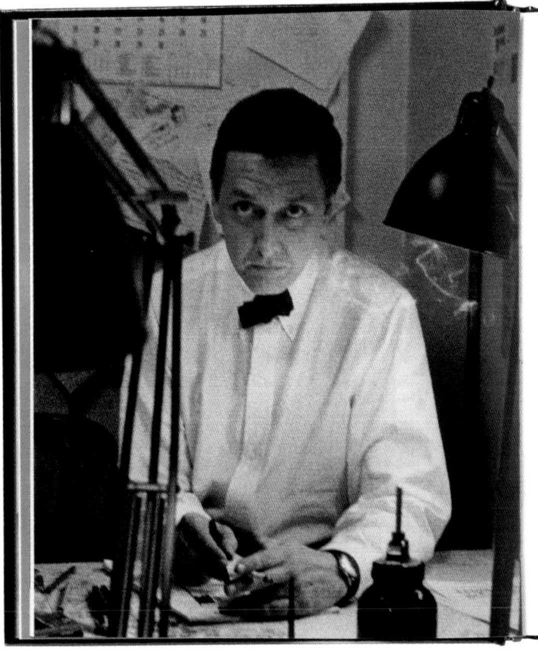

1950–1960 New York

1951 **Leaves Chicago for New York.**

1951–56 **Works as a freelance graphic designer in New York for clients including George Nelson, then the Design Director of Herman Miller, Edgar Bartolucci and Bob Cato.**

Edgar Bartolucci — A few years after I left Chicago I started a design business in New York with Bob Cato, a company called BC Associates. Brownjohn had a drug problem and he came out from rehabilitation to see us. He needed a job, so he worked for us on and off. I remember that a cigarette was a permanent fixture in his hand; his drafting paper was always getting burnt.

Bob Cato — Bj was belligerent, anti-social ... He never wanted you to find anything out about him, he wouldn't give anything away. He had a keen wit and extraordinary sense of humour. We had terrible fights, but he was absolutely wonderful and adorable. He had a keen and available mind, he worked hard not to work.

Edgar Bartolucci — Bob Cato started working full time for CBS in 1955 so he left the company and I tied in with a display manufacturer by the name of Lane Displays. Harold Lane and I were partners and we changed the company name to Instore Advertising. Sometimes Brownjohn worked for us steadily for two or three months, but then he would get interested in something else and disappear. He would always come back, eventually. I didn't even know whether he had an apartment, because he would often end up sleeping in the office. We would come in and find him asleep on a drafting table. He would say, 'Well, I worked late and I didn't feel like going.' Truthfully, we didn't know. He had a key to the place. We had nothing that could be stolen, so it wasn't a matter of who you gave the key to.

Early 1950s **Becomes a friend of Charlie Parker, Miles Davis, Stan Getz and others.**

Dick Davison — My brother was a jazz musician and so I was involved with jazz musicians most of my life. Bj was attracted to them too. We went to the Half Note, where probably the most loaded jazz musicians in the world were playing. John Coltrane and Miles Davis, guys who were really zonked. We all liked that kind of thing.

Ivan Chermayeff — A little before we were in business together, I was spending the summer as a waiter in the first-class carriage of the *Bermuda* [*The Queen of Bermuda*, Furness Bermuda Line]. On my days off, I used to leave the ship and spend time

27

Brownjohn's biography is told almost entirely in quotes from his colleagues, friends and family.

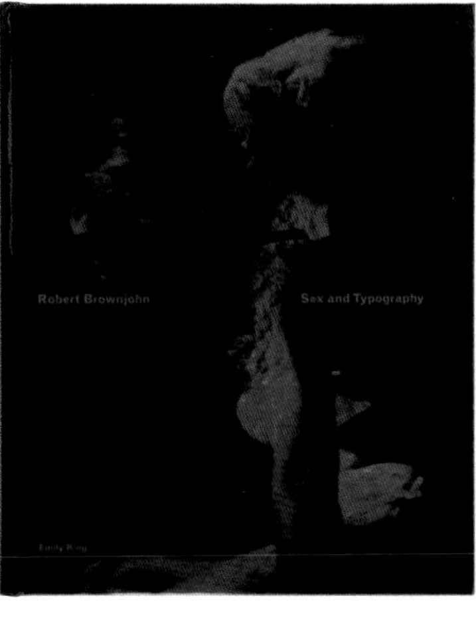

The cover is printed black and red on a gold paper.

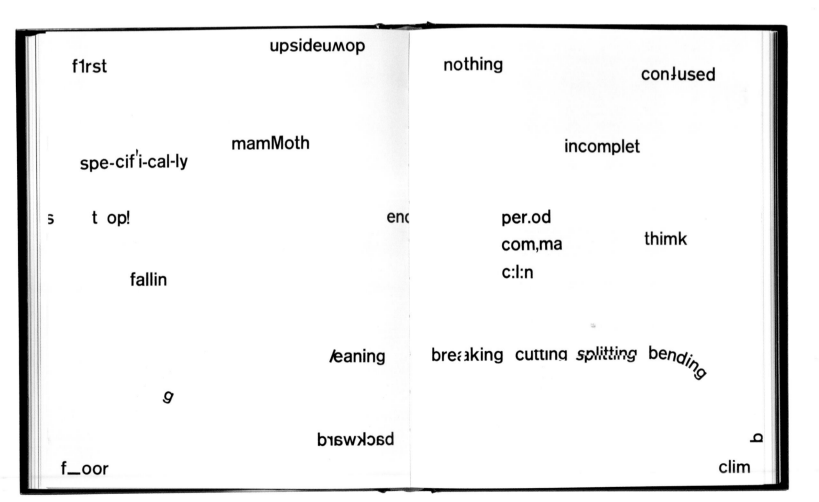

upsideuʍop

f1rst

mamMoth

spe-cif'i-cal-ly

s t op!

enc

fallin

/eaning

g

bɿɒwʞɔɒd

f_oor

nothing

conɟused

incomplet

per.od

com,ma

thimk

c:l:n

breaking cutting splitting bending

b

clim

Further Reading

Aicher, Otl, *Typographie*, Ernst & Sohn Verlag, Berlin, 1988

Amstutz, Walter (ed.), *Who's Who in Graphic Art*, Amstutz and Herdeg Graphis Press, Zurich, 1962

Baines, Phil and Andrew Haslam, *Type & Typography*, Laurence King Publishing, London, 2002

Barton, Bruce and Craig James, *Thirty Centuries of Graphic Design*, Watson-Guptill, New York, 1987

Bierut, Michael, Jessica Helfand and Steven Heller (eds.), *Looking Closer 3: Classic Writings on Graphic Design*, Allworth Press, New York, 1999

Blackwell, Lewis, *Twentieth-Century Type: Remix*, Laurence King Publishing, London, 1998

Bos, Ben and Elly (eds.), *AGI: Graphic Design Since 1950*, Thames & Hudson, London and New York, 2007

Bringhurst, Robert, *The Elements of Typographic Style*, Hartley & Marks, Vancouver, BC, 1992

Carter, Sebastian, *Twentieth Century Type Designers*, Trefoil, London, 1987

Constantine, Mildred (ed.), *Word and Image*, exh. cat., Museum of Modern Art, New York, 1968

Diethelm, Walter, *Signet, Signal, Symbol*, ABC Verlag, Zurich, 1970

Eskilson, Stephen J., *Graphic Design: A New History*, Laurence King Publishing, London, 2007

Evans, Harold, *Pictures on a Page: Photo-Journalism, Graphics and Picture Editing*, Heinemann, London, 1978

Friedman, Mildred and Phil Freshman, *Graphic Design in America: A Visual Language History*, Harry N. Abrams, New York, 1989

Frutiger, Adrian, *Signs and Symbols: Their Design and Meaning*, Studio Editions, London 1989

Garland, Ken, *Graphics Handbook*, Studio Vista, London, 1966

Gentleman, David, *Design in Miniature*, Studio Vista, London, 1972

Gill, Eric, *An Essay on Typography*, Lund Humphries, London, and David R. Godine, Boston, 1988

Gottschall, Edward M., *Typographic Communications Today*, MIT Press, Cambridge, Massachusetts, 1989

Gray, Nicolete, *A History of Lettering: Creative Experiment and Letter Identity*, Phaidon Press, London, 1986

Heller, Steven and Louise Fili, *Stylepedia: A Guide to Graphic Design Mannerisms, Quirks, and Conceits*, Chronicle Books, San Francisco, 2006

Heller, Steven, *Merz to Emigre and Beyond: Avant-Garde Magazine Design of the Twentieth Century*, Phaidon Press, London, 2003

Kinross, Robin, *Modern Typography: An Essay in Critical History*, Hyphen Press, London, 1992

Lawson, Alexander, *Anatomy of a Typeface*, David R. Godine, Publisher, Boston, 1990

Lee, Marshall (ed.), *Books for our Time*, Oxford University Press, New York, 1951

Lewis, John, *The Twentieth Century Book: Its Illustration and Design*, Studio Vista, London, 1967

Livingston, Alan and Isabella, *Dictionary of Graphic Design and Designers*, new edition, Thames & Hudson, London, 2003

Lupton, Ellen and J. Abbott Miller, *Design Writing Research: Writing on Graphic Design*, Princeton Architectural Press, New York, 1996

McAlhone, Beryle and David Stuart, *A Smile in the Mind: Witty Thinking in Graphic Design*, Phaidon Press, London, 1996

McLean, Ruari, *Magazine Design*, Oxford University Press, London, 1969

Meggs, Philip B., *Six Chapters in Design: Saul Bass, Ivan Chermayeff, Milton Glaser, Paul Rand, Ikko Tanaka, Henryk Tomaszewski*, Chronicle Books, San Francisco, 1997

Müller-Brockmann, Josef, *A History of Visual Communication*, Hastings House, New York, 1981

Müller-Brockmann, Josef and Shizuko, *History of the Poster*, ABC Verlag, Zurich, 1971

Ogilvy, David, *Ogilvy on Advertising*, Vintage Books, New York, 1983

Opie, Robert, *The Art of the Label: Designs of the Times*, Simon and Schuster, London, 1987

Poynor, Rick, *The Graphic Edge*, Booth-Clibborn Editions, London, 1993

Ricci, Franco Maria and Corinna Ferrari (eds.), *Top Symbols and Trademarks of the World*, seven vols., Deco Press, Milan, 1973

Roberts, Lucienne, *Drip-Dry Shirts: The Evolution of the Graphic Designer*, AVA, Lausanne, 2005

Rosen, Ben, *Type and Typography: The Designer's Type Book*, Reinhold Publishing Corporation, New York, 1963

Rothschild, Deborah, Ellen Lupton and Darra Goldstein, *Graphic Design in the Mechanical Age: Selections from the Merrill C. Berman Collection*, Yale University Press, New Haven and London, 1998

Shaughnessy, Adrian, *How to be a Graphic Designer Without Losing Your Soul*, Laurence King Publishing, London, 2005

Simon, Oliver, *Introduction to Typography*, Faber & Faber, London, 1945

Spiekermann, Erik and E.M. Ginger, *Stop Stealing Sheep & Find Out How Type Work*, Adobe Press, Mountain View, California, 1993

Index

Page numbers for specific captions and illustrations are in *italics*.

Picture Credits

The author and Laurence King Publishing Ltd would like to thank all the publishers, art directors, authors, designers, editors and estates who have granted permission to reproduce images in this book. Every effort has been made to contact copyright holders, but should there be any errors or omissions in the credits provided on the relevant page or below, Laurence King Publishing Ltd would be pleased to make the appropriate alteration in any subsequent printing of this publication.

Lo Studio Boggeri: 1933–1981 and *The Language of Graphics* reproduced by permission of Mondadori Electa S.p.a.

A Constructed Roman Alphabet: A Geometric Analysis of the Greek and Roman Capitals and of the Arabic Numerals by David Lance Goines reprinted by permission of David R. Godine, Publisher, Inc., copyright © 1982 by David Lance Goines.

All photography by Nick Turner, except pages 12–13 Amy Wu.

The books *Die Neue Typographie* (pages 14–15), *Manuale Typographicum* (pages 20–21), *Semiologie Graphique* (pages 48–49), *Mise en Page* (pages 74–75), *Colour in Advertising* (pages 76–77) and *Typography* (pages 84–85) are from the collection of St Bride Printing Library, London.

Acknowledgements

In collecting my own graphic design library and in my envious perusals of those of friends and colleagues I had often thought that it would be useful to have as a resource a book that contained the finest examples of this publishing niche. I am grateful to Angus Hyland at Pentagram, whose encouragement led me to proposing this book idea to Laurence King Publishing. That the book comes into being is a result of the interest and enthusiasm of Laurence King and Jo Lightfoot, and their confidence in commissioning a novice writer, for which I am much indebted.

My editor at Laurence King, John Jervis, has been an enormous help at all stages of the book's development, helping to give the book focus and providing me with a sounding board for my numerous ideas and questions. His unflappable patience in the face of the glacial progress of the book's writing was particularly appreciated. Thanks are also due within Laurence King to the work of Lesley Henderson in her help on accumulating correct bibliographical information and to Simon Walsh for his skill in production matters.

This collection of books could not have been put together without the generous help of many people who kindly lent books from their own collections for me to study and photograph. I would like to thank Dan Adams, Andy Altmann, Eric Baker, Tony Brook, Matt Dennis, Marion Deuchars, Alan Dye, Simon Esterson, Nick Finney, Angus Hyland, Darrel Rees, Aude Van Ryn, Ben Stott, John Turner, Matthew Wilson and Ian Wright. A few of the books have been sourced from the St Bride Printing Library: my thanks go to its librarian Nigel Roche for his keen interest and help in facilitating the photography of these books.

The photography of this book has been undertaken tirelessly by Nick Turner. This was a demanding task incorporating different formats, an extended time-frame and numerous locations. He has kept a consistent quality to the images, which has helped to unify the look of the book.

Tony Brook's publication *Spin 2: 50 Reading Lists* was the starting point for the inclusion of the 'Ex Libris' lists that are a feature of this book. I am most grateful to Tony for his permission to appropriate his idea for inclusion here and to the designers who spared their time to supply lists of favourite books: Andy Altmann, Henk van Assen, Eric Baker, André Baldinger, Michael Bierut, Tony Brook, Matthew Carter, Wim Crouwel, Mario Eskenazi, Simon Esterson, Vince Frost, George Hardie, David Hillman, Angus Hyland, Quentin Newark, Peter Saville, Adrian Shaughnessy and Gabriele Wilson.

Lastly my thanks goes to my family Angela and Orson for their support and tolerant acceptance of my bookish interests.